HISTORICAL
SOUTHERN FAMILIES

Volume I

by

John Bennett Boddie

Baltimore

GENEALOGICAL PUBLISHING COMPANY

1967

Originally Published

Redwood City, California, 1957

Reprinted

Genealogical Publishing Company

Baltimore, 1967

Library of Congress Catalog Card Number 67-29833

TABLE OF CONTENTS

iii

EXPLANATION OF ABBREVIATIONS

A.C.	Alumni of Cambridge by Venn.
A.O.	Alumni of Oxford by Foster.
A.P.R.	Albemarle Parish Register.
B.J.	Journals of the House of Burgesses.
Bell	Old Free State
Boddie	Designations used by others to denote "17th. Century Isle of Wight" or "Colonial Surry".
Brown	Brown's Abstracts of Somerset England Wills in 6 volumes.
Burgess	Revolutionary Soldiers of Virginia.
Chapman or C.	Mrs. Blanch Adams Chapman's Abstracts of Elizabeth City County, or Isle of Wight.
C.M.	Mrs. Chapman's Marriages of Isle of Wight.
C.S.W.	Mrs. Chapman's Wills of Southampton.
C.P.	Cavaliers and Pioneers (Abstracts of Virginia Land Grants), by Mrs. Nell M. Nugent.
do.	Ditto; meaning the same reference as previously shown.
D.A.B.	Dictionary of American Biography.
D.B.	Deed Book.
dsp.	Died single person.
dvp.	Died before parent.
D.N.B.	Dictionary of National Biography.
E.	Essex.
Foster	Alumni Oxoniensis, by Foster.
Fleet	Abstracts of Virginia County Records, by Beverly Fleet
G.E.C.	The Complete Peerage by G.E. Cokayne.
G.B.	Grant Book.
Harl.	Harleian Society Publications.
Hasted	Hasted's History of Kent County, England.
Hathaway	North Carolina Historical and Genealogical Register.
Hayden	Virginia Genealogies, by Hayden.
Heitman	Historic Register of Officers, American Revolution, by F.B. Heitman.
Hotten	Original Lists of Immigrants to America, by Hotten.
I.P.M.	Inquests Post Mortem.
J.H.B.	Journals of the House of Burgesses.
K.G.	King George County, Virginia.
L.B.	Land Book at Virginia State Library.
M.C.B.	Magna Carta Baron.
M.C.G.C.	Minutes of Court and Council.
M.	do.

N.N.	Northern Neck Land Grants.
N.E.G.R.	New England Genealogical and Historical Register.
Nash	Nash's History of Worcestershire.
O.	Orders.
O.B.	Order Book.
P.B.	Patent Book.
P.C.C.	Prerogative Court of Canterbury Wills, England.
P.G.	Prince George County.
P.R.	Patent Rolls of England.
P.W.	Prince William County.
R. or Reg.	Register of Parish.
R.B.	Record Book.
S.	Stafford County.
17C.	Seventeenth Century Isle of Wight County.
S.P.	St. Paul's Parish or Parish Register of Stafford County.
sp.	Single person.
S.P.R.	St. Paul's Parish Register, Stafford County.
S.P.	Calendar of State Papers of England.
S.P.Col.	Calendar of State Papers, Colonial.
S.V.F.	Southside Virginia Families, Vol. I or II.
Sweeney	Abstract of Rappahannock Wills, by Sweeney.
T.	Tylers Magazine
Tylers	do.
V.B.	Vestry Book.
Vic. His.	Victorian Histories of the Counties of England.
V. or V.M.	Virginia Historical Society Magazine.
W.	William and Mary College Quarterly.
W.M.	do.
W.B.	Will Book.

Abbreviations are not üniform because some chapters were written before Dr. Swem's Index was published using W. and V. to designate the above magazines. Also, other persons contributing used other forms of abbreviations which were not changed.

A CORRECTION OF MISTAKES APPEARING IN
SOUTHSIDE VIRGINIA FAMILIES, VOL. II

p. 1: John Arrington, d. S'ampton Co., Va. (will dated 4-26-1761) was the son of William Arrington and his wife Jane Peddin. They probably should be omitted. Their daughter, Ann Arrington, m. Thomas Holt (p. 280).

p. 27: Charles Barham's second wife was Ann Arrington, widow of John Arrington, above, pp. 1, 280.

p. 47: Daniel Powell was the son of Zachariah Powell and his wife, Mary SMITH, not Jones as stated. Jemima Powell m. Patrick H. Branch about 1829 or 1830 and not in 1839 or 40 as stated.

p. 54: "Children of first or second marriages" should read Children of John Branch and his wife Rebecca Bradford - (see Haywood: John Branch 1782 - 1863 pp. 1-5).

p. 106: Rebecca Elizabeth Dickens (b. 1826) who m. John J. Keeter. They were the parents of a fourth child who was omitted in the list of their children. She was Margaret Ann Keeter who m. her cousin Robert Patrick Dickens, son of Balaam Dickens and his wife Susan Ann Branch (p. 114)

p. 112: Elizabeth Smith, widow of Matthew Dickens (b. ca. 1777-8) m. WILLIAM DICKENS, son of JOSEPH DICKENS who d. 1802. It appears correctly on p. 102.

p. 114: Robert Patrick Dickens m. (1) Jan. 25, 1885 (not Jan. 1 as stated), his cousin, Margaret Ann Keeter, fourth child of John J. Keeter and his wife Rebecca Elizabeth Dickens p. 106 and correction above.

p. 114: Joshua should read Joseph Numa Dickens. He is living unmd. and not d. s. p. as stated. On line 4 the date should be 1876 not 1874.

p. 114: Teressa Hope Dickens m. William Marion Mann, not William Morton Mann as stated. It appears correctly on p. 323.

p. 115: Ella Jemima Dickens (b. 1874) was the daughter of Balaam Dickens and his wife Susan Ann Branch (p. 114). They had a son Willie Dickens (b. 1870) also, who was omitted in the list of children. He moved with his family to South Carolina where he died.

p. 116: The name Foxworth also appears as Foxworthy in Overwharton Parish Register.

p. 117: Nancy Dickens Mills (b. 1805) should be NANCY DICKENS. She was a child of the 1st marriage of Rebecca Green. It appears correctly on p. 106 and elsewhere.

1

p. 118: May Green should be MARY GREEN.

p. 127: Estalle should be ESTALEE and Gardlin should be SAND-LIN.

p. 278: Thomas Holt, son of Randall Holt (2) and Elizabeth Hansford, had a son THOMAS HOLT who was omitted from the list of children on page 279 - see will Surry Co., Va. Book 1730 - 1738, p. 86. It was evidentally this THOMAS HOLT who remained in Surry County and whose inventory was recorded in 1775 and whose daughter m. Henry COCKE and not the THOMAS HOLT, son of William Holt and his wife Elizabeth Seward, for as stated William Holt in his will gave his son Thomas Holt "all my Land on the South Side of Nottoway River whereon he now lives." Therefore, Thomas Holt, Son of William, lived on the south side of Nottoway River and was therefore the Thomas Holt who died in Southampton County (on the southside of Nottoway River) in 1788 since no other Thomas Holt who could be his son has been found living on the "South Side of Nottoway River". see pp. 279-80.

p. 279: Thomas M. Mann, Jr. should be William Marion Mann, Jr.

p. 280: Harvey Holt m. Elizabeth, widow of Britton Jones and had issue Rebecca Holt who m. James Hux and had issue.

p. 282: The children and grandchildren of Ira David Wood and his wife Lucy Della Savage are incorrectly given. It should be as follows:
Children of Ira David and Lucy Della (Savage) Wood:
  (1) Evelyn Ray Wood (b. Dec. 31, 1905) m. Robert Edward Shervette Jr. Mar. 24, 1935. Res. Enfield, N.C.
      Children:
      a.   Robert Edward Shervett III, b. Oct. , 1937
      b.   Gera-Lu Shervett b. May 1, 1942
  (2) Ira David Wood, Jr. (b. May 3, 1916) m. Bettie Winstead. Res. Enfield, N.C.
      Children:
      a.   Ira David Wood III
      b.   Carol Winstead Wood
  (3) Carroll Thomas Wood, b. Aug. 28, 1918, d. in France, Aug. 1, 1944, of wounds received in battle near St. Lo.

p. 282: James Watsob Parker should be James WATSON Parker.

p. 284: Mary Elizabeth Parker was born at "Rose Hill" Sept. 12, 1866 (not Oct. 6th as stated). She died Oct. 6, 1908 - see p. 322.

p. 286: Picto should be Picot.

p. 312: Charles Griffin should be Charles Gaffin.

p. 320: Charlity should be CHARITY.

p. 323: Samings should be SAVINGS.

p. 324: Line 5, Beta Chemical Fraternity should read Beta Beta Beta, Honorary Biology Fraternity and Gamma Sigma Epsilon, Honorary Chemical Fraternity.

p. 340: Benjamin Greeb should be Benjamin Grubb and he mar-
Jane, sister of John Hardy of Halifax County, N.C. Elizabeth
Hardy, daughter of Hugh and Bethea Hardy and granddaughter of
John Hardy of Halifax married John Whitaker of that county and
moved to Wake County, N.C. (Hal. Co., D.B. 15, p.348).

p. 110: William Hux was son of 'James (not Wm.) and Nancy Hux.

p. 127: Line 2, b.ca. 1784 should be b.ca.1774.

Southside Virginia Families Vol. I

p. 265: Mary Mennet should be MARY BENNETT.

LIST OF COLONISTS

"THE ARK" AND "THE DOVE"

Leonard Calvert (the Gov.).
George Calvert
Thomas Cornwallis, Esq.
Jerome Hawley, Esq.
Richard Gerard (son of Sir
Thomas Gerard, K.B.)
Edward Wintour
Frederick Wintour (sons of
the Lady Anne Wintour)
Henry Wiseman (son of Sir
Thomas Wiseman, Bart)
John Saunders
Edward Cranfield
Henry Greene
Nicholas Fairfax
John Baxter
Thomas Darnall
Capt. John Hill
John Medcalf
William Saire
William Ashmore
Thomas Allen
John Ashmore
William Andrews
James Barefate
John Bowlter
Richard Bradley
John Briant
Dr. John Briscoe
Ralph Bean
Henry Bishop
Henry Briscoe
William Browne (Brown)
Thomas Beckworth
Anam Benam
Christopher Carnot (Carnock)
Mrs. Ann Cox
Thomas Charinton
Thomas Cooper
John Curke
John Carle
Richard Cole
Richard Duke
Peter Draper
William Edwin (Edwyn)
Richards Edwards
John Elkin
Robert Edwards
Cuthbert Fenwick
Lewis Fremonds (Freeman)
William Fitter (Fidler)
Thomas Green
Thomas Gervais (Grigsta)
Stephen Gore
John Games (Gaines)
Richard Gilbert
Thomas Griston (Grigston)
Thomas Heath

John Halfhead
Nicholas Harvey (Harvie)
Mr. John Hollowes
(Hellis)
John Hollis
Thomas Hodges ("Gent")
Benjamin Hodges
James Hockley (Hickley)
John Hillierd (Hilliard)
John Hill
Richard Hills
Thomas Harrington
John Holden (Holdene)
Mary Jennings
Henry James
Richard Kenton
Samuel Lawson
Richard Lowe (Loe)
Richard Lusthead
Roger Morgan
John Marlburg
Thomas Munns (Minns)
Charles Middleton
Fra. Molcto
John Nevill
Richard Nevill
Richard Orchard
John Price, Sr.
Michael Perril
Thomas Price
Nicholas Perrie
Robert Pike
Lodwick Price
John Price, Jr.
Mr. Rogers
Francis Rabnett
John Robinson
Mr. William Smith
A. Smith
Thomas Smith ("Gent")
Mathias Sousa
Robert Simpson
Thomas Stratham
Robert Shirleys (Shorley)
Stephen Sammon (Sammion)
(Salmon)
Mr. Robert Smithson
John Thomson
James Thornton
Richard Thompson
Mathias Tousa
Andrew White
Capt. Robert Wintour
(Winter)
Roger Walter
Evans Watkins
John Ward
Mathias Zause

GOODRICH OF RAPPAHANNOCK AND CHARLES CITY COUNTY

This article is a correction of "Goodrich of Isle of Wight" appearing in "Southside Virginia Families", Vol.1, p.217.

It seems that there were two Charles Goodriches living in Virginia at the same time. One was a son of Capt. John Goodrich of Isle of Wight and the other one was a son of Colonel Thomas Goodrich of Rappahannock.

Colonel Thomas Goodrich imported himself, Anne his wife, seven negroes and four other persons to Lower Norfolk County, for whom he received a Certificate from the Court of that county June 17, 1652, for 1250 acres. (14V 91) Seven of these headrights Goodrich assigned to Peter Sexton, viz., himself, wife Anne and five negroes. (NEHR 47-194) On March 31, 1653, Peter Sexton was granted 350 acres for the transportation of those seven persons, Thomas Goodrich, Anne Goodrich and five negroes. (C.P. 275) Thomas Goodrich testified in court at Lower Norfolk, in 1654, that he was aged 40. That would place his date of birth in the year 1614. (25 W (I) p.38.) He soon moved to the south side of the Rappahannock River where on June 10, 1657, as "Major Thomas Goodrich" he patented 600 acres of land. (C.P. 347) He also patented 400 acres in the same place, Mar. 16, 1657/58, as "Lt. Colonel" Thomas Goodrich. He patented 1134 acres and 2000 acres with the same designation, and in the same place on June 12, 1664. (Id. 397-517) He joined Nathaniel Bacon in "Bacon's Rebellion" in 1676 and was appointed by him Lt. General in charge of forces along the Rappahannock and Potomac. When the Rebellion collapsed the General was sentenced by a Berkeley Court Martial to be hanged, but on the intervention of influential friends and loyal members of the House of Burgesses he was allowed to go free if he "with a rope around his neck and on his knees did beg his life from the Governor and Council upon payment of a fine of 50,000 pounds of tobacco". (Hening 1660-1682 Vol. 2, pp. 377-378)

Colonel Thomas Goodrich made his will Mar.15, 1678/9, same probated April 3, 1679. He bequeathed "to eldest son BENJAMIN 300 acres of land on the riverside bought of Clement Thresh: to son JOSEPH ½ of the dividend of land called "Matapony' containing 1800 acres; to son CHARLES tract of land containing 400 acres joining upon the dividend I settled on Hoskins Pocoson; to daughter ANNE 900 acres of land being a moiety of the dividend called 'Matapony'; to son PETER 800 acres part of dividend called Hoskins Pocoson; to daughter KATHRINE 800 acres part of the dividend of 4000 aforesaid. (Sweeney, Rap. Wills p.77)

Anne Goodrich married Colonel John Lightfoot, Member of the Council, Commander in Chief of King and Queen County Militia.

Benjamin Goodrich, eldest son, of James City County, in

5

1703 deeded to William Aylett of King and Queen part of the tract of land Col. Thomas Goodrich willed to his son Joseph, and Joseph in his will bequeathed the tract to his son Danby Goodrich, who, dying in his minority, the tract passed to Joseph's eldest brother, Benjamin Goodrich.

It is evident that JOSEPH GOODRICH had another son, Thomas, who died a minor, for in the P.C.C. Administrations in England granted Nov. 20, 1703 to Sir Abstrubs Danby, Kt., "Uncle on the mother's side and next of kin" it is proven that Joseph[2] married a sister of Sir Abstrubs Danby, whose mother was Anne, daughter of John Culpepper, brother of the first Lord. (32V 61.)

Three of Benjamin Goodrich's children are evidently mentioned in the following law suit:

"Robert Goodrich, living in James City and Thomas Ravenscroft, next friend to Anne Goodrich, and Elizabeth Goodrich, infant orphans of Benjamin Goodrich; versus the petition of Phillip Ludwell for an acre of land on Chickerhouse Creek, James City, Nov. 17, 1719. (27 W (I) 210)

Thomas Ravenscroft had married Elizabeth Hamlin, daughter of Ann Goodrich and John Hamlin of Prince George County. (V.H.G. 219)

Anne Goodrich, widow of Col. Thomas Goodrich, married Col. Edward Hill of "Shirley", Charles City County, about 1680. (Rap. Records) Col. Hill was one of the most important men of his time. He was a Member of the Council, Attorney General, 1679, Speaker of the House of Burgesses, 1691, and in 1697 Judge of the Admiralty Court for Virginia and North Carolina. In 1680, both Benjamin and Joseph Goodrich, as heirs of Col. Thomas Goodrich, signed a receipt to Col. Edward Hill, as marrying Anne, executrix of Col. Thomas Goodrich, decd.; and in the same receipt provided for what might in the future be given Charles, Peter and Catharine, orphans (minors) of the said Col. Thomas Goodrich. (7 T 60.)

This was Col. Edward Hill's second marriage. His first was to Elizabeth, daughter of Sir Edward Williams and wife Elizabeth_____. Elizabeth, widow of Sir Edward Williams, married secondly, _____Howe, and made her will as "Elizabeth Howe of St. Giles, Cripplegate, London, widow" dated April 18, 1677, probated May 30, 1677 as follows: ". . . to my son-in-law Edward Hill, now of Virginia L 5 which Mr. Baker, a mercer of St. Lawrence Lane, London, owes me; to my grand daughter Elizabeth Hill the Table Diamond Ring; to my grand daughter Henrietta Maria Hill, my necklace of pearls; to my grand daughter Sara Hill my Rose Diamond Ring; to my daughter, their mother, Elizabeth Hill, a Gold Seal Ring; to my said grandchildren L 150; to my grandchildren not specified a gold Hoop ring each. My son-in-law to come over to England or his executors to receive...... The rest among my grandchildren...Exrs.: Edward Hill and my maid Sarah Alcorne." (Hale 49) (V 14-171) Sir Edward Williams and his wife Elizabeth had two children: (1) Henry Williams married Mary, daughter of John Walbrioff of Hannamloch; (2) Elizabeth, married Edward Hill of Virginia. (10V 107). Henry Williams probably died without children.

Anne (Goodrich) Hill died about 1696 for in that year Col. Hill married Tabitha, widow of Major General John Custis of

Arlington, Va., and eldest daughter of Col. Edmond Scarburgh ? (Hening 2-319)

Charles Goodrich, a minor at the time of his mother's marriage, evidently moved with his mother to Charles City. Probably owing to the influence of Col. Hill he was appointed High Sheriff of Charles City in 1687. (O.B. 1687-95, p.104) As Sheriff, in January 1690, he arrested a Quaker, James Denson, for not appearing at Muster, and Charles sued the said Denson as follows: "Capt. Charles Goodrich v. James Denson, defendant, declares that the plaintiff did lately seize the sum of 300 lbs. tbco. as a fine for his non-appearance at Muster, as the law directs since the the defendant hath grossly abused the plaintiff, etc. (Id. 357)

The Military officers for Charles City in 1699 were: Edward Hill, Colonel; Edward Hill, Jr., Lt. Colonel; Charles Goodrich, Major. (Crozier Col. Militia 1651-1776) Capt. Charles Goodrich was a Burgess for Charles City on April 24, 1696. He held 900 acres, as "Major Charles Goodrich" in 1704 and "Charles Goodrich" of Isle of Wight was holding 80 acres. Evidently Charles Goodrich of Isle of Wight as "Charles Goodrich, Sr., and his son "Charles Goodrich, Jr." witnessed the will of Francis Rayner in Isle of Wight Sept. 29, 1716. (G.B. p.9; C 11-p.2)

Ann Goodrich, daughter of Charles Goodrich of Prince George married John Hamlin and among their children was a son named Peter, more reminiscent of the Rappahannock Goodrich's; also Ann Goodrich Hamlin had an only brother named "Edward" who might have been named for Col. Edward Hill.

I am advised that it is stated in the "Memorials of the Goodrich Family", that Lt. Commander Casper Goodrich, U.S.N., went to England and on examining the Goodrich papers found that John Goodrich who came to Virginia in 1635 was the second son of Sir Richard Goodrich, High Sheriff of Yorkshire in 1580-1592, and his wife Muriel, daughter of Lord William Eure. This John Goodrich was said to be the father of Thomas Goodrich of Rappahannock. There seems to be no evidence to support this as far as Thomas Goodrich is concerned; but John Goodrich of Isle of Wight seems to have been the John Goodrich who came over on the ship "George", August 21, 1635, from Gravesend, England, for on March 5, 1697/8 in Isle of Wight John Goodrich testified that he was aged 80 years or there abouts. (V.H.G.-217) His date of birth would be about 1618, and Thomas Goodrich about 1614. If any kin they were probably brothers.

These facts concerning the family of Colonel Goodrich of Rappahannock, later Essex, were kindly given to me by Mr. C.H. Hamlin, of 590 Ludlow Ave., Cincinnati 20, Ohio.

The Goodrich family of England mentioned above is shown in the Visitations of Yorkshire, 1584/5 and 1612 by Foster, also those of Gloucester 1569, p. 5; Lincolnshire Pedigree, Harleian Vol. 51, p.415; Misc. Gen. & Heraldry, 4th series, Vol.5-p.205

Some effort should be made to compare from the parish registers, the date of birth of John Goodrich, the second son, mentioned above with that of John Goodrich of Isle of Wight. Also contemporary wills of members of the family at that time should be examined.

BALDWIN of ISLE of WIGHT

A William Baldwin was living in Isle of Wight at the time of the massacre in 1622. The Indians first appeared at the house of George Harrison, half a mile from Baldwin's. Then they set fire to a tobacco house as a ruse, and as the people rushed out of Harrison's house in order to quench the flames, many of them were slain. Thomas Hamor was writing a letter and did not go out with the others, but seeing the commotion rushed out and received an arrow in his back. Thereupon he, with twenty-two others, fled to Baldwin's house, leaving their own to burn. There William Baldwin and the others valiantly defended the house until the Indians gave up and departed. (17 C-35)

Baldwin, the next year, was living at Elizabeth City when the census was taken, evidently having gone there for safety. In February 1645 he was an officer of the Isle of Wight company under Captain John Upton that marched against the Indians and destroyed their corn fields and burned their habitations. (Id-99)

A William Baldwin, very probably his son, signed a petition to His Majesty in Behalf of Governor Berkeley in 1676 praising his administration. (17 C-161) He was therefore a Loyalist.

He married in Sept. 6. 1679, Mrs. Elizabeth Barlow, widow of Thomas Barlow whose will was recorded April 9, 1679. (BK A-179) As Mrs. Elizabeth Baldwin she presented an inventory of Thomas Barlow's estate on June 9, 1679 (Id 200).

Mr. Lundie Barlow, in his chapter on the Barlow family which will appear in Volume II of this series, states that Elizabeth was probably a sister of George and Thomas Moore. They were sons of John Moore, Burgess of Isle of Wight 1640 (5V233). John Moore patented 300 acres on the western Branch of Nansemond River March 11, 1664, 200 acres granted John Bryan March 18, 1662, who sold to said Moore and 100 acres for the transportation of John Moore's wife and John Clarke. (C.P. 480) John Moore probably died in Nansemond leaving wife Ann who afterwards married a Mr. Baron and then Anthony Matthews.

Anthony Manthews and his wife Ann for love and affection to James Baron, son of Ann and son-in-law to Anthony, give him 300 acres on the Blackwater, if said James Baron die the land to John Moore, eldest son to Anne Matthews. (17 C. 572; Admin. and Probate, p. 54; C1 32). John[2] Moore, son of John[1] Moore and wife Ann, died in 1688, leaving a daughter Elizabeth who was probably the wife of William Baldwin.

William Baldwin was granted 57 acres of land in 1688 and he and his wife Elizabeth sold that in 1693. (17C-109) He died before

June 27, 1737, when his estate was appraised and admitted to record. Inventory of his estate was recorded in 1737 (W.B. 4-106).

William[3] Baldwin, only known child of William[2] Baldwin, was born in Isle of Wight. He moved first to North Carolina but later moved to Amelia where he patented land April 20, 1739. He died about 1755 for his will was dated April 14, 1755 (W.B.1-161-2). He was married twice. The name of his first wife is unknown. His second wife was named "Susannah", last name also unknown.

He had five children by his first wife: (1) John m. Elizabeth -------(See later); (2) Elizabeth; (3) Mary; (4) David. By his second, his children were (5) Benjamin, (6) Sarah.

John[4] Baldwin, son of William[3] Baldwin, was born and died in Amelia. His will was recorded Sept. 27, 1770. His children mentioned in the will were: (1) John; (2) Elizabeth Whitworth; (3) Mary Smith; (4) Martha Atkins; (5) Edith Baldwin; (6) Prudence Baldwin; (7) Lucy Baldwin; (8) Damaris Baldwin; (9) George Baldwin, he to be executor.

George[5] Baldwin, son of John[4] Baldwin, was born in Amelia County, Va.; died in 1817, in Amelia County, Va.; married Rachel--------- and had children: (1) Joseph; (2) Nancy; (3) William, m. Nancy Williams, (4) George W., m. Elizabeth Vaughn; (5) Lewis; (6) Sally, m. Henry Wingo; (7) Polly, m. Thomas Williams (See later); (8) John.

Mary (Polly) Baldwin was born Feb.17, 1789, in Nottoway County, Va.; died Nov. 10, 1849, in Yalobusha County, Miss.; married Dec. 10, 1807, in Amelia County, Va., Thomas Williams, born Sept. 26, 1785, in Nottoway County, Va.; died Jan.28, 1850, son of Philip Williams and Martha Motley.

Children:
I. Sarah Elizabeth Ann Williams, b. Dec. 30, 1827; m. Samuel Harrison Garner (See later).
II. Philip Williams, Jr., m. Elizabeth Woodson;
III. Thomas Williams;
IV. Elizabeth Williams;
V. Nancy Williams;
VI. Joel Motley Williams;
VII. William Armstead Williams.

Sarah Elizabeth Ann Williams was born Dec. 30, 1827, in Lauderdale County, Ala.; died Dec. 29, 1902, in Grenada, Miss.; married April 4, 1847, in Yalobusha County, Miss., Samuel Harrison Garner.

Children:
I. John Garner;
II. Mollie Garner, m. McNeill;
III. Walter Garner, b. April 4, 1865; m. Dodie Sherman (See later).

Walter Williams Garner, son of Samuel Harrison Garner, was born April 4, 1865, in Granada, Grenada County, Miss.; died in Granada, Miss; married April 4, 1895, in Granada, Miss., Dodie Sherman, born Sept.23, 1871, Grenada, Miss., daughter of Henry Boyce Sherman and Cora Buffaloe.

Children:
I. George Merrill Garner, b.Sept. 9, 1896; m. Ruth Stokes;

II.   Sam Hall Garner, m. Martha Leigh;
III.   Walter Williams Garner, Jr., m. Thelma Jackson.

George Merrill Garner, son of Walter Williams Garner, was born Sept. 18, 1896. In Grenada, Miss.: married Aug. 20, 1924, Grenada, Miss., Ruth Stokes, b. Aug. 17, 1903, Grenada, Miss., daughter of Archibald Wade Stokes and Ludie Eggelston Williams.

Children:
I.   George Merrill Garner, Jr., b. March 26, 1930, m. Mary Alice McRee.
II.   Wade Stokes Garner, b. Jan. 28, 1932.

BARKER - BRADFORD - TAYLOR of Flowerdieu Hundred

(Continued from page 78, S. V. F. Vol. I)

Henry Boen Bradford, son of Henry Bradford and his wife Sara Crowell, was a first cousin of Governor John Branch of Florida. With the exception of one brother and sister, he and his entire family moved to Tallahassee, Florida, about 1843. Henry was born Oct. 30, 1791, in Halifax County, N. C., died Nov. 24, 1852, in Leon County, Florida; married (1) Ann Harris, (2) on May 1, 1833, in Leon County, Fla., Eliza Jones Taylor, a great granddaughter of Judge Benjamin Waller of Williamsburg, Va., daughter of John Taylor and Elizabeth Jones. Mr. Bradford was a planter in Leon County, Florida, and a member of the Methodist Church.

Children:
I. John Richard Bradford, b. Feb. 8, 1834, m. Nannie Taylor;
II. Henry Crowell Bradford, b. Oct. 20, 1836, died Dec. 25, 1841;
III. Eliza Jones Bradford, b. Aug. 19, 1838, died Sept. 25, 1841;
IV. William Lewis Bradford, b. Oct. 16, 1840, died July 23, 1841;
V. Sarah Ann Eliza Bradford, b. Nov. 5, 1842, m. Samuel Miles Parkhill;
VI. Virginia Alice Bradford, b. March 7, 1845, m. Samuel Parkhill Chaires (See later);
VII. Mary Ella Taylor Bradford, b. June 6, 1848, died Sept. 26, 1852;
VIII. Henry Waller Bradford, b. Mar. 11, 1851, died Oct. 26, 1862.

Virginia Alice Bradford, born March 7, 1845, Leon County, Fla., died Oct. 11, 1868, Clay Landing, Levy County, Fla., married Dec. 18, 1861, Verdura Plantation, Leon County, Fla., Samuel Parkhill Chaires, born Sept. 12, 1841, Leon County, Fla., died Dec. 7, 1928, Chaires, Leon County, Fla.

Children:
I. Samuel Parkhill Chaires Jr., b. Oct. 21, 1862, died Nov. 28, 1863;
II. Henry Bradford Chaires, b. July 19, 1864, m. Lilla Hightower;
III. Waller Taylor Chaires, b. Feb. 28, 1866, died April 5, 1867;
IV. Annie Green Chaires, b. Jan. 4, 1868, m. John Howell Patterson (See later).

Annie Green Chaires, born January 4, 1868, Brooksville, Hernando County, Fla., died March 10, 1944, Tallahassee, Leon

11

County, Florida, married April 22, 1889, John Howell Patterson, born Oct. 21, 1866, at Lloyd, Jefferson County, Fla., died July 22, 1928, Chaires, Leon County, Fla.

Children:

I.   Mary Alice Patterson, b. Oct. 11, 1890, m. Hubert Theodore Cotten;

II.   Howell Gwynn Patterson, b. Jan. 13, 1893, m. Margaret Lucretia Beard;

III.   John Bradford Patterson, b. July 20, 1895, m. Frances Rebecca Lingo;

IV.   Lila Corinth Patterson, b. Nov. 29, 1897, m. Charles Aubrey Dawson;

V.   Emmie Green Patterson, b. Oct. 3, 1900, m. James Munro Phillips;

VI.   George Lester Patterson, b. Aug. 4, 1906, m. Amelia Maud Goodbody (See later).

George Lester Patterson, 905 E. Park Avenue, Tallahassee, Fla., was born Aug. 4, 1906, at Chaires, Leon County, Fla., married Sept. 30, 1947, Thomasville, Thomas County, Ga., Amelia Maud Goodbody, born Dec. 14, 1907, Tallahassee, Fla., daughter of Albert George Goodbody and Francis Maud Craig. Mr. Patterson was educated in Florida and Iowa and is a member of the Episcopal Church. He is an auditor in Chaires, Fla.

BUTLER of SOUTH CAROLINA
(Continued from V. H. G. p. 32)

Captain James Butler, born 1723, Prince William County, Virginia, died Nov. 7, 1781, in the Cloud Creek Massacre, Edgefield County, S.C. (See V.H.G.-11), married Mary Simpson, born in Virginia. Capt. Butler was educated in Loudon County, Va. He was a member of the Protestant Episcopal Church and resided in Virginia and in the 96th District, S.C. Capt. James, a patriot, with his four sons during the Revolution were imbued with the principle that, come what would, they would battle for the rights of the colonies to the death. He entered the Snow Camp Expedition 1775 under General Richardson (See South Carolina in the Revolutionary War). After this, he was with General Williamson in his expedition against the Cherokee Indians in 1779. Refusing to swear allegiance to British Authority, was by a British officer placed in irons, then thrown in Ninety Six jail, from whence he was transferred to Charleston, where he was confined in the "provost" for 18 months, released in winter 1781. With his second son, James Butler, Jr., a lad of but 19, he was massacred at Clouds Creek, November 7, 1781 (See V.H.G.-11,12).
Children:
I. William Butler, b. Dec. 17, 1758, m. Behethland Foote Moore (See later);
II. James Butler, b. Mar. 2, 1761, killed with father at Clouds Creek, Nov. 7, 1781.
III. Thomas Butler, b. Nov. 4, 1763, m. Miss Grigsby;
IV. Nancy Butler, b. Sept. 27, 1765, m. Elisha Brooks;
V. Elizabeth Butler, b. Dec. 17, 1776, m. Zachariah Smith Moore;
VI. Stanmore Butler, b. Dec. 17, 1768, m. Ann Patience Youngblood.
VII. Sampson Butler, b. Feb. 6, 1769, married - childless;
VIII. Mason Butler.

General William Butler, born Dec. 17, 1759, Prince William County, Virginia; died Nov. 15, 1821, near Saluda, Saluda County, S.C., m. June 3,1784, at Edgefield, Edgefield Co.,S.C., Behethland Foote Moore, b.Dec.28,1764,Fauquier Co.,Va., d.Dec.2,1853, Edgefield,S.C.,daughter of Capt.Francis Moore and Frances Foote.

General William Butler, before his majority, served under General Lincoln at the battle of Stono as a lieutenant and afterwards under Count Pulaski. He also served under Watson and Ryan at Dean Swamp and Orangeburg. He was made a captain of Mounted Rangers in February 1781, within two months after coming of age, and in a year had become a man of recognized reputation and influence. He surprised and dispersed in 1782 the invading

13

band of Tories, which, under the famous William Cuningham, had penetrated the Up Country and in the hot pursuit which ensued that notorious partisan leaded owed his life to the fleetness of his horse. In 1788 William Butler was chosen as a member of the convention of the state of South Carolina called to consider the adoption of the Federal Constitution, against which he voted. He also was a member of the convention of 1790 which framed the constitution of the State. He was elected by the Legislature Sheriff of the District of Ninety Six in 1791, and in that capacity received General George Washington. In 1796 he was elected a member of Congress and served until 1810 when he retired in favor of John C. Calhoun. In 1812 he was offered the position of brigadier-general in the United States service which he declined, saying "I can be a major-general and stay at home". In 1814 he was given command of all the State forces in South Carolina. General Andrew Jackson, with whom he was intimate in early life, then at New Orleans, sent him word that while both were militia generals which ever was attacked would do his duty. He was a Methodist.

Children:

I.   James Butler, b. Mar. 25, 1785, m. (1) Miss Mays, (2) Eliza Kennedy;
II.   George Butler, b. Sept. 25, 1786, bachelor;
III. William Butler, b. Feb. 1, 1790, m. Jane Tweedy Perry;
IV.   Frank Moore Butler, b. Sept. 25, 1793, m. Louise Ford;
V.   Andrew Pickens Butler, b. Nov. 18, 1796; m. (1) Susan Ann Simpkins, (2) Harriet Hayne;
VI.   Pierce Mason Butler, b. Apr. 11, 1798, m. Miranda Julia DuVal (See later);
VII. Emmala Butler, b. Aug. 24, 1800, m. Edmund Bacon;
VIII. Leontine Butler, b. Apr. 8, 1802.

Father, General William Butler, Mother, Behethland Foote Butler, sister and brothers, with one exception, lie buried in the family burial ground near the old house where they lived and the children were all born. Dr. William Butler, the third son, was graduated at the South Carolina College and served as a surgeon in the United States Navy, being present in that capacity at the battle of New Orleans, 1814. He lies buried at Fort Gibson, Arkansas, where he died September 24, 1850.

Colonel Pierce Mason Butler, born at Mount Willing, Edgefield County, S.C., April 11, 1798; died Aug. 20, 1847, at Churubusco, Mexico; married May 22, 1826, at Fort Gibson, Territory of Arkansas, Miranda Julia DuVal, born Baltimore, Maryland; died July 9, 1862, at Edgefield, S.C. Colonel Butler was Governor of South Carolina, soldier and planter. He was educated at Edgefield and Abbeville. Through the influence of John C. Calhoun, he was assigned to the Fourth Infantry, United States Army, as a Second Lieutenant August 13, 1819. He was transferred to the Seventh Infantry on December 13, and became a First Lieutenant March 1, 1822, this original commission signed by James Monroe, President, and John C. Calhoun, Secretary of State, is at the Caroliniana Library, Columbia, South Carolina. He became a Captain December 16, 1825. He resigned from the service October 1, 1829. Took part in the Black Hawk War. Was president of the first bank of the state. Lieutenant Colonel in Seminole War. When asked if he would run for governor he said that "the office should seek the man, not the man the office," was elected governor 1836.

"It's a damn long time between drinks," said Edward B. Dudley, Governor of North Carolina, to Pierce Mason Butler, Governor of South Carolina, in 1838, at the home of Mrs. ˜Nancy Ann Jones, about midway between Raleigh and Durham, N.C. (Dictionary of American History, Vol. IV., p. 145).

Agent for the Cherokee Nation at Fort Gibson, Arkansas when asked to organize the Palmetto Regiment in the Mexican War, his wife protested, but he said that he had been called and "that it is not only necessary that a man must live, but he must do his duty." Fell mortally wounded at Churubusco, Mexico, August 20, 1847. His watch and letter seal was returned to his family by his slave, valet and bodyguard, who accompanied his body back to South Carolina. After Colonel Butler was killed, members of his regiment marked each piece of lumber in a stack, removed them, dug his grave where the lumber stood, disposed of excess dirt, replaced each piece as it was. This was done under darkness, his body remaining there until removed to his native state. All this was done to keep the Mexicans from mutilating his body. The State of South Carolina gave every man in the Palmetto Regiment a medal, silver to the enlisted men, gold to the officers. Also the State of So. Carolina presented a gold jeweled sword to his oldest son, "William Loudon Butler as a tribute to the memory of his father, Pierce M. Butler, Colonel of the Palmetto Regiment in the War with Mexico 1847". Colonel Pierce M. Butler, by family tradition, served as governor of Florida for six months during Andrew Jackson's absence. While he would have been quite young at the time, and had later been somewhat discounted, some members of the family who have since passed on never ceased to insist that it was true. I have added this note for what it is worth, take it or leave it.

Children:

I. Behethland Butler, b. 1829, m. John Edmund Bacon;
II. Emmala Butler, b. 1831, m. Abner Perrin;
III. William Loudon Butler, b. 1835, served as a Major of the 19th Louisiana Volunteers, killed at Chickamauga, Sept. 20, 1863, while in command. The story of his death goes: Major Butler had sat under a tree, a private sat down beside him saying "I, sir, will sit between you and the enemy in order to shield you". Shortly thereafter the private was killed. Major Butler was killed later that day while leading the regiment into action.
IV. Pierce Mason Butler, b. 1835; m. Permelia Catherine Goode (See later).
V. Andrew Pickens Butler, b. 1838, m. Maria Burt;
VI. Edward Julian Butler, b. 1845, was killed at the battle of Malvern Hill, July 1, 1862. When his body was returned home his mother died from shock - they are buried in the same grave.

Captain Pierce Mason Butler, born 1835, Edgefield, Edgefield County, S.C.; died Minden, Webster County, La.; married July 17, 1862, Edgefield, S.C., Permelia Catherine Goode (Kate), born Sept. 29, 1844, Edgefield, S.C.; died Oct. 11, 1869 Minden,

Webster County, La., daughter of Samuel Freeman Goode and
Mary A. Gomillion. Captain Butler was graduated June 1860 from
North Carolina College, Chapel Hill, N.C. He was a planter and
soldier and a member of the Protestant Episcopal Church. He
commanded a company of the Edgefield Hussars in Hampton's
Legion during the Civil War.

Children:
I.   Edward Julian Butler, b. Apr. 15, 1863, d. 1864.
II.   Pierce Mason Butler, M.D., b. Jan. 14, 1865, d. 1933, a
      Bachelor.
III. Samuel Goode Butler, b. Oct. 26, 1866; m. Sara Shapard
      (See later)
IV.   Julian Deval Butler, M.D., b. March 11, 1869, m. Cleora
      Gilmer.
      Children:
      1. Nelda Butler, b. Aug. 14, 1903; m. Francis Carrigan.
      2. Jewell Butler, m. John McCullough.

Samuel Goode Butler, born Oct. 26, 1866, Minden, Webster
County, Louisiana; married Nov. 6, 1895, Shelbyville, Bedford
County, Tenn., Sara Shapard, born May 31, 1874, Shelbyville,
Tenn.; daughter of David Green Shapard and Martha Jane Allen.
Mr. Butler was educated at Minden and Nashville and is a retired
Pharmacist, residing in Shelbyville. He is a Methodist.

Children:
I.   Samuel Goode Butler, b. Sept. 8, 1896;
II.   Sara Butler, b. Jan. 12, 1898, m. Andrew J. Grigsby, Jr.
III. Martha Butler, b. Dec. 27, 1899, m. J. Lawson Hutton;
IV.   Catherine Permelia Butler, b. Jan. 22, 1907;
V.   Pierce Mason Butler, b. Feb. 15, 1910; m. Susan C.
      Jones (See later).
VI.   Dorothy Allen Butler, b. Dec. 8, 1916, m. Porter Hick-
      erson.

Pierce Mason Butler, born Feb. 15, 1910, at Shelbyville,
Tenn.; married January 14, 1939, at Huntsville, Madison County,
Ala., Susan Cheatham Jones, born Apr. 5, 1917, at Nashville,
Tenn., daughter of Foster Jones and Harriet Clark Barton. Mr.
Butler was educated in Shelbyville and Nashville and has an LLB
degree. He is an Accountant and a member of the Presbyterian
Church. To Mr. Butler is due credit for furnishing this interest-
ing account of his family.

Children:
I.   Susan Barton Butler, b. Oct. 26, 1942;
II.   Sara Shapard Butler, b. Apr. 26, 1947;
III. Julia Duval Butler, b. Nov. 19, 1953.

HILL and HARRINGTON of NORTH CAROLINA
(Continued from Vol. II, p. 168, Southside Virginia Families)

Charles Harrington was born about 1720, and died after May, 1771 and before July 19, 1773, at Chatham, N.C. In 1747, in Fayette District, N.C., he married Agnes, the daughter of Tabitha and Robert Hill. She was born about 1730 and died in Chatham about 1797.

Charles Harrington, Sr., was wounded in the Battle of Alamance, May 1771, and died somewhat later of his wounds. His wife Agnes was "billed" for caring for one of the Regulators, referred to in the "true bill" as "..idle, loose, and dissolute person of evil character" as of 19 July, 1773, when the government was still making it unpleasant for any Regulators who yet remained in the Colony.

Children:

I.   John Harrington, b. ante 1743, m. Frances (Fanny) Bust;
II. Drury Harrington, b. 1751, m. Rachel Petty;
III. Whitmel Harrington, b. 1799, m. Sarah Rowe;
IV. Thomas Harrington, b. 1760, m.   Higdon;
V.   Charles Harrington, Jr., b. 1748, m. Patience Braysdale;
VI. Philamon Harrington, b. cr. 1757, m. Frances Harmon; (See later)
VII. Mary Harrington, b. ante 1756, m. Abner Landrum;
VIII. Tabitha Harrington, m. Robert Johnson.

Philamon Harrington was born about 1757 probably in Edgecombe County, N.C., and died between May 8, 1803, when his will was dated, and Aug. 1803, when it was probated at Chatham, N.C. It was probably there that he married, about 1780, Frances (Fanny) Harmon, born about 1760. (She had six children under 16 by 1790). She died sometime after 1822, when she had signed a deed in Hickman County, Tenn..

Several sons of Charles Harrington were patriots or soldiers in the Revolution, and Philamon is known to have furnished supplies as is shown by cancelled vouchers. (Book C, p. 100, #3720 Voucher 3079 - Book 1 - No. 4975- October 10, 1783)

Children, taken in order from Philamon's will:

I.   Nancy Harrington, b. cr. 1784, m. William Maddox (Mattocks).
II. William Harrington, b. cr. 1782 (67 years old in 1850 Hickman County census).
III. Polly (Mary) Harrington, b. cr. 1798, m. Enos Coleman (See later).
IV. Drury Harrington, b. 1788, m. Mary Maddox (Mattocks).
V.   Larany Harrington, b. cr. 1786, m. James McCaleb, Jr.
VI. Dempsey Harrington, b. cr. 1790. No information.

VII.   Robert Harrington, b. cr. 1797, m. Sallie Anderson.
VIII.   Elizabeth Harrington, b. cr. 1800, probably m.
       Tucker.
IX.   Sallie Merriman Harrington, b. July 1801, probably died
      young.
    Polly (Mary) Harrington, born in Chatham, N.C. about 1798,
and died about 1840 in Hickman County, Tenn., was the daughter
of Frances Harmon and Philemon Harrington. In 1814 or 1815 in
Hickman County she married Enos Coleman who was born about
1796 in either Wilkes or Ashe County, N.C., and died 1830 or
1831 in Hickman County, Tenn. He was a land owner and con-
stable.
      Children:
I.   John Coleman, b. cr. 1815
II.   Elizabeth Coleman, b. cr. 1815; twins, m. Evan Shelby.
III.   Ureula Euzitta Grisella Drucilla Coleman, b. cr. 1817,
       m. Harrington.
IV.   Zill Coleman, b. ca. 1819-1822, m. (1) Fannie Neal,
       (2) Mrs. Harriet McCurdy Lucas
V.   Ephraim Coleman, b. cr. 1823, was alive in 1847
VI.   Caledonia P. Coleman, b. May 7, 1825, m. Thomas H.
       Lancaster (See later)
VII.   Alexander Coleman, b. March 26, 1827, m. (1) Mary
       Ann McCune, (2) Sallie Jean Foster
VIII.   James W. Coleman, b. March 26, 1827, twins, m.
       Louisa Tharkington?
IX.   Emiline Coleman, b. cr. 1829, m. D. B. Griggs
X.   Caroline Coleman, b. cr. 1829, twins, d. before 1830.
    Caledonia P. Coleman was born May 7, 1825, in Hickman Co.,
Tenn., and died Oct. 12, 1899, at Temple, Texas. She was a
daughter of Mary Harrington and Enos Coleman. About 1845 she
married Thomas Hamilton Lancaster, who was born Sept. 8, 1813,
in Franklin County, N.C., and died April 5, 1867, near Temple,
Texas. He was a rancher and lived in Hickman and Perry Coun-
ties, Tenn., and Bell Co., Texas.
      Children:
I.   Felix Napolen Lancaster, b. Nov. 23, 1846, m. Margaret
       (Peggy) Bigham
II.   William Enos Lancaster, b. Dec. 2, 1848, d. Dec. 18,
       1852.
III.   James Hamilton Lancaster, b. Nov. 29, 1850, m. Alberta
       Haseltine Golden.
IV.   Benjamin A. Lancaster, b. Sept. 14, 1852, d. in infancy
V.   Lucinda Emmaline Lancaster, b. Jan. 21, 1854, m. Dan-
       iel Webster Moore.
VI.   Louisa Elizabeth Lancaster, b. Oct. 26, 1855, m. Thos.
       Franklin Childers.
VII.   Charlotte Caroline Lancaster, b. Nov. 18, 1858, m.
       Miniard H. Gilliam.
VIII.   Mary Catherine Lancaster, b. Nov. 18, 1858, twins, m.
       Dr. John Miller Phipps (See later).
    Mary Catherine, the daughter of Caledonia Coleman and Thom-
as Hamilton Lancaster, was born Nov. 18, 1858, near Temple,

Texas, and died April 18, 1918, at Austin, Texas. On Nov. 24, 1880, near Temple, she married Dr. John Miller Phipps, who was born Sept. 8, 1852, at Stony Point, Tenn., and died May 14, 1925. Dr. Phipps was educated at King College, Bristol, Tenn., and Jefferson Medical College in Philadelphia. He retired early from the medical profession and engaged in Real Estate in Temple.
Children:
I.   Ida May Phipps, b. Nov. 5, 1881, m. James Wm. Bonner.
II.   Georgia Gwendolyn Phipps, b. Nov. 11, 1883, m. Geo. Mahan Cruteinger.
III.   John Miller Phipps, daughter, b. April 9, 1888, m. James T. Ramage (See later).

John Miller Phipps Ramage, (Mrs. J. T.) whose present address is General Bruce Dr., Route 5, box 123, Temple, Texas, was born April 9, 1888, near Temple, Texas, where on Sept. 2, 1913, she married James Toliver Ramage, son of Carolina Robinson Towles and James Blakely Ramage, who was born July 27, 1887, near La Fayette, Ala., and died Oct. 25, 1950, at Temple, Texas. Mrs. Ramage was educated at N. T. S. T. College, Denton, Texas; Baylor College (Fine Arts) Belton, Texas; and Marks Conservatory, New York.

CLARK of SURRY and ISLE of WIGHT COUNTIES, VIRGINIA

by B. C. Holtzclaw

The tradition in the Clark family is that the original immigrant to Virginia was a Scotsman. If so, the name should properly be spelled Clarke, and many of the descendants of the family do spell it thus. However, others, including many of my own immediate family spell it Clark (without the "e"), and this is the way it is spelled in the Family Bible of my great-great-grandfather, William Clark (1763-1831).

Thomas[1] Clarke first appears in the records of Isle of Wight County, Va., June 14, 1662, when he, Richard Penny, and Thomas Parker appraised the estate of John Brewer (Chapman, "Wills", I, 15). He was dead by April 9, 1675, when Elizabeth, his relict, was appointed his administratrix, her securities being Richard Penny and Humphrey Marshall (id., p. 101). Richard Penny was the father and Humphrey Marshall was the nephew of Elizabeth Clarke. Elizabeth Penny is mentioned as early as Jan. 1, 1651/2, when William Jewry left a bequest to Elizabeth, daughter of Richard Penny (id., p. 1). She married (2) after Thomas Clarkes's death a Mr. Noyall, and as "Elizabeth Noyall" witnessed in 1695 the will of her brother-in-law, James Patridge (id., p. 6). The mother of Elizabeth and wife of Richard Penny was named Mary, as shown by a deed March 11, 1666/7 (Boddie "17th Cent. I. of W.Co.", p. 548). The Isle of Wight records show that Richard Penny lived for a time in Nansemond County and that he was active in the troubles connected with Bacon's Rebellion in Isle of Wight County. Richard Penny died in Isle of Wight County in 1694. His will, dated April 14, 1693, and probated June 9, 1694, mentions his eldest daughter Frances Patridge; daughter Elizabeth Noyell, grandchildren, Elizabeth and Thomas Clarke; son John; grandson Richard Penny; granddaughter Mary, daughter of John Penny; granddaughter Mary, daughter of Will Penny; Elizabeth, daughter of Will Penny; son Will; daughter Mary, wife of Robert Marshall; and grandson Richard Grey (Chapman I, p. 50).

Thomas[2] Clarke of Isle of Wight was born about 1650-55, and died about 1700. He married about 1670-75 Elizabeth, daughter of James Sampson, who was apparently a widow Brown at the time of the marriage, and had a son John Browne, b. 1669. Thomas[2] Clarke was probably the son of Thomas[1] Clarke and Elizabeth Penny, and identical with the grandson Thomas Clarke mentioned in Richard Penny's will. There is some slight doubt about this identification, as it would mean that Elizabeth Penny must have married Thomas[1] Clarke almost immediately after 1651, when as "Elizabeth Penny" she was left a bequest by William Jewry, must have borne her son Thomas very shortly, and that Richard Penny must

have been a very old man, around 80-85 years old, when he died
in 1694. However, the assumption seems reasonable. Thomas
Clarke and his wife Elizabeth Sampson had three children; Sampson, Thomas, and Grace Clarke, who married Robert Reynolds,
Jr., of Surry County. The proof regarding the family of Thomas[2]
Clarke and his wife, Elizabeth Sampson, is indirect, but seems
to be fully confirmed by the following records regarding the Samp
son and Barcroft families and their descendants:

(1) Charles Barcroft was the grandfather of Elizabeth (Sampson) Clarke. He was granted 300 acres in Isle of Wight County,
Feb. 10, 1637) C. & P., p. 80). On June 17, 1647, Elizabeth
Barcroft was granted 1200 acres of land in Isle of Wight County
(id. p. 166). This was Charles Barcroft's daughter, Elizabeth,
who married James Sampson, for her son, James Sampson, Jr.,
still held this 1200 acres in the Quit Rent Rolls of 1704. Mr. Barcroft claims land for importing Charles Barcroft for the 4th time,
indicating that he made frequent trips to England. Mr. Barcrofts
will was dated March 12, 1654, and leaves his property to his son
William and wife Magdalen (Chapman I, 3), but he apparently did
not die until 1661, for administration on his estate was granted his
son-in-law, George Moore, Sept. 23, 1661 (id., p.89). George
Moore married Jane, daughter of Charles Barcroft, so that the
latter had three children, William, Jane and Elizabeth. The son
William apparently died unmarried, as he disappears from the
records. George Moore, who married Jane Barcroft, was usually
known as Lieutenant George Moore, was born in 1632, and died
in 1714. From his will and other documents, he had four daughters:
(1) Magdalen Moore, who married Thomas Carter and had sons
George and Thomas Carter; (2) Eleanor Moore, who married
Richard Piland. (Richard died in 1695, his will mentioning his
wife and 5 children, two of these being George and Thomas Piland
mentioned in George Moore's will and two others probably being
James and Richard Piland, who appears in documents in Surry and
Isle of Wight in connection with their relatives, the Clarkes,
Browns, Wilsons, etc.); (3) Ann Moore married Thomas White
and had issue, Jane, John, Moore Thomas, William and Henry
White; and (4) a daughter who married a Williams and had sons
Samuel and John Williams mentioned in George Moore's will (Chap-
man, Wills, I, 79-80; "Marriages", pp. 9, 41, 54; D.B.1, p.161).

(2) James Sampson first appears in the records of Isle of Wight
County, in 1664, when he signed as "James Sampson of Steven-
heath Parish in County Middlesex, Shipwright" (D. & W. No.1, p.
21). On Dec. 3, 1666, he and his wife, Elizabeth, receipted
George Moore for Elizabeth's share of the estate of her father,
Charles Barcroft (id., p. 84). Elizabeth Barcroft Sampson was
still living March 15, 1669/70, when she witnessed the will of
Thomas Wooten (Chapman, Wills, I, 14), but died before her husband's death in 1689. James Sampson's will, dated Feb. 4, 1688/9
and probated in Isle of Wight County, April 9, 1689, leaves a
rather large estate to the following legatees: daughter Margaret,
wife of Nicholas Wilson; Mr. George Moore and his wife; son James
Sampson; "my daughter Clarke"; John Browne; and in a codicil
mentions that his deceased wife on her death bed requested that
he take notice that she left her two daughters, Margaret and Eliza-

beth, 300 acres apiece of the land, which the testator desired to
be done provided the law permitted (Chapman, Wills I, p. 43).
This land was obviously the 1200 acres granted to Elizabeth Barcroft in 1647. Apparently the law did not permit its disposal to
the daughters, for the son James Sampson still owned the 1200
acres in 1704, as mentioned previously. This son, James Sampson, Jr., died in Isle of Wight County in 1728. His will, dated
Nov. 30, 1727, and probated March 25, 1728, mentions a son
Barcroft Sampson, and daughters Margaret, Elizabeth, and Anne,
wife of Nicholas Derring (Chapman, II, 36). Margaret, daughter
of James and Elizabeth (Barcroft) Sampson, married Nicholas
Wilson, who died in 1696 (appraisement Dec. 9, 1696). This
couple had three children; James, Anne, and Sampson Wilson
(Chapman, Wills, I, 49; I. of W.D.B. I, p. 42). Margaret Wilson
died in Isle of Wight County about 1698, her nuncupative will
mentioning her son James, stating that Mr. Moore and James
Sampson should have nothing to do with her estate, and appointing
Thomas Clarke and John Browne her executors (Chapman, I, 54).
Thomas Clarke gave bond for the guardianship of James Wilson,
July 20, 1698 (D.B. 1, p. 264). The above records show that Elizabeth Sampson, the "daughter Clarke" of James Sampson's will,
was the wife of Thomas [2] Clark. Thomas [2] Clark died between
1698 and 1701. He may have been still living March 22, 1700,
when Thomas Clarke witnessed the will of John Page (Chapman I,
p. 61), though this Thomas may have been his son, Thomas[3]. He
was certainly dead by April 25, 1701, when Elizabeth Clark, widow, was granted administration on the estate of William Wilmott
(Chapman I, 114).

(3) John Browne, mentioned in James Sampson's will, was a
grandson, as he calls Nicholas and Margaret Wilson "uncle" and
"aunt" in a deposition made in 1694 (Boddie, 17 Cent., p.616).
The deposition shows that he was born in 1669. As James Sampson
had only the two daughters, Elizabeth Clarke and Margaret Wilson,
John Browne was probably a son of Elizabeth Clarke by a first
marriage. This view is confirmed by the will of Grace Reynolds,
widow of Robert Reynolds, Jr., in Surry County in 1711. The
will, dated Dec. 15, 1711, and probated Dec. 19, 1711, mentions
a bequest to Sarah Brown, a mulatto woman; leaves the bulk of
her property to her daughter Mary Reynolds; but in case Mary
should die, the property to go to her kinswomen, Hester Brown,
daughter of John Brown, Mary Clark, daughter of Sampson Clark,
and Susannah Clark, daughter of Thomas Clark (Surry D. & W.,
1709-14, p. 92). Thomas and Sampson Clarke, mentioned in the
will, were living together in one household in Surry County in
1699. The name Sampson indicates a connection with the Sampson family of Isle of Wight, and the above will connecting them
with John Brown strengthens the hypothesis. Thomas and Sampson Clarke were sons of Thomas[2] Clark and his wife Elizabeth
Sampson, and John Brown was their half-brother. Grace Reynolds
was probably a whole sister of the Clarkes and a half-sister of
John Brown. My reason for assuming this is that Robert Reynolds,
Jr., Grace's husband, first appears as a tithable in Surry County
in the family of his father, Robert Reynolds, Sr., in 1692, which
would put his birth in 1675 or 1676. The Clarke brothers were

both tithables and presumbably of age in 1699, which would put
their births around 1675 and 1677. Grace Reynolds was probably
somewhat younger, since she married a man born about 1675-6.
She was apparently, therefore, a daughter of Thomas[2] Clarke
and Elizabeth Sampson.

The relationship is further confirmed by the fact that Thomas[3]
Clarke, in his will in 1728 which will be cited below, states that
Nehemiah Joyner was to occupy some of the Clark land during the
life of his (Nehemiah's) wife. Nehemiah Joyner married Elizabeth,
daughter of John Brown, so that if the above hypothesis is correct,
she was Thomas[3] Clark's half-niece. John Brown died in Surry
County in 1714, his inventory being handed in by his widow, Elizabeth Brown, June 6, 1714. He left one son and four daughters,
Sylvester Brown, Hester Brantley, Grace, wife of John Warren,
Elizabeth, wife of Nehemiah Joyner, and Susannah Brown, as
shown by the following records: (1) Bertie County, N.C., D.B.
"C", p. 168, shows that in 1727 Susannah Brown, John Warren
and Grace his wife, and Sylvester Brown of Bertie County made
a deed of gift to their sister Elizabeth Joyner of all their right
to 256 acres granted July 28, 1713, to "John Brown, our father,
deceased". (2) The will of Hester Brantly, probated in 1727 in
Surry County, Va., mentions her daughters Priscilla and Elizabeth; sisters Elizabeth Joyner and Grace Warren; and appoints
James Wilson and James Piland executors (D. & W. 1715-30,
p. 274). This is obviously the "kinswoman", Hester daughter of
John Brown, mentioned in Grace Reynold's will. The connection
with the Sampson and Barcroft families is further shown by the
names of the executors of Hester Brantly. James Wilson was a
son of Margaret (Sampson) Wilson, and James Piland was a grandson of George and Jane (Barcroft) Moore. (3) That the sister,
Elizabeth Joyner, in the above records was the wife of Nehemiah
Joyner, is shown by a deed in Isle of Wight County May 16, 1729,
in which Nehemiah and Elizabeth his wife deeded land to Abraham
Stevenson (D.B. 4, p. 148).

Sampson[3] Clarke, son of Thomas[2] and Elizabeth (Sampson)
Clarke, moved to Surry County, where he was living as head of a
household in 1699 along with his brother, Thomas[3] Clarke. Sampson is shown alone in the tithables of 1700-1702, his brother having temporarily moved back to Isle of Wight County. He was executor of Grace Reynolds (mentioned above as a sister) and handed
in an account of her estate Dec. 17, 1712 in Surry County. (D. &
W. 1709-14, p. 130). After this he disappears from the records
of Surry County. In addition to his daughter Mary, mentioned in
in Grace Reynolds' will, he was almost certainly the father of
James Sampson Clark, who married Joyce --------, and died
in Surry County in 1752. His will, probated in 1752, mentions his
wife, Joyce, and children; Lucy, Ann, Patty, Sampson, William,
James, Mary, Elizabeth, Sarah and Mary. The widow, Joyce Clark,
died in Surry County in 1775. Her will, dated July 28, 1773, and
probated Feb. 28, 1775, mentions her sons Sampson and James;
daughters Mary White, Elizabeth Gwaltney, Lucy Harris, Martha
Lancaster, and Winny Davis; grandchildren William, James, and
Sampson Clarke and Lucy Thompson; and makes James Davis
her executor. Some of the descendants of James Sampson Clarke

and his wife Joyce were as follows:

(1) Their daughter, Winifred Clarke, married James Davis; their daughter Mary Davis married James Gwaltney, Jr.; William Gray Gwaltney was a son of this couple, and by his wife Sarah Holland, he had a daughter, Oceana Winifred Gwaltney, who married Samuel Edwin West; and this last couple were grandparents of Mr. James G. W. MacClamroch of Greensboro, N.C.

(2) Sampson Clarke, son of James Sampson and Joyce Clarke, died in Surry County in 1778. His will, dated June 10, 1776, and probated Feb. 24, 1778, mentions sons William and James Clarke; daughters Mary, Sarah, and Anne; wife Martha and Thomas Gwaltney, exrs. The following statement regarding Sampson Clarke and his descendants was made by Miss Polly Clarke about 1880, when she was about 85 years old, to her nephew George T. Clarke (grandfather of Ashton W. Clarke of Newport News, Va.):

"Sampson Clarke, son of James Sampson Clarke, was my grandfather. His wife was Patsy (Martha) Bell, a sister of Benjamin Bell; and his children were William Clarke, James Clarke, Polly Parsons wife of Joe Parsons, Annie Parsons wife of Henry Parsons, and Sallie Clarke. He lost his life in the Revolution. I don't know whether or not he died or was killed. I have heard my grandmother say that he came home once on a furlough, returned to the army, and never came back any more. James Clarke (son of Sampson Clarke) was the father of Col. James S. Clarke. William Clarke (son of Sampson) was my father. His wife, my mother, was Sallie Gwaltney, daughter of Patrick Gwaltney and Millie his wife. My father's and mother's children were Sampson Clarke, Champion Clarke, Wilmouth Clarke, Willis Clarke, Polly Clarke, Watson Clarke, William Clarke, Ann Rogers wife of John Rogers, Patrick Clarke, Fielding Clarke, Merit Clarke, Simmons Clarke, and James Clarke. My brother Willis Clarke's wife was Zillah Delk, daughter of James and Martha Delk. Their children were two girls that died unnamed, George Talbert Clarke, and Sarah Virginia Gwaltney, wife of Leonard H. Gwaltney." Mr. George T. Clarke adds to the above account: "William Clarke (son of Sallie Gwaltney Clarke) married Mrs. Ann Blow, widow of Henry Blow, and had one daughter, Martha Ann Clarke, who married William W. Parsons and had eight children. ------ Patrick Clarke, (son of William and Sallie Gwaltney Clarke) married Rhoda Williams and died without children. "

(3) Miss Polly Clarke, in the statement quoted above, mentions in the first paragraph that her great-grandparents were James Sampson and Joyce Clarke, and that they had the following children: Sampson Clarke, James Clarke, Sallie Thompson wife of Joel Thompson, Rebecca Lancaster wife of James Lancaster, Winnie Davis wife of James Davis, Mollie White wife of William White, Patsy Pendleton, Lucy Harris wife of Harman Harris, and a daughter who married a Pleasants.

(4) Miss S. Elizabeth Clarke, Route 3, Box 8, Washington, N.C., wrote me in 1933 that she was a descendant of James Simpson Clarke (b. March 12, 1797), who was son of James Sampson Clarke (born in Virginia, died in 1820 in North Carolina). Mrs. Duncan McLeod Moore (Elizabeth Clarke), P.O. Box 747, Washington, N.C., another descendant, writes that James Simpson

Clarke married Martha Ann Elizabeth Lanier, and that the tradition was that James Sampson Clarke and a brother William came to Pitt County, N.C., from Virginia. This James Sampson Clarke, who died in 1820 in North Carolina, was probably son of James Clarke, son of James Sampson and Joyce Clarke.

Thomas[3] Clark, son of Thomas[2] and Elizabeth (Sampson) Clarke, was brobably born about 1677-78. He first appears in the family of his brother Sampson Clarke in Surry County in 1699, but moved back to Isle of Wight County for a few years thereafter. He was married by August 29, 1700, when he and his wife Susannah witnessed a deed from Rebecca Gutridge of Isle of Wight County, to John Prison of Surry (Surry D. & W. 1694-1709, p. 215). Thomas Clarke was an appraiser of the estate of John Wilkton in Isle of Wight County August 9, 1701 (Chapman, I, 60), and is shown as a Cornet in that county in 1702, in a list of magistrates and militia who prepared an address of loyalty to Queen Anne of England (Boddie, 17th Cent., p. 169). There is no present clue to the maiden name of Susannah, wife of Thomas[3] Clarke, except the bare possibility that she was a daughter of George Williams of Isle of Wight County, who in his will, dated Aug. 26, 1737, and probated Feb. 25, 1744, leaves his property to his wife Elizabeth; sons George, Thomas, and Roland; and a plantation to his grandson Thomas Clark (who may have been Thomas[4] Clark, son of Thomas[3]). Thomas Clark deeded this land in Isle of Wight County to Nicholas Williams Oct. 13, 1748. I am not at all sure, however, that this Thomas Clark was identical with the son of Thomas[3]. All the evidence points to this George Williams as being a son of a Roland Williams, who died in Isle of Wight County in 1679, and left two children, George and Mary, both of whom were minors and left in the guardianship of friends. Now we have mentioned that Susannah, wife of Thomas[3] Clark, was married to him by 1700, and it is difficult to see how a boy who was under guardianship in 1679 could have had a daughter who was married just 21 years later. All that can be said is that it is barely possibly that Susannah, wife of Thomas Clark, was a daughter of this George Williams. In favor of the hypothesis is the fact that if the Thomas Clark of George Williams' will was not Thomas[4] Clark, son of Thomas[3] and Susannah, it is hard to tell who else it could have been, for there is no other Thomas Clark revealed by the records from 1744-48, except Thomas[4].

Thomas[3] Clark moved back to Surry County by 1713, for Thomas Pittman of Isle of Wight deeded to Thomas Clark of Surry, planter, 150 acres in Lawnes Creek Parish Nov. 17, 1713 (D. & W. 1709-14, p. 164). He remained in Surry County until November 19, 1723, when he deeded the above land to Thomas Morland of Isle of Wight, and his wife Susannah relinquished her dower in it (D. & W. 1715-30, p. 501-2). The family then moved to Bertie County, N.C., just across the border from Isle of Wight Co., Va., and Thomas[3] Clark died there in 1728. The will of Thomas Clarke, dated April 25, 1728, leaves a bequest to his son Thomas Clarke; leaves the rest of his estate to his wife, and at her death or marriage to be divided among his 9 children, Thomas, Elizabeth, Mary, Lewis, William, John, Matthew, Grace and Bridget; mentions his two plantations on the county line adjoining Thomas Boykin, and that his wife is not to falsify the promise made to Nehemiah Joyner that he should possess some of the land during his (Nehemiah's) wife's life; appoints his wife and son Thomas executors; witnesses, Nehemiah Joyner and Ellis Braddy (N.C. Wills to 1760, Bertie County, Vol. VI., p. 51, at Raleigh). The wife Susannah Clark was still living on Feb. 13, 1732/3, when she deeded 50 acres near the county line adjoining Thomas Boykin to James Joyner (probably a son of Nehemiah and Elizabeth Brown Joyner) (Bertie Co. D.B. "D", p. 29).

Thomas[4] Clark, son of Thomas[3] and Susannah Clark, was born in Isle of Wight Co., Va., about 1702-5, and died in Southampton Co., Va. in 1752. He married Sarah Norwood, daughter of Richard and Elizabeth Norwood of Isle of Wight Co. (for her ancestry see V.H.G. pp. 333ff). Thomas Clark's will, dated Dec. 1, 1750, and probated in Southampton Co. Feb. 13, 1752, leaves a rather large personal estate and considerable areas of land in Lunenburg Co., Va., to his wife Sarah, daughter Frances, and sons John, James, Jesse, Jordan Thomas, and Carter Clark (Southampton W.B. "A" p. 72). All the sons moved to Lunenburg Co., Va. (later Mecklenburg Co.) almost immediately after their father's death. James Clark married Hannah --------- and died in Mecklenburg Co. in 1785, while his wife Hannah died in the same county in 1809, both their wills being extant in the Mecklenburg records. Their children were: (1) Sarah Clark who married Abel Farrar Aug. 11, 1789; (2) Elizabeth Clark who m. David Holmes Jan. 15, 1790; (3) Jordan Clark; and (4) Diana Clark who married George W. Brame April 9, 1804, and had a son James H. Brame mentioned in her mother's will. Jesse Clark died unmarried in Mecklenburg Co. in 1770, his will, dated Dec. 24, 1769, and probated March 12, 1770, leaving all his property to his brothers John, James and Carter Clark (W.B. I, p. 59). Jordan Thomas Clark apparently died unmarried in Mecklenburg Co. in 1767, and on April 14, 1767, John, James and Carter Clark deeded to Jesse Clark a negro belonging to the estate of Jordan Thomas Clark (Mecklenburg D.B. 1, p. 459). Carter Clark, the youngest of his brothers, was an Ensign and later a Lieutenant in the Mecklenburg Co. mil. in 1778, during the Revolution, and married Martha Farrar in Mecklenburg Co., Nov. 9, 1778. He died in Mecklenburg Co. in 1828, his will, dated Dec. 13, 1827, and probated Jan. 21, 1828, showing the following children: (1) Frances Clark; (2) Lucy Clark, (3) Jesse Clark (b. 1781-2); (4) Sarah Clark m. Martin Jones; (5) Elizabeth O.R. Clark m. Milton Robinson; (6) Thomas N. Clark, deceased when his father made his will, leaving a widow Wilmouth Clark; and (7) George N. Clark.

John[5] Clark, son of Thomas[4] and Sarah (Norwood) Clark, was born in Isle of Wight Co., Va. The date of his birth was 1728 according to the D.A.R. Line of Mrs. Hattie Nisbet Latta, a descendant of his daughter, Sarah (Clark) Harvey, who joined the D.A.R. many years ago on John Clark's record as a Revolutionary soldier in South Carolina (D.A.R. Lineage Book, Vol. XX, p. 39). John Clark died in Edgefield County, S.C. in 1794. His will shows that his wife was named Judith and a series of notes made over 75 years ago on the Clark and Harvey families by

Rev. Thomas Boykin, a descendant, gives her maiden name as Mallett. The notes include a letter written by John and Judith Clark's grandson, Judge James Clarke (b.1798) of Atlanta, Ga., and the information about Judith's maiden name no doubt came from Judge Clarke. The statement in the notes was confirmed by a great-granddaughter, Mrs. Fannie Keene, who stated that Judith, wife of John Clark, was French, that she was named Mallett, and that her father was Etienne Mallett. Judith Mallet, daughter of Etienne (Stephen) and Olive (Magdaleine (Salle) Mallet was born Sept. 2, 1736 at the Huguenot colony at Manakintown, then in Goochland Co., Va. The father, Stephen Mallett, moved to Lunenburg Co., Va., about 1750, and Judith Mallett and John Clark were probably married there about 1755 (for further ancestry, see the Mallet and Salle Families). Mr. Boykin's notes further state that John Clark had a brother named Carter Clark, who lived in Mecklenburg Co., Va., which further confirms the connection of this Clark family with Thomas[4] Clark and his sons, mentioned in the preceding paragraph.

John[5] Clark first appears in the Virginia records in 1736, when his uncle, William Norwood, left him land in Isle of Wight Co., as as small child. The land fell into Southampton Co. on the organization of that county, and in 1763, as "John Clark of Lunenburg Co.", he deeded the land away. Between April 14, 1767, when he and his brothers James and Carter deeded the negro from Jordan Thomas Clark's estate to Jesse Clark, and Dec. 3, 1767, John Clark moved from Mecklenburg Co., Va., to Granville Co., S.C. I(later Edgefield Co.). On the latter date John Clark of Granville Co., S.C. sold Carter Clark of Mecklenburg Co., Va., 300 acres on Allen's Creek in Mecklenburg Co. (Mecklenburg D.B. 2, p. 5); and on Nov. 12, 1770, no doubt in connection with the settlement of his brother Jesse's estate, John Clark of Granville Co., S.C., appointed James Clark his attorney for collecting debts in Mecklenburg Co. (D.B. 2, p. 540). According to his grandson, Judge James Clarke, John Clark settled about 16 miles north of Hamburg, S.C. on Stephens Creek. During the Revolution he served as a soldier in the South Carolina troops. In Rev. Thomas Boykin's notes, it is stated that John Clark was killed by marauders in his house in 1777; and my father's cousin, Ben Carter, told me that he had heard from his own grandfather, Benjamin W. Clark (another grandson of John Clark), that John was called to the door of his house and shot by Tories. This testimony seems certain, so far as John Clark's being shot and wounded is concerned. However, he could hardly have been killed, as his will, dated 1779 in Edgefield Co., S.C., was not probated until 1794, which must have been the date of his death. The will, dated July 7, 1779 and probated at the March Term, 1794, in Edgefield Co., leaves 8 negroes and considerable landed property to his wife Judith, her property to go later to sons Jeremiah and Jesse and "the child that my wife is now big with"; son Thomas; son John; son William; son James; daughter Frances Clark; daughter Rebeckah Clark; and appoints the wife Judith and son Thomas executors. It is possible that John Clark died from his wounds in 1779, and that the will was not probated until 1794, possibly on the death of his wife. However, there was a Judith Clark who died in Edgefield Co. in 1815, her estate being administered by John Adams and payments made to Willoughby and Elizabeth Clark, minors, under the guardianship of Thomas Dozier. This may possibly have been Judith, wife of John Clark, and the minor Clark children may have been her grandchildren, children of Jeremiah or Jesse Clark. John Clark's will does not mention the eldest daughter, Sarah Clark, who had already married James Harvey at the time the will was written. However, Sarah is a well attested daughter, being mentioned in the Boykin notes, and also by Judge James Clark in 1876, he being both her nephew and her husband's great-nephew. The Boykin notes also mention a daughter Elizabeth, who was probably the unborn child mentioned in John Clark's will. Of the other children, Thomas lived and died in Edgefield Co., S.C., and so apparently did John. James Clark moved to Green Co., Ga. with his brother William, and died there. According to the Boykin notes, either Elizabeth or Frances married a Mr. Christopher, while Rebecca married an Ousley and lived in Auburn, Ala.

Sarah [6] Clark, daughter of John and Judith Clark, married prior to 1779 James Harvey, son of Thomas and Rachel Harvey, who was born in Virginia about 1755 and died in Hancock Co., Ga. in 1807. Sarah (Clark) Harvey died in Hancock Co. in 1813. James Harvey, like his father Thomas Harvey and his brothers, John, Evan, Michael and Richard Harvey, served in the Revolution in South Carolina and Georgia (see Harvey Family), and received land-grants in Georgia for his Revolutionary services (see D.A.R. Lineage Book, XX, 39; Salley "Stub Indents to Rev. Claims in S.C."; Candler "Rev. Records of Ga.", II, pp. 555 and 677; Knight "Ga. Roster of the Rev.", p. 383; Smith "Story of Ga. and Ga. People", p. 617). James Harvey lived for several years in Wilkes Co., Ga., but was in Greene Co. in 1792, and by 1802 was in Hancock Co., where he died. His will was dated Jan. 16, 1807 and his appraisement occurred on Nov. 4, 1807 (Hancock Co. W.B. "C", pp. 429 and 432). The will mentions his wife Sarah and children Judith, Lucy, Mary, Rebecca, John, Elizabeth, Jeremiah, Richard, Epsy, Leroy, and Asenath; makes his wife Sarah, son-in-law Thomas Cooper and son John Harvey executors; and was witnessed by his brothers, John Harvey, Sr., and Michael Harvey, Sr. The inventory of Sarah (Clark) Harvey was dated Jan. 21, 1813 (Hancock W.B. "G", p. 158). I have no record of the descendants of the sons of James and Sarah (Clark) Harvey. Of the daughters, the eldest, Judith Harvey, married Thomas Cooper, Jr., of Eatonton, Ga., a prominent member of the Baptist Church and a wealthy man in his day. They were parents of Congressman Mark. A. Cooper of Georgia; ancestor of the Nisbet family; and grandparents of Rev. Thomas and Rev. Samuel Boykin, distinguished Baptist ministers of Atlanta, Ga. Of the other daughters, Lucy married Edmund Low; Mary married Bennett Hillsman; Rebecca married William Williams; Elizabeth married a Mr. Johnston; Epsy married Benjamin Rutherford; and Asenath died young.

William[6] Clark, son of John[5] and Judith (Mallett) Clark, was born in Lunenburg Co., Va. in 1763 and died in Putman Co., Ga. Jan. 16, 1831. On Oct. 23, 1792 he married (probably in Greene Co., Ga., where her father was living at the time) Mary Harvey, daughter of Evan Harvey and his wife Charity Powell, and niece of James Harvey who married his sister, Sarah Clark (see Harvey, Powell, and Williams Families). She was born Sept. 22, 1776, probably in Edgefield Co., S.C., and died Nov. 8, 1830 in Putnam Co., Ga., William Clark was a soldier in the Revolution under Gen. Elijah Clarke and on Oct. 1, 1784 was granted land in Washington Co., Ga. for his services (see also, Smith "Story of Ga. and the Ga. People", p. 614, where William Clark is cited as a soldier). This land fell into Greene Co. on the organization of that county and William Clark lived there for a number of years, but later moved to Putnam Co., Ga. and was one of the first settlers there. William and Mary Clark were faithful members of the Baptist Church, and built a large and commodious home in the Kinderhook Neighborhood in Putnam Co., where their youngest son, Benjamin W. Clark, later lived. I saw the house in my youth, but it has since been burned. Further details regarding William and Mary Clark and their family will be found in the biography of their son, Rev. John H. Clarke, in "Georgia Baptists, Historical and Biographical" by J. H. Campbell (p. 492 ff), but will be omitted here through lack of space. The children of William and Mary Clark were the following (dates of birth, etc. being taken from their Family Bible, which is now in my possession):

I. Jeremiah[7] Clark, b. Jan. 11, 1794, d. April 5, 1849, married four. times, his first wife being a Miss Henderson and his second a widow, Mrs. Abercrombie. He had the following children:
    1. Benjamin Clark, lived and died in Lumpkin Co., Ga.
    2. William Clark, Baptist missionary to Africa, who had two sons, Jeremiah, a lawyer in Texas, and Harvey, Baptist missionary to Japan.
    3. James Clark, never married
    4. Jeremiah Clark, Baptist minister in Texas
    5. Elizabeth Clark, m. Dr. Kingman of Jones Co., Ga.
    6. Emma Clark who m. (1) William B. Carter and (2) Mr. Moseley.

II. Rev. John[7] Harvey Clark, son of William[6] and Mary Clark, was born Nov. 30, 1796 in Greene Co., Ga., and died Apr. 23, 1867 at Henderson, Houston Co., Ga. He married in Putnam Co., Ga., Dec. 28, 1820 Elizabeth Kendrick (b. 1805, d. after 1878), daughter of James and Tabitha (Rogers) Kendrick (see Kendrick Family). He joined Enon Baptist Church in Putman Co. about 1828, and was one of the charter members of Ramoth, Baptist Church along with his wife on the organization of that church in 1836. He served for several years as a deacon at Ramoth, but was finally ordained to the Baptist ministry there Nov. 13, 1847. He was a pastor for several years in Putnam, Jones and Baldwin Cos., but moved to Houston Co., Ga. in 1854, and later served churches in that county, Macon, Dooly and Lee Cos. The children of Rev. John H. and Elizabeth (Kendrick) Clark were the following:
    1. James M. Clark, lawyer and judge, of Americus, Ga., m. Miss Williams and left issue.
    2. Mary Ann Clark, b. 1826, m. John P. Key (b. 1816) of Putnam Co. and had

- (1) John W. Key, b. 1843
- (2) James M. Key, b. 1845
- (3) Henry M. Key, b. 1847
- (4) Elizabeth W. Key, b. 1850
- (5) William Key, b. 1852
- (6) Howell Key, b. 1855
- (7) Mary Ann Key, b. 1858, m. Mark Green
- (8) Ella Key, b. 1860
- (9) Ada Key who m. Frank Freeman

3. Charity C. Clark, b. 1828, m. John Smith
4. Benjamin Clark, b. 1833, m. Miss Walker
5. Sarah Clark m. a Walker also
6. Judson J. Clark, b. 1839, d.s.p.
7. Isabella S. Clark, b. 1842, m. Mr. Henderson and had two sons, Lucius and James Henderson of Hawkinsville, Ga.
8. Frances Clark, b. 1847, m. Mr. Keene.

III. Judge James[7] Clarke, son of William[6] and Mary Clark, was born Aug. 28, 1798, and died after 1876 in Atlanta, Ga. He married (1) in 1822 Martha Alexander of Putnam Co., Ga. and had one son, William Alexander Clark, who died in 1834. Judge Clarke married (2) Permelia S. Wellborn of Putnam Co., a sister of Congressman Marshall S. Wellborn, by whom he had:

1. Elizabeth Clarke, m. Edward E. Rawson of Atlanta
2. Mary Clarke, m. Sidney J. Root of Atlanta
3. Judge John Thomas Clarke of Cuthbert, Ga., lawyer and distinguished jurist, who later became a Baptist minister
4. Amelia Clarke m. Moses Cole of Atlanta
5. Judge Marshall J. Clarke of Atlanta
6. Alice Clarke m. Dr. Joseph P. Logan of Atlanta
7. Eugenia Clarke, never married.

IV. Jesse[7] Clark, son of William[6] and Mary Clark, b. June 4, 1800, died young.

V. Charity[7] Clark, b. Dec. 15, 1802, d. Aug. 11, 1867 in Houston Co., Ga., married Ephraim Jones Kendrick (b. 1797 in Washington Co., Ga., d. 1854 in Houston Co., Ga.) son of Martin and Jane (Whitehead) Kendrick, of Putnam Co., Ga. (see Kendrick Family). They had:

1. William Kendrick, moved to Texas before the Civil war and left a family at Plantersville, Tex.
2. Sarah Kendrick, m. Allen Greene of Jones Co., Ga., and they moved to Texas also
3. Jane Malvina Kendrick m. Hardy Brown and left one daughter, Charity Frances Brown, who m. Capt. Anderson of Hawkinsville, Ga., and left several children
4. Mary Kendrick, m. Mr. Casham and had two children, Jones Casham (b. 1849) and Sarah Casham
5. Martin van Buren Kendrick, b. 1824, m. Eliza Brown (b. 1826) and had Francis Kendrick (b. 1848) and Hollis Kendrick
6. John Kendrick, b. 1829, m. Mary Hodges of Houston Co., and had one child, Theodosia Kendrick of Haw-

kinsville, Ga., who never married
7. Eliza Caroline Kendrick, b. 1832, m. Mr. Faulkner
   and had two children:
   (1) Frances Faulkner who m. Dr. Kezar of Elko, Ga.,
       (whose first wife was her aunt, Elizabeth Kendrick)
       and had:
       a. Lucille Kezar who m. Clinton D. Cooper of
          Perry, Ga., and had two children:
          (a) Clinton D. Cooper, Jr.
          (b) Frances Cooper
       b. Edna Kezar
       c. Ed Kezar
   (2) Eugenius Faulkner, never married
8. Civility Coates Kendrick, b. Sept. 14, 1834, m. John
   Henry of Hawkinsville, Ga. and had:
   (1) Edwin Jones Henry of Hawkinsville
   (2) Cora Elizabeth Henry
   (3) Susan Emma Henry
   (4) Amanda Louisa Henry who m. Loy Caldwell of
       Hawkinsville, Ga., and had several children, a-
       mong them Miss Emma Caldwell of Hawkinsville.
9. Permelia Elizabeth Kendrick, b. 1836, first wife of
   Dr. Kezar, left no children
10. Benjamin Campbell Kendrick, b. 1829, of Unadilla,
    Ga., m. (1) Mattie Cater of Perry, Ga., and (2) Nan-
    nie Peacock of Dooly Co., Ga.
    Children of first wife:
    (1) Eugenia Kendrick, m. Mr. Vaughan, a Methodist
        minister, lived in California and had several chil-
        dren
    (2) Elizabeth Kendrick, m. Judge Henderson of Vi-
        enna, Ga.
11. James Dawson Kendrick, b. 1843, m. Mildred Brown
    and had two sons:
    (1) Col. William Kendrick, U.S. Army, m. Mary
        Neal and had two daughters, one of whom, Neal
        Kendrick, lives in Atlanta, Ga.
    (2) Dawson Kendrick of Ft. Valley, Ga.
12. Amanda Louisa Kendrick, b. 1845, m. Henry Ander-
    son of Hawkinsville, Ga. and had two children, Susan
    Charity Anderson and Walter Anderson, both of whom'
    died unmarried.
13. Martha Virginia Kendrick, b. 1847, died young

VI.   Evan[7] Harvey Clark, son of William[6] and Mary Clark,
       b. June 25, 1806, died young.
VII.   Benjamin[7] Williams Clark, son of William[6] and Mary
       Clark, was born in Putnam Co., Ga., July 9, 1810, and
       died there July 4, 1886, while attending services at Ramoth
       Baptist Church, of which he and his first wife were char-
       ter members in 1836, and of which he had been a deacon
       since 1848. During the War between the States he went
       to defend Atlanta among the old men and boys called up
       by Gov. Brown at the last for that purpose. Benjamin W.

Clark married (1) Oct. 25, 1832, Julia Caroline Kendrick (b. 1813, d. Jan. 19, 1850), daughter of James and Tabitha Rogers Kendrick of Putnam Co. (see Kendrick Family) He married (2) Sept. 2, 1851, Permelia A. Haughton (b. 1813, d. April 1, 1885). By his second marriage, he had one son, Benjamin Willis Alexander Clark, b. Nov. 12, 1855, who died unmarried as a young man. Benjamin W. Clark lived all his life in the home and on the plantation of his father, William[6] Clark, and is buried in the Clark family burying ground there, along with his two wives, his father and mother, William and Mary Clark, and his first wife's parents, James and Tabitha Kendrick. A tablet to his memory stands in Ramoth Church. By his first marriage to Julia Caroline Kendrick, Benjamin Williams Clark had the following children:

1. Mary Etta[8] Clark, b. Oct. 28, 1833, d. Oct. 2, 1926, m. May 1, 1849, Henry Macon Holtzclaw (b. Dec. 29, 1826, d. April 6, 1892). Her descendants are given in "The Genealogy of the Holtzclaw Family", published in 1936.
2. William[8] Clark, M.D., b. Aug. 31, 1835, d. Aug. 15, 1862, while serving in the Confederate Army as a surgeon, m. Oct. 18, 1859, Annie E. Williams. They had two children:
   (1) William Augustus Clark, b. Oct. 25, 1860, of Jeffersonville, Ga. and had a son, Gus Clark, Jr.
   (2) Annie Clark, died unmarried
3. Virginia[8] Ann Judson Clark, b. Feb. 10, 1838, d. in Atlanta, Ga., in her late eighties; m. (1) Dec. 19, 1854, in Putnam Co., Ga., George W. Walker, by whom she had:
   (1) Julia Walker, m. Mr. Allen and had three children,:
      a. Emily Allen, wife of Dr. Hull of Atlanta, Ga.
      b. George Allen
      c. Virginia Allen
   (2) Linda Walker, m. George Sullivan and had two sons, Clark and Neal Sullivan
   (3) Georgia Walker, died young.
   Virginia A. J. Clark m. (2) June 8, 1864, in Perry, Ga., Dr. Leonidas D. Carpenter and moved to Atlanta. Their children were:
   (4) Robert Carpenter, married but had no children
   (5) William Carpenter, died unmarried
   (6) Henry Eugene Carpenter, who m. Annie Bond, of Montezuma, Ga., and had 5 children.
4. Adeline[8] Elizabeth Clark, b. April 24, 1841, died about 1900-1905 near New York City, m. Oct. 26, 1865 William Bennett Carter, Jr., a Kendrick descendant (see Kendrick Family). They had one son, Bennett Cook Carter, who m. Mamie Roquemore of Putnam Co. and had two children, Adeline Carter (now Mrs. Phillips of Cuthbert, Ga.) and Clark Carter.

5. Julia[8] Frances Clark, b. Feb. 21, 1844, in Putnam Co., Ga., d. Feb. 1885 in Atlanta, Ga., m. (1) May 23, 1866, Robert Holmes of Hayneville, Ga., by whom she had one child, Lena Holmes, who died young. She married (2) Jabez T. Richards of Atlanta, Ga., Sept. 8, 1874. Their children were: Erma Richards, Marietta Richards, Harold Richards and Lucy Richards.

6. Emma[8] Louisa Clark, born March 1, 1848 in Putnam Co., Ga., died in New Jersey, aged 93 or 94, married Dec. 15, 1869 Henry L. Cook of Eatonton, Ga., who died September 14, 1885, in his 39th year. They had two children:

(1) Susie Cook who m. Thomas Fetherston and had:
   a. Thomas Cook Fetherston
   b. Frank R. Fetherston
   c. John Holtzclaw Fetherston
   d. George Cutler Fetherston
   e. Henry L. Fetherston
   f. Robert Fetherston
   g. Benjamin Clark Fetherston

(2) Addie Cook who m. Mr. Bayley and had two daughters. All these families live in New Jersey.

KENDRICK of GLOUCESTER CO., VA, and NORTH CAROLINA
by B. C. Holtzclaw

John[1] Kendrick was probably the progenitor of the family, being born approximately 1675-80 and dying some time after 1721 in King William Co., Va. He is shown in 1704 as the owner of 100 acres of land in Gloucester Co., Va. (VM 32, p. 282)1 on Aug. 16, 1708, he gave a power of attorney to Capt. Henry Harrison to recover a debt from Will Browne in Surry Co., Va. (D. & W. 1693-1709, p. 406); his daughter Mary was christened March 27, 1709 in Gloucester Co. (Abingdon Psh. Reg.); and on March 14, 1721, Henry Fox of King William Co. deeded to John Kendrick of Abdingdon Parish, Gloucester Co., land in King William Co. (Record Bk. 1, p. 34, King William).

William[2] Kendrick was born in 1704 and his wife, Sarah Jones, was born in 1715, according to the Family Bible record of their grandson, Richard Fox, now in the possession of Mrs. Rose Freeman Ferrell of Anson, Tex., a descendant. He was probably the son of John[1] Kendrick above. It is not improbable that a deed in Hanover Co., Va., dated May 21, 1730, from Henry Fox of King William Co., and Joseph Fox of Hanover Co. to William Hendrick of King William Co. for 400 acres on which Joseph Fox lived at the time (Records 1733-35, p. 208, Hanover) refers to William[2] Kendrick, as the names Hendrick and Kendrick were frequently confused in copying the old records. There were later Kendricks in Hanover Co., who were probably nephews of William[2] Kendrick and grandsons of John[1] Kendrick: Robert Kendrick, who is shown as early as 1761, was a Revolutionary soldier, born in Hanover Co. in 1747, who later moved to Mecklenburg Co., Va., and finally to Tennessee; the latter's brother, James Kendrick, who appears with him in numerous records in Mecklenburg Co., Va., and Abel Kendrick, another Revolutionary soldier, who was born in Hanover Co. in 1759, later moved to South Carolina, and finally to Georgia. Two of the children of William[2] Kendrick married Foxes, a fact which also contributes to the plausibility of the view that the above deed was to Kendrick rather than Hendrick. According to a very reliable family tradition, William Kendrick was a surveyor by profession. Years ago Miss Mittie Hook, a great-granddaughter of Isham Kendrick, youngest son of William, wrote me that she had an old hickory nut in her possession, carved with the name "William Kendrick", and she had been told that her ancenstor, William Kendrick, was a surveyor.

By 1735 William[2] Kendrick had moved to Isle of Wight Co., Va., where he witnessed a deed on Feb. 18, 1735, from William Bowers to Edward Morgan (D.B. 4, p. 518). He must have moved almost immediately to North Carolina, for on Nov. 20, 1744, he "proved his rights" for the importation of only 3 persons into the colony (N.C. Col. and State Rec., IV, 1705), probably himself, his wife, and his eldest son, James, who was born about 1734. On Feb. 2, 1739, he petitioned for 300 acres in Edgecombe Co., N.C., (same, IV, 446), which was granted him Feb. 22, 1739 (Grant Bk. 4, p. 109). On April 7, 1743 he sold this land to Edward Jones, who was probably his brother-in-law (Edgecombe D.B. 5, p. 149), and on April 11, 1743 was deeded land on Six Pound Creek by John Grant (same, p. 150), Edward Jones being a witness. This land fell into Granville Co. on the organization of that county and on March 25, 1759, he was granted 500 acres on Six Pound Creek in that county (Grant Bk. 11, 431; Granville D.B. "A", 267). Edward Jones died in Granville Co. in 1750, his will mentioning the following children: Sugars, James, Edward, Daniel, Sarah, Obedience and Rebecca Jones, and Priscilla Mason; he was from Isle of Wight Co., Va. and his wife was Abigail, daughter of John Sugars (Isle of Wight D.B. 5, p. 45; Chapman "Wills", II, 32). On Sept. 2, 1751, William Kendrick was deeded by John Martin 200 acres in Granville Co. from the estate of Edward Jones (D.B. "A", p. 540). The close association between Edward Jones and William Kendrick probably indicates that Edward was a brother of Sarah Jones, William's wife. If so, they were probably the children of Rebecca West, widow, of the Lower Parish of Isle of Wight Co., Va., who on Nov. 21, 1719, made a deed of gift to her four children, Edward Jones, Obedience Jones, James Jones ("when he is 20, he being 11 years old in February next"), and Sarah Jones ("she being 5 years old last July") (I. of W. Great Book, p. 311). There is so far no clue to the name of Rebecca West's first husband, Jones, nor her second husband, "West". The names Rebecca, Obedience, James and Sarah, all occur in the families of both Edward Jones and William Kendrick, which strengthens the above view. The deed shows that Sarah Jones was born in July, 1714, which makes a slight discrepancy, as 1715 is given as the birth-date of Sarah Jones Kendrick by her grandson, Richard Fox. However, this discrepancy does not seem too serious. There was an Edward Jones of Isle of Wight Co., who married Deborah, daughter of William Exum, and died in 1730, leaving among other heirs a son Edward and a daughter Sarah (Chapman, Wills, I, 60 and II, 53), but the family names do not correspond so well, so that it is probable that this older Edward Jones was an uncle of Edward Jones of Granville Co., N.C. and of Sarah Jones Kendrick.

William[2] Kendrick appears in numerous deeds in Granville Co., N.C. (D.B. "B", pp. 37, 250, 246, 388; "C" pp. 88, 440; "E", pp. 86, 88). He was apparently a Justice of Granville Co. in 1751, when he is styled "Gent." in a deed. His land fell into' Bute Co. (later Warren Co.) on the organization of that county, and William Kendrick died there in 1777. His will, dated Jan . 12, 1776 and probated at the May Court, 1777, in Bute Co., mentions children John, James, Mary, Sarah, Rebecca, and Martha (to each of whom he leaves 1 shilling, they being already married and probably previously provided for); grandson Benjamin Thornton; son Jones a plantation; son Isham a plantation after wife's death, and appoints wife Sarah and friend Capt. Philip Buford executors (Warren Co. W.B. 2, p. 119). Sarah Jones Kendrick died early in 1796 at the age of 81. Her will, dated May 23, 1793, and probated in Warren Co. at the Feb. Court, 1796, leaves most of her property to Benjamin Thornton, but directs that her clothing be divided among her three daughters, Mary Fox, Rebecca Nicholson, and Martha Wood (Warren Co. Book 8, p. 236). In addition to the 8 children mentioned in William Kendrick's will, there was a Benjamin Kendrick who witnessed deeds to and from William Kendrick in 1762 (Granville D.B. "E", pp. 86 and 88), who was probably another son and died before his father. The two eldest children James and John Kendrick, who were old enough to be in the Granville Co. militia in 1754 and were born about 1733-4 and 1735-6 respectively; the next child was Mary, who was born in 1738 (Family Bible); Benjamin was of age in 1762, and was apparently born about 1740. The daughter Martha was born in 1747 (Family Bible). Jones and Isham were the youngest children, Jones being born about 1750 and Isham about 1755. Of the children mentioned in the wills, there is no further record of Rebecca Nicholson. The daughter, Sarah, was living in 1776, when her father's will was written, but seems to have been dead at the time of her mother's will in 1793. She was probably the mother of the grandson Benjamin Thornton, mentioned in both wills. This Benjamin Thornton was probably the father of the Rev. Benjamin Thornton, an early Baptist minister is Georgia, whose biography in Campbell's "Georgia Baptists, Historical and Biographical" states that he was the son of Benjamin and Sarah Thornton and was born Aug. 15, 1801, in Warren Co., N.C. The other children of William[2] and Sarah (Jones) Kendrick will be treated below. In addition, there was a Martin Kendrick, closely associated with James[3] Kendrick, eldest son of William and Sarah, in Chatham Co., N.C. in later years, who may have been a son of William and Sarah not mentioned in the will. We shall devote a paragraph to him later. He was certainly a kinsman of James[3] Kendrick, as the name Martin appears later among James' descendants, as well as among the descendants of Jones[3] Kendrick, son of William and Sarah.

James[3] Kendrick, son of William[2] and Sarah (Jones) Kendrick was born about 1733-4, probably in Isle of Wight Co., Va. He was probably the eldest son of this couple, being the child brought into the Colony of North Carolina with them about 1735. He and his brother John were old enough to be in the Granville Co. militia Oct. 8, 1754, in the Great Muster for the French and Indian War (N.C. Col. and State Rec., Vol. 22, p. 373). This shows that they were over 16 years of age, but as their sister Mary was born in 1738, they were obviously born a few years earlier, James about 1733-4 and John about 1735-6. The tax-lists of Granville Co., N.C. shows James as a tithable in 1755 in William Kendrick's family, his brother John having probably moved elsewhere at this time. James must have married during this same year, 1755, Susannah, daughter of Israel and Sarah Roberson of Granville Co., for John Kendrick, their eldest son, was appointed constable in his father's militia district in Chatham Co., N.C. at the November Court, 1777, showing that he was of age, and probably born in 1756, certianly not later than that date.

Israel Roberson (Robertson, Robinson, Robyson), the father
of Susannah Kendrick, was born in Prince George Co., Va.,
about 1698-1700, as his eldest son, Matthew, was born in 1720,
and Israel himself was not too old to serve as an Ensign in the
Granville Co., N.C. militia in the General Muster Oct. 8, 1754
(N.C. Col. and State Rec., Vol. 22, p. 372-3). He served in the
same company, Capt. Richard Coleman's, as James[3] and John[3]
Kendrick, and the list of militiamen shows also Israel's sons,
Matthew (Sergeant), Israel, Jr., and John Robinson. Prince
George Co., Va. records indicate practically conclusively that
Israel Roberson and his brothers, John and Edward Roberson,
were sons of Nicholas Roberson of Bristol Parish and grandsons
of Matthew Marks of Martins Brandon Parish, Prince George
Co., thus connecting them with two of the founders of the first
Baptist Church established in Virginia (cf. Ryland, "The Baptists
of Virginia", pp. 2-5). Probably at the request of Matthew Marks,
in 1714 the General Assembly of the General Baptists of England
sent to Virginia the Rev. Robert Norden to become pastor of a
Baptist congregation, and at the Prince George Co. Court June
14, 1715, Robert Norden, "an Anabaptist preacher", took the
oath of allegiance, and Matthew Marks' home was authorized as
a meeting house for the Baptists (O.B. 1714-20, p. 20). At the
next court, July 12, 1715, "On the motion of Nicholas Robertson
it's ordered that his house be recorded a publick meeting house
for the Sext of Anabaptists" (p. 25). Matthew Marks had lived in
Charles City Co., Va. (later Prince George) at least since June,
1691, when he was summoned before the court for not going to
church, indicating that he was probably already a Baptist and
opposed to worshipping in the Established Church (Charles City
Orders, 1687-95, p. 348). He was a comparatively wealthy man
and was the owner of 1500 acres in Prince George Co. in 1704
(VM 28, p. 344). He died in Prince George Co. in 1719. The will
of Matthew Marks of Martins Brandon Parish, dated Aug. 15, 1719
and probated at Merchants Hope Oct. 13, 1719, leaves land to
Edward, son of Edward Marks; to John Robyson; to Israel and
Edward Robyson; to John Marks son of Israel Marks; to his daughter Mary Davenport; states that Robert Norden (the Baptist minister mentioned above) is to have a room reserved for him in
the house as long as he remains in Virginia and is to have the
plantation until Edward Marks comes of age; and appoints Robert Norden and John Avery executors (D. & W., 1713-28, p. 358).
An account of the estate in 1720 shows that the daughter was the
wife of George Davenport, and mentions a parcel of books "belonging to the Baptist minister, not belonging to Marks" (p. 470).
It is unfortunate that the will mentions no relationships except
the daughter, Mary Davenport. However, it seems practically
certain that the Marks and Roberson legatees were grandsons.
The legatee, Edward Marks, was the son of an Edward Marks
who died prior to 1714, his widow Martha in that year being the
wife of James Bell (O.B. 1714-20, p. 6). She was a sister of
William Santain, whose will, dated Dec. 31, 1716 and probated
May 14, 1717, mentions his wife; James Bell and Martha his
wife ("my sister"); and her children, Edward Marks and James

Bell (D. & W. 1713-28, p. 162). John Marks, the other Marks legatee, was the son of Israel Marks who died in 1718, and his wife Elizabeth, who was a daughter of Richard Pigeon, who also died in 1718 (D. & W. 1713-28, pp. 250 and 288). Edward Marks, Sr., and Israel Marks were almost certainly sons of Matthew Marks. The names Israel and Edward Roberson among the legatees, the fact that Israel Roberson's eldest son was named Matthew, and the fact that the three Roberson brothers were left together 200 acres of land (the same as Edward Marks and the daughter Mary Davenport), indicate very strongly that their mother was a daughter of Matthew Marks, who had predeceased her father.

That the three Roberson brothers were sons of Nicholas Robertson is, also, practically certain, for both John and Israel Roberson had sons named Nicholas, John Roberson witnessed a deed made by Nicholas Roberson in 1718, all four men lived in Bristol Parish, Prince George Co., and Nicholas Roberson is the only Roberson shown in the records who was of an age to have been their father. Nicholas Roberson first appears in the Charles City Co. records in Feb., 1687/8, when he recorded his mark for cattle (Charles City Orders, 1687/8, when he recorded his mark for cattle (Charles City Orders, 1687-95, p. 109), indicating that he was of age, so born about 1665-7. On April 21, 1690, he and Nicholas Darrell were granted jointly 289 acres of land (Patent Book 8, p. 55). We have indicated that his first wife was a daughter of Matthew Marks. His second wife was Jane Tillman, daughter of Roger and Susannah Tillman of Prince George Co. The will of Susannah Tillman, aged 69 years, was dated Nov. 19, 1716, and probated in Prince George Co. Mar. 12, 1716/17 (D. & W. 1713-28, p. 144). It mentions sons Thomas Parham, George Tillman, and John Tillman; daughters Jane Robinson and Christian Abernathy; granddaughter Mary Bethell; and grandson Robert Abernathy. Susannah Tillman's son, Thomas Parham, in his will dated Feb. 15, 1716/17 and probated May 14, 1717, mentions as legatees: Nicholas Robyson (100 acres of land), John Tillman, William Pettypool, Sr., sons Thomas and William Parham, daughters Amy Jones, Elizabeth Tucker, Phoebe, Susannah, and Jane, and wife Elizabeth (D. & W. 1713-28, p. 168). On May 12, 1718, Nicholas Robertson of Bristol Parish deeded the land left him by Thomas Parham to George Tillman, the land having originally been patented by Roger Tillman, father of George (same, p. 228), and Jane Robyson, wife of Nicholas, relinquished her dower in the land Nov. 14, 1721 (p. 501). The deed was witnessed by John Robyson and George Davenport (husband of Mary Marks). This is the last appearance of Nicholas Roberson in the records. Nicholas Roberson was probably the son of Edward Robinson and wife Ann of Charles City Co. This Edward Robinson was administrator of Francis West in 1679 (Charles City Orders, 1677-79, pp. 359, 390), and died late in 1689 or early in 1690, his wife Anne being appointed his administratrix (Chas. City Records, 1689-90, p. 86; Orders 1687-95, p. 274). Edward Robinson was the son of Christopher Robinson of Bristol Parish, then in Henrico Co., Va., who first appears in the records in 1642 in a grant to John

Ewens, Jr., in Charles City Co. (C. & P., p. 139), and on Feb. 23, 1652, was granted 600 acres of land in Henrico Co., Va. along with John Sturdevant (C. & P. p. 273). Christopher Robinson was dead by Aug. 31, 1663, when Francis Burrill gave bond for the administration of his estate (VM, 18, p. 196). On Oct.19, 1677, Edward Robinson and Anne, his wife, he being son and heir of Christopher Robinson, decd., late of Bristol Parish, Henrico Co., deeded the land he inherited to Nicholas Dyson and Richard Kennon (Henrico D. & W. No. 1, p. 25). Another son of Christopher Robinson was Christopher, Jr., who on June 4, 1681, receipted his mother, Mrs. Frances Burrell, for his inheritance from his father (same, p. 179). Henry Robinson, who witnessed the deed from Edward mentioned above, was probably another son.

Of the three brothers, John, Israel, and Edward Roberson, mentioned in Matthew Mark's will, Edward was probably the youngest, born about 1700-02. He was of age March 14, 1722/3, when Israel Robinson, Sarah his wife, and Edward his brother, deeded away the land left jointly to Israel and Edward by Matthew Mark's (D. & W. 1713-28, p. 967). Edward Roberson had a survey of land in 1772 in Prince George Co. which was confirmed to him by patent in 1726 (D. & W. 1713-28, p. 762; Va. Patent Bk. 13, p. 68). He appears to have moved to North Carolina, where he petitioned for land in 1739 and again in 1745, in Edgecombe Co. (N.C. Col. and State Rec., IV, 348). After this there is no further record of him. John Roberson, the eldest brother, was probably born about 1695-98. Chamberlayne's "Vestry Book and Register of Bristol Parish", shows the births of John Roberson's six children by his wife Mary as follows: (1) Nathanael, b. June 21, 1723, bapt. Aug. 21 (p.357); (2) Abraham b. July 21, 1725 (p. 357); (3) Frances b. Mar. 3, 1726/7 (p.358); (4) Mark b. June 23, 1729 (p.358); (5) Edward b. Dec. 22, 1731, bapt. April 23, 1732 (p. 359); and (6) Robert born June 10, 1734 (p. 360). John Robyson and Mary his wife on Feb. 6, 1719, deeded away the land that had been left him by Matthew Marks (D. & W. 1713-28, p. 384), and a survey of 250 acres was made for him in Prince George in 1722 (p. 762). During the years 1728-1750 he received land-grants in Prince George, Brunswick, and Lunenburg Cos., Va. (Patent Bk. 13, pp. 122, 457; 15, p. 135; 17 p. 123; 29, p. 238). John Roberson, Mary his wife, and his sons John and Nicholas appear in a number of deeds in Brunswick Co., Va. and apparently lived in that county for several years. Bell's "Sunlight on the Southside" shows that from 1748 to 1752 John Roberson and his sons, John, Nicholas, Abraham, Nathaniel, Mark, Edward and Robert, were all living in Lunenburg Co., and deeds to and from them show their residence there later in the 1750's. The son Abraham died there in 1762 (W.B. 2, p. 47). The son, Nathaniel, died in Mecklenburg Co., Va. in 1792, his will, dated June 14, 1792 and probated Oct., 1792, mentioning his wife Elizabeth, sons Benjamin, Mark and John, daughter Frances Robinson and her sons Elijah and Pleasant Robinson, daughter Keziah Johnson and her sons William and John Johnson, daughter Patty Robinson and her sons Charles and Leonard Robinson; and daughter Molly Paschall (Mecklenburg W.B. 3, p.128).

John Roberson, Sr., moved to Granville Co., N.C. some time about 1760 and died there in 1774. His will, dated April 8, 1773 and probated in Granville Co. at the May Court, 1774, mentions his daughter Sarah Short, sons John and Nicholas, Mark Roberson's youngest child, granddaughter Ruth daughter of Abraham Roberson, Robert Roberson, James Mitchell, Nathaniel Roberson, granddaughter Susannah Roberson, wife Mary; "my seven children", Sarah, John, Nicholas, Nathaniel, Frances, Mark, and Robert, residuary legatees after wife's death; Edward Roberson, Miles Williams and Charles Eaton, executors.

Israel Roberson, the father of Susannah wife of James Kendrick, by his wife Sarah had the following children recorded in Chamberlayne's "Vestry Book and Register of Bristol Parish, Va.": (1) Matthew b. Nov. 22, 1720, bapt. April 20, 1721 (p. 356); (2) John, b. May 8, 1723, bapt. Aug. 21 (p. 357); (3) Israel b. Nov. 14, 1725 (p. 357); (4) David b. Aug. 19, 1728 (p. 358); (5) Nicholas b. Sept. 12, 1731, bapt. Nov. 7 (p. 359); and (6) Charles b. July 24, 1733 (p. 360). In addition to the above 6 children, Israel Roberson's will shows that he had two other children, Susannah Kendrick, and George Roberson. The will names the above 6 children in the exact order of their births, then names Susannah Kendrick, and finally George, thus indicating that Susannah was the next youngest child, and George the youngest. This indicates that Susannah was born about 1735-6, and George about 1737-39. I do not know why the births of these last two children are not shown in the Bristol Parish Register, for Israel was still living there as late as 1739. It is possible that by the time of their birth, Israel had returned to the Baptist faith of his father and grandfather. Israel Roberson and David Williams were processioners in the parish in 1731 and 1735, and Israel and his brother John Roberson were processioners there in 1739 (Chamberlayne, pp. 55, 57, 77, 92, and 99). It is possible that a George Robinson, born Dec. 6, 1740, who is strangely recorded as son of Martha and Sarah Robinson, was really Israel's son, George. However, Israel's eldest son, Matthew, had a son named George, so that it seems somewhat more likely that Martha above was a corruption of the name Matthew, and that this George was Matthew's eldest son. There is no positive evidence of the maiden name of Sarah, Israel Roberson's wife, though it is possible that she was a Williams and sister of David, Charles, and George Williams, who were bringing children for baptism in Bristol Parish about the same time as the Robersons. Israel and Sarah had sons named David, Charles, and George, which were apparently not Roberson family names, and may indicate that they were named for these Williams men, their uncles.

We have alluded to the deed May 14, 1722/3, in which Israel Roberson, Sarah his wife, and his brother Edward sold the land left them by Matthew Marks (Prince Geo. Co. D. & W. 1713-28, p. 967). Israel Roberson had other surveys for land in that county in 1722 and 1726 (same, pp. 761 and 1026). From 1726 to 1749 Israel Roberson had grants of land in Prince George, Brunswick, and Lunenburg Cos., Va. and his sons Matthew and David in Lunenburg Co. (Va. Patent Bks. 13, p. 41; 14, pp. 83 and 309; 29, pp. 21 and 29; and 31, p. 151). Israel, however, never seems,

like his brother John, to have lived in Brunswick or Lunenburg
Co., though his sons Matthew and David lived in Lunenburg, Va.
for several years from 1748 to 1755 (Bell, "Sunlight on the South-
side", pp. 73, 167, 188; Lunenburg D.B. 3, p. 91 and 7, p. 128).
Israel Roberson seems to have moved directly from Prince
George Co., Va. to Edgecombe Co., N.C., where he was
granted 600 acres of land Nov. 24, 1744 (N.C. Col. & State Rec.,
Vol. IV, p. 708). This was the section of Edgecombe which later fell into Granville Co., N.C. and all his sons later joined
him in Granville. We have mentioned that Israel, Sr., was an
Ensign, his son Matthew a Sergeant, and his sons Israel, Jr.,
Nicholas and John privates in the Great Muster of Granville Co.
militia Oct. 8, 1754 (same, Vol. 22, pp. 372-3). Israel Roberson owned large areas of land in Granville Co., N.C. and appears in numerous deeds there from 1749 to 1759, three of them
deeds of gift to his sons Matthew, Nicholas and Israel (D.B.A,
p. 221; D.B. "B", pp. 352, 427, 469; D.B. "C:, pp. 130, 176,
631, 634, 635). The will of Israel Roberson, dated Dec. 4, 1758
and probated in Granville Co. Aug. 12, 1760 was not recorded in
the books there, but is original will No. 59 in the Clerk's Office.
It makes bequests to the son Matthew Roberson and Matthew's
daughter Mary; sons John, Israel and David Roberson, and David's son Israel; son Nicholas and Nicholas' daughter Abby; son
Charles and Charles' son Julius; daughter Susannah Kendrick;
son George Roberson property after the death of "Sarah Roberson my beloved wife the mother of George"; and appoints David
and George Roberson executors. The son George Roberson died
unmarried in 1761. His will, dated Aug. 22, 1761 and probated
at the Nov. Court, 1761, mentions his mother Sarah Robertson;
my brother Charles' son Julius; my sister Susannah Kendrick's
son John Kendrick; my brother David's son Matthew; my brother
Matthew's son George; my brother Nicholas' son Charles; my
sister Susannah Kendrick; my brother Israel's son Joel and daughter Sarah; and appoints "my brother Matthew Roberson and James
Kendrick" executors. The only other son of Israel and Sarah
Robertson who left a will was David, who moved to Tryon Co.,
N.C., and as "David Robertson" left a will dated July 8, 1771,
now on file in the Clerk's Office of Lincoln Co., N.C. It mentions his wife, Frances Robertson; children Matthew, Molly,
Israel, Isacc, Isham, James, David, Abner, Sally, John and
Betty Robertson; brother Charles Robertson and the latter's
youngest son, George. The brother Matthew Robertson was a
witness.

James[3] Kendrick, who married Susannah Roberson, was given
a deed of gift of land by his father, William[2] Kendrick, Mar. 4,
1758 in Granville Co., N.C. (D.B. "C", p. 440), but deeded this
land back to his father Feb. 8, 1762 (D.B. "E", p. 86). In the
same year, 1762, he was deeded land in Orange Co., N.C. (later
Chatham Co.) by William Churton (Chatham D.B. "C", p. 315),
and moved almost immediately to that county. He had landgrants
in Chatham Co. from 1778 to 1782 totaling over 1500 acres (N.
C. Grant Books 30, pp. 49, 63 and 156; Book 36, p. 452; Book
48, p. 11). He appears in numerous deeds in Chatham Co. from
1772 to 1784 (Book A, p. 83; Book B, pp. 100, 249, 250, 251,

477, 476; Book C, pp. 366 and 455). On April 26, 1783, he deeded
land to Burwell Kendrick, whom we shall see later to have been
a son (Book C, p. 481); and on April 9, 1784, he made a deed to
William Kendrick, calling William a son in the deed (Bk. C, p.
458). On Sept. 22, 1784, James Kendrick and his wife, Susannah,
in four deeds, sold all the remainder of their land in Chatham
Co. to Benjamin Watts (Bk. C, pp. 315-319), and moved almost
immediately to Wilkes Co., Ga., where James Kendrick appears
in the tax-list of 1785. The above four deeds were witnessed by
his son John Kendrick.

James[3] Kendrick had a fairly prominent public career in
Chatham Co., N.C. He was appointed a Justice of the county
Aug. 12, 1774 (N.C. Col. and State Rec., Vol. IX, p. 1027).
During the Revolution he was a captain of the Chatham Co. Militia in 1777 and 1778, and probably in later years, as shown by
the following excerpts from the Chatham Co. Court Minutes,
1774-79, which are preserved at Raleigh, unpaginated: (1) Aug.
Court, 1777 - James Kendrick is appointed assessor in District
No. 5; (2) Nov. Court, 1777, John Kendrick is appointed constable
in Capt. Kendrick's District; James Kendrick and John Thompson are appointed patrollers in District No. 5; (3) Feb. Court,
1778 - Capt. Kendrick's District is to be divided and John Thompson is appointed to administer the State oath in Capt. Kendrick's
District; (4) August Court, 1778, Friday, Aug. 15 - Ordered that
the clothing to be found by the different companies in the county
be proportioned as follows (here follows a list of 12 captains,
among them:) - James Kendrick's Company: 6 hats, 24 linens,
12 cloths, 12 shoes, 12 stockings. The North Carolina Revolutionary Accounts at Raleigh show numerous payments to James
Kendrick, some of them mentioning him as from Chatham Co.,
and practically all being allowed by the Auditors of Hillsborough
District, in which Chatham was located, the payments being
dated from 1780 to 1783 (Book C, pp. 100, 103 and 138; Book I,
p. 25, Book XI, p. 50; Book XII, p. 10; Book IX, p. 59; Canceled
Voucher No. 1097). Canceled Voucher No. 266, dated April 26,
1781, was a very large payment of over 3000 pounds, and is accompanied by a note from the Chatham Co. Court, dated Nov.,
1780, saying that this was due for James Kendrick's services
as Assessor in Districts No. 5 and 6 in Chatham Co. James
Kendrick's Revolutionary services are also proved by Georgia
records, which cite him as a Revolutionary soldier (Smith "Story
of Ga. and Ga. People", p. 628; Knight "Ga. Roster of the Rev."
p. 400).

As mentioned, James[3] Kendrick moved to Georgia about 1784,
and is shown in Wilkes Co., Ga. in the tax-list of 1785 with $7\frac{1}{2}$
polls, 13 slaves, 100 acres in Wilkes Co. on the Ogeechee River,
and 250 additional acres in Wilkes (Davidson "Wilkes Co.", II,
p. 62). James Kendrick's three older sons, John, William, and
Burwell, who were already married, did not move to Georgia
with their father in 1784. However, John and Burwell Kendrick
appear in Wilkes Co., Ga. in 1787 as witnesses to a deed, Burwell being a J. P. James[3] Kendrick's fourth son, James, Jr.,
married in Wilkes Co. about 1788-9 (his first child was born
about 1790) Tabitha, daughter of Drury and Tabitha Rogers, and

either he or his father was identical with a James Kendrick who witnessed a sale of slaves in Wilkes Co. in 1791 (Davidson, II, p. 118). However, the whole family moved to Washington Co., Ga. in the 1790's, where James[3] Kendrick had four land-grants, a soldier's grant of 150 acres Oct. 4, 1785 (Land Plat Bk. "K", p. 305); another 150 acres July 14, 1787 (Ga. Grant Bk. "NNN", p. 620); 140 acres Aug. 5, 1794 (Bk. "EEEE", p. 683); and 438 acres Sept. 21, 1796 (Bk. "YYYY", p. 454). The last grant in 1796 was made to James Kendrick, Sr., showing that his son, James, Jr., had moved to Washington Co., Ga. by that date. James' son, William Kendrick, sold out in Chatham Co., N.C. in 1791, and probably moved to Washington Co., Ga. in that year, though he is not mentioned in the records until 1798, when he was appointed a Captain of Militia in Washington Co. in place of his brother, Burwell Kendrick, who had moved to Montgomery Co., Ga. in 1793, the son John Kendrick was appointed a Justice of the Peace in Washington Co., and the son Burwell was granted land there. The last mention of James[3] Kendrick is in the 1796 grant, and he probably died soon afterwards, probably about 1797-8, for in 1798 the son Burwell Kendrick moved to Montgomery Co. and a grandson, Benjamin Kendrick, son of William, moved from Washington Co., Ga. to Louisiana. James[3] Kendrick was certainly dead by 1803-5, for although all his sons and their families appear in the list of all heads of families, widows, and orphans, made as an eligibility list for the Lottery of 1806, James[3] Kendrick's names does not appear. In addition to John, William, Burwell, and James, Jr., mentioned above, James[3] Kendrick had three younger sons, Benjamin, Martin, and Jones. The son John died in 1802 and Benjamin died as a young man about 1804. The 1803-5 list of eligibles for the lottery shows James[3] Kendrick's posterity as follows: William Kendrick, Martin Kendrick, Jones Kendrick, Martha Kendrick (widow of John), Tabitha Kendrick (widow of Benjamin), and Benjamin Kendrick's Orphans, all in Washington Co.; Burwell Kendrick in Montgomery Co.; and James Kendrick (Jr.) in Hancock Co. The actual winners in the Land Lottery of 1806 from the family were: Martin Kendrick, Jones Kendrick and James Kendrick (son of William) in Capt. Jones Kendrick's District, Washington Co., Ga.; James Kendrick (Jr.) in Baldwin Co. (which had been formed from Hancock); and Burwell Kendrick in Parks District, Wilkes Co., Ga. (whither he had moved about 1805-6 from Montgomery Co.). There was a Susannah Kendrick, widow, who had a lucky draw in 1806, living in Wilkes Co. in the same district at Burwell Kendrick. This may have been Susannah (Roberson) Kendrick, the widow of James[3], who had moved to Wilkes with her son Burwell. This Susannah Kendrick of Wilkes drew land in Jasper Co., Ga., which on Aug. 1, 1808 she deeded to William Foard of Tatnall Co., Ga. (Jasper Co. D.B. 1, p. 205). If she was identical with Susannah (Roberson) Kendrick, she must have died soon after this date, for she would have been over 70 years of age in 1808.

As indicated in the preceding paragraph, James[3] Kendrick and Susannah Roberson had seven sons, as follows: (1) John[4] Kendrick, b. ca. 1756, d. 1802 in Washington Co., Ga.; his widow, Martha Kendrick, and children moved after 1805 to Putnam Co., Ga., where Martha died in 1822; (2) William[4] Kendrick, b. ca. 1758 (his first child Benjamin was born 1778-9), lived in Washington Co., Ga. 1798-1809, moved to Morgan Co., Ga. in 1810, thence to St. Helena Parish, La. in 1818, where he died in 1838; (3) Burwell[4] Kendrick, b. ca. 1760-62 (certainly of age in 1783 when his father deeded him land in Chatham Co., N.C.), moved to Wilkes Co., Ga. 1793-1798, in Montgomery Co., Ga., 1798-1805, in Wilkes Co., Ga. 1806-14, then moved to Morgan Co., Ga. with his brother, William, where he died 1817; (4) James[4] Kendrick, b. ca. 1765-67 (he was married in Wilkes Co. 1788-9), in Washington Co. 1796, in Hancock in 1805, in Baldwin Co. 1806, his land there falling into Putnam Co. on the organization of that county, died in Putnam 1831-2; (5) Benjamin[4] Kendrick, b. ca. 1768-70 (married about 1790, first child born 1792), died about 1804 in Washington Co., Ga., his widow and orphans in Hancock Co., Ga. in 1806, children living in Putnam Co. later along with James[4] Kendrick, Martin[4] Kendrick, and the widow and children of John[4] Kendrick; (6) Martin[4] Kendrick, b. 1772 (tombstone record), living in Washington Co., Ga. 1805-6, in Putnam Co., Ga. in 1808 (along with families of his brothers James, John and Benjamin), died in Putnam 1812; (7) Jones[4] Kendrick, b. 1778, appears in the records of Washington Co. Ga. 1796-1808, moved to Wilkes Co., Ga., in 1810 to join his brother Burwell, died there in 1845.

In addition to the above 7 sons, James[3] Kendrick had at least one daughter, Sarah Kendrick, who married Aaron Tomlinson and lived in Washington Co., Ga. Her husband was a Revolutionary soldier, Aaron Tomlinson, who was residing in Jordan's District of Washington Co. in 1827 and as such, drew land in the Lottery of that year. Although the families of her 7 brothers will be treated later on at length, all that is known at present about her descendants is that she had a daughter, Ann Tomlinson, who married Elijah Butts. Their daughter, Lavinia Butts of Macon, Ga., married in 1853 John F. Lewis and had issue: Elijah Banks Lewis, Mrs. Eva Leonard, R. G. Lewis, Sherry Lewis, John F. Lewis, Mattie Lewis (Mrs. W. A. Dodson of Americus, Ga.), Pearl Lewis (Mrs. John C. Holmes), and William M. Lewis. Elijah Banks Lewis, the eldest son of the above marriage, lived in Montezuma, Ga., was born Mar. 27, 1854 in Dooly Co., Ga., was a member of the Georgia Senate 1894-5, and U.S. Congressman from the Third Georgia District, from the 55th through the 66th Congress of the United States.

Since the records of Washington County, Ga. have all been destroyed and there is no will extant of James[3] Kendrick, it may be well to give further evidence that the above 7 brothers and their sister, Sarah Tomlinson, were children of James[3] Kendrick and Susannah Robertson. That this is the case is indicated very strongly by the fact that they all appear in Washington Co., Ga. along with James[3] Kendrick (who was the only Kendrick of an age to be their father in that county), and by the way in which they followed one another around and settled in the same Georgia counties, as indicated above. However, there is a very strong family tradition, emanating from the grandchildren of the above

7 men, also confirming the fact that they were brothers. It is as follows:

(1) John[4] Kendrick is a proved son of James[3] Kendrick and Susannah Roberson, since he is mentioned in George Roberson's will in 1761 as "my sister Susannah Kendrick's son John Kendrick". His widow and children moved to Putnam Co., Ga. I knew personally there Mr. David Lawrence, a grandson of Meredith Kendrick, son of John[4], and he knew of the kinship to the families of James[4], Martin[4], and Benjamin[4] Kendrick who resided in Putnam, and talked to me of them long before this geneology had been perfected.

(2) William[4] Kendrick is another proved son of James[3], since his father mentions him as a son in deeding him land in 1784 in Chatham Co., N.C. Sarah Longmaid, a great-granddaughter of William[4] Kendrick above, married John West Kendrick, a grandson of Jones[4] Kendrick. In a letter written in 1900 she states her great-grandfather, William Kendrick, and her husband's grandfather, Jones Kendrick, were brothers; and that they had other brothers and sisters, among them Martin[4] Kendrick of Putnam Co. and Sarah Kendrick who married Aaron Tomlinson of Washington Co.

(3) Burwell[4] Kendrick was deeded land by James[3] Kendrick in 1783 in Chatham Co., N.C., and although the deed does not call him a son as in the case of William 4, the deed offers strong evidence for this. Burwell[4] and William[4] Kendrick had the same military service in the Revolution in North Carolina and were paid exactly the same amounts for their services; in addition, the two of them signed a bond of John[4] Kendrick in Chatham Co., N.C. in 1785, indicating close relationship. Dr. W. C. Kendrick of Dawson, Ga., a grandson of Burwell[4] Kendrick, in his biography "Memoirs of Georgia" (Vol. 2, p. 879), states that his grandfather, Burwell[4] Kendrick, was a brother of Jones[4] Kendrick of Wilkes Co., Ga. If Jones[4] Kendrick was a brother of William[4] Kendrick, as stated by Mrs. John West Kendrick above, then Burwell[4] was also a brother of William[4], and they were all three sons of James[3] Kendrick. Dr. W. C. Kendrick goes on to add that the father of Burwell and Jones Kendrick was a Captain in the Revolutionary War, a statement which is correct and applies only to James[3] Kendrick. He adds incorrectly that the father's name was Burwell Kendrick, Sr., which has caused many a headache in the nearly 50 years sporadic investigation of the Kendrick genealogy, through the effort to find an imaginary and nonexistent Capt. Burwell Kendrick, Sr. of the Revolutionary War who was old enough to be the father of the seven brothers mentioned.

(4) James[4] Kendrick had two children who married Clark brothers in Putnam Co., Ga. and a son of Martin[4] Kendrick married the Clark sister. This is my own family, and I knew intimately many of the children of these three marriages. They all knew one another well, were fairly well informed about the family, and all agreed that their respective grandparents, James and Martin Kendrick of Putnam Co. were brothers. Mrs. John West Kendrick mentions Martin[4] Kendrick as a brother of William[4] Kendrick, a proved son of James[3] Kendrick. If this is the

case, then James[4] Kendrick was also a son. Further evidence is the grant to James[3] Kendrick as James Kendrick, Sr. in Washington Co. in 1776, proving that he had a son, James, Jr.

(5) Mr. John M. Harrison of Atlanta, Ga., a descendant of Benjamin[4] Kendrick, knew of the relationship of his Kendrick family through the statement of older members, to descendants of John[4] Kendrick (the Goodes), of Martin[4] Kendrick (the Cloptons), and of Jones[4] Kendrick (an aunt of the Harrisons and a granddaughter of Benjamin[4] Kendrick married a son of Jones[4] Kendrick).

(6) Grandchildren of Martin[4] Kendrick all stated that he was a brother of James[4] Kendrick, as indicated in paragraph (4) above. In addition, Cousin Civility Henry, a granddaughter of Martin[4], knew intimately Mrs. Lavinia (Butts) Lewis in Hawkinsville, Ga., and the two ladies called each other cousin on the ground that Mrs. Lewis' mother was a Tomlinson and her grandmother was a Kendrick. This confirms the statement of Mrs. John West Kendrick in 1900 that Sarah Tomlinson and Martin[4] Kendrick were brother and sister of her ancestor, William[4] Kendrick.

(7) John Roberson Kendrick, a grandson of Jones[4] Kendrick, stated that his grandfather had a brother named William and another named Burwell, in a letter in 1909. Miss Christine Brown of Sharon, Ga. wrote that her grandmother (another grandchild of Jones[4] Kendrick) gave the names John, William, and Burwell as brothers of her grandfather, Jones Kendrick. Mrs. George A. Dure of Macon, Ga., another granddaughter of Jones[4] Kendrick, in a letter in 1922, stated that her grandfather had brothers William, Burwell, and Benjamin Kendrick. Mr. A. T. Kendrick, another grandson, mentioned the names John and William as brothers of his grandfather, Jones[4] Kendrick, and said that he was positive that his father (son of Jones[4]) was a first cousin of Sarah (Kendrick) Clopton, daughter of Martin[4] Kendrick, the families having known each other well in Alabama. Finally, Miss Elizabeth Mayes of Americus, Ga., a great-great-granddaughter of Jones[4] Kendrick, wrote in 1949 that her mother, who was still living, remembered distinctly being told by her grandfather, Rev. Green Marshall Kendrick (youngest son of Jones[4]), that the father of Jones[4] Kendrick (i.e., Rev. Green M.'s grandfather) was a Captain in the Revolutionary War, though Mrs. Mayes could not remember whether his name was John or James. Again, this tradition fits James[3] Kendrick alone.

Family names also confirm the above tradition among the seven brothers mentioned. William[4], Burwell[4], James[4], and Jones[4] Kendrick all had sons named James and daughters named Susan or Susannah. Benjamin[4] also had a daughter, Susannah. Jones[4] Kendrick's second son was named James Roberson Kendrick in honor of his father and mother presumably, and the name Roberson persisted in his branch of the family; he also had a daughter Susannah R. Kendrick, the middle initial no doubt standing again for Roberson in honor of his mother Susannah Roberson. He also had a son named Aaron Tomlinson Kendrick, no doubt for his sister Sarah's husband. Martin[4] Kendrick named one of his sons Jones, and Burwell[4] and James[4] both had grandsons named Jones Kendrick. Benjamin[4] Kendrick named one of his sons Burwell, and Burwell[4] reciprocated by naming one of his sons Benjamin. William[4] and James[4] Kendrick both had sons named Isham, probably for James[3] Kendrick's brother Isham, their uncle.

The above discussion of relationships has been somewhat tedious, but seemed necessary to prove the names of the children of James[3] Kendrick and Susannah Roberson. The seven sons and their families will be treated later.

John[3] Kendrick (William[2], John[1])

John[3] Kendrick was probably the second son of William and Sarah (Jones) Kendrick and was born about 1735-6. He died in Mecklenburg Co., Va. in 1811. His wife was Amy Fox, daughter of Richard Fox and his wife Hannah Williamson of Lunenburg and Mecklenburg Co.'s, Va. Their marriage must have occurred about 1758 or 1759, as on Sept. 4, 1759 Richard Fox made a deed of gift to his son-in-law, John Kendrick, in Lunenburg Co. (D.B. 5, 485). Richard Fox died in Mecklenburg Co., Va. in 1771. His will, dated Jan. 10, 1771 and probated May 13, 1771, mentions his grandchildren, Amy, James, Joseph, John, Mary Ann and Isaac Burchett and their father Joseph Burchett; sons Jacob, Richard and Isham; daughters Sarah Price, Nancy Fox, Amy wife of John Kendrick, Hannah and Ann; wife; and appoints Jacob Fox and John Kendrick executors (Mecklenburg W.B. 1, 94; O.B. 3, p.3). A son not mentioned in the will was William Fox, who married Mary Kendrick, sister of John. On June 10, 1765 Richard Fox acknowledged a deed in Mecklenburg Co. to his son, William Fox (O.B. 1765-8, p. 34). A deed in Macklenburg Co., dated Feb. 7, 1777, shows that the son, Isham Fox, had died under age and without issue and his land was deeded to William Davis by his brothers and sisters, namely, William, Jacob, Richard and Anne Fox, and John Kendrick and Amy his wife of Mecklenburg Co., Va.; Joseph Price and Sarah his wife and David Towns and Hannah his wife of Bute Co., N.C.; Samuel Jones and Mary his wife of Georgia; and Luke Matthews and Lucy his wife of Brunswick Co., Va. (D.B. 5, p. 21). Richard Fox's wife was Hannah, the daughter of John Williamson, who died in Surry Co., Va. in 1732. John Williamson's will, dated Jan. 30, 1731 and probated in Surry Co. May 17, 1732, mentions his daughters, Elizabeth, wife of Hollum Sturdevant, Susannah wife of John Rottenbury, Edith Williamson, and Hannah, wife of Richard Fox; son Cuthbert (under 20); and brother Cuthbert Williamson (Surry D. & W. 1730-38, p. 196). The parentage of Richard Fox has not been proved, though it has been stated for many years and is not improbable in view of the evidence, that he was a grandson of Henry Fox of King William Co., Va. and his wife Anne West, daughter of Col. John West and Ursula Croshaw and granddaughter of Gov. John West of Virginia (VM I, 424; 8, 362; W (1) 21, 262ff, W (1) 26, 133ff). Henry Fox and Anne West married about 1689 and had two proved sons, John and Thomas Fox. The articles from the "Virginia Magazine" and the "William and Mary Quarterly" cited above state that Thomas Fox married

Mary Tunstall and that Richard Fox was a son of this couple. It seems more probable, however, that he was a son of Henry Fox, mentioned in the articles as probably a third son of Henry and Anne (West) Fox. This Henry Fox was Sheriff of King William Co. in 1725 and vestryman of St. John's Parish in 1730. We have mentioned Henry Fox's deed to John[1] Kendrick in 1721, and his joint deed with Joseph Fox to William Hendrick or Kendrick in 1730. Henry Fox moved to Brunswick Co. soon after 1730 and was a Justice there in 1732, possibly also a Burgess (Journal of House of Burgesses, 1727-40, pp. vii, viii, 136, 149, 152, 155 and 185). His last appearance in Brunswick Co. was in 1735, when "Henry Fox of North Carolina" deeded his land in Brunswick Co. to John Davis (Brunswick D. & W. 1, p. 159). There is no further record of this Henry Fox after his removal to North Carolina; but since this member of the Fox-West family moved south of the James River, like Richard Fox, it seems not improbable that he was Richard's father. Richard himself was deeded land in Brunswick Co. in 1736 (D. & W. 1, 296), and William Fox, who appears in deeds in Brunswick from 1743 to 1769, may have been another son of Henry and a brother of Richard.

John[3] Kendrick was in the Granville Co., N.C. militia along with his brother James in 1754 (N.C. Col. & State Rec., Vol. 22, p. 373), but is not shown in the tax list of 1755 there, having probably moved already to Virginia, where he was certainly living in 1759, when Richard Fox made him a deed of gift of land. John Kendrick and Amy his wife appear in numerous deeds in Mecklenburg Co., Va. During the Revolution, he was appointed First Lieutenant in Capt. James Lewis' Company on Oct. 13, 1777 (Mecklenburg O.B. 4, p. 374) and took oath as a militia officer May 11, 1778 (p. 403). He later became a Captain and saw active service, as proved by the statement of James H. Kidd of Virginia (then living as an old man in Georgia) that he served two months in 1780 under Capt. John Kendrick (McAlister "Va. Militia in the Rev. War", Sec. 172, p. 144). The Land Tax Lists of Mecklenburg Co. also refer to him as Capt. John Kendrick in 1782, 1787 and 1789. John[3] Kendrick also owned land in Warren Co., N.C., being deeded land there by his brother-in-law William Wood in 1786, which he sold in 1799 (Warren D.B. 9, p. 58; D.B. 18, p. 119). The marriage bonds of Warren Co., N.C. show that five of his children married there, namely John, Betsy, Keziah, Lucy and Obedience. John[3] Kendrick died in Mecklenburg Co., Va. in 1811. His will, dated Oct. 16, 1807 and probated July 15, 1811, mentions his wife Amy, daughter Molly Cunningham, deceased, and her children, Keziah, Jacob, Rebecca Jones, George and Sally K. Baird, and "my grandson" John Cunningham; children of son William, deceased, names not given; daughters Sarah Patrick and Keziah Stevens; son John; daughter Betsey Price; son James; daughter Obedience Dinkens; daughter Lucy Dinkins; grandsons Greenberry and Asa Stevens; and John Stevens (Mecklenburg W.B. 7, p. 115). In addition to the children mentioned in the will, there was another son, Bennett Kendrick, who was born about 1777-8 (first shown as a tithable in his father's family in 1794, showing that he was 16),

who entered the Methodist ministry in 1799, and died unmarried
April 5, 1807 in South Carolina (see Lee "Short History of
Methodism"). Of the daughters, Mary Kendrick married a Cunningham and predeceased her father, as indicated by the will.
Elizabeth Kendrick married John Price Oct. 10, 1787 in Warren
Co., N.C. Keziah Kendrick married John Stephens Jan. 11, 1791
in Warren Co., N.C. and had two sons, Greenberry and Asa
Stephens, mentioned in John Kendrick's will. Obedience Kendrick,
said to have been born in 1773 by one of the later descendants of
the family, married (1) John Osborne in Warren Co., N.C. (date
not given in the marriage bond), and she married (2) Joshua Dinkins. There is a somewhat fuller record of the other children, as
follows:

Sarah[4] Kendrick, daughter of John and Amy (Fox) Kendrick,
was born in 1761 according to her descendant, Jesse L. Warner,
627 S. 8th St., W., Salt Lake City, Utah, from whom the following information about her descendants was obtained. She married
Sept. 29, 1779 in Mecklenburg Co., Va. John Patrick, who made
a large land entry in Kentucky April 10, 1784 and died near Rich-
ardsville, Warren Co., Ky. in 1816. John Patrick's will, dated
Aug. 29, 1816 and probated in Warren Co. at the Dec. Court,
1816, mentions his wife Sarah; sons James, Allen, Wiley and
Green; daughter Nancy (under age); children William, John, Luke,
Betsy and Polly; Sally Boseman; grandchildren Wiatt, John and
Catherine McFadin; daughter Betsy Taylor; Polly Tarrants; ap-
points John Patrick and William Taylor executors.

The children of John and Sarah (Kendrick) Patrick were:
I. William Patrick
II. Polly Patrick, born Feb. 21, 1788, d. in Ky. Dec. 23,
1853, m. Terry Tarrants, and had a daughter, Sally Tar-
rants who m. John Mannons.
III. Luke Patrick, m. April 20, 1812, Levena Carson
IV. John Patrick, m. May 8, 1811, Polly Mitchell
V. Elizabeth Patrick, b. Dec. 9, 1795, d. Oct. 25, 1880 in
in Harrisville, Weber Co., Utah; m. (1) Mar. 11, 1811
in Warren Co., Ky. William Taylor (b. March 21, 1787
in Edgecombe Co., N.C., d. Sept. 9, 1839 near Warsaw,
Hancock Co., Ill., son of Joseph Taylor, Jr. and his wife,
Sarah Best; m. (2) Feb. 3, 1846 James Allred.
Issue of first marriage.
1. John Taylor, b. Dec. 7, 1812 in Warren Co., Ky., d.
Feb. 7, 1896, m. April 3, 1834 Eleanor Burkett.
2. Allen Taylor b. Jan. 17, 1814 in Warren Co., Ky. d.
Dec. 5, 1891, m. (1) Sept. 5, 1833 Sarah Lovisa Allred;
m. (2) Jan. 1, 1850 Hannah Egbert; m. (3) Elizabeth
Smith; m. (4) Mar. 27, 1857 Phoebe Ann Roberts.
3. Julia Ann Taylor b. Feb. 9, 1815, d. May 16, 1898, m.
Oct. 11, 1832 Isaac Allred.
4. Mary Ann Taylor b. Mar. 22, 1818, d. Sept. 5, 1842,
m. (1) May 29, 1834 Robert McCord; m. (2) Nov. 2,
1839 Jordan P. Hendrickson.
5. Louisa Taylor b. Oct. 19, 1819, d. Jan. 11, 1853, m.
Nov. 12, 1840 Hosea Stout.

6. Elizabeth Ann Taylor b. Nov. 30, 1821, d. Mar. 9, 1906, m. (1) Oct. 4, 1841 Samuel Driggs; m. (2) John Criddle.
7. Sarah Kendrick Best Taylor b. Aug. 24, 1823, d. April 27, 1909, m. Oct. 29, 1843 Thomas Dobson.
8. Joseph Taylor b. June 4, 1825, d. Aug. 11, 1900, m. (1) Mar. 24, 1844 Mary Moore; m. (2) Jane Lake; m. (3) Anna Maria Harris; m. (4) Caroline Madson.
9. Pleasant Green Taylor, b. Feb. 8, 1827, d. May 16, 1917, m. (1) Feb. 2, 1847 Clara Lake; m. (2) July 5, 1853 Mary Eliza Shurtliff; m. (3) April 6, 1857 Jane Narcissus Shurtliff; m. (4) June 20, 1858 Sarah Jane Marler.
10. William Warren Taylor, b. Dec. 13, 1828, d. Feb. 20, 1892, m. (1) Julia Aner Carbine; m. (2) May 17, 1862 Mary Adelia Carbine; Eugenia Elmire Taylor, a daughter of the first marriage m. Samuel H. Roundy; their daughter Josephine Roundy m. Jesse Payton Warner; and their son, Jesse Lenard Warner, is the source of the information regarding the Patrick family.
11. Levi Taylor b. Sept. 3, 1830, d. April 6, 1909, m. July 23, 1853 Emeline Owen.
12. Nancy Jane Taylor b. May 17, 1833, d. March 19, 1900, m. July 11, 1857 Jonathan Smith.
13. Amanda Melvina Taylor b. Jan. 28, 1835, d. Oct. 22, 1845.
14. James Caldwell Taylor, b. Feb. 27, 1837, d. Nov. 7, 1907, m. (1) Jan. 8, 1860 Sarah Maria Hyde; m. (2) Oct. 15, 1885 Lucy Jane Lake.

VI.   Sally Patrick m. (1) July 22, 1801 Jonathan McFadden; m. (2) June 22, 1809 Jacob Boseman; issue of first marriage, Wiatt, John and Catherine McFadden.

VII.   Wiley Jones Patrick b. Mar. 4, 1802, d. Mar. 1851, m. Jan. 10, 1829 Margaret Shortle Reynolds (b. April 10, 1809, d. Mar. 1862).
       Issue:
       1. John Patrick
       2. Allen Patrick
       3. Jane Wilmot Patrick, b. July 18, 1835, d. 1879, m. Edward Carrington Campbell.
       4. James Patrick
       5. Wiley Jones Patrick, Jr., b. Jan. 3, 1840, d. Aug. 18, 1913, m. (1) Elizabeth Ann Withers (information from Mrs. Laura Lee Patrick Munger, Bowling Green, Mo.)

VIII. Allen J. Patrick, b. 1803, m. Dec. 15, 1822 Lucinda Mitchell.

IX.   James Patrick, m. April 20, 1816 Martha E. Lanier

X.   Ludson Green Patrick, b. July 18, 1805, d. 1879, m. Mar. 28, 1824 Magdalene Bellar (d. 1887), daughter of James Bellar.
       Issue:
       1. Eli Bellar Patrick m. Aug. 4, 1851 Rachel Combes.

2. John Patrick, d. Jan. 20, 1904, m. Mary Combes.
3. Nancy Jane Patrick, b. 1827, d. 1890, m. (1) Alexander Mosley; m. (2) Alexander Adams.
4. William B. Patrick, d. Jan. 31, 1913, m. Eliza Jane Shanks.
5. Eliza Ann Patrick, b. 1834, m. (1) Hyrum Withers; m. (2) Robert Sparks.
6. James Arthur Patrick, d. 1913, m. (1) Kate Whiteside; m. (2) Mittie Vaughan.
7. Mary Magdalene Patrick, b. Sept. 2, 1844, d. Aug. 4, 1925, m. 1865 William Threlkeld.
8. Sarah Elizabeth Patrick, b. Nov. 24, 1847, d. Dec. 31, 1920, m. Sept. 9, 1868 John Franklin Hawkins (information from Hawkins descendants and Belle Threlkeld Vance of Paris, Mo.)

XI.   Nancy Patrick, d. Nov. 1833.

John[4] Kendrick, eldest son of John[3] and Amy (Fox) Kendrick, was born in Lunenburg Co., Va. about 1764 and married Martha Dinkins in Warren Co., N.C. about 1784. The above dates were given by his descendant, Hon. Greene Kendrick of Waterbury, Conn., who began investigation of the Kendrick genealogy over 50 years ago, and accumulated a great amount of material before his death. The marriage of John Kendrick and Martha Dinkins is found in the marriage bonds of Warren Co., N.C., though no date is given. John[4] Kendrick seems never to have lived after his marriage in Virginia, but moved soon afterward to Mecklenburg Co., N.C., where he and his family appear in the Census of 1790 and later years. He died in Mecklenburg Co., N.C. in 1823. His will, dated Sept. 18, 1823, mentions lands adjoining Frederick Dinkins and Joshua Dinkins, decd., appoints Joseph Smith executor, and names the following children. William, John F., James, Ephraim, Green, Thomas, Amy Smith, Mary Bowden, and Lucy. Of these children, John[5] Fox Kendrick was born in 1788, married Elizabeth Daniel, and died in 1833; their son was Richard Greene Kendrick (1823-1913) who married Esther Fairess; the son of Richard Greene Kendrick was John Fox Kendrick (1853-1897), who married Martha Irwin. The last couple were the parents of Julia Kendrick (Mrs. T. W. Bethea) of Dillon, S.C., from whose D.A.R. line the above data was taken. Greene[5] Kendrick, son of John[4] and Martha (Dinkins) Kendrick, was born in North Carolina in 1798, married in 1824 Anna Leavenworth of Waterbury, Conn., moved to Connecticut in 1831, was Lieutenant-Governor of Connecticut in 1851, Governor of Connecticut in 1853, was Speaker of the House of Representatives three terms, was Senator and Congressman from Connecticut, and died at Waterbury in 1873. They only son of Greene[5] Kendrick was John[6] Kendrick, who was born at Charlotte, N.C. May 27, 1825, married in 1849 Marion Marr of New York City and Athens, Ga., Member of Congress 1871-2, Mayor of Waterbury four terms, graduate of Yale in 1843, and died on his birthday, May 27, 1877. John[6] Kendrick had three children: (1) John (1850-1895); (2) Green Kendrick, b. May 31, 1851, Mayor of Waterbury two terms, Representative and Speaker of the House in Connecticut, M.A. (1872) and LL.B.

(1875), Yale University, married and had one daughter; and (3) Kate Kendrick, b. Sept. 6, 1853, d. April 17, 1861.

William[4] Kendrick, son of John[3] and Amy (Fox) Kendrick, was born 1768-9, as he is first shown as a tithable in his father's family in 1785, showing that he was 16 years of age. He moved to Mecklenburg Co., N.C. with his brother John, and is shown there in the Census of 1790 with a family consisting of 1 male, and two females; and in 1800 with a family consisting of 1 male b. 1755-74, 1 female b. 1774-84, and 2 males b. 1790-1800. He was dead by 1807 when his father's will was written. The will mentions William's children, but does not give their names. It is probable that Richard Kendrick, who is shown in Mecklenburg Co., N.C. in the Census of 1820 living by himself and born 1794-1804, was a son.

James[4] Kendrick, son of John[3] and Amy (Fox) Kendrick, was born 1772-3, as he first appears as a tithable in his father's family in 1789. He married Dec. 12, 1797 in Mecklenburg Co., Va. Elizabeth Wright, John Wright being the security (Marriage Bonds), and died in Mecklenburg Co., Va. between May and June 1811. His will dated May 16, 1811 and probated June 17, 1811, mentions land and slaves in Tennessee (with the indication that he was planning to move there), and leaves his property to his wife Elizabeth, and his three children, Dennis, James and Polly Kendrick, all under age. The family apparently did not move to Tennessee, but to North Carolina, where Elizabeth Kendrick appears in deeds, one of them to her son, Dennis Kendrick, in Granville Co. (D.B. X, p. 37; Z, p. 274; W, p. 37; 1, p.254). The son, James, was probably identical with a James Kendrick who married Susan Green in Warren Co., N.C. Aug. 30, 1827 (Warren Co. Marriage Bonds). The son, Dennis S. Kendrick, died in Mecklenburg Co., Va., where he left a will, mentioning his wife Nancy and three sons, John, James, and Delacy Kendrick (Mecklenburg W.B. "U", pp. 87 and 314).

Lucy[4] Kendrick, daughter of John[3] and Amy (Fox) Kendrick, was born in 1775 in Mecklenburg Co., Va., and died in Canton, Miss. She married Jan. 5, 1796 in Warren Co., N.C. James Dinkins. James and Lucy (Kendrick) Dinkins lived in Charlotte, N.C. where James Dinkins died. After his death, Lucy moved to Mississippi in 1841 with her eldest son, Lewis, and is buried at Canton, Miss. (information regarding the family sent in by her great-great-granddaughter, Mrs. W.E. Stevenson (Mabel C.), of Moorheard, Miss.)

Issue of James and Lucy (Kendrick) Dinkins:

I. Lewis[5] Dinkins, b. 1798, m. (1) Harriet Ervin, daughter of Col. Alexander Ervin who fought in the Revolution in North Carolina (N.C. Col. & State rec., Vol. 21, p. 366 and Vol. 24, pp. 535 and 538); m. (2) Elizabeth Patterson. By the first marriage he had:

1. James A. Dinkins, b. 1822, d. 1893, m. Margaret Washington, and had:

(1) Harriet[7] Dinkins, b. 1846, d. 1930, m. William J. Cameron; their daughter, Mabel Cameron, m. W. E. Stevenson, lives at Moorhead, Miss., and has

two children, Pauline Stevenson who m. M. J. Shaw, and Cameron Stevenson who m. Clara Johns.
  (2) Lewis[7] Dinkins, died young.
  (3) Rufus[7] Dinkins
  (4) John[7] Fox Dinkins
  (5) Elizabeth[7] Dinkins
  (6) Henry[7] Dinkins
  (7) Paul[7] Dinkins
  (8) Edwin[7] Dancy Dinkins
  (9) Lolah[7] Dinkins
2. Margaret[6] Dinkins m. William E. Dancy
3. Elizabeth[6] Dinkins m. Charles B. Galloway and was mother of Bishop Charles B. Galloway of the M.E. Church, South.

Issue of 2nd marriage:

II. Sarah[5] Dinkins, b. 1800, m. William Branch.
III. Louisa[5] Dinkins, b. 1802, m. (1) Richard Dinkins and (2) Alfred Galloway.
IV. Rufus[5] Dinkins, b. 1804, killed in a duel at Canton, Miss., in 1837.
V. Lucinda[5] Dinkins, b. 1812, m. Lewis Slaughter.
VI. Alexander[5] Hamilton Dinkins, b. 1815, m. Cynthia Springs and had:
  1. Capt. James[6] Dinkins, m. Sue Hart and had:
    (1) Lynn[7] Dinkins, d.s.p. in New Orleans
    (2) Miriam[7] Dinkins, m. Mr. Robinson, lives in New Orleans, and has a son James Dinkins Robinson of Memphis, Tenn.
  2. Lee[6] Dinkins m. Kate McWillie and had several children.

Mary[3] Kendrick (William[2], John[1])

Mary[3] Kendrick, eldest daughter of William[2] and Sarah (Jones) Kendrick, was born April 12, 1738, probably in North Carolina, and died prior to 1795 in Mecklenburg Co., Va. She married about 1758-9 William Fox (b. Feb. 13, 1732, d. 1783), son of Richard and Hannah (Williamson) Fox of Mecklenburg Co., Va., and brother of Amy Fox who married John[3] Kendrick. William Fox's will, dated Sept. 4, 1783 and probated in Mecklenburg Co., Va. Nov. 10, 1783, mentions sons Arthur, Richard, William and Henry, daughter Mary Kendrick Fox; son Benjamin; daughters Sally Jones Fox, Johannah, Priscilla and Betsy Fox; wife Mary; and appoints the wife, Mary, and John Kendrick executors. The following is known about these children:

I. Arthur[4] Fox was born in 1761, married Mary Young, daughter of Richard Young, and moved to Mason Co., Ky., where he died about 1793 (will dated Sept. 19, 1793, W.B. 2, p.9). He had three children, Betsy, Polly and Arthur Fox. Arthur[5] Fox married June 14, 1814 Lucretia Taylor.
II. Richard[4] Fox, b. Mar. 2, 1764, married Mary Blanton (b. Oct. 20, 1772), and died Jan. 10, 1833 (dates from his family Bible, now in the possession of Mrs. Rose Freeman Ferrell of Anson, Tex., a descendant, the Bible also giving the birth-dates of his father and mother, and of his grandfather and grandmother, William[2] Kendrick and Sarah

(Jones) Kendrick. Mrs. Ferell gives the children of Richard Fox and Mary Blanton as follows:

1. Lucy[5] Fox m. (1) Mr. Sullivan and (2) Mr. Morrison, and left issue:
2. Mary Fox m. Robert Brenham and left issue.
3. Elizabeth[5] B. Fox, b. Aug. 13, 1792, d. Jan. 9, 1832, unmarried.
4. Dr. Newton[5] Fox, died 1856, lived at Hopkinsville, Ky. and left issue.
5. Sidney[5] L. Fox m. (1) Miss Pruett and (2) Miss Hearndon.
6. Martha[5] Fox, b. March 15, 1800, died July 24, 1864, m. March 8, 1825 D.C. Freeman and left issue, Mrs. Ferrell being one of the descendants.
7. William[5] Kendrick Fox, died unmarried.
8. Richard[5] L. Fox, b. June 5, 1804, d. April 14, 1845, m. 1830 Sarah Ann Williams, his cousin, and left issue.
9. Eliza[5] Fox b. Jan. 29, 1807, d. Jan. 6, 1831, m. William McBride, no issue.
10. Julia[5] Ann Fox, born 1809, m. Milton Withers and left descendants in Missouri.

III. William[4] Fox, twin of Richard, b. Mar. 2, 1764, d.s.p.

IV. Henry[4] Fox, moved to Warren Co., Ky., where his will is recorded (W.B. 2, p. 206). According to a descendant, Mrs. Lillie Osborn of Bowling Green, Ky., Henry Fox married (1) a Miss Kendrick from Virginia and (2) Sarah Parks of North Carolina, and had the following children by his two marriages.
I Issue of first marriage:
1. William[5] Fox, d.s.p. in Texas.
2. Sallie[5] Ken'rick Fox, m. Thomas Stone, moved to Athens, Ala. and later to Carr Co., Tex., where they died, leaving issue.
3. John[5] Fox, m. Jane Smith and lived at Glasgow, Barren Co., Ky.
4. Arthur[5] Fox m. Rachel McGraw, lived in Warren Co., Ky., later moved to Paradise, Muhlenburg Co., Ky., where both died, leaving several children, among them Mrs. Sarah Eliza McDaniel.
5. Elizabeth[5] Fox, m. Daniel Stone and had 14 children, lived and died in Warren Co., Ky.
6. Martha[5] C. Fox, married three times, among the husbands being a Mr. Harris, lived and died at Huntsville, Ala.
7. Jane[5] Fox, m. James Buttersworth and lived at Bowling Green, Ky., later moved to Athens, Ala., where she died, leaving issue.
8. Margaret (Peggy)[5] Woods Fox, m. William McCracken and lived in Athens, Ala., where she died, leaving issue.

By his second marriage to Sarah Parks, Henry[4] Fox had the following children:
9. Benjamin[5] Fox, married and lived in northern Kentucky.

10. Madison[5] Fox
11. Priscilla[5] Fox m. Mr. Tipton and lived and died in Morgan Co., Mo.
12. Julia[5] Ann Fox m. John Hess and lived and died in Bowling Green, Ky., leaving issue.
13. Henry[5] Jones Fox of Bowling Green, Ky., b. March 17, 1812, d. 1899, m. June 14, 1837 Elizabeth Lowry; their daughter, Sarah Jane Fox (b. 1838, d. Dec. 1922), m. William M. Porter and they were the parents of Mrs. Osborne.

V.   Mary[4] Kendrick Fox was living in Mason Co., Ky. Dec. 17, 1795, when she gave a power of attorney to Samuel Hopkins of Mecklenburg Co., Va. to settle all matters relative to the estates of her deceased father and mother, William and Mary Fox (Mecklenburg W.B. 7, p. 101). Apparently she never married, and is said to have returned to Mecklenburg Co., Va. and died there.

VI.   Benjamin[4] Fox m. Martha Norvell May 9, 1792, In Mecklenburg Co., Va.

VII.   Sally[4] Jones Fox is probably identical with a Sally Fox who m. Thomas Nowell Oct. 12, 1790 in Mecklenburg Co., Va.

VIII.   Joanna[4] Fox m. Samuel Holmes, according to Mrs. Ferrell.

IX.   Priscilla[4] Fox m. James Taylor Dec. 9, 1801, in Mecklenburg Co., Va.

X.   Betsy[4] Fox, no information.

Martha[3] Kendrick (William[2], John[1])

Martha[3] Kendrick, daughter of William[2] and Sarah (Jones) Kendrick, was born in Edgecombe Co., N.C. Jan. 7, 1747 and died in Randolph Co., N.C., Feb. 14, 1831. She married May 28, 1764 William Wood (b. 1737 on the Eastern Shore of Maryland or Virginia, d. April 26, 1804 near Farmer, Randolph Co., N.C.). The Woods moved to Randolph Co., N.C. about 1779. William Wood was a Captain in the Revolutionary War from North Carolina (N.C. Rev. Accts., Bk. A, No. 42), and the following D.A.R. memberships are based on his record: Nos. 134, 189; 144,064; 154,135; 188,954; and 372,064. The data concerning this family come from Mrs. Sam H. Burchard, 811 St. Lawrence St., Gonzales, Tex., a descendant. Mrs. Burchard gives the children and descendants of William Wood and Martha Kendrick as follows, the dates being taken from Family Bibles.

I.   Sarah[4] Wood, b. Jan. 25, 1765, no further information.
II.   Disey[4] Wood, b. Dec. 11, 1767, d. May 31, 1837, m. Whitlock Arnold and lived at Toms Creek, Randolph Co., N.C. Their children were:
1. Wood[5] Arnold m. Porry Hoover
2. John[5] Arnold, m. Patsy Steed
3. William[5] Arnold m. Betsy Lewis
4. Penuel[5] Wood Arnold m. (1) Hannah Jackson and (2) Mrs. Cynthia Rush Sheets, a widow.
5. Larkin[5] Wood Arnold, m. Celia Foust and moved to Indiana.

6. Nancy[5] Arnold m. John Ingram.

7. Fannie[5] Arnold m. Absalom Foust.

III.   Burrell[4] Wood, b. April 4, 1770, d. May 1, 1847, m. Margaret Burkhead and lived in Davidson Co., N.C., where he died without issue. His nephew, Gray Wood, lived with him and inherited his property.

IV.   Penuel[4] Wood, b. Jan. 22, 1772, d. Jan. 8, 1841, m. (1) Miss Smithson and (2) Sarah Kimball. According to Mrs. Burchard, who is a descendant of the second marriage, Sarah Kimball was the daughter of Buckner Kimball (b. 1746, d. 1812 in Granville Co., N.C.), who was a Captain in the Revolution. Buckner Kimball was the son of Peter Kimball and Winnie Gilliam, and the grandson of Joseph Kimball. Buckner Kimball's wife was Pattie Harriss, daughter of West Harriss. The children of Penuel Wood and his first wife were:

1. Wiley[5] Wood, m. Linny Hall

2. Nancy[5] Wood, b. Sept. 5, 1800, d. July 6, 1878, m. Feb. 17, 1827 Allen Kearns

3. Priscilla[5] Wood m. John Wilborn

4. Rena[5] Wood m. William Ridge

5. Patsy[5] Wood m. (1) Ebenezer Laughlin and (2) Billy Lewis

6. Sallie[5] Wood m. John Kirk

7. Disey[5] Wood m. Winslow Thornburg

8. Peggy[5] Wood m. Solomon Burns

9. Rebecca[5] Wood m. Willis Carter and moved to Illinois.

10. Jincy[5] Wood m. Isham Luther

11. Josephine[5] Wood m

12. Samantha[5] Wood.

Mrs. Burchard gives the children of the second marriage to Sarah Kimball as follows:

13. William[5] Wood b. Jan. 8, 1806, d. Oct. 8, 1844, m. March 23, 1826 Henrietta Andrews, daughter of Richard and Martha Andrews of Randolph Co., N.C. They had:

(1) Harriss Kimball Wood, b. April 4, 1827, d. May 19, 1923 in Gonzales, Texas, m. Jan. 3, 1855 Nancy Jance Parchman (b. Nov. 24, 1837 in Lawrence Co., Tenn., d. Jan. 24, 1918 in Gonzales, Texas, and had 8 children:

a. J. W. Wood b. Oct. 3, 1855, d. Nov. 8, 1926, unmarried.

b. L. P. Wood b. June 1, 1859, d. Sept. 4, 1928, m. Lillie Nunn.

c. Vida Wood b. March 2, 1861, d. Oct. 27, 1913, unmarried.

d. Ora Wood, born March 10, 1863, d. Nov. 20, 1929, unmarried.

e. Dula Wood, b. March 14, 1865, d. Nov. 5, 1936, unmarried.

f. Willie Wood, b. March 11, 1867, d. August 2, 1923, m. W. B. Jackson.

g. Rue Wood, b. March 13, 1869, died July 21, 1895, m. J. T. Cardwell.

h. Lilla May Wood, b. March 24, 1871, still living, m. June 17, 1896 Robert Crooke Botts and has one daughter, Lillian Fay Botts, b. July 22, 1897, who m. August 22, 1917 Sam Houston Burchard and has two daughters, Margaret May Burchard, b. Oct. 8, 1920, m. Sept. 8, 1950 Valin Ridge Woodward, Jr., and Frances Jane Burchard, b. Oct. 28, 1925, m. Aug. 22, 1946 Clarence Arthur Wilson.

(2) James[6] Madison Wood b. Nov. 15, 1829

(3) Laura[6] Ann Wood, b. Feb. 18, 1832, died July 4,
(4) 1872, m. August 31, 1852 Robert Thomas Nixon.

(4) Elmira[6] Wood, b. Sept. 14, 1834, d. Oct. 1897, m. May Foster.

(5) Alexander[6] Norman Wood b. Nov. 13, 1837, d. June 19, 1869, unmarried.

(6) Simon[6] Wood, b. July 22, 1841, d. Dec. 22, 1850

(7) William[6] Barney Wood b. April 16, 1844, d. Feb. 12, 1921, m. Keziah McAnelly.

14. Burrell[5] Wood m. Dorinda Burkhead.

15. Penuel[5] Wood, Jr., b. Dec. 13 or 17, 1812, died Aug. 8 or 12, 1881 at Ashboro, N.C., m. 1833 Dorinda Burkhead (b. Aug. 17, 1816, d. April 16, 1903) and had:

(1) Franklin[6] Harriss Wood b. Aug. 19, 1836, d. Oct. 2, 1913, m. Oct. 23, 1858 Elizabeth Pearce.

(2) Julia[6] Ann Wood m. McNair

(3) Thomas[6] J. Wood m. Sadie Christian

(4) William[6] Penn Wood m. Henrietta Hunter.

(5) Eunice[6] Roxanna Wood m. James R. Pearce.

(6) Nannie[6] Wood m. George Reed.

(7) Sarah[6] Frances Wood m. Dr. Person.

(8) James[6] Henry Bascom Wood, b. May 1, 1853, d. Feb. 21, 1892, m. Miss Rountree.

r. Rebecca[4] Wood b. Sept. 6, 1773, m. Clement Arnold, and had: William Arnold, John Arnold, Rebecca Arnold, Patsy Arnold and Nancy Arnold.

I. William[4] Kendrick Wood, b. April 27, 1775, died April 3, 1834, m. Rachel Robbins and had:

1. Kendrick[5] Wood m. Eliza Jackson.
2. Eliza[5] Wood m. William Lassiter.
3. Mealy[5] Wood m. William Laughlin.
4. Lindy[5] Wood m. Matthew Skeen.
5. Patsy[5] Wood m. Daniel Thompson and moved to Ky.
6. Betsy[5] Wood m. Lane Alton.
7. Nancy[5] Wood m. Ezra Crow.
8. Josiah[5] Wood m. Polly Griffin.
9. Spencer[5] Wood m. Nancy Skeen.
10. William[5] Wood m. Miss Harris.

II. Nancy[4] Wood b. Aug. 2, 1777, m. a Tucker and died without issue.

III. Dorcas[4] Wood b. Dec. 16, 1778, m. (1) William Lee and

had a daughter Polly Lee who m. Wesley Hancock; m. (2) Harriss Kimball (1778-1825), son of Buckner Kimball, and had Joel Kimball and Patsy Kimball who m. a Crowell; she m. (3) Henry Cross, by whom she had no children.

IX. Martha[4] Jane Wood b. June 2, 1782, d. Jan. 5, 1856, m. Hezekiah Nailor and had:
1. Calvin Nailor m. a Miss Lewis and moved to Ill.
2. Sallie Nailor m. Herbert Nance.
3. Lena Nailor m. Jesse Steed.
4. Nettie Nailor m. Edwin Steed.

X. Elizabeth[4] Wood b. Nov. 15, 1783 m. Ransom Harriss son of West Harriss, and lived in Davidson Co., N.C. Their children were:
1. Patsy Harriss m. (1) Jacob Gass and (2) Jack Finch.
2. Lindy Harriss m. Hoke Skeen.
3. Betsy Harriss m. Sam Lewis.
4. Tappena Harriss m. Madison Ward.
5. Calvin Harriss, unmarried, moved to S.C.
6. Mumford Harriss m. Martha Workman.
7. Jason Harriss m. Lucile Henley.
8. Ransom Harriss m. Margaret Ward
9. Turner Harriss m. Chloe McKoy.

XI. Jones[4] Kendrick Wood b. July 6, 1790, d. Sept. 5, 1880 in Randolph Co., N.C., m. May 3, 1812 Ruth Dunn Loftin b. April 28, 1793, d. March 28, 1869.
Issue:
1. Sabrina[5] Wood b. April 15, 1813, d. 1906, m. Oct. 5, 1837 John Garner.
2. Peninah[5] Wood, b. Jan. 22, 1815 m. Eldridge Carter
3. Gray[5] Wood, b. Oct. 8, 1816, d. March 25, 1877 in McCracken Co., Ky., m. (1) April 18, 1844 Martha Birkhead and (2) May 29, 1854 Martha Ann Cotten
4. Elizabeth[5] Wood, b. May 31, 1818, d. March 4, 1892, m. Abner Coltrane.
5. Hilah[5] Wood b. Feb. 18, 1820, d. April 4, 1855.
6. William[5] Wood, b. Sept. 11, 1821
7. Nancy[5] Wood b. Aug. 25, 1823, d. 1912, m. John Schwab Aug. 19, 1856.
8. Hill[5] Wood b. April 1, 1825
9. Dorinda[5] Wood b. July 16, 1827
10. Marquis[5] Lafayette Wood b. Oct. 23, 1829, d. Nov. 25, 1893, m. (1) Sept. 19, 1859 Ellen E. Morphis (b. Jan. 7, 1835, d. Mar. 16, 1864), m. (2) Mar. 2, 1869 Carrie V. Pickett (b. Dec. 3, 1843, d. Oct. 29, 1871), and m. (3) Nov. 22, 1875 Mrs. A. A. Robbins (b. Nov. 18, 1833, d. Mar. 9, 1890); Marquis Lafayette Wood was a member of the N.C. Methodist Conference from 1855 to 1893, was for 7 years a missionary to China, and was President of Trinity College for 2 years. His children were:
(1) Edwin[6] Herbert Wood b. July 13, 1861 in Shanghai, China, d. April 1, 1884 in N.C.
(2) Charles[6] Albert Wood b. Oct. 17, 1863 in Shanghai, m. Patty Mann.

(3) Frances[5] Loftin Wood b. Dec. 24, 1869, m. Walter L. Steele.

(4) Thomas[6] Pickett Wood, b. July 29, 1871, m. Lila Phillips

(5) Margaret[6] Graves Wood b. Dec. 17, 1872, m. Lar-ry C. Lawrence.

11. Rufus[5] Jones Wood b. July 1, 1831, d. Nov. 22, 1846

12. Sarah[5] Wood, b. July 13, 1833 m. Aug. 10, 1851 Tur-ner Harris

13. John[5] Wesley Wood, b. July 14, 1834, m. Sept. 16, 1858 Sarah Nance.

14. Virgil[5] Stewart Wood b. Sept. 29, 1836, d. at Peters-burg, Va. while serving in the Confederate Army.

Jones[3] Kendrick (William[2], John[1])

Jones[3] Kendrick was apparently the next to the youngest child of William[2] and Sarah (Jones) Kendrick, and was probably born about 1750. He died in Maury Co., Tenn. about 1816-17. His wife was named Margaret, but there is no clue to her last name. He served in the Revolution in North Carolina and payment of 16 pounds, 0 shillings and 8 pence was allowed him by the Auditors of Hills-borough District in Aug., 1782 (N.C. Rev. Accts., Book C, p. 8; N.C. Co. and State Rec., Vol. 19, p. 526). On April 7, 1778 he sold land in Warren Co., N.C. left him by his father to Lew Tucker (Warren D.B. 7, p. 8), and in Dec. 1778 entered 640 acres of land in Orange Co., N.C., which was granted him Oct. 5, 1782 (N.C. Grant Bk. 49, p. 36). The tax returns of Orange Co. show Jones Kendrick there in 1779 and 1780 (though in the 1780 tax list he is called Jones Hendricks instead of Jones Ken-drick); but he sold his land there on June 21, 1784 to James Williams (Orange D.B. 2, p. 58), though again the Clerk copied the name as Hendrick instead of Kendrick. There seems no doubt that the same James Williams to whom Jones Kendrick sold his land had received on Oct. 27, 1783 a grant of 5000 acres in what later became the State of Tennessee, but was then a part of North Carolina, which he transferred to Jones Kendrick and the warrant (No. 535) was issued in the name of Jones Kendrick July 10, 1784. The above s proved by the records of Maury Co.' Tenn., where the land was located (Maury Co. D.B. 1-E, Nos. 208 and 211; Tenn. Grant Bk. F, pp. 207 and 302.) The transactions mentioned may indicate a family connection between Jones Kendrick and James Williams, so there is a possibility that Jones' wife Margaret was a Williams.

Jones[3] Kendrick moved away from Orange Co., N.C. soon after 1784, and followed his brother, James[3] Kendrick, to Ga., where he was living at least from 1792 to 1802. Blair's "Early Tax-Digests of Georgia" shows John Kindrick with 390 acres, 1 poll, and 5 slaves, adjoining Duberry in Col. Alexander's Dis-trict of Wilkes Co., Ga. in 1793. The same volume shows that the name John Kindrick is an error for Jones Kendrick; for War-ren Co. was formed from Wilkes in 1794, and the tax-digest for Warren in that year shows Jones Kendrick with 1 poll, 5 slaves,

and 390 acres adjoining Duberry, exactly the same taxable properly as for "John" in 1793. The somewhat incomplete county
records of Warren Co. show that on June 30, 1798, Jones Kendrick and wife, Margaret U. Kendrick, deeded away 290 acres
in Warren Co. on Williams Creek, the land having been deeded
to Jones Kendrick April 3, 1792. On Dec. 6, 1796 Jones Kendrick was granted 72 acres in Washington Co., Ga., the same
county in which James[3] Kendrick and his family lived (Grant
Book ZZZZ, p. 103). This grant may have been to Jones[4] Kendrick, son of James and nephew of Jones[3], but as Jones[4] Kendrick was only 18 years of age in 1796, it seems more probable
that the grant was to his uncle. The Index lists the above grant
in the name of James Kendrick, but the grant itself shows the
name Jones. On Oct. 7, 1799 Janet Kendrick married John Lawrence in Warren Co., Ga. Janet was probably a daughter of
Jones[3] Kendrick. The last appearance of Jones[3] Kendrick in the
Warren Co. records is on Mar. 29, 1802, when he deeded the
remainder of his land there Ichabod Cox. He probably moved
about this time to Maury Co., Tenn. to occupy his large land-
grant there. The Warren Co. tax-digest of 1805 shows no Jones
Kendrick, though it does show a William Kendrick with 1 poll,
who was probably a son. This William Kendrick later appears in
Maury Co., Tenn. in the Census of 1820, and had moved by 1830
to Lauderdale Co., Ala., where he is shown along with Olsemus
Kendrick, a proved son of Jones[3] Kendrick.

Over 35 deeds in Maury Co., Tenn. shows that Jones[3] Kendrick had at least two sons, Olsemus Kendrick and Jones Kendrick,
Jr., and probably daughters who married respectively John Elliott, Joshua Orr, and William Weems. Practically all these
deeds are from the 5000 acre grant to Jones Kendrick in 1784,
and in several of them he is called Jones Kendrick, Sr., to distinguish him from his son, Jones, Jr. Unfortunately he left no
will, and the records show no list of heirs. Jones[3] Kendrick last
appears on Nov. 29, 1816, when he deeded 200 acres from the
5000 acre tract to Joshua Orr, John Elliott being a witness.
(Maury Book 1-J, No. 143). He died in 1816 or 1817, as on Feb. 5,
1818 Alsimus Kendrick, administrator of the estate of Jones Kendrick, decd., deeded $82\frac{2}{3}$ acres from the 5000 acre tract to
Charles Weems, administrator of William Weems, decd. (Book
1-H, No. 67). John Elliott and Joshua Orr were witnesses to this
deed, as well as to a later deed Feb. 5, 1819 from Olsimus, as
administrator, to Charles, as administrator. (No. 90, same
book), for 22 acres. Jones[3] Kendrick was probably a member of
Lauderdale Co., Ala., admr. of Jones Kendrick, decd., deeded
to the Baptist Church of Fountain Creek 1 acre of land, it being
agreeable to an obligation that Jones Kendrick, Sr., gave to the
church Feb. 17, 1811 (Book 1-M, p. 285). The following deeds
indicate something of the family connections: (1) Jan. 5, 1814,
Jones Kendrick, Sr., of Maury Co. to Olsimus Kendrick 300
acres; test; John Elliott and Jones Kendrick, Jr. (Book 1-E, No.
422, p. 373). (2) John Elliott witnessed a deed from Jones Kendrick to Samuel Jemison Feb. 3, 1814 (same p, 375). (3) Jones

Kendrick to William Weems 415 acres on Fountain Creek, test, John Elliott (same, p. 371). (4) Jones Kendrick, Jr. witnessed a deed from Jones Kendrick, Sr. to Lemuel Prewitt June 10, 1814 (Book 1-F, No. 16, p. 15). (5) Jan. 1815, Jones Kendrick, Sr., to John Elliott 150 acres; Olsimus Kendrick as witness (same, No. 60). (6) Feb. 12, 1815, Jones Kendrick to John Elliott 22 acres; Jones Kendrick, Jr. a witness (same, No. 139, p. 146). (7) Oct. 15, 1814, Jones Kendrick, Sr., to Jones Kendrick, Jr., 200 acres; John Elliott and Joshua Orr witnesses (same, No. 220). (8) Feb. 14, 1815, Jones Kendrick to William Weems 98 3/4 acres; Charles Weems a witness (same, No. 390, p. 380). (9) Aug. 15, 1815, Jones Kendrick, Sr. to Joshua Orr 500 acres; John Elliott and Jones Kendrick, Jr. witnesses (same, No. 225). (10) April 21, 1816, Olsimus Kendrick, John Elliott, and Joshua Orr to J. Reid 100 acres on Fountain Creek; Sarah J. Elliott a witness (perhaps she was Sarah Jones Kendrick, daughter of Jones[3] Kendrick) (Book 1-G, No. 20). (11) Jones Kendrick, Jr. and Joshua Orr witness to a deed from Jones Kendrick to Alexander Montgomery Jan. 11, 1816 (same No. 49). (12) Oct. 5, 1814, Jones Kendrick to John Elliott 50 acres; Jones Kendrick, Jr., and Olsimus Kendrick witnesses (same, No. 132). (13) John Elliott witness to a deed Sept. 30, 1819 from Olsimus Kendrick, admr. of Jones, decd., to Armstrong Redding (Book 1-H, No. 318). (14) on Oct. 18, 1820, Olsemus Kendrick of Lauderdale Co., Ala. to Nancy Weems of Maury Co., Tenn. 13 acres; test, John Elliott, Charles Weems (Nancy Weems was perhaps the widow of William Weems, mother of Charles, and daughter of Jones[3] Kendrick) (Book 1-J, No. 690). (15) July Court, 1820, Olsemus Kendrick of the State of Alabama, admr. of Jones Kendrick, decd., and Charles Weems, admr. of William Weems, decd., 56 acres to James Warden (Book 1-L, p. 548). (16) Jan. 5, 1814, Jones Kendrick to Olsimus Kendrick a deed of four negroes, test, John Elliott (Book 1-M, p. 473). (17) Jones Kendrick, Jr. to his daughter Elizabeth Kendrick deed of gift of negro girl; test, Joshua Orr, John Elliott; recorded Aug. 8, 1828 (same, p. 475). (18) Aug. 20, 1829, Jones Kendrick to Joshua Orr bill of sale for a negro girl, John Elliott a witness (Book 1-N, p. 508). (19) Aug. 8, 1822, Jones Kendrick and James Elliott deed a slave to William Kid in Lauderdale Co., Ala. (Lauderdale W.B. "A", p. 134). (20) Jan. 24, 1820, James Elliott was one of the sureties for Alsenius Kendrick as County Surveyor in Lauderdale Co., Ala. (Orphans Court Bk., p. 7). The James Elliott of the last two records could have been a son of John Elliott of Maury Co., Tenn.

The above records indicate rather strongly that in addition to Alcimus and Jones Kendrick, Jr., Jones[3] Kendrick, Sr., had three daughters, Sarah J., the wife of John Elliott, Nancy, the wife of William Weems, and the wife of Joshua Orr. Other daughters were probably Janet Kendrick, previously mentioned, who married John Lawrence in 1799 in Warren Co., Ga., and Judith (Juda) Kendrick, who married William Welch Feb. 8, 1816, in Maury Co., Tenn. (Maury Co. Marriage Bonds). Other sons were probably: (1) William Kendrick, shown in Warren Co., Ga. in 1805, in Maury Co., Tenn. in the Census of 1820, and in

Lauderdale Co., Ala., in the Census of 1830, with a fairly large family in both Census records. Alsimus Kendrick was also living in Lauderdale Co., Ala. in 1830 with a large family. The Census shows that William and Alcimus were born between 1770 and 1780. (2) John Kendrick, indicated by the Census as born about 1785-90 approximately, was living in Maury Co., Tenn. in 1820. He was perhaps another son. (3) Thomas Kendrick, probably another son, was living in Maury Co., Tenn. in the Census of 1820, 1830, and 1840, with a wife and several children. He appears in numerous deeds in Maury Co. from 1818 to 1852, though he is not shown in the county in the Census of 1850. The Census records indicate that he was born 1780-90. (4) Martin Kendrick is shown with his family living in Lauderdale Co., Ala. in 1830 along with William and Alsimus Kendrick, and was the only Kendrick living in that county in the Census of 1840. He was probably born about 1800, as the 1830 Census shows him born 1800-10 and the 1840 Census as born 1790-1800. He may have been the youngest son of Jones[3] Kendrick. The name Martin is significant, since it also occurs in other branches of the family of William[2] Kendrick.

Isham[3] Kendrick (William[2], John[1])

Isham[3] Kendrick was probably the youngest son of William[2] and Sarah (Jones) Kendrick and born about 1755 in Granville Co., N.C. He died March 17, 1881 in Spartanburg Co., S.C. He married (1) Oct. 31, 1781 in Warren Co., N.C. Elizabeth Tucker (Warren County Marriage Bonds), and (2) April 17, 1788 in the same county Elizabeth Duncan (b. 1770-71 in Virginia, d. ca. 1853 in Cherokee Co., Ga.). Isham Kendrick served in the Revolution in North Carolina, as shown by the Revolutionary Accounts at Raleigh, one payment being for the loss of a gun (N.C. Rev. Accts. Book IV, p. 104, folio 1; Book V, p. 8, folio 2; Book VIII, p. 97, folio 3; Book XI, p. 15, folio 3; Book B, p. 62; Book IV, p. 51, folio 2; and page 54, folio 2 - the last two payments to "I. Kendrick", the others to "Isham"). Revolutionary War Pension Claim R 5862 in the Veterans Administration at Washington shows that Isham Kendrick married Elizabeth Duncan April 17, 1788 in Warren Co., N.C. and died March 17, 1818 in Spartanburg District, S.C., age not shown. His widow, Elizabeth Kendrick, applied for a pension July 4, 1850 and was then 79 years of age and living in Cherokee Co., Ga. She had previously lived in Greenville and Spartanburg Districts, S.C. She stated that Isham Kendrick, while residing in Warren Co., N.C., enlisted and served about 12 months as a private with the North Carolina troops, a part of the time in Capt. Sterling Clack's Company and under Major Charles Davis, and that he was in the battles of Cowpens and Hillsborough. The cliam was not allowed, as the widow failed to furnish proofs according to law. However, Isham Kendrick's service is proved by the above payments from North Carolina. Reference is made in the pension claim to a son, Alston Kendrick; and in 1850 the widow's sister, Mrs. Alsey Wood, aged 71 years, testified in Greenville Dist., S.C. in behalf of the widow.

Isham Kendrick appears in three deeds in Warren Co., N.C. from 1783 to 1792 (D.B. 8, p. 214; D.B. 12, p. 116; D.B. 13, p. 231). He was living in Warren Co. in 1790, the census showing himself and wife, and 2 males born 1774-90 in his family. Presumably these two males were his sons by his first marriage to Elizabeth Tucker, but they must have died young, as all the children who shared in Isham's estate in South Carolina seem to have been by the second marriage. It is uncertain just when he moved to South Carolina, as the Census returns of 1800 and 1810 show the family in neither Warren Co., N.C. nor Spartanburg Co., S.C. The widow, Elizabeth Kendrick, is shown in 1820 in Spartanburg Co. with a family consisting of 1 female b. before 1775 (herself), 1 male and 1 female b. 1794-1804, and 2 males and 1 female b. 1804-10. Isham Kendrick appears in three deeds in Spartanburg Co., S.C. in 1812 (D.B. "N", p. 200; D.B. "P", pp. 106 and 107). As mentioned, he died in 1818. Probate Box 16, package 8 in the office of the Probate Judge of Spartanburg Co. shows the widow and heirs of Isham Kendrick as follows: (1) Account of the estate in 1818 by the widow shows daughter Rosey, son Alston, and daughter Elizabeth; (2) Elizabeth Kendrick and Page Rork were administrators of the estate in 1819; (3) Page Rork as one of the legatees receipted Elizabeth Kendrick for his part of the estate in 1822; (4) Rosannah McDavid, Jefferson Kendrick, John McMakin, James Robertson, Alston W. Kendrick, John M. Lister, and Elizabeth Kendrick gave receipts for their parts of the estate in 1827; (5) A letter from L.M. Hook, Jan. 9, 1854, to D.W. Moore mentions his brother-in-law, A.J. McMakin, and asks for all documents on the Isham Kendrick estate and deeds by Mrs. Elizabeth Kendrick up to 1839, to be used at the ensuing term of "our Superior Court". This L.M. Hook married a daughter of John McMakin and Jane Kendrick (daughter of Isham and Elizabeth), and Elizabeth Kendrick was living in his family in the Census of 1850 in Cherokee Co., Ga., which shows them as follows: L.M. Hook, b. 1814 in S.C.; A.W. Hook (female) b. 1827 in S.C.; three daughters all born in Georgia, M.J. in 1843; L.M. in 1845; and L.O. in 1849; and A. Kendrick (a mistake for E. Kendrick), an aged female 80 years of age, born in Virginia. The letter indicates that the family moved to Cherokee Co., Ga. in 1839 and that Elizabeth Kendrick died there about 1853. The daughter, M.J. Hook, b. 1843, is probably identical with Miss Mittie Hook, who wrote me years ago about the hickory nut in her possession which had belonged to her ancestor, William Kendrick, and was carved with his name, mentioned previously in the section on William[2] Kendrick. In 1828 Elizabeth Kendrick made a deed of gift of slaves to her children, Alston W. Kendrick, Isham J. Kendrick, John McMakin, John M. Lister, Edward Edwards, and John McDavid (Spartanburg D.B. "EE", p. 82); and deeds in 1828 and 1829 show the heirs of Isham Kendrick as Elizabeth Kendrick, the widow, James Robertson and Polly J. Robertson, John McMakin and Jane McMakin, John McDavid and Rosannah McDavid; John M. Lister and Abigail H. Lister, Edward Edwards and Elizabeth W. Edwards, Alston W. Kendrick and Isham J. Kendrick (D.B. "EE", pp. 83-4-5). In addition to the above two sons and five daughters of Isham Kendrick, the probate package shows that there was another daughter who married Page Rork prior to 1819, and received her share of the estate in 1822. The McMakins, as mentioned, moved to Cherokee Co., Ga. The McDavids also moved to Georgia, where Rosannah (Kendrick) McDavid died near Marietta. The son, Isham Jefferson Kendrick, was usually called Jefferson, according to Mrs. Walter M. Finlay, 102 Vannoy St., Greenville, S.C., a descendant of his brother, Alston Wood Kendrick, and she states that he died in Spartanburg Co., S.C. and is buried at the intersection of the two Tyger Rivers. He appears in deeds in Spartanburg Co. in 1840 and 1846 (D.B. "Y", p. 44; D.B. "Z", p. 358).

Alston[4] Wood Kendrick, son of Isham and Elizabeth (Duncan) Kendrick, was born Jan. 21, 1801 and died June 12, 1863 in Spartanburg or Greenville Co., S.C. He married Oct. 27, 1828, Susannah Few (b. Feb. 1, 1803, d. Dec. 3, 1884), and had two children:

I.   William[5] Isham Kendrick, b. April 28, 1835, d. May 27, 1892; m. (1) Sept. 25, 1859 Mary Ann Barton; m. (2) Nov. 18, 1862 Mrs. Julia (Gilreath) Rea (b. Sept. 8, 1836, d. Feb. 14, 1884); and m. (3) Jan. 4, 1885 Mary E. Rosamond. William I. Kendrick had no children by the third marriage. He had the following six children by his first two marriages, only the first being by his first wife:

1. Benjamin[6] Kendrick, died in infancy.
2. Charles Kendrick, who died April 7, 1884.
3. Anna[6] Kendrick, born Oct. 15, 1867, died Feb. 25, 1947, m. Dec. 9, 1890 John Wesley Watson Walker (b. Jan. 1, 1852, d. April 13, 1916), and had issue:
    (1) Willie Kendrick Walker, b. June 5, 1892, m. Aug. 28, 1947 Walter Marshall Finlay (b. July 9, 1890, at Asheville, N.C.), and resides at 102 Vannoy St., Greenville, S.C.
    (2) Edyth Walker, b. Feb. 1, 1897, M.E. (Duke University), teacher at Carolina College, Cullowhee, N.C.
    (3) Lillie Janette Walker, b. Feb. 25, 1900, died May 6, 1914.
4. John[6] W. Kendrick, b. June 16, 1871, d. April 25, 1936, m. April 16, 1896 Cora Taylor.
5. Mary[6] Eveline Kendrick b. June 25, 1873, m. July 16, 1896 Frederick Gibson James, M.D.
6. Fannie[6] Kendrick, b. Dec. 6, 1875, d. Dec. 22, 1937, m. July 21, 1897 Thomas E. Roe.

II.   Rachel[5] M. Kendrick, b. 1840, d. Nov. 7, 1922, m. 1863 Dr. Benjamin Franklin Few of Greer, S.C. (b. May 11, 1830, d. 1923), and had issue:

1. Robert Alston Few, b. 1865, d. 1897, Methodist minister, S.C. Conference.
2. William Preston Few, for many years a member of the Faculty of Trinity College, Durham, N.C., then President 1910-24, and first President of Duke University.
3. Sallie Leona Few, m. 1894 Martin Luther Merchant, and d. 1898.

4. Ignatius Pierce Few, m. 1894 Fannie Cannon; they were the parents of 11 children, one of whom is Benjamin F. Few, President of Liggett and Myers Tobacco Co., and another is Rev. E.C. Few, Methodist minister.
5. Ellie Few, unmarried, lives at the old home in Greer, South Carolina.

Martin[3] Kendrick

Martin[3] Kendrick may have been a son of William[2] Kendrick hose name was inadvertently omitted from William's will among ιe older children who were left only 1 shilling, as he was fairly losely associated with James[3] Kendrick and his three older sons, ohn, William and Burwell, in Chatham Co., N.C., married a ister of William[4] Kendrick's wife, and the name Martin persisted ι the families of both James[3] Kendrick and his brother, Jones[3] endrick, proved sons of William[2]. Martin Kendrick must have een born about 1745, as his wife, Susannah Thompson, was born ι Surry Co., Va. Nov. 16, 1749 (Albemarle Parish Reg.). She as the eldest daughter of William and Hannah (Bell) Thompson f Chatham Co., N.C. Information about the Thompson family ·ill be given in the section on William[4] Kendrick, who married ιsannah's youngest sister, Ann Thompson. It is probable that lartin Kendrick and Susannah Thompson were married in Chatam Co. about 1770, as the witnesses to a deed dated Dec. 11, 771 from John Thompson, eldest son of William and Hannah, to is brother William Thompson, are given as Balaam Thompson ι brother of John and William), Martha Hendrick, Susannah Henrick, and Sarah Thompson (an unmarried sister of John and Wil-.am Thompson) (Chatman D.B. "A", p. 88). Though the records f Chatham Co. contain a few references to a Hendrick family ιere, the names Martha and Susannah do not appear among the lendricks, and it is highly probable that the above names were ιiscopied by the Clerk and should be Martin Kendrick and Susannah .endrick, particularly as the deed seems to have been a family ffair and as the Thompson brothers were connected with Martin endrick in a number of later deeds in Chatham Co. Except for ιe above reference, the first appearance of Martin Kendrick in ιe Chatham Co. records was on Jan. 11, 1772, when he witnessed deed from John Davis to James[3] Kendrick (D.B. "A", p. 83).

Martin[3] Kendrick is given as a Tory Captain in Chatham Co. uring the Revolution by Col. David Fanning in a long list of offiers who "received their appointments from Major Ferguson in outh Carolina in July, 1780, but joined all according to their ates" (N.C. Col. & State Rec., Vol. 22, p.197). It is doubtful ·hether he accepted this appointment or ever was a Tory, but if o, he changed to the partiot side before the end of the Revolution, or the Revolutionary accounts show payments to him for Revo-.ıtionary services, one from Moore Co., which adjoined Chatham N.C. Rev. Accts., Book C, p. 127; Book IX, p. 108; Loose caneled voucher No. 5747). He was appointed road overseer August , 1775, recorded his mark for cattle at the Nov. Court, 1777, nd was sued in a land case by John Wilcox at the Aug. Court, 1778

(Chatham Co. Court Minutes 1774-9). He entered 640 acres of land in Chatham Co. on Cedar Creek, adjoining James[3] Kendrick and his son, John[4] Kendrick, on March 29, 1779, and this land was granted him Oct. 23, 1782 (N.C. Grant Book 48, p. 44; Chatham Co. D.B. "B", p. 443). He deeded some of this land to Thomas Galloway in 1785, John Thompson being a witness to the deed (D.B. "D", p. 287); was deeded land by John[4] Kendrick in 1782 (D.B. "C", p. 464); witnessed a deed from William Thompson to Simon Terrell (who married his wife's sister Sarah) in 1787 (D.B. "D", p. 249); was granted 33 acres in Moore Co. Dec. 10, 1790 (Grant Bk. 77, p. 68); deeded away the balance of his land in Chatham Co. Aug. 12, 1793 to Thomas Galloway (D.B. "G", p. 92); and last appears in the Chatham Co. records in Dec. 1793, when he was sued by Richard Kennon. It is uncertain what became of Martin Kendrick after this. He may have moved to Moore Co., N.C., where all the county records have been destroyed, and appears to have died before 1800, as the Census records for that year show him in neither Chatham nor Moore. The Census of 1790 shows Martin Kendrick living in Chatham Co. with a family consisting of 2 males born before 1774 and 7 females. This would indicate that he and Susannah Thompson had 1 son (b. before 1774) and 6 daughters. The son was probably a William Kendrick who in shown in Chatham Co. in 1800 with a family consisting of 1 male and 1 female b. 1774-84, and 2 females b. 1790-1800. This William Kendrick was granted $25\frac{1}{2}$ acres of land in Chatham Co., which he deeded June 9, 1801 to John Hays (D.B. "L", p. 329' "N", p. 20). After this the Kendrick family disappears from Chatham Co. and there is no further information about the descendants of Martin[3] Kendrick.

John[4] Kendrick (James[3], William[2], John[1])

John[4] Kendrick was born about 1756, the eldest child of James[3] and Susannah (Roberson) Kendrick, in Granville Co., N.C., and died Dec. 14, 1802 in Washington Co., Ga. He married Martha Montgomery, daughter of John and Mary (Wilcox) Montgomery of Chatham Co., N.C., who died in Putnam Co., Ga. in 1882. The grandfather of Martha (Montgomery) Kendrick was Alexander Montgomery of Orange Co., N.C., who died in 1767 in that county. His will, dated July 27, 1767, mentions his wife; sons Alexander, Michael, James, and John Montgomery; daughters Ann and Mary; and son-in-law Robert Barnett of Amherst Co., Va. John Montgomery, the father of Martha, is mentioned a number of times in "The Colonial and State Records of North Carolina" around the time of the Revolutionary War. He was appointed on a committee with John Thompson by the Provincial Congress to inquire into the iron works in Chatham Co. owned by John Wilcox (Vol. 10, p. 949); sold a saw-mill to the iron works (Vol. 12, pp. 166-7 and 336); and was appointed on the Board of War on provisions and revolutionary supplies in Chatham Co. (Vol. 14, pp. 442-3). The Chatham Co. records show John Montgomery and his wife Mary in two deeds in 1788 (D.B. "D", p. 418; D.B. "F", p. 1). The first deed was witnessed by John Wilcox, John Thompson, and

William Thompson; the second by Pendleton Gaines (who was possibly a son-in-law). Dr. Jerome Dowd of the University of Oklahoma, who was descended from John Montgomery through his grandmother, Anna Maria (Gaines) Dowd, stated that Mary Montgomery, wife of John, was named Wilcox, that she was a sister of John Wilcox, who witnessed the deed above and owned the Chatham Co. iron-works which played a rather important part in North Carolina during the Revolution, and that John and Mary Wilcox were descendants of Thomas Wilcox, who lived near Philadelphia and owned the first paper mill in America. Judging by his will and the Census of 1790, which shows him with 18 slaves, John Montgomery was a rather wealthy man. He died in Chatham Co., N.C. in 1818. His will, dated Jan. 28, 1818 and probated in Chatham Co. (Chatham Co. Wills, p. 89, folio 4, N.C. Dept. of Archives and History at Raleigh), mentions his daughter Ann McKay; granddaughter Mary P. Mebane wife of Robert Mebane; wife, " all the plate and household furniture she brought me", daughter Eleanor Woodside of Pennsylvania and her son Robert Woodside; daughter Martha Kendrick of Georgia; daughter Elizabeth Gaines; daughter Deborah Debrutz; daughter Margaret Waudill; Peregrine Brooks, son of Abner Brooks; "all my negroes to have a suit of coarse black cloth as moarning"; "I also leave $100 to be placed in the hands of Archd. McBryde and William Tyson and to be paid over by them to such person as shall be selected by James Gaines and Abner Brooks to examine, collect, revise and digest the manuscript writings I have left and on making such collection to have them printed and published". Archibald McKay, one of the witnesses to the will, was probably the husband of the daughter Ann McKay. A codicil mentions a grandson, John Montgomery, son of the Daughter Elizabeth Gaines, "provided he shall continue my name, John Montgomery"; John's brother, William Montgomery Gaines; and mentions again the daughter Martha, grandson Robert Woodside, and the daughter Eleanor.

John[4] Kendrick was a Lieutenant in the Revolutionary troops under Gen. Butler and on Sept. 30, 1781, in a skirmish with the British and Tories at Brown Marsh, was wounded in the breast very severely. The wound incapacitated him to such a degree that he appealed for assistance, first to the Auditors of Hillsborough District and later to the Legislature of North Carolina. The County Court of Chatham Co. endorsed the petition, and he was finally granted a pension by the State of North Carolina. The North Carolina Colonial and State Records have a number of references to the matter (Vol. 18, pp. 122, 126, 173-4, 351 and 420; Vol. 19, pp. 526, 528, and 697; Vol. 20, pp. 192, 199, 236, 317, 418-19, and 425). The petition was made first about 1784 and was granted finally in 1787. John Kendrick also testified in 1784 to the innocence of Col. Alston in the death of Thomas Taylor, a Tory (Vol. 17, p. 399; Vol. 20, p. 73). The following payments to John Kendrick from the North Carolina Revolutionary Accounts at Raleigh also show his Revolutionary services, one of them mentioning that he was from Chatham Co., another being endorsed by him at "Lt. John Kendrick", and two others indicating that the

claim or pension had been transferred as an obligation to the
Federal Government (though some of these are in the name of
"J. Kendrick" rather than "John Kendrick"): Book IX, p. 61,
folio 2; Canceled Vouchers No. 4815 and 4971; Book V, p. 31;
Book IX, p. 59; Book VI, p. 51; Book IV, p. 54, folio 2. There
were several Revolutionary soldiers named John Kendrick in
Georgia after John[4] Kendrick moved there, but the reference to
"John Kendrick, Lieut" in Knight's "Georgia Roster of the Revolution" (p. 420) probably refers to him. That John[4] Kendrick was
a Lieutenant from North Carolina, received a pension of $150 a
year from the Federal Government, was transferred from North
Carolina to Georgia, and died in Georgia Dec. 14, 1802, is
shown on page 514 of the "Pension Roll of the American Revolution", Vol. III, Senate Documents 1st. Session 23rd Congress,
1835 (See also, Saffell "Revolutionary Record", p. 551).

John[4] Kendrick first appears in the records of Chatham Co.,
N.C. on Nov. 3, 1775, when he witnessed a deed from Matthew
Capps to his father, James[3] Kendrick (D.B. "B", p. 100). At
the November Court, 1777, he was appointed Constable in Capt.
Kendrick's District and Collector in District No. 5 (which was
also his father's district) (Chatham Co. Court Minutes, 1774-9).
On July 1, 1779 he was granted 199 acres in Chatham Co. (N.C.
Grant Bk. 30, p. 111), on March 30, 1780 he was granted 150
acres (Grant Bk. 36, p. 394), and on Oct. 9, 1783 he was granted
another 200 acres (Chatham D.B. "C", p. 226). These grants
were all adjoining the land of his father, James[3] Kendrick. Probably due to financial pressure due to incapacity from his wound
and before the granting of his pension, John[4] Kendrick disposed
of this land successively in three deeds, one to Martin[3] Kendrick
Dec. 24, 1782, one to James White Nov. 10, 1783, and the last
one from John Kendrick and Martha his wife to Daniel Dowd July
23, 1784 (D.B. "C", pp. 293, 464, and 480). John[4] Kendrick was
still living in Chatham Co., N.C. at the July Court, 1785, when
his brothers, Burwell and William Kendrick signed a bond for
him. He had moved to Wilkes Co., Ga., by 1787, when he and
his brother Burwell witnessed a deed there. He moved with his
father and brothers soon after this to Washington Co., Ga., where
he was appointed a Justice of the Peace Dec. 17, 1793 (Minutes
of Exec. Council of Ga., 1793-96, p. 32), and died there Dec. 14,
1802. John[4] Kendrick's widow, Martha Kendrick, was still living
in Washington Co. in 1805, when with other Kendricks she is mentioned as one of the eligibles for the Land Lottery of 1806. She
and her family soon moved to Putnam Co., Ga., however, joining her brothers-in-law, James[4] and Martin[4] Kendrick. She was
taxed for 3 slaves in Putnam in 1813, and appears in the Census
of 1820, with a family consisting of only two females, one born
before 1775, one born 1794-1804. Martha Kendrick died in Putnam Co., Ga. in 1822, her will being dated May 3, 1822 and probated in the same year. It leaves her daughter Betsy A. Kendrick
one-fifth of the estate; one-fifth to her four grandsons John W.,
William B., Walton T., and Robert M. Carter; $5.00 to her son-
in-law, Lewis Wright; and one-fifth each to Meredith Kendrick,
John Monk, and Priscilla Goode. John Monk and Priscilla Goode

were appointed executors, and the will was witnessed by Harvey
Kendrick (son of Benjamin[4] Kendrick), Richard Wright, and Silas
Monk. The children of John[4] Kendrick and Martha Montgomery
were the following:

I. Mary[5] Kendrick, daughter of John[4] and Martha (Montgomery)
    Kendrick, was probably born about 1785, as her eldest son,
    William B. Carter, was born in 1805. She probably died be-
    tween 1830 and 1840 in Putnam Co., Ga. Her first husband
    was John Carter, son of Josiah Carter, a Revolutionary
    soldier who died in Putnam Co., Ga., in 1827. John Carter
    was dead by 1820, at which time Mary (Kendrick) Carter
    was married to her second husband, Lewis Wright. The
    Census of 1820 for Putnam Co. shows Lewis Wright with a
    family consisting of one male and one female b. 1775-94,
    3 males b. 1804-10, and 5 males b. 1810-20. Lewis Wright
    died before 1830, for the Census of that year shows Mary
    Wright as head of the family, which consisted of 1 female
    b. 1790-1800, 1 male b. 1810-15, 1 male b. 1815-20, and
    2 females b. 1820-25. By her first marriage Mary Kendrick
    had the following children:

    1. John[6] W. Carter, who m. Elizabeth Langford Dec. 16,
       1329 in Putnam Co., Ga. It is possible that his first wife
       died almost at once and that he is identical with a John
       W. Carter who married in Wilkes Co., Ga. Nov. 22,
       1830 Elizabeth[5] Caroline Kendrick, daughter of Jones[4]
       Kendrick. However, this is uncertain.

    2. William[6] Bennett Carter, b. 1805 (Census), was Ordin-
       ary of Putnam Co. from 1830 until his death in 1867. He
       died April 13, 1867. His first wife was Ariadne E. Aber-
       crombie, whom he married in Putnam Co. Oct. 3, 1830.
       According to my father's cousin, Ben C. Carter, who
       was her grandson, she was a daughter of Wylie Aber-
       crombie and granddaughter of Charles Abercrombie, an
       officer in the Revolution. Cousin Ben also stated that
       William[6] B. Carter's paternal grandmother was named
       Mollie Anthony. After his first wife's death, William B.
       Carter m. (2) Jan. 27, 1857 Susan Emma Clark of Put-
       nam Co., daughter of Jeremiah Clark (see Clark Family).
       She m. (2) May 12, 1870 Joseph A. Moseley of Eatonton.
       The Census of 1850 shows William B. Carter, merchant,
       b. 1805 in Georgia, living at Eatonton with his wife, Ari-
       adne (b. 1813), and the following children: Leonard, b.
       1833; Thomas b. 1835; Savannah b. 1837; William b. 1839;
       Edgar b. 1841; Robert b. 1844; Mark b. 1846; and Aber-
       crombie b. 1849. William B. Carter was in the mercan-
       tile business in the firm of Harvey and Carter, as well
       as being Ordinary of the County. His estate was adminis-
       tered by Thomas G. Lawson June 18, 1867. The records
       from the Estate Book show Lizzie H. Carter, Sydney A.
       Carter, and Thomas W. Carter as minor heirs in later
       years; and Minute Book C, p. 201, shows that Evan Har-
       vey was appointed guardian of Mark A., Elizabeth H., and
       Sydney A. Carter Aug. 5, 1867. Of the children of William

Bennett Carter, Thomas W. Carter died in 1881. Savannah Carter m. (1) Mr. Ross and (2) March 8, 1881, Sandy Suther. William Bennett Carter, Jr., married Oct.
26, 1865 Adeline Elizabeth Clark, a cousin, daughter of
Benjamin W. and Julia[5] Caroline (Kendrick) Clark, and
granddaughter of James[4] Kendrick (see Clark Family).
They had one son, Bennett Cook Carter, who married
Mamie Roquemore, and had two children, Addie Carter
who married Vernon Phillips and lives in Cuthbert, Ga.,
and Clark Carter.

3. Walter[6] T. Carter.

4. Robert[6] M. Carter, b. 1813, a minister. He married
Martha L. Collingsworth in Putnam Co. Dec. 7, 1837.
His family is shown in Putnam Co. in the Census of 1850
as: Robert M. Carter, Minister, b. 1813, Martha L.
Carter b. 1820, David Carter b. 1842, William C. Carter b. 1845, Mary F. Carter b. 1847, and Robert Carter
b. 1850 (1 month old).

By her second marriage to Lewis Wright, Mary[5] Kendrick
had:

5. Benjamin[6] Harvey Wright, b. Feb. 7, 1819, d. April 28,
1903, m. Emily Eubanks Tompkins and moved to Carroll
Co., Ga. Their children were: Tompkins Wright; Benjamin Wright; Emma Wright; Katherine Wright; Nicholas
Wright; Ada Wright; and William Carter Wright. William
Carter Wright was born in Carroll Co., Ga. Jan. 6, 1866
and died June 11, 1933. He married (1) Pauline E. Arnold,
who died in 1918; he m. (2) Mrs. Rosa May F. Bunn. By
his first wife he had: Evelyn Wright (now Mrs. William
Banks of Newnan, Ga.), Arnold Wright, William C. Wright,
and two children who died young. William Carter Wright
was U.S. Congressman from the Fourth Ga. District
from 1917 to 1933.

6. and 7. Martha[6] Wright and Elizabeth[6] Wright. One of
these daughters married Hilary Cherry, the other a Mr.
Goodyear. Both lived in Macon, Ga.

II. Priscilla[5] Kendrick married a Goode and her husband died
prior to 1820, for the Putnam Co. Census of that year shows
Priscilla Goode as head of a household consisting of 1 female
b. 1775-94, 2 females b. 1804-10, and 1 male and 1 female
b. 1810-1820. She had moved to Bibb County by 1832, for
the "Cherokee Land Lottery" shows Priscilla Goode, widow,
living in Candler's District, Bibb Co., who drew land in
Murray Co. One of her daughters was probably a Priscilla
Goode who was the mother of Dr. James Alexander Thornton,
who married Mollie Harrison, a descendant of Benjamin[4]
Kendrick. Mollie (Harrison) Thornton's nephew, Mr. John
B. Harrison of Atlanta, Ga., stated that his aunt and her
husband knew that they were kin through the Kendricks.

III. Meredith[5] Kendrick was born in 1790 (Census) in Wilkes or
Washington Co., Ga. and died after 1850 in Putnam Co.,
Ga. He married (1) Sept. 5, 1814 in Putnam Co. Charity
Harvey (b. 1797), daughter of Evan and Charity (Powell)

Harvey of Putnam Co. (see Harvey, Powell and Williams Families). After her death he married (2) Sept. 28, 1833 Mariah Stevens (b. 1811-Census), who was still living in 1850. Deeds in Putnam Co. show that Meredith Kendrick was closely associated with Harvey Kendrick (son of Benjamin[4] Kendrick), Jones Kendrick (son of Martin[4]), and the descendants of James[4] Kendrick. He was a wealthy man and left to each of his two daughters by his first marriage over 1000 acres of land and an ample home, one of which is still in the possession of a great-great-grandson. These daughters were:

1. Civility[6] Kendrick, b. 1814, m. Allen Lawrence in 1838 in Putnam Co., Ga. The family is shown in 1850 next to Meredith Kendrick in the Census as follows: Allen Lawrence, Jr., b. 1814 in Ga., C.C. Lawrence (female) b. 1814 in Ga., William Lawrence b. 1838, four daughters, C. Lawrence b. 1840, S. Lawrence b. 1842, M. Lawrence b. 1844, and A. Lawrence b. 1846, and a son, M.K, Lawrence b. 1850 (4 mos. old). The Census shows Civility (Kendrick) Lawrence's middle initial as "C", which indicates that she was named for Civility (Harvey) Coates, her mother's sister (see Harvey Family). Mr. A. J. Rosey gave the names of the children of Allen and Civility (Kendrick) Lawrence to Miss Lillie Odum, Route 4, Eatonton, Ga., as follows: Maria Lawrence m. William T. Stewart; Charity Lawrence m. David Lawrence, Sarah Lawrence m. James L. Stewart; Molly Lawrence m. Dave Dawson; Addie Lawrence d.s.p.; Meredith Kendrick Lawrence m. (1) Annie Lawrence dr. of Charles Lawrence and (2) "Gyp" Wiggins; and Lula Lawrence, never married. These names correspond pretty well to those given in the 1850 Census, except that the son William was not mentioned by Mr. Rosey and propably died young; and there is some doubt as to whether the "M. Lawrence" who was born in 1844 was Maria or Molly.

2. Sarah[6] Kendrick (Sally) was born in 1818 (Census) and married Sept.16, 1833 in Putnam Co. James Lawrence. The following list of names of the children of James and Sarah (Kendrick) Lawrence were given by Mr. Rosey to Miss Odum, the dates being taken from the Census:

    (1) Laura Lawrence, b. 1848, m. Terry Dismukes;
    (2) Martha Lawrence b. 1850 m. John Francis Williams;
    (3) Samuel Lawrence b. 1856, d.s.p.
    (4) Sadie Lawrence b. 1846 m. Thomas Wooten;
    (5) a daughter who m. Mr. Jenkins;
    (6) a daughter who m. Mr. Sparks;
    (7) a daughter, "Make", who m. (1) Mr. Rainey and (2) Major Anderson;
    (8) David Lawrence b. 1846 m. (1) "Make" Lawrence (2) Johnnie Philips. David Lawrence had a daughter by his first marriage, who m. Will Philips, and several daughters by his second marriage.

IV.   Salive[5] Kendrick, daughter of John[4] and Martha (Montgomery)

Kendrick, married John Monk, probably as his first wife. The biography of M.K. Monk (did these initials stand for "Meredith Kendrick"?) of Lumpkin, Ga. in "Memoirs of Georgia" states that he was born Sept. 15, 1819, the son of John and Salive (Kendrick) Monk; and that John Monk married four times and reared 15 children, of whom 7 were stepchildren. One of John Monk's wives was Elizabeth Kendrick, whom he married in Putnam Co. July 22, 1830. This Elizabeth Kendrick probably belonged to another numerous family of Kendricks who resided in Putnam Co. from its organization until about 1830 or 1835. They were related to Hezekiah Kendrick, a Revolutionary soldier, who was probably born in Maryland, and were a very large family connection. They lived in another district from our Kendricks and appear to have been unconnected with our family.

V.   Elizabeth[5] A. (Betsy A.) Kendrick, youngest daughter of John[4] and Martha (Montgomery) Kendrick, was unmarried in 1822, and is probably identical with a Betsy Kendrick who married William Benson May 29, 1823 in Putnam Co. (Book D. p. 63).

William[4] Kendrick (James[3], William[2], John[1])

William[4] Kendrick, apparently the second son of James[3] and Susannah (Roberson) Kendrick, was born in Granville Co., N.C. about 1758 (his eldest son, Benjamin, was born 1778-9, his elder brother John was born about 1756, and the Census of 1830 shows him as born 1750-60). He married (1) about 1777-8 in Chatham Co., N.C. Ann Thompson (some descendants give her name as Eliza Ann or Elizabeth Ann), daughter of William and Hannah (Bell) Thompson of Chatham Co., N.C. She died in Washington Co., Ga. about 1800, and William Kendrick m. (2) about 1800-5 Margaret Watt or Watts from near Milledgeville, Ga. William Kendrick died in St. Helena Parish, La. Feb. 26, 1838. His second wife, Margaret Watt, died in Livingston Parish, La., in 1845. There is no clue to the parentage of Margaret Watt, though one wonders whether she may not have been a daughter of Benjamin Watts, to whom James[3] Kendrick finally deeded all his land in 1784 in Chatham Co., N.C. Margaret (Watt) Kendrick's age is given as between 50 and 60 in the 1840 Census of Livingston Parish, La., so she was born 1780-90.

The ancestry of Hannah Bell, mother of Ann (Thompson) Kendrick, has been given in Boddie's "Southside Virginia Families" Vol. I, pp. 35ff and p. 48ff). She was the daughter of John and Hannah Bell of Surry Co., Va.; the granddaughter of John Bell and Ann Bennett of Surry Co.; the great-granddaughter of Richard Bennett, Jr., of Isle of Wight Co., Va.; the great-great-granddaughter of Richard Bennett, Sr., and wife Anne of Isle of Wight Co.; and the great-great-great-granddaughter of Thomas and Alice Bennett, Thomas Bennett having been a member of the Virginia House of Burgesses in 1632. William Thompson, the father of Ann (Thompson) Kendrick, was born about 1720 or 1721 in Surry Co., Va., as he was granted land there in 1742 and was married to Hannah Bell by 1742 or 1743 (their eldest son was born in 1744). The grant was for 350 acres on the north side of Three Creeks and near Plowmans Swamp, and was dated July 30, 1742 (Grant Bk. 20, p. 425). The births of the four eldest children of William and Hannah (Bell) Thompson were given in the Albermarle Parish Register, from 1744 to 1749. In 1746 2 acres of the above land was appraised for a mill, William Thompson, Sr. being an appraiser; and in 1748 William Thompson, Jr., deeded the 2 acres to John Morgan for a mill (Surry O.B. 1744-9, pp. 244 and 293; D.B. 5, p. 321). William Thompson is again called William Thompson, Jr., on Sept. 15, 1751, when he was ordered to procession land (Albemarle Psh. Vestry Bk., p. 71). The above records indicate the William Thompson was a son of another William Thompson; and if so, it must have been a William Thompson of Albemarle Parish, Surry Co., Va., who died in 1752, and whose will, dated Dec. 28, 1751 and probated April 21, 1752, leaves all his property to his wife Mary, daughter Mary Killebrew, and son James (Surry D. & W., 1735-54, p. 757). This William Thompson Sr., was probably from Prince George Co. originally, for William Thompson was granted 1316 acres in Prince George Co. in 1747 (Grant Bk. 28, p. 301), and William Thompson, Jr., was granted 2000 acres in the same county Aug. 20, 1748 (Grant Bk. 26, p. 588). The account of the estate of Thomas Clifton, decd., in Prince George Co. in July, 1726 by Mary Clifton, the widow, contains an item, "By William Thompson's children's legacy' and mentions a payment to Chappell Thompson (Prince George Co. D. & W. 1713-28, p. 903). Thomas Clifton's will, dated Dec. 11, 1724 and probated in Prince George Jan. 12, 1724/25, mentions only his son William, daughter Elizabeth, wife Mary, and "my youngest daughter" (same p. 577). It is possible that the youngest daughter was Mary, wife of William Thompson, Sr. In spite of the fact that William Thompson, Sr., of Surry does not mention a son, William, Jr., in his will in 1751, it seems highly probable that William, Jr. (who married Hannah Bell) was his son. I thought in previous years that William Thompson, father of Ann Kendrick, was a son of John Thompson, who died in Surry Co. in 1755, and whose will mentions a son William; that he was grandson of William Thompson who died there in 1732; and was great-grandson of Rev. William Thompson, early minister of Surry Co. However, this John Thompson of 1755 was apparently unmarried when his father's will was written in 1732, while our William Thompson must have been born at least as early as 1721; a discrepancy in time which seems to make the identification impossible. In addition, the William Thompson who died in 1732, was still under age in 1699 and it is not proven that he was married to his wife, Martha Moseley, until 1708, so that it is hard to see how he could have had a grandson born as early as 1721. William Thompson and Martha Moseley did have a son William, who is mentioned in the will of his uncle Samuel Thompson in 1721; but this son seems to have died young, for he is not mentioned in his father's will in 1732, and the wording of the will seems to indicate rather specifically that all the children and grandchildren (only two of the latter) are mentioned.

William Thompson (Jr.), who married Hannah Bell, sold his
land in Surry Nov. 25, 1751, his wife signing the deed (D.B.
6, p. 423), and moved to Brunswick Co., Va., where he was
deeded land in 1752 (D.B. 5, p. 163), was granted land in 1753
(Grant Bk. 32, p. 27), and on Aug. 24, 1761, in a joint deed with
Hannah his wife finally sold out again (D.B. 7, p. 11). James
Thompson, son of the William who died in 1752, signed the Surry
deed in 1751, which is another indication that William Thompson
(Jr.) was a son of William Thompson who died in 1752. William
Thompson may have moved to North Carolina before he sold out
in Brunswick Co., Va. in 1761, for the Orange Co., N.C. deeds
show that he was deeded land there in 1758. He was certainly living in Orange Co. in 1764, for he was deeded land there in May
and November of that year. He was a Justice of Orange Co. in
1768 and took various depositions there in that year in the months
of April and May (N.C. Col. and State Rec., Vol. 7, pp. 773-7,
779 and 782). William Thompson's land fell into Chatham Co., N.
C., on the organization of that county, and he died there between
1771 and 1773. He owned an interest in a saw-mill in Chatham Co.
and in the iron works which were later sold to John Wilcox and were
of great importance during the Revolution. He may have been dead
by Dec. 11, 1771, when his eldest son, John Thompson, deeded
land to the youngest son, William (Chatham D.B. "A", p. 88). He
was certainly dead by Jan. 30, 1773, when John and Balaam Thompson, admrs. of William Thompson's estate, deeded to John Mont-
gomery $\frac{1}{4}$ interest in the iron-works and $\frac{1}{2}$ interest in a saw-mill
that he had owned on Deep River (D.B. "A", p. 331). William
Thompson's wife, Hannah, died in Chatham Co., N.C. in 1788,
mentions son John Thompson; daughter Susannah Kendrick and her
husband; daughter Mary Self; daughter Sarah Terrell and her husband; daughter Ann Kendrick and her husband; son William Thompson; deceased husband, William Thompson; and makes her sons
John and Balaam Thompson executors. The children of William
and Hannah (Bell) Thompson, as gathered from the Albemarle Parish Register and from the will (which appears to name the daughters in order of ther age) were:

I.   John Thompson, b. June 24, 1744, christened Aug. 19, 1744,
      m. Susannah -------- (cf. Chatham D.B. "D", p. 219), and
      died in Chatham Co., N.C. in 1811. John Thompson was a
      Justice of Chatham Co. in 1774, 1775 and later years (N.C.
      Col. & State Rec., Vol. 7, p. 89; Vol. 9, pp. 1027 and 1169);
      was a delegate in 1775 from Chatham Co. to the Provincial
      Congress (same, Vol. 10, pp. 165, 167, 173, 500, 502, and
      523); was a member of the Committee of Safety of Hillsborough
      District (same, Vol. 10, p. 215); and represented Chatham
      Co. in the Convention of 1789 (Vol. 22, pp. 37, 47, and 48).
      His will, dated June 3, 1808, and probated in Chatham Co.
      in 1811, names only a deceased daughter Martha, her son
      Jerry, and a son William, though it alludes to other children
      without mentioning their names.

II.   Balaam Thompson, b. Oct. 13, 1745, bapt. Dec. 15, 1745,
      m. Olive ------- (see Chatham D.B. "B", p. 35), Justice
      of Chatham Co. in 1775 and later years (N.C. Col. & State

Rec. Vol. 9, p. 1169; Vol. 23, p. 993), last appears in Chatham Co. in 1793.

III. William Thompson, b. Aug. 10, 1747, bapt. Nov. 8, 1747, last appears in Chatham Co. in a deed in 1797.

IV. Susannah Thompson, b. Nov. 16, 1749, bapt. March 18, 1749/50, m. ca. 1770 Martin[3] Kendrick.

V. Mary Thompson, b. approximately 1751-2, m. Mr. Self, probably Parrish Self who was deeded land in Chatham Co. in 1787 and 1789 (Chatham D.B. "D", pp. 227 and 645).

VI. Sarah Thompson, b. approximately 1753-4, m. Simon Terrell (cf Chatham D.B. "B", p. 225; D.B. "D", pp. 32 and 84). Simon Terrell was the son of Timothy Terrell, who died in Orange Co., N.C. in 1763, his will, dated Feb. 1, 1763, mentioning his wife, sons Solomon, Micajah, Nimrod, Simon, Moses, Daniel, Richard, and Aaron; and daughters Jemima, Ruth, Millie, Mary, Betty, and Cuzziah. Simon and Sarah Terrell were still living in Chatham Co., N.C. in 1790, but moved later to Georgia, where their son William Terrell married in Morgan Co. in 1817 his first cousin, Sarah Kendrick, daughter of William[4] and Ann (Thompson) Kendrick.

VII. Hannah Thompson, b. approximately 1756-7, m. Aaron Terrell, brother of Simon (cf. Chatham D.B. "D", p. 503).

VIII. Ann Thompson, b. ca. 1758-9, m. William[4] Kendrick.

William[4] Kendrick first appears in the North Carolina records in 1780, when he was paid for Revolutionary services (N.C. Rev. Accts. Book "B", p. 297). He received another payment in 1783, exactly the same as to his brother, Burwell Kendrick, indicating that they saw the same service (Book I, p. 18, folio 2! Canceled Voucher No. 4823). On April 9 and April 20, 1784, he received two deeds from James[3] Kendrick, in one of which James Kendrick calls him his son (Chatham D.B. "C", pp. 455 and 458). In July, 1785, William Kendrick and Burwell Kendrick signed the bond of their brother, John Kendrick, in Chatham Co. (from loose documents in the Court House), and Burwell deeded to William in 1786 the land which the father, James, had deeded to Burwell (D.B. "D", p. 419). William Kendrick deeded away this latter piece of land in 1788 (D.B. "F", p. 258); was living in Chatham Co. in 1790 with a family consisting of 1 male b. before 1774, 1 male b. 1774-90, and 3 females (Census); and last appears in the records of Chatham Co. on March 1, 1791, when he deeded the rest of his land to Charles McGee (D.B. "E", p. 306). He moved soon after this to Georgia, joining his father and brothers in Washington Co., and on March 26, 1798 was appointed Captain in the Second Battalion of Washington Co. Militia in room of Burwell Kendrick, who had removed to Montgomery Co., Ga. (Min. Exec. Counc. of Ga., p. 255). He is shown along with other Kendricks in 1805 among the list of eligibles in Washington Co. for the coming lottery, and in the Lottery of 1806 itself his son, James[5] Kendrick, received a lucky draw, perhaps transferred to him by his father. In 1808 and 1809 William Kendrick was deeded land in Morgan Co., Ga. (Morgan D.B. "A", p. 444; "B", p. 196), and removed there about 1810, appearing in deeds from 1810 to 1818 (D.B. "C", pp. 74 and 119; D.B. "D", p. 177; D.B. "F", pp. 38, 221 and 421). William

Kendrick was a Justice of the Inferior Court of Morgan Co. from May 28, 1812 to Oct. 27, 1813.

In 1818 William[4] Kendrick moved from Morgan Co., Ga. to St. Helena Parish, La. His eldest son, Benjamin Kendrick, had gone to Louisiana as early as 1798, according to his tombstone; and his son-in-law, Robert Fluker, who witnessed a deed from William Kendrick in Morgan Co. and married his daughter, Susan, preceded him to Louisiana. The whole family moved to that State, except his son, James, who remained in Washington Co., Ga.; the daughter Sarah and her husband William Terrell, who moved to Gwinnett Co., Ga.; and the daughter Rebecca and her husband, Gooderum Davis. The Davises, however, moved to Louisiana in the early 1820's, so that only James and Sarah remained permanently in Georgia. The following letter from William Kendrick's son, Kenyon Thompson Kendrick, to his brother-in-law and first cousin, William Terrell of Carnesville, Ga., dated from St. Helena Parish, La. June 4, 1818, gives details of the trip: "Dear Sir: I now write to inform you of the many difficulties which I have had to encounter with in getting to this part of the world. We set out from Georgia on the 17th of February and reached R. Fluker's on the 15th of April. The weather was extremely unfavorable and the roads intolerably bad. We were several times winterbound and had to take our wagons to pieces and carry them over on logs. We repaired several bridges and built one flat and dug down the banks of the Chattahoochee 60 feet. - The Indians were extremely dangerous, they were murdering on all sides of us daily; the first depredation was within 12 miles of our camp, and the second was before us 25 miles, and the third 4 miles. Our camp was viewed more than once, and there was nothing saved us from an attack only our company made a very formidable show. - There were several families with my father and our arms consisted of 4 guns, 5 pistols, and 10 Tomahawks. When we reached Fort Claborn, we stayed 2 nights and one day to lay in some provisions; after we were supplied and all ready, we again took up the line of march, but discovered that Tony had given us the slip and was gone. The family crossed the Alabama, and continued their march for the Louisianas, and I in pursuit of Tony, I was determined to have him at the risk of my own scalp. I followed him four days and then turned back, being convinced that I was ahead of him. The fifth day I made a great day's travel in order to reach a fort that night, and on my arrival to my great mortification I found it vacated. It was then dark - I rode about a mile farther and struck camp. I had fed my horse and was sitting by my fire broiling my meat and thinking of Georgia - I turned for a stick for the purpose of taking off my meat and discovered that the fort was enveloped in flames; my meat was an object, I took care of that, then knocked out my fire, went about three hundred yards farther, and went to sleep within 200 yards of the house of Ogle where there were nine persons murdered a few days previous. The sight of this was enough to raise indignation in the breast of the most constitutional coward; and to cause him to take up the weapons of revenge. The floor was covered with blood, and the tracks of the infants hands in blood all over the floor. ---- I am, Yours truly, K. T. Kendrick."

The above letter, along with the following others, from which excerpts will be given, were preserved by Mrs. Sarah (Kendrick) Terrell and inherited by her granddaughter, Mrs. George S. King of Atlanta, Ga.: (1) Letter from Susan Fluker to Sarah Terrell, Aug. 4, 1818 hopes that Mr. Terrell and Mr. Davis will move to Louisiana; mentions her brother James from whom she hopes to hear; sends regards to her Uncle and Aunt Terrell and her cousin Hannah; congratulates Sarah on her new-born son, to be called W.K. T.; and says that she herself has 6 children with the 7th at hand. (2) Letter from same to same, from Red Bluff, St. Helena, La. June 17, 1835 mentions the death of her brother Kenyon, who left a widow, a very fine woman, two little children by his first wife and an infant by the last; mentions her old father, still living but helpless and confined to bed 3 months with rheumatic gout; that all her father's youngest set of children were married, except two, William and John; that Gooderum Davis, her sister Rebecca, and their family were well; that her eldest daughter, who married Adville Atkins, had died and left a little daughter, that Adville had married her sister Rebecca's eldest daughter and "Becky" had taken the grandchild; and that she had 8 children then living, Baldwin the eldest aged 22, Jemima 18, George 17, Owen 14, Elizabeth Ann Thompson, 12, Susan 10, Rebecca and Elizabeth quite young. (3) From same to same April 16, 1849: that her children lived near her and were doing well; that her daughter Eliza who married Mr. H. Edwards had 3 children, 2 sons and a daughter; that Susan, her next oldest daughter, who married Amos Kent, had 5 children, 3 sons and 2 daughters; that Elizabeth, her youngest daughter, who married Dr. A. B. Taylor, had a son about 3 months old and that Dr. Taylor was a young physician who stood high and had a very fine practice; that her granddaughter, Ann Atkins, married about 8 months previously Mr. A. D. Woodward, a very worthy young man; that her eldest son George lived within 2 miles and had 2 children, a son and a daughter, that her youngest son, Owen, had gone to California; that Goodrum Davis' family were doing well and all his children married; that Kenyon's widow had not married again and that Kenyon's son James lived in Tennessee and his daughter Theresa in Arkansas; mentions the heirs of her brother James and brother Kenyon in connection with her father's estate; and that poor James Harvey (who married her half-sister) had been unfortunate, two of his daughters and their children having been drowned the preceding summer in Lake Pontchartmain when the steamboat they were in burned. (4) Letter from E. S. Longmade of Sandersville, Ga. (who married a daughter of William[4] Kendrick's son James) to Kenon Terrell of Lawrenceville, Ga., son of Sarah (Kendrick) Terrell, June 10, 1849, mentions the claim in Louisiana (to William[4] Kendrick's estate) and William Kendrick and James Mays (his brothers-in-law), who then resided in Baker Co., Ga. (5) Letter from Goodrum Davis of St. Helena, La., to Sarah Terrell of Lawrenceville, Ga., August 12, 1850, calls her sister; states that Kennon Kendrick's daughter Theresa married a Mr. McDermit, moved to Arkansas, had died leaving 5 children, that one of the children had died since the mother's death, that McDermit had married again, and was

a very pious man, doting on his children; that James Kendrick
(son of Kenyon) lived in Nashville, Tenn., married and doing
well; that 6 of her father's youngest children were living and
"scattered all over the world"; that Matilda (widow of Kenyon
Kendrick) had never married again; that he had 21 grandchildren
living and 12 dead; and that Robert and Susan Fluker and their
children were well. (6) Letter from same to same, May 13, 1857,
announcing the death of her sister, Susan Fluker, on May 3, a
sudden death, and that Fluker was taking it hard; that W. K. Davis (his son) lost his eldest daughter on April 3! and that "sister
Gillet" (his own sister) informed him of the death of her brother,
John, on Nov. 15, last.

Mrs. Rebah Tillery Smith, Greensburg, La., a descendant
of William[4] Kendrick through his daughter Rebecca, who married
Gooderum Davis, writes of William Kendrick: "Capt. Kendrick
stood erectly and his young grandson, William Kendrick Davis,
my grandfather, who was born in Georgia in 1820 and brought to
Louisiana when 3 years old, disliked to ride on horseback behind
his grandfather, because he leaned back too far." William Kendrick was granted land in St. Helena Parish, La. as early as
1807 (La. Land Office), but did not occupy it until 1818. He and
his family are shown in the Census there for the years 1820 and
1830, the latter Census showing that he was born between 1750
and 1760. Mrs. Tillery, who examined the county records carefully, states that William Kendrick's signature is first shown in
the records of St. Helens Parish on May 25, 1819, and that his
first purchase was two tracts of land on the west side of the Tick-
jaw River in E. Feliciana Parish. He was instrumental in getting
the county seat located at Greensburg, La., which was near his
own lands, in 1834, and in 1837 he and his wife, Margaret, gave
to the town the lot on which the Court House was later located.
William[4] Kendrick died in St. Helenea Parish, La. Feb. 26, 1838.
His second wife, Margaret (Watt) Kendrick, La., in 1845, James
Harvey, her son-in-law, being appointed her administrator April
28, 1845. Mrs. Smith writes that the county records show that
William Kendrick's property amounted to over $30,000 at the public
sale in July, 1838, including 700 acres adjoining the town of Greens-
burg; that the records show as heirs Rebecca Davis, wife of
Goodrum Davis, Susan Fluker, wife of Robert Fluker et al; David
Fluker of E. Feliciana Parish, tutor of the heirs of Kennion Ken-
drick, decd., to wit, Theresa and James, absent heirs, in 1844,
James Kendrick and Sarah Terrell, widow of William Terrell,
both of Georgia, and James H. Kendrick of Tennessee (son of
Kenyon Kendrick); two minor heirs, William C. and John Watt
Kendrick; that Farrish C. Kendrick of Mississippi and Isham
Kendrick (who was his father's overseer at the time of the latter's
death) were also sons, as well as Benjamin Kendrick, who built
the mansion, "Asphodel", in East Feliciana Parish.

The descendants of William[4] Kendrick have been interested in
the family history for over 50 years, and various lists of his children, some of them sent to Hon. Greene Kendrick of Waterbury,
Conn., many years ago when he started work on the genealogy,
agree to the names of 13 children by his two wives, as follows:

Benjamin Kendrick b. 1778-9; James Kendrick b. 1780; Kenyon
Thompson Kendrick; Susan Kendrick b. 1790; Rebecca Kendrick
b. 1795; Sarah Kendrick, b. June 1797; Isham Kendrick; Mary
Elizabeth Kendrick; Farrish Carter Kendrick b. 1810; Reuben
Kendrick; Tucker Kendrick; William C. Kendrick; and John Watt
Kendrick, b. 1820. Some of the lists add the name of Matilda
Kendrick, mentioned in Goodrum Davis' letter to Sarah Terrell,
but she was the second wife of Kenyon T. Kendrick. All the lists
agree that Benjamin Kendrick, b. 1778-9, who built "Asphodel",
was a son; but if so, William[4] Kendrick had two sons named Benjamin apparently, one by the first wife and one by the second,
Mrs. Julia Henning of Jackson, Miss., a granddaughter of Farrish Carter Kendrick, writes that William[4] Kendrick had a son
named Benjamin who married Julia Cargill Warner, and that a
long time after her grandfather's death, his brothers, Benjamin
and John, visited in her father's home. Deeds recorded in St.
Helena Parish, La. show that there was a younger son, Benjamin, to whom William[4] Kendrick deeded 640 acres of land June
7, 1830 (D.B. "D", p. 57), which land Benjamin Kendrick and
his wife, Mary Permelia, deeded away June 13, 1836. William[4]
Kendrick and Margaret his wife, also, deeded slaves to this
Benjamin Kendrick on Feb. 12, and Feb. 18, 1835. These deeds
show that there certainly was a younger son, Benjamin Kendrick,
in St. Helena Parish, La. with his father, as the elder Benjamin
Kendrick lived in East Feliciana Parish, and his wife was named
Caroline. Mary Permelia Kendrick must have been the first wife
of Benjamin Kendrick II, and Julia Cargill Warner the second.
Of the children mentioned, Benjamin I, Kenyon, James, Susan,
Rebecca and Sarah were by the first marriage to Ann Thompson;
Mary Elizabeth, Farrish C., Reuben, Tucker, William C., John
W., and Benjamin II, were by the second marriage to Margaret
Watt. There is some doubt as to whether the son Isham was by
the first or second marriage. Nothing is known of him, except that
he married Matilda W. Bradford Sept. 5, 1832 in St. Helena Par-
ish, La. and was overseer for his father at the time of the latter's
death in 1838. Nothing further is known of Reuben, Tucker, and
William C., either, except that William C. was a minor when his
father died. Mary Elizabeth, probably the eldest daughter by the
second marriage, as her husband was appointed administrator of
Margaret (Watt) Kendrick in 1845 and Margaret lived with them in
Livingston Parish, La., after William[4] Kendrick's death, married
James H. Harvey in St. Helena Parish May 8, 1820. James H.
Harvey is perhaps identical with James H., son of Charles Harvey of Jefferson Co., Ga. (see Harvey Family). Nothing further
is known of this family, except that two of the daughters and their
children were drowned in Lake Pontchartrain in the summer of
1848, as mentioned in the letter of Susan Fluker to Sarah Terrell
in 1849.

Benjamin[5] Kendrick, son of William[4] and Ann Thompson Kendrick, was born in Chatham Co., N.C. in 1778 or 1779, moved
to East Felicians Parish, La. in 1798, and died there May 26, 1838.
The above dates are from his tombstone at "Asphodel", which
states: "Here lie the remains of Benjamin Kendrick, a Native of·

Georgia. He departed this life on the 36th day of May, 1838, in the 60th year of his age & for 40 years a citizen of Louisiana. He was not more beloved for the kindness and humbleness of his heart then respected for the honesty and righteousness of his character." The tombstone must be in error in stating that Benjamin was a native of Georgia, of course, though he no doubt moved from Washington Co., Ga. to Louisiana. Benjamin Kendrick married Caroline M. Pollard (b. 1795, d. Dec. 25, 1833 - dates from her tombstone at "Asphodel"). He was a wealthy man and built "Asphodel" in East Feliciana Parish, one of the great plantation houses of Louisiana, which is still standing and is mentioned in Spratling's and Scott's "Old Plantation Houses of Louisiana" and in the Saxon's "Old Louisiana". The house was completed in 1833, the year that his wife died. The great naturalist, Audubon, stayed at "Asphodel" while painting his birds, and did a number of portraits of the family as a way of paying his board.

Isabella[6] Ann Kendrick, only child of Benjamin[5] and Caroline (Pollard) Kendrick, was born Jan. 27, 1816, and died at "Asphodel" Dec. 27, 1875. She married May 29, 1834 David Jones Fluker (b. June 14, 1809, d. 1854), a nephew of Robert Fluker who married Susan[4] Kendrick and probably a son of David and Sarah (Harvey) Fluker of Georgia and Louisiana (see Harvey Family). The children of this couple were:

I   Sarah Caroline Fluker, b. Dec. 16, 1835, m. (1) Oct. 16, 1856 Joseph Glover Logan and had three daughters, Mel, Julia and Lulu who m. William C. Bentley. Sarah C. (Fluker) Logan m. (2) June 26, 1878 at Pulaski, Tenn, her cousin, James Harvey Kendrick, son of Kenyon[4] Kendrick, and died March 11, 1885;
II.   Benjamin K. Fluker, b. April 3, 1838;
III.   Horace Fluker, b. Nov. 10, 1839;
IV.   Mary Williams Fluker, b. Dec. 9, 1842, m. Oct. 11, 1865, James L. Bradford.
V.   John Fluker b. Jan. 5, 1845;
VI.   Isabella Augusta Fluker, b. Nov. 19, 1846, m. Jan. 6, 1869 John W. Leake;
VII.   David Jones Fluker, b. Oct. 10, 1848;
VIII.   Horace Fluker b. June 25, 1850;
IX.   Calhoun Fluker, b. May 6, 1852;
X.   William Sully Fluker, b. Oct. 5, 1853;
XI.   Louisiana Estelle Fluker, b. June 29, 1855.

James[5] Kendrick, son of William[4] and Ann (Thompson) Kendrick, was born in 1780 and died in 1845 in Washinton County, Ga. These dates are taken from a penciled card in the Georgia Department of Archives, Rhodes Memorial Hall, Atlanta, Ga., which states that he left 4 children. His wife may have been a Miss Davis, as he had a daughter Ann Davis Kendrick. James[5] Kendrick does not appear in the list of eligibles for the lottery of 1806, but in the actual lottery he had a lucky draw in Baldwin Co. His residence then was Capt. Kendrick's (i.e., his uncle, Capt. Jones[4] Kendrick's) District, Washington Co. The land fell into Jones Co. and he sold it to Job Taylor Aug. 7, 1809. He was deeded more land in 1815 in Jones Co. by Farrish Carter of

Baldwin Co., which he sold in 1816; and was deeded land in Pulaski Co., Ga. in 1814, which was not recorded until 1856 (Pulaski D.B. "M", p. 181). The tax-digest of 1825 shows James Kendrick of Washington Co., Ga. with 27 slaves and 2800 acres of land in various counties. He had 5 land-grants in Washington Co., two in 1816, one in 1817 and two in 1820 (Ga. Grant Bk. K-5, p. 574; p. 575; Bk. N-5, p. 58; Bk. O-5, p. 111; Bk. 22, p. 246). The minutes of the Executive Council of Georgia show that he was Sheriff of Washington Co. 1805-7, Tax Collector 1807-9. In 1816 he was a trustee of Sandersville Academy (Ga. Laws, 1815, p. 50). He represented Washington Co. in the State Legislature 1820-21, and the card at Rhodes Memorial Hall states that he was District Surveyor under Gov. Troup. James[5] Kendrick's children were:

I.   William[6] W. Kendrick, b. 1814 (Census), living as a single man in the family of his brother-in-law, James J. Mays, in Baker Co. in 1850. Dougherty Co. was formed from in 1852 and W. W. Kendrick was appointed First Lieutenant of the Dougherty Hussars Dec. 11, 1860, and was Justice of the Inferior Court there from 1854 to 1865.

II.   Caroline[6] S. Kendrick, b. 1817, m. James J. Mays and moved to Baker, later Dougherty Co., Ga. The 1850 Census for Baker Co. shows the family as: James J. Mays, b. 1811, Caroline S. Mays b. 1817, James Williams Mays, b. 1838, Sarah Ann Mays b. 1845, L. Taylor Mays b. 1847, George W. Mays b. 1849, Thomas F. Mays b. 1831 and William W. Kendrick b. 1814. "Savannah and South Georgia", p. 870, states that Judge Kendrick J. Hawkins of Dublin, Ga. was born in Washington Co., Ga., in 1871, the son of William A. Hawkins and Mary Mays of Dougherty Co., Ga. He was probably a grandson. The marriage of Caroline Kendrick and James J. Mays took place April 20, 1836, in Washington County, Ga.

III.   Ann[6] Davis Kendrick, b. 1818-18, m. Edward Sevey Longmade of Washington Co., Ga., a native of Canada and a lawyer. The 1850 Census of Washington Co. shows the family as: E. S. Longmade b. 1816 in L. Canada, Ann D. Longmade b. 1817 in Ga., Sarah Longmade b. 1845, and Missouri Longmade b. 1847. Sarah F. Longmade, the daughter, married John West Kendrick, a grandson of Jones[4] Kendrick. The Census of 1870 shows both these families living at Sandersville as follows: (1) Edward Longmade b. 1816 in Canada, lawyer, Anna D. Longmade b. 1818 in Ga., James or Jane Longmade b. 1852; (2) John West Kendrick b. 1842, Sarah F. Kendrick b. 1843, James Kendrick b. 1863, Mittie Kendrick b. 1865, and Buena Vista Kendrick, b. 1867.

IV.   Elizabeth[6] Kendrick m. John S. Longmade Aug. 10, 1843 in Washington Co.

Kenyon[5] Thompson Kendrick, son of William[4] and Ann (Thompson) Kendrick, was born about 1805 according to descendants, but this date seems too late, as he was a grown man in 1818 and his son James H. Kendrick was born in 1824. The Census of 1840 for West Feliciana Parish, La. shows him as the head of a large

household containing 2 males and 1 female b. 1780-90, 1 male
b. 1790-1800, 3 males and 1 female b. 1800-10, 1 male and 1 female b. 1820-25, and 1 female b. 1825-30, so that he could have
been any one of the older males mentioned. He married (1) Mary
Theresa Fluker, sister of David Jones Fluker who married Isabella[6] Ann Kendrick, daughter of his brother, Benjamin[5] Kendrick.
Mary Theresa and David Jones Fluker were nephew and niece of
Robert Fluker, who married Kenyon's sister, Susan Kendrick. They
were probably children of David Fluker (b. April 28, 1774) and his
wife Sarah, daughter of Rev. John Harvey (see Harvey Family),
as James H. Kendrick, son of Kenyon and Mary Theresa, was an
heir in the partition of the estate of Sarah Fluker, decd., in East
Feliciana Parish, La. Jan. 2, 1841 (D.B. "I", pp. 74-5). Kenyon
T. Kendrick married (2) Matilda Cook (b. 1807, d. after 1850-
Census). That her maiden name was Cook is indicated by the fact
that she signed her name Matilda C. Kendrick in a deed in E.
Feliciana Psh. in 1838 (D.B. "J", pp. 357-364). Kenyon T. Kendrick was Sheriff of St. Helena Parish, La. 1823-27, but later
lived in Feliciana Parish, where he died in 1834. Descendants state
that he died of yellow fever, contracted one night when he stopped
over at his sugar refinery on the way back from a trip to New Orleans. He seems to have been a rather wealthy man. He had a son
and a daughter by his first marriage, James Harvey Kendrick and
Theresa Kendrick, who were under the guardianship of their uncle
David Jones Fluker, and lived in their minority at "Asphodel".
There was a child by the second marriage who apparently died
young. East Feliciana Parish records show a meeting Oct. 28,
1834 regarding the minor heirs of K. T. Kendrick, decd. (D.B.
"D", pp. 269-91), and a receipt for sale of property from the estate, dated Aug. 6, 1835, and signed by D. J. Fluker, Tutor for
the minor heirs of estate of K.T. Kendrick, and Agent for Matilda
Kendrick. The daughter, Theresa Kendrick, married a Mr. Mc-
Dermott, moved to Arkansas, and died there prior to 1850, leaving 5 children.

James[6] Harvey Kendrick, son of Kenyon[5] T. and Mary Theresa
(Fluker) Kendrick, was born in Louisiana in 1824 and died in 1886
in Nashville, Tenn. He married (1) about 1843-4 Sarah Bateman
(b. 1820, d. Nov. 10, 1855 at Tullahoma, Tenn.), daughter of
Henry and Mary (Hill) Bateman. His third wife was Sarah Caroline
(Fluker) Logan, eldest daughter of David Jones Fluker and Isabella[6] Ann Kendrick, daughter of Benjamin[5] Kendrick. He had the
following children, all by his first wife:

I. Mary[7] Theresa Kendrick, m. 1865 Arthur Dickson Wharton.
    Arthur D. Wharton graduated second in his class at Annapolis
    in 1860. He was born July 19, 1840, d. April 3, 1900, and was
    the son of William H. Wharton and his wife, Priscilla Dick-
    son. Arthur D. Wharton resigned his commission in the U.S.
    Navy at the beginning of the Civil War and served with dis-
    tinction in the battles of Vicksburg and Mobile Bay in the Con-
    federate Navy. Issue:
    1. Minnie C. Wharton (d. 1944) m. Payton Robertson (d.
       1948) and had a son Arthur Dickson Robertson who m.
       Darien Jones, lives in Tampa, Fla., and has 2 daughters
       and a son.

2. Harvey Wharton b. 1868, d. Oct. 1950, unmarried.
3. Arthur Dickson Wharton, Jr., b. July 22, 1871, m. July 5, 1894 Katherine White of Murfreesboro, Tenn. and has 6 children: Frank White, Arthur D., Jr., Katherine, Walter, Harvey and Joe Wharton.
4. Mary Kendrick Wharton m. William J. Smith, no children.
5. Louise Frances Wharton m. Mr. Ricketts, no children.
6. John Houston Wharton m. Minnie App, had three children, Elizabeth, J. Houston, Jr., and Eugenia, moved to Oregon, where he died.

II. Thomas[7] Fluker Kendrick m. Sarah Clark, and had issue:
1. Minnie Kendrick, d. s. p.
2. Henrietta Kendrick m. John H. Reeves and had one son;
3. Adelle Kendrick m. Joseph Orgill, lived in Memphis, Tenn. and had a son Joseph, Jr. and a daughter Florence who m. Thomas J. O'Brien in 1929.

III. Frank[7] Bateman Kendrick ran off aged 15 and joined the Confederate Army. He married twice. By his first wife he had issue:
1. Loulie, d. s. p.
2. Belle;
3. Henry, who moved to Texas.
By his second wife, Margaret Kane, he had:
4. Frank, d. s. p.;
5. Samuel Watkins Kendrick, a Baptist Minister;
6. Yeatman, who married and went to California;
7. Maggie who m. Mr. Vester, has a son and a daughter and lives at Ann Arbor, Mich.

IV. James[7] Harvey Kendrick, Jr., b. Jan 14, 1848, d. Jan. 1, 1914, m. Jan. 14, 1868 Jane Lytle Foster, b. Sept. 14, 1848, died May 31, 1911, daughter of William Lytle and Susan Cheatham Foster. They had six children:
1. Susan Cheatham Kendrick, b. Jan. 20, 1869, died March 23, 1906, m. Sidney Goode and had Kendrick Goode and Susan Goode.
2. Jane Foster Kendrick, b. July 4, 1871, m. Matthew Benson and had one son, Matt, Jr.
3. James Harvey Kendrick b. Oct. 6, 1876, m. Claire Williams Sept. 10, 1919. The live at Battle Creek, Mich., and have a son, James Harvey Kendrick, Jr., who is married and has three children; and a daughter Anne Bryant Kendrick, b. June 18, 1924, who m. Robert Ferguson and has one child.
4. Edith Kendrick b. June 4, 1878 m. Bentley Lewis and died in New Orleans.
5. Thomas F. Kendrick b. July 14, 1880, m. May ------, and died in Chattanooga, Tenn., July 4, 1945. He had 5 children:
   (1) Tom, a Lieut-Commander in the Navy;
   (2) James lives in New Orleans:
   (3) John, a Chief in the Navy;
   (4) Dorothy Louise, who lives in Chattanooga, Tenn.
   (5) Jennie Ruth who m. Henry Williams.

6. Marion Kelly Kendrick, b. Sept. 14, 1884, m. June 29, 1916 Mary Douglas Causey at "Crownes", King William County, Va., and had the following children:
   (1) Evelyn Douglas Kendrick, b. June 22, 1917, m. May, 1939 John Rankin Kinney, has a daughter, Lois Wharton Kinney b. March 8, 1941;
   (2) James Causey Kendrick b. Sept. 8, 1918;
   (3) Elizabeth Dandridge Kendrick, .b.June 21, 1920, m. Dec.30,1945 William Wallace Woolford,III,of Galveston,Tex., and they have one child, Mary Douglas Woolford, b. June 30, 1947.

V. Sarah[7] Kendrick m. Yeatman Hardcastle. They had three children:
   1. Kendrick Crossman Hardcastle m. Amanda Gant, daughter of Judge Gant of Nashville; they have one son, Kendrick, Jr., who m. June 15, 1931 Elizabeth, daughter of Dr. and Mrs. Frank P. Bachman of Nashville, and has 2 sons, and a daughter Sarah Gant Hardcastle who m. April 9, 1929 George Folsom McCandless.
   2. Sarah Hardcastle m. Charles Short Kinkead of Louisville, Ky., and had three daughters,
      (1) Sarah, m. Sept. 1916 Jesse A. Pittman and has no children;
      (2) Anne Eastin m. Albert Stockell Nov. 2, 1921 and has three daughters, Anne, Sara and Alice;
      (3) Eunice Jackson m. Blair Trimble June 12, 1929 and has 2 sons, Blair, Jr., and Charles Kinkead.
   3. Walter Hardcastle, m. Martha Ezell, lives at Nashville, Tenn., and had three children, Martha, Sallie and Walter, Jr.

Susan[5] Kendrick, daughter of William[4] and Ann (Thompson) Kendrick, was born in Chatham Co., N.C. in 1790 and died in St. Helena Parish, La. at the family home, "Red Bluff", on May 3, 1857. She married Col. Robert Fluker (b. in North Carolina Oct. 1, 1783, died at "Red Bluff" June 5, 1863 or 1864), who is said by descendants to have served in the War of 1812. The following Family Bible record of Robert Fluker's parents, brothers and sisters, written by Robert Fluker himself, was sent in by a descendant, Mrs. Elizabeth (Taylor) Davidson of Birmingham, Ala.: "David Fluker was born March 30th, 1732; Jemima Fluker was born Nov. 14, 1739; George Fluker was born April 19th, 1759; Nancy Fluker was born Sept. 27th, 1760; William Fluker was born May 24th, 1762, Winney Jones Fluker was born July 7th, 1764; Betty Taylor Fluker was born Dec. 27th, 1765; Patty Fluker was born Aug. 27th, 1767; Sukey Fluker was born July 3rd, 1769; Mary Ann Fluker was born March 8th, 1771; Baldwin Fluker was born Sept. 18th, 1772, David Fluker was born April 28th, 1774; Holton Fluker was born Jan'y ---, 1776; John Fluker was born June 20th, 1777; Jemima Fluker was born April 3rd, 1779; Prissey Fluker was born May 25th, 1781; Robert Fluker was born Oct. 1st, 1783." Of the above children, Baldwin Fluker married a Miss Whitehead, a sister of Martin[4] Kendrick's wife, Jane Whitehead, as shown by the will of Sally Irwin in 1808 in Putnam Co., Ga.; and David Fluker married Sarah, daughter of Rev. John and Margaret Harvey of Washington Co., Ga. (see Harvey

Family). It is possible that Robert Fluker married (1) Eliza Irwin, before he married Susan[5] Kendrick. This is indicated by the following records: (1) Sally Irwin, in her will in 1808 in Putnam Co., Ga., leaves a bequest to her nephew David Fluker, son of Robert Fluker. This will will be given in the section on Martin[4] Kendrick. (2) Mrs. Elizabeth (Taylor) Davidson, a great-granddaughter of Robert and Susan (Kendrick) Fluker, wrote: "years ago my grandmother (i.e., Elizabeth Fluker, youngest daughter of Robert and Susan) gave me the names of her brothers and sisters and her mother's brothers and sisters. I wrote them down. She said her mother was Susan Kendrick, who married Col. Robert Fluker, and that Susan's father was Capt. William Kendrick and her mother was Eliza Irwin." Now there is ample evidence that Susan Kendrick's mother, the wife of William[4] Kendrick, was Ann Thompson, and Susan herself named one of her daughters Eliza Ann Thompson Fluker. The only way that I can solve the above puzzling statement is that Mrs. Davidson in some way confused William[4] Kendrick's wife with an Eliza Irwin who was perhaps the first wife of Robert Fluker. (3) The 1850 Census for St. Helena Parish, La. shows B. M. Fluker b. 1808 in Ga., Harriet Fluker b. 1826, and Josephine Fluker b. 1848 living in the family of Robert Fluker (b. 1784 in N.C.) and Susan Fluker (b. 1790 in N.C.). This B. M. Fluker was not Baldwin Fluker (b. 1813), son of Robert and Susan, for Susan's letters and the list of children of Robert and Susan given by Mrs. Davidson state that Baldwin died young. It looks very much as though B. M. was a son of Robert by a first marriage. (4) David A. J. Fluker married Laura Lee March 4, 1836, according to Mrs. Mamie Kent Ellis, of Kentwood, La., a granddaughter of Robert and Susan (Kendrick) Fluker, who was still living at the age of 82 in 1951. The Census of 1850 shows living right next to Robert and Susan Fluker: D. A. J. Fluker b. 1806 in Ga., Lauren Fluker b. 1816 in La., Elizabeth Fluker b. 1838, Sarah Fluker b. 1840, Robert Fluker b. 1842, George Fluker b. 1846, and James Fluker b. 1848. It looks very much as if this David A.J. Fluker were the eldest son of Robert Fluker, and the "nephew David son of Robert Fluker" mentioned in Sally Irwin's will.

The fourteen children of Robert and Susan[5] Kendrick Fluker, some of them mentioned in Susan Fluker's letters to her sister, Sarah Terrell, and others given in Mrs. Davidson's list from her grandmother, were as follows:

I.   Sarah Fluker m. Adville Atkins and left one child, Ann Atkins, who m. A. D. Woodward in 1848;

II.   Mary Ann Fluker, d. young;

III.   Baldwin Fluker, b. 1813, d. young;

IV.   James Fluker, d. young;

V.   Jemima Fluker, b. 1817, m. Sam R. Hughes and died before 1849, leaving two children, R. T. Hughes b. 1840 and Jemima Hughes b. 1843 who were living in the family of Robert and Susan Fluker in 1850;

VI.   George Fluker b. 1818, m. Martha Collingsworth and had Robert, Anna, Amos, Elizabeth Saunders, and George Fluker.

VII.   Owen Fluker, b. 1821, moved to California, m. a Miss D'Armond.

VIII. Eliza Ann Thompson Fluker, b. 1823, m. H. Edwards and left issue.

IX.   Susan Fluker b. 1825 m. Amos Kent and had 13 children, of whom the youngest, Mrs. Mamie Kent Ellis, was living at Kentwood, La. in 1951, aged 82.

X.   Robert Fluker

XI.   Rebecca Fluker

XIII William Fluker, who d. Sept. 8, 1833.

XIII. Margaret Fluker

XIV. Elizabeth Fluker, b. 1831, d. 1909, m. (1) Nov. 9, 1847 Dr. (later Gen.) A.B. Taylor; m. (2) Mr. Redd and had one son; (3) m. Mr. Miller, by whom she had two children. By her first marriage, Elizabeth Fluker had three sons, Marion Taylor, Leland Taylor, and Rev. Eugene Augustine Taylor, a Baptist minister. Rev. E.A. Taylor m. Margaret Jordan and they had: Eugene Taylor, Frances Taylor, and Elizabeth Taylor, who m. Dr. M. T. Davidson and lives in Birmingham, Alabama. Elizabeth (Taylor) Davidson's children were: Frances Davidson m. Philip Cole and was living in Nashville, Tenn., in 1930; Mildred Davidson; and Leland Taylor Davidson, Mayor of Louisville, Ky. when he died Feb. 16, 1948. Leland T. Davidson m. Edith Somers of Albemarle Co., Va. and had four daughters, Mrs. J. Davis Marret of Louisville, Ky., Mrs. James T. Skelley, Jr., of Wilmington, Del., Mrs. Albert E. Hulbert, and Edith Taylor, both of Louisville.

Rebecca[5] Kendrick, daughter of William[4] and Ann (Thompson) Kendrick, was born in 1795 and died in St. Helena Parish, La. in 1845. She married, probably in Morgan Co., Ga. and certainly prior to 1818, Gooderum Davis (b. 1789 in Georgia, d. 1873 in St. Helena Psh., La.). The Davises moved from Georgia to Louisiana in 1823 or 1824, as stated in affidavits made in 1870 by Gooderum Davis and his eldest son, William Kendrick Davis, that they were residents of Louisiana and had had no office in the Confederate Government. The following were the children of Rebecca[5] Kendrick and Gooderum Davis, as sent from the Family Bible by Mrs. Rebah Tillery Smith, Greensburg, La., a descendant:

I.   Sarah Ann Davis b. Jan. 9, 1814, d. young.

II.   Nancy Davis, b. Nov. 15, 1815, d. Nov. 1869, m. (1) Adville Atkins Nov. 17, 1833; m. (2) James Boykin.

III. Emily Amanda Davis b. Sept. 30, 1817, m. Aug. 25, 1835 John W. Leonard and moved to Colorado, where she died after 1879.

IV. William Kendrick Davis b. Jan. 15, 1820, d. April 22, 1899, m. (1) Oct. 29, 1845 Sarah Ann Jane Cain, by whom he had all his children, Mrs. Smith being a granddaughter; m. (2) March 22, 1880 Mrs. Mary Womack.

V.   Thomas Kinion Davis b. Nov. 17, 1821, m. (1) Nov. 27, 1846 Lucy Jane Burton; m. (2) Missouri Chambers of New Orleans.

VI.   Diocletian Davis (later known as Dio C. Davis), b. Sept.

19, 1824, d. Nov. 9, 1903, m. (1) Missouri Ann Kent.
VII.   Almira Jane Davis b. Nov. 12, 1826, m. March 8, 1843,
Carter Thompson, son of Hezekiah and Sally (Berry)
Thompson.

Sarah[5] Kendrick, daughter of William[4] and Ann (Thompson) Kendrick, was born in Washington Co., Ga. in June, 1797 and died in Lawrenceville, Ga., after 1857. She married April 4, 1817 in Morgan Co., Ga. her first cousin, William Terrell, son of Simon and Sarah (Thompson) Terrell, who died prior to 1830, as Sarah Terrell was listed as head of the family in the Census of that year for Gwinnett Co., Ga. We have mentioned the letters from her relatives in Louisiana, preserved by Mrs. Terrell and inherited by her granddaughter, Mrs. George S. King of Atlanta. Among these relics is also preserved an invitation to Miss Sarah Kendrick to a ball in honor of the end of the War of 1812 at Madison, Ga. March 11, 1815. The Census of 1830 shows Sarah Terrell's family as consisting of 1 female b. 1790-1800, 1 female b. 1815-20, 2 males and 2 females b. 1820-25. The Census for 1840 for Gwinnett Co. shows Sarah Terrell with a family consisting of 1 female b. 1790-1800, 2 females b. 1820-25, and 1 male, b. 1825-30. William and Sarah (Kendrick) Terrell had at least two sons, William Kendrick Terrell b. 1818, mentioned in a letter from Susan (Kendrick) Fluker in that year, who probably died young; and Kenyon Terrell, b. 1826, unmarried in Gwinnett Co. in the Census of 1850, to whom E. S. Longmade wrote in 1849 concerning the estate of William[4] Kendrick in Louisiana. Sarah Terrell had two granddaughters who lived in Atlanta, Ga., Mrs. George S. King and Mrs. James P. Williams (who married first Dr. J. A. Leconte).

Farrish[5] Carter Kendrick, son of William[4] and Margaret (Watt) Kendrick, was born in 1810 in Washington or Morgan Co., Ga., and died in Copiah Co., Miss., after 1850. According to Mrs. Julia Hennington of Jackson, Miss., daughter of his eldest son, John, Farrish Carter Kendrick married (1) Samantha Goff, (2) Martha Cook and (3) Sue Shadwick. The Census of 1850 for Copiah Co., Miss., shows: Farrish Kendrick b. 1810 in Ga. with his second wife, Martha Kendrick, b. 1815 in Miss., with the following children, all born in Miss.: Margaret A. Kendrick b. 1836; John H. Kendrick, born 1838; Matthew W. Kendrick b. 1841; Jane E. Kendrick b. 1842; Albert B. Kendrick b. 1844; Catherine Kendrick b. 1846; and William C. Kendrick b. 1848. Mrs. Hennington states that Margaret, John and Matthew were children of the first marriage; Jane Elizabeth, Katie, Albert and James Monroe by the second marriage; and there was one son, Pipkin Kendrick, by a third marriage.

John[5] Watt Kendrick, son of William[4] and Margaret (Watt) Kendrick, was born in St. Helena Parish, La. in 1820, and married in that parish Nov. 17, 1842 Ann Catherine Reames (b. 1825 in La.). The Census of 1850 shows the family in St. Helena Parish with the above birth dates for the parents and the following children: Martha A. Kendrick, b. 1844, John C. Kendrick b. 1846, William C. Kendrick b. 1848, and Elizabeth H. Kendrick b. 1850 (3 months old).

Burwell[4] Kendrick (James[3], William[2], John[1])

Burwell[4] Kendrick, third son of James and Susannah (Roberson) Kendrick, was born in Granville or Orange Co., N.C. about
1760-62, not later than 1762, as he must have been 21 when his
father, James[3] Kendrick, deeded him 640 acres of land April
26, 1783 (Chatham D.B. "C", p. 481). He died in Morgan Co.,
Ga. in 1817. His wife was a Miss Dowd. Her grandson, Dr. W.
C. Kendrick of Dawson, Ga., stated in his biography in Harden's
"Savannah and South Georgia" that his "grandfather, James Burwell Kendrick, was born and reared in Virginia, and there married Mary Dowd, who was born in Ireland and at the age of ten
years crossed the ocean with her parents, who settled in Virginia."
The above statement seems to be in error in several respects:
Burwell Kendrick never appears in the records as James Burwell Kendrick, and he had a brother James[4] Kendrick; he was
born and reared in North Carolina, not Virginia; the Dowds, too,
settled in North Carolina, not Virginia; and Burwell Kendrick's
wife was named Catherine, as shown by a deed in Chatham Co.,
N.C. Feb. 6, 1784 (D.B. "C", p. 471; Chatham Court Minutes,
1781-5, p. 49, folio 4). Of course, her name may have been
Mary Catherine. She was probably a daughter of Conner Dowd,
who first appears in the North Carolina records in 1761, or
possibly one of Connor's brothers, Owen and John Dowd, who
came over from Ireland a few later than Conner. Dr. Jerome
Dowd of the University of Oklahoma, a great-great-grandson
of Conner Dowd through his eldest son, Cornelius Dowd, got out
a manuscript account of the Dowd family which I have seen. He
states that Owen and John Dowd came over in 1763. Conner
Dowd first lived in Orange or Chatham Co., N.C., where his
first land grant was on Deep River May 10, 1761. From 1761 to
1772 he had 14 land-grants and became quite wealthy. According
to Dr. Dowd he married (2) around 1770 a Highland Scottish woman, Mrs. Mary Shields, and moved around that time to Campbelltown (later Fayetteville) in Cumberland Co., the center of
the Highland Scotch settlement to which Flora MacDonald and
her husband, Alan MacDonald, came in 1775. Conner Dowd had
a prosperous mercantile establishment there and the Fayetteville
records show that in 1780 he owned 3559 acres of land, 3 lots in
Campbelltown, 1 lot in Chatham, 12 negroes, 6 horses, 31
cows, a stock in trade of 13,030 pounds, and cash in hand 1300
pounds. Conner Dowd joined his Highland Scottish neighbors in
opposing the rebellion of the colonists in 1775 and 1776, supported
their forces with supplies, and after the defeat of the loyalists
at Moore's Creek, Feb. 27, 1776, was arrested and imprisoned
at Halifax along with other loyalist leaders. He remained in prison
until May 3, 1776, when his wife Mary gave bond for him in the
sum of 1000 pounds and he was released. He was order Aug. 23,
1776, to sell salt to the Revolutionary forces, but it is reported
that he refused to do so, and in November of that year he fell
under an act, confiscating all the properties of the Tories. It
appears from later records that his property was not actually con-
fiscated, but that he was restrained from all business transactions,

ying or selling, and late in the Revolution, in disgust he returned
Ireland, where he died. After this his wife Mary moved back to
e old home on Deep River (Chatham Co., later Moore Co.), and
1784 whe petitioned the General Assembly to be allowed to trans-
t business and use Conner Dowd's property for the benefit of herself
l children, and the permission was granted Nov. 11, 1789 (see
r the above Ashe "History of N.C.", pp. 520 and 561; N.C. Col.
d State Rec., Vol. 10, pp. 559, 602, 704, and 839; Vol. 15, p.
Vol. 19, pp. 548, 551, 631, 639, 644, 658, 696; Vol. 21, pp.
8, 342, 356, 393-4, 399, 710 and 720; Vol. 24, pp. 639-40;
l. 25, p. 46). The records of Moore Co., N.C., where Mary
wd lived in her later years, have all been destroyed, but the
cords of Chatham Co., N.C. show nearly 50 deeds in which the
mily was involved, three from 1772 to 1776 involving Conner
wd of Cumberland Co., himself; ten from 1785 to 1798 by the
eriff of Chatham Co. for land that belonged to Conner Dowd, ten
id-grants to Conner Dowd from the State of North Carolina from
83 to 1798; fifteen deeds to and from Mary Dowd of Moore Co.,
fe of Conner Dowd, from 1786 to 1797, one of which is a joint
ed with Cornelius Dowd (who was eldest son of Conner); and nine
eds to and from Cornelius Dowd, in one of which Patrick Dowd,
other son of Conner, was a joint grantor. Conner Dowd appears
have been still alive in 1797, when Mary Dowd still syled herself
ife of Conner Dowd" (D.B. "J", p. 433). Mary Dowd may have
en still living as late as 1810, when a female born before 1765 is
own in the family of her son, Samuel Dowd, in Chatham Co.,
C.

Since all the records of Moore Co., N.C., have been destroyed,
re is sóme uncertainty about the children of Conner Dowd. Dr.
rome Dowd states that the children of the first wife (name unknown)
re O'Connor Dowd, Patrick Dowd, and Ann Maria Dowd (informa-
n from H.F. Seawell of Carthage, N.C., a descendant). That
re was a Conner or O'Connor Dowd, Jr., is shown by a deed in
atham Co. Nov. 10, 1786 from Mary Dowd of Moore Co. to Ju-
h Dowd of Chatham Co. for 100 acres which had been granted to
nner Dowd, Sr., by the State (Chatham D.B. "D", p. 176). The
cords also indicate Patrick as a son, for he witnessed deeds
ide by Mary Dowd in 1790 and 1791 (D.B. "E", pp. 215 and 217),
d in 1793 made a joint deed with Cornelius Dowd to Aaron Tyson
.B. "G", p. 118). Dr. Dowd states that Conner Dowd's second
fe, Mary, was a widow, who had been married three times be-
re, first to Overton, second to Dunlop, and third to Shields; and
it Conner and Mary Dowd had four children, Cornelius, Richard,
muel, and a daughter who married James Dalrymple (a descen-
it of the last being Judge James Dalrymple McIver). I think that
rnelius was eldest son of the first marriage, and that there was
ther son James by the first marriage, and that the children of
second marriage were: Jane Dowd, b. Dec. 23, 1772, Rosanna
wd, b. March 20, 1774, Richard Dowd b. June 2, 1775, Laura
wd b. Aug. 20, 1776, Margaret Dowd, b. Jan. 27, 1778, John
wd, b. April 17, 1779, and Samuel Dowd, b. about 1781. My
asons for the above are as follows: (1) Dr. Dowd states that Wil-.
m Carey Dowd, a descendant of Cornelius Dowd, possessed a

gold watch which had come down to him from Cornelius Dowd, the eldest son of Conner Dowd. The Census of 1810 shows Cornelius Dowd in Moore Co. as born prior to 1765, a date which is apparently previous to the marriage of Conner Dowd to Mary Shields, and the Census of 1790 shows him with two daughters in the family born prior to 1790, which indicates again that he was born about 1760-65. A good deal of Conner Dowd's land was deeded to Cornelius Dowd by the Sheriff of Chatham Co. in 1788 and 1789 (D.B. "C", p. 522 and p. 548). Finally, Cornelius Dowd and John Montgomery on Jan. 11, 1793 deeded to John Alston 400 acres from the Conner Dowd estate (D.B. "G", p. 34), which land had been deeded to John Montgomery from the estate by the sheriff of Chatham Co. in 1791 (D.B. "E", p. 199). It looks as though Cornelius Dowd was the eldest son and heir, and that it was felt that he had to sign this deed with John Montgomery in order to make it unquestionably legal. (2) Mary Dowd, Cornelius Dowd and Patrick Dowd (still unmarried) are the only ones of Conner Dowd's family shown in the Census of 1790, all in Moore Co. James Dowd appears in Moore Co. along with Cornelius and Patrick in 1800 with two children born prior to 1800, and the Census returns of 1800 and 1810 shows him as born between 1765 and 1774. It looks as though he was the youngest son of Conner Dowd by his first marriage. (3) Dr. Jerome Dowd gives the six children; Jane, Rosanna, Richard, Laura, Margaret and John Dowd above, who were born between 1772 and 1779, as children of Samuel Dowd, son of Conner and Mary Dowd, and states that the births were recorded in an old account book of Samuel Dowd's. Now the only positive birth date of a child of Samuel Dowd was that of his son, Atlas Samuel Dowd, who was born Jan. 19, 1819. Further, Samuel Dowd is not shown in the Census until 1810 in Chatham County with only one child born prior to 1800 and two born 1800-10. The Census returns of 1810 and 1820 show his own birth as between 1775 and 1784. He was too young, therefore, to have been the father of children born between 1772 and 1779, and the evidence indicates that he was the youngest son of Conner and Mary Dowd, born about 1781, and that the children whose births were in the account book were really the children of Conner and Mary Dowd. This view is confirmed by the fact that Mary Dowd is shown in Moore Co. in 1790 with a family consisting of 3 males born 1774-90 (probably Richard, John and Samuel above) and five females (probably herself, Jane, Rosanna, Laura and Margaret above); that Richard Dowd witnessed deeds of Mary Dowd in Chatham Co. in 1790 (D.B. "G", pp. 32 and 71) and that he is first shown as head of a family in Chatham Co. in 1800, the Census returns of 1800, 1810, and 1820 showing his birth as 1774-5, corresponding exactly to the date in the account book, June 2, 1775; that Rosanna Dowd (b. Mar. 20, 1774 according to the account book) witnessed a deed of Mary Dowd in Chatham Co. in 1793 (D.B. "H", p. 95); that John Dowd (b. April 17, 1779 according to the account book) does not appear as head of a family in Chatham Co. until 1810, his age being given as born 1765-84; and that Samuel Dowd, too, does not appear in the Census until 1810.

Cornelius Dowd (eldest son of Conner Dowd by his first marriage, if the above is correct) is shown as head of a family in Moore Co., N.C. in 1790, 1800 and 1810. He was Clerk and Sheriff of Moore Co. (N.C. Col. & State Rec., Vol. 21, pp. 1065 and 1075); represented Moore Co. in the Conventions of 1788 and 1789 (Vol. 22, pp. 2, 6, 26, 27, 30; Vol. 35, pp. 22, 40, 40, 46 and 49); and was a Member of the N.C. Assembly from Moore Co. from 1791 to 1809 (cf. Vol. 21, pp. 879, 908, 930, 937, 941, 946, 965, 970, 980, 999, 1003, 1004, 1006, 1012, 1013, and 1015). Unfortunately Dr. Jerome Dowd in his account of the family did not give a list of the children of Cornelius Dowd, but mentions only one son, his grandfather Willis Dickerson Dowd, who was born in 1802, lived on a farm 3 miles from Carthage, N.C., was a General in the Mexican War, and married Ann Maria Gaines, who was a granddaughter of John and Mary (Wilcox) Montgomery of Chatham Co., N.C., parents of Martha Montgomery who married John[4] Kendrick. Willis D. and Ann Maria (Gaines) Dowd had 7 children: (1) Clement Dowd, father of Dr. Jerome Dowd; (2) Ann Maria Dowd m. a Dunlop; (4) Emily Dowd m. W. E. Allen; (5) Henry Dowd m. Miss Smith; (6) James Cornelius Dowd b. Nov. 25, 1836, died Nov. 26, 1898, m. Oct. 3, 1860 Henrietta Rives (b. Jan. 23, 1843, died June 30, 1895), and had 12 children; a descendant, William Carey Dowd, b. 1893, possesses Conner Dowd's gold watch; (7) Charles Dowd m. Sallie Little. According to Dr. Dowd, Richard, son of Conner and Mary Dowd, died in 1851, and a deed recorded at Hillsboro, N.C. (Book C, p. 246) gives his children as: (1) Cornelius Dowd b. Oct. 1, 1800; (2) Sally Dowd m. a Jenkins; (3) May Dowd m. a Bright; (4) Mary Dowd; (5) Alexander Dowd b. Nov. 28, 1806; (6) Alfred Dowd; and (7) John Dowd. Again according to Dr. Dowd, the children of Samuel Samuel Dowd, son of Conner and Mary, according to his will recorded at Hillsboro (Book 6, p. 320), were (1) Thomas Swain Dowd, eldest son, father of J. A. Dowd of Silver City, N.C.; (2) Atlas Samuel Dowd b. Jan. 19, 1813, d. Dec. 20, 1905; his son was John Watson Dowd, b. Aug. 15, 1842, d. Feb. 5, 1906, m. Feb. 19, 1873 Mary Watson Lipscomb; John Watson Dowd gave Dr. Jerome Dowd the old account book of his grandfather, Samuel Dowd, containing births of the 6 Dowd children discussed above, b. 1772-1779; (3) Horace Q. Dowd; (4) Jane Dowd m. David Bennett; (5) Rosanna Dowd m. Aaron Emerson; (6) Margaret Dowd m. Josiah A. Fox; (7) Leah Dowd m. William Patterson; (8) Mariah Dowd m. Charles A. Foushee; (9) Sophia Dowd m. William Edwards; (10) Ruth Dowd m. William P. Wrenn; (11) Elizabeth Dowd m. Allen Jones.

Paschal's "History of North Carolina Baptists" states that Conner Dowd was a Baptist, having been first a member of Deep River Church, and after the dissolution of that church, of Haw River Church (founded 1764); and remarks on the fact that he was the only prominent Baptist in North Carolina known to have been a Tory (p. 379). Purefoy's "History of the Sandy Creek Baptist Association" shows the following other members of the family who were members of Baptist Churches in Chatham and

Moore Co's.: Cornelius, Conner (Jr.?), Samuel, John, Richard, Atlas, Willis, William, W. D., and P. W. Dowd.

Owen Dowd, brother of Conner, by his wife Judith, had a son, Conner Dowd, who served in the Revolution, according to the D.A.R. papers of Conner's daughter, Mrs. Hannah Dowd Vanderford, which also state the name of Conner's parents above. According to these papers, Conner Dowd was born in Ireland Oct. 18, 1757 and died at Zaleski, O. March 31, 1839. He enlisted in Dec., 1779 in Chatham Co., N.C., married there Feb. 28, 1799 Hannah Graves (who died July 24, 1861), the ceremony being performed by Sherwood White, elder of Bear Creek Baptist Church, moved later to Randolph Co., N.C., and finally to Athens, Ohio, where he was pensioned in 1834 and died. Conner and Hannah (Graves) Dowd had seven children: (1) Alexander; (2) William; (3) Charles; (4) Conner; (5) Hannah, born July 9, 1815, m. a Vanderford, lived in Cincinnati, and finally moved to Indiana; (6) John; (7) Owen. Owen Dowd, father of this Conner Dowd, may have been a Tory, like his brother Conner, for Sabine's "American Loyalist" mentions "Doud of North Carolina, Captain in Loyal Militia, killed 1781 in attack of McNeal on Hillsborough". His widow, Judith Dowd, was deeded land in Chatham Co., N.C., by Mary Dowd, wife of Conner, in 1786 (D.B. "D", p. 176), and was deeded land there by John Thompson in 1789 and by John Montgomery in 1795 (D.B. "D", p. 578; D.B. "G", p. 363). Judith Dowd made a petition to the N.C. General Assembly 1788-90, but the nature of the petition is not stated, though it may have been in connection with her deceased husband (N.C. Col. & State Rec., Vol. 21, pp. 292, 298, and 645). Judith Dowd is shown in Chatham Co. in 1790 with a family consisting of 4 males b. before 1774 and 3 females. Three of the sons were probably Owen, Charles and Conner Dowd, all of whom were living in Chatham Co. in the Census of 1800. Judith disappears from the Census in 1800, but is perhaps identical with a female b. before 1755 in the family of Charles Dowd in that year. Julius Dowd, who was a Revolutionary soldier in North Carolina (Col. & State Rec., Vol. 17, p. 207), was perhaps the fourth son indicated in Judith's family in 1790.

John Dowd, brother of Conner and Owen, seems never to have moved to Chatham Co., but is probably identical with a John Dowd shown in Richmond Co., N.C., in the Census of 1790 with sons born before 1774. The same Census shows younger men, John Dowd in New Hanover Co. with a family, and Thomas Dowd in Fayetteville, a single man, who were probably his sons. The son John seems to have been a Revolutionary soldier and to have moved to Georgia, for the Cherokee Land Lottery of 1832-5 in that State shows John Dowd, Revolutionary soldier, living in Warren Co., Ga., who had a draw of land in Murray Co.

Catherine Dowd, wife of Burwell[4] Kendrick, was probably a daughter of Conner Dowd by his first marriage, as Patrick Dowd (along with Burwell's brother, John) witnessed Burwell's deed to William[4] Kendrick, when he sold out his land in Chatham Co. Dec. 26, 1786 (D.B. "D", p. 419), and Catherine named one of her sons James Cornelius Kendrick, probably in honor of her brother, Cornelius Dowd.

Burwell[4] Kendrick saw service in the Revolution in North Carolina, being paid 13 pounds 10 shillings on Sept. 9, 1783, the same date and amount as to his brother, William Kendrick, indicating that they saw the same service (N.C. Rev. Accts, Book I, p. 18, folio 2! Canceled Voucher No. 4822). He was deeded land in Chatham Co. by James Kendrick April 26, 1783 (D.B. "C", p. 481); deeded part of the land with wife Catherine to John McIntyre Feb. 6, 1784 (D.B. "C", p. 471; Court Min. 1781-5, p. 49, folio 4); deeded more of the land to Thomas Galloway Feb. 5, 1785 (D.B. "C", p. 472); recorded a promissory note from John Stroud March 19, 1785, and with William Kendrick signed the bond of his brother John Kendrick in July, 1785 (loose documents); finally deeded the remainder of his land to William Kendrick Dec. 26, 1786 (D.B. "D", p. 419); and last appears in the records of Chatham Co. in May 1787, when he sued Jeremiah Barnes (loose documents). He had probably moved to Wilkes Co., Ga. with his brother John prior to the mention of the above suits, however, for John Kendrick and Burwell Kendrick (the latter as J.P.) witnessed a deed in 1787 from William Campbell of Wilkes to Abednego Turner of Greene Co., the deed being recorded in Greene Co., Ga. Burwell Kendrick moved to Washington Co., Ga. about 1790 with his father and brothers, and was granted 550 acres of land there Aug. 31, 1793 (Ga. Grant Bk. "AAAA", p. 376). He was a Captain of Militia in Washington Co., Ga., but about 1797-8, probably on the death of his father James[3] Kendrick, he moved to Montgomery Co., Ga. The Minutes of the Executive Council of Georgia show that on March 26, 1798 William Kendrick was appointed Captain of Militia in Washington Co. in room of Burwell Kendrick, who had removed to Montgomery Co. (p. 255), and Burwell Kendrick, Esq., was appointed Captain of the 6th or Silver Bluff Co. in Montgomery Co. Sept. 3, 1798 (p. 155). Blair's "Early Tax Digests of Georgia" shows him in Montgomery Co. in 1798 with 5 slaves and 200 acres in Washington Co.; he was a Grand Juror there Oct. 18, 1804 (Montgomery Superior Court Minutes); was granted 400 acres of land there June 11, 1805 (Grant Bk. F-5, p. 35); and his residence is listed as Montgomery Co. in the list of eligibles, 1805, for the Land Lottery of 1806. He was deeded land in Wilkes Co. by Thomas Gafford May 10, 1806, however (Wilkes Co. D.B. "XX", p. 529), and had moved there by that year, for Blair (op. cit) shows that his land was held by other people in Montgomery Co. in the tax-lists of 1805 and 1806, and he was residing in Parks District of Wilkes Co. in the Land Lottery of 1806, being a lucky drawer. He sold the land which had been deeded him in 1806 to Jacob Bull on Feb. 16, 1810 (Wilkes D.B. "YY", p. 68). His brother, Jones[4] Kendrick was a witness to this deed, and Jacob Bull was Jones' father-in-law. His brother, William[4] Kendrick, had moved to Morgan Co., Ga. in 1810, and some time between 1810 and 1816 Burwell Kendrick moved to that county, too. The Wilkes Co. tax-lists show Burwell Kendrick with property in Wilkes in 1811, 1812, 1813 and 1814 (6 or 7 slaves, and 1812 shows him with 660 acres of land, presumably in Wilkes Co., and $202\frac{1}{2}$ acres in Laurens Co.). It is doubtful whether he was still living in Wilkes Co. in these years, however, for the 1811 tax record has at the end the ambiguous statement: "to who given - J. Kendrick"; 1813 has: "who granted: S. P. Kendrick"; and 1814 has: "given to J. Kendrick". "J. Kendrick" was probably his brother Jones. Burwell Kendrick was probably still living in Wilkes March 10, 1811, when his daughter Patsy married John Garrett there. He was certainly in Morgan Co. when his daughter, Catherine Kendrick, married Joel Garr there Sept. 24, 1816. He died in Morgan Co., Ga. in 1817. John Garrett and William Kendrick were appointed administrators of Burwell Kendrick, decd., in Morgan Co. May 5, 1817 and gave bond May 15 (Court Minutes 1808-23, p. 184); at a sale July 1, 1817 Catherine Garr and John Garrett each purchased a negro from the estate (Admin.'s Returns, "B", pp. 171-2); and John Garrett, as administrator, made a partial return from the estate Sept. 7, 1818, showing legacies paid to B. D. Kendrick ($300), William Kendrick ($324), J. C. Kendrick ($280), Richard Maddox ($280), and Susannah Kendrick ($600) (Adm.'s Returns, "B", p. 258).

It is possible that Burwell Kendrick married a second time in Wilkes Co., and that his widow either returned to Wilkes prior to 1820, or never moved from there permanently. If this is the case, his second wife was probably a Susannah Kendrick who, on Sept. 22, 1822, deeded all her property to her daughter, Louisa Kendrick, to go to Louisa after her death. This deed was recorded in Wilkes Co. Oct. 18, 1823, probably indicating the death of Susannah; and the daughter, Louisa Kendrick, married Sherror S. Little in Wilkes Co. Feb. 18, 1824 (Davidson "Wilkes Co.", II, 345). That Susannah Kendrick may have been the second wife and widow of Burwell Kendrick is indicated by the following: (1) the ambiguous statement at the end of Burwell's tax assessment in Wilkes Co. in 1813: "who granted: S. P. Kendrick", may refer to a wife Susannah; (2) in 1818 Susannah Kendrick received as her legacy twice as much as the other legatees, which may indicate that she was the widow and had a minor child; and (3) the Census of 1820 for Wilkes Co. show a "B. Kindreck" with a household headed by a woman born before 1775, two females practically grown, and 4 children, a record which may refer to the family of Burwell[4] Kendrick.

The following were the children and descendants of Burwell[4] Kendrick and his wife, Catherine Dowd:

Martha[5] Kendrick, born probably about 1785, married 1805 Richard Maddox, as his second wife, and died in Morgan Co., Ga. in 1828. Richard Maddox died in Wilkes Co., Ga., about 1820, and was one of 5 brothers who came from Wales about 1790 and settled in Georgia. The above dates and the following information about the family come from Miss Leila Kendrick of Columbus, Ga., a great-granddaughter, now deceased. The Land Lottery of 1827 shows Richard Maddox's Orphans living

in Wilkes Co., Ga., but the Cherokee Land Lottery shows that
Martha Kendrick's son, Thomas Maddox, and her sons-in-law,
Reuben and Marlin Wheelus, were living in Morgan Co., Ga.,
1832-5. Issue of Richard and Martha (Kendrick) Maddox:

I.   Nancy[6] Maddox, b. about 1807 (the Census of 1850 says
1810), married about 1822 Allen T. Garrard (b. 1800-Cen-
sus), and died in Wilkes Co., Ga., in 1889. The 1850
Census of Wilkes Co. shows the children of this couple
as:

1. George A. Garrard b. 1828;
2. Sarah Garrard b. 1833;
3. Louisa Garrard b. 1834;
4. Nancy Garrard b. 1836;
5. Martha E. Garrard b. 1838;
6. Mary Garrard b. 1840;
7. William Garrard b. 1842;
8. John Garrard b. 1844;
9. James Garrard b. 1846;
10. Margaret Garrard b. 1848.

II.   Sarah[6] Maddox, b. about 1809, m. 1825 Reuben Wheelis
in Morgan Co., Ga., d. 1881 in Drew Co., Ark.

III.   Rebecca[6] Maddox b. about 1811, m. 1827 in Morgan Co.,
Ga., Marlin Wheelis, d. 1885 in Meriwether Co., Ga.

IV.   Thomas[6] Maddox b. Oct. 12, 1813, d. Oct. 28, 1889 in
Muscogee Co., Ga., m. 1833 in Morgan Co., Ga. Minerva Weston Wheelis (b. 1820, d. 1882). Thomas Maddox lived most of his life in Talbot Co., Ga. and was a
neighbor and close friend of Benjamin Burks Kendrick
there, who is to be discussed later, and two of whose
children married children of Thomas Maddox. The children of Thomas and Minerva (Wheelis) Maddox were:

1. Sarah[7] Ann Maddox, b. 1835, d. 1854, m. a Hinson;
2. Mary[7] Frances Maddox b. 1837, d. 1890, m. (1) a
Bridges and (2) a Collins;
3. George[7] Allen Maddox, b. 1839, killed 1862 in Civil
War;
4. Thomas[7] Asbury Maddox b. 1840, d. 1919, m. Mollie Garrard;
5. Nancy[7] Elizabeth Maddox, b. 1845, d. about 1919,
m. Joseph Hunn;
6. John[7] Matthews Maddox, no descendants.
7. William[7] Fletcher Maddox, no descendants;
8. Levice[7] Green Maddox, b. 1842, d. 1923, m. William
Thomas Kendrick (b. 1842), son of Benjamin Burks
Kendrick and had:
   (1) Fannie[8] Weston Kendrick, b. 1869, d. 1905, m.
(1) Guss Brooks and (2) Bunn Rentz;
   (2) Henry[8] Binns Kendrick b. 1871, m. Cornelia
Birdsong;
   (3) Leila[8] Burks Kendrick, b. 1873, d.s.p.;
   (4) Thomas[8] Clarence Kendrick b. 1875, m. Marlin
Oregon Morton and had two sons, T.C. Kendrick,
Jr., (b. 1907) and Sam Morton Kendrick (b. 1909);

    (5)   Effie[8] Rochelle Kendrick b. 1877 m. Henry Rentz;

    (6)   William[8] Walter Kendrick b. 1879, m. Pearl Story;

    (7)   Lizzie[8] Clifford Kendrick b. 1882 Pittman Sylvester Brownlee;

    (8)   Benjamin[8] Burks Kendrick b. Oct. 16, 1884, B.A. (Mercer), Ph.D. (Columbia), Professor of History for many years at N.C. Woman's College, m. Nov. 24, 1909 Elizabeth Shields and had 5 children:

        a. Benjamin Burks Kendrick, Jr.,

        b. Margaret Shields Kendrick (Mrs. William J. Horney, Jr.),

        c. John Whitfield Kendrick,

        d. David Stewart Kendrick,

        e. Janet Joanna Kendrick.

  9.   James[7] Stephens Maddox b. 1856, d. 1888, m. Miss James;

  10.   Leonora[7] Weston Maddox, b. 1856, d. 1887, m. a Bridges;

  11.   Clifford[7] Eoline Maddox b. 1860, d. 1883, m. Benjamin C. Kendrick b. 1847), son of Benjamin Burks Kendrick, and had a daughter, Eva P. Kendrick, b. 1879;

  12.   Sephronia[7] Catherine Maddox b. 1863, d. 1896, m. J.M. Thornton.

V.   George[6] Maddox, b. about 1815, m. 1838 Martha Johnson in Chambers Co., Ala., d. 1893 in White Co., Ark.

VI.   John[6] Maddox, b. about 1817, m. 1839 Ailey Harlan in Coweta Co., Ga., d. 1896 in Faulkner Co., Ark.

The father of Benjamin Burks Kendrick, two of whose children married daughters of Thomas[6] Maddox, was Sheldrake Kendrick, who first appears in the jury list of Columbia Co., Ga. in 1794 along with John, Thomas, Hezekiah, Nathaniel, and Robert Kendrick (the first four being Revolutionary soldiers and probably from Maryland, as John Kendrick certainly was). Sheldrake Kendrick was living in Wilkes Co., Ga. April 28, 1801, when he is mentioned in the Minutes of the Inferior Court (p. 315). However, he had moved back to Columbia Co. by 1805, when he is mentioned among the list of eligibles for the lottery of 1806, and in the lottery itself had a lucky draw in Baldwin Co. (later Jasper Co.). Sheldrake Kendrick was born about 1770-72 and married about 1802 Nancy Burks, who died in Talbot Co., Ga. in 1854. Sheldrake died in Jasper Co., Ga., about 1817, as the records of the Ordinary's Office there show the inventory and appraisement of Sheldrake Kendrick, decd., by James L. Burks, and signed by Nancy Kendrick and Robert Kendrick, administrators; and an account of the estate for the year 1817 by Robert Kendrick, administrator, handed in Jan. 10, 1820. Jasper Co. deeds show that Nancy Kendrick, admx. of Sheldrake, sold land there in April 1821, and she drew a parcel of land in Dooly Co. in the Lottery of 1821 as "Nancy Kendrick, widow", of Jasper Co. The Census of 1830 shows

Nancy Kendrick as head of a family in Jasper Co., along with her son Burks Kendrick, but they all moved to Talbot Co., Ga., about 1832, when Benjamin B. Kendrick (i.e. Burks) is shown as a resident in the Cherokee Gold and Land Lotteries. The children of Sheldrake and Nancy (Burks) Kendrick, according to their great-granddaughter, Miss Leila Kendrick, were:

I.   Rebecca Kendrick b. about 1803, m. Aug. 10, 1828 Daniel Trussell in Jasper Co., Ga.

II. Virginia Kendrick b. about 1805, m. March 1, 1821, Mastin Hatcher in Jasper Co., Ga.

III. Benjamin Burks Kendrick, b. 1807, d. in Talbot Co., Ga., m. (1) Feb. 4, 1830 Frances Lloyd, m. (2) prior to 1850 Ann Trussell (b. 1817);

IV. Elizabeth Kendrick b. about 1809, m. Feb. 2, 1824 John Folds in Jasper Co.

V.   Sarah Kendrick, b. about 1811, m. Dec. 25, 1830, Henry Christopher Binns in Jasper Co.

VI. Robert Sheldrake Kendrick, b. about 1813, married twice, his second wife being Martha Crouch of Talbot Co., Ga., whom he married Nov. 7, 1883. The Census of 1860 for Barbour Co., Ala., shows a Robert S. Kendrick, b. 1815 in Georgia, with a wife Elizabeth, b. 1819 in Ga., who may be identical with this Robert Sheldrake Kendrick. The Barbour Co. Census shows the following children in the family of Robert S. and Elizabeth Kendrick: Henry T. b. 1836; Daniel b. 1840; Samuel b. 1842; Mary A. b. 1844; Rebecca b. 1846; Texanon b. 1850; Columbus b. 1853; and William H. b. 1851. The same Census shows a young married man, B. E. Kendrick (b. 1837 in Ga.) with wife Mary R. (b. 1844 in Ala.) who may have been another son of Robert S. Kendrick.

Benjamin Burks Kendrick, son of Sheldrake and Nancy (Burks) Kendrick, had by his first marriage to Frances Lloyd the following children:

I.   Robert Kendrick, b. 1831, shown in Talbot Co., Ga., in 1880 with wife Mary A., b. 1836, a son Homer b. 1871, and two daughters, Minnie (b. 1876) and Rashear (9 mos. old); probably identical with a Robert Sheldrake Kendrake who married Mary Brooks and whose daughter, Ida Frances Kendrick, b. 1860, m. John Wesley Woodall of Lamar Co., Ga.;

II.   John Kendrick b. 1832;

III. Nancy Jane Kendrick, b. 1835, m. 1856 Dr. William Callaway Kendrick, son of James[5] Cornelius Kendrick and grandson of Burwell[4] Kendrick;

IV.   Elizabeth Kendrick b. 1837;

V.   Sarah Kendrick b. 1838;

VI.   William Thomas Kendrick, b. 1842, m. Levice Green Maddox, daughter of Thomas[6] Maddox;

VII. Joseph Kendrick b. 1844;

VIII. Benjamin C. Kendrick b. 1847, m. Clifford Eoline Maddox, daughter of Thomas[6] Maddox.

Three of Benjamin Burks Kendrick's children married de-

scendants of Burwell[4] Kendrick; Burks Kendrick and Thomas[6]
Maddox were neighbors and "claimed kin"; and Miss Leila Ken-
drick, granddaughter of the two, stated that the family were
very positive about the relationship, namely, that Sheldrake
Kendrick was a son of Jones Kendrick, that this Jones Kendrick
was a brother of Burwell[4] Kendrick, and that the two men were
both sons of Capt. Burwell Kendrick of the Revolutionary War.
We have mentioned previously that there is no trace of a Capt.
Burwell Kendrick of the Revolutionary War, and that Burwell[4]
Kendrick and his brother, Jones[4] Kendrick, were sons of James[3]
Kendrick and his wife, Susannah Roberson. Sheldrake Kendrick,
father of Benjamin Burks Kendrick, must have been born as
early as 1770-72, as he was a grown man in Columbia Co., Ga.
in 1794; he could not, therefore, have been a son of Jones[4]
Kendrick, brother of Burwell, for Jones was not born until
1778. I suspect that the tradition given by Miss Leila Kendrick
is entirely a mistake, and that Sheldrake Kendrick did not be-
long to our family of Kendricks at all, but to the group of Kendricks from Maryland with whom he first appears in Columbia
Co., Ga. in 1794. The view is strengthened by the fact that
Robert Kendrick (b. 1831), son of Benjamin Burks Kendrick,
stated in the Census of 1880 that both his parents were born in
South Carolina, where none of our Kendricks settled except
Isham[3] Kendrick. However, although Sheldrake Kendrick could
have been a nephew of Burwell[4] Kendrick and a son of Burwell's
brother, Jones, the tradition in Miss Leila Kendrick's family is
so positive, that it seems possible that he was a son of Jones[3]
Kendrick, uncle of Burwell, who later moved from Warren Co.,
Ga. to Tennessee. However, there is not the slightest document-
ary evidence of this. Whatever the truth is regarding the parentage of Sheldrake Kendrick, it is almost certain that he was
a brother of Robert Kendrick, who appears with him in Columbia Co., Ga., in 1794 in the list of jurors and in the same county in 1805, as a single man with only 1 draw in the list of eligibles for the 1806 lottery, and who was joint administrator with
the widow, Nancy Kendrick, on Sheldrake's estate in Jasper
Co., Ga., 1817-20. According to a card in the Adjutant-Gen-
erals Office at Washington, D.C., Robert Kendrick served in
the Seminole War, 1817-18, in Capt. James Hendon's Company
of Georgia Volunteers from Feb. to May 1818. He had moved
to Conecuh Co., Ala., by 1820, and is shown there in the Census of that year, as well as the one for 1840. He probably died
there between 1840 and 1850. Robert Kendrick had at least two
sons: (1) Sheldrake Kendrick, b. 1808, shown in Butler Co.,
Ala. in the Census of 1840 and in Conecuh Co., Ala., in 1850
with a wife Levicey (b. 1823) and the following children: Martha b. 1830; John b. 1832; Robert b. 1832; Josiah b. 1833;
Mary b. 1835; Ramsey b. 1838; Thomas b. 1840; Asa b. 1842;
Wesley b. 1844, and Richard b. 1847; (2) Josiah Kendrick b.
1810, shown in the 1850 Census of Conecuh Co., Ala. with wife
Jane, b. 1815 in S.C., and the following children: John b. 1832,
Sheldrake b. 1834, David b. 1836, Mary b. 1838, Jefferson b.
1840, Nancy b. 1843, and Elizabeth b. 1848.

Patsy[b] Kendrick, b. probably about 1790-93, m. John Garrett March 10, 1811 in Wilkes Co., Ga. John Garrett is shown with a family in Wilkes Co., Ga. in the Census of 1830, but had apparently died prior to 1832-5, the time of the Cherokee Land Lottery, for that lottery shows John Garrett's orphans, living in Morgan Co., Ga.

William[5] Kendrick, son of Burwell[4] and Catherine (Dowd) Kendrick, may be identical with a William B. Kendrick, who married Mittie M. Hawes in Wilkes Co., Ga., Feb. 2, 1814, and appears briefly in the records of Walton Co., Ga. at Social Circle in 1828. He is probably identical with a William Kendrick, Sr., b. 1795, who appears in Baker Co., Ga. in the Census of 1850 with a wife, Ceney, b. 1805 (perhaps his second wife), and the following children: George Washington Kendrick b. 1827, Andrew J. Kendrick b. 1831, Ruffin T. Kendrick, b. 1832; William N. Kendrick b. 1843; John P. Kendrick b. 1845; and Benjamin L. Kendrick b. 1849. Ruffin T. Kendrick, son of this William Kendrick, was a physician and is shown in the 1880 Census for Dougherty Co., Ga. with a wife Drusilla, b. 1834, and children, Charles W. b. 1859, Della B. b. 1863, Andrew J. b. 1864, Electra B. and Mattie Kendrick, b. 1868. Ruffin Kendrick was living in Berrien Co., Ga. in 1890.

B.D.[5] Kendrick, son of Burwell[4] and Catherine (Dowd) Kendrick, is probably identical with a Benjamin D. R. Kendrick who married Elizabeth Kyle Feb. 22, 1824 in Tuscaloosa, Ala. This was probably a second marriage, for the Census of 1830 for Tuscaloosa Co., Ala., shows B.D.R. Kendrick (b. 1790-1800) with four children, 2 born 1815-20 and 2 born 1820-25. He may have moved to Texas, for B. D. Kendrick received a grant of 320 acres in Augustine Co., Tex., June 6, 1839.

Catherine[5] Kendrick, daughter of Burwell[4] and Catherine (Dowd) Kendrick, married Joel Garr Sept. 24, 1816, in Morgan Co., Ga. This Joel Garr was probably the son of Michael Garr, who died in Elbert Co., Ga. in 1797, leaving a minor son, Joel. Two Revolutionary soldiers, Lewis and Joel Garr, who lived in Morgan Co., were probably his uncles. Joel Garr (Jr.), who married Catherine Kendrick, died in Morgan Co. prior to 1827, for the Lottery of that year shows Joel Garr's orphans, and the Cherokee Land Lottery, 1832-5, shows Catherine Garr, widow, in Morgan Co., Ga.

James[5] Cornelius Kendrick, son of Burwell[4] and Catherine (Dowd) Kendrick, was born May 12, 1801 in Wilkes or Montgomery Co., Ga. and died in Dec., 1883 at Dawson, Terrell Co., Ga. He married about 1819-20 Mary Butler (b. 1804, d. 1877), daughter of John and Nellie (Walden) Butler of Greene Co., Ga. A card in the Adjutant-General's Office at Washington, D.C., shows that James C. Kendrick, No. 554, served in Capt. Terry Runnells Company of the Second Georgia Militia in the Seminole War, 1817-18, from Feb. 13 to May 5, 1818. He made application for bounty land for service in this war and received land for his services. In 1856, Allen Garrard (who married his niece Nancy Maddox) made affidavit that he served with James Cornelius Kendrick and that they were both from

Wilkes Co. James C. Kendrick is shown in Morgan Co. in the Lottery of 1820, in the Census of 1830, and in the Cherokee Land Lottery, 1832-5. He had moved to Sumter Co., Ga., by 1850, and his family is shown there in the Census of that year. He finally moved to Terrell Co., Ga., where he died the first week in December, 1883. His will, dated Nov. 5, 1877 and probated in Terrell Co. April 14, 1884, mentions his sons, Burwell J., W.C., James K., Benjamin, John T., and Isaac Kendrick; his daughters Miriam K. West, Melissa Harper, and Catherine Fuller; his granddaughters Sillobata, Willetie, and Sarah Mary Harper, Cornelia Fuller McNair, and Katherine Fuller Stargill; and his grandson Isaac Fuller. James Cornelius Kendrick was for many years a Baptist minister, but in his old age left the Baptists and became a Universalist. The children of James C. and Mary (Butler) Kendrick, as shown by the will, the Census of 1850, and direct family tradition and Bibles, were:

I. Butler[6] Kendrick, b. about 1820, died young.
II. Burwell[6] Jones Kendrick, b. Sept. 23, 1823 in Morgan Co., Ga., died April 13, 1912 in Waco, Texas, m. Margaret Diana Bond (b. 1826, living aged 92 in 1920 in Waco), moved to Texas about 1870; issue:
  1. John[7] D. Kendrick, b. 1847, m. Mary Erath, daughter of George B. Erath, a native of Vienna, Austria, who came to Texas with a company of Rangers from Tennessee about 1837, was a surveyor, fought at San Jacinto, was a member of the Texas Congress, and settled at Waco in 1849 (Hyer "Land of Beginning Again", pp. 243, 363, 367, and 368). Issue:
    (1) Minnie Kendrick, born 1873;
    (2) Hampton Kendrick born 1874;
    (3) Erath Kendrick born 1876;
    (4) Clifford Kendrick born 1878;
    (5) Burwell Kendrick born 1880;
  2. James[7] Marcellus Kendrick, born Dec. 12, 1848 in Meriwether Co., Ga., m. Laura Ish (born in Tenn.)
    (1) Edwin Ish Kendrick born 1877;
    (2) Susan Kendrick born 1880 (unmarried and living in 1920 at Route 5, Waco, Texas);
    (3) Helen Kendrick;
    (4) Robert Toombs Kendrick;
    (5) Benjamin Hill Kendrick;
    (6) Hester Kendrick;
    (7) Blanche Kendrick.
  3. William[7] Kendrick, b. 1852, d.s.p. 1871;
  4. Eugenia[7] Kendrick, b. 1852;
  5. Mary J. Kendrick, b. 1854, m. W. J. Buster;
  6. Lucy[7] A. Kendrick, b. 1857, m. G. W. Bolger;
  7. Meredith[7] Kendrick, b. 1859, m. Eddie Connolly;
  8. Alice[7] Kendrick, b. 1864, m. John Buster;
  9. Maggie[7] L. Kendrick, b. 1867, d. 1951, m. James Isaac Kendrick of Virginia, no relationship known.
III. John[6] Kendrick born Sept. 23, 1823, twin of Burwell Jones.

IV.   James[6]Kenyon Kendrick, b. 1825.

V.   Catherine[6] Kendrick b. 1827, m. a Fuller and was mother
       of Isaac Fuller, Cornelia Fuller McNair, and Catherine
       Fuller Cargill, mentioned in 1883 in thier grandfather's
       will.

VI.   William[6] Calloway Kendrick, M.D., b. May 17, 1831,
       died July 25, 1913 at Dawson, Ga.; graduate New York
       U. Medical School 1856; practised medicine at Talbotton,
       Ga., several years, then moved to Fort Smith, Ark., but
       returned to Georgia to enter Confederate Army; Surgeon,
       12th Ga. Regt., C.S.A., with rank of Captain; moved
       after the war to Webster Co., Ga., and finally to Terrell
       Co., 1888-98; Baptist deacon for 20 years; member of
       Board of Education and trustee of College in Terrell Co.,
       m. (1) March 25, 1855, Nancy Jane Kendrick, daughter of
       Benjamin Burks Kendrick of Talbot Co., Ga. (b.1835,
       d. 1875), and had one son, Herschel[7] Kendrick, b. 1856,
       d.s.p. 1877; m. (2) July 11, 1876 Emma Foster (b. 1854,
       d. 1937), daughter of Newitt and Catherine (Woolbright)
       Foster, and had:
       1. James[7] Burwell Kendrick, b. Aug. 19, 1877, d. Jan.
          18, 1947, m. Addie Ensign (b. 1884, died 1919), daugh-
          ter of Charles A. and Nancy (Proctor) Ensign, and had:
          (1) Louise[8] Ensign Kendrick, b. July 9, 1909, m.
               1930 Robert Ogden Persons, of Forsyth, Ga., and
               has two sons, Robert Ogden Persons, Jr., b. Nov.
               4, 1931, and George Ogden Persons, b. Feb. 24,
               1935.
          (2) Josephine[8] Ensign Kendrick b. Aug. 26, 1911, un-
               married.
       2. Juanita[7] Kendrick, b. 1879, m. Dr. Thomas Meri-
          wether.
       3. May[7] Belle Kendrick m. Roy D. Smith;
       4. Mary B. Kendrick, unmarried;
       5. Lessie[7] Estelle Kendrick m. William Calloway Page.

VII.   Meredith[6] Kendrick, b. 1834, d. June 4, 1861, Solicitor-
       General of the Tallapoosa Circuit March 19, 1860, Major
       in Confederate Army and killed at Pine Mountain near
       Marietta, Ga., m. Emily Jones, daughter of Thomas
       Jones of Newnan, Ga., who m. (2) Rev. James Stacy; no
       children.

VIII. Benjamin[6] Kendrick b. 1837, d. 1862, Captain in Confed-
       erate Army and killed at Big Gap Creek, Tenn.; m. Liz-
       zie Hopkins and had one child, Tallulah Kendrick.

IX.   Melissa[6] Kendrick, b. 1840, m. Dec. 1, 1863 in Sumter
       Co., Ga., William J. Harper and had the three daughters
       mentioned in their grandfather's will. She m. (2) Enoch
       Johnson of Sumter Co.

X.   Miriam[6] Kendrick, b. 1843, m. Mr. West.

XI.   Isaac[6] Kendrick, b. 1845, a Confederate soldier.

James[4] Kendrick (James[3], William[2], John[1])

James[4] Kendrick, son of James[3] and Susannah (Roberson) Kendrick, was born in Orange Co., N.C. about 1765-70, as his first child was born about 1790, showing that he was married about 1788-9, and as the Putnam Co., Ga. Census of 1830 shows him as born between 1760 and 1770; died in the Kinderhook neighborhood of Putnam Co., Ga. in 1831 or 1832; and married about 1788-9 in Wilkes Co., Ga., Tabitha Rogers (b. 1770-72 in Johnston Co., N.C., d. Oct.-Nov., 1833 in Putnam Co., Ga.), daughter of Drury and Tabitha Rogers of Wilkes Co., Ga., granddaughter of Joseph and Mary Rogers of Northampton Co., N.C., great-granddaughter of William and Elizabeth (Cartwright) Rogers of Surry Co., Va., and great-great-granddaughter of William and Mary Rogers of Surry. An account of the Rogers family is shown in Boddie's "Southside Virginia Families" (Vol. II, pp. 357-363). There are only a few corrections and additions to be made to that account, due to new information, as follows: (1) John Rogers, the immigrant ancestor, did not marry Mary, sister of Richard Booth, though his wife was named Mary; Mary Booth was the wife of John **Rogers**, Jr., as shown by a deed in 1722 in Isle of Wight Co., **Va.** from John Rogers, now called "Sr.", and his son John **Rogers**, Jr., son of Mary Booth (D.B. 2, p. 500). (2) There are erroneous statements about James[4] Kendrick: he did not die 1817-20, but 1831-2, and Burwell and Catherine Kendrick were his brother and sister-in-law, not his parents. (3) Drury Rogers and his family suffered a great disaster in 1779, when a fort he had constructed in Wilkes Co. on the Ogeechee for protection during the Revolution was burned and all his property plundered by a party of about 100 Creek Indians and their Tory allies, and the family had to flee to the Savannah River. Drury Rogers, his daughter Talitha, and several neighbors were carried away captive by the Indians, but were shortly allowed to escape. After the U.S. Government made a treaty with the Creeks, from the years 1802 to 1824, Brittain Rogers made a claim for this property to the Government, and a number of documents and affidavits connected with the claim are preserved at the Georgia Department of Archives in Atlanta. These documents show that Burwell Rogers, third son of Drury, was living in Conecuh Co., Ala., in 1822; that Drury's daughter, Talitha Stokes, was also living in that county; and that Talitha (probably the eldest daughter) was apparently already married in 1779 to a Mr. Lee, having married later her second husband, Samuel Stokes. (4) A deed from Drury's eldest son, Brittain Rogers, in Hancock Co., Ga. in 1822 shows that his full first name was Albritton Rogers. Brittain Rogers' birth was Oct. 11, 1761 (not 1781, as given in the Rogers family account).

James[4] Kendrick came to Georgia in 1784 with his father, James[3] Kendrick, and as mentioned, married about 1788-9 in Wilkes Co., Ga. He may have continued to live in Wilkes until the death of his mother-in-law, Tabitha Rogers, in 1793, but was apparently living in Washington Co., Ga. in 1796, when his father was granted land as James Kendrick, Sr. The list of eligibles for the 1806 land lottery shows that he was living in Hancock Co., Ga. in 1805, and in Aug. 1805 James Kendrick, yeoman, was involved in a suit in Hancock Co. involving his assault and battery on Joel Hurt, Esq. The difference must have been patched up, however, for the Hurts were intimate friends of the Kendricks in Putnam Co. There was a Mrs. Hurt there whom my grandmother Holtzclaw, James Kendrick's granddaughter, always called "Auntie Hurt", and her daughter, who married a wealthy man named Winter from Augusta, was an intimate friend of my grandmother and was mother of the late Mrs. Norman Miller of Hawkinsville. The families always called one another cousin, and there may have been some relationship through the Kendricks. James Kendrick was a lucky drawer in the Lottery of 1806, his residence at that time being Baldwin Co., Ga., in that section which later became Putnam. He appears as grantor in 5 deeds in Putnam Co. from 1805 to 1813, the first, dated Dec. 2, 1805, showing his residence still in Hancock Co., and the second, in 1810, being a deed to his brother-in-law, John Rogers (Putnam D.B. "B", p. 130; "C", p. 285; "D", p. 114; "E", p. 152; and "M", p. 391). He does not appear later in the deeds of Putnam Co., though the tax-list of 1817 shows him with 14 slaves and property on Little River. My grandmother Holtzclaw told me years ago that the family moved for a short time to Tennessee, but soon returned to Putnam; and since the Census of 1820 shows James Kendrick's family in Putnam, but does not show a man in it old enough to have been himself, it is possible that he was still temporarily in Tennessee at that time. He was still living, however, for the Putnam tax digest of 1822 shows James Kendrick, Sr. with land in Appling Co., Ga. and the Census of 1830 shows him with a family consisting of 1 male b. 1760-70, 1 female b. 1770-80, 1 male b. 1800-10, 2 females b. 1810-15, and 1 female b. 1815-20. In 1831 James Kendrick listed land in Jones, Lee and Coweta Counties, being then a resident of Putnam, but whether this was James[4] Kendrick or his son, James, Jr., is uncertain. He probably died about 1831 or 1832 intestate. My grandmother told me many years ago the names of her father and mother, Benjamin W. and Julia C. (Kendrick) Clark, and of her grandparents, William and Mary (Harvey) Clark and James and Tabitha (Rogers) Kendrick; she stated that James Kendrick was one of the first settlers of Putnam Co., a statement confirmed by Smith's "Story of Georgia and the Georgia People" (p. 263); gave me the names of James Kendrick's children as Drury, Tabitha Holland, Isham, Susan Stubbs, James, Elizabeth, wife of Rev. John H. Clark, Celia Mullins, Julia C., wife of Benjamin W. Clark (her mother and father), and Catherine Baisden; stated that her grandfather Kendrick died before she was born, but that her mother told her that her grandmother Kendrick (Tabitha Rogers) died only a few days after she, my grandmother, was born on Oct. 28, 1833; and that her Kendrick grandparents, along with her Clark grandparents, were all buried in the Clark family burying ground on the Clark plantation where she was born and reared. There was an old slave, Reddick, who was inherited by Julia C. (Kendrick) Clark from her

father, James Kendrick, who was a charter member of Ramoth
Baptist Church along with his master and mistress and the latter's brother and sister, John H. and Elizabeth (Kendrick)
Clark, and who, during Sherman's march to the sea and B. W.
Clark's absence to defend Atlanta, slept with an axe each night
before the room of my great-aunts to defend them against the
Federal soldiery - an act which did not prevent the soldiers
from appropriating the girls' silk dresses and racing with them
fastened to the pommels of their saddles as standards.

Drury[5] Kendrick, son of James[4] and Tabitha (Rogers) Kendrick, was born about 1790 in Wilkes or Washington Co., Ga.
and married Hannah Holland Dec. 3, 1812 in Putnam Co., Ga.
Drury Kendrick moved to Monroe Co., Ga., after his marriage,
and was appointed Captain of Militia there Nov. 9, 1825. He was
on the Grand Jury in Harris Co., Ga. in 1828, appears there in
the Census of 1830, and was living there 1832-5, when he drew
land in the Cherokee Gold Lottery. The family in 1830 contained
1 male and 1 female b. 1790-1800, 1 male b. 1810-15, 1 male
and 1 female b. 1815-20, 2 males and 1 female b. 1820-25,
and 2 females b. 1825-30. There is no further record of Drury
Kendrick after 1835, though it is possible that he moved to Texas, where his son, John Rogers Kendrick, moved later. A
grandson of this John Rogers Kendrick, Mr. Andrew Kendrick
of Pocatello, Idaho, years ago sent his grandfather's Family
Bible record and a list of the children of Drury and Hannah (Holland) Kendrick to U.S. Senator John B. Kendrick of Wyoming,
giving the names of the children as Amelia, Georgia, Kenyon,
John Rogers, Isaac, William, and James. Kenyon[6] Kendrick
was the eldest child, born in 1811 according to the Census of
1850, but this is obviously a mistake, as the parents were not
married until 1812. He married Charlotte Hardy in 1839 in Monroe Co., Ga., appears there in the Census of 1840, deeded land
there in 1843, and was still living in Monroe Co. in 1850, when
the Census shows K. B. Kendrick (b. 1811), his wife Charlotte
(b. 1820), and the following children: James b. 1840, William
b. 1842, Mar. (Mary?) b. 1845, John b. 1848, and Sallie b.
1850 (3 mos. old). The only other child of Drury Kendrick of
whom anything is known was John[6] Rogers Kendrick, born Sept.
27, 1817, died about 1899, m. May 10, 1838 Cornelia Todd in
Monroe Co., Ga. (she was born Nov. 15, 1819, and died in 1901).
John Rogers Kendrick appears in Monroe Co., Ga. in the Census of 1840 and deeded land there in 1843. His children were:

I.   Erastus A. Kendrick, b. March 22, 1839, killed in Civil
       War;
II.   Mary E. Kendrick b. July 6, 1841, died about 1895, m.
       Edward Fry;
III.   Julia E. Kendrick b. 1843;
IV.   Joseph M. Kendrick b. 1846;
V.   Hester E. Kendrick b. 1848, m. G. W. Williams;
VI.   Cornelia E. Kendrick b. 1850 m. W. R. Williams;
VII.   Kenyon B. Kendrick b. 1853, m. Ella McVicker, lived in
       Texas, and they were parents of Andrew Kendrick who
       sent this record;

VIII.   Harvey R. Kendrick b. 1855, m. Amelia McVicker;
IX.   Rebecca H. Kendrick b., 1857, m. John Scott;
X.   Sarah H. Kendrick b.. 1859, m. T.B. Holland;
XI.   Manassas Kendrick b. 1861.

Tabitha[5] Kendrick, daughter of James[4] and Tabitha(Rogers)
Kendrick, was born in 1792 (Census) in Washington or Wilkes
Co., Ga., died after 1872, probably in Columbus, Ga. She married Dec. 24, 1812 in Putnam Co., Ga. Samuel Holland (b.1790
in Tenn., died Dec. 7, 1865 in Newton Co., Miss.). According
to Tabitha Holland's pension application (WO 9020, WC 4170) in
the National Archives at Washington, D.C., her husband, Samuel Holland, served in the War of 1812, being enlisted Oct. 12,
1814 at Eatonton, Putnam Co., Ga. and served until Mar. 15,
1815, when he was honorably discharged at Savannah; Samuel
and Tabitha were married Dec. 24, 1812 at Crossroads, Putnam
Co., Ga., by Benjamin Wright, J.P.; Samuel Holland applied
for bounty land Nov. 20, 1850 from Russell Co., Ala., giving
his age as 64 years; he applied again for bounty land March 28,
1855, giving his age as 63 years; and residing at that time in
Columbia Co., Fla.; he died in Newton Co., Miss. Dec. 7,
1865, affidavits being given from Erastus Holland and Thomas
S. Matley that they were present at the death, and that Tabitha
was the widow; and Tabitha Holland applied for a pension July
3, 1872, then residing at Columbus, Ga., and in that year was
granted the pension. Samuel Holland was living in Monroe Co.,
Ga. in 1830, the Census of that year showing his family as consisting of 1 male and 1 female b. 1790-1800, 1 female b. 1810-
15, 3 females b. 1815-2-, 1 female b. 1820-25, and 1 male and
1 female b. 1825-30. The Census of 1840 shows that he was residing at that time in Russell Co., Ala., and he was still living
there in 1850, when the Census shows: Samuel Holland, aged 60,
b. in Tenn., Tabitha Holland aged 58, b. in Ga.; Hetta Holland
aged 21, Colquitt Holland aged 18, and Thacker Holland aged 16.
In the bounty land applications above Samuel Holland gave his
birth as 1786 in 1850 and 1792 in 1855; probably the Census date,
1790, is the correct one. Other children of Samuel and Tabitha
(Kendrick) Holland, besides Hetta, Colquitt and Thacker above,
were probably: (1) Erastus Holland, who was present at Samuel's
death, and whose family is shown in Russell Co., Ala., close to Samuel's as: Erastus Holland aged 38 and Salona Holland aged 30,
both born in Tenn., William Holland aged 15, Cynthia Holland
aged 12, Louisa aged 10, Adeline aged 9, Hetta aged 7, Mary
aged 5, and James aged 3, all born in Ga. (if Erastus' age is
given correctly, however, he could not have been a son, as
Samuel and Tabitha were not married until 1812); (2) perhaps a
daughter who married Thomas S. Matley, the other man who
made affidavit that he was present at Samuel Holland's death;
(3) perhaps William Holland aged 23 living in Russell Co., Ala.
in 1850 in the family of Stafford Gibson; and (4) perhaps Elizabeth Holland, aged 24, living in Russell Co. in 1850 in the family of Anderson Baldwin. Other Hollands living in Russell Co.,
Ala. in 1840 and 1850 were probably brothers of Samuel (James
b. 1805, David b. 1800-10, and William b. 1803).

Isham[5] Kendrick, son of James[4] and Tabitha (Rogers) Kendrick, was born in 1794 (Census of 1860 - the Census of 1850 gives it 1792, but this is improbable unless he was a twin of Tabitha), married Sept. 6, 1827 in Putnam Co., Ga., Ann Strubbs (b. 1800), daughter of Frank Stubbs of Eatonton, Ga. and his wife Miss Booth, and granddaughter of James Stubbs, a Revolutionary soldier, and his wife Mary Eliza Scott, daughter of Col. James Scott of Prince Edward Co., Va. (data from Mrs. Eunice B. Stubbs, Ordinary of Putnam Co., Eatonton, Ga., who has a genealogy of the Stubbs family). Both Isham Kendrick and Nancy his wife died after 1860, probably in Smith Co., Tex. The Putnam Co. Census of 1820 shows Isham Kendrick as a single man, b. 1794-1804; he was a Captain of Militia in Putnam in 1826 and 1827; listed land in Houston Co. in 1827; and drew land as a soldier in the Lottery of 1827. He probably moved to Harris Co., Ga. with his brother, Drury, a few years later, for the Census returns of 1830 and 1840 apparently show his family there, though 1830 lists him as "Gam Kendrick" and that of 1840 as "J. Kendrick". The Census of 1850 shows Isham Kendrick and his family in Macon Co., Ala., and that of 1860 shows him in Smith Co., Texas. The two Census returns show the following children of Isham[4] and Nancy Stubbs Kendrick: (1) James F. Kendrick b. 1830, unmarried in 1860; (2) Mildred Kendrick b. 1830; (3) Drury Kendrick, b. 1832, married to Ann (b. 1825) in 1860, she being perhaps a widow Dixon, as the Census shows two Dixon children in the family, Sarah aged 10 and Thomas aged 5; (4) Isham Kendrick b. 1833; (5) Kenyon Kendrick b. 1835; (6) William Kendrick b. 1837; (7) Sarah Kendrick b. 1839; (8) Maria Kendrick b. 1841; and (9) Jones Kendrick b. 1844-5. It is possible that there was an older son, Granville Kendrick, b. 1828, who is not shown in the family in 1850 in Macon Co., Ala. and may have been living elsewhere. Granville Kendrick is shown in 1860 in Smith Co., Texas with a wife, Jane, b. 1838 in Ala., and two children, Cicero b. 1857 and Elizabeth, b. 1860 (1 mo. old). Granville had the same address as Isham Kendrick (Jamestown P.O.), but the Census returns of 1830 and 1840 show no son born prior to 1830 in Isham Kendrick's family, and there was a William Kendrick (b. 1784 in South Carolina), living at Jamestown P.O. in 1860, who may have been Granville's father or grandfather.

Susan[5] Kendrick, daughter of James[4] and Tabitha (Rogers) Kendrick, was born in 1799 (Census), probably in Washington Co., Ga., and died in Copiah Co., Miss., some time after 1850. She married in Putnam Co., Ga. Jan. 22, 1818 John Stubbs (b. 1798), son of Frank Stubbs of Eatonton and brother of Ann or Nancy Stubbs who married Isham[5] Kendrick. John Stubbs was known as Jack, moved to Copiah Co., Miss., and is said to have been a patron of the races in Natchez, Vicksburg and Memphis. The Stubbs genealogy and the Copiah Co. Census of 1850 show the children of Susan Kendrick and John Stubbs as:

I.   John[6] Stubbs, b. 1819, d. 1863 at Crystal Springs, Miss., m. Phoebe Campbell, who died 1878 of yellow fever, and had issue: John, Logan, Elwell, Susie (m. Mr. Sturges),

Emma (m. Mr. Jones), and Mildred (m. Mr. Bloomfield). The Copiah Co. Census of 1850 shows John L. Stubbs, b. 1819 in La., Matilda A. Stubbs, b. 1834, John F. Stubbs b. 1848, and Martha W. Stubbs b. 1850 (6 mos. old). The Census names do not correspond to those above sent from the genealogy, but perhaps there was a second marriage, and the birth in "La." in the Census could be a mistake for "Ga.".

II.   Martha[6] Clements Stubbs, b. 1821 at Eatonton, Ga., m. Moody Stackhouse and had two children:

1. Beatrice[7] Stackhouse, b. 1847, m. (1) 1865 Dr. Henry G. Stackhouse who d. 1877; m. (2) Hampton England who d. 1886; and m. (3) W. T. Matheney; she had 5 Stackhouse children: Blanche, Cordelia A., Camilla, Legrand Brickell Stackhouse and Henry Coma Stackhouse;

2. John[7] Stubbs Stackhouse, b. 1854, m. 1887 Ellen Coor.

III.   Ann[6] Stubbs, b. 1823, d. 1884, m. Mr. Broomfields of Baltimore, Md.

IV.   Louisa[6] B. Stubbs, b. 1825 (Census).

V.   Susan[6] Stubbs, b. 1827 (Census).

VI.   Mildred[6] Stubbs, b. 1836 (Census).

James[5] Kendrick, son of James[4] and Tabitha (Rogers) Kendrick, was born about 1800 or 1801 in Washington or Hancock Co., Ga. He lived in his father's family, unmarried, up to the latter's death. The Census of 1820 shows him as b. 1794-1804 and that of 1820 shows him as b. 1800-10. He was probably born about 1800, as the Lottery of 1821 shows a lucky draw to James Kendrick of Putnam in Dooly Co., and in 1822 James Kendrick, Jr. listed land in Putnam and Dooly Co's. James Kendrick listed land in Capt. Isham Kendrick's District in 1826, and in 1831 the tax-list of Putnam shows James Kendrick as owner of land in Jones, Lee and Coweta Co.'s. It is uncertain whether the James Kendrick of 1826 and 1831 is the son or the father, but probably the son. After 1831 there is no further record of James[5] Kendrick.

Elizabeth[5] Kendrick, daughter of James[4] Kendrick and Tabitha Rogers, was born in 1805 (Census) in Hancock Co., Ga., married in Putnam Co., Ga. Dec. 28, 1820 Rev. John Harvey Clark, son of William and Mary (Harvey) Clark, and died after 1878. Her family and descendants are given in the article on the Clark family in this volume.

Celia[5] Kendrick, daughter of James[4] and Tabitha (Rogers) Kendrick, was born about 1810 in Putnam Co., Ga. James Kendrick's family is shown in 1830 with two unmarried daughters in it, born 1810-15, One of these was my great-grandmother, Julia C. Kendrick, who was born 1812-13, and as my grandmother Holtzclaw told me that her aunt Celia was just older than her mother, Julia C., 1810 would be about the correct date for Celia's birth. Celia Kendrick married some time after 1830 Major Pleasant J. Mullens of Putnam Co. They were members of Ramoth Baptist Church, and many years ago I spent the night in the house built by Major Mullens (then owned by his granddaughter, Cousin Molly Gorley), and remember the magnificent boxwood leading up to the house. Pleasant and Celia Mullens had the following children:

I.   Catherine[6] Mullens, m. Dr. King. Miss Lilla Odum, Route 4, Eatonton, Ga., wrote me several years ago that a daughter of the Kings married Ed Freeman, and that other children, she thought, were Rivers, Ira, and Nannie King.

II.   Mary[6] Mullens, b. 1836 (Census), m. Henry Lawrence (b. 1830) of Putnam Co., son of Allen Lawrence and Mary L. Coates and grandson of Henry and Civility (Harvey) Coates (See Harvey Family). Their children were:
   1. Molly[7] Lawrence m. Mark Gorley and had three children, Clyde Gorley who m. William K. McCrea, Nona Gorley who m. Ben Harper, and Nat Gorley who m. Effie Tyler;
   2. Lula[7] Lawrence m. Charles Leonard and had: John Leonard and Mrs. Mary Lou Bozeman (both of Eatonton), Cephas Leonard, Henry Leonard, Ruth Leonard, Mrs. Marjorie Barber, and Mrs. Hannah Powell;
   3. Puella[7] Lawrence m. William Dennis and had: Plunkett and William Dennis (both of Eatonton), Charles Dennis of Alexandria, Va., Mrs. Marie McDade, and Frank Dennis;
   4. John[7] Lawrence m. Sydney Dismukes.

III.   Blandina[6] Caroline Mullens, b. May 5, 1843 in Putnam Co., Ga., d. Nov. 1, 1918 in Forsyth, Ga., m. April 14, 1859 Eugene Rufus Roberts (b. Oct. 9, 1837, d. June 10, 1920 at Forsyth); issue:
   1. Carrie[7] E. Roberts, b. Aug. 30, 1864, d. July 5, 1928, m. 1881 Thomas R. Talmadge (b. Aug. 3, 1858, d. June 23, 1931), and they were parents of Eugene Talmadge, Governor of Georgia, and grandparents of his son, Herman Talmadge, also Governor;
   2. Lucile[7] Roberts m. 1890 John H. Gay and moved to Miami, Fla.;
   3. Count[7] Pulasky Roberts m. Lucile Robertson and moved to Texas;
   4. Sarah[7] R. Roberts m. 1899 B. Frank Holder;
   5. Lilla[7] Roberts m. 1897 Claude F. Chambliss;
   6. Eyleen[7] Roberts m. 1903 John Oscar Elrod;
   7. Inez[7] M. Roberts m. 1904 Julius B. Smith and lives in Miami, Fla.

Julia[5] Carolina Kendrick, daughter of James[4] and Tabitha (Rogers) Kendrick, was born 1812-13 in Putnam Co., Ga., and died Jan. 19, 1850 aged 37 years (Clark Family Bible). She married Oct. 25, 1832 Benjamin Williams Clark of Putnam Co., son of William and Mary (Harvey) Clark, and her descendants are given in the article on the Clark family. Her eldest daughter, Mary Etta Clark, married Henry M. Holtzclaw and they were my grandparents. An account of the Holtzclaw family is given in Boddie's "Southside Virginia Families", Vol. I, pp. 144-5, as well as in the longer Holtzclaw Genealogy, published in 1936. I shall only add her material regarding my daughter and her family not published in these earlier accounts. My daughter, Alnita Hasselle Holtzclaw, married William Thomas Dyall of Ottumwa, Ia., June 7, 1947. They live in Lancaster, Pa. and have two children, Ruth Cornelia Dyall b. Jan. 6, 1949 and Hewitt Wood Dyall b. Dec. 18, 1949.

Catherine[5] Kendrick was born about 1815 in Putnam Co., Ga., the youngest child of James[4] and Tabitha (Rogers) Kendrick, and died in Schley Co., Ga., Aug. 12, 1884. There is some doubt about her birthdate, as the Census of 1850 gives it as 1817, that of 1860 as 1812, and that of 1870 as 1815. 1812 is bound to be wrong, as her next older sister, Julia C. Kendrick, was born in that year or 1813. The 1830 Census of Putnam Co. shows one daughter in James[4] Kendrick's family born 1815-20, so 1815 or 1817 is the correct date. Catherine Kendrick married in 1832 Thomas Jefferson Baisden (b. 1810 at Baisden's Bluff, McIntosh Co., Ga., d. Aug. 17, 1894 at La Cross, Ga.), son of Solomon Baisden, who died about 1825 (administration on the estate of Solomon Baisden, decd., late of McIntosh Co., Ga. was granted to James Govan in Chatham Co., Ga. Jan. 17, 1826 (File No. 189, Chatham Co.). There is some doubt about Solomon Baisden's birth-date, for his obituary states that he was 88 years old when he died in 1894, which would put his birth in 1806; however, the Census consistently gives it as 1810, which is probably correct. The Land Lottery of 1827 shows a draw for Solomon Baisden's orphans, of Chatham Co. The land was in Troup Co., Ga., and Thomas Baisden appears there in the Census of 1830, a single man, b. 1810-15. By 1840 his family is shown in Sumter Co., Ga., and again in the Census of 1850; and Thomas J. Baisden in 1842 was appointed a trustee of Farmer's Academy in Americus. Schley Co. was formed from Sumter in 1857, and Thomas J. Baisden's family is shown there in the Census of 1860, 1870 and later years. The children of Thomas Jefferson and Catherine (Kendrick) Baisden, as gathered from family records, census returns, ets., and sent in by a descendant, Louis A. Baisden, 1316 Whittier Place, N.W., Washington 12, D.C., were as follows:

I. John[6] Randolph Baisden, b. Sept. 14, 1833 at La Cross, Ga., d. Sept. 7, 1883 near Shellman, Ga., Confederate soldier, m. Dec. 18, 1855 in Talbot Co., Ga. Lavonia Ann Mathews (b. July 17, 1836 in Pike Co., Ga., d. Feb. 9, 1895 at Searight, Ala.); issue:

 1. Francis[7] Lawrence Baisden, M.D., b. Oct. 1, 1856 at La Cross, Ga., d. 1934 or 1935, m. (1) Nov. 28, 1884 M. Belle Shanklin (b. Aug. 28, 1864, d. Dec. 24, 1890); m. (2) Sept. 30, 1891 Annie Bedford Lynch (b. Jan. 29, 1867, d. 1913). Issue of first marriage:

  (1) John[8] Randolph Baisden b. Sept. 19, 1885, d. Oct. 11, 1886;

  (2) Robert[8] Emory Baisden b. June 21, 1888, d. 1945;

  (3) E. T.[8] Baisden, b. Oct. 28, 1890, d. about 1943, m. Lucille Lowe and had E. T. Baisden, Jr., b. June 28, 1894.

Issue of second marriage:

(4) Anna[8] Lee Baisden, d. aged 6;

(5) Asa[8] Randolph Baisden m. Margaret Vonadore of Valdosta Ga.;

(6) William[8] Lawrence Baisden m. Igee ------;

(7) Flora[8] Lee Baisden, b. April 25, 1898, m. (1) June 5, 1923 in Norfolk, Va., Hobson Haigh (b. July, 1890 in Penn., d. Sept. 19, 1945), m. (2) M. M. Hussey, and by first marriage had:

   a. Eleanor[9] Haigh b. June 7, 1924 at Daytona Beach, Fla., m. July 23, 1943 Nelson P. Hobdell, Jr. and had Nelson P. Hobdell, III, b. Aug. 9, 1947 and Johnny Leroy Hobdell, b. Dec. 4, 1950;

   b. Mary[9] Judith Haigh b. May 30, 1926, m. Nov. 13, 1949 Andrew F. Dexter and had Kathyleen Eva Dexter b. July 3, 1953;

   c. Joseph[9] F. Haigh, b. July 3, 1929 at Deland, Fla., m. Sept. 12, 1953 Sarah Ruth Hinkle;

(8) Albert[8] Sidney Baisden b. Jan. 11, 1900 at Hull, Ga., m. Dec. 22, 1921 in Norfolk, Va., Sidneth Charlotte Harrington (b. Nov. 23, 1899 in Bachelor, N.C.) and had:

   a. Albert[9] Sidney Baisden b. June 30, 1935

   b. Leroy[9] Grancis Baisden b. Sept. 15, 1940

(9) Felix[8] Lynch Baisden b. June 18, 1902 in Brandon, Fla., m. July 2, 1946 Mary Edith Elison in Shreveport, La.;

(10) Gladys[8] Lavonia Baisden d. aged 1 yr.;

(11) Frederick Francis[8] Baisden, d. 1949-50.

2. George[7] Rousseau Baisden, b. Sept. 27, 1858 at La Cross, Ga., d. Dec., 1949 at Los Angeles, Calif., m. (1) Nov. 19, 1890 Alva L. Rhodes (b. July 24, 1875) m. (2) Alma ------. Issue, all by first marriage and born in Texas:

(1) U. T. Baisden

(2) Athan Baisden

(3) Jessie Baisden

(4) Georgia Baisden m. Lindsey Albright

(5) Topsy Baisden m. Willard F. Miller and d. Jan. 1941 leaving a son, Willard F. Miller, Jr., b. ca. 1930;

(6) Helen Baisden m. Mr. Zimmermann

(7) Travis Baisden.

3. Thomas[7] Edwin Baisden, b. Oct. 9, 1860 at La Cross, Ga., d. 1939 at Andalusia, Ala., m. Dec. 23, 1891 Mrs. Lorena Hart Crumpler (b. Oct. 2, 1869 in Covington Co., Ala., d. Jan. 31, 1953 at Tifton, Ga.); Issue:

(1) R. D.[8] Basiden b. Jan. 27, 1893, m. ca. 1920 Mrs. Ann Christian;

(2) Tison[8] Edwin Baisden b. March 18, 1894, m. ca. 1920 Ruth Lowe and has a daughter, Eva Lowe

Baisden and a son; res. Columbus, Ga.
- (3) Edna[8] Baisden m. Ross Stanton, lives at Columbus, Ga., and has Edwin, Fred, and Ross Stanton, Jr.;
- (4) Wilma[8] Baisden m. John Will Woodham, res. Brundidge, Ala., and has two children, Robert Alan Woodham who m. June 10, 1950 Patricia Beth Dillon, and Lorena Woodham who m. Dec. 27, 1953 James Jordan Plaster;
- (5) Fred[8] Baisden, lives in Miami, Fla.;
- (6) Mildred[8] Baisden m. 1935 Stewart McRae, lives in Tifton, Ga.

4. John[7] Randolph Baisden, Jr., b. Aug. 23, 1865, d. Oct. 5, 1866.

5. Joseph[7] Sidney Baisden b. Sept. 3, 1867, d. Aug. 6, 1869;

6. James[7] Kendrick Baisden, b. July 11, 1869, lives in Houston, Tex., m. (1) Kate Shelton and (2) ca. 1906 Daisy Belle Yarborough (b. May 18, 1883 in Liberty Co., Texas, d. Aug. 9, 1930); issue by second marriage:
- (1) James[8] Kendrick Baisden, Jr., b. Nov. 19, 1907, d. Dec. 3, 1907;
- (2) Reuben[8] Kendrick Baisden b. March 22, 1909, d. Dec. 18, 1953, m. June 6, 1944 Ruby Faulk and has a daughter, Susan Kendrick Baisden, b. July 3, 1948;
- (3) Daisy[8] Lavonia Baisden b. Sept. 9, 1917, m. Sept. 3, 1937 Paul Ray Goalsby and has a son, Michael Scott Goalsby b. Oct. 7, 1947.

7. Britt[7] Mathews Baisden b. Sept. 10, 1873 in Talbot Co., Ga., d. July 28, 1938 in Covington Co., Ala., m. (1) April 7, 1897 Josephine Adams (b. Jan. 28, 1874 in Covington Co., Ala., d. March 4, 1914 in Santa Rosa Co., Fla.), m. (2) April 5, 1923 Mrs. K. Adams Brown (b. 1891 in Fla.).
Issue of first marriage:
- (1) Thomas[8] Edwin Baisden b. Oct. 14, 1899 in Covington Co., Ala., d. Oct. 28, 1900;
- (2) Lavonia[8] Ann Baisden b. Feb. 2, 1903 in Covington Co., Ala., m. July 8, 1938 Thomas Bibb Cottle and has a son Thomas Bibb Cottle, Jr., b. April 22, 1939;
- (3) Lawrence[8] Albert Baisden b. June 28, 1905 in Fla., m. Dec. 22, 1927 in Covington Co., Ala., Eula Mae Shehane (b. Aug. 1, 1903) and had:
  - a. Albert[9] Lawrence Baisden, Jr., b. Nov. 17, 1928, d. Dec. 20, 1928;
  - b. James[9] Kenneth Baisden b. June 29, 1930;
  - c. Gene[9] Arthur Baisden b. April 23, 1932;
  - d. Martha[9] Nell Baisden b. Nov. 1, 1933;
  - e. Winnie[9] Mae Baisden b. Sept. 28, 1935;
  - f. Betty[9] Sue Baisden b. Feb. 6, 1938.
- (4) Bessie[8] Lee Baisden b. Sept. 11, 1907 in Santa

Rosa Co., Fla., d. May 31, 1908;

(5) Arthur[8] Mathis Baisden b. Dec. 31, 1909 in Santa Rosa Co., Fla., m. May 5, 1940 Mary Ann Coak and had: Stephen[9] Arthur Baisden, b. Sept. 23, 1942;

(6) Louis[8] Alma Baisden b. Jan. 18, 1912 in Santa Rosa Co., Fla., m. Dec. 16, 1939 Caroline Josephine Leonardo; res. 1316 Whittier Place, N.W., Washington 1 2, D.C.

Issue of second marriage of Brit Mathews Baisden:

(7) Verna[8] Rebecca Baisden b. Jan. 18, 1912 in Santa Rosa Co., Fla., m. about 1944 William Kuchko.

8. Nyda[7] Kate Baisden b. June 25, 1876 in Talbot Co., Ga., res. Andalusia, Ala., m. Sept. 22, 1897 Marion Athan Boyett (b. Feb. 26, 1871) and had:

(1) Marion[8] Athan Boyett, Jr., b. Dec. 15, 1903 at Searight, Ala., m. (1) Margaret Knox and had John[9] Knox Boyett b. April 1928, m. Dec. 28, 1952 Faye Anderson; he m. (2) Florence -------- and had Marion[9] Athan Boyett (a daughter), b. Dec. 9, 1950.

II. Richard[6] P. Baisden, son of Thomas J. and Catherine (Kendrick) Baisden, was born July 1836 at La Cross, Ga. and died in Ellis Co., Tex. He m. Dec. 17, 1856 in Sumter Co., Ga. Permilia C. Hays (b. 1838-9). Present members of the family are W. S. Baisden, No. 1 Nonesuch Rd., Dallas, Texas, G.K. Baisden, Ennis, Texas, and a grandson W. S. Baisden, Kileen, Texas. The Census of 1860 and 1870 for Schley Co., Ga. show the following children of Richard and Permilia Baisden: Irene, b. 1858; Ada, b. 1859; George W. b. 1860, d. before 1870; Robert b. 1866; Josephine b. 1868; and Ida b. 1870.

III. Josephine[6] Baisden, daughter of T. J. and Catherine, was born in 1841 at La Cross, Ga., and died Oct. 23, 1918; she m. (1) Mr. Fulton, who was killed in the Civil War; (2) Nov. 14, 1868 Tom R. Royal (b. Aug. 12, 1837); and (3) Dec. 19, 1878 Charles B. Hudson, Solicitor-General of the Americus Circuit. By her second marriage Josephine Baisden had one daughter, Katie Eudora Royal, b. Oct. 28, 1870, m. 1888 Tom Hudson. The Hudson's had two children, Gertrude Hudson who m. Carl Hawkins and had two sons, Carl, Jr., and Thomas Hawkins, and Charles Hudson who m. Clara Willis Prather and had Charles Jr., and Billy Hudson.

IV. Joseph[6] Algernon Sidney Baisden, son of T. J. and Catherine (Kendrick) Baisden, b. June 12, 1840 (date given by Mr. L. A. Baisden, but the Census consistently shows his birth as 1842), m. Nov. 14, 1864 Fannie Darkins Matthews (Mathis), sister of the wife of his brother, John Randolph Baisden, and died Feb. 3, 1913. His wife was born July 2, 1843 and died Jan. 29, 1912. Their children were:

1. Albert[7] Victor Baisden, b. Dec. 15, 1865, d. Jan.

1919, no issue;

2. Annie[7] Lee Baisden, b. March 19, 1867, d.s.p. Mar. 29, 1887.
3. Lula[7] Darkins Baisden, b. April 14, 1870, unmarried;
4. Herbert[7] Sidney Baisden, b. Jan. 30, 1872, m. Dec. 25, 1895 Lillie Archer, and had issue: Carrie Frank, Archer, Flora May, Melvin, and Bert Baisden;
5. Nyda[7] Randolph Baisden, b. May 19, 1873, m. March 29, 1899 Wade C. Stevens in Atlanta, Ga., and had: Joe Frank Stevens and Gladys Stevens, who m. Clift H. Williams;
6. Frank[7] Mathews Baisden, b. March 12, 1875, d. Feb. 1943; m. Marie Doyle; issue: Marie, Frank Mathews, Jr., and Doyle Baisden;
7. Clifford[7] Jerome Baisden, b. June 28, 1877, m. Mrs. Mina Johnson White, d. in Atlanta, Ga.; no issue.
8. Lillie[7] May Baisden b. Aug. 2, 1880, m. July 11, 1900 in Atlanta Rev. Wesley Fletcher Patch, res. 1954 Houston, Texas. Issue:
   (1) Charles Elbert Patch, b. June 21, 1901, m. Ruth -------- and had Charles Elbert, Jr., b. 1930, and Wallis Patch, b. 1936;
   (2) Annie Mae Patch, b. July 23, 1903, m. William R. Dixon and had Bobby, b. 1936, and Francis, b. 1942;
   (3) Clifford Baisden Patch, b. Dec. 3, 1907, m. Anna Dean Turner and had Clifford B., Jr., b. 1937, and Anna Katherine Patch, b. 1945;
   (4) Thomas Carter Patch, b. July 10, 1910, m. Meda Gore;
   (5) Sidney Baisden Patch, b. 1912, d. aged 6 mos.;
   (6) Wesley Fletcher Patch, Jr., b. Feb. 5, 1913, m. Alice Lee Triplett and had Martha Ann b. 1940, Mary Alice b. 1941, William Wesley b. 1945, Jettye Lillian b. 1947, and Cheryl Patch, b. 1949;
   (7) William Harrison Patch, b. Dec. 14, 1918, m. Mary Elizabeth Dendy and had Betty Joyce b. 1942, Ronald Harrison Patch b. 1947;
   (8) Mary Frances Patch b. July 23, 1923, m. Marion P. Beard and had twins, Carolyn and Catherine Beard, b. 1947.

V. Elizabeth[6] Baisden, daughter of T. J. and Catherine (Kendrick) Baisden, b. 1845 at La Cross, Ga., m. George Walker; issue: Augustus, Eula, Ardie, Hattie, Pearl, Charles (d. young), Eva, Mattie, Bess, Dewhart, and Garrett Walker.

VI. Zachariah[6] Taylor Baisden, son of Catherine[5] Kendrick and T. J. Baisden, was born Aug. 5, 1845 at La Crosse, Ga., and died Jan. 27, 1916 at Greenville, Ala. He married Elizabeth Hubert (b. March 4, 1847, d. Oct. 18, 1923). He was a Confederate soldier, serving in Co. B, 5th Ga. Reserves (Nat. Archives, R.G. 109, Packet No. 89). His three brothers, John Randolph Baisden, Richard

P. Baisden, and Joseph A. S. Baisden, also served in the Confederate Army: John Randolph in Co. E, 56th Regt. Ala. Partisan Rangers (same, Packets No. 28 and 53); Richard P. in Co's. H, B, and D, 46th Ga. Inf. (Packet No. 97); and Joseph A.S. in Co's. A and K, 4th Ga. Inf. (Packet No. 72). The father, Thomas Jefferson Baisden, helped to organize and supply young men in Schley Co. for the Confederate Army. He had had previous military experienced, as he was appointed Captain of the Home Guard of Baldwin Co., Ga., Jan. 12, 1829. The children of Zachariah[6] Taylor and Elizabeth Hubert were:

1. Homer[7] Z. Baisden, b. ca. 1867 in Schley Co., Ga., d. June 29, 1914 at Greenville, Ala., m. June 16, 1891 Odie Kilgore (b. June 5, 1871, d. July 11, 1932), Issue:
    (1) Iver D. Baisden b. June 12, 1892, d. Nov. 6, 1909;
    (2) Bennie Baisden, b. Aug. 27, 1895, m. Maud Heaton, no children, res. Greenville, Ala.

2. Carrie[7] C. Baisden, b. Nov. 12, 1870 in Schley Co., Ga., d. Dec. 6, 1944 at Pensacola, Fla.; m. (1) Arthur Dow Johnson, (2) Mr. Mitchell, and (3) Mr. Belser; issue (only by first marriage):
    (1) Bessie Johnson b. Jan. 29, 1892, d. July 13, 1893;
    (2) Thomas Carl Johnson, m. Lois Belser and had one son, Thomas Carl Johnson, Jr., who m. Betty Cage and had a son Elmore Johnson.
    (3) Arthur Dow Johnson, Jr.

3. Claudius[7] Baisden, b. Dec. 13, 1874 in Schley Co., Ga., d. Nov. 11, 1941 in Greenville, Ala.; m. (1) Lillie Norris and had several children, among them Claude[8] S. Baisden, Beach Haven near Pensacola, Fla., who m. Myrtice Lloyd and has three children, Claude III, Donald and Edward; m. (2) Annie Laurie Potts, by whom he had two children, Homer[8] and Helen[8] Baisden; m. (3) Katie Lee Whidden, now Mrs. Johnson of Greenville, Ala., no issue.

4. Estella[7] Baisden, b. April 7, 1878, d. June 20, 1910 at Greenville, Ala., m. Joe Dickerson; issue:
    (1) Thomas Jefferson Dickerson;
    (2) Lewis Dickerson;
    (3) Claudie Dickerson;
    (4) Hubert Dickerson;
    (5) Gertrude Dickerson m. Fred Mostyn.

5. Cora[7] Eunice Baisden, b. ca. 1879, m. George B. Hughey, res. 1400 E. Lee St., Pensacola, Fla.; children, George B. Hughey, Jr., and an adopted son, Lucius Hughey.

6. Zachariah[7] Taylor Baisden, b. ca. 1880, d. 1949 in Pensacola, Fla., m. (1) Belle Russell; issue:
    (1) John[8] Stark Baisden, res. 1818 E. Strong St., Pensacola, Fla.
    (2) Eunice[8] Baisden, died young;
    (3) Russell[8] P. Baisden;

(4) Mary[8] Baisden m. Mr. Urso;

(5) Zachariah[8] Taylor Baisden m. Eula Hall; res. Ferry Pass, Pensacola, Fla.;
Issue:
a. Zachariah Taylor b. 1941;
b. Virginia b. 1943;
c. Sarah b. 1948.

(6) Faye[8] Baisden m. Arthur Marshall.

VII. Catherine[6] Baisden, daughter of T.J. and Catherine (Kendrick) Baisden, died unmarried Nov. 11, 1872.

VIII. Thomas[6] Jefferson Baisden, Jr., son of T. J. and Catherine, b. Jan. 19, 1850 in Schley Co., Ga., d. May 1904 in Americus, Ga., m. 1872 Arie Ann Winifred Murphy (b. Dec. 19, 1855, d. Feb. 13, 1918); issue:

1. Roy[7] Thomas Baisden, b. Sept. 18, 1874, m. Sept. 22, 1896 Mary Louise Schmidt (b. Feb. 17, 1875, d. May 2, 1937) and had:

(1) Roy[8] Thomas Baisden, Jr., b. Dec. 6, 1897, m. June 21, 1920 Mary Louise Rivers (b. July 8, 1898); no issue;

(2) Otelia[8] Pauline Baisden, b. Jan. 16, 1900 at Milledgeville, Ga., m. June 15, 1918 James Mitchell Salter, Jr. (b. July 8, 1895, d. April 21,1951) and had:
a. James[9] Mitchell Salter, III, b. Nov. 27, 1920, m. Dec. 30, 1945 Mary Jewell Teresi (b. July 1, 1922); issue:
   (a) J. M. Salter, IV, b. June 30, 1949 at Milledgeville;
b. Mary[9] Jane Salter, b. Sept. 23, 1926, m. Dec. 22, 1949 Joseph William Deckard (b. Oct. 15, 1921);

(3) George[8] Henry Baisden, b. Aug. 21, 1901, m. Feb. 17, 1927 Helen Louise Haynes (b. June 9, 1903); issue:
a. Betty[9] Ann Baisden, b. Oct. 14, 1927;
b. George[9] Henry Baisden, Jr., b. Nov.25, 1930;
c. Pauline[9] Louise Baisden, b. Sept. 14, 1932, m. Feb. 2, 1951 Otto Conn Morrison (b. June 6, 1931),
d. Joe[9] Thomas Baisden, b. Dec. 26, 1937, all at Milledgeville, Ga.

(4) Emma[8] Louise Baisden b. Jan. 2, 1904, m. June 25, 1926 at Milledgeville William Clayton Pace (b. Oct. 5, 1886) and had:
a. Otelia[9] Louise Pace b. Aug. 31, 1935
b. William[9] Baisden Pace b. June 30, 1939, both at Hendersonville, N.C.

(5) Frederick[8] Haug Baisden b. Sept. 9, 1907 at Milledgeville, Ga., m. Sept. 6, 1925 Velma Winifred Langford (b. Oct. 24, 1907) and had:
a. Winifred[9] Pauline Baisden b. Sept. 11, 1928, m. Feb. 23, 1945 James Travis Paul, Jr.,

(b. March 15, 1926) and had James Travis
Paul III, b. Dec. 16, 1950;
b. Roy Thomas[9] Baisden III, b. Oct. 7, 1932 at
Milledgeville, Ga.;
(6) John[8] Rupert Baisden, b. Nov. 7, 1911, m. July
4, 1937 Myrtle Arlene Dennard (b. June 7, 1912)
and had:
a. John[9] Douglas Baisden b. Feb. 19, 1945;
b. Frederick Haug Baisden II, b. Feb. 14, 1950,
both at Milledgeville.
2. Charlie[7] Wynn Baisden b. Jan. 30, 1877 in Schley Co.,
Ga., died July 20, 1950 in Americus, Ga.; m. (1) Oct.
30, 1895 Lorin Battelph Smith (b. Oct. 10, 1866, d.
Jan. 27, 1919) m. (2) Eston Buchanon.
Issue of first marriage:
(1) Katherine[8] Smith b. Sept. 25, 1898 in Americus,
Ga., m. Oct. 28, 1925 Themmer Wilson Stewart
and had:
a. Thomas[9] Wilson Stewart b. Oct. 23, 1926,
m. 1949 Priscilla Ann Maybe;
(2) Lorin[8] Baisden Smith b. July 30, 1900 at Americus, Ga., m. May 20, 1926 Judy Bryan and had
a. Leela[9] Ann Smith b. June 7, 1929, m. 1951
John Bridge;
(3) Charles[8] Wynn Smith b. July 11, 1902 at Americus, Ga., m. (1) Elizabeth McNaughton and (2)
1951 Mary Elizabeth Jones;
(4) Elizabeth[8] Smith b. July 3, 1908 at Americus,
Ga., m. June 12, 1927 James Rodgers Buchanan
(b. March 9, 1904) and had:
a. Elizabeth[9] Jane Buchanan b. Aug. 7, 1928 at
Americus;
b. James[9] Rodgers Buchanan, Jr., b. March 11,
1932 at Americus;
(5) Mike[8] Smith b. Jan. 11, 1911, m. Elizabeth
Poole and had:
a. Mike[9] Smith, Jr., b. May, 1928;
b. Lorin[9] Smith;
(6) William[8] Evans Smith b. July 25, 1917 at Americus, m. June 4, 1941 Lucile Snyder and had:
a. Susan[9] Wynn Smith b. July 25, 1943 at Americus;
b. Elizabeth[9] Jane Smith b. Oct. 5, 1950, at
Americus.
3. Willie[7] Belle Baisden b. July 20, 1878 in Schlay Co.,
Ga., d. June 2, 1936 at Ft. Valley, Ga., m. Dec. 5,
1900 Albert James Evans (b. Feb. 2, 1875, d. Mar.
4, 1949); issue:
(1) Ruth[8] Evans b. Dec. 22, 1901 at Ft. Valley, m.
March 1, 1928 Joseph William Larimore (b. Apr.
5, 1887) and had:
a. Ann[9] Evans Larimore b. Dec. 5, 1931 at St.
Louis, Mo.

b. Joseph[9] William Larimore, Jr., b. Dec. 7, 1937 at St. Louis,, Mo.;

(2) Christine[8] Evans b. April 20, 1903 at Ft. Valley, Ga., m. May 27, 1926 at Ft. Valley Edwin Thompson Murray (b. May 21, 1893);

(3) Albert[8] James Evans, Jr., b. Oct. 1, 1904 at Ft. Valley, m. Oct. 25, 1951 Mary Jane Brooks at Nashville, Tenn., and had:
a. James[9] Albert Evans b. June 6, 1953;

(4) Willie[8] Baisden Evans b. Dec. 7, 1908 at Ft. Valley, d. Sept. 19, 1910 at Americus;

(5) Charles[8] Baisden Evans, b. Jan. 19, 1912 at Ft. Valley, m. Nov. 15, 1938 Sarah Eunice Hooten, and had:
a. Sarah[9] Elaine Evans b. Sept. 10, 1941 at Ft. Lauderdale, Fla.
b. Charles[9] Baisden Evans, Jr., b. April 6, 1951 at Macon, Ga.

(6) Mary[8] Jane Evans b. Jan. 22, 1914 at Ft. Valley, m. June 24, 1936 Rev. James Marcellus Lichliter (b. April 1911) and had:
a. Mary[9] Christie Lichliter b. July 26, 1940 at St. Louis, Mo.;
b. Bruce[9] Evans Lichliter b. March 20 at St. Louis.

5. Ethel[7] Lynn Baisden b. Feb. 19, 1884 at Schley Co., Ga., m. Oct. 20, 1904 in Macon, Ga., Samuel Robert Heys (b. Feb. 15, 1884 in Sumter Co., Ga.); issue:

(1) Ann[8] Heys b. Nov. 24, 1906 at Americus, Ga., m. May 6, 1933 Malcolm Nash (b. Mar. 13, 1903) and had:
a. Malcolm[9] Nash, Jr., b. Feb. 2, 1936 at Americus, Ga.

(2) Samuel[8] Robert Heys, Jr. b. Aug. 31, 1910 at Americus, Ga., m. Nov. 15, 1936 Ruba Elizabeth Gammedge (b. June 21, 1909), and had:
a. Jo Ann[9] Heys b. June 21, 1941 at Americus;
b. Ruba[9] Elizabeth Heys b. Sept. 20, 1943 at Athens, Ga.

(3) Thomas[8] Baisden Heys b. Nov. 3, 1917 at Jasper Co., Ga., m. July 15, 1939 in Atlanta, Ga., Mary Jo Dozier (b. April 30, 1917 in Jasper Co., Ga.) and had:
a. Thomas[9] Baisden Heys, Jr. b. Dec. 7, 1946 in Atlanta;
b b. Samuel[9] Robert Heys III b. May 28, 1950 in Chattanooga, Tenn.

IX. Emma[6] Gertrude Baisden, daughter of T. J. and Catherine (Kendrick) Baisden, b. April 23, 1853 in Schley Co., Ga., d. July 7, 1916, m. Nov. 13, 1873 Lucius Winston Dixon, b. Sept. 14, 1851, d. Sept. 28, 1898; issue:

1. Earnest[7] Winston Dixon, b. Oct. 16, 1874, d. April 2, 1930.

2. Thomas[7] Baisden Dixon, b. July 21, 1880, d. July 13,

1907 in Schley Co., Ga.;
3. Annie[7] Eugene Dixon, b. Sept. 19, 1881, m. Jan. 18, 1906 Cleveland Hamilton Burt (b. Nov. 12, 1882); issue:
  (1) Annie[8] Gertrude Burt, b. Nov. 4, 1906, m. June 4, 1933 Cleveland Bell Strange (b. July 31, 1883) and had:
    a. Robert Burt Strange, b. Jan. 13, 1936.
4. Josephine[7] Dixon, b. April 28, 1883, m. Dec. 18, 1902 Cullen Lazarus Battle (b. Aug. 4, 1880, d. Nov. 27, 1945); issue:
  (1) Lucius[8] Winston Battle, b. Aug. 31, 1903, m. Dec. 9, 1932 Louise Elrod (b. Nov. 30, 1905) and had:
    a. L. W. Battle, Jr., b. June 19, 1934;
  (2) Thomas[8] Jefferson Battle, b. June 10, 1909;
  (3) Mary[8] Dixon Battle b. June 10, 1909;
  (4) Cullen[8] Lazarus Battle, Jr., b. Sept. 29, 1911, d. Oct. 16, 1912;
  (5) Emma[8] Gene Battle, b. Jan. 11, 1913, m. June 1, 1932 William L. Easterlin (b. Oct. 5, 1912) and had:
    a. William L. Easterlin, Jr., b. Feb. 18, 1933;
    b. Paul Cullen Easterlin b. Jan. 17, 1937;
  (6) Josephine[8] Battle, b. June 20, 1914, m. May 14, 1936 Joseph Colquitt Logan (b. Nov. 14, 1915), and had:
    a. Jo Ann Logan, b. Nov. 15, 1943;
    b. J. C. Logan, Jr., b. March 11, 1947;
  (7) Charles[8] Thomas Battle, b. Nov. 17, 1915, m. April 1), 1947 Ann McMickle (b. June 22, 1928) and had:
    a. Charles Lester Battle, b. Nov. 19, 1947;
    b. Deborah Gene Battle, b. April 20, 1948;
  (8) Margaret Battle, b. Mar. 27, 1918, m. April 16, 1945 George Williams (b. Sept. 7, 1906) no issue.

Benjamin[4] Kendrick (James[3], William[2], John[1]).

Benjamin[4] Kendrick, son of James[3] and Susannah (Roberson) Kendrick, was born in Orange Co., N.C. about 1768-70, as he was appointed Lieutenant of Militia in Washington Co., Ga. in 1792 (showing that he was of age), his first child was born in 1792 (indicating his marriage as 1790-91), and his next younger brother, Martin Kendrick, was born in 1772. On Feb. 14, 1792, Benjamin Kendrick was appointed Second Lieutenant of the 12th Company of Washington Co., Ga. Militia. His first wife was Ruth Harvey (b. 1773-4), the second daughter of Rev. John and Margaret Harvey (see Harvey family). They had four children, Harvey, b. 1792, Burwell, b. 1793, Susan b. 1797, and Isaac b. 1799. Rev. John Harvey in his will in 1822 left a negro to Isaac Kendrick, son of his daughter Ruth, decd.; his

son, James Harvey, in his will in 1808, left bequests to his
niece and nephew, Susan and Burwell Kendrick; on March 2,
1812 in Jones Co., Ga. Isaac Harvey (son of Rev. John) was
appointed guardian of Susan Kendrick, orphan of Benjamin,
decd.; and in 1815 in Putnam Co. Harvey Kendrick was appointed
guardian of Isaac Kendrick, minor son of Benjamin Kendrick,
decd. Ruth (Harvey) Kendrick died about 1799-1800, and Benjamin Kendrick married (2) Tabitha --------. He died about
1804 in Washington or Hancock Co., Ga., and on March 16,
1805 Tabitha Kendrick in Hancock Co. was appointed guardian
to her two daughters, Sally and Mary Kendrick, orphans of
Benjamin Kendrick, decd. Tabitha Kendrick and the Orphans
of Benjamin Kendrick are shown in Washington Co., Ga., in
1805 in the list of eligibles for the Land Lottery of 1806; and
the actual lottery of 1806 shows them in Hancock Co. Of the
two daughters by the second marriage, Sally Kendrick is probably identical with a Sally Kendrick who married Walker Chatham in Putnam Co., Ga. in 1818; and Mary Kendrick with a Mary
Kendrick who married John Foreman in Putnam Co. Jan. 13,
1822. The following is known of the four children of Benjamin
Kendrick by his first marriage to Ruth Harvey.

I.   Harvey[5] Kendrick was born April 14, 1792 in Washington
      Co., Ga., died April 12, 1849 in Matagorda Co., Tex.,
      and married July 5, 1815 in Hancock Co., Ga. Maria G.
      Hall (b. 1798, d. Oct. 3, 1850 in Matagorda Co., Tex.).
      Harvey Kendrick first appears in the records Dec. 22,
      1808, when at the age of 16, he witnessed a deed in Mor-
      gan Co. to his uncle, William[4] Kendrick, then residing
      in Washington Co., Ga. He was appointed Lieutenant of
      Militia in Putnam Co., Ga. May 21, 1813 and Captain
      Feb. 18, 1817. He and his brother, Burwell Kendrick,
      bought land in Putnam Co. in 1816 and were assessed for
      taxes there in 1817; Harvey's family is shown there in
      the Census of 1820; he drew land in the Lottery of 1821;
      and appears in deeds there in 1823 and 1824. He owned
      land in Monroe Co., Ga., which he deeded away in 1826;
      was living in Houston Co., Ga. in the Census of 1830;
      along with his brother Burwell and his sister, Susan Har-
      rison; and drew land as a resident of Bibb Co. in the
      Cherokee Gold Lottery of 1832. About 1835 Harvey Ken-
      drick moved to Texas, was granted land there Jan. 6,
      1938 in Eastland Co., and his son, Benjamin H. Kendrick,
      was granted land there in Gillespie Co. somewhat later.
      He was a merchant of Matagorda, Tex., and a member of
      the firm of Alford & Kendrick, which supplied the Missis-
      sippi Company of Volunteers in 1836 and the ships, "Lib-
      erty" and "Durange", in Matagorda Bay in 1838. He was
      Senator in the 3rd, 4th, 5th and 8th Congresses of the Re-
      public of Texas and described as "a most worthy and es-
      timable man among the pioneers of the country" at a gath-
      ering at Austin in Oct., 1839 to welcome President Mira-
      beau B. Lamar. The Matagorda Co. Census of 1850 shows
      Harvey Kendrick's family as follows: B. H. Kendrick,

b. 1821, Maria Kendrick b. 1798, Burwell Kendrick b. 1793, Susan R. Collingsworth, b. 1823 (all b. in Georgia), George Collingsworth b. 1842, S. H. Collingsworth b. 1844 (both b. in Texas), and Alford H. Clopton, b. 1828 in Georgia, student of medicine. The son B. H. Kendrick, b. 1821, was named Benjamin. The daughter, Susan Rebecca Kendrick, b. 1823, married Capt. George Morse Collingsworth, Collector of the Port of Matagorda, on June 5, 1837. G. M. Collingsworth was living in Matagorda Co. as late as 1854, and was a surveyor. Alford Clopton, b. 1828, in Harvey Kendrick's family in 1850, was the son of Alford and Sarah (Kendrick) Clopton, the latter being a daughter of Martin[4] Kendrick.

II. Burwell[5] Kendrick, son of Benjamin[4] and Ruth (Harvey) Kendrick, was born in Washington Co., Ga. in 1793 (Census), died on or about the last day of Sept., 1853 in Matagorda Co., Tex., and married Lucy --------, from whom he was separated in 1829. He apparently had no children. Burwell Kendrick made tax-returns in Putnam Co., Ga. in 1813, bought land in Jones Co., Ga., in 1818, was appointed First Lieutenant of Militia in Jones Co. March 9, 1819, and was in the same county in the Census of 1820. He was back in Putnam in the Lottery of 1821 and was apparently living there in 1829, when he petitioned the Legislature for a divorce from his wife Lucy. In the Census of 1830 he was living in Houston Co., Ga. along with his brother Harvey and sister Susan Harrison. Burwell Kendrick arrived in Texas in April, 1835 and was granted land there in Matagorda Co. in Jan., 1838. His will, dated Dec. 29, 1852 and probated at the November Term, 1853 in Matagorda Co., states that he had given the lower quarter of his land to Alice Dudley Denison, daughter of James Denison; gives one quarter to his nephew, Benjamin H. Kendrick; the next quarter to his niece, Susan R. Collingsworth; and the last quarter to Burwell Kendrick Harrison (another nephew); Susan R. and George M. Collingsworth residuary legatees; Benjamin H. Kendrick executor (Will Book, p. 49). John W. McCamly, one of the witnesses, testified that Burwell Kendrick died on or about the last day of December, 1853 (Minute Book C, pp. 187-8).

III. Susan[5] Kendrick, daughter of Benjamin[4] and Ruth (Harvey) Kendrick, was born Dec. 5, 1797 in Washington Co., Ga., died Jan. 26, 1872 in Macon, Ga., and married Feb. 9, 1815 at Eatonton, Ga. William Harrison (b. 1788, d. June 1, 1870 at Macon, Ga.). William Harrison purchased land in 1814 in Jones Co., Ga., and he and his family were living in that county in the Census of 1820. About 1822 they moved to Houston Co., Ga., and are shown there in the Census of 1830. They were living in Bibb Co., Ga., in 1837 when their son, Burwell Kendrick Harrison, went to Randolph-Macon College with his cousin, David Clopton (son of Sarah Kendrick and grandson of Martin[4] Kendrick). In 1841 William Harrison moved to Florida, and lived at

Port St. Jo, Appalachicola, and on a farm in Franklin Co., until 1869, when he and his wife went to live with their daughter, Mrs. Flanders, in Macon, where they died and were buried.

The children of Susan[5] Kendrick and William Harrison' were:

1. Robert[6] G. Harrison, b. Dec. 10, 1815, d. Aug. 8, 1835.
2. Burwell[6] Kendrick Harrison, b. Jan. 2, 1818, d. Jan. 6, 1860, m. Oct. 1840 Eliza Woodson Robertson. They were grandparents of Mr. John M. Harrison of Atlanta, Ga., who contributed a great deal of time and research to the Kendrick genealogy, and is now dead. The children of Burwell K. Harrison, according to a record in Lampasas Co., Tex. in 1877, in which they deeded away the land left their father by his uncle, Burwell Kendrick, were: W. H. Harrison, Archer B. Harrison, John T. Harrison, Robert B. Harrison, James L. Harrison, Eva Harrison, and Mary Harrison, all residing at the time in Stewart Co., Ga.
3. Benjamin[6] Kendrick Harrison, b. Jan. 26, 1820, d. June 9, 1863, killed in Civil War at Morganfield, Ky.
4. Mary[6] Bryan Harrison, b. Dec. 3, 1821, d. July 4, 1889, m. 1840 James J. Flanders of Macon, Ga.
5. Sarah[6] Maria Harrison, b. Aug. 6, 1824, d. March 6, 1850, m. (1) Alexander Patton and (2) John Bull Kendrick, son of her great-uncle, Jones[4] Kendrick.
6. Reuben[6] Luckey Harrison, b. Nov. 22, 1830, d. July 20, 1877, m. July 23, 1856 Martha Taliaferro Hunter.
7. Francis[6] Embro Harrison, b. Jan. 20, 1834, d. June 6, 1911, m. Jan. 20, 1867 Elizabeth W. Hunter.
8. William[6] C. Harrison b. Jan. 26, 1837, d. Dec. 18, 1845.

IV. Isaac[5] Kendrick, son of Benjamin[4] and Ruth (Harvey) Kendrick, was born Feb. 9, 1799 in Washington Co., Ga., d. Sept. 12, 1842 in San Augustine Co., Tex., and married May 2, 1820 in Jones Co., Ga., Phoebe Tucker Moreland (b. 1803, d. Aug., 1863). Isaac Kendrick was living in Putnam Co. in the Lottery of 1820 and bought land there in 1822, which he sold in 1825. He bought land in Monroe and Jones Co. in 1826, was in Jones Co. in the Census of 1830, and in 1834 sold his land there to Alford Clopton (who m. Sarah Kendrick, daughter of Martin[4] Kendrick). He petitioned for land in Texas May 28, 1835, stating that he had a wife and 6 children at the time, and land was granted him in Cherokee Co. June 3, 1835. Isaac Kendrick died, however, in San Augustine Co., Tex., though his family moved to Cherokee Co. shortly after his death. His eldest son, John Harvey Kendrick, received a grant of land in Wood Co., Tex. March 29, 1847. Isaac and Phoebe (Moreland) Kendrick's children were:

1. John[6] Harvey Kendrick, b. Jan. 30, 1821, died Jan. 20, 1860, m. (1) Feb. 2, 1841 Hetty H. Smith; m. (2)

July 20, 1856 Anna Maye. By his second wife, John Harvey Kendrick was the father of U. S. Senator John B. Kendrick of Wyoming, who years ago sent in this record of his grandfather's family from the Family Bible.

2. Martha Ann Kendrick, b. Aug. 31, 1822, d. March 1, 1854, m. (1) Aug. 15, 1839 B. H. Hawkins; m. (2) Jan. 2, 1844 Dr. William Sharp.

3. Benjamin Kendrick, b. Aug. 13, 1826, d. June 5, 1848.

4. Sarah Jane Kendrick, b. Oct. 26, 1828, d. 1855; m. Jan. 7, 1847 James S. Bloomfield.

5. Francis Moreland Kendrick, b. Sept. 5, 1831, d. Jan. 26, 1862, m. Oct. 9, 1851 Araminta Smith (in John Harvey Kendrick's family in 1850, aged 16, and probably a sister of John Harvey's first wife).

6. Isaac Tucker Kendrick, b. Oct. 17, 1833, d. May 3, 1920, m. Emma Meeks.

7. Susan Rebecca Kendrick, b. Jan. 11, 1839, d. June 11, 1874, m. Dec. 25, 1856 Dr. James Marion Brittain.

8. Amanda[6] Ruth Kendrick, b. March 23, 1841, d. Sept. 11, 1842.

Martin[4] Kendrick (James[3], William[2], John[1])

Martin[4] Kendrick, son of James and Susannah (Roberson) Kendrick, was born in Chatham Co., N.C. in 1772 and died in Putnam Co., Ga. in 1812 (dates from his tombstone). He married about 1792-3 in Washington Co., Ga. Jane Whitehead of Burke and Jefferson Co's., Ga. Reason and Thomas Whitehead were granted land in St. George's Parish, Ga. 1761-74; C. Whitehead was granted land there 1784-90; and Thomas and John Whitehead were granted land in Burke Co., Ga. 1786-90 (Smith "Story of Ga. and Ga. People", p. 607). Reason Whitehead died in Jefferson Co., Ga. in 1781. His will, dated Aug. 28, 1780 and probated Feb. 26, 1781, mentions wife Jane; eldest son John and second son Reason; eldest daughter Elizabeth, second daughter Sarah, third daughter Catherine, fourth daughter Jane, and fifth daughter Mary; and makes Jacob Whitehead and Hugh Irwin executors (Jefferson Co. W.B. "A", p. 1). Hugh Irwin, the executor, may have been married to one of the daughters, probably the eldest daughter Elizabeth, for the will of Sally Irwin, dated July 27, 1800 and probated in Putnam Co., Ga. Oct. 4, 1808, mentions her uncle, John Whitehead, Esq.; half-brother and sister, Jared and Rebecca Irwin; nephew David Fluker son of Robert Fluker; aunts Jane Kendrick and Mary Fluker; uncle Martin Kendrick; cousin Jones Kendrick; uncle Baldy Fluker; aunts Jane Kendrick and Patsy Whitehead (Putnam W. B. "A", p. 3). The will shows that Sally Irwin's father had married a second time; that her uncle John Whitehead's wife was named Martha (Patsy); that Jane Whitehead, 4th daughter of Reason Whitehead, had married Martin Kendrick (though grandchildren of Martin and Jane had stated this to me long before these wills were discovered); that Mary Whitehead,

he 5th daughter, had married Baldwin Fluker (b. Sept. 18, 1772),
on of David and Jemima Fluker; and that probably a sister of Sally
rwin had married Robert Fluker, brother of Baldwin, who later
narried Susan, daughter of William[4] Kendrick (see section on
Villiam[4] Kendrick and his daughter Susan, wife of Robert Flu-
ter).

Martin[4] Kendrick was living in Washington Co., Ga. in the
District of his brother, Capt. Jones Kendrick, in the list of
eligibles, 1805, and in the Lottery of 1806. He must have moved
about 1806 or 1807 to Putnam Co., Ga. He died there in 1812,
his widow, Jane Kendrick, being appointed administrator Jan.
1, 1813. Alford Clopton, their son-in-law, became the admin-
strator a little later, giving bond for $50,000 for an estate show-
ng 28 slaves and land in Putnam, Wilkinson and Laurens Cos.,
is indicated by the tax digests. Returns in 1822 show payments
o Jones Kendrick, John Kendrick, John as agent for Jane Kendrick and as guardian for Eliza Kendrick (to whom he was appointed guardian Jan. 10, 1820). Later returns show the heirs as
Jones Kendrick, Sarah Clopton, John M. Kendrick, and Eliza C.
Kendrick; and much later, a son-in-law, William Redd. Jane
Whitehead) Kendrick died in Putnam Co. in 1830, leaving a will
vhich mentions as heirs Jones Kendrick, Sarah Clopton, John M.
Kendrick and Eliza C. Redd; and making John Kendrick and the
son-in-law William A. Redd executors. In the settlement, the
case was transferred to Troup Co., Ga. Sept. 6, 1830.

Sarah[5] Kendrick, daughter of Martin[4] and Jane (Whitehead)
Kendrick, was born in Washington Co., Ga. in 1794 (Census),
married June 25, 1812 in Putnam Co., Ga. Dr. Alford Clopton
b. 1787 in Virginia), and both died in Alabama after 1850. The
Cloptons lived for some time in Jones Co., Ga., but had moved
to Macon Co., Ala. by 1850, where the Census of that year and
other records show their children as:

I. Ann[6] Green Clopton m. Joseph Barnett Wiley of Jones Co.,
    Ga. They had at least two children:
    1. Eugenia Clopton Wiley who m. James Henderson Blount
       of Clinton, Jones Co., Ga., for many years U.S. Con-
       gressman from Georgia; they were parents of Mrs.
       Walter D. Lamar of Macon, Ga. (Eugenia Dorothy Blount),
       distinguished publicist and clubwoman; and
    2. Col. Charles Moses Wiley of Macon (b. July 30, 1841),
       who m. Juliette Reid.
II. Eliza[6] Clopton, b. 1817, who m. a Fort, was probably a
    daughter, as she is shown in the family of Alford Clopton
    in Macon Co., Ala. in 1850 with children: Mary Fort b.
    1834, Robert b. 1839, Louisiana b. 1842, George b. 1845,
    and Sarah b. 1847.
III. Martin[6] Clopton, b. 1819, living with parents in 1850.
IV. David[6] Clopton, b. 1820, m. Martha E. Ligon (b. 1830),
    living in Macon Co., Ala. in 1850 with one child, Sarah W.
    Clopton, b. 1848. David Clopton went to Randolph-Macon
    College in 1837 with his cousin, Burwell Kendrick Harrison
    (son of Susan Kendrick Harrison and grandson of Benjamin[4]
    Kendrick), graduated at the head of his class, was a lawyer,
    U.S. Congressman from Alabama, member of the Confed-

erate Congress, and Judge of the Supreme Court of Alabama.

V. Nathaniel[6] Clopton, b. 1825, was probably a son, as he was living in Macon Co., Ala. in 1850 with a wife Letitia, b. 1827, and a son Sydney b. 1848.

VI. Alford[6] Clopton, b. 1828, living in 1850 in Matagorda Co., Tex. in the family of his cousin, Harvey Kendrick, son of Benjamin[4] Kendrick.

VII. James Osgood Andrews Clopton, b. Nov. 11, 1830, d. 1863, A. B. (University of Ala.), lawyer, enrolled at U. of Ala. 1850 from Notasulga, Macon Co., Ala., as son of Dr. Alford and ------ (Kendrick) Clopton.

John[5] Martin Kendrick (called "Uncle Martin" by his nieces and nephews, but John or John M. in documents), lived with his sister Eliza Redd, and died unmarried. He is probably identical with a John Kendrick who was Colonel of Militia in Troup Co., Ga. from 1828 to 1835, served in the Creek Indian War of 1836, and whose tombstone at La Grange shows his birth in 1795 and his death in 1837.

Ephraim Jones[5] Kendrick (always called "Jones"), son of Martin[4] and Jane (Whitehead) Kendrick, was born in Washington Co., Ga. in 1797 (Census), died in 1854 in Houston Co., Ga., and married Charity Clark of Putnam Co., Ga., daughter of William and Mary (Harvey) Clark. Their family and descendants are given in the article on the Clark family in this volume.

Eliza[5] C. Kendrick, daughter of Martin[4] and Jane (Whitehead) Kendrick, was born in Putnam Co., Ga. in 1808 (Census), died in Columbus, Ga. after 1850, and married about 1829-30 William A. Redd (b. 1803 in Greene Co., Ga.). The Redds moved before 1830 to Troup Co., Ga. with Eliza's brother, John Martin Kendrick, but moved to Muscogee Co., Ga. before 1840, and died after 1850 at Columbus. Their children, from the 1850 and 1860 Census, were:

1. Charles[6] Redd, b. 1831 in Troup Co., married and left two children, Mrs. Felder Pou of Columbus, Ga. and William A. Redd of Flora, Ala.

2. William[6] Redd, b. 1836 in Troup Co., Ga. His family is probably identical with the following somewhat incorrect account from the 1860 Census of Muscogee Co.: William Redd Sr., aged 31, Eliza P. Redd aged 29, Annie Redd b. 1857, and Henry Redd b. 1860 (aged 3 mos).

3. John[6] Redd b. 1840 in Muscogee Co., Ga.

4. Frank[6] Redd, b. 1845 in Muscogee Co., Ga.; he had a daughter, Willie Franc Redd who m. Joseph R. Estes of Birmingham, Ala.

Jones[4] Kendrick, (James[3], William[2], John[1])

Jones[4] Kendrick, youngest son of James and Susannah (Roberson) Kendrick, was born Dec. 16, 1778 in Chatham Co., N.C. and died Feb. 21, 1845 in Wilkes Co., Ga. He married (1) about 1798 (their first child was b. 1799-1800) Susan Vail Bull (b. 1781 in Maryland, d. Sept. 30, 1829 in Wilkes Co., Ga.); and after her death, he married (2) Aug. 26, 1830 in Wilkes Co., Ga. Mrs.

Nancy M. Powell, nee Nancy Marshall Williams (b. Nov. 12, 1791, d. Dec. 26, 1855), who had previously been married to John R. Anderson and later to Nelson Powell, both of Wilkes Co. The dates above are taken from the tombstones of Jones Kendrick and his two wives in the family burying ground on his plantation in Wilkes Co. The statement that the first wife, Susan Vail Bull, was born in Maryland comes from two of her sons, William Bull and Jones Jackson Kendrick, the information being given in the Census of 1880. By his first wife Jones Kendrick had 10 children, b. 1799-1818, Jacob Bull, James Roberson, Martin, William Bull. Aaron Tomlinson, Tillman Franklin, John Bull, Easter Caroline, Jones Jackson, and Susannah R. Kendrick. By his second marriage he had only one son, Rev. Green Marshall Kendrick, b. 1834, a Methodist minister. The first wife, Susan Vail Bull, was almost certainly the daughter of Jacob Bull and wife Rennes of Warren and Columbia Cos., Ga. There were Bulls in Harford Co., Md. from 1734 to 1778, and in the latter year William Bull, Jacob Bull (son of Jacob), and Jacob Bull (son of John) took the oath of allegiance in that county to the American cause. It is uncertain which of the Jacob Bulls in Harford Co. in 1778 was the one who moved to Georgia, but he was probably one of them. Jacob Bull, the father of Susan Kendrick, was living in Columbia Co., Ga. from 1794 to 1798. Two deeds in 1794 show that his wife was named Rennes Bull; in two deeds in 1796 he calls himself Jacob Bull, Sr., indicating that he had a son, Jacob, Jr.; and in three deeds from 1796 to 1798 he made deeds of gift of slaves and property to his son, Jesse Bull. The son Jesse Bull withdrew from the bench of Columbia Co. July 1, 1811, and died here in 1817, his wife Martha being appointed his administratrix in November of that year, and his heirs being shown in 1820 as Martha Bull, the widow; minor children, Orville R., Amanda M., Jesse and Mary; and two married daughters, Elizabeth wife of Edward Short and Matilda wife of James Reese (they married Mar. 12, 1817). Edward Short was administrator of the estate of William Bull, decd., Jan. 10, 1820, and an Edward Bull married Sarah Warden in Columbia Co., Ga. June 8, 1817, but it is uncertain whether William and Edward were sons or grandsons of Jacob Bull, Sr. The latter seems to have moved about 1800 to Warren Co., Ga., where was the recipient of 6 deeds from 1800 to 1812. His last appearance in the records is on Dec. 24, 1816, when he deeded away all his Warren Co. land to Dunwoody Harrison of Columbia Co. Warren Co. records are rather incomplete, particularly as to wills, and there appears to be no record of the death, will, or administration of Jacob Bull, Sr. That he was the father of Susan (Bull) Kendrick is indicated by the fact that she named her eldest son Jacob Bull Kendrick and two other sons had the middle name, Bull; as well as by the fact that her husband, Jones[4] Kendrick, in a note in 1816 concerning his administration of the estate of James Willis, Sr. in Wilkes Co., says: "In the spring of 1815, while I was in the service of the U.S. (i.e., in the War of 1812), Mr. Jacob Bull received for me from sundry persons the sum of $331.75".

The ancestry of Nancy Marshall Williams, second wife of

Jones[4] Kendrick, has been traced in Boddie's "Southside Virginia Families" (Vol. II, pp. 382-388). She was the daughter of Drury and Tabitha (Marshall) Williams, granddaughter of William and Mary Williams of Goochland Co., Va. and of William and Phoebe (Farmer) Marshall of Cumberland Co., Va.; great-granddaughter of Alexander and Elizabeth (Worsham) Marshall of Henrico Co., Va.; great-great-granddaughter of John and Mary (Wynne) Worsham of Henrico; and great-great-great-granddaughter of Major Joshua Wynne and his wife Mary Jones, who was daughter of Major Peter Jones and his wife Margaret, daughter of Maj.-Gen. Abraham Wood. The only error in the article seems to be the statement that Nancy Marshall Williams, daughter of Drury and Tabitha Williams, was born in April, 1774, while her tombstone and other records give it as Nov. 12, 1791. Nancy (Williams) Kendrick's youngest son was born in 1834, which makes 1774 an impossible date for her birth. It is possible that Drury and Tabitha Williams had two daughters named Nancy, of whom the first, born in 1774, died young.

Jones[4] Kendrick first appears in the records July 17, 1799, when he was commissioned Lieutenant in the Washington Co. regular militia, and he was commissioned Captain of the same May 9, 1801. He was residing in his own district of Washington Co. in the eligibility list of 1805 for the land lottery, and had two lucky draw in the Lottery of 1806, one in Baldwin and one in Wilkinson Co. He was still living in Washington Co., Ga. July 1, 1808, when he sold land in Morgan Co., but was deeded land in Wilkes Co. on Feb. 20, 1810 and Mar. 3, 1810 (Wilkes D.B. "YY", pp. 301 and 502), and moved there in that year. He was commissioned Captain of Militia in Wilkes Co. Mar. 9, 1813 and again on Aug. 17, 1814. He saw active service as a Captain in the Georgia Militia from Nov. 21, 1814 to May 20, 1815 in the War of 1812 (Adjutant-General's Office); was away from home in the spring of 1815 "in the service of the U.S.", according to his own statement quoted previously in connection with his first wife's father, Jacob Bull; and was in the Fourth Regiment under Gen. Booth in the army of Gen. Andrew Jackson, according to his granddaughter, Eliza Jane (Kendrick) Walker, in "Other Days", a book of reminiscences about the family and Jones Kendrick's prosperous plantation in Wilkes Co. before the Civil War. (This book, in manuscript, with copies of original letters, documents, etc. is in the Alabama Department of Archives and History, and has been published in the "Alabama Historical Quarterly". It states: "His (i.e., Jones Kendrick's) plantation was like a village, so numerous were the cabins for his servants and the various houses required in the management of a large country place of that period".) There is a bulky file in the National Archives at Washington (Bounty Land Files, Warrant No. 55, 347, Jones Kendrick, War of 1812, Captain under Col. Booth, Can. No. 1179, Bundle 95), which shows the application of Nancy M. Kendrick, Jones Kendrick's widow, for bounty land for his services in 1855, a renewed application of her son, Greene Marshall Kendrick, in 1869, and includes statements of Jones Kendrick's services as above, date of his second marriage, his death and the death of his widow, births of his 8 living children taken from the Family Bible, a certificate from the Third Auditor's Office in Washington stating that Jones Kendrick served as a Captain in a Company of Georgia Militia from Nov. 21, 1814 to May 20, 1815, and a letter from Senator Robert Toombs, stating his close association with Jones Kendrick as a neighbor.

Jones Kendrick was a wealthy and prominent man in Wilkes Co. He represented the county in the Georgia Legislature in 1820 and 1821, and in the State Convention in 1833. In 1825 he owned 35 slaves and 1575 acres of land in various counties, an estate which was increased later. His will, dated Jan. 15, 1845 and probated Mar. 3, 1845, is on file in the Ordinary's Office of Wilkes Co., and recors of his estate are in the Georgia Department of Archives and History at Atlanta. He died Feb. 21, 1845 after a long and rather terrible illness following the amputation of a leg (without anaesthesia), injured when a limb being cut from a tree fell across it as he sat on his horse. Five doctors cut off the leg with Jones Kendrick strapped down and the pain so awful that some of the doctors even then had to hold him (from Dr. Ripley Stevens, Washington, Ga.).

Jacob[5] Bull Kendrick, son of Jones[4] and Susan (Bull) Kendrick, was born in Washington Co., Ga. about 1799. He married (1) about 1827 Frances Harris of Wilkes Co., Ga., and (2) Jan. 25, 1841 Eleanor Semmes in Wilkes Co. There is no record of Jacob Bull Kendrick's death. His children by the first marriage were:

I. James[6] Kendrick, b. 1829, shown in the Taliaferro Co., Ga. Census of 1850 with wife Mary (b. 1828 in Va.), and children, Gilchrist aged 2 and William aged 8 months. This family moved to Virginia later, or perhaps to Tennessee.

II. Robert[6] Tomlinson Kendrick, b. Nov. 19, 1830, d. Jan. 16, 1916 at Sharon Ga., m. Frances Ellen Summers (b. 1828); member of Ga. House of Representatives from Taliaferro Co.: issue :
1. Frances Ellen Kendrick b. 1850 m. William Arnett;
2. Sarah C. Kendrick b. 1852 m. Ivey;
3. Mary Crooks Kendrick b. 1854 m. George Lewis Moore;
4. William R. Kendrick b. 1856;
5. James Albert Kendrick b. 1858 m. Effie Cleo Moore;
6. Susan Beulah Kendrick b. 1858 m. (1) William Graham, (2) Brad Thompson;
7. Edward L. Kendrick m. Sarah Keating; and
8. Thomas Felix Kendrick b. 1866, m. (1) Lillis Beall Stone, m. (2) Caroline Garrett of Wilkes Co.; his children were:
(1) Della Kendrick who m. Martin Leary
(2) Annabelle Kendrick m. George Anderson Stirling.

III. James[6] Albert Kendrick, moved to Virginia.

IV. Mary[6] Ann Kendrick, b. Dec. 16, 1833, d. after 1904, m. (1) James Beder Proctor of Wilkes Co. and had one child, Allie Proctor, who m. Jay Brown of Morristown, Tenn. and had a daughter, Carrie Brown, who m. Ben R. Stewart;

Mary Ann m. (2) in 1864 Rev. Henry Waugh, and had one son, Henry Waugh, newspaper man in New York.

V. Susan[6] Kendrick, m. (1) Mr. Moore; lived for some time with her uncle, Aaron[5] Tomlinson Kendrick; m. (2) Peter W. Reddick and lived in Lumpkin Co., Ga. and at Cuthbert, Ga.

James [5] Roberson Kendrick, son of Jones[4] and Susan (Bull) Kendrick, was born in 1801 (Census) in Washington Co., Ga. and died 1853 in Macon Co., Ala. He married June 13, 1830 in Columbia Co, Ga. Nancy Semple Coleman (b. 1810), daughter of Thompson and Elizabeth (McFarland) Coleman of Pittsylvania Co., Va. and Wilkes Co., Ga., and granddaughter of James Mc-Farland of Maryland. The James R. Kendricks lived on the Coleman land in Columbia Co., Ga. until about 1845, when they moved to Macon Co., Ala. Issue:

I. Sarah[6] Ann Thompson Kendrick, b. May 5, 1831, m. 1848 Richard Dobbs Spaight Bell of Columbus. Ga. "Other Days" mentions her visiting her father's cousin, Eliza Kendrick Redd of Columbus, Ga. (daughter of Martin[4] Kendrick).

II. Elizabeth[6] Susan Kendrick, b. April 20, 1833, d. Mar. 25, 1835.

III. James[6] Coleman Kendrick, b. Jan. 13, 1835, d. young.

IV. Eliza[6] Jane Kendrick, b. Oct. 20, 1836, d. 1923, m. (1) 1853 in Macon Co., Ala. James Cook Lewis (b. 1839, d. 1862). Col. Lewis died of fever while in the service of the Confederate Government. She m. (2) Capt. John Absalom Walker (b. May 9, 1827 in Putnam Co., Ga.), son of John Hedge and Elizabeth Hunter (Wooldridge) Walker, and had one child, Anne Kendrick Walker, newspaper woman and historian of Alabama and New York City, who published her mother's reminiscences, "Other Days".

V. John[6] West Kendrick, b. June 30, 1838, graduate of Talmadge College, m. Dec. 17, 1861 Sarah F. Longmaid (b. April 27, 1844), daughter of Edward Sevey and Ann Davis (Kendrick) Longmaid of Washington Co., Ga. and great-granddaughter of William [4] Kendrick. Their children were:
1. James E. Kendrick b. 1863;
2. Mittie A. Kendrick b. 1865 m. H. O. Bassett;
3. Buena Vista Kendrick b. 1867 m. Cameron I. Daw;
4. Willie Kendrick (daughter);
5. John L. Kendrick, d. unmarried;
6. Charles Kendrick; and
7. Daisy M. Kendrick m. T. E. Davis.

VI. Margaret[6] Matilda Kendrick, b. May 20, 1842, d. s. p.

VII. William[6] Jones Kendrick, b. April 6, 1844, d. young.

VIII. Buena Vista[6] Kendrick, b. June 5, 1847, d. aged 12.

Martin[5] Kendrick, son of Jones and Susan (Bull) Kendrick, was born about 1803-4, and married in Putnam Co., Ga. Oct. 2, 1831 Elizabeth Jenkins. Mrs. George A. Dure of Macon, his niece, wrote in 1922: "I had an uncle named Martin Kendrick who married a lady from Putnam Co. He was in the Mexican War. I always understood that he had one child. Don't remember if it was a son or a daughter." Martin Kendrick was living in Wilkes

Co., Ga. 1832-5 and drew land in the Cherokee Gold Lottery. He was either in ill health or away in the Mexican War in 1845, when his father wrote his will, which leaves "to my son John B. Kendrick certain negroes out of which John B. is to pay $200 yearly to my son Martin Kendrick for a period of three years, if my son Martin lives so long."

William[5] Bull Kendrick, son of Jones[4] and Susan (Bull) Kendrick, was born Jan. 12, 1806 in Washington Co., Ga., and died April 18, 1888 near Sharon, Ga. He married Dec. 22, 1830 Ann Prather Shaw (b. Dec. 23, 1813, d. Aug. 26, 1891), daughter of Charles and Margaret (Prather) Shaw of Columbia Co., Ga. William B. Kendrick received a deed of gift of land in Columbia Co. in 1831 from his father, and owned 7000 acres there in 1850. He moved some time later to Taliaferro Co., Ga., owned a great deal of property there, was an ardent supporter of the Confederacy, and is said to have equipped a company in the Confederate Army.
Issue:

I. Charles[6] Shaw Kendrick, b. Oct. 28, 1831, d. June 14, 1896, M. D. University School of Medicine, Augusta, Ga.; never married; lived at Sharon.

II. William[6] Gabriel Kendrick, b. Nov. 26, 1833, d. after 1899; m. Miss Boyd. Issue:
1. Morgan Kendrick, a daughter, m. Robert Jackson and had one child, Gabriella Jackson, who m. a Crawley and had Hoyt Crawley, Cecile Crawley (m. Walter Harper), and Claudine Crawley (m. Pat Mell Saggus);
2. Hubert Kendrick.

III. William[6] Bull Kendrick, b. April 9, 1836, d. June 19, 1905, at Sharon Ga., m. Sept. 30, 1858 America Catherine Johnson (b. Aug. 28, 1840, d. Mar. 4, 1906), dr. of W. F. Johnson of Thomson, Ga. Issue:
1. Beulah[7] Catherine Kendrick m. Mr. Davis, went west, had two children, Charlie Davis and Nita Davis (m. Cecil Moore, a first cousin) of Dallas, Tex.
2. Leonora America Kendrick, b. April 12, 1867, d. April. 20, 1949 at Sharon, Ga., m. Feb. 20, 1895 Linton Stephens Jackson, no children.
3. Eola Lee Kendrick, b. May 10, 1869, m. June 8, 1892 George T. Moore of Sharon, Ga.; issue:
 (1) Richard[8] Cecil Moore, b. May 2, 1893, d. about 1940, m. Nov. 16, 1917 Nita Davis, his first cousin, res. Dallas, Tex.
 (2) Irad Roland Moore b. Aug. 2, 1894, of Atlanta, Ga.;
 (3) Beulah[8] Moore, b. Jan. 26, 1896, m. Oct. 30, 1920 Wyman Frederick Dozier, no children;
 (4) Grace[8] Moore b. Aug. 9, 1898, d. Aged 10 mos.;
 (5) Mary[8] Lee Moore, b. Dec. 27, 1899, d. Aug. 9, 1903; and
 (6) Frederick Moore, b. Sept. 30, 1901, d. aged 26 mos.

IV. Matilda[6] Jane Kendrick, b. Jan. 23, 1838, d. Nov. 27, 1852.

V. Aaron[6] David Kendrick, b. Sept. 11, 1839, d. Nov. 17, 1922 at Sharon, Ga., m. July 4, 1865 Katherine Amanda

McCord (b. Jan. 11, 1839, d. Dec. 12, 1914), dr. of John and Julia (Harden) McCord; issue:

1. William[7] Lovelace Kendrick, b. July 4, 1866, m. Feb. 11, 1899 Mary O'Keefe, dr. of Daniel and Ann (Sullivan) O'Keefe of Banteer, Co. Cork, Ireland; no children.

2. John[7] McCord Kendrick, b. May 20, 1868, d. April 25, 1950 at Sharon, Ga., m. Feb. 28, 1893 Martha Belle Johnson (b. Jan. 11, 1870, d. Oct. 2, 1951), dr. of James and Martha (Granada) Johnson of Thomson, Ga.; issue:

    (1) Harry[8] Carlton Kendrick, b. Dec. 23, 1893, of Atlanta, Ga.

VI. James[6] Ruffin Kendrick, b. July 24, 1841, killed at the Battle of Atlanta, near Decatur, July 22, 1864; color-bearer, First Ga. Regt., Hardee's Corps, under Gen. Hood.

VII. Susannah[6] Lovelace Kendrick, b. Mar. 13, 1843, d. Jan. 29, 1924, m. Nov. 24, 1859 Rev. Felix Persons Brown (b. Nov. 11, 1832, d. Oct. 3, 1909 at Sharon, Ga.), son of Dr. Washington and Cynthia (Walker) Brown of Lunenburg Co., Va. and Warren Co., Ga. Mr. Brown was a Methodist minister, North Georgia Conference. Issue:

1. Mary[7] Ann Brown, b. Sept. 8, 1860, d. April 14, 1944 in Atlanta, Ga., m. Jan. 24, 1893 Eugene Augustus Moore of Atlanta, and had one child, Lucille Brown Moore, b. Feb. 23, 1894, d. Oct. 19, 1945, a musician of note in Atlanta.

2. Lawrence[7] Ruffin Brown, b. June 28, 1862, d. Nov. 26, 1931 at Sharon, Ga., M.D. University School of Medicine, Augusta, Ga., m. Nov. 3, 1891 Mary Albina Davidson (b. Oct. 16, 1871), dr. of Dr. Arthur Chase and Ada (Mershon) Davidson of Sharon; issue:

    (1) Lloyd[8] Davidson Brown, b. July 28, 1892, d. Feb. 17, 1950, graduate U. of Ga. (1912), Captain First World War, Major-General Second World War, m. (1) Sept. 10, 1919 Benita Allen, dr. of Judge John Troup and Harriet (Hendrix) Allen of Milledgeville, Ga. and had Allen[9] Davidson Brown, b. Oct. 11, 1925, of Savannah, Ga.; m. (2) Katherine Green of Washington, Ga., no issue;

    (2) Gladys[8] Alline Brown, b. Oct. 11, 1893;

    (3) Lawrence Hartwell Brown, b. Dec. 14, 1895, d. Aug. 19, 1949, m. (1) Alice (Clapp) Vredenburgh of Selma, Ala., no issue, m. (2) Erma Carl, dr. of Alfred and Emma (Ruppert) Carl of Smith's Ferry, Mass. and had (a) Mary[9] Emma Brown, b. Nov. 10, 1944, and (b) Lawrence[9] Carl Brown, b. Aug. 5, 1946;

    (4) Christine[8] Davidson Brown, b. Sept. 21, 1897, of Sharon, Ga., who has contributed much to this

genealogy;

(5) Ruth[8] Lovelace Brown b. Jan. 13, 1899, m. Dec. 27, 1929 Thomas Markham Brinkley, son of William O. and Augusta (Hardaway) Brinkley of Warrenton, Ga., Col. U.S.A., one child, Ruth[9] Brown Brinkley, b. Sept. 11, 1937;

(6) Felix[8] Bartelle Brown, b. Oct. 18, 1900, M.D., m. Sept. 20, 1930 Edith Winston Pilcher, dr. of Dr. William Wyman and Katherine (Burkhalter) Pilcher of Warrenton, Ga., no children;

(7) Arthur Davidson Brown, b. Oct. 3, 1904, m. April 2, 1938 Louise Briscoe Brooks, dr. of Robert Faust and Gladys (Crawford) Brooks of Lexington, Ga., living at Sharon, Ga. with two children, (a) Mary[9] Louise Brown, b. Oct. 13, 1940, d. Mar. 8. 1942, and (b) Serena[9] Crawford Brown, b. Jan. 28, 1950;

(8) Walter Edward Brown, b. May 9, 1907, M.D., Savannah, Ga., m. April 27, 1935 Neva Malone Barber, dr. of Charles Guinn and Grace (O'Neal) Barber of Savannah, two children, (a) Sharon[9] Mershon Brown, b. June 17, 1937 and (b) Walter[9] Edward Brown b. Dec. 11, 1939;

(9) Kendrick[8] Mershon Brown, b. Dec. 9, 1910, d. July 29, 1936.

VIII. John[6] Roberson Kendrick, b. May 22, 1846, d. May 12, 1926 near Sharon, Ga., Company K, First Ga. Regt., C.S.A., wounded twice, member of Ga. Legislature, m. Mar. 8, 1871 Cynthia Elizabeth Brown (b. Nov. 3, 1846, d. Jan. 16, 1910), dr. of Thomas Marion and Mary (Hall) Brown of Warren Co., Ga.; issue:

1. John[7] Ruffin Kendrick, b. Mar. 8, 1872, of Sharon, Ga., m. (1) Octavia Stone, dr. of Welcome and Elizabeth (Meadows) Stone of Raytown, Ga., no issue; m. (2) Dec. 19, 1916 Mabel Claire Andrews, dr. of William Marcus and Miranda Clay (Hubert) Andrews of Hancock Co., Ga. and had Robert[8] Marcus Kendrick, b. July 25, 1920, d. in infancy.

2. Mary[7] Lovelace Kendrick, b. Nov. 16, 1873, m. Wesley Wright, son of John and Anna (Stone) Wright of Raytown, Ga.; lives in Atlanta and has two children, Elizabeth and Margaret Wright.

3. William[7] Marion Kendrick, b. Dec. 4, 1875, d. Dec. 20, 1950 at Sharon, Ga., m. Nov. 10, 1904 Rosalie Stone (b. Sept. 6, 1882), dr. of John and Anna (Lewis) Stone of Raytown, Ga. and had: (a) John[8] Marion Kendrick, b. Mar. 22, 1909, d. Feb. 6, 1951, and (b) Lewis[8] Brown Kendrick, b. June 28, 1913, of Sharon, Ga.

4. Annie[7] May Kendrick, b. Mar. 10, 1878, of Sharon, Ga., m. Oct. 28, 1902 Owen Gordon Stone and had Nellie Kendrick Stone, b. Nov. 7, 1905, m. Sept. 3, 1927 Burton Middlebrooks of Atlanta, Ga., one son,

Burton Stone Middlebrooks, b. Feb. 9, 1931.

5. Elizabeth[7] Brown Kendrick, b. June 8, 1887, of Atlanta, m. (1) Mr. Mayo and (2) Aug. 4, 1913 Arthur W. Cline, no children.

IX. Lovelace[6] Kendrick, b. June 1, 1848, d. Sept. 28, 1852.
X. Ann[6] Elizabeth Kendrick, b. July 17, 1850, d. April 6, 1900, m. Jan. 17, 1872 George Washington Hardaway Brown (b. Aug. 26, 1846, d. Jan. 24, 1908), son of Dr. Washington Hardaway and Dorcas (Thigpen) Brown; issue:

1. William[7] Charles Brown, b. Feb. 7, 1873, d. June 1, 1896.

2. Jesse[7] Roberson Brown, b. July 13, 1876, d. about 1939 in Sharon, Ga., m. (1) Jan. 4, 1900 Annie Moore (b. Oct., 1877, d. May 21, 1906) dr. of Lucius and Anne (Moore) Moore of Hillman. Ga. and had three children:

  (1) Lucia[8] Elizabeth Brown, b. Dec. 28, 1900 m. Charles Massey;

  (2) Nina[8] Louise Brown, b. July 6, 1903, m. Dr. Paul Sanders; and

  (3) Mary[8] Jesse Brown, b. Feb. 17, 1905, m. Dr. Laurie L. Dozier and lives at Tallahassee, Fla. with two children, Laurie L. and Richard Dozier;

Jesse R. Brown m. (2) Jan. 6, 1909 Alma Harris (b. 1884), dr. of Jack Harris of Warren Co., Ga. and had (4) George William Brown, b. Mar. 23, 1910, m. Jan. 6, 1932 Beulah Flynt, dr. of Lamar and Ethel Maude (Sturdevant) Flynt, and has three children, (a) Kathleen[9] Brown m. John Kinsey, (b) George[9] Harris Brown, and (c) Jesse[9] Lamar Brown.

3. Ella[7] Aurie Brown, b. Sept. 21, 1877, m. July 14, 1897 George Christopher Frederick Brown, son of Andrew Black and Catherine Maddox (Snow) Brown of Hogansville, Ga., living at Valdosta, Ga. with three children:

  (1) Evelyn[8] Kendrick Brown, b. Nov. 26, 1902, m. Leonard Hoge. no children;

  (2) Andrew[8] George Brown, b. May 16, 1907, M.D., m. June 29, 1932 Louise Lorraine Wilson, dr. of Solon Wilson of Bartow, Fla.; and (3) Katherine Elise Brown, b. Dec. 2, 1909, m. William Gaffney, no children.

4. Anne[7] Lovelace Brown, b. about 1880, m. Eli Litchfield, lives in Arkansas, two children, Martha and George Litchfield.

Aaron[5] Tomlinson Kendrick, son of Jones[4] and Susan (Bull) Kendrick, was born Jan. 23, 1808 in Washington Co., Ga., and died Aug. 13, 1892 at Leon, Ala. He married Sept. 18, 1830 in Columbia Co., Ga. Eleanor Lucinda Nesbitt (b. Sept. 4, 1815), dr. of Hugh Nesbitt of Augusta, Ga. and his second wife, Lucinda O'Keefe (who were married Feb. 7, 1810 in Richmond Co., Ga.). Aaron T. Kendrick lived for some time in Stewart

Co., Ga., then moved about 1852 to Alabama, first to Barbour
Co., then to Greenville, and finally to Leon, Ala. Five of his·
sons served in the Confederate Army and were wounded, according to a letter from A. T. Kendrick, Jr. to a niece: "Five of
us were in the Confederate Army and four of us were wounded.
I was wounded in the head before I was 17 years old - on April
5, 1865. Brother Joel was wounded July 28, 1864, the day
your uncle Rob was wounded, and your uncle Ruffin was killed
in Atlanta, Ga. Brother John was wounded in the head at the
7 days battle before Richmond and at the siege of Vicksburg
that lasted 48 days. Billie was wounded 13 times in 4 years
and one time left on the battlefield as dead." Issue of Aaron
Tomlinson and Eleanor Kendrick were:

I.   Joel[6] Cloud Kendrick, M.D., b. 1833 in Warren Co.,
     Ga., d. 1905 at Greenville, Ala., m. Ann Riviere,
     served Co. C, 37th Ala. Regt., C.S.A.; issue:
     1. William[7] Thomas Kendrick, M.D., of Montgomery,
        Ala., m. Marie Antoinette Dixon, dr. of Capt. George
        and Narcissa (Judkins) Dixon; issue:
        (1) Marie[8] Antoinette Kendrick, b. April 15, 1879,
            m. Joseph C. Duckworth of Greenville, Ala., and
            had two children, Kenneth Duckworth and William
            Dixon Duckworth;
        (2) Ann[8] Cloud Kendrick m. Thomas S. Sharp of
            Greenville, Ala., two children, Ann Kendrick
            Sharp and Thomas Kendrick Sharp;
        (3) William[8] Dixon Kendrick of Birmingham, Ala.,
            unmarried; and
        (4) Eugenia[8] Drue Kendrick m. Dr. W. E. Patton,
            one child, Barbara Lewis Patton.
     2. Joel[7] Beder Kendrick, died about 1895, m. Etta
        Byrnes and had one child, Etta Byrnes Kendrick who
        m. a Johnson and lives in New York.
     3. Wesley[7] Kendrick, d. young.
     4. Edward[7] Kendrick, d. about 1910, unmarried.
     5. John[7] Kendrick, M.D., m. Katharine Lane, one child,
        Katharine Lane Kendrick.
     6. James[7] Kendrick, M.D., m. Bertha Flowers and had
        two children, Mary Kendrick, and James Kendrick,
        Jr., M.D.
II. William[6] Bull Kendrick, b. 1838 in Warren Co., Ga.,
     lived at Raleigh, N.C., d. 1914 in Atlanta, Ga., m.
     Nannie Nesbitt, a cousin: three children: Nesbitt Ken-
     drick, d. young, Gerald Kendrick, and Hugh Kendrick.
III. John[6] A. Kendrick, b. 1841 in Warren Co., Ga., moved
     to Texas, m. Merced Anderson of California; killed in
     Mexico 1878, no children.
IV. Jones[6] Kendrick, b. 1842, d. young.
V.   Caroline[6] Kendrick, b. 1844, d. young.
VI. James[6] Evans Kendrick, M.D., b. Dec. 18, 1847 in War-
     ren Co., Ga., d. Feb. 18, 1920 at Luverne, Ala., m.
     Fannie Riley (b. May 2, 1848, d. Aug. 14, 1936); issue:
     1. Buena May[7] Kendrick, b. Sept. 6, 1873, d. Sept. 21,

1901, m. Dec. 24, 1891 Charles Russell Bricken, Judge, Court of Appeals, Montgomery, Ala.; issue:
  - (1) Beryl[8] Richardson Bricken, b. July 26, 1893, m. Feb. 25, 1930 Peterson Bryant Jarman (b. Oct. 31, 1892), Congressman from Ala. and Ambassador to Australia, no issue;
  - (2) Charles[8] Russell Bricken, Jr., b. Sept. 26, 1895, m. Dec. 22, 1944 Mary Wilson Wilcox (b. Dec. 7, 1900);
  - (3) Isabel Bricken, b. Oct. 2, 1897, m. James H. Dunklin, Jr. (b. April 28, 1897) and had: (a) Isabel[9] Dunklin, b. April 19, 1923 and (b) James[9] H. Dunklin, III, Dec. 28, 1925.

2. Fletcher[7] Comer Kendrick, b. Dec. 3, 1875, d. Sept. 14, 1905, unmarried.

3. Lena[7] Kendrick m. Richard Hayne Parks, lives Troy, Ala., issue:
  - (1) Evelyn[8] Parks, b. Jan. 3, 1892, d. June 9, 1940, m. Lewis Dyrenforth, no issue;
  - (2) James[8] Kendrick Parks, b. Jan. 28, 1894, d. 1928, unmarried; and
  - (3) Julia[8] Hayne Parks, b. Feb. 20, 1896, m. O. W. Landergren, res. Pittsfield, Mass.

4. Bishop[7] Marvin Kendrick, b. Dec. 1, 1877, d. July 21, 1938, m. Margaret Parks (b. July 31, 1881, d. Sept. 7, 1916); issue:
  - (1) Margaret[8] Frances Kendrick, b. Nov. 21, 1908, d. Aug. 7, 1952, m. William B. Mills (b. Aug. 11, 1899), one child, Anna Margaret Mills, b. Dec. 30, 1943;
  - (2) Marvin[8] Hayne Kendrick, M.D., b. Nov. 29, 1910, m. Sept. 6, 1941 Barbara Barrett Truesdell (b. May 25, 1917), dr. of Dr. Edward Delavan and Henrietta (Norton) Truesdell, and had (a) Barbara[9] Barrett Kendrick b. Aug. 8, 1942, (b) Marvin[9] Hayne Kendrick b. Aug. 20, 1946, (c) Eleanor[9] Parks Kendrick b. July 25, 1948, and (d) Susan[9] Stanton Kendrick b. Feb. 24, 1952;
  - (3) James[8] Evans Kendrick, b. Jan. 10, 1913, m. Martha Naomi Sims (b. July 14, 1920), and had: (a) Mary[9] Martha Kendrick b. Mar. 27, 1944 and (b) Laura[9] Carol Kendrick b. Feb. 3, 1949;
  - (4) Mary[8] Eleanor Kendrick, b. Aug. 29, 1916, m. John Hardy Whichard (b. Sept. 15, 1916), one child, Mary Irene Whichard, b. May 2, 1949.

VII. Aaron[6] Tomlinson Kendrick, Jr., b. 1848 in Barbour Co., Ala., d. July 24, 1930 in Greenville, Ala., m. (1) Almira Dunklin and had: (1) Claude[7] Kendrick and (2) Mary[7] Kendrick who m. Joe T. Rhodes. He m. (2) May Campbell (who d. May 19, 1889) and had (3) Kenneth[7] Kendrick b. May 19, 1889, d. April 27, 1916; (4) Joel[7] Kendrick; and (5) May[7] Morning Kendrick m. W. T. Dickson. He m. (3) Willie White (b. Mar. 10, 1853, d. Feb. 11, 1950) and had (6) Aaron[7] Tomlinson Kendrick, III.

VIII. George[6] Pierce Kendrick, b. Dec. 4, 1856, in Barbour Co.,
Ala., m. Mattie J. Sikes (b. Sept. 24, 1858, d. Dec. 3,
1924); issue:
1. Waverly[7] Briggs Kendrick, b. April 21, 1878, m. Milo
Asenath Webster (b. April 16, 1884, d. Oct. 28, 1951),
and had:
(1) George[8] Herbert Kendrick, b. Oct. 20, 1904, m.
Lena Drain Hoskins, one child, Anne[9] Kendrick,
b. Dec. 15, 1929; he m. (2) Betty Nelle Fussell
on Sept. 1, 1946 and had two children, Jane[9] Webster Kendrick b. Jan. 17, 1948 and Katherine[9] Kendrick b. July 17, 1950.
2. Comer[7] B. Kendrick b. Dec. 25, 1879, d. May 5, 1883.
3. Clara[7] Mae Kendrick, b. 1882, m. Robert W. Webster;
one daughter, Nettie Mae Webster m. Carl Lang and
has a daughter Ann Lang.
4. Mary[7] Kendrick, b. about 1883, m. Arthur Salmon of
Birmingham, Ala., two sons, Robert Salmon and Arthur Salmon.
5. Mattie[7] Sikes Kendrick, b. abt. 1884, m. Franklin
Stoddard and had James Stoddard and Franklin Stoddard,
Jr.
6. Nellie[7] Gray Kendrick, b. 1885, m. Col. J. S. Lucas,
U.S.A., one son, William Lucas.
7. Bernice[7] Kendrick, b. abt. 1887, m. J. S. Kendall, no
issue.
8. James[7] Cloud Kendrick, b. 1898, m. Mary Petry Kelly
of Montgomery, Ala., one daughter, Mary Petry Kendrick.
9. Lucille[7] Kendrick, b. abt. 1900, m. Charles L. Bird
and had Martha Jane Bird and Charles L. Bird, Jr.
IX. Texas[6] Kendrick, died aged 12.
X. Susan[6] Kendrick, d. young.
XI. Edward[6] N. Kendrick, b. Dec. 4, 1860, d. Aug. 18, 1869.

Tillman[5] Franklin Kendrick, son of Jones[4] and Susan (Bull)
Kendrick, was born Sept. 30, 1810 in Wilkes Co., Ga. and died
Sept. 30, 1891 at Raytown, Ga. He married Nov. 18, 1830 in
Wilkes Co., Ga. Elizabeth Booker (b. 1811-Census), who was
probably daughter of Richard Booker (b. 1777 in Va.) and his
wife Elizabeth (b. 1788 in Va.) of Wilkes Co., as two of Tillman
Kendrick's children, Evaline and George, were living in Rich-
ard Booker's family in the Census of 1850. Issue:
I. Franklin[6] W. Kendrick, b. 1831, d. Nov. 24, 1898 in
Taliaferro Co., Ga., m. (1) Susan MacWilliams of Decatur, Ga.; m. (2) Caroline --------. Issue of first
marriage:
1. Tillman[7] Kendrick b. 1858.
2. Susan[7] Kendrick b. 1861, d. after 1939 in Taliaferro
Co., Ga., m. B. M. C. Bell and lived in Columbia
Co., Ga.; issue: Arthur Bell, Ada Bell m. Pritchett,
Leonard Bell, Grady Bell, and Thomas Bell.
3. James[7] F. Kendrick b. 1862.

4. Edgar[7] P. Kendrick, b. 1865, married twice, his second wife being Frances Florence Moore (b. 1864, d. July 18, 1939); children (all by first wife):
   (1) Joel[8] F. Kendrick of Norwood, Ga., m. Eunice Burt, one child, Sally Kendrick;
   (2) Robert[8] L. Kendrick, m. Miss Hadden, one child, Edgar Lamar Kendrick;
   (3) Mrs. R. D.[8] Burt of Moultrie, Ga.; and
   (4) Georgia[8] Kendrick, m. W. Anderson Wagnon of White Plains, Ga.

II.   Anna[6] Kendrick m. William Moore, lived near Raytown, Ga. and had two children:
   1. Walter[7] Moore, d. about 1946, married and had 4 children, Ruth, Annie Lizzie, William Moore, and one other.
   2. Beatrice[8] Moore m. Tobias Kendrick and lives at Chattanooga, Tenn.

III.   Evaline[6] Kendrick b. 1838.
IV.   George[6] A. Kendrick b. 1840.
V.   William[6] Kendrick.

John[5] Bull Kendrick, son of Jones and Susan (Bull) Kendrick, was born July 22, 1812 in Wilkes Co., Ga., and died after 1880, probably in Columbia Co., Ga., where he was living with his son Zachariah in that year. John Bull Kendrick married (1) June 23, 1831 in Wilkes Co., Ga. Sarah Ann Powell (b. July 4, 1818, d. Nov. 24, 1844 in Wilkes Co.), daughter of his stepmother, Nancy M. Kendrick, by her second husband, Nelson Powell. Nelson Powell was probably a son of Cader or Lewis Powell and grandson of Moses and Mary (Williams) Powell of Wilkes Co. (see Powell and Williams Families). John B. Kendrick married (2) about 1848 his second cousin, Mrs. Sarah Maria (Harrison) Patton, daughter of William and Susan (Kendrick) Harrison and granddaughter of Benjamin[4] Kendrick, his uncle. By her he had one son, William Harrison Kendrick, b. 1849, killed by lightning while on his wedding trip at the age of 22. After the second marriage John B. Kendrick married (3) Charlotte Wright of Union Springs, Ala.; (4) a lady in Mobile, Ala., by whom he had one daughter who m. Mr. Dandy; and (5) he married again in New Orleans (this information from his nephew, Aaron T. Kendrick, Jr.). It has been reported that the daughter born of the fourth marriage was named Lilias. The children of John B. Kendrick by his first wife, Sarah Ann Powell, were:

I.   Zachariah[6] Kendrick, b. 1832, living in Columbia Co., Ga. in the Census of 1880, with wife Amanda (b. 1838), and children: Ora b. 1859, Cephas b. 1862, Phoison (?) b. 1865, James b. 1866, Georgia b. 1871, and Allison b. 1874.

II.   Cornelia[6] Kendrick, b. abt. 1833, m. as his first wife Capt. George Augustus Dure, no issue.

III.   Julia[6] Kendrick, b. 1835-6, d. 1929 in Macon, Ga., m. Dec. 22, 1857 as his second wife Capt. George Augustus Dure (b. 1832 in Savannah, Ga., d. 1908 in Macon, Ga.); issue:

1. Cornelia[7] Dure.
2. Anna[7] Dure m. Frank Coburn.
3. George[7] Powell Dure.
4. Emma[7] Dure.
5. Lily[7] Dure.
6. Leon[7] Sebring Dure, b. Oct. 8, 1874 in Brunswick, Ga., d. Jan. 10, 1948 in Macon, Ga., m. July 26, 1906 Kathleen McGregor (b. June 6, 1886), and had two children:
   (1) Leon[8] Sebring Dure, Jr., Major, Second World War, Burma Theatre, Bronze Star, b. June 27, 1907 at Macon, m. Jan 15, 1928 Katherine Mac-Kean (b. May 1, 1909 at Macon), and has two sons: (a) Leon[9] Sebring Dure, III, b. Jan. 22, 1930 at Macon, and (b) Kendrick[9] Dure, b. Aug. 7, 1938 at Richmond, Va.; and
   (2) Mary[8] Dure, b. April 3, 1909 at Macon, Ga., m. June 15, 1925 Buford Sandford Birdsey (Lt. U.S.N., Second World War, citation, b. May 1, 1906 at Macon), and has one son, Buford Sandford Birdsey, Jr., b. Aug. 14, 1941 at Macon: res. 1261 Jefferson Terrace, Macon, Ga.
7. William[7] Dure, d. young.
8. Julia[7] Dure, d. young.
9. Jasper[7] Dure, d. young.

IV. Ann[6] Marshall Kendrick, b. 1838 in Wilkes Co., Ga., d. s. p.

V. Lucius[6] Franklin Kendrick, b. 1841, living in Columbia Co., Ga., Census of 1880, served in Confederate Army and lost an arm, m. about 1870 Mary Elizabeth Marshall and had issue:
1. John[7] P. Kendrick b. 1872.
2. Naomi[7] A. Kendrick b. 1875.
3. Leila[7] B. Kendrick b. 1877.
4. Martha[7] Ray Kendrick b. 1879.
5. Julia[7] Kendrick m. Mr. Lucky and lived at Grovetown, Ga.

VI. Susan[6] Kendrick b. Nov. 15, 1844, d. at birth, buried with mother.

Easter[5] Caroline Kendrick, daughter of Jones[4] and Susan (Bull) Kendrick, was born in Wilkes Co., Ga. June 24, 1814 and died in Texas. She married Nov. 22, 1830 in Wilkes Co. John W. Carter, who also died in Texas. Their only known child was Mary Carter, mentioned in the will of Jones[4] Kendrick, who m. (1) Mr. Hargraves and (2) Mr. Young. She had one daughter who m. Mr. Casey, and had two sons, William and John Casey, living in 1916 in San Antonio, Texas.

Jones[5] Jackson Kendrick, son of Jones[4] and Susan (Bull) Kendrick, was born in Wilkes Co., Ga. Aug. 13, 1816 and died in 1900 at Calvert, Robertson Co., Tex. According to his nephew, A. T. Kendrick, Jr., Jones J. Kendrick first moved to Alabama, where he was a member of the State Senate from Geneva and surrounding counties; then moved to Texas (Calhoun Co. 1854,

Jackson Co. 1858, and finally to Robertson Co.), where he was a "rich lawyer and judge". The Census of 1880 for Calbert, Tex. shows that his wife was named Mary, probably a widow Parker, as Etta Parker, aged 18, was living in their family; however, Jones J. Kendrick left no children.

Susan[5] R. Kendrick, daughter of Jones[4] and Susan (Bull) Kendrick, was born in Wilkes Co., Ga. May 16, 1818. She married in Wilkes Co. Dec. 16, 1834 Charles N. Simpson, and they moved to Stewart Co., Ga., later to Cuthbert, Ga., where both probably died. In addition to several daughters, they had the following sons:

I.   Jones[6] Simpson, died in the Confederate service.
II.   Charles[6] Simpson, b. 1844 (Census), m. Jessie Bibb Key (b. 1852), living in Randolph Co., Ga. in 1870, still living 1916 at Cuthbert; issue:
     1. Key[7] Simpson b. 1870.
     2. Charles[7] Simpson m. Miss Brantley of Troy, Ala. and had issue.
     3. Jessie[7] Key Simpson m. Judge Arthur Foster of Troy, Ala. and died Aug., 1952; a son, Arthur Key Foster lives in Birmingham, Ala.
     4. Stella[7] Simpson, d. s. p.
III.   Robert[6] Simpson, living at Cuthbert, Ga. 1916.

Green[5] Marshall Kendrick, teacher and Methodist minister, only son of Jones[4] Kendrick and his second wife, Nancy Marshall Williams, was born in Wilkes Co., Ga. Sept. 3, 1834, and died at Augusta, Ga. Jan. 11, 1908. He married (1) Oct. 2, 1851 Olivia Prudence Stovall (b. Nov. 16, 1832, d. 1898 at Augusta, Ga.), daughter of Stephen Stovall of Lincoln Co., Ga.; and (2) in 1901 Ada E. Storey, by whom he had no children. Issue of first marriage:

I.   Lucius[6] W. Kendrick, b. Aug. 10, 1852, d. Aug. 23, 1857.
II.   Thomas[6] Edward Kendrick, b. May 17, 1854, d. April 7, 1905 at Sharon Ga., m. Mar. 16, 1881 Sarah Bertha Davidson (b. Dec. 13, 1856, d. Jan. 14, 1889), dr. of Dr. Paul Chase Davidson by his second wife, Sarah Jane Dyer; issue:
     1. Marshall[7] Davidson Kendrick b. July 30, 1883, d. at birth.
     2. Hildegarde[7] Davidson Kendrick b. Sept. 24, 1888, m. William J. Lunsford, lives at Sharon, Ga., four children, Mary, Davidson, Olivia and Martha Lunsford.
     3. Helen[7] Olivia Kendrick, b. Sept. 6, 1891, m. Fred Hall, issue: Fred, Jr. Sarah, Margaret, Claire, and Jane Hall.
     4. Florence[7] Estelle Kendrick, b. Oct. 1, 1893, m. Bert C. Lyons, lives Thomson, Ga., no issue.
III.   William[6] Marshall Kendrick, b. May 11, 1856, m. Lillian Richards, dr. of Vernon Richards of Augusta, Ga., one daughter, Lillie Kendrick, m. Clarence Reynolds and lives at Mayfield, Ga.
IV   Stephen[6] S. Kendrick, b. Sept. 7, 1857, d. Feb. 25, 1858.
V.   Walter[6] Barnett Kendrick, b. Feb. 20, 1859, d. June,

1905, m. Anna Moffett; a daughter, Annie Claire Kendrick, m. a Mayes, and their daughter, Elizabeth Mayes, lives at Americus, Ga.

VI. Emmett[6] S. Kendrick, b. Sept. 17, 1860, m. Nelle Burnett.

VII. Emily[6] Anna Kendrick, b. May, 1862, m. (1) Mr. Amoss of Augusta, Ga. and had a daughter, Olivia Amoss, who m. Fred Wood; she m. (2) Ernest Pounds.

VIII. Nancy[6] Estelle Kendrick, b. May, 1864, m. Mr. Moffett.

IX. Mary[6] Lee Kendrick, b. June, 1865, d. July 17, 1900.

X. Jane[6] Olivia Kendrick, b. Feb. 3, 1867, d. Nov. 6, 1867.

XI. Lucy[6] Florence Kendrick, b. Jan., 1868, m. Mr. Latimer.

XII. Marion[6] Abbott Kendrick, b. Aug. 1, 1869.

XIII. Ruth[6] May Kendrick b. May 7, 1870, m. Dr. J. E. Prather of Americus, Ga.

XIV. Sidney[6] Albert Kendrick, b. Feb. 25, 1873, of Atlanta, Ga.

MALLETT AND SALLE OF MANAKINTOWN, VA.

Stephen Mallett, or Etienne Malet, with his wife ("Theph. Mallott and wife"), was among the French settlers who came in the first ship in 1699 to Manakintown, Henrico Co., Va. (Brock "Huguenot Emigration to Va.", p. 45). He died in Henrico Co., Va. in 1712. His will, written in French was dated April 2, 1712 and probated June 2, 1712. It states that he was a native of Bordeaux in Guienne, and leaves his property to his three children, Etienne, Marie and Suzanne. It is probable that he was born in 1674, the son of Jacob Malet and Madeleine Aidelot, nephew of another Etienne Malet, and grandson of Etienne Malet and his wife Anne Bergoin of Montauban, France, as indicated by the following records from the French Church of Threadneedle Street, London (Vol. XIII, Publications of the Huguenot Society of London): (1) p. 50. Etienne Maillet, native of Montauban, son of Etienne Maillet and Anne Bergoin, and Ester Coquart, native of London, daughter of Antoine Coquart and Marie Corvillé, were married July 8, 1673. (b) Jeanne, daughter of the above, was baptized Feb. 14, 1677. (p. 222.) (c) Rachel, daughter of the above, was baptized Nov. 5, 1684. (p. 272.) (d) Estienne Malett, son of Jacob Malett and Madelenne Aidelot his wife, was baptized Sept. 9, 1674; witnesses, Etienne Malet and Marie Aidelot (p. 212). The child Etienne just mentioned could easily have been born in Bordeaux and not christened until his parents came to London, perhaps in haste because of persecution. Montauban is up the Garonne River from Bordeaux. Of the children of Etienne Malet of Manakintown, Marie or Marian Mallett died unmarried and her land was inherited by her brother Stephen (Etienne), as shown by a deed from him May 19, 1741 in Goochland Co. (D.B. 3, p. 475). The daughter Suzanne probably married Tobit Lafitte of Manakintown, where the church records show that "Janne, wife of Tobit Lafitte and daughter of Etienne and Marie Mallet, died in her ----teenth year, Dec. 15, 1722 (Brock, p. 110). The original church records from which the above was copied are now at the Huntington Library, and the Librarian there wrote some time ago that the manuscript is torn or defaced at the place where the wife's name is written, so that it could easily have been the end of the name "Suzanne", rather than the name Janne. That this is the case is indicated by the fact that Ester Lafitte, daughter of Tobit, was godmother to Ester Mallett, daughter of Etienne[2] Mallett, showing probable kinship. The above record, if interpreted thus, shows that the wife of Etienne[1] Malett was named Marie.

Stephen[2] Mallett, son of Stephen[1] Mallett, was born in 1706-7, as he is first shown as a tithable in 1723, when 16 years old. (VM 12, 251). He married between April 16, 1728 and July 4, 1728 Olive Magdalen Salle, daughter of Abraham Salle and his wife Olive Perrault of Manakintown. This is shown by the church records, which show Olive Salle as a godmother on the first date and Olive Mallet in the same capacity on the latter date (Brock, pp. 80, and 81). The marriage is proved by a document dated Mar. 31, 1747, in which Stephen Mallett of Goochland Co. acquits Magdaleine Salle (widow of Abraham Salle, Jr., who was eldest son of Abraham Salle, Sr.) for goods left his wife, Olive Magdaleine, by her father's will (Henrico Co. D.B. 1744-8, p. 273). Stephen[2] Mallett was a churchwarden of King William Parish in 1733, 1737, 1742 and 1748, and vestryman from 1737 to 1750 (VM, 13, pp. 74, 178, 180, 182, 183, 184, 185, 188, etc.). In 1750 he and his family moved to Lunenburg Co., Va. to that section which later became Mecklenburg Co., and Stephen[2] Mallett and his two sons, Stephen, Jr. and William, appear in a number of deeds and other records in Lunenburg in the 1750's. The last appearance of Olive Mallett, wife of Stephen[2], is in 1762 (Lunenburg O.B., 1761-2, p. 237), and she probably died soon afterwards. The last positive reference to Stephen himself is on Aug. 4, 1769, when John Burton acknowledged a debt to Stephen Mallett, Sr., John Farrar, and Stephen Mallett, Jr. in Mecklenburg Co. (D.B. 2, p. 366). Stephen[2] Mallett probably died about 1770-71 in Mecklenburg Co., Va. Mecklenburg Co. Order Book 3 shows that Carter Clark sued Stephen Mallett in 1772 and 1773 (pp. 333 and 463), and O.B. 4 shows that Stephen Mallett sued James Clark in 1774 (p. 283). Stephen[2] Mallett's daughter Judith had married John Clark, who moved to South Carolina in 1767, and Carter and James Clark were John's brothers (see Clark Family). It is probable that the Stephen Mallett referred to in the above suits was Stephen[3] Mallett and that the suits were in regard to property connected with the estate of Stephen[2], though there is no further record of his death. Stephen[2] Mallett and his wife, Olive Magdaleine Salle, had the following children:

I.   Marie[3] Mallet, b. Mar. 8, 1730, bapt. May 20, 1730; godparents, William and Elizabeth Salle, and Susanne Billiebo (Brock, p. 84).

II.   Etienne[3] Mallet (Stephen[3] Mallett). b. Nov. 25, 1731; godparents, Peter Salle, Jean Pierre Billiebo, and Magdaleine Salle (Brock, p. 86). Stephen[3] Mallett must have married quite early, as we shall see later that his eldest son, Stephen[4], must have been born about 1750-51. His wife's name was Rachel (Lunenberg Co. O.B. $2\frac{1}{2}$ B, p. 584). He first appears in the records in 1752, when Julius Nichols deeded land to Stephen Mallett, Sr. and Jr. in Lunenburg Co., and when his father petitioned for him to be authorized to build a mill (O.B. 2, p. 528; O.B. $2\frac{1}{2}$ A, p. 35). He served in the French and Indian War in Capt. James Gunn's Co. (Mecklenburg Co. O.B. 5, p. 13). Stephen[3] Mallett appears in numerous deeds in Mecklenburg Co., being called after 1770 Stephen Mallett, Sr. to distinguish him from his son Stephen[4] Mallett. On Oct. 10, 1779 and Nov. 20, 1779 he made deeds of gift of land and a mill to his son, Zachariah Mallett (D.V. 5, p. 498

and p. 533), and on Dec. 14, 1789 was excused from levies because of his age (O.B. 7, p. 464). He probably died between 1790 and 1800. The Mecklenburg Co. records indicate that he had the following four sons:

1. Stephen[4] Mallett, Jr., m. Mary ------- (O.B. 5, p. 110), and served in the Revolutionary War from Mecklenburg Co. (Eckenrode "List of Rev. Soldiers from Va.", p. 295, and Supplement, p. 204). He had at least the following children:
   (1) Isaac Mallett, b. 1770-71 (tithable first in his father's family 1787);
   (2) Jesse Mallett b. 1774-5 (tithable 1791);
   (3) Joseph Mallett, b. 1775-6 (tithable 1792); and
   (4) Sally Mallett, who along with her brothers Isaac and Joseph was paid by her father as witness in a law-suit Mar. 15, 1792.

2. Zachariah[4] Mallett m. Mary, daughter of Hugh Noel of Lunenburg Co. prior to 1777 (Mecklenburg D.B. 5, p. 153; O.B. 4, p. 384; Lunenburg Co. W.B. 1, p. 320). He had the following sons as shown by the tithables lists:
   (1) William Mallett, b. 1777-8;
   (2) Howell Mallett b. 1778-9; and
   (3) Thomas Mallett b. 1782-3, M. Feb., 1804 Betsy H. Allgood in Mecklenburg Co.

3. William[4] Mallett, who was deeded land in Mecklenburg Co. in 1781 (O.B. 5, p. 98), and is shown as head of a household up to 1794.

4. Jacob[4] Mallett, on whose estate Stephen[4] Mallett, Jr. and Zachariah[4] Mallett administered in 1791 (O.B. 7, p. 648).

III. Guillaume[3] Mallet or William [3] Mallett, b. Jan. 28, 1773-4 (Brock, p. 89). William Mallett was deeded land in Lunenburg Co. by his father April 3, 1750, when he was only 16 years old (D.B. 3, p. 229), and deeded the land back to his father in 1756 (D.B. 4, p. 325). He married in Lunenburg Co. Rachel Baker, daughter of William Baker of Lunenburg Co., who died about 1752. Zachariah Baker was appointed guardian of James, Judith, William, and Sarah Baker, orphans of William Baker, decd. at the Oct. Court, 1752 in Lunenburg Co. (O.B. 2½A, pp. 292-3). The daughter Rachel must have been already married to William Mallett. That she was a daughter is proved by the testimony of Stephen Mallett, Jr. and Henry Avey in Mecklenburg Co. in Dec., 1789, that "Rachel Mallett, before she married her late husband, William Mallett, decd., is own sister to William Baker, late of South Carolina, decd". (O.B. 7, p. 466). This shows that William Mallett was dead by 1789. He may have died in Mecklenburg Co. prior to 1777, as on August 11, 1777, the Court of Mecklenburg Co. bound out Priscilla Mallett, an orphan, to John Farrar (O. B. 4, p. 365), and unless she was a daughter of William[4]

Mallett, it is hard to place this Priscilla. However
this may be, the widow Rachel Mallett and her two sons,
James and William Mallett, were living in Randolph Co.,
N.C. in the Census of 1790, the sons being married and
heads of families of their own. In 1792 Rachel Mallett
gave a power of attorney to her son James in Edgefield
Co., S.C. to settle for the inheritance from her brother,
William Baker. The sons, William and James, were
living in Edgefield Co., S.C. up to 1810, but later moved
to Baldwin Co., Ga., and their descendants to Hinds Co.,
Miss. Mr. L. E. Mallette of Greenwood, Miss., is a
descendant of William[4] Mallette.

IV.   Judith[3] Mallet, b. Sept. 2, 1736; godparents James
      Goss, Elizabeth Salle, and Magdaleine Salle (Brock, p.
      93). She married John Clark (see Clark Family).
V.   Ester[3] Mallet, b. Nov. 27, 1738; godparents Jacques
      Faure, Ester Laffitte, and Ann Oge (Brock, p. 97).
VI.   Elizabeth[3] Mallet, b. Jan. 20, 1740-41; godparents,
      Jean Chastain, Charlotte Chastain, and Ann David (Brock,
      p. 101).
VII. Marie[3] Magdaleine Mallet b. Oct. 10, 1742; godparents
      Matthew Bingley, Judith Salle, and Mariane Salle (Brock,
      p. 102).

Salle

Abraham Salle was born at St. Martin, Ile de Re, Aunix,
France, the son of Jean and Marie Salle (Baird "Huguenot
Emigration to America", I, 308). He was probably the most
important member of the Huguenot colony at Manakintown. He
was a merchant, was Clerk of King William Parish, a Captain
of militia, and a Justice of Henrico Co., Va. (VM 2, 5; 11,
294,299; 12,247; Va. Patent Bk. 10, 253). He first moved to
New York, where he petitioned the Governor and Council for
denization in 1700 (Baird, I, 308); and his two eldest sons by
his wife, Olive Perault, were born there, Abraham on Sept. 3,
1700 and Jacob on July 28, 1701 (Collections of the Huguenot
Soc. of Amer., I, 77 and 83). His wife was probably daughter
of sister of Daniel Perrault or Perreau, who was Commander
of the ship "Peter and Anthony", which brought 169 French Refugees to Virginia in 1700 (Brock, p. 14 and 16). By Nov. 10,
1701, Abraham Salle had moved to Manakintown, as the list of
French refugees on that date shows: "Merchant Suillee, below
ye Creek, his wife and 2 children, and one negro woman" (Brock,
p. 48). A letter from Abraham Salle to George I of England soon
after the latter's accession is still extant (VM34, pp. 159-60).
It asks that the French settlers in Virginia be granted land in
some more fertile spot, possibly in Ireland. Abraham Salle died
at Manakintown in 1720. His will, dated Aug. 9, 1718, and probated in Henrico Co. in March, 1719/20 (Henrico Misc. Records,
II, 513; Brock, p. 74) gives his nativity in France as cited above,
requests to be buried by his wife, and leaves slaves, land, and
considerable property to his sons Abraham, Jacob, Isaac, Wil-

liam and Peter, and to his daughter Olive Magdaleine. The will leaves to his heirs all his interest in the estates of his late father, mother, brother, sister, father-in-law and uncle in France or England, and appoints the sons Abraham, Jacob, and Isaac executors. The children of Abraham and Olive (Perault) Salle were:

I.   Abraham Salle, Jr., b. Sept. 3, 1700 in New York City, d. 1731 in Henrico Co., Va., m. ca. 1720 Magdalen Amonet, who d. 1756 in Chesterfield Co., Va. Their children, as shown by the wills, church records, and other documents, were:
1. Abraham Salle III;
2. Magdalen Salle m. William Wooldridge;
3. Olive Salle.
4. Judith Salle b. Nov. 9, 1726 (Brock, p. 80).
5. Elizabeth Salle b. Mar. 13, 1728 (p. 82), unmarried in 1756.
6. Mariane Salle b. Aug. 20, 1731 m. Charles Clarke.

II.   Jacob Salle, b. July 28, 1701 in New York, d. unmarried in 1720 soon after his father (shown in the tithables 1719, but not in 1720).

III.   Isaac Salle is shown to have been b. 1703-4 by the tithables lists, and was still living Feb. 21, 1729/30, when he was godfather to one of his brother William's children (Brock, p. 83), but is mentioned as dead in his brother Abraham's will, dated Feb. 3, 1730/31 (Henrico D. & W. No. 1, p. 292).

IV.   William Salle was born 1706-7 (first tithable 1723). He married twice, his first wife being named Elizabeth and his second Magdalen. His children by the first wife as shown by Brock were:
1. Elizabeth b. July 4, 1728;
2. Elizabeth b. Feb. 21, 1729/30;
3. William b. April 17, 1732;
4. William b. May 8, 1734;
5. Isaac b. July 27, 1739.
The children by his second wife were:
6. Isaac b. April 22, 1741;
7. Peter b. July 13, 1743;
8. John b. Nov. 2, 1745;
9. Olive b. Nov. 5, 1749.

V.   Peter Salle, b. 1708-9 (first tithable in 1725), m. Frances Bondurant and d. in Cumberland Co., Va., in 1752. His wife d. in Powhatan Co. in 1777. Both left wills. Their children were:
1. Isaac Salle b. Oct. 5, 1734;
2. Abraham Salle b. Nov. 18, 1736;
3. Marie Salle b. Oct. 1, 1741 m. Mr. Reddy;
4. Jacob Salle b. Feb. 9, 1743/4.
5. Joseph Salle b. March 9, 1745/6;
6. Judith Salle b. Oct. 25, 1749.

VI.   Olive Magdaleine Salle b. ca. 1710-11, m. 1728 Etienne[2] Malet.

POWELL AND WILLIAMS OF NANSEMOND CO., VA.
and NORTH CAROLINA

George[1] Powell and his wife Ann appear in Bertie Co. deeds from 1719 to 1726 (Chowan d. B. F, p. 20; Bertie D.B. "A", pp. 22, 30-32, and "B", pp. 79 and 174). He was probably from Nansemond Co., Va., the son of an earlier George Powell who is mentioned as having sold land to Col. John Lear of Nansemond Co. in the latter's will in 1695 (Grimes "N.C. Wills and Inv.", p. 283). George Powell died in Bertie Co., N.C. in 1736, his will, dated March 24, 1735/6 and probated at the May Court, 1736, leaving all his property to his four sons, Cader, Lewis, George and Moses Powell (Grimes "Abstracts",p. 298).

Moses[2] Powell was probably the youngest son of George[1], born about 1725-30. He married prior to 1751 Mary, daughter of Anthony Williams of Duplin Co., N.C. The Williams family was, also, from Nansemond Co., Va., where Lewis[1] Williams, Mary's great-grandfather, was granted land in 1682 (Va. Pat. Bk. 7, p. 170). North Carolina records show that Lewis Williams was granted land in Chowan Co., N.C. in 1697; that he had trouble with the Meherrin Indians in 1707; that he was a vestryman of the Southwestern Parish of Chowan Co.; that he had a son, William Williams, who was living in Isle of Wight Co., Va. in 1706, and a daughter Elizabeth who married James Rutland (Hathaway, I, pp. 85, 89, 92, 93, 94, 99, 102, 290 and 304; II, pp. 208 and 643). He died in Chowan Co., N.C. in 1717, his will, dated Oct. 1, 1716 and probated April 16, 1717, mentioning his son Anthony and the latter's wife Martha; grandsons Anthony and Lewis Williams, John and Lewis Jones, Charles Sawell, John and Joshua Pritchett, and John Williams (son of William); wife Mary; and daughter Priscilla West (Grimes, p. 411; Hathaway, I, 502). Anthony[2] Williams, son of Lewis[1], married Martha Bush, daughter of William and Martha Bush of Chowan Co., and died in Chowan in 1718. William Bush was originally from Isle of Wight County, Va., where he was granted land in 1682, which he sold early in 1683 and moved to North Carolina (I. of W. D. & W., 1662-1715, p. 506; D.B. 1, p.39). The will of William Bush, Sr., dated April 5, 1716 and probated in Chowan Co. at the Oct. Court, 1716, mentions his sons, John and William; daughters Mary Early, Martha Williams, Rose Winns, Eleanor McLendon, and Elizabeth Bush; and wife Martha (Grimes, p. 58; Hathaway I, 185). The will of Anthony[2] Williams, dated Dec. 3, 1717 and probated in Chowan Co. at the April Court, 1718, mentions his sons, Lewis, William, John and Anthony; daughters Sarah, Mary and Eleanor; brother-in-law John Early; and wife Martha (Grimes, p. 408; Hathaway, I, p. 502). Anthony[3] Williams, son of Anthony[2], moved to Duplin Co., N.C., where he died in 1752. His will, dated July 3, 1751, and probated at the April Court, 1752, mentions his sons, Stephen and Benjamin; brother John; daughter Mary wife of Moses Powell; grandson Cader Powell; cousin Anthony Beverly; daughters Penelope, Pherabee, Easter and Civility Williams; and wife Mary (Grimes, p. 408; Hathaway I, p. 502).

Moses[2] Powell, who married Mary Williams above, was still living in Duplin Co., N.C. Oct. 7, 1766, when he appears in the militia of that county in the General Muster (N.C. Col. and State Rec., VII, 263). He was granted land in what later became Edgefield Co., S.C. in 1762, and probably moved there soon after 1766. By 1774 he was living in Georgia, Wilkes Co., and last appears in the records on Feb. 14, 1791, when Moses Powell, Sr., of Wilkes Co., Ga., deeded to Thomas Holsel of Edgefield Co., S.C., 100 acres in Edgefield which had been granted him June 1, 1762 (Edgefield D.B.8, p. 102). On Sept. 29, 1773, 400 acres of land on the Ogeechee River in Georgia was granted to "Moses Powell, with a family of three sons and one daughter, aged 17 to 7 years of age", and on the same date 100 acres was granted to "Cader Powell of South Carolina with a wife and a son 2 months old" (Davidson "Early Records of Ga., Wilkes Co.", I, 7). On Aug. 24, 1774, Moses Powell was living in Georgia, for on that date he signed a protest of the inhabitants of St. Paul's Parish against the resolutions passed Aug. 10, 1774 by the patriots on the coast (Candler "Rev. Rec. of Ga.", I, 23). However, Moses Powell, his sons Cader and Lewis, and probably also his sons, Benjamin and Moses, Jr., all served in the Revolutionary War in Georgia. Their Revolutionary service is shown in Knight's "Georgia Roster of the Revolution" as follows: (1) Moses Powell, pp. 143, 213, 390; (2) Cader Powell, pp. 143, 273; (3) Lewis Powell, pp. 143, 207, 210, 272, 390, 444; (4) Benjamin Powell, pp. 143, 425.

Davidson's "Early Records of Georgia, Wilkes Co." shows the children of Moses[2] Powell as Cader Powell, Penelope Lamar, Charity Harvey, Lewis Powell, Moses Powell, Jr., and Benjamin Powell, in the following records: (1) The tax-list of 1785 shows Moses, Kader, Lewis and Moses, Jr. (II, 61, 63, 64). (2) Moses Powell, Sr., deeded to his sons Moses, Jr., and Benjamin on July 2, 1789, all his property, which is to go to them at the death of Moses, Sr. (I, 266). Cader Powell and Charity Harvey witnessed this deed. (3) The will of Benjamin Powell, dated Dec. 9, 1823 and probated Jan. 5, 1824, leaves most of his estate to his wife Mary Powell, but leaves bequests to his brothers, Lewis and Moses Powell, and $1 each to the heirs of his deceased brother, Cader Powell, and his deceased sisters, Penelope Lamar and Charity Harvey (II, 147). Benjamin Powell's wife was named Mary Lybas, as her will, dated July 30, 1825, and probated Sept. 5, 1825, leaver her property to her brother Charles Lybas (II, 148).

Moses[2] Powell, Sr., probably died in Wilkes Co., Ga., between 1791 and 1800. The deed of gift in 1789 to his two younger sons would indicate that his wife Mary was dead at the time. There is a bare possibility that she may have survived him, as a Mary Powell's will was probated in Wilkes Co. Dec. 2, 1816, though the will has been lost (Davidson, I, 216). It is more probable, however, that this Mary Powell who died in 1816 was the widow of the son, Cader Powell. Of the other children of Moses[3] and Mary (Williams) Powell, besides Benjamin above, we have the following information. (1) Cader Powell, the eldest son, was born about 1750-51, as he is mentioned in his grandfather Williams' will; was married prior to 1773 when he moved to Georgia with his father, and died prior to 1823. His wife was perhaps the Mary Powell who died in 1816. There is no further information regarding the children of Cader Powell, but it is not improbable that Nelson Powell and his brother Benjamin Powell of Wilkes Co., Ga., were his sons. Nelson Powell married Dec. 19, 1816 in Wilkes Co., Ga., Nancy Marshall Williams Anderson (b. Nov. 12, 1791), widow of John R. Anderson, who became the third wife of Jones Kendrick (b. 1778) after Nelson Powell's death; and their daughter, Sarah Ann Cornelia Powell married John B. Kendrick, son of Jones by his first marriage (see Kendrick Family). The sons of John R. Anderson are shown to have been named John and Edward Anderson, in accounts handed in by Nelson Powell from 1816 to 1818. In 1822 and 1823 Nelson Powell administered on the estate of Lewis McLendon in Wilkes Co., and paid certain amounts from the estate to himself, to Benjamin Powell and to Mary Powell. He died in Wilkes Co., Ga., in 1825, his will, dated Feb. 22, 1825 and probated Mar. 15, 1825, mentioning his wife Nancy; children Sarah Ann, Willis and Tabitha Powell; and appoints among his executors his brother, Benjamin Powell, and his brother-in-law, Jesse Williams (Davidson, II, 147). Nelson Powell's brother, Benjamin Powell, married Mary Burdett Sept. 7, 1824 in Wilkes Co. (2) Penelope Powell, daughter of Moses[2] Powell, was married prior to 1773 to a Lamar, as the 1773 record shows only one unmarried daughter to Moses Powell's family. This was certainly Charity Powell Harvey, who did not marry Evan Harvey until 1774. Penelope Powell was probably the second child, b. ca. 1753-4, and her husband was probably William Lamar, who made a deed in Greene Co. in 1789 which was witnessed by Evan Harvey, husband of her sister Charity. (3) Charity Powell was the unmarried daughter in the family of Moses Powell when he came to Georgia in 1773, being probably the child 17 years old, so born in 1756. She married Evan Harvey March 3, 1774 (see Harvey Family). (4) Lewis Powell was probably the fourth child of Moses[2] Powell, born about 1758-60, as he certainly served in the Revolutionary War. He was still living in 1823 when his brother Benjamin's will was written. (5) Moses Powell, Jr., was probably the fifth son, and probably identical with the Moses Powell who was a private in Capt. John Hill's Co., Elijah Clarke's Regt., at Fort Martin May 1 to Aug. 3, 1782 (Card Index File of Rev. Soldiers, Ga. Dept. of Archives, Atlanta). Both he and his father seem to have served in the Revolution, and if this is the case, he was probably born about 1762-3. He and his wife Sally, along with his brother Cader Powell, were members of Williams Creek Bap-

tist Church in Warren Co., Ga., prior to 1791 (D.A.R. Hist.
of Warren Co., II, p. 258). Moses Powell, Jr., finally moved
to Jasper Co., Ga., where he died in 1821. His will, dated
Aug. 23, 1821, mentions his wife, Sarah; sons George, William,
Evan and Benjamin (the last named a minor); daughters Nancy
Respass, Catherine Maddox, Martha Marchman, Charity Mc-
Michael, Sarah Goolsby and Civility Marks; grandson Moses,
son of William Powell, and granddaughter Almirah McMichael.
(6) Benjamin Powell, who died without issue in 1824 in Wilkes
Co., was probably the youngest son, aged 7 in 1773, so born
1765-6.

HARVEY FAMILY of LUNENBURG CO., VA.

There were four Harveys who appear as heads of families in Lunenburg Co., Va. from 1750-1760, who were closely associated with one another in deeds and other records, and were probably brothers. They were John Harvey, Thomas Harvey, William Harvey, and Charles Harvey. John, William and Charles moved to South Carolina during the 1760's or 1770's, Thomas alone remaining in Virginia. We shall therefore treat of Thomas and his family first.

Thomas[1] Harvey was probably born about 1705-10, as there is evidence that his eldest son, John, was born about 1730-35, and he died in Charlotte Co., Va. in 1782. His wife was named Elizabeth, as shown by a Cumberland Co., Va., deed in 1750 and a Charlotte Co. deed in 1774. He first appears in the records in 1741, when he was deeded land in Goochland Co., Va. He lived in that county up to about 1745, but was residing in Cumberland Co. in 1750. He appears in Lunenburg Co. in 1752 with a family of 6 tithables, among them his eldest son, John. In 1747 he was granted large tracts in Goochland Co., and in Lunenburg and Bedford Co.'s in 1767. The will of Thomas Harvey, Sr., dated April 29, 1782, and probated Aug. 5, 1782 in Charlotte Co., mentions his sons William, Thomas, and Blasingame Harvey; daughters Sarah Howl, Frances Harvey, Elizabeth Paulet, and Drusilla Harvey; son John Harvey; and directs that his lands in Georgia be divided among his eight children. John[2] Harvey, the eldest son of Thomas, was a Captain of Militia in Lunenburg Co. in 1756 in the French and Indian War. He married Ann Richardson, daughter of John Richardson of Amelia and Cumberland Co.'s, and died in Charlotte Co. in 1813, his will mentioning his wife Ann, and sons William, Thomas and Isham. The sons William and Thomas are apparently identical with a William and Thomas Harvey who married, respectively, Agnes and Barbara Walton, daughters of Simeon Walton of Amelia Co., William in 1789 and Thomas in 1779. Isham, son of John[2] Harvey, married Drusilla, daughter of his uncle Thomas[2] Harvey. William[2] Harvey, son of Thomas[1], was a Captain of Militia in Charlotte Co. during the Revolution, and died there in 1809. His will mentions his wife Drusilla, son Jack D. Harvey, and daughters Elizabeth Paulet, Frances Overton, wife of William Overton, Polly Richardson, and Sallie Harvey. Thomas[2] Harvey died in Charlotte Co. in 1812. His will mentions his son Nathan Harvey and daughters, Sarah, wife of Martin Hancock, Drusilla, wife of Isham Harvey, Elizabeth, wife of Pleasant Jennings, Susannah, wife of William Thornton, and Polly, wife of Douglas Hancock. Blassingame[2] Harvey, son of Thomas[1], moved to Georgia, where he was a Captain in the Revolution and died in Jefferson Co. in 1800. His will mentions his son Thomas Harvey; daughter Betsy Tuberfield Harvey, wife of Blassingame Harvey, Jr., and her 5 children; son John Harvey; son Billy Blassingame Harvey; and daughters Polly Key, Sally Paulett, and Frances Blackman. The wife's name is not mentioned in the will, but other records in Jefferson Co., Ga., show that it was Drusilla. Frances[2] Harvey married Charles Harvey, son of Charles Harvey, Sr., and probably her first cousin. Charles and Frances Harvey also moved to Jefferson Co., Ga., where he died in 1800. His will mentions his son Blassingame Harvey, son James H. Harvey; son John Holcomb Harvey; daughters Elizabeth French, Sally and Susannah Harvey; and wife Frances. The son James H. Harvey seems to have moved to Louisiana and to have been identical with the James H. Harvey who married there Mary Elizabeth Kendrick, daughter of William Kendrick (see Kendrick Family).

William[1] Harvey appears in the Lunenburg list of tithables in 1748 and 1749 along with John[1] Harvey, and in 1752 along with Thomas[1] and Charles[1] Harvey. He is mentioned in the Lunenburg and Bedford records as late as 1762. In the latter year there is mention in Lunenburg of a William Harvey, Jr., which indicates that he had a grown son, b. ca. 1740-41, so he himslef must have been born ca. 1710-20. William Harvey moved to South Carolina some time in the 1760's, and had four land-grants in Craven Co. He later moved to Edgefield Co., where his brother John had moved, also, and died there in 1788. His will, dated Dec. 1, 1787 and probated in Edgefield Co. Oct. 15, 1788, mentions ִِis wife Elizabeth, Hillary Phillips, and son Zephariah Harvey, whom he appoints executors; sons and daughters Matthew, Mary and James; to wife "the chest I gave Dick" (indicating a son Richard, decd.); the heirs of Micajah Andrews; Zephariah, John, William, Nehemiah, Thomas, Eleanor and Liney, "my loving wife, sons and daughters"; "the bed called Sally's to Sarah Andrews"; daughters Ann and Elizabeth. The will indicates that a daughter had married Micahah Andrews, who died in Edgefield Co. in 1786, his administrators being William and Elizabeth Harvey.

Charles[1] Harvey is shown in Lunenburg Co. as head of a family in 1752 along with Thomas and William Harvey. He was granted land in Lunenburg Co. in 1761 and again in 1763, in that section of Lunenburg which later became Charlotte Co. Charles Harvey, Jr., appears in the Lunenburg Co. records in 1762 and 1764, which indicates that he was a grown man, b. ca. 1740-41, so that his father must have been born about 1710-20. This Charles Harvey, Jr., seems to be the one who married Frances, daughter of Thomas[1] Harvey, and to have died in Georgia. Charles[2] Harvey had moved to Craven Co., S.C. by 1772 along with his brothers, John and William Harvey. He had two land-grants in Craven Co., and made a deed of land there in 1772. He appears to have been the Charles Harvey who was appointed a magistrate of the District of Queensborough in Georgia on July 2, 1776 (Candler, Rev. Rec. of Ga., I, 149), for Charles Harvey, Jr. was still living in Charlotte Co. at the time. Another son of Charles[1] Harvey was probably James Harvey, who was granted land in Lunenburg Co., Va., in 1758, appears in Lunenburg in 1762, was deeded land in Bedford Co., Va. in 1764, but deeded this land away to John Harvey, son of Thomas[1], in 1765, moving in that year to Berkeley Co., S.C., where he was deeded land in 1765 and received land-grants amounting to 550 acres in 1772. It is possible that another son of Charles[1] Harvey was Thomas Harvey of Brunswick Co., Va., who was deeded land in that county in 1764 and died there in 1781. Thomas' will mentions sons Thomas, John, Twiford and Raleigh Harvey. The wife's name is not shown in the will, but other records show it to have been Ann. Ann Harvey died in Brunswick Co. in 1782, her will mentioning her four children, Tryford, Raleigh, Ann and Judith Hust. This Thomas Harvey of Brunswick Co. may not have been connected with the Lunenburg Harveys; but if he was, he must have been a son of Charles.

John[1] Harvey was probably the eldest of the four Harvey brothers of Lunenburg, b. about 1700-1705. He first appears in the Virginia records in 1742, when he was granted land in Brunswick Co. (Book 20, p. 426, Va. Land Patents). He was granted land in Lunenburg Co. in 1749 (Book 29, p. 91) and in Bedford Co. in 1756 (Book 32, p. 668). He was head of a family in Lunenburg Co. in 1748, 1749 and 1750 along with William[1] Harvey, but with his wife Mary deeded the land away in 1750 and moved to Bedford Co. (Lunenburg D.B. 2, p. 24). He appears in the Bedford Co. records from 1752 to 1756, but in 1755 and 1756 he and Mary his wife deeded away all their large land-holdings in the county, amounting to over 1000 acres (Bedford D.B. 1, pp. 38, 43, 47, 62 and 76), and apparently moved to South Carolina. John Harvey had been granted land in that colony on Jan. 9, 1752 in "Crv. Co." (probably Craven). He had four other grants in Craven Co., S.C. amounting to 550 acres from 1768 to 1774, and two grants in Granville Co. (which later became Edgefield) amounting to 400 acres in 1770 and 1773. He had moved to Granville Co. from Craven by Nov. 13, 1767, when Samuel Fry deeded 200 acres to John Harvey, planter, of Granville Co. This deed was witnessed by John Harvey, Jr., presumably his son. On Feb. 20, 1775 John Harvey of Granville Co. deeded 100 acres in that county to James Thompson. It is impossible to know whether this last deed was that of John Harvey, Sr., or John Harvey, Jr., as John, Sr., may have died in the meantime. The above two deeds are in the Mesne Conveyances at Charleston, and the destruction of South Carolina records prior to about 1785 makes it impossible to determine more accurately the death of John[1] Harvey. The land-grants in Craven and Granville Co. are in the index all bracketed under the name, John Harvey, showing that they were granted to one man. In addition to John Harvey, Jr., mentioned in the 1767 deed, John[1] Harvey probably had two other sons, Michael[2] Harvey and Thomas[2] Harvey.

Michael[2] Harvey is shown in the tithables of Lunenburg Co. in the years 1748 and 1749, not as an independent tithable like John[1] and William[1] Harvey, but among the tithables of Paul Paulson. He was probably a young man, born about 1730-32, working for Paulson. Apparently he never moved to South Carolina, but seems to be identical with a Michael Harvey who died June 13, 1805 in Randolph Co., N.C. According to a descendant, Mrs. Ethel H. S. Russell of Mesa, Ariz., Michael Harvey and his wife Elizabeth had the following children:

I.   Lydia Harvey b. May 31, 1761, d. July 9, 1803, m. John Hobson.
II.   Jesse Harvey, b. Dec. 31, 1762, m. Keziah Ward.
III.   John Harvey, b. June 8, 1765.
IV.   Michael Harvey b. Aug. 17, 1767.
V.   Margaret Harvey b. Jan. 17, 1769.
VI.   William Harvey b. Feb. 12, 1771.
VII.   Sarah Harvey, b. Mar. 12, 1773.
VIII. Elizabeth Harvey b. April 3, 1775.
IX.   Mary Harvey b. Jan. 8, 1779.
X.   Jane Harvey b. Dec. 23, 1780.

Thomas[2] Harvey was probably also a son of John[1] and Mary Harvey. According to D.A.R. Lineage Book, XX, p. 39, he was born about 1730, a date which can not be far wrong, as his eldest son, John[3] Harvey was born in Virginia in 1749 or 1750. The D.A.R. line referred to states correctly that Thomas Harvey and his four sons, John, Evan, James and Michael Harvey, were all soldiers under Gen. Elijah Clarke; adds that Gen. Clarke said of Thomas that "he was a brave soldier"; and says that his wife was named Rachel. Thomas[2] Harvey never appears in Lunenburg Co. from 1748 on along with the other Harveys mentioned. He had probably already married before John[1] Harvey moved to Lunenburg, and remained in Brunswick Co., Va., where his father had his first land-grant, or else moved to North Carolina. Like John[1], William[1], and Charles[1] Harvey, he received land-grants in Craven Co., S.C., being the recipient of 6 grants in that county from 1765 to 1774. The first of these grants, dated July 15, 1765, was for 300 acres in "Williams 69 T.V.", which may be Williamsburg Township. The other five, totaling around 1000 acres, were all in Craven Co., the first being dated June 6, 1766 and the last Nov. 18, 1774. The index brackets the grants under the one name, Thomas Harvey, showing that they were all granted to one man. Salley's "Stub Indents to Revolutionary Claims in South Carolina" shows three payments to Thomas Harvey, one Oct. 2, 1784 to Capt. Thomas Harvey, late of Col. Hammond's Regiment (Books L-N, p. 77); another Nov. 26, 1785 to Mr. Thomas Harvey for the hire of a store and cellar for the Commissary of prisoners in 1780 (Books Y-Zm p. 67); and another May 21, 1786 to Thomas Harvey for the loss of a horse at the siege of Augusta (Books Y-Z, p. 167). It is not certain that all these payments were to Thomas[2] Harvey, as he had a son and cousin (son of William[1]) in South Carolina named Thomas Harvey, also. However, his Revolutionary services are proved from records in Georgia, which show that he, along with his sons, John, Evan, and Michael were granted land in 1783 "in a list brought down by John Harvey" (Candler, "Rev. Rec. of Ga.", II, 555); that he was granted land as a soldier in 1784 (Knight "Ga. Roster of Rev.", p. 263); and that he was in the list of soldiers and certified troops (Candler, IV, 383; Knight, p. 383; Smith "Story of Ga.", p. 617).

Thomas[2] Harvey, along with his sons, John, Evan, James and Michael, are all shown living in Wilkes Co., Ga. in 1785. The land granted them for Revolutionary services in Washington Co. fell into Greene Co. on the organization of that county, and the records show that Thomas[2] Harvey died in that county about 1792. On Feb. 29, 1792 John Harvey of Washington Co., Ga., Michael, Evan, and James Harvey of Greene Co., Ga. applied for letters of administration of the estate of Thomas Harvey, decd., of Greene Co., and they were granted April 3, 1792. (Greene Co. Court Minutes). A partial account of the estate, dated Jan. 1794 (p. 56 of the first Greene Co. Minute Book) shows payments to Ruth Harvey, Sally Harvey, Michael Harvey and John Harvey for what was apparently their share of the estate. Thomas Harvey's land fell into Hancock Co., Ga. on the organization of that county in 1793, and on Dec. 29, 1802 John, James, Michael and Evan Harvey of Hancock Co., admrs. of Thomas, decd., finally sold the land that had been granted Thomas in 1783.

In addition to John, Evan, James, Michael, Ruth and Sally Harvey, shown to be children of Thomas[2] Harvey by the above records, there were three other sons, Richard, Thomas and Nathan Harvey, all of whom predeceased their father, as shown by the following records: Richard Harvey died in Richmond Co., Ga., in 1781. His will, dated May 19, 1781 and probated Sept. 24, 1781, mentions child in esse; wife Mary; brothers Thomas and Nathan Harvey; wife Mary and friend Henry Graybill, exrs.; and Evan and James Harvey were appraisers of the estate ("Hist. Coll. Ga. Chapters D.A.R., II, 8). Richard Harvey was living in 96th Dist., S.C. in 1779, when he and James Harvey (son of Thomas[2] Harvey) witnessed the will of Dionysius Wright (same, work, p. 18). That Richard Harvey and his brothers, Thomas and Nathan Harvey, were brothers of John, Evan, Michael and James Harvey and sons of Thomas[2] Harvey, is shown by old 96th Dist., S.C. records at Abbeville, S.C., which show that John Harvey was appointed administrator of his brother, Thomas Harvey, in 1782 (W.B. "A & B", p. 9). Richard, Thomas, and Nathan Harvey were apparently younger brothers of John, Evan, James and Michael, as Richard was a young married man when he died in 1781, and Thomas apparently died young and unmarried. There is no further record of Nathan Harvey, who also probably died before his father. Richard Harvey, like his father and brothers, also served in the Revolution in South Carolina and Georgia, as Salley shows a payment to him in South Carolina June 23, 1785 for militia service, and the heirs of Richard Harvey were granted a soldier's grant in Washington Co., Ga. in 1784 (Candler IV, 225). A land order in Wilkes Co., Ga. in 1783 indicates that the unborn child of Richard Harvey's will

was named James Harvey and that the widow Mary had married
a man named Manna: "Ordered that James Harvey have 400
acres of land in lieu of an old land warrant of Marry Manna his
mother on the Beaverdam of Ogeechee".

John[3] Harvey, son of Thomas[2], was born in Virginia 1749-
50 and died in Clarke Co., Ga. in 1823 in his 74th year (these
dates being drawn from the date of probate of his will and his
biography in Jesse Mercer's "History of the Georgia Baptist
Denomination", published in 1836). His first wife was named
Margaret, as shown by a Greene Co., Ga. deed in 1788. His
second wife, whom he married about 1802 in Hancock Co.,
Ga., was named Patsy (Martha), and she married (2) about
1826 William McKay or McCoy in Clarke Co. John[3] Harvey
first appears in the records on Jan. 13, 1775, when "John Harvey of South Carolina with a wife and daughters aged three and
one year old" was authorized to take up 200 acres by the Georgia Land Court at Wrightsboro, Ga. Salley's "Indents" shows
that he was paid Aug. 23, 1785 and April 11, 1787 for militia
service in South Carolina during the Revolution and for a horse
lost in the service. His Revolutionary service and land-grants
as a Revolutionary soldier are shown by numerous records in
Georgia (Candler, II, 555; Knight "Ga. Roster", pp. 98, 262,
264, 265, 275, 314, and 417; Land Lottery of 1821, which shows
John Harvey, Revolutionary soldier, in Clarke Co.). John Harvey lived in Wilkes Co., Ga. with his father and three brothers
from 1784 to 1789. In the latter year he moved to Washington
Co., Ga.; was in Hancock Co., Ga. in 1802; and in 1808 moved
to Clarke Co., Ga., where he died. He was a pioneer Baptist
minister in Georgia, being called "a very distinguished and use-
ful minister in his day" in "The History of the Baptist Denomination in Georgia", published in 1881. He was a delegate to the
Georgia Baptist Association in 1802 and 1807, and was President of the Powellton Conference in 1802. John[3] Harvey's will,
dated Nov. 30, 1822 and probated in Clarke Co. July 27, 1823,
mentions the following legatees: (1) daughter Mary, decd.,
and her daughter Patsy; (2) daughter Ruth, decd., and her son
Isaac Kendrick; (3) son James, decd.; (4) daughter Rachel and
her son John Parrott; (5) daughter Sally; (6) son John; (7) son
Isaac; (8) son Willis; (9) three young sons, Elijah, Israel and
Willis, when they come of age; (10) daughter Claremond; (11)
wife Patsy, and at her death, property to be divided among the
four youngest children, Elijah, Israel, Willis, and Claremond.
The last four children were obviously children of the second
wife, Patsy, whom he married about 1802, as indicated by
deeds of gift made by him in May, 1802 in Hancock Co. to his
sons Isaac and John, and his grandchildren Patsy Talbot, Isaac
Kendrick, and John H. Parrott; and by a deed in Oct. 1803 from
John Harvey and Patsy his wife to their sons, John and Isaac
Harvey. The other children mentioned in the will were by the
first wife, Margaret. Of these older children, Mary was the
eldest (the three year old daughter mentioned in 1775, so born
about 1771-2). She married in 1787 Rev. Edmund Talbot, a
distinguished early Baptist minister (for their family see WM,

1st Series, IX, 258). Ruth Harvey was the second daughter (the one who was one year old in the 1775 record, so b. 1773-4). She married Benjamin Kendrick, son of James and Susannah (Roberson) Kendrick (see Kendrick Family for descendants). The son James Harvey died unmarried in Baldwin Co., Ga. in 1818. His will, dated Jan., 1808 and probated March 7, 1808, mentions his two brothers, John and Isaac Harvey; his sister, Sarah Fluker, wife of David Fluker; his nephew Burwell Kendrick; and his niece Susan Kendrick, both these children to be schooled. The daughter, Sarah Kendrick, married David Fluker, son of David and Jemima Fluker. This couple seems to have moved to East Feliciana Parish, La., along with other Fluker and Kendrick relatives, where Sarah Fluker died about 1841. They were probably the parents of Mary Theresa Fluker who married Kenyon Thompson Kendrick, and of David Jones Fluker, her brother, (b. 1809), who married Isabella Ann Kendrick, Kenyon's niece (see Kendrick Family). John Harvey, son of Rev. John[3] Harvey, moved to Jones Co., Ga., while his brother Isaac moved to Putnam Co., Ga., where he married Sally Napier 1808-16.

Evan[3] Harvey, son of Thomas[2] Harvey, was born in Virginia about 1751-52. He was probably the second son, as he was married to his first wife, Charity Powell, daughter of Moses and Mary (Williams) Powell, in St. Paul's Parish, Ga., March 3, 1774 (see Powell and Williams Families). The above date, along with dates of birth of children, etc., shown later, are from Evan Harvey's Family Bible. Charity (Powell) Harvey was born about 1756, and died Jan. 8, 1798. Evan Harvey married (2) in Hancock Co., Ga., Dec. 10, 1799, Ursula Jackson, known as "Tersh", said to have been a niece of Andrew Jackson. She was born Jan. 11, 1772 and died in Jasper Co., Ga. after 1850 (see Census of 1850, family of her youngest son, Evan Harvey). Evan Harvey served in the Revolution in South Carolina and Georgia under Gen. Elijah Clarke with the other members of his family. He was paid for militia service in South Carolina June 23, 1785 (Salley, Vol. 3, p. 260) and received land grants in Georgia for services in that State (Candler "Rev. Rec. of Ga.", II, 677; Smith "Story of Ga. and Ga. People", p. 618; Knight "Ga. Roster of Rev.", pp. 216, 326, and 383). Evan Harvey was living in Wilkes Co., Ga. in 1785, in Greene Co. in 1792, in Hancock in 1802, in Baldwin in 1807, and in Putnam Co. finally, his land falling into these various counties as they were organized. He died in Putnam Co., Ga. in 1814, his will, dated Oct. 4, 1812 and probated Dec. 12, 1814, mentioning his wife "Tersh", and all the following children except Sarah (who probably died young) and Evan (who was born after the will was written). Evan[3] Harvey and his first wife, Charity Powell, had the following children:

I. Mary Harvey b. Sept. 22, 1776. m. William[6] Clark (see Clark Clark Family).
II. Sarah Harvey b. June 4, 1780, apparently died young.
III. James Harvey b. Sept. 14, 1782.
IV. Moses Harvey b. April 14, 1784, m. the daughter of Mr.

Ichabod Cox of Jones Co., Ga. and left issue; "an exemplary member of the Baptist Church", according to his nephew, Judge James Clarke of Atlanta.

V.   Civility Harvey b. Feb. 15, 1786 m. Henry Coates of Putnam Co.; had one daughter, Mary L. Coates (b. 1805), who m. Allen Lawrence (b. 1796), and had the following children: (1) Adeline Lawrence m. Mr. Vaughan; (2) Henry Lawrence b. 1830 m. Mary T. Mullens, a Kendrick descendant (see Kendrick Family); (3) Evan H. Lawrence b. 1834; (4) Jeremiah Lawrence m. a Gorley; (5) Jackson Lawrence m. a Williams; (6) Cynthia Lawrence m. a Walker; (7) Civility Lawrence m. Rev. Edgar Jewell, a Baptist minister; (8) Mary Lawrence d. young.

VI.   Thomas Harvey b. April 15, 1788, m. Frances Coleman July 24, 1810 in Baldwin Co., Ga., and moved to Mississippi about 1810-15.

VII.   Benjamin Harvey b. May 13, 1790.

VIII. Richard Harvey b. Dec. 19, 1791, m. Rebecca Reid 1808-16 in Putnam Co.; moved to Mississippi with his brother Thomas.

IX.   Penelope Harvey b. Aug. 9, 1794, d. in Putnam Co., Ga., Sept. 1853, m. Nathanael Coates, brother of Henry Coates who married her sister Civility. They had four children; James, Alfred, Charity (who m. Mr. Adams) and Leslie Coates.

X.   Charity Harvey b. Dec. 1797, m. Meredith Kendrick (see Kendrick Family).

Evan[3] Harvey had by his second wife, Ursula Jackson:

XI.   Susannah Harvey b. Nov. 23, 1800, m. Robert Young; had six children, all of whom died young.

XII.   William Harvey, b. Dec. 1, 1802.

XIII. Joseph Harvey, b. Dec. 9, 1804

XIV. John Harvey b. Sept. 2, 1806.

XV.   Michael Harvey b. May 30, 1809.

XVI. Nancy Harvey b. Sept. 5, 1811, m. March 21, 1833 Freeland Buckner (b. May 8, 1802), son of Avery and Mary Buckner. They had six children:
1. Avery J. Buckner, b. Nov. 1, 1834;
2. Susan H. Buckner b. May 30, 1837;
3. William C.D., b. March 5, 1839;
4. Charity J., b. Dec. 30, 1841;
5. Mary F. b. March 5, 1844;
6. Sarah U. b. May 23, 1846.

XVII. Evan Harvey, Jr., b. April 24, 1814, m. Sarah -------- (b. 1807), and lived in Jasper Co., Ga.

James[3] Harvey, son of Thomas[2] Harvey, was born about 1755 and married Sarah Clark about 1777-79 in Edgefield Co., S.C. Like his father and brothers, he was a soldier in the Revolution. His wife was the daughter of John[5] and Judith (Mallett) Clark and a sister of William[6] Clark who married Mary, eldest daughter of Evan[3] Harvey. The descendants of James and Sarah (Clark) Harvey are given in the section on the Clark family.

Michael[3] Harvey, son of Thomas[2] Harvey, married Rebecca, who was apparently the daughter of Pinkethman Hawkins, as the couple had a son named Pinkethman Harvey and Michael[3] Harvey administered on the estate of Pinkethman Hawkins in 1782 in Abbeville Co., S.C. (Will Bk. "A" and "B", p. 9). This Pinkethman Hawkins was originally from Lunenburg Co., Va., and was appointed Captain of Militia there in 1756 in the French and Indian War. Michael Harvey's service in the Revolution is shown in Candler (II, 555), Smith (p. 617), and Knight (pp. 263, 265 and 383). He was living in Greene Co., Ga. in 1792, in Hancock in 1802, and in Baldwin in 1807. He died in Baldwin Co., Ga., in 1810. His sons, Pinkethman, William and Michael Harvey Jr., are shown in the tax-lists of Baldwin Co. from 1807 on to 1819. Michael[3] Harvey's will, dated March 30, 1810 and probated in Baldwin Co. June 4, 1810; mentions his wife Rebecca; sons William, Stephen and Michael; son Pinkey; daughter Elizabeth Howell (the home place adjoining William Howell, who was probably her husband); daughter Sally Barksdale; and daughters Polly, Martha and Rachel Harvey. Of the younger children of Michael[3] Harvey, Stephen was under age in 1807 and 1808, as he does not appear in the tax-lists of those years. He married Ann Barksdale Oct. 14, 1819 in Baldwin Co. The daughter Rachel was still under the guardianship of her brother William in 1819. Michael Harvey, Jr., was an older son and probably identical with a Michael Harvey who married Polly Clower in 1796 in Warren Co., Ga. Another son was probably Thomas Harvey, whose orphans and widow, Rebecca Harvey, are shown in Hancock Co., Ga. in the Land Lottery of 1806. In 1803 and 1805 Evan Harvey, orphan of Thomas Harvey, decd., was entrusted to the guardianship of Michael Harvey; and Rebecca and Verlinda Harvey, orphans of the same, were placed under the guardianship of William Spencer (Hancock Co. Court Minutes).

PETERSON AND THWEATT of PRINCE GEORGE

by B. J. Kincaid

John Peterson settled on Baylie's Creek in Charles City County, Virginia, prior to 1677. After 1702, this section became Prince George County. The parentage of John Peterson and where he came from are not known. As early as 1624, a John Peterson owned 100 Acres at the falls of the James River (Hotten). In 1661 and 1662, a John Peterson, Jr., "Merchant of Bristol, England", appears in the records of Rappahannock County, Va. In 1670, a John Peterson was naturalized by the Virginia Assembly. (Henning 2, p. 308). A Christian Peterson was naturalized the following year.

John Peterson of Charles City seems to have married a daughter of Col. Henry Soane of James City County, Speaker of the House of Burgesses 1660-1661. On 11/24/1652, Henry Soane was granted 297 acres in James City for transporting Henry Soane, Sr., Henry Soane, Jr., John Soane, Judith Soane, Sr., Judith Soane, Jr., and Eliza Soane to Virginia. (Patent Book 2, 352). The following record is on file in Henrico County:

"Whereas, by order of the Henrico Court, dated ye first June last, I was ordered and appointed to set out and divide the saw mill, divideth; of land on the north side of Swift Creek in ye said county between John Peterson, son and heir of John Peterson, dec'd.; Capt. Peter Field; and ye orphans of Capt. Henry Randolph (Vizt.), the lower most fourth part to the orphans, the next one-fourth part to Capt. Field and ye uppermost part to John Peterson which I have accordingly done in the presence of Capt. William Randolph and Mr. Richard Kennon, the whole containing 416 acres as also the particular parts being on the above plot, plainly laid, sworn and demonstrated, this 28th day of July, 1693, signed John Soane."

Judith Soane, daughter of Col. Henry Soane, married (1) Henry Randolph and (2) Peter Field.

From this record it would appear that John Peterson married a daughter of Henry and Judith Soane, probably the Elizabeth Soane mentioned in the land grant of 1652, and had issue one son, John Peterson, that survived.

John Peterson, the emigrant, may have died relatively young. On June 25, 1678, the suit of John Peterson vs. John Coggin was dismissed, the plantiff being ill. (Charles City O. B. 1677-1679, p. 308). John Peterson died soon thereafter; for, on 2/19/1679 (ibid: p. 354), Abraham Odium and his wife petitioned the Court of Charles City - "that John Peterson, lately dec'd., sometime before his death, declared it to be his desire that the said Odium should have the management and tuition of his children and their

158

estate; therefore,he, the said Odium, prays commission of administration may be granted unto him -- he giving security that the mill and plantatiou be kept in good repair and order, the mill to be kept at work for the benefit of the orphans, and that the said Odium bring in a true and perfect inventory of the said estate at the next court..."

The relationship of Odium to John Peterson is not known. An Abraham Odium is listed in the rent rolls of Nansemond Co. in 1704. Odium mismanaged the estate and the following records appear in the court held Dec. 3, 1679 (ibid-417):

"Whereas the estate of John Peterson, dec'd., consisting of a mill and other perishable things, which, without great care taken thereof, and whereas Abraham Odium, now in possession of the said estate, cannot find security for administration - nor doth take such care as is needful for preserving the sd. estate, which being seriously considered by the court, doth think fitt to remove the estate and put the same into the care of Mr. Henry Batte; but Mr. Batte, objecting that ye mill, being the most considerable part of the estate, is daily exposed to ye violence of the Indian enemy, who, by fire,or otherwise, may destroy ye same. If, therefore, the court will grant and allow that, in case of such fire, or otherwise, done by the Indians to the sd. mill, that the proper estate of him, the said Batt, may not be lyable to make ye same good to the orphan, when of age, that then he would accept administration upon ye said estate and of the guardianship of the orphan, to which the court consents and agree to, with that reservation - commission of administration is granted to Capt. Henry Batt on the estate of John Peterson, dec'd., for the performance of which office Maj. John Stith becomes security."

John Peterson (2), second of the name, only surviving issue of John Peterson and his wife, Elizabeth Soane, appears on the Charles City Jury list in 1694; and, hence, he was born at least prior to 1673. He died in Isle of Wight in 1731. The name of his wife (or wives) is not known. Since he had a son named Batte, it has long been assumed that he married a member of the Batte family. However, this connection cannot be authenticated by existing records. The will of Henry Batte has been destroyed and it is possible that he had an older daughter, not mentioned in the will of Henry Batte, Jr., (S.V.F.1-26), who could have married John Peterson. It seems probable that John Peterson named his son Batte out of gratitude to Capt. Henry Batte who became his guardian (see above) and saved his estate from ruin. It would appear from John Peterson's will, that he married (1) or (2) a widow named Brown, the mother of Jeremiah and Burrell Brown, mentioned in his will. John Peterson was a Justice of the County Court for Prince George (Order Book 1714-1720, p. 187).

On November 12, 1723, John Peterson of Bristol Parish sold to John Fitzgerald the water grist mill and corn mill called Froghole mill on Bailey's Creek in Prince George County, three tracts of land (1) 118 acres, as by deed dated Jan. 26, 1677, from Francis Whittington to John Peterson, the feoffer, as heir at law to sd. John Peterson, dec'd; (2) 60 acres, as by deed dated October 11, 1703, from Henry Batte to John Peterson, the feoffer,

which said land descended to sd. Henry Batte, as heir at law to
his father, Henry Batte; and (3) 95 acres purchased by John
Peterson, the feoffer, by deed dated May 12, 1703 (P. George
Deeds, 1713-1728, p. 658). This was the mill built by the first
John Peterson. Fitzgeralds, on Froghole Millpond, was the
site of the Prince George County Court for many years.

On Jan. 10, 1723, John Peterson, Sr. of Isle of Wight Co.,
deeded to his son, John Peterson, Jr., of Prince George, two
tracts of land, 100 acres at the head of Froghole Millpond,
Bristol Parish, and a tract on west run (P. G. Deeds 1713-1718,
p. 679). John Peterson, Sr., built another mill on Bailey's
Creek and this property continued in the possession of his descendants until about 1870.

From 1715 until his death in 1731, John Peterson (2) acquired, by purchase and patent, several thousand acres of land
in Isle of Wight County, later Brunswick, on both sides of the
Meherrin River and moved to that section to live about 1723.
He seems to have resided in what is now Greensville County.
His will, dated March 1, 1731, probated January 24, 1731-32,
Isle of Wight, (B. 3, p. 292), mentions sons, John and Batte;
daughters, Mary Spain, Judith Thweatt and Ann Thweatt; grandson, John Eppes; Jeremiah Brown, Burrell Brown, John Smith
and Mathew Parham. The last four named persons were devised
tracts of land in the will; but their relationship to John Peterson,
if any, is not known. John Eppes, grandson of John Peterson,
may have been the son of a daughter who predeceased her father;
or issue, by a previous marriage, of one of the three daughters
mentioned above.

John[2] Peterson had issue:

I.   John[3] Peterson, of whom later;
II.   Batte Peterson of whom later;
III. Mary Peterson, m. William Spain of Prince George.
      Issue (B. P. R.):
      1. John[4] Spain, born March 22, 1721.
      2. William Spain, Jr., born March 9, 1723.
      3. Joshua Spain, born July 10, 1725.
      4. Eliza Spain, born May 30, 1731.
      5. Batte Peterson Spain, born September 9, 1733.
IV.   Judith Peterson m. John Thweatt, of whom later;
V.   Ann Peterson m. James Thweatt, whose identity is un-
      known to this writer.

John Peterson[3], son of John[2] Peterson and ----------. A
John Peterson in Prince George married Frances (surname
unknown); and had two children whose births are listed in the
Bristol Parish Register. By 1732, a John Peterson had married
Martha Thweatt and had issue. There is disagreement among
the genealogists of the Peterson family as to whether this rep-
resents father and son; or whether it is the same John Peterson
who was married twice. This point cannot be clarified in the
fragmentary records of Prince George County. Figures, after
names, indicating the generation, after the first John Peterson,
are omitted hereafter in this branch, because of the uncertainty
indicated above. In 1723, John Peterson[3], Jr., was Adm. of
Mary Eppes, widow of John Eppes. It is possible that John Pe-

terson, Jr.'s, wife was related to this Mary Eppes.

Issue of John and Fanny Peterson from B.P.R.:

I. Nathaniel, born November 12, 1720. Nothing further known.
II. William, born October 25, 1723. Nothing further known.

By 1731, a John Peterson married Martha Thweatt, according to a family memoir left by John Herbert Peterson. The grandson of this couple, John Peterson, died in October, 1773. According to the same authority, and from the Parish Register, John Peterson and Martha Thweatt, whose parentage is unknown, had issue:

I. Nathaniel, born April 25, 1732, N.F.K.
II. Martha, born circa 1734, married Robert Batte.
III. Peter, born prior to 1741.
IV. Mary, m. Francis Poythress.
V. Frances, born 1745, m. James Parsons, but had no issue.
VI. John, born 1749, died 1773, unmarried (Va. Gazette, Feb. 1773).
VII. Thos. Peterson, born circa 1751, of whom later.

Thomas Peterson, son of John, born circa 1751, died 1788. On Jan. 30, 1778 he sold to John Sturdivant, Jr., 200 acres in Brunswick County, "a moiety of a tract of 400 Acres, sold by Lewis Parham to John Peterson; and devised to Thomas Peterson by the last Will and Testament of his father, John Peterson, dec'd., on record in the County Court of Prince George". (Brunswick Co. D.B. 13, p. 55). Thomas Peterson married Elizabeth Claiborne, daughter of Col. Augustine Claiborne of Sussex (V.H.G.). The marriage bond was dated, Sussex County, June 15, 1775. The will of Thomas Peterson, June 24, 1782/ Sept. 8, 1789, left his whole estate to his wife Elizabeth, and appointed his friends, Maj. William Claiborne and John Cocke of Sussex County, Executors (P.G. W & D B. 1787-1792, Part 1, p. 305). According to the Prince George Tax Lists, he left an estate of 600 acres. Elizabeth Claiborne, wife to Thomas Peterson, was born in 1758 and died in 1794. They had issue:

I. John Herbert Peterson, of whom later.
II. Thomas Peterson, married Sarah, daughter of Col. Peter Eppes of Prince George County, and died without issue in 1809.
III. Augustine Peterson (1783-1803), no issue.
IV. Ann Peterson, died young in 1794.

John Herbert Peterson, (Circa. 1777-1829), son of Thomas Peterson, married April 9, 1795, his first cousin, Mary Herbert Harrison, daughter of Charles Harrison and Mary Herbert Claiborne. John H. Peterson lived on the original Peterson property on Bailey's Creek, Prince George County. About 1828 he wrote an interesting memoir on the Peterson and Claiborne families.. While incorrect, as far as the early generations are concerned, it gives a great deal of information on John Peterson's immediate contemporaries. This manuscript was published in W 2 (2) pp. 1-20.

John H. Peterson and Mary H. Harrison had issue:

I. John Augustine Peterson, of whom later.
II. Lucy Ann Peterson, b. 1801, d. Oct. 1828, married

William H. Young. No issue.

III. Maria Harrison Peterson, married John Prentiss, son of William Prentiss of Petersburg, and had: John Peterson, Thomas Augustine and Maria Prentiss.

See carefully prepared articles in Southside Virginia Families, Boddie, 1955, by Dr. Claiborne Thweatt Smith, Jr., Chapel Hill, N.C. of progeny of John Augustine Peterson (1798-1879). Dr. Smith also prepared nearly all of this Peterson work.

Batte[3] Peterson, b. circa 1700, resided in Brunswick County, Va. John Peterson of Prince George deeded land to his brother, Batte Peterson, April 18, 1750 (Brunswick Co. D.B. 4, p. 148). Batte Peterson deeded 920 acres to his son, John Peterson, March 28, 1750 (Brunswick D.B. 4, p. 137). He died intestate in Brunswick County in 1751 or 1752. The inventory of his estate, dated March, 1752, was signed by John Peterson, who appears to have been his only son, and perhaps his only child. There is no indication as to the name of the mother of his child or children. He was Captain of Militia in Brunswick County (Order Book 3, p. 452, October 6, 1748).

Batte[3] Peterson had issue:

I. John Peterson, of whom later;
and some genealogists believe that he had:

II. Martha Peterson, who married Timothy Thorpe, whose will, Sept. 5, 1763-Oct. 13, 1763, Book 2, pp. 59-62, mentions wife, Martha; sons, Peterson and Timothy, daughter, Betty Atherton, Mary Person, Lucy Simmons and Temperance, Silva and Patty Thorpe; granddaughter, Martha Jarrell. Peterson Thorpe married Mary Person and moved to Granville Co., N.C., where he left numerous descendants. On August 14, 1766, John Peterson of Brunswick gave Peterson Thorpe of Southampton 420 acres in said County, which might indicate relationship above;
and possibly:

III. Christian Peterson.

John[4] Peterson, only known son of Batte[3] Peterson (Circa 1720-1769) lived on the Meherrin River in Brunswick County. A marriage agreement between John Peterson and Boyce Brewer was recorded in Brunswick County February 28, 1765. The name of a previous wife of John Peterson, the mother of his children, is not known. In 1759 his first wife's first name was Martha (Brunswick D.B. 6, p. 451). From the given names of her children, and from the fact that she had a son named Kinchen, it is possible that she was a Kinchen or of Kinchen descent. The will of John Peterson, May 16, 1763-Jan. 23, 1768, was recorded in Brunswick County, where he was Captain of Militia (Order B. 3, p. 452, 1748).

He had issue:

I. Batte[5] Peterson, of whom later.

II. William Peterson. On September 25, 1794, he, as "William Peterson of Northampton Co., N.C.", deeded to Kinchen Peterson, Jr., all the land in Greensville Co., Va., devised to sd. William "by his father John Peterson"

(Greensville D.B. 2, p. 208). He seems to have died in Northampton Co. intestate. He married (1) Sally Williamson, Southampton Co. (M.B. 4/7/1765); and (2) Sarah Bass, age 35, Greensville (M.B. March 11, 1797.) No record of issue.

III. John Peterson moved to Northampton County, N.C. He married Martha, daughter of Thomas Barrett of Northampton (M.B. 1770-1808, p. 2), and died intestate in 1799. He was a member of the North Carolina Constitutional Convention in 1788; and was sheriff of Northampton County. The will of his widow, Martha (Bertie Co., N.C., Jan. 30, 1805/1808) mentioned her sons, Henry, Thomas, Jacqueline and Robert Peterson. Henry Peterson represented Northampton in the N.C. assembly in 1797. His will was probated in Bertie in 1811.

IV. Kinchen (5) Peterson also moved to Northampton County, N.C. He married Ann Stanton. No issue. His will, dated Aug. 5, 1796, Northampton Co. March 1799. (Proof for Ann Stanton, sister of Frederick Stanton, Northampton D.B. 12, p. 25).

V. Temperance Peterson married Henry Taylor (M.B. Dec. 20, 1768), and had issue.

VI. Mary Peterson - N.F.K.

VII. Martha Peterson married Joseph Gurley, Southampton Co. (M.B. May 11, 1772). Nothing further known.

VIII. Patience Peterson, nothing further known.

IX. Rebecca Peterson married (1) Peterson Thweatt, (2) Jesse Grigg, May 27, 1783.

X. Elizabeth Peterson m. James Thweatt, of whom later.

XI. Lucy Peterson married Edwin Lundy (M.B. Feb. 3, 1788); nothing further known.

Batte[5] Peterson, son of John[4], lived in Greensville County, Virginia, formed from Brunswick and Southampton. He married Mary Taylor, daughter of Etheldred Taylor and Patience Kinchen of Southampton County, Va. (M.B. Dec. 15, 1762). She was the sister of Henry Taylor who married Batte's sister, Temperance Peterson (V 22, pp. 446-447, 23V., p. 105). His will, 1795, was probated in Greenville Co. (W.B. 1, p. 269). They had issue:

I. Mason[6] Taylor Peterson, married Person Turner (M.B. Feb. 16, 1796).

II. Ann Peterson married Joseph Turner (M.B. Feb. 19, 1785).

III. John Peterson, died in Hancock County, Ga., in 1806, apparently on a visit, as his family remained in Greensville. His will, made in Georgia, and probated in Greensville Co. Va. (W.B.2, p. 126) devised one-third of his estate to his wife and two-thirds to his children, not named. In 1810 Simon Turner gave a legal title to land conveyed from Joseph Turner to John Peterson, dec'd., to Dolly, widow of John Peterson, and the four children listed below. (Greensville D.B. 4, p. 147). John Peterson married (1) Miss Greenway, daughter of Dr. James

Greenway of Dinwiddie County, and sister to his brother Kinchen's wife. Dr. Greenway was a physician and a noted botanist. John Peterson married (2) Dolly Sturdivant, Sussex (M.B. 1801). The issue is uncertain, but the children were probably by the first wife.

1. Rebecca[7] Ann Peterson, nothing further known.
2. Batte Peterson, nothing further known.
3. Mary Greenway Peterson married Littleberry Robinson (M.B. Dec. 14, 1818).
4. Martha Dixon Peterson married Charles R. Eaton (M.B. Nov. 18, 1820).

IV. Kinchen Peterson married Martha Greenway, daughter of Dr. James Greenway. The will of Kinchen Peterson, dated 1819, appears in Greensville Co. W.B. 3, p. 137. They had issue:

1. Dr. John[7] Peterson, died unmarried, in Northampton Co., N.C. in 1826.
2. Eliza M.G. Peterson, nothing further known.
3. Margaret G. Edwards Peterson, m. John H. Edwards ((M.B. Oct. 5, 1816).
4. Mary Ann G. Peterson, married Richard Malone (M.B. April 1, 1833).
5. Martha Dixon G. H. Peterson m. Joseph Crump (M.B. Sept. 10, 1824).

C. Peter Peterson, Greensville Co., Va., m. Elizabeth Barham Newsome, daughter of Randolph Newsom of Southampton Co., Va. (1755-1819) and his first wife, Sarah Mason. The will of Peter Peterson, dated 1819, was probated in Greensville Co. (W.B. 3, p. 101). The will of his wife, Elizabeth, dated 1848, was probated in W.B. 8, p. 349. They had issue:

1. Sarah[7] Mason Peterson, m. John Norfleet Blunt, (M.B. May 28, 1822). They resided at "Belmont", in eastern Greensville, and had 9 children, among whom Ann Eliza (1825-1862) m. Robert Ridley.
2. Mary E. L. Peterson m. Edward Drinkard (M.B. June 2, 1828).
3. Ann P. Peterson, posthumous child, m. John M. Rives (M.B. July 25, 1833).

The name, James Thweatt (Thweat) occurs many times in the few available documents in Henrico, Charles City and Prince George Counties, Virginia, between 1670 and 1760. The emigrant was likely James Thweat who received Patent, April 22, 1670, for 600 acres in Charles City County, "S. Side Appomattock River, on Bayleyes Creeke, adjoining Robert Coleman, Jr.", for 12 Headrights, including James Thweate. This is the earliest evidence found of a Thweatt in Virginia. On March 15, 1672-73, he was granted 550 acres, again on "S. Side of Appomattock River in Charles City County, adjoining his former grant (of 600 acres ?) and also adjoining Robert Coleman; and on Baylies Run, and extending to ye Blackwater", for 13 Headrights, of which "James Thweate" was one. On April 20, 1682, he and "Mr. Henry Bates" (one Thweatt genealogist believes this was Capt. Henry Batte) were granted 673 acres, 2 road and 6 poles in Charles City County on S. Side of James River "in the Parish of Jordanes (?)", adjoining Jon. Evingame, Wm. Edmonds and Edward Adington, "crossing the great swampe", for 14 Headrights. On April 20, 1689, James Thweat, Sen'r., was granted 673 acres in Charles City County, Bristol Parish "on S. Side of Appomattock River, adjoining Henry Batte (?) & Edward Birchett", for 3 Headrights. On April 24, 1703, James Thweat was granted 234 acres, 3 Rood, 10 Poles, in "Bristole" Parish, Henrico County, on "N. Side of Appomattock River", for 5 Headrights. This land had previously been part of a Patent of 784 Acres, 3 Rood, 10 Poles, to George Archer, September 25, 1671; and Archer deserted it. On the same day, James Thweat was granted 223 Acres, 2 Rood, in Birstol Parish, Henrico County, "on N. Side of Appomattock River", for 5 Headrights, "adjoining Col. Thomas Ligon, George Archer and Major Genr. Wood, on old Town River."

It is impossible for this writer to state that the foregoing Patents were issued to the same James Thweatt, although it seems likely that one man received all of them. He cannot identify certainly the James Thweatts who received the next Patents listed:

1. October 31, 1716, 180 Acres in Isle of Wight County, to James Thweatt of Prince George County, on N. Side of Meherin River, on East side of Island Swamp.

2. September 5, 1723, 300 Acres in Prince George County, to James Thweatt, Jr. of Prince George County, on both sides of Butterwood Swamp, adjoining James Anderson and Thomas Nunnally.

3. November 5, 1730, 360 acres in Brunswick County to James Thweatt, Jr., of Prince George County, on S. Side of Little Nottoway River, below Batt's ford, on Horsepen Branch.

4. July 10, 1745, 103 Acres in Prince George County to James Thweatt on upper side of Butterwood Swamp, adjoining his own and Wm. Coleman's lines. He might have been James Thweatt, Jr. (9/5/1723, 300 acres above). He also might be James Thweatt who married Sarah Sturdivant, and son of John Thweatt and Judith Peterson.

5. September 10, 1755, 205 acres in Brunswick County, to James Thweatt, (County of residence not shown) on Occaneechy Swamp, 125 Acres having been granted, February 20, 1733, to Robert Ellice, and adjoining Wm. Batts, Eades Smith, Thos. Smith, James Parham. This might be also James Thweatt who married Sarah Sturdivant.

Since so many of the records of Charles City and Henrico Counties, 1670-1730, and of Prince George County, 1704-1715, and after 1730, are destroyed, we have not been able to trace the disposition of the thousands of acres patented and purchased by one or several James Thweatts, 1670-1735.

CHARLES CITY COUNTY ORDERS, 1677-1679:
p. 168. "Judgment for Thomas Swann, vs. James Thrate, Circa. 1677".

p. 170. "James Thrate" was a Trial Juror, Circa. 1677, "Richard Wathen vs. Mary Rose."

p. 164. "James Thrate" was a Trial Juror, Ca. "1678."

p. 301. "George Holton, June 3, 1678, servant to James Thweat, Judged att twelve years of age."

p. 320. "Daniel Sanbourn, bein sued by Robert Bolling, p'lt. & appearing by his attorney, James Thweatt, prays a reference, w'ch upon promise to produce six hundred & fifty pounds Tob. & Casq., with cost of.....in his hands & ......, Aug. 15, 1678."

p. 339. "Nonsuite granted Mr. Thweet vs. Mr. Bolling, noe cause of accon appearing. 12/3/1678."

CHARLES CITY COUNTY ORDERS, 1687-1695:

p. 226. "This Courte requests Capt. Henry Batte to divide ye difference between Judith, ye relict of Jno. Lee, dec'd., & James Thweatt, it being a very inconsiderable matter. Court of 8/5/1689 (or of Sept. following)."

p. 371. "To Ja. Thweat, the Levey in Anno., 1691, (December) 1 Wolves' head, 200 :lbs. Tobo:"

p. 433. "To James Thwait, at a Levy Courte 11/3/1692, a Woolf, 200 lbs. Tobo."

p. 440. "James Thweat, Joshua Wynn and John Mayes 'with the advise of Capt. Henry Batt, were Survey'rs of the highways in these parts --- a new great road insteed of that over Frogg hole dam'."

p. 444. "James Thweat & John Mayes assigned by the Justices, as Overseers for the Highways for Appomattox, 1/3/1692-93."

p. 458. "Uppon the Compl't of James Thweat, Survey'r of the Highways of the lower precinct of Bristoll Parish, against Edward Hughes, 6/5/1693, for stopping upp the highway, threw the inhabitants on the South side of Baylies Runn, have been a long time Wanted to pass to Church and the river. Ordered. that the said Edward Hughes either leave a sufficient land for the highway affors'd, or otherwise ...... "

p. 482. "Mr. James Thweat & Mr. Robt. Tucker for Apamatox (Assigned by the Court, Surveyors for the Highways). Levy Court, December (?), 1693."

PRINCE GEORGE COUNTY ORDERS AND RETURNS OF EXE- CUTIONS, 1714-1720:

p. 358, Part 2. "James Thweatt signed as Corroner, 11/4/1714."

p. 101. "James Thweatt took deposition of Appraisers of Estate of James Boreman, 11/13/1716."

p. 101. "James Thweatt took deposition of Appraisers of Estate of Robert Birchet, 11/13/1716."

p. 102. "James Thweatt took deposition of Appraisers of Estate of ------------. Appraisers: Wm. Stainback & George Woodcliffe, 11/15/1716."

p. 104. "James Thweatt took deposition of Appraisers of property attached for debt for Mathew Smart, Jr., under order of the Court of 11/13/1716."

p. 104. "James Thweatt took deposition of Appraisers of property attached for debt for George Rives, 11/15/1716, under order of the Court of 11/13/1716."

p. 104. "James Thweatt took deposition of Appraisers of property attached for debt for Robert Bolling, 11/15/1716, under order of the Court of 11/13/1716."

p. 105. "James Thweatt took deposition of Appraisers of property attached for debt for Peter Wynne, 11/15/1716-11/13/1716."

p. 105. "James Thweatt, Justice, gave verdict against Henry Ledbetter for Hugh Lee, 2/5/1716-17."

p. 117. "The Sheriff makes return of the appraisement of the Estate of Hubbard Gibson attacht. for James Thweatt, 4/9/1717. Appraised by William Batte, Robert Poythress & Edward Mitchell, the appraisers first sworn by me, John Peterson."

p. 119. "James Thweatt Vs. Mathew Sturdivant, 4/9/1717, Dismissed, neither party appearing."

p. 142. "David Crawley Vs. James Thweatt, 8/13/1717, Pl't failing to prosecute, case is dismissed."

p. 142. "George Robertson Vs. James Thweatt, action of debt, 8/13/1717. Thomas Simmons became Special Bail for the said debt, whereupon Oyer of the Plt's Bond is granted him and time till the next Court to consider same."

p. 147, Pt. 1. "Judgment of 16352 lbs. Tobacco was given George Robertson Vs. James Thweatt, 9/10/1717, 'Unless he shall appear at the next Court and answer the said Action'." No further reference to this was found.

p. 143. "James Thweatt and John Peterson, Gents," were among Justices, "9/10/1717."

pp. 187, 188, pt. 2. "James Thweatt, 6/10/1718, sworn Sheriff. He, John Simmons and David Crawley gave Ł 1000 Sterling, Bond."

p. 197, Pt. 2. "On petition of Hugh Lee, it is ordered that James Baugh be overseer of the Nottoway River Road from John Coleman's, on Appomattox River, to the South end of Blackwater Bridge, and that the male labouring titheable persons of Capt. James Thweatt, Henry Thweatt, John Thweatt, David Crawley, Thomas Gregory, Edward Burchett, James Anderson, Edmond Browder, Daniel Vaughn & Thomas Spain assist in clearing the said road, 8/12/1718."

p. 359, Pt. 2. "James Thweatt, Sheriff, signed Execution, 7/8/1718, Cornelius Fox Vs. Wm. Wallis."

p. 220, Pt. 2. "James Thweatt," Court, 12/10/1718, For Wolves Killed,"100 Lbs. Tobo:".

p. 220, Pt. 2. "James Thweatt," Court, 12/10/1718, "Sherr: for the County Service, 1 year, 1080 lbs. Tobo:"

p. 266, Pt. 2. "More goods attached of Est. of David Colyshaw, for John Peterson, P. one James Thweatt, Sheriff, Ł 1:16:9, 6/9/1719. Appraised 6/8/1719 by Henry Wm. Batte."

p. 275, Pt. 2. "In the action bro't by Thomas Goodwyn, ag'st. John Poythres for Ł 34:6:3 due by acco't., the def't being arrested and not appearing nor any security returned for him, on the Motion of the Plt'f's Atty., Judgement is granted him ag'st the said def'd't, and James Thweatt, Sherr: for the sd. sum and costs, unless the said Def't. shall appear at the next Court and answer the said action. 7/14/1719."

p. 276, Pt. 2. "Honor Coleman (the wife of Francis), letter of Atty. to Edward Goodrich, was proved by Oaths of James Thweatt and Richard Smith, witnesses thereto, and ordered to be Recorded. 8/11/1719."

p. 292, Pt. 2. "On the petition of James Baugh, it is ordered that Geo. Rives, Wm. Eaton, Jno. Thweatt, Henry Thweatt, James Thweatt, Thos. Gregory & Daniel Vaughn be summoned to the next Court to answer the same. '11/10/1719."

p. 294, Pt. 2. "James Thweatt, as Sheriff, apparently collected the necessary money from Est. of Stephen Cater (?), as his attachments were dismist. for failure to prosecute. 11/10/1719."

p. 297, Pt. 2. "To James Thweatt, Sherr: 11/11/1719, For the County Service & Casks, 1080 Lbs. Tobacco."

p. 297, Pt. 2. "Ord. that James Thweatt, Sher: of this Co. pay the several claims of 4673 Lbs. Tob:, At a Court, 11/11/1719."

p. 304, Pt. 2. "Apparently James Thweatt's term of office as Sheriff was expiring soon, or had expired. See Court, 3/8/1719-20."

p. 309, Pt. 2. "The Attach. awarded James Thweatt, Sherr: Vs. Est. of Wm. Jackson, is cont. until the next Court, 3/8/1719-20."

p. 325, Pt. 2. "James Thweatt Vs. Est. Wm. Jackson, 6/14/1720, the Attach. dismist, neither party appearing in Court."

p. 346, Pt. 2, "Drury Bolling Vs. James Thweatt, 1/10/1720-21. James Thweatt defaulted, Ł 5:11:5 and John Peterson was his Security. Remanded to next Court."

p. 347, Pt. 2. "James Thweatt, Court, 1/11/1720-21, was paid 100 lbs. Tobacco for killing one wolfe."

p. 350, Pt. 2. "Ord. that a road be cleared from Peter Wynne's to James Thweatt's p'antation, whereon Edward Burchett formerly lived, the Antient & most convenient way, and that John Peterson be overseer. 2/14/1720-21."

p. 353, Pt. 2. "James Thweatt Vs. John Inglas, 2/14/1720-21, dismist. Plt. failed to prosecute."

p. 14. "Robert Munford and James Thweatt, present, Court, May 10, 1715." (Did not say for what. They likely were Justices.)

p. 24. "John Peterson & William Batte against Richard Flint, indebtedness of Ł 30 Sterling, Bill, March 14, 1714-15, they having obtained an attachment under the hand of James Thweatt, one of his Majesty's Justices. Court of June 14, 1715. Pl't'fs to have bill & costs, etc."

p. 45. "On motion of James Thweatt, it is entered that he refused to allow the Burgesses the tobacco above levied and allowed them. Court of December 13, 1715."

p. 51. "John Poythress and James Thweatt and others appearing in Court, take the usual oaths, sign the tests and are, accordingly, sworn Justices of this County, pursuant to a Commission of the Peace (?), etc., dated the 8th day of December, 1715. Court of 3/13/1715-16."

p. 53. "Ordered that Capt. James Thweatt, administer the oath of Constable to Henry Thweatt, and that Thomas Clay,

present Constable, summon the said Henry Thweatt to appear
before the said James Thweatt for that purpose. Court of April
13, 1716."

p. 56. "The action depending between James Thweatt and George
Still, neither party appearing, dismissed, Court of 4/13/1716."

p. 87. "James Thweatt, present as one of the Justices, Court
of 11/13/1716."

p. 89. "James Thweatt, Assignee of David Duke, made com-
plaint that Hubbard Gibson stands indebted to him, Assignee,
the sum of 16 good, well drest Doe skins, etc., by Bill dated
11 July, 1711, Court of 11/13/1716."

p. 93. "James Thweatt and John Peterson, Justices, Present,
Court of 11/13/1716, Court for laying County Leavy."

p. 94. "To James Thweatt, Coroner for ye Inquist of John Nesbitt, 133 pounds of tobacco, Court of 11/13/1716."

PRINCE GEORGE COUNTY DEEDS, ETC., 1713-1728:
Deeds of James Thweatt (Grantor or Grantee):

Pt. 1, pp. 49, 50. "James Thweatt, etux, Judith, L. & R. to
John Cureton, 200 acres, 4/8-9/1715."

Pt. 1, pp. 56, 57. "James Thweatt, etux, Judith, L. & R. to
Edward Mitchell, 40 acres, 6/13-14/1715."

Pt. 2, pp. 197, 198. "James Thweatt, etux, Judith, L. & R.
to Wm. Eaton, 200 Acres, 1/11-12/1717-18."

Pt. 4, pp. 528, 529. "James Thweatt only, Mtg. to David
Crawley & John Simmons, of 4 Slaves, for being James Thweatt's
security as Pr. Geo. Sheriff, 10/16/1721."

Pt. 4, pp. 715-17. "James Thweatt only, Deed to John Thweatt,
60 Acres, 6/8/1724."Pt. 4, pp. 717, 718. "J

Pt. 4, pp. 717, 718. "James Thweatt, etux, Judith, Deed to
Samuel Jordan, 90 Acres, 6/8/1724."

Pt. 6, pp. 985, 986. "James Thweatt, only, Deed to his son,
Miles Thweatt, 10 Acres, 5/8/1727."

p. 51. "James Thweatt, Wit., L. & R., 5/10/1715, John Price
to Samuel Lee."

p. 98. "James Thweatt, Wit., L. & R., 2/14/1715-16, Nathan-
iell Urvin to David Crawley."

p. 106. "James Thweatt, Wit., L. & R., 4/10/1716, Mathew
Anderson to James Anderson."

p. 113. "John Peterson and William Batte, Administrators,
Est. of Joseph Holycross, 6/12/1716, Appraisers, John Thweatt,
James Thweatt."

p. 138. "James Thweatt, Wit., L. & R., Henry Mayes to Daniel Nance, 2/12/1716-17."

p. 141. "James Thweatt, Wit., Bond, Mathew Anderson to
Daniel Nance. 2/12/1716-17."

p. 184. "James Thweatt, Wit., Deed, William Grigg to John
Peterson, 8/13/1717."

p. 189. "James Thweatt & Daniel Sturdivant, Wit., Writ, James
Parram to Lewis Green, 10/8/1717."

p. 193. "James Thweatt, Wit., Deed, James Parram to Lewis
Green, 11/12/1717."

p. 194. "James Thweatt, Wit., L. & R., Wm. Temple to Sam
Temple, 11/12/1717."

p. 203. "James Thweatt, Wit., L. & R., Wm. Mayes to Buller Herbert. 1/14/1717-18."

p. 237. "James Thweatt. Wit., Deed of L. Mathew Marks to Thomas Harrison, 7/8/1718."

p. 255. "James Thweatt, Wit., Deed, John Womack to Hannah Headworth, 10/14/1718."

p. 341. "James Thweatt, Wit., Letter of Attorney, Honor Coleman, to 'my trusty friend, Edward Goodrich', to relinquish dower in deed, Francis Coleman to Wm. Persons, 4/14/1719."

p. 349. "James Thweatt & James Thweatt, Jr., Wit., L. & R., James Anderson to Richard Cureton, 9/7/1719-9/8/1719."

p. 377. "James Thweatt. Wit., L. & R., Thomson Stapley to George Stell, 12/7-8/1719."

p. 471. "James Thweatt, Jr., & James Thweatt, Sr., Wit., Letter of Attorney, James Parham to Lewis Green, Jr., 6/13/1721."

p. 500. "James Thweatt & James Thweatt, Jr., Wit., Deed, Francis Coleman to Jno. Coleman, 11/14/1721."

pp. 505-6. "James Thweatt, Jr., Wit., L. & R., James Thweatt only to Samuel Jordon, 12/29-30/1721-1/9/1721-22."

p. 521. "James Thweatt, Wit., L. & R., Jno. Ledbetter to Rich. Ledbetter, 3/13/1721-22."

p. 523. "James Thweatt, Wit., L. & R., Richard Ledbetter to Wm. Ledbetter, 3/13/1721-22."

p. 525. "James Thweatt, Wit., L. & R., Moses Beck to Joseph Lanthrope, 3/13/1721-22."p

p. 531. "James Thweatt, Wit., L. & R., Wm. Stainback to Jno. Hill, 4/10/1722."

p. 533. "James Thweatt, Wit., Deed, Ann Carter & Jno. Hill to Wm. Stainback, 4/10/1722."

p. 719. "James Thweatt & Miles Thweatt, Wit., Let. of Atty., John Clay of N.C. to Maj. Robt. Munford, to sell land in Pr. George to Henry Thweatt, 9/2/1723."

p. 645. "James Thweatt, Wit., L. & R., Thos. Clay to James Batt, 10/7-8/1723."

p. 680. "James Thweatt, Chris. Roberson, Wm. Mattox, Wit., Deed, Jno. Peterson to his son, John Peterson, 2/11/1723-24."

p. 689. "James Thweatt, Wit., Deed, Edw. Mitchell to Chas. Williams, etux, Elizabeth, 3/10/1724."

p. 690. "Jas. Thweatt & Miles Thweatt, Wit., Deed, Edw. Mitchell to Sam Jordan, 3/10/1723-24."

pp. 704-6. "James Thweatt, John Thweatt & John Fitzgerald, Wit., Deed of R., Thos, Nunneley, etux, Elizabeth, to John Peterson, 5/9-12/1724."

pp. 703-4. "James Thweatt, Wit., Deed, Thos. Nunneley to John Thweatt, 3/29/1724-5/12/1724."

p. 721. "James Thweatt, Wit., Deed of R., John Clay of N.C. to Henry Thweatt, 9/3/1723-6/9/1724."

p. 769. "James Thweatt, Wit., Deed, John Stroud to Rich. Massey, 11/10/1724."

p. 776. "James Thweatt, Wit., Deed, Andrew Beck, Sr., to his son, Andrew Beck, Jr., 1/12/1724-25."

p. 927. "James Thweatt & James Sturdivant, Wit., will, David Crawley, 3/21/1725-26/9-13-1726., Appraisers: Thos. Hardaway and Wm. Parsons."p'

p. 831. "James Thweatt, Wit., L. & R., Joshua Poythres to Wm. Poythres, 7/13/1725."

p. 855. "James Thweatt, Wit., L. & R., Geo. Williams to Henry Willson, 2/8/1725-26."

p. 877. "James Thweatt & John Thweatt, Wit., L. & R., Isaac Hall, Hall Hudson & Elizabeth Hudson to Daniel Sturdivant, 5/10/1726."

p. 891. "James Thweatt, Sr., & James Thweatt, Jr., Wit., Deed, James Williams to Charles Williams, 6/14/1726."

p. 893. "James Thweatt, Sr., & James Thweatt, Jr., Wit., Deed, Chas. Williams to James Williams, 6/14/1726."

p. 939. "James Thweatt, Wit., Deed, Instance Hall to John Lewis, 3/13/1726-27."

p. 983. "James Thweatt & Miles Thweatt, Wit., L. & R., Edw. Mitchell etux Margaret, to Samuel Jordan, 5/9/1727."

pp. 1100 - 2. "James Thweatt & Daniel Sturdivant, Wit., L.& R., Chichester Sturdivant to his sons, Jno. Sturdivant & Thomas Sturdivant. 5/8/1728-5/14/1728. Gifts."

AMELIA COUNTY, DEED BOOK 1:
pp. 114-117: "Miles Thweatt, etux Sarah, sold 360 acres, 5/11/ 1738-5/12/1738, to Wm. Jordan, all of Pr. Geo. County, on S. side, Little Nottoway River, adj. Sam'l. Jordan (which seems to be the land patented 11/5/1730 in Brunswick by James Thweatt, Jr.)"

AMELIA COUNTY, ORDER BOOK 3, 1751-1755:
p. 230 (or 236). "James Thweatt, Pl't., Vs. William Baldwin, Def't. 5/23/1755, Court. This day, came the parties, and, with the assent of the Pl't. the Defendant acknowledged himself to have afsumed to pay the said Pl't. Five Pounds and six Pence. Therfore, it is considered by the Court that the said Pl't do recover Judgment against the said William Baldwin for the same, with Costs and a Fee."

AMELIA COUNTY, ORDER BOOK 4, 1755-1757:
pp. 42, 43. "James Thweatt and John Dabney, Vs., John Mann, Def't. 3/25/1756, Judgment Ł 3:1:7 & Costs awarded Plaintiffs."
p. 84. "James Thweatt & John Dabney Vs. Chas. Hamlin, 7/22/ 1756, Ł 1:15:6½ for Plaintiffs & Costs & Lawyer's Fee."

AMELIA COUNTY, ORDER BOOK 6, 1760-1763:
p. 32. "This petition of Est. of James Thweatt, by Wm. Thweatt, Executor, Vs. Lodowick Talley, for debt 7/1760, is continued to next Court at the Def't's Motion, & Costs."
p. 32. "The petition of Est. of James Thweatt, by Wm. Thweatt, Executor, Vs. Charles Hamlin, for debt, on hearing the parties, is dismist, 7/1760."

ISLE OF WIGHT COUNTY, GREAT BOOK, VOL. 2, 1715-1726:
p. 336. "James Thweatt, Nathan Anderson, John Johnson, & Jno. Ingles, Wit., Power of Atty., Judith Thweatt to Col. Arthur Smith, to relinquish her right of dower in 180 acres, sold

by her and her husband, (another) James Thweatt, 10/29/1717, to John Johnson." See Patent 10/31/1716, previously mentioned.

BRUNSWICK COUNTY, DEEDS:

Bk. 1, p. 452. "Mary Thweatt, Wit., Deed, Thomas Williams to Wm. Batte, both of Pr. Geo. Co., 7/22/1738, 150 Acres on Meherrin River." (Mary Thweatt is unidentified).

Bk. 6, pp. 98, 99. "Robt. Batte deeded, 1/20/1757, 170 acres to James Thweatt (both of Pr. Geo. Co.), adj. Jno. Thweatt, Jno. Davis, Eades Smith, Jno. Peterson, Wm. Batte & Jno. Thweatt (again) and James Thweatt (different from buyer?) on Meherrin River."

Bk. 12, p. 143. "James Thweatt, of Dinwiddie, & Peterson Thweatt, of Brunswick, to Thos. Thweatt, of Pr. George., Deed, 12/28/1776-1/27/1777."

GREENSVILLE COUNTY, DEED BOOK 1. 1781-1792:

pp. 48-49. "James Thweatt (identity unknown), Benj. Jordan & Thos. Turner, wit., Deed, 8/28/1781-7/24/1783, Thos. Smith, to Jno. Peterson Thweatt and Peterson Thweatt (sons of Peterson Thweatt), 100 acres on S.W. side of Occaneechy Swamp, where Peterson Thweatt, deceased, lived."

Several James Thweatts, 1659-1755.

1. Deposition. November 12, 1707 (Va. Mag. 7, p. 342): "Prince George County - SS: James Thweatt, aged sixty-four years or thereabouts, swore, saith: That he hath known the River now called Nottoway River for the space of about Eight and forty years or more and then it was called by the name of Nottoway River and by no other name that the Deponent knows or has heard. That when the Deponent was first acquainted in these parts, the chief town of the Nottoway Indians was on the South side of the River where Maj. Wynn's Quarter now is, about three miles above the mouth of Monksneck Creek, and some few of them lived at Rowonte, which is about four miles up Monksneck Creek; and two or three familyes of them at Tonnatorah, which is on the North side of the River. And that they lived at some of these places. and at Cottashowrock and thereabouts, till about five or six and twenty years ago, and then they removed and setled and grew Town upon Atyamonsock Swamp at place now called the Old Town. That about forty-eight years ago the Meherin Indians lived upon Meherin River at Cowachahowkon, and some of them at Unote, and about four and twenty years ago they lived some of them at Unote and some at Taurara, but how long they lived there after then, he cannot particularly remember. And further this Deponent saith not.

Novemb. 12, 1707   JAMES THWEATT

Sworn before us: B. Harrison, Jr., John Hardyman."

This places James Thweatt, likely the emigrant, probably in Charles City County by 1659, at the age of 16.

2. Patents to James Thweatt, April 22, 1670, and March 15, 1672/73, in each of which James Thweate is listed as a Headright. In this second listed patent, the Headright, James Thweate, may have been (a) the father of the Patentee, or (b), the son of the Patentee, or (c), the Patentee himself who had returned

from a trip to Europe with colonists whose passage, with his
own, he had paid.

3. Patent to James Thweat, Sen'r., 4/20/1689, which indicates
that a kinsman, possibly his son, was about 18 (or 21?) years
of age.

4. "Lycence Granted Mr. James Thweate for marryage with
'Mistress' Judith Soane ...... Marryage Lycences to be returned to O'ber Gen'll Court, A.D. 1702, O'ber 24, 1702."

5. Prince George County Quit Rent Roll, 1704, showing 715
Acres owned by James Thweatt, and 100 Acres owned by James
Thweat, Jr.

6. Patent, 10/31/1716, 180 Acres, Isle of Wight County, to
James Thweatt of Pr. Geo. County.

7. Patent, 9/5/1723, 300 Acres, Pr. George County, to James
Thweatt, Jr., of said County.

8. The 300 Acres above had been Surveyed, 3/27/1721, for
Capt. James Thweatt (Pr. Geo. Co. Surv. Platt Bk., 1711-1724.)

9. Patent, 11/5/1730, 360 Acres, Brunswick County, to James
Thweatt, Jr. of said County.

10. Patent, 7/10/1745, 103 Acres, Pr. Geo. County, to James
Thweatt (County of residence was not shown).

11. Patent, 9/10/1755, 205 Acres, Brunswick County, to James
Thweatt (County of residence was not shown).

12. Br. Par. Reg. 11/23/1721. "It is ord'r'd, and Cap't Bullard
Herbert is hereby Elected Vestryman, for this P'ish in the room
of Cap't Ja. Thweat, he, the s'd Thweat haveing, for these two
years past, neglected Appearing at the Vestries".

13. Ibid, p. 56, 8/3/1731. "Ord'red yt Edward Mitchell & James
Thweat procession Between ye Butterwood & Whiteoak to the
Extent ......". Ibid, p. 82, 2/9/1735. "...... and James
Thweatt Procession Between Butterwood and white Oak......".
Ibid, p. 93, 8/20/1739. "...... and James Thweatt Procession
Between Butterwood and white Oak."

It seems likely that James Thweatt who made a Deposition,
11/12/1707, Pr. Geo. Co., at the age of 64, was the emigrant
of this family and hereafter he is designated as James Thweatt,
the emigrant. It must be remembered, however, that he was
aged 16 when he first knew "the River now called Nottoway".
Therefore, he may have been brought to Virginia by a parent,
his parents, or as a ward of another Colonist. Since most early
Chas. City Co. records are destroyed, we cannot know the full
facts. We do not believe that James Thweatt, Jr., listed in the
Quit Rent Roll of 1704 in Pr. Geo. Co., as owning 100 Acres,
made the Deposition.

We do not know that James Thweatt, Jr., was son of James
Thweatt, the emigrant. Men living at the time were designated
as "Jr.", also, because an elder kinsman of the same name
lived in the same vicinity or County. As an illustration, living'
concurrently with James Thweatt and James Thweatt, Jr., in
1704, was Henry Soane, Jr. His father was not Henry Soane,
but Capt. William Soane. James Thweatt, Jr., may have been
a grandson of James Thweatt, the emigrant.

The first Thweatt marriage found is "Lycence Granted Mr.

James Thweate for marryage with Mistress Judith Soane......
Marryage Lycences to be Returned to O'ber Gen'll Court A.D.
1702. 9ber 24 1702" (p. 279, Henrico County Deeds, etc.,
1693-1704.) It seems likely that "Mistress Judith Soane", daughter, as is shown later, of Capt. William Soane, was, in fact,
a spinster. There seems to be evidence that spinsters were, at
times, designated as "Mistress". This writer does not know
which James Thweatt married Judith Soane. For this record,
there seems to be no point in speculating as to his identity.
Well informed students of this family believe that the emigrant,
having been widowed, with several small children, Henry, John,
James, and possibly others, married Judith Soane. Other well
informed students believe that the second James Thweatt married Judith Soane. We have no documentation of any issue by
this marriage.

We are faced, then, with our inability to identify positively,
by documentation so far revealed, children or grandchildren
of James Thweatt, the emigrant, despite what our personal be-
liefs are. In like manner, we cannot determine the relationship
to each other or to James Thweatt, the emigrant, of these contemporaries: Henry Thweatt; John Thweatt; James Thweatt, Jr.;
Drury Thweatt; James Thweatt, who married Ann Peterson
(Bristol Parish Records); James Thweatt, who married Mary
--------- (B.P.R.); Miles Thweatt; William Thweatt; Martha
Thweatt, who was married to a John Peterson; Agnes Thweatt,
who married, 1737, Thos. Hardaway, Jr.; and James Thweatt
of Prince George County, who, with Christopher Martin of
Chesterfield County, on 5/2/1750, bought a ½ Acre Lot in Wit-
tontown, from Richard Witton of Lunenburg County (Chester-
field County, Deeds, Book 1, 1749-1753, p. 98).

It is impossible for this writer to name the mother of the
children of James Thweatt, the emigrant, or to state whether
he had multiple marriages. We have scant evidence that he had
issue (Patent to James Thweat, Sr., 4/20/1689). We simply
assume that he was the progenitor of the two great families of
Thweatt descendants who can, documentarily, be traced to (1)
Henry Thweatt, who married Hannah Stanley, Ca. 1715, and to
(2) John Thweatt, who married Judith Peterson, Ca. 1715-19.
Henry Thweatt and John Thweatt may have been sons of James
Thweat, the emigrant. We do not believe that they were sons of
James Thweatt, Jr. (Quit Rent Rolls, 1704, 100 Acres).

It seems likely that John Thweatt married, first, Elizabeth
Soane, daughter of Capt. William Soane, whose widow was
Mary ------, of Henrico County, Ca. 1710-1714. Capt. William
Soan's will, 1714, Henrico Co., indicates that his widow was
not mother of his children. He bequeathed a slave to his son-
in-law, John Thweatt. We believe that John Thweatt married,
second, Judith Peterson. Capt. William Soane did not name
any children of John Thweatt and Elizabeth Soane. We have no
evidence of any children. Capt. Wm. Soane named his daughter,
Judith Thweatt, in his will, however. John Thweatt married
Judith Peterson about 1719. Her identity was clearly established
in the will (I. of W. Co., 1732) of her father, John Peterson.

We have photostats of the wills of John Thweatt (1/5/1758-6/12/1759, Brunswick Co. Deeds, etc.; 1759-60; pp. 84, 85, 86) and of his widow, Judith Thweatt (10/12/1770-6/28/1773, Brunswick Co. Will Book 4; 1761-1777; pp. 162, 163). Issue (all recorded in Bristol Parish Register except Mary, whose identity is proven in the wills of her parents.):

I.   John, Bap 4/17/1720, (1/11/1770-?).
II.   John, (3/21-? -6/10/1722).
III.   James, Bap. 5/20/1722, (3/12/1722-ante 1/5/1758), m. ante 1745, Sarah Sturdivant, whose parents are unknown, of whom later.
IV.   Elizabeth, Bap. 5/24/1724 (3/11/1724-?), m. ante 1/5/1758, ------Birchett (possibly Edward, Jr.)
V.   John (8/22/1726-?)
VI.   William, Bap. 3/4/1727-28 (9/11/1727-? /1763, Will, 3/16/1763-8/11/1763, Southampton Co. , Bk. 1762-1772, pp. 47, 48, 49), Mar. (Lic. , 7/18/1754) Jane, daughter Ephraim Parham.
VI.   Martha, Bap. 12/17/1732 (10/20-1732-?), m. Ca.1755, Joseph Goodwyn, son of Thos. Goodwyn, Surry Co.
VII.   Mary (Ca. 1734-?), m. post 1/5/1758, Urvin Brown, son of Burrell Brown, who received a legacy of land from John Peterson (d. 1732), father of Judith Peterson,above.
VIII.   Judith, Bap. 7/23/1743 (6/9/1743-?), Mar. Bond 10/12/1770, Brunswick Co. , to James Goodwyn, son of John Goodwyn and Winifred Tucker.

Because of the destruction of the records of Dinwiddie County, we know little about James Thweatt, son of John and Judith (Peterson) Thweatt. He predeceased his father, as the latter's will shows. James Thweatt probably died intestate, as his father, John Thweatt, left land to James Thweatt's sons, John and Peterson, seemingly more than John Thweatt's legacy of 90 Acres to John Thweatt, brother of James and Peterson Thweatt. We presume that the eldest son, John, of James Thweatt and Sarah Sturdivant received, by primogeniture, all the land that his intestate father left. We do not know the parents or any others of the family of Sarah Sturdivant. She possibly was a great-granddaughter of the emigrant John Sturdivant, who married the relict of Samuel Woodward of Henrico County. It seems likely that sons of John Sturdivant and Mrs. Samuel Woodward (born Sarah Hallam), were Daniel Mathew, Chichester and Hallam (or Hollam). Sarah Sturdivant, who married James Thweatt, ante 1745, was likely a granddaughter of one of these four brothers. Issue: (the first 3 recorded in Bristol Parish Register):

I.   John (6/12/1745-11/15/1802), Bap. 7/28/1745. (Will 5/5/1795-4/25/1803, Brunswick Co. , Bk. 6, p. 498) m. Ca. 1765, Edith Parsons, daughter of Capt. Wm. Parsons and Mrs. Samuel (Mary Batty) Markham.
II.   Tabitha (5/27/1749-? ? 1805, Hancock Co. , Ga. Mar. (Bond, Brunswick Co. , 8/29/1769) John Hamilton, Rev. Sol. of Amelia Co. , Va. (1745-1829, Hancock Co. , Ga.) (son of John Hamilton of Surry Co.), of whom later.

III.   James (4/3/1752-9/17/1814) (W.D. 9/5/1814, appraised 2/6/1815, Hancock Co., Ga.) m. (1) 4/3/1777, his cousin, Elizabeth Peterson, mother of his children, b. 1761, in Va. d. 5/11/1806 in Hancock Co., Ga., daughter of John Peterson (d. 1769) of Brunswick Co., Va., the name of the mother of whose children, we do not know; (2) Susannah----------, who survived him; of whom later.

IV.   Thomas, probably a Rev. Sol., m. Betty ------ and probably died without issue. Betty subsequently, Ca. 7/12/1786, m. Nathaniel Dunn, and (3) Ca. 1800, m. Thomas Galt.

V.   Peterson, (Ca.1755, Will, 8/25/1779-9/27/1779, Brunswick Co. Will Book 5, 1778-1795, pp. 74, 75), m. his cousin (and the sister of the first wife of his brother, James), Rebecca Peterson, who bore him two sons.

VI.   Sarah, (b. Dinwiddie Co., where she mar., Ca. 1786, John Mitchell, Esq. (8/25/1745, Sussex Co., Va. -1/3/1804, Hancock Co., Ga.)

Tabitha Thweatt, daughter of James Thweatt and Sarah Sturdivant, was likely born in Prince George or Brunswick County. After the service, in the Revolution, of her husband, John Hamilton, they joined the families of her brother, James Thweatt, and her sister, Sarah Mitchell, in Hancock Co., Ga. Issue:

I.   Marmaduke (9/22/1770-11/18/1832) m. Elizabeth Scott (d. 12/25/1837). No issue.

II.   John (1773-1806), unmarried.

III.   Sarah Thweatt (11/28/1775-7/30/1850), m. Maj.Robt. Raines (1766-1816). Issue.

IV.   James Thweatt, b. 1777, unmarried.

V.   Martha, died at birth.

VI.   Frances (1/22/1781-2/28/1827), m. 12/2/1802, Brig. General David Blackshear (9/31/1764-7/4/1737). Issue.

VII.   Thomas Peterson (1782-1831), m. Elizabeth Freeman, Capt. of Art. in Creek War. Issue.

VIII.   George (1784-dsp. 1880) m. Elvira Evans.

IX.   Mary Ann Tabitha (1/17/1788-3/23/1870), m. 11/15/1804 George White Hayes, Esq. (11/24/1783-9/14/1849) of Charlotte Co., Va., and Clarke Co., Ga., of whom later.

X.   Major William (1789-Ca.1870) Aide to Gen. Blackshear in Creek War, father of 14 children, 3 by (1) Mary Bryan (1791-1828), and 11 by (2) Elizabeth Bryan (1796-1875), daughters of Edward Bryan of Twiggs Co., Ga.

XI.   Col. Everard (12/4/1791-1/12/1847), Secretary of State of Georgia, m. 10/31/1816, Mary Hazard Floyd (10/1/1795-10/?/1888), daughter of Gen. John Floyd and Isabella Maria Hazzard. Issue.

Mary Ann Tabitha Hamilton (1-17/1788-3/23/1870), m. 11/15/1804, George White Hayes, Esq. (11/23/1783-9/14/1840), son of Capt. Richard Hayes (Am. Rev.) and ---------. They settled and died in Thomas County, Ga. Issue:

I. Elizabeth White (9/5/1805-8/30/1806)
II. John Richard (11/4/1808-11/13/1846), m. 1/24/1832, Sarah Ann Wiley (b.1806-8/29/1881). Issue.
III. James Thweatt (3/25/1811-1/29/1878), m. 8/7/1832 Julie Ann Hadley (9/13/1802-2/3/1863). Issue.
IV. Mary Ann Tabitha (7/25/1812-?), m. 7/17/1827, Wm. H. Reynolds. Issue.
V. William Everard (11/13/1815-12/3/1889), m. 12/21/ 1836, Jane L. Hardin. Issue.
VI. Martha Hamilton (8/26/1817-10/19/1818).
VII. Marmaduke Hamilton (1/8/1819-1898), m. (1) 10/30/ 1839, Sarah Ann Munson (1823-1866) of whom later. m. (2) Mrs. Eliza (Mitchell) Cagle.
VIII. George White (6/16/1822), m. Mary Ray. Issue.
Marmaduke (Duke) Hamilton Hayes lived in Thomas County, Georgia, and in Coushatta, Louisiana, where he died.
Issue by Sarah Ann Munson:
I. George Hamilton (9/14/1840-5/31/1842).
II. Mary Ann Tabitha (10/22/1842-11/16/1910), m. 6/1/ 1865, John Edwin Dickey (5/6/1840-9/29/1913), son of Shadrach Edward Dickey and Susannah E. Harvin, both of Sumter, S.C., and Thomas County, Ga. More of this family later.
III. Martha Munson (11/1/1844).
IV. John Richard (5/24/1847-1908), m. 1863 Martha Platt (1845). Issue.
V. Theodosia Eugenia (10/4/1849), m. Samuel A. Vickers. Issue.
VI. Angelina Chaires (6/7/1852), m. 1870, Thomas W. Howell (1834). Issue.
VII. Ella Alice (6/11/1854), m. 1870, Dr. Henry Bryant (1835). Issue.
VIII. Belle Hamilton (1/24/1857), m. John Slayton. Issue.
IX. Sarah Duke (5/29/1859), m. John Ringgold McGould-rick. Issue.
X. Octavia.
Issue by Mrs. Eliza (Mitchell) Cagle:
XI. Eudora, m. John Martin. Issue.
XII. Eunie May, m. Henry Martin. Issue.
Mary Ann Tabitha Hayes, m. John Edwin Dickey, son of Shardrach Edward Dickey and his first wife, Susannah E. Harvin, who were children, respectively, of William Nelson Washington Dickey and Mary Atkinson, and of John Edwin Harvin and --------White, all of Sumter District, South Carolina.
Issue:
I. Mary Hayes (3/28/1866-8/6/1936), m. 4/15/1891, as his third wife, Henry Cumming Quarterman.
II. William Heir (4/8/1868-1893), unmarried.
III. Walter Lee (12/12/1873-12/31/1873).
IV. Ida Belle (10/26/1871-8/29/ 1874).
V. John Edwin (12/4/1874-3/26/1912), m. May, 1904, Virginia Warren.
VI. Leroy Hamilton (11/1/1877) m. 12/14/1905, Mamie Butler.

VII.   Mitchell Harvin (1/26/1883) M. Elizabeth Pratt.

Mary Hayes Dickey and Henry Cumming Quarterman had issue:

I.   Mary Bell (5/8/1892-9/21/1948), m. 4/22/1922, Benjamin Jefferson Kincaid (4/18/1894-). He m. (2), 4/15/1954, Mrs. Wm. Dewey (Gretchen Hand) Hilsabeck.

II.   Ellen Leona (8/23/1893) M. 1923, George Bradford Field. No issue.

III.   Theodosia (12/23/1899) m. 1924, Wade Morrow. Issue.

IV.   Hattie Hayes (11/26/1896-9/26/1898).

.   Mary Belle Quarterman and Benjamin Jefferson Kincaid had issue;

I.   Mary Hayes (8/6/1923), m. (1) 12/20/1943, Wayman Horace Little, (2) 9/13/1949, Charles Bernard Karl Schultz.

II.   Benjamin Jefferson (2/15/1926), unmarried, 1956.

Mary Hayes Kincaid had no issue by her 1st. marriage.
By Charles Bernard Karl Schultz:

I.   Michael Karl Schultz (8/6/1950)

II.   Roderick Kincaid Schultz (1/2/1954)

James Thweatt (4/3/1752, Va. - 9/14/1814, Ga., where his will is on file), buried near Sparta, Ga. p m. (1) 4/3/1777, in Va. Elizabeth Peterson (1761-5/11/1806, in Hancock Co., Ga.), daughter of John and Martha (Kinchen) (Traditional) Peterson. On 7/15/1788 James Thweatt bought land on Ogeechee River, Wilkes Co., Ga. The Inventory of his estate showed that he owned considerable wealth. (His second wife was Susanna ------; by whom he probably had no issue.)

     Issue:

I.   Uriah (1/13/1781-11/10/1815), m. 1814, Jones Co., Ga., Harriet Napier, sister of Leroy Napier.

II.   Rev. Thomas (9/23/1786-2/2/1853), m. (1), 10/13/1807, in Hancock Co., Ga., Temperance Seegars Turner of Soarta, Ga; (2), 8/28/1821, Catherine A.S. Hammil, with issue by both.

III.   Eliza (3/14/1785-1/?/1851), m. (1) Alexander Devereaux, by whom she had no issue; (2) Michael Kennan, and had 4 children.

IV.   Kinchen Peterson, of whom hereafter.

V.   Dr. James (8/17/1793-4/4/1867, at his home, "Bolinbroke", Monroe Co., Ga., 16 miles from Macon), a graduate of the University of Georgia and Surgeon in War of 1812; .m. 4/26/1815 Frances Flanders Moore, daughter of Thomas and Nancy (Walton) Moore.

VI.   Mary Thweat (Polly) (8/6/1797-9/7/1874), m. (1) 11/3/1814, Gen. Wm. Flewellen of Jones Co., Ga.; (2) Rev. Isaac N. Johnson, 11/24/1842.

Kinchen Peterson, (6-4/1789-in Upson Co., Ga., 1/13/1849, and is buried in the old part of Glenwood Cemetery at Thomaston, Ga.); m. (1) Elizabeth (Betsy) Reese (b. 12/31/1796), daughter of Joel and Rebecca (Harris) Reese; (2) Eliza R. Harris (6/19/1802-10/12/1848, and is buried beside her husband). He died intestate. His estate was administered by James' Thweatt and

Robert M. Jackson. He is shown in the 1820 Census of Jones
Co., Ga. Land records show that he sold out in 1834. He moved
to Upson County, where he is listed in the 1840 Census. (Mason
Turner, orphan daughter of Dred Turner, was ward of James
Thweatt (d. 9/14/1814), and after his death was ward of above
Kinchen Peterson Thweatt).

Issue:

I.   Martha Jane (Matt) (4/3/1824-6/16/1900), m. 11/15/1842,
        Dr. John Smith Searcy (3/20/1820-4/13/1896), son of
        Wm. Searcy and Sarah Smith.
II.   James, b. ca. 1825, m. 12/12/1849, Elizabeth Virginia
        Flewellen, in Upson Co., Ga.
III.   Eliza Ann, (12/2/1827-8/27/1839), buried in family plot
        in Thomaston.
IV.   Kinchen Peterson, Jr., b. ca. 1831; m. 4/27/1852, Up-
        son County, Ga., Eugenia L. Flewellen, daughter of
        Thomas M. and Frances Flewellen.
V.   Benn, lived at Fort Valley, Ga., m. and had issue.
VI.   Sarah Antoinette (2/13/1836-12/21/1877 in Talbot Co.,
        Ga.) of whom hereafter.
VIII   Virginia , m. Wick (Wyche) ? Jackson. No further record.

William Harris Searcy (Monday, 5/30/1825-Monday, 1/26/
1915) lived and died in Talbot Co., Ga.; son of William and
Sara (Smith) Searcy. On 2/6/1856 he m. Sarah Antoinette Thweatt,
2/13/1836-12/21/1877, in Talbot Co., Ga. Both Sarah and William Searcy are buried in Searcy Cemetery, Talbot Co., Ga.
William H. Searcy m. (2) in Talbot Co., Ga. on Tuesday, 4/15/
1879, Missouri M. Maxwell (by whom no issue) in ceremony
performed by his brother, Dr. John Smith Searcy. (William H.
Searcy, who m. Sarah Antoinette Thweatt, and Dr. John Smith
Searcy, who m. Matt Thweatt, were brothers. The Thweatt
girls were half-sisters. Daniel Bartlett Searcy, first cousin to
the Searcy boys, m. Camilla Thweatt, the dau. of Dr. James
Thweatt, and first cousin to Sarah Antoinette and Matt.) Wm.
H. Searcy had issue by his first wife only, all born in Talbot
Co., Ga.:

I.   William Harris, b. Ca. 1859; m., Talbot Co., Ga.,
        12/29/1881, Kate Maxwell. Issue.
II.   Daniel Bartlett (8/16/1861-11/6/1943), m. Allie King
        (11/17/1865-2/1/1940).
III.   Martha Victoria, b. 9/3/1863, m. 1883, Talbot Co.,
        Ga., Dr. J. A. Leonard, As of 1/10/1956, she is living.
IV.   James Kinchen (8/20/1865-5/19/1910), of whom hereafter.
V.   Virginia Ella (twin to James) 8/20/1865-ante 1955), m.
        Walter Maxwell.
VI.   Sarah Aurelia, d. in infancy.

The last will and testament of William Harris Searcy is
recorded in Talbot Co., Ga., on June 7, 1915. It names daughters, Mattie and Ella, the heirs of his son, Kinch, and his son,
D.B. Filed with the will is a codicil dated 7/10/1913, naming
daughter-in-law, Allie King. The home place is still in the
hands of descendants (only a few years ago the woodland was
sold).

James Kinchen Searcy, (Talbot Co., Ga. 8/20/1865-Atlanta, Ga., 5/19/1910); buried in Butler, Ga.; m. 12/16/1904, Sara Fletcher Wallace (Redbone, Talbot Co., Ga., 11/29/1882-10/ 11/1953), dau. of Arch Steele and Frances (Walker) Wallace.

James Kinchen Searcy graduated from Mercer University, Macon, Ga., June, 1896, as B.A. He taught school in North Georgia, at Culloden and in Taylor County.

     Issue:
I.   Unnamed Stillborn son, 1905.
II.   Mable Antoinette, m. 1928, Joseph Stanford Brown of Howard, Ga.
III.   James Kinchen, Jr. (Butler, Ga., 6/20/1909-living, 1/10/1956); m. 10/5/1940, Clinton, Hinds Co., Miss., Margaret Lynn Stovall (1/19/1911, Lake, Scott Co., Miss.) dau. of Gilbert Spencer and Emma (Pruitt) Stovall. Issue:
    1. Sara Margaret (3/13/1942, Jackson, Hinds Co,, Miss.-3/24/1942, Jackson, Miss., buried, Clinton, Miss.
    2. James Kinchen, III (Monroe, Ouachita Parish, La., 2/5/1944).
    3. Judith Louise Mary (1/11/1947, Vicksburg, Warren Co., Miss.)

****

James Thweatt, unidentified, married Ann Peterson, (supra; will of John Peterson, 1731-1732, I. of W. Co.). B.P.R. shows issue, of whom nothing further has been found:
I.   Frances, Bap. 4/8/1726 (12/25/1725-)
II.   Christian, Bap. 5/31/1730 (2/9/1729-)
III.   Martha, Bap. 11/14/1731 (9/29/1731-)
IV.   Elizabeth (8/5/1734-)

****

James Thweatt, unidentified, m. Mary -------- (supra). B.P.R. shows issue, of whom nothing further has been found: Mary.

****

Benjamin Jefferson Kincaid, Sr., 1779 Micanopy Avenue, Miami 45, Florida, January 1, 1956, acknowledges that he is deeply obligated to many Thweatt descendants, but especially to those who have contributed substantially to the purchase of hundreds of pages of photostats of deeds, wills, bonds, orders, and other legal documents of Southside Virginia Counties and of Northampton and Edgecombe Counties, N.C. They most patiently studied all records and expressed opinions: Mrs. James Kinchen Searcy, Jr., 2009 North Upland St., Arlington, 7, Va.; Lawrence B. Gardiner, 1863 Cowden Avenue, Memphis 4, Tenn.; and Dr. Claiborne Thweatt Smith, Jr., N.C. Mem. Hospital, Chapel Hill, N.C.

LAWRENCE of ISLE of WIGHT COUNTY, VIRGINIA
and
EASTERN NORTH CAROLINA

Robert Lawrence, son of Sir John Lawrence, merchant of London, appears to be the first of this family in Virginia. He obtained a patent of 100 acres of land on Lawne's Creek, Isle of Wight, and another one of 200 acres "adjacent to the widow Bennett and Mr. Hardy, August 25, 1642". He was a Justice for the County of Nansemond in 1659-60. His wife was named Elizabeth. (17th C. 491).

Children:

I.   Robert Lawrence, Jr., born 1639. It appears that he married Mrs. Jane Gay, widow of Henry Gay. He was granted 625 acres of land on the west side of the Chowanoke River, in North Carolina, in 1663, thus becoming one of the first Virginia settlers to migrate to North Carolina. However, he returned to Virginia and made his will, Isle of Wight, April 20, 1720, which is only partially preserved. All names are missing from the will except that of Robert Lawrence, III, and son-in-law Henry Gay, son of Mrs. Jane Gay. (Great Book 2, p.59)

    1.   Robert Lawrence, III, m. his cousin Sarah Exum, daughter of Jeremiah and Ann Lawrence Exum. Children:

        (1) Jeremiah Lawrence, made his will in Isle of Wight, where he died unmarried in 1756. (W. B. 6, p. 246)

        (2) Samuel Lawrence, m. a daughter of Jacob Darden I.

        (3) Ann Lawrence, m. (1) Edward Eley, son of Robert and Martha Daughtry Eley, III, and m. (2) William Joyner.

        (4) John Lawrence wife's name unknown, made his will in Isle of Wight, March 2, 1757, and died the following year, leaving two children, Samuel and Ann Lawrence who m. Elisha Ballard. (W. B. 6, p. 313).

        (5) Robert Lawrence IV, m. Ann Council, daughter of Hardy and Susannah Council. He made his will in Newport Parish, Isle of Wight, November 1, 1743. (W.B. 4, p. 522). Children:

            a. Hardy, m. Martha Gay;

            b. Robert, V., m. Sarah Eley, daughter of Robert and Cherry Eley, March 23, 1786;

            c. George, m. Sarah Beale, January 13, 1792;

            d. Charles; e. Sarah; f. Priscilla.

See Nicholson's "Herald & Genealogist; Vol. IV", for a more complete study of the family.

    (6) A daughter, m. Jacob Darden II, and left two children, Jacob and Charles Darden.

II.   George Lawrence received a patent of 120 acres on Western Branch of Nansemond, July 10, 1680. He also received a patent of 830 acres on the Blackwater in Nansemond for the transportation of 13 persons, and the record shows he owned 400 acres in Nansemond in 1704. The Nansemond fire destroyed further record of this family. (17th Cent. 492)

III.   Henry Lawrence made his home in Nansemond County. His wife's name is unknown. He had two sons, Michael and Thomas. His daughter, Isabella, m. Thomas Page, son of Thomas Page, of Isle of Wight, January 15, 1702, at the home of Frances Denson, widow. Rebecca Page, daughter of Thomas Page, married Thomas Gay, son of Mrs. Jane Gay Lawrence, November 11, 1699/1700. (17th Cent. 493)

IV.   John Lawrence, I, patented 625 acres of land on the west side of the Chowanoke River, in North Carolina, next to his older brother, Robert Lawrence, September 25, 1663. He made his will in Nansemond County, January 2, 1696. His wife, Mary, signed her name at Quaker Meetings as "Mary Lawrence, Widow", after 1700. (17th Cent. 494)

Children:

1.   Priscilla Lawrence, m. Matthew Whitfield, of Nansemond County, and moved to Bertie County, North Carolina.

2.   Mary Lawrence, m. John Thomas, of Nansemond County. She was his second wife. His first wife may have been the daughter of Michael Rogers, of Isle of Wight, who made his will April 5, 1710. John Thomas moved to Bertie County, North Carolina, where he made a deed to Colonel Thomas Pollock of 208 acres of land on the west side of Chowan River, "right to said land by my now wife, daughter of John Lawrence, deceased". This was the land patented by John Lawrence in 1663. (17th Cent. 495)

3.   John Lawrence, II, m. Margaret Murphy (See later).

4.   Ann Lawrence, m. Jeremiah Exum, who was one of the Justices of the County Court of Isle of Wight in 1693-94. He made his will September 3, 1712, and died in 1720. (Great Book 2, p. 21) Ann Lawrence Exum made her will, Isle of Wight, February 3, 1726/27 and it was recorded March 27, 1727. (W.B. 3, p. 19).

Children:

(1)   Elizabeth.

(2)   Mary, m. (1) Jacob Ricks (Southside II, p. 295) and m. (2) Barnaby Mackquinny (McKinnie), son of Michael and Elizabeth McKinnie, and moved to Bertie County, North Carolina, where he was a Justice of the Peace in 1724, a Judge of the General Court in 1725, and a member of the General Assembly from Edgecombe County in 1735.

(3) Jane, m. William Outland. One son, Richard Exum Outland, is named in the will of Ann Exum.

(4) Mourning, m. William Scott and left a son, Exum Scott.

(5) Christian, m. Colonel George Norsworthy, son of Tristram Norsworthy. She was his second wife, his first wife being Martha Pitt, daughter of Colonel John Pitt.

(6) Sarah, m. Robert Lawrence. (See above). Others mentioned in the will of Ann Exum were: granddaughters Katoren Godwin, and Ann Murphy; also, grandson Jeremiah Lawrence.

5. Robert Lawrence, m. Elizabeth, family name unknown, of Nansemond County and moved to Bertie County, North Carolina. Children:

(1) Humphrey, m. Ann Ashley and had issue: Frederick, Reuben, David, Ann and Nathaniel. (W.B. "A", p. 156)

(2) Robert;

(3) George, m. Sarah, family name unknown, and had issue: Ann, Sarah, Joshua, and George. (Grimes p. 209).

(4) William, m. Ann, family name unknown, and had issue: Joseph, Patsey, Prudence, and William. (W.B. "F", p. 317).

(5) Elizabeth, m. Samuel Sprewell, no issue (W.B. "D", p. 85).

(6) Thomas, m. Elizabeth, family name unknown, and had issue: Thomas, Asa, Williamson, George, Elizabeth, and Zebulon (W.B. "A", p. 33).

(7) John, m. Jane, family name unknown, and had issue: Abner, Robert, Obadiah, and John (W.B. "D", p. 88).

(8) Martha, m. a Parker.

6. Elizabeth Lawrence died before February 9, 1708, and willed her land to her sister Priscilla.

7. The will of John Lawrence names two sons-in-law, Henry Sanders and Richard Taylor, but the names of his daughters are omitted, indicating that they were deceased.

. John Lawrence, II, son of John and Mary, m. Margaret Murphy, daughter of William and Sarah Holladay Murphy of Isle of Wight. Sarah Holladay was the daughter of Anthony and Mrs. Ann Brewer Holladay. John Lawrence made his will in Newport Parish, January 27, 1738, and it was recorded April 23, 1739. (W.B. 4, p. 226). Margaret Murphy Lawrence made her will in the same county September 26, 1746, and same was recorded February 7, 1750 (W.B. 5, p. 296).

Children:

I. John Lawrence, III, m. Martha Ricks (see later).

II. William Lawrence m. (1) Penelope Browne, daughter of Dr. Samuel Browne, and had one daughter, Penelope; m. (2) Sarah Applewhite of Isle of Wight. He made his will in Newport Parish, September 8, 1756, and it was recorded June 2, 1757 (W.B. 6, p. 269). Sarah Applewhite Lawrence made her will, Newport Parish, October 6, 1762, and died in 1762 (W.B. 7, p. 209).

Issue by second marriage:

1. John Lawrence, m. Mary Bridger, daughter of Colonel James "The Elder" and Susanna Bridger, January 13, 1773, and as Colonel John Lawrence, made his will, Isle of Wight, in November 1787, and it was recorded January 3, 1788 (W.B. 10, p. 88). Issue: William, Salley, John, m. Sarah Groce, December 26, 1791, and Peggy. Also mentioned in his will, brother Mills Lawrence, and Elisha Lawrence Ballard.
2. Molley.
3. . Ann.
4. Salle.
5. Mills Lawrence, who was Captain of a Company of Militia, Isle of Wight, on June 5, 1777. He made his will in Isle of Wight in 1814, and died unmarried in 1816.

III. Margaret Lawrence, m. (1) John Daughtry, son of William Daughtry, who made his will in Isle of Wight, April 28, 1742, and died without issue in 1749; and m. (2) Thomas Langford.

IV. Priscilla, untraced, may have died young.

V. Mary Lawrence, m. Robert Carr, who made his will, Isle of Wight, May 10, 1734, recorded May 26, 1735.

Issue:

1. Elizabeth Darden;
2. Robert Carr, Jr., who married Elizabeth Vasser, daughter of Nathan Vasser, Southampton County, Virginia (W.B. 4, p. 59).

VI. Sarah Lawrence, m. William Moore.

VII. Elizabeth Lawrence, untraced.

John Lawrence, III, eldest son of John and Margaret Murphy Lawrence, m. Martha Ricks, daughter of Abraham and Mary Bellson Ricks, Isle of Wight, June 9, 1740, at Pagan Creek Meeting House. His will was made, Isle of Wight, March 30, 1772, and recorded May 7, 1772 (W.B. 8, p. 150).

Children:

I. Ricks Lawrence, m. (1) Lilly Waddrop, April 10, 1788, daughter of John and Nancy Ann Cocke Waddrop of Nansemond County. He m. (2) Rachel Wilkinson, January 16,

q 1794. His will, made July 18, 1797, was recorded in Isle of Wight February 5, 1798. (W.B. 11, p. 92). His wife's name is not mentioned in the will indicating that she was deceased. Legatees: (1) Marcia Ricks, and (2) Polly Strickland; nephews, Robert and Thomas Lawrence, sons of Robert Lawrence, Sr. of North Carolina, and niece, Nancy Newby.

II. Elizabeth Lawrence, m. Mr. Pretlow.

III. John Lawrence, IV, m. Mary Duke. (See later)

IV. Mary Lawrence, m. Thomas Newby who made his will,

Isle of Wight, March 27, 1797, recorded February 5, 1798 (W.B. 11, p. 91).

Issue:
1. Anne, m. James Stanton,
2. Mary,
3. John Newby.

V. Robert Lawrence, Isle of Wight, m. Milicent Copeland, of Hertford County, North Carolina, June 18, 1775, at Rich Square Meeting House. They moved to Rich Square in 1777 where they joined the Rich Square Society of Friends. In 1798 they removed to Virginia and joined the Western Branch Society of Friends. Robert Lawrence died September 30, 1807 (Hinshaw I. p. 245).

Children:
1. Martha Lawrence, was "reported married to Morris Nixon, March 22, 1823." On February 19, 1833, she
w was accepted for membership in the Short Creek Society of Friends, Mt. Pleasant, Jefferson County, Ohio.
2. Mary Lawrence, joined Short Creek Society of Friends, in Ohio.
3. Samuel Lawrence, untraced.
4. Demcy Lawrence, untraced.
5. Robert Lawrence, reported married in 1811, Isle of Wight, and on May 25, 1822, requested that his daughter, Ann D., a minor, be placed under the care of Friends, Western Branch Preparative Meeting. Ann D. joined the Short Creek Society of Friends in 1833, and m. Mr. Test, of Ohio, 1844.
6. Thomas Lawrence, Isle of Wight, m. (1) Isabella Harris, daughter of Thomas and Clotilda Harris, at Cedar Creek Meeting House, Hanover County, Virginia, May 12, 1822. They had one son, Robert Barclay Lawrence, b. July 24, 1823, m. Tacy Bates of Ohio in 1850 and had six children. Isabella Harris Lawrence died about 1824, and Thomas Lawrence m. (2) Deborah Pretlow in 1826. They moved to Ohio and were accepted for membership at Short Creek Monthly Meeting, February 19, 1833 (Hinshaw IV, p. 237).

Issue:
(1) Thomas, Jr.;
(2) Julia Ann Wilkerson;
(3) Deborah Ricks, m. William J. Harrison;
(4) Ricks;
(5) Margaret J., m. Samuel Harrison;
(6) Mary Ann, m. Oliver Flanner;
(7) Martha;
(8) Murray.

John Lawrence, IV, son of John and Martha Ricks Lawrence, Isle of Wight, m. Mary Duke, daughter of John and Sarah Peele Duke, at Rich Square Meeting House, November 20, 1768. John Lawrence made his will in Northampton County, North Carolina, where he died October 23, 1796 (W.B. 2, p. 135). Mary Duke Lawrence made her will in Northampton County and died there in 1817. John Lawrence was a soldier in the American Revolution, for his name was "on the list for commanding officer, Colonel Allen Jones, May 20, 1775."(Hinshaw I, p. 245)

Children:

I. John Lawrence, V., b. September 14, 1771, d. December 28, 1816. He m. Margaret Nixon (d. September 2, 1819), daughter of Zacharias and Mary White Nixon, at Little River Meeting House, Pasquotank County, North Carolina, January 22, 1797. In 1814, disowned by Society of Friends "for selling two of his black people."

Issue:

1. Ann, b. November 13, 1797.
2. Mary Duke, b. February 8, 1800, m. Thomas Barrow, son of Thomas and Millea Smith Barrow, and had William Barrow, M.D. (V.H.G. p. 353).
3. Margaret, b. March 4, 1802.
4. Martha Elizabeth, b. June 29, 1804.
5. Rebecca John, b. October 30, 1806;
6. William, b. February 29, 1809, d. March 8, 1809;
7. Catherine R., b. March 3, 1810, m. Mr. Nichols.
8. Deborah, b. July 13, 1813, d. June 14, 1821.

II. Ricks Lawrence, b. December 26, 1774, d. June 3, 1824. He married Sabrina Toole Boddie, daughter of Willie and Jane Boddie, of Northampton County, November 3, 1803. After his death, his wife, with her brother Willis Henry Boddie, moved to Mt. Pleasant, Maury County, Tenn., where she died August 6, 1867.

Issue:

1. Maria Anne Caroline Boddie, b. September 6, 1804, m. James Moore Granberry, December 25, 1825.
2. Matilda Ricks, b. January 28, 1806, m. Lemuel Long, November 23, 1823.
3. Jane Toole, b. March 17, 1809, m. Dr. Simon Peter Frierson.
4. Sabrina Boddie, b. December 26, 1811, m. John Mourning Francis, December 26, 1832, at Columbia, Tenn.
5. Martha Willie, b. April 10, 1814, m. Benjamine R. Harris.
6. Willie Willis, b. June 10, 1817, d. September 6, 1821.
7. John David, b. August 23, 1819, d. September 2, 1825 (Boddie & Allied Families, p. 39).

III. Nancy (Ann) Lawrence, b. April 2, 1777, m. Exum Scott, son of William and Elizabeth Scott, of Nansemond County, Virginia, at Rich Square Meeting House, June 25, 1794. Nancy Scott died in Virginia, for it was reported at the Virginia Yearly Meeting, Society of Friends, May 21, 1827 that "Ann Scott, deceased, of Nansemond Co., bequeathed to Yearly Meeting the sum of $1,000.00. The residuary legatees of this will were: Samuel Jones,

Thomas, Mary and David Lawrence, William I., Joseph
M., Catherine and Margaret I. Lewis".

IV. Exum Lawrence, b. November 5, 1779, d. January 21,
1815.

V. David Lawrence, b. June 10, 1782, transferred his membership from Rich Square to Western Branch, December
26, 1812. He married Sophia Pretlow, in June 1816, and
died in Nansemond County, December 16, 1827.

VI. Jonathan Lawrence, twin brother of David, b. June 10,
1782. He moved his membership from Rich Square to
Western Branch Society of Friends, May 28, 1814, and
died in Virginia, December 20, 1814.

VII. Mary (Polly) Lawrence, born about 1785, was living at
the date of the writing of her mother's will, August,
1815. No further record.

VIII. Sarah Lawrence, b. January 18, 1787, d. January 6, 1826,
leaving her estate to David Lawrence, brother.

IX. Thomas Duke Lawrence, b. January 21, 1789, m. Mary
Bailey Powell (see later).

X. Martha Lawrence, b. April 16, 1791, m. Mr. Randolph,
d. June 1, 1816.

XI. Josephus Duke William Lawrence, b. 1793, m. Elizabeth
R. Powell, daughter of Jesse and Charity Harrell Powell,
of Northampton County, January 6, 1831. Disowned by
Society of Friends, Jan. 1818, "for lack of plainess and
keeping a fiddle". He made his will, Northampton Co.,
December 10, 1834, and died shortly thereafter.(W.B.
4, p. 126). Issue:

1. William Thomas Lawrence, born January 23, 1834.
He married Sarah, family name unknown, about 1856,
and died prior to 1878.
Issue:

(1) Alice May Lawrence, b. August 14, 1857, m.
Julian Pendleton, of Scotland Neck, about 1885,
and d. January 27, 1920.
Issue:

a. William Thomas, b. January 21, 1886, d.
January 31, 1944, unmarried.

b. George Edmund, b. September 20, 1887, m.
Neda Taylor, daughter of O.K. and Minnie
Edmondson Taylor, of Whitakers, North Carolina, September 23, 1908.
Issue:
(a) Alice May,
(b) Minnie Edmondson,
(c) Neda Taylor
(d) George Edmund, Jr.

c. Virginia Pendleton, b. September 28, 1893,
d. April 9, 1935, m. A. Claude Yandle, and
had issue:
(a) Jeannette,
(b) Ella May,
(c) Francis,
(d) A. Claude, Jr.

(2) Catherine (Kate) Lawrence, b. 1858, d. 1926,
m. Walter C. Pendleton. They had one son,
Walter Lawrence Pendleton, b. 1877, d. 1929,
unmarried.
(3) Amanda P. Lawrence, b. 1871, d. March 1887.
(4) Charles W. Lawrence;
(5) William E. Lawrence;
(6) Louis M. Lawrence, died unmarried, as did
Charles W. and William E.

Thomas Duke Lawrence, son of John and Mary Duke Lawrence, m. Mary Bailey Powell (b. Jan. 1, 1800, d. May 21, 1854), daughter of Jesse and Charity Harrell Powell, October 16, 1817, Northampton County. On April 16, 1814, disowned by Society of Friends "for attending muster". He purchased his first tract of land in Halifax County, North Carolina, from John H. Anthony, February 16, 1833, after which he moved to Halifax County, where he made his will, January 1, 1863 (W. B. 5, p. 108). He died near Scotland Neck, July 3, 1863.

Children:

I. Martha Eliza Lawrence, b. November 15, 1818, m.
Benjamin Whitmel Cotten, of Bertie County, February
26, 1840. She made her will in Halifax County, Oct.30,
1889, and died in 1892 (W.B. 7, p. 245).
Issue:
1. Mary Foreman Cotten, b. 1843, d. October 28,1862.
2. Joseph R. Cotten, M.D., b. Aug. 12, 1845, m. Anna Baker Paull, daughter of W. H. and Cornelia A.
Paull, of Scotland Neck. Dr. Cotten d. May 16, 1877.
Issue:
(1) Mary, b. September 16, 1868, m. William H.
Josey, of Scotland Neck.
(2) Etta, m. Captain Gus S. White, of Scotland Neck.
(3) Nannie, m. Charles Speed, of Scotland Neck.
(4) Mattie W., b. December 6, 1875, m. Dr. Charles Anthony Beck, son of Robert and Eleanor
Townley Beck, of Wilmington, Delaware.
3. Whitmel Lawrence Cotten, m. Susan Emily Bryan,
daughter of Joseph and Louisa Higgs Bryan. He died
near Scotland Neck in 1914.
Issue:
(1) Charles Mabry, b. October 27, 1868, m. Lelia
Cherry, and d. June 10, 1947.
(2) Joseph Walter, married and left issue.
(3) Wayland Bryan, b. 1870, d. February 10, 1956,
unmarried.
(4) Mary Foreman, b. June 4, 1873, m. Joseph L.
Barnes, d. December, 1942.
(5) Ethel, m. Floyd C. Patterson.
4. Thomas Cotten, d.s.p.
5. James Cotten, m. Louise Morrisett and had issue:
(1) Lillian;
(2) Joseph Whitmel.
6. Martha (Pattie) Cotten, died unmarried.

7. Elizabeth L. Cotten, m. Captain Zack G. Vinson, and had issue.

8. Susan Cotten, m. Mr. Walker.

II. Louisa Ann Lawrence, b. December 29, 1820, d. February 2, 1892, m. Thomas K. Harris, son of Hamlin Harris of Northampton County, October 3, 1837.
Children:

1. Hamlin Duke Harris, b. 1840, d. January 24, 1865, unmarried.

2. William Benjamine Harris, m. (1) Theodora Pittman, daughter of Beverly T. and Elizabeth Pittman, of Edgecombe County, January 25, 1893. They had one son, Reddin Hamlin, b. March 21, 1895, m. Sarah Blumberg, Dec. 12, 1916. William Benjamine Harris m. (2) Louise Estell Millikin, March 2, 1898.
   Issue:
   (1) Ruth Bernice, b. February 24, 1899, m. Lee F. Cooper, d. April 30, 1925.
   (2) Isabel Norma, b. February 24, 1899, unmarried.
   (3) William Thaddeus, b. December 4, 1901, m. Inez Watson, d. October 1, 1955.
   (4) Benjamine Franklin, b. December 4, 1901, m. Evolyn Gentry.

3. Mary (Molly) Harris, m. David Crockett Gatling, and died at age 27 in Hertford County. Her remains were interred at the family homestead in Halifax County.
   Issue:
   2 (1) Thomas Duke Gatling, d. Portsmouth, Virginia.
   (2) Lula Gatling, m. Benjamine Davis, d. Rich Square.
   (3) Molly Gatling, m. Everette Baum, d. Rich Square.
   (4) Nannie Gatling, m. Luther Davis, d. Texarkana, Texas.

4. Susan Elizabeth Harris, b. 1847, m. Henry H. Raspbury in 1862, and died of Diphtheria, December 18, 1863, at the home of Daniel Herring in Duplin Co., North Carolina, while her husband was in the Confederate Army.

5. Anna J. Harris, died unmarried.

6. Della Lawrence Harris, b. June 9, 1861, m. Lemuel Edmund DeBerry, son of Lemuel James and Catherine DeBerry, December 28, 1881, d. September 5, 1947.
   Issue:
   (1) Archie Addison, b. November 13, 1882, d. Aug. 29, 1954, m. Maude Parrish, daughter of Luther T. Parish, Richmond, Virginia, September 28, 1915. They had one daughter, Mildred Mae.
   (2) Elizabeth Stanton, b. February 2, 1884, died unmarried July 26, 1912.
   (3) Thomas Hamlin, b. June 9, 1886, d. September 2, 1951, m. Marie Winnicke, daughter of Os-

car Winnicke of Minnesota, March 31, 1928.
Issue:
a. Delphia Kathleene,
b. Marie Lois DeBerry.

(4) Herman Milford, b. November 12, 1888, m.
Connie Weeks, daughter of William H. and
Mary Imogene Weeks, April 1, 1914.
Issue:
a. Milford Fergerson, b. February 12, 1915,
d. December 3, 1940.

(5) Early Lawrence, b. March 21, 1892, m. Mattie LeNeave, daughter of James Harper LeNeave
of LaGrange, North Carolina, May 11, 1924.
Issue:
a. Nina Mae,
b. Yvonne LeNeave,
c. Lemuel Early.

(6) Naomi Harris, b. April 14, 1895, m. Albert
Jackson Green, son of James Leonard Green,
of Grover, North Carolina, February 5, 1913.
Issue:
a. Bettie Beverly,
b. Edith DeBerry,
c. Gladys Lucille,
d. William Albert.

III. John Thomas Lawrence, b. April 22, 1822, m. (1)
Ann Rosanna Allen, daughter of Colonel Daniel B. and
Lucretia Faulcon Allen of Warren County, North Carolina, December 30, 1845. John T. Lawrence was one
of the founders of the Scotland Neck Baptist Church,
and the Dawson Baptist Church near Scotland Neck.
He enlisted in the Confederate States Army, April 23,
1861, for a period of one year, and was a Corporal,
Company "G", 41st Regiment, the "Scotland Neck
Mounted Riflemen". He was discharged January 14,
1862, for James L. Harding, a substitute for the war.
Ann Allen Lawrence, b. June 1, 1829, d. November
25, 1872. John T. Lawrence m. (2) Lucy V. Coppedge, daughter of William D. and Henrietta I. Coppedge, of the Cedar Rock section of Franklin County,
North Carolina, May 20, 1875, and died at Dawson
February 20, 1898. Lucy Coppedge Lawrence died
without issue November 15, 1915, in Louisburg, North
Carolina.
Children:

1. Josephus Faulcon Lawrence, b. March 1, 1847, m.
Emily Ann Whitehead, daughter of William Whitehead
of Halifax County, October 15, 1873. He enlisted in C.
S. A., April 16, 1864, at Halifax, and was a private
in Company "K", 2nd. N. C. Junior Reserves, and
served for the duration of the war. He died near Enfield,
North Carolina, May 23, 1922.
Children:

(1) Rosa Anna Lawrence, b. November 14, 1874, m.
Charles N. Parks, son of A.J. and Beady Parks,
of Halifax County, February 17, 1892.
   Issue:
   a. Leonard David, b. Sept. 2, 1893, d. June 1, 1920.
   b. Minnie Lawrence,
   c. Ruth Allen,
   d. Sarah Elizabeth,
   e. Nannie Lee,
   f. Blanche Macon,
   g. Edna Earle,
   h. Lena Alice,
   i. Andrew Jackson.

(2) William Edwin Lawrence, b. April 29, 1877, m.
Jessie Ellen Messenger, daughter of Warren E.
and Annie Johnson Messenger, of Halifax County,
April 25, 1909, and d. October 1940.
   Issue:
   a. Emily Ann,
   b. William Edwin, Jr.
   c. Joseph Faulcon,
   d. Manford Messenger,
   e. Lynwood Allison,
   f. Infant, d. January 27, 1923.
   g. Landon Lawrence.

(3) Thomas Duke Lawrence, b. October 14, 1878, m.
Ethel Pittman, daughter of Ruffin A. and Martha
Green Pittman, of near Enfield, December 10, 1902,
and d. June 11, 1944.
   Issue:
   a. Lucille Willard,
   b. Elizabeth Glenn,
   c. Leona Pittman,
   d. Thomas Duke, Jr.,
   e. James Ruffin.

(4) John Eaton Lawrence, b. May 22, 1882, m. Elizabeth Pittman, daughter of Ruffin A. and Martha
Green Pittman, December 19, 1906, and d. Dec.
1, 1933.
   Issue:
   a. Katherine Pittman;
   b. John Allen;
   c. Jesse Macon, b. June 14, 1914, d. Mar. 22, 1944.

(5) Mary Elizabeth Lawrence, b. May 22, 1884, m. (1)
Lemuel Wesley Barnhill, son of William Burton
Barhhill, of the Dawson section of Halifax County,
October 1, 1905. She marrried (2) Robert Lawrence
Simmons, November 24, 1920. She was his third
wife. Robert Lawrence Simmons left issue by first
and second marriage, but no issue by third. He
died July 20, 1952.
   Issue of Mary Elizabeth and Lemuel Barnhill:
   a. Daniel Lawrence;

       b. Paul Raymond;

       c. Lemuel Wesley, Jr., b. October 18, 1913, d. Aug. 2, 1949.

       d. Emily Gertrude.

      Lemuel Wesley Barnhill, Sr., d. Oct. 7, 1916.

  (6) Paul Allen Lawrence, b. February 12, 1888, m. Anna Lou Thorne, daughter of George T. and Anna Rebecca Ricks Thorne, of Enfield, April 29, 1917. They had one daughter, Doris Hazel Lawrence.

2. Mary Lucretia Lawrence, b. April 13, 1849, m. Noah Biggs, son of Harry and Crissey Gurganus Biggs, of Martin County, North Carolina, April 22, 1873. Noah Biggs enlisted in Company "G", 41st. Regiment, C.S.A., October 29, 1861. Their only child, Annie C. Biggs, b. January 25, 1874, m. James Allen Pittman (d. Jan. 29, 1924), their foster son, about 1907. There were two other foster children: (1) Tyler B. Wheeler, m. Lillian Timberlake, of Louisburg, and (2) Emily Sawyer, m. William Herbert McDowell, of Scotland Neck. Mary Lawrence Biggs d. July 7, 1925.

3. Martha Allen Lawrence, b. December 25, 1850, m. Captain Whitmel Hill Anthony (d. November 1, 1904), son of Charity Barnes and Colonel Whitmel Hill Anthony, I, of the Hill's Cross Roads section of Halifax County, February 22, 1871. Captain Anthony was in command of Company "B", 9th Regiment, 1st. Cavalry, C.S.A., composed of Northampton County men. He was wounded near Dinwiddie Court House, Virginia, March 29, 1865. Whitmel H. Anthony, II, represented Halifax County in the General Assembly in 1888. Martha Allen Lawrence Anthony d. February 21, 1907, at Hill's Cross Roads, near Scotland Neck.

      Issue:

  (1) Whitmel Hill Anthony, III, b. November 6, 1872, m. Josephine Jones, daughter of Andrew Jackson and Amanda Rogers Jones, of Granville County, North Carolina, March 4, 1899, d. November 7, 1951, Weldon, N.C.

      Issue:

      a. Whitmel Hill, IV,

      b. Marion Childress, b. Oct. 30, 1902, d. infant,

      c. Margaret Childress, b. Nov. 30, 1903, d. May 20, 1949.

      d. Elizabeth Lawrence,

      e. Katherine Gregory,

      f. Evelyn Josephine,

      g. Nan Elliott,

      h. John Anthony.

  (2) John Allen Anthony, b. November 11, 1876, m. Bessie Lee Riddick, daughter of William Thomas and Georgeanna Steptoe Biggs Riddick, of Scotland Neck, November 11, 1902, d. April 2, 1943, Florence, S.C. He was a veteran of the Spanish American War.

Issue:
a. Bessie Lee, b. February 8, 1904, d. June 20, 1929.
b. Mattie Cecelia
c. Doris Allen, b. February 8, 1907, d. July 18, 1908.

(3) Mattie Lawrence Anthony, b. August 22, 1880, m. William Thurston Van Landingham (d. November 29, 1920), son of Micajah Thomas Van Landingham, of Hinkerville, Kentucky, January 29, 1902, d. January 11, 1922, in Scotland Neck.
Issue:
a. William Thurston, Jr., b. November 5, 1902, d. September 27, 1920.
b. Whitmel Lawrence,
c. Martha Lawrence,
d. John Robert,
e. Mary Elizabeth (see later),
f. James Atherton, b. Feb. 28, 1915, d. infant,
g. Annie Christine, b. February 28, 1915, d. infant,
h. James Allen,
i. Mildred Elise.

4. Sarah E. Lawrence, b. Oct. 31, 1852, d. June 2, 1853.
5. John Duke Lawrence, b. June 3, 1854, m. Mary (Molly) Edwards (d. January 24, 1953), daughter of Salathial Wren and Rebecca Ann Jordan Edwards of Scotland Neck, January 21, 1881, d. Scotland Neck, December 19, 1937.
Children:
(1) Ernest Wren Lawrence, b. October 31, 1882, m. Ida Messenger, daughter of Warren E. and Annie Johnson Messenger, of Tillery, N. C., July 31, 1902.
Issue:
a. Wren Edwards,
b. Helen Mae.

(2) Leonard Duke Lawrence, b. March 1, 1885, d. September 5, 1887.

(3) Annie Edwards Lawrence, b. June 6, 1890, m. Isaac Ferd Harrison, son of Joseph Albert and Cottie Bateman Harrison, of Scotland Neck, Oct. 7, 1915.
Issue:
a. Henry Lee,
b. Ferd Lawrence.

(4) James Douglas Lawrence, b. August 7, 1899, m. Grace Locke, daughter of Lucion Sidney and Lula Whitehead Locke of Enfield, May 28, 1921.
Issue:
a. Mary Lou,
b. Marjorie Craig,
c. Ann Douglas,
d. Glenn Duke.

6. William James Lawrence, b. October 7, 1856, d. Oct. 8, 1874.

7. Christopher B. Allen Lawrence, b. December 4, 1858, m. (1) Marie Antoinette Manford, daughter of James and Mary Law Manford, of Luling, Texas, September 22, 1886. Marie Antoinette Manford Lawrence died 1911, and Christopher A. Lawrence m. (2) Mrs. Blanche Snaverly, daughter of Larkin D. and Mary Jane Dodson Secrest, of Columbus, Texas, March 20, 1913, by whom he had no issue. Christopher Allen Lawrence d. December 31, 1937, San Antonio, Texas, and was buried in Luling, Texas.

Children:

(1) John Manford Lawrence, b. Oct. 9, 1887;
(2) Martha Antoinette Lawrence, b. August 19, 1889, and had issue.
(3) Mary Elizabeth Lawrence, b. December 7, 1892, m. Harry Stebbins.

8. George Powell Lawrence, b. January 2, 1861, d. Aug. 22, 1889, Luling, Texas. Unmarried.

9. Lellie Whitten Lawrence, b. December 26, 1862, m. James Monroe Tillery (d. September 7, 1923), son of John B. and Martha Dunn Tillery, of Tillery, April 4, 1884. Lellie Lawrence Tillery d. September 2, 1921, in Scotland Neck.

Children:

(1) John Lawrence Tillery, b. March 13, 1885, d. Oct. 1885.
(2) Alice Pauline Tillery, b. March 10, 1886, m. Chas. J. Shields, son of James Griffin and Margaret Whitmore Shields, d. May 10, 1947.
   Issue:
   a. Fay Memory,
   b. Frank Percival,
   c. Angeline Katherine.
(3) Ruby Ernestine Tillery, b. January 31, 1888, m. Hugh Johnson, son of Dr. R. M. and Pattie Shields Johnson, of Scotland Neck, October 18, 1910. Hugh Johnson d. April 12, 1955, Raleigh, N.C.
   Issue:
   a. Ruby Tillery,
   b. Hugh Johnson, Jr.,
   c. James Tillery.
(4) James Lawrence Tillery, b. October 22, 1889, m. Georgette Braud, daughter of Monsieur and Madam Jean Braud, of Nates, France, February 19, 1919. James Lawrence Tillery died without issue, March 3, 1953, in Florida.
(5) Lellie May Tillery, b. January 14, 1893, d. June 16, 1908.
(6) Katherine Elizabeth Tillery, b. January 26, 1895, m. William A. Quinerly, son of John William and Lena Kilpatrick Quinerly, of Ayden, N.C., November 5, 1919. No issue.
(7) Annie Allen Tillery, b. December 13, 1897, d. February, 1899.

(8) Robert Wells Tillery, b. March 18, 1901, d. July 7, 1902.

10. Ida Dandridge Lawrence, b. September 28, 1864, d. January 15, 1866.

11. Ada Alston Lawrence, b. November 23, 1867, m. Joseph Ranson Holliday, son of Major Jesse Gray and Ann Ivey Holliday, of Dawson community, January 8, 1890. Ada Lawrence Holliday d. August 29, 1917, and Joseph R. Holliday m. (2) Elizabeth Eleanor Cherry, daughter of William Rodney and Elizabeth Eleanor Moore Cherry, of Scotland Neck, April 5, 1921. He died in Scotland Neck, January 20, 1930.

Children:

(1) Annie Mary Holliday, b. January 12, 1891, died June 14, 1892.

(2) Jesse Lawrence Holliday, b. July 3, 1895, m. Mary Joyce, daughter of Robert Francis and Alice Garrett Joyce, of Stoneville, N.C., December 28, 1921. He died without issue, May 30, 1952.

(3) Joseph Allen Holliday, b. December 6, 1900, d. July 18, 1902.

(4) Donald Vann Holliday, b. January 29, 1904, m. Gladys Taylor, daughter of Henry Clay and Henrietta Bridges Taylor, of Louisburg, October 25, 1930. Residence, Enfield. They have one daughter, Betty Bridges Holliday, b. October 3, 1931, m. William Bryan Waddell, son of Dr. Robert Lee and Rose Evelyn Fulmer Waddell, of Galax, Virginia, June 20, 1952. William B. Waddell is now an Ensign in the U.S. Navy and stationed in Hawaii.

(5) Dennis Hutson Holliday, b. January 29, 1904, m. Mary Eugenia Elliott, daughter of Joseph F. and Sarah Effie Winslow Elliott, of Hertford, N.C., May 9, 1938. Residence, Enfield. They have one son, Dennis Hutson Holliday, Jr., b. June 9, 1948.

12. Daniel Allen Lawrence, b. June 13, 1869, m. Hattie Clark, of Weldon, N.C., who died without issue July 30, 1905. He m. (2) Constance Evelyn Saum, daughter of John W. and Ella F. Saum, of Strasburg, Virginia, May 25, 1911. Daniel Lawrence moved to Luling, Tex., in 1912. He married (3) Mrs. Clara Francis Beaty in 1922. He died January 2, 1938, in Sinton, Texas, and was buried in Luling.

Issue of Daniel and Constance Lawrence:

(1) Allen Saum Lawrence, b. July 7, 1913, m. Apolline Cobb, daughter of Delaney Whitehurst and Lucia Pauline Dow Cobb, of Jourdanton, Texas, July 9, 1938. They have one son, Allen Saum Lawrence, Jr., b. April 3, 1943. Residence, Sinton, Texas.

(2) Constance Ellen Lawrence, b. September 23, 1918, m. Frank George Eisenhauer, June 11, 1949.

Issue:

a. Gary Frank,
b. Gregg Allen.

13. Robert Edwin Lawrence, b. October 22, 1872, d. December 14, 1874.

IV. William Josephus Lawrence, son of Thomas Duke and Mary B. Powell Lawrence, b. February 5, 1824, m. Annie F. Shields, daughter of Charles C. and Felicia Norfleet Young Shields, of Scotland Neck, March 20, 1851. He d. September 21, 1856.

Children:

1. Olivia Norfleet Lawrence, b. July 31, 1853, m. Dr. William Owen McDowell, son of Dr. Archibald McDowell, of Murfreesboro, N.C., December 18, 1877. Olivia Lawrence McDowell d. June 7, 1923.

Children:

(1) Charles Lawrence McDowell, b. October 9, 1878, m. Annie Maria Kitchin, daughter of Captain W.H. and Anne Maria Arrington Kitchin, of Scotland Neck, December 12, 1905. They had one son, Dr. William Kitchin McDowell. Charles Lawrence McDowell d. June 16, 1938.

(2) Archibald McDowell, b. May 7, 1880, d. June 3, 1897.

(3) William Herbert McDowell, b. December 17, 1882, m. Emily S. Biggs, daughter of Isaac Paul Sawyer, and foster daughter of Noah and Mary Lawrence Biggs, December 25, 1912. No issue.

(4) Harry Lee McDowell, b. November 14, 1889, m. Dorothy Marian Dunn, daughter of Charles Wells Dunn, of Scotland Neck, October 11, 1916. They had one son, Harry Lee McDowell, Jr. Harry Lee McDowell, Sr., died October 12, 1918, and Dorothy Dunn McDowell died in Scotland Neck, Jan. 10, 1933.

(5) James Allison McDowell, b. June 3, 1894, m. Mary B. Ashcraft, daughter of Kenan Wilson Ashcraft, June 23, 1920. No issue.

(6) Norfleet Owen McDowell, b. March 4, 1897, m. Margaret Joyner, daughter of William H. Joyner of Garysburg, N.C., October 23, 1922. They have one son, Norfleet Owen McDowell, Jr.

2. Charlie Thomas Lawrence, b. March 21, 1855, m. Annie Rebecca Camp, daughter of James Oscar and Carrie Virginia Jackson Camp, of Scotland Neck, and died April 21, 1903.

Children:

(1) Annie O. Lawrence, b. November 4, 1879, died June 20, 1882.

(2) William Oscar Lawrence, b. December 20, 1881, m. Kate Dunn, daughter of William Arrington and Kate Speed Dunn, of Scotland Neck, April 17, 1906.

Issue:

a. John Elmore,

b. William Oscar, Jr.

William O. Lawrence, Sr., died in Scotland Neck, September 8, 1950.

(3) Blanche Lawrence, b. August 2, 1882, m. Dr. Joseph Powell Wimberly, son of Joseph Powell and Frances Wimberly, of Battleboro, N.C., October 29, 1902. They had one son, Joseph P. Wimberly, Jr. Blanche Lawrence Wimberly died in Battleboro, February 19, 1950. Dr. Joseph P. Wimberley died August 14, 1942.

(4) Charlie Thomas Lawrence, II, b. May 4, 1885, m. Eliza Tripp Shaw, daughter of Robert Bonner and Eliza Tripp Shaw, of Washington, N.C., June 10, 1907, and died in Scotland Neck, September 19, 1947.
Issue:
a. Dr. Charlie Thomas, III, M.D.
b. John Graham,
c. Ann Bonner.

(5) James Shields Lawrence, b. December 18, 1899, m. Jule O'Brian.

(6) Olivia Norfleet Lawrence, m. Samuel Arrington Dunn, son of James Leonidas and Dorothy Miriam Dunn, of Scotland Neck, February 3, 1915. She was his second wife. His first wife was Huldah Edmondson Josey, who died in Scotland Neck, August 9, 1908. Her children were: Marietta and Samuel Arrignton Dunn, Jr.
Children of Samuel and Olivia Dunn:
a. Nancy Elizabeth
b. Charles Wells Dunn.
Samuel Arrington Dunn, Sr., died in Scotland Neck, May 14, 1935.

(7) Carrie Virginia Lawrence, m. Alvin Paul Kitchin, son of Captain W.H. and Annie Maria Arrington Kitchin of Scotland Neck, January 2, 1907. He represented Halifax County in the Lower House of the General Assembly in 1909 and the Senate in 1911.
Children:
a. Alvin Paul, Jr.,
b. Charlie Lawrence, died at age three,
c. Travis Camp,
d. Frances Jane Kitchin.
Alvin Paul Kitchin, Sr., died June 28, 1923.

V.   Mary Elizabeth Lawrence, daughter of Thomas Duke and Mary B. Powell Lawrence, was born in Northampton Co., February 20, 1826, and died in Water Valley, Mississippi, February 16, 1905. She married William Ruthven Avent, son of Benjamine W. Avent, of Wilmington, N.C., about 1859, and they moved to Water Valley within a year or two. She was his second wife. His first wife, Rebecca Harvey Avent, of Halifax County, bore him three children: (1) Eddie Ruthven, b. July 8, 1849, died May 8, 1919; (2) John Lawrence, b. April 12, 1851, died in Grenada, Mississippi, December 28, 1934; (3) Alice Winifred, b. August 6, 1854, m. T. A. Hale, of Water Valley.
Children by second marriage of William Ruthven Avent:

1. Elizabeth Avent, b. April, 1862, m. C.P. Shaw, son of John Shaw of Water Valley, and died in Natchez, Mississippi in 1935.
   Issue:
   (1) Willie
   (2) Lawrence
   (3) Lillian, m. Best Vincent.
2. Mary Avent, b. June 1864, m. W.S. Cook, son of Hiram Cooke of Water Valley. They made their home in Oklahoma City, Oklahoma, where she died March 24, 1944.
   Children:
   (1) Ehren, m. Dr. S.E. Frierson, of Oklahoma City;
   (2) Louise Susann, m. (1) A.G. Elfut, and m. (2) John (Jack) Ford.
   (3) William Hiram Cook, was drowned July 4, 1933, in Oklahoma City.

VI. Sarah Imogene Lawrence, daughter of Thomas Duke and Mary B. Powell Lawrence, b. February 27, 1831, m. David Crockett Gatling and resided in Rich Square, N.C., where she died May 24, 1891. She was his second wife. His first wife was Mary (Molly) Harris, daughter of Thomas K. and Louisa Ann Lawrence Harris (above). Issue: (1) Willie, (2) Eddie Gatling.

VII. James Hiram Lawrence, son of Thomas Duke and Mary B. Powell Lawrence, b. August 8, 1833, d. December 14, 1907, m. (1) Mary N. Brady (d. May 29, 1869) of Tarboro, N.C., about 1858. Children: (1) Edwin C., b. February 22, 1859, d. January 10, 1865; (2) Mary E., b. August 16, 1867, m. Rufus C. Lassiter, and died without issue February 15, 1916; (3) James N., b. April 9, 1869, d. August 21, 1869. James H. Lawrence m. (2) Mary Biggs (died 1877), daughter of Joseph D. and Elizabeth Davis Biggs. of Martin County, about 1871.
   Children of second marriage:
1. Elizabeth Davis Lawrence, b. December 8, 1872, m. Eugene Thomas Whitehead, son of Joseph H. and Eliza Gray Whitehead, of Scotland Neck, November 23, 1892, and died in Scotland Neck September 12, 1950.
   Children:
   (1) Mary Eliza Whitehead, b. May 22, 1894, died August 16, 1895.
   (2) Irene Gray Whitehead, born October 8, 1895, m. Richard David House, son of William Lawrence and Sally Mitchell House of Scotland Neck, April 11, 1917.
   (3) Gertrude Biggs Whitehead, b. December 31, 1897, m. John Calhoun Riddick, son of Albert C. and Willie Allsbrook Riddick, of Martin County, April 21, 1920.
   (4) Louise Lawrence Whitehead, b. August 23, 1900, d. June 12, 1901.
   (5) Eugene Thomas Whitehead, II, b. December 23, 1902, m. Elizabeth Farmer, daughter of Reginald

Leo and Mary Moore Farmer, of Wilson, N.C.,
November 28, 1934. Elizabeth Farmer Whitehead
died in Scotland Neck, February 14, 1952.

(6) James Lawrence Whitehead, b. July 15, 1904,
died June 26, 1905.

(7) Joseph Leartes Whitehead, b. September 22, 1905,
m. Katherine Shields, daughter of Frank P. and
Mollie Tillery Shields, of Scotland Neck, August
21, 1929.

(8) Landon Lawrence Whitehead, b. May 23, 1907.
Unmarried.

(9) Elizabeth Lawrence Whitehead, b. May 25, 1912,
died July 30, 1912.

2. Landon Z. Lawrence was killed in Lula, Mississippi,
November 16, 1894.

3. Robert Lee Lawrence, died in California, November 3,
1895.

4. Louisa Biggs Lawrence, died at age 19 years.

James Hiram Lawrence m. (3) Annie Elizabeth Montague,
daughter of Dr. Henry W. and Annie Elizabeth Jones Montague, of Wake County, N.C., on November 8, 1882. Annie
Montague Lawrence died in Scotland Neck, August 29, 1916.
No issue.

VIII. Charity F. Lawrence, daughter of Thomas Duke and Mary
B. Powell Lawrence, b. May 6, 1836, m. Lafayette L.
Moore, of Enfield, N.C., and died in Arkadelphia, Arkan-
sas, December 28, 1872, and was buried in the Masonic
Cemetery.
Children:

1. Sarah Moore, m. Harry Lyner, of Water Valley, Mississippi. Their daughter, Lois Lyner, m. Mr. Sea-
mons, of Memphis, Tennessee.

2. James Moore, born in Coffeeville, Mississippi, in
1866, made his home in Woodson, Texas.

3. John Moore, born about 1868, was deceased prior to
1933.

4. Willie Moore, born about 1870, made his home in New
Orleans, La.

The above data was prepared by Dennis Hutson Holliday,
Enfield, North Carolina, April, 1956.
(Added by the Author)
Mary Elizabeth Van Landingham, the daughter of Martha
Lawrence Anthony and Wm. Thurston Van Landingham, was
born Nov. 24, 1912 at Scotland Neck, N.C., and married there
Oct. 8, 1938, Claude Franklin Goldsmith, the son of Janie Ada
Coone and James Warren Goldsmith, who was born in Winston-
Salem, N.C., Nov. 25, 1905, educated in public schools in
Winston-Salem, Charlotte and Marion, N.C. and the North Caro-
lina State College in Raleigh, N.C., and is now Secretary and
Buyer of Cross Cotten Mills Co., in Marion, N.C. His present
address is Box 529, Marion, N.C. Issue: (a) Claude Franklin
Goldsmith, Jr., born August 26, 1945; (b) James Whitmel Gold-
smith, born March 12, 1948.

FRIZZELL of ISLE of WIGHT

Several Frizzell families settled in Virginia about the middle of the Seventeenth Century and it is difficult to determine their relationship. William Frizzell was a headright of James Pope who patented 1000 acres in Westmoreland Jan. 28, 1662 (C P 509). John Frizzell patented 104½ acres in the same county Feb. 9, 1663 (C P 483). Two persons bearing the same name are later found in Isle of Wight County. John Frizzell, on Mar. 4, 1667, bought land of Nicholas Cobb (17C-551). He and Ann, his wife, sold the land in 1673 (Id 569). On October 9, 1671, he appraised the estate of Arthur Lewis (C-1-15). Both he and William Frizzell appraised the estate of John Wale (Id 23). This was apparently the first time William Frizzell's name appears in the records. John Frizzell Jr. appraised the estate of Jane Valentine in 1677 (Id 22). On March 9, 1680, John Frizzell witnessed a power of attorney (17C-556).

It is very probable that this John Frizzell Jr. was the John Frizzell, son of William Frizzell who made his will Aug. 19, 1692, same probated April 10, 1693. He gave son William land in the lower parish adjoining William Frizzell. "If son dies bequests to be divided with rest of my children, daughters Mary, Elizabeth, and wife Susannah personalty she to be executor". (C-1-49)

William Frizzell, father of John, decd., made his will Oct. 25, 1706, probated March 30, 1706-07. He gave 100 acres to grandson William Frizzell, son of JOHN FRIZZELL deceased (grandson William Frizzell was under age). He also mentions granddaughters Mary and Elizabeth Frizzell and Susan Pope. Also daughter Isabella who married Thomas Sawyer.

On April 6, 1693, John Portis gave to his daughter Susannah Thomas, wife of John Thomas, land for life. Susannah was formerly the wife of John Frizzell, decd., "and if she die before her son Will Frizzell is of age of 18, then her grandson Will Frizzell is to possess it." (17 C-609)

It seems that John Frizzell, the elder, evidently moved to Maryland for he disappears from the county records and is said to be the father or grandfather of John Frizzell who married about 1720 Elizabeth Gale, daughter of John Gale. John Gale made his will in Maryland Dec. 31, 1730. The Gale family was also from Isle of Wight (See "17th Century" and Chapman's Wills). They had a son, Gale Frizzell, who married Susannah --------, in Baltimore County, Maryland, in 1742.

Children:

I.   Elizabeth Frizzell, b. Feb. 4, 1743, m. Capt. Lance Todd.

II.   Sarah Frizzell, b. Jan. 25, 1745

III.   John Gale Frizzell, b. July 1748, m. Rebecca Bryson (see later).

IV. Thomas Frizzell, b. Jan. 12, 1750.

John Gale Frizzell was born July 1748 in Baltimore, Maryland, and married Rebecca Bryson. He served in the Revolutionary War from Chesterfield District, S.C. under Capt. Deason and Gen. Sumpter. He was given land for his services on the PeeDee River in Anson County, N.C. near Wadesboro.

Children:

I. James Frizzell, b. 1790, m. Rebecca Flowers
II. Thomas Bryson Frizzell, fought and was massacred at Goliad in Texas in the Mexican War.
III. David Frizzell, went to Kentucky.

James Frizzell was born 1790 on the Hiwassee River in Cherokee Country, then North Carolina, now Tennessee; died Jan. 1873 in Bell Buckle, Bedford County, Tenn; married 1810 Rebecca Flowers, born near Knoxville, Tenn., died in Bedford Co., Tenn.

Children:

I. William Frizzell, b. 1816, m. Ana Hayes; went to Arkansas.
II. Jacob Frizzell, b. 1818, m. Elizabeth Brewer; went to Kentucky.
III. Nathan Frizzell, b. 1820, m. Anna Hopper, went to Kentucky.
IV. John Frizzell, b. Feb. 1, 1822, m. Mary Chaffin (see later).
V. Mary Frizzell, b. 1824, m. Jesse Thomas, to Missouri.
VI. Polly (Mary) Frizzell, b. 1826, m. Pleas Jacobs, to Arkansas.
VII. Hannah, b. 1828, m. Andrew Rushing, to Kentucky.
VIII. James Frizzell, b. 1831, unmarried.
IX. Thomas, b. 1836, unmarried.
X. Mahaley, b. 1839, m. Green Majors, to Tennessee.
XI. Elizabeth (Bettie), b. 1840, m. James Keele, to Tenn.

John W. Frizzell was born Feb. 1, 1822, in Bell Buckle, Bedford County, Tenn.; died June 5, 1861, Bell Buckle, Bedford Co., Tenn.; married June 28, 1849, in Bell Buckle, Tenn., Mary Chaffin, born July 24, 1826, m. Bell Buckle, Tenn., died May 23, 1859, Bell Buckle, Tenn., daughter of Archer Chaffin (son of Nathaniel Chaffin) and Frances Fears, daughter of William Fears. The Chaffins and Fears were from Charlotte County, Virginia.

Children:

I. Jessie Edwin Frizzell, b. Oct. 25, 1857, m. Catherine Malinda Blair (see later).
II. Thomas Fears Frizzell, b. Dec. 25, 1855, m. Sallie Mosley.
III. Archer Chaffin Frizzell, b. Mar. 27, 1852, m. Charlie Sutton.
IV. Julia Coleman Frizzell, b. Oct. 3, 1850, m. Albert Latimer.

Jessie Edwin Frizell, was born Oct. 25, 1857 in Bell Buckle, Bedford Co., Tenn.; died Jan. 6, 1952, Beech Grove, Coffee County, Tenn.; married July 4, 1880 Bell Buckle, Tenn., Catherine Malinda Blair, born Jan. 6, 1857, Bell Buckle, Tenn.; died June 24, 1929, Beech Grove, Coffee County, Tenn., daughter of Robert Doak Blair and Sarah Dillard.

Child:

I.   Lucile Frizzell, b. Oct. 2, 1882, m. Herbert Jacobs.

Lucile Frizzell was born Oct. 2, 1882, Beech Grove, Coffee County, Tenn.; married Oct. 9, 1904, Murfreesboro, Rutherford County, Tenn., Herbert Jacobs, born Nov. 22, 1883, Beech Grove, Coffee County, Tenn., died Jan. 24, 1950, Nashville, Tenn., son of Dallas Polk Jacobs (son of Clinton Jacobs) and Ann Belle Mankin, daughter of John Mankin. Mrs. Jacobs resides at Tuckaway Farm, Beech Grove, Tenn.

Children:

I.   Blair Jacobs, b. June 6, 1907, m. Ruby Provence.
II.   Merle, b. Oct. 23, 1909.
III. Dallas Luke Jacobs, b. June 30, 1911, m. Leona McMichael.
IV. Catherine Frizzell Jacobs, b. Oct. 5, 1914.
V.   Robert T. Jacobs, b. Apr. 22, 1917.
VI. Eleanor Doak Jacobs, b. Aug. 11, 1920, m. Edgar Raoul Ibe.
VII. Lucile Frizell Jacobs, b. Dec. 10, 1922, m. Mell Marbury.
VIII. Nancy Jane Jacobs, b. Sept. 7, 1926, m. James Dow Blake.

GILLIAM

This name has been variously spelled Guilham, Gillham, Guilliam, etc. The first mention of the name appears in a patent granted Joseph Royall August 20, 1642, in Henrico County for the transportation of 12 persons, among whom were John and Thomas Guilham (C.P. 130). They are undoubtedly the John, aged 21, and Thomas Gillam, aged 18 years, who sailed from Gravesend, England, bound for Virginia on August 21, 1635, on the "George", master, John Severne. (Hotten-124). They were probably brothers.

On October 1, 1687, the following deed was made by Henry Randolph, II, to Mrs. Margery Guilliam: "To all to whom these presents shall come Greetings; Whereas he Henry Randolph, late of this county of Henrico, deceased, did, by virtue of the General Court bearing date ye 21 of September, 1571, make out and patent a tract formerly deserted by Mr. John Guillam as by ye patent for ye same dated at James Citty ye May 17, 1673 may plainly appear; and the said Randolph did assign over ye said land unto Mrs. Margery Guyllam, relict of ye said John, her heirs and assigns forever on 16 July 1673, but before ye same was acknowledged in Court or ratified accordingly did depart this life., Now I, Henry Randolph, son and heir of ye before mentioned deceased Henry Randolph, out of filial duty and reverence I bear to ye memory of my said deceased father, do grant unto Margery Briggs, late relict of ye aforesaid John Guilliam and assignee of Mr. Henry Randolph and assign forever that piece, parcel and tract of land situated, lying or being in Bristol Parish in ye county of Charles Citty on ye southside of Appamattox River as in contained herein ye bounds in ye before mentioned patent granted ye said Henry Randolph."

Mrs. Margery Gilliam married, secondly, cr. 1680, Henry Briggs (1635-1686) of Surry County. (See S.V.F. 1, 104-108). Mrs. Margery Gilliam-Briggs died in 1688, for on Oct. 20, 1688, the following order was entered in Surry Court: "Whereas Margery Briggs, late of this county, dying and leaving an estate and divers goods, John Gilliam, Hinchia Gilliam and Francis Maybury, by right of his wife Elizabeth, are granted administration rights."

Children of John[1] and Margery Gilliam:

I.   Elizabeth[2] Gilliam m. (1) ------ West; m. (2) William Bevin; (3) Francis Mayberry. She mentions sons John and Francis West in her will dated 1713. Francis West made his will in Isle of Wight, Oct. 8, 1715, and named cousin Francis West, son of John West and the rest of the children of John West. (C-1-85)

II.   John Gilliam, m. Sarah ------, who died Feb. 23, 1769. John made his will in Surry, Aug. 9, 1738, probated Sept. 20, 1738 (B. 8-902). He owned 1000 acres in Prince George in 1704. Charles Gilliam also held 200 acres there in 1704.

Children mentioned in will:

1. John[3] received plantation on Roanoke in Carolina. He married Ann Mason.
   Children, A.P.R.:
   (1) Mary Gilliam, 12/9/43; Joseph Mason, Phœbe Mason, Mary Gilliam.
   (2) John Gilliam, 2/29/48; John Morre, Wm. Rachael, Eliz. Prichard.
   (3) Elizabeth Gilliam, 9/22/55; Mason Bishop, Mary Glover, Rebecca Mason.
   (4) Hinchae, 7/2/53; John and David Mason, Mary Mason.
   (5) Howell, 12/14/60; Holman Southall, Wm. Dansey, Jr., Mary Gilliam.

2. Hinchea Gilliam, given 150 acres next to mill in Surry. His will was probated April 20, 1737, names wife, extrx; sons: Hinchea, John, Samuel; daughters: Elizabeth and Ann Gilliam; and brother John[3]. Hinchea married Mary --------.
   Children of Hinchea and Mary Gilliam (A.P.R.):
   (1) John Gilliam, b. 1/22/1745;
   (2) Lucy, b. 3/25/48;
   (3) Mary, b. 2/9/52;
   (4) Sarah, b. 3/9/55;
   (5) Lucy, b. 1/5/57;
   (6) Peggy, b. 3/23/59;
   (7) Edna, b. 1/29/64.

3. Burwell[3] Gilliam, given 150 acres on south side of Great Branch. His wife was Anne ------.
   Children of Burwell and Anne Gilliam (A.P.R.)
   (1) Patty, b. 11/25/1746;
   (2) Franky, b. 10/22/47;
   (3) William, b. 10/11/49;
   (4) Anne, b. 3/3/52;
   (5) Rebecca, b. 1/3/55;
   (6) Moses, b. 11/17/56;
   (7) Miles, b. 2/21/59;
   (8) Wyatt, b. 4/6/62.

4. Levy[3] Gilliam, given one negro. He m. Elizabeth.
   Children of Levy and Elizabeth Gilliam (A.P.R.)
   (1) Prissilla, b. 2/4/49;
   (2) Lucy, b. 10/13/52;
   (3) Anslem, b. 4/7/54;
   (4) Harris, b. 4/22/56;
   (5) Levi, b. 6/23/58;
   (6) Sally, b. 8/16/61.

5. Isam[3] Gilliam, b. Feb. 25, 1733, given remainder of estate after death of wife to be divided with Hanselle[3]. He m. Pricilla;
   Children of Isam and Pricilla Gilliam (A.P.R.)
   (1) Margery, b. 3/11/1763;
   (2) Patty, b. 7/9/68;
   (3) Burwell, b. 1/20/72;
   (4) Prissilla, b. 9/1/74.

6. Hansille[3] Gilliam; daughters: Amy; Mary; Millie; Tabitha; Lidia, b. March 27, 1736.

III. Hinchea[2] Gilliam (John[1]) held 658 acres in Surry in 1704.
He married Fortune Flood, daughter of Walter Flood and
wife Anne Browne, daughter of Col. William Browne.
(See p. 306, V.H.G.) Captain Hinchea Gilliam died in 1734,
will being probated Nov. 20, 1734. Children mentioned in
will were: Hinchea, plantations where I now live; Walter,
plantation where he now lives and 200 acres next to Rock-
on Swamp; Thomas, 200 acres and land after wife's death;
Charles, plantation where he now lives and 200 acres next
to Benjamin Harrison; daughters, Priscilla and Lydia
Gilliam.

Mrs. Fortune Gilliam's will was probated in Sussex
in 1754. She mentioned only four sons in her will: CHARLES
(see later); THOMAS; WALTER and WILLIAM.

Children of Hinchea and Fortune Gilliam (A.P.R.)
1. John[3] Gilliam, b. ca. 1696-1738, m. ca. 1717 Sarah
------, d. 1770.
2. Hinshaw[3] Gilliam, b. ca. 1698-1737, m. ca. 1725
Faith Briggs. Their children were: (A.P.R.) (see
p. 108 S.V.F., Vol. I)
(1) Hinchea[4], b. July 30, 1729 (see later).
(2) Anne, b. April 6, 1731
(3) John, b. April 12, 1733.
(4) Samuel, b. July 9, 1736.
(5) Elizabeth, mentioned in her father's will.
Hinchea[4] Gilliam, son of Faith Briggs and
Hinshaw[3] Gilliam, married Amy ------. He made
his will Dec. 12, 1768, probated April 20, 1769.
Amy Gilliam made her will in 1772. Children from
A.P.R., who were under age at parents death:
a. John[5], b. Feb. 16, 1755, died unmarried; mentioned his two brothers Hinchea and William in
his will dated Sept. 23, 1776, probated 1777.
b. Lucy, b. Nov. 12, 1765, died young.
c. Hinchea, b. April 17, 1759.
d. William, b. Jan. 1, 1762.
3. Walter[3] Gilliam, b. cr. 1700-1758; m. Sarah (Bolling?)
4. Thomas Gilliam, b. ca. 1702-1790; m. (1) 1723, Mary
(Clements?); (2) 1784, Selah Sorsby (1744-179-).
5. William Gilliam, b. ca. 1704-1764. (see later)
6. Charles Gilliam, ca. 1706-1767. (see later)
7. Priscilla Gilliam
8. Lydia Gilliam

William Gilliam, son of Captain Hinchea Gilliam and wife,
Fortune Flood, lived in the southern part of Surry County which
in 1753 became Sussex County, Va. He married, 1725, Susanna
Green, daughter of Lewis Green, Jr., of Prince George County,
Va. Thier children were:
I. Margery[4] Gilliam, b. ca. 1726, m. 1742 Capt. Richard
HILL (see Hill) 1720-1775.
II. Capt. William Gilliam, 1728-1765, m. (1) 1752 Mildred

Hill, d. Feb. 5, 1753, reported by William Gilliam, Jr.;
m. (2) ca. Mary--------. Mary, widow of William Gilliam,
d. Oct. 20, 1771, reported by Richard Hill.

III. Amy Gilliam m. Lewis Tyus of Brunswick County, Va.
IV. Frances Gilliam, m. Thomas Evans of Dinwiddie County, Virginia.
V. Jane Gilliam, m. Robert Jackson of Sussex County, Va.

Charles[3] Gilliam, son of Hinchea and Fortune Flood Gilliam,
married Mary, daughter of John and Amy Clanton. Their children were (A.P.R.):

I. Fortune[4] Gilliam, 6/16/1742, d. same day, reported by Burwell Gilliam.
II. Lydia[4] Gilliam, 11/25/44.
III. John Gilliam, 4/14/51.
IV. Phoebe, twin;
V. Jordan, 9/2/57.

A William Gilliam, who may have been the William, Jr.,
(above), who had evidently moved away from Surry before 1771,
and had a wife named Hannah, made his will in 1789 in Newberry,
S.C. He had a land grant of 500 acres, 2-15-1769 in South Carolina from his Excellency, the Right Honorable Lord Charles
Greville Montagu, under the great seal of the Province. In 1772
he deeded 250 acres of this original grant on Bush and Saluda
Rivers in Berkley Co., S.C. to Jonathan Taylor. Gilliam styled
himself as from the "Parish of Mark's, Wheel Right" in the deed
which is in Charlestown, S.C. In his will he named children:
Ann; Mary; Hannah; and John, not of age. He left son William
part of this same land.

William[2] Gilliam; son of Hannah and William[1] Gilliam, was
born in Goochland County, Va., where his father may have lived,
and died in Newberry, S.C. William Gilliam was said to have
been a soldier in the Revolution. His will, dated 1816, is in the
Probate Judge's Office, Newberry, S.C.

Children:
I. James S. Gilliam, b. 1768.
II. Elizabeth R.S. Gilliam, m. Clement Nance.
III. John Taylor Gilliam.
IV. William Gilliam.
V. Jacob Faris Gilliam, 1788-1836, m. Mary Massey (see later).
VI. Reuben Gilliam, 1793-1858, m. Mary Coleman Sims.
VII. Robert Glen Gilliam, m. Eusebia Blackburn.
VIII. Drucilla Ann Goodman Gilliam, m. J.P. Neel.
IX. Nathan Sims Gilliam.
X. Sarah Thompson Gilliam.

Jacob Faris Gilliam, son of William[2] Gilliam and Ann Sims,
was born June 27, 1788, in Newberry, S.C., where he died
August 6, 1836. In 1814 in Newberry he married Mary Massey,
who was born there Jan. 1, 1801 and died there Sept. 19, 1843.

Children:
I. William C. Gilliam, b. June 10, 1818, m. Elizabeth Turner.
II. Drucilla Ann Gilliam, b. Nov. 4, 1815, m. James B. Wilson.

III.   Pettus Wales Gilliam, b. Jan. 16, 1827, m. Harriet C.
       Wilson (see later).
   Pettus Wales Gilliam, son of Mary Massey and Dr. Jacob
Faris Gilliam, was born Jan. 16, 1827, at Newberry, S.C. and
died Sept. 3, 1884, at Hot Springs, Ark. In 1846, at Newberry,
S.C., he married Harriet Caldwell Wilson, who was born there
Feb. 26, 1832, and died in Hot Springs, Ark. March 27, 1879.
Pettus Wales Gilliam was in the Confederate Army.
       Children:
I.   William Clement Gilliam, b. Aug. 2, 1847, m. Almania
       Bell (see later).
II.   Sarah Colin Gilliam, b. 1866, m. John H. Clifton.
III.   Mary Elizabeth Gilliam, b. 1868, m. Thomas White.
   William Clement Gilliam, son of Harriet Caldwell Wilson
and Pettus Wales Gilliam, was born Aug. 2, 1847, at Newberry,
S.C., and died Dec. 17, 1911 at Hot Springs, Ark. On Oct. 8,
1868, at Colonia, Ark., he married Almania Bell, who was born
near Corinth, Miss., Dec. 30, 1845, and died Jan. 25, 1922, at
Hot Springs, Arkansas. Mr. Gilliam was a farmer, Tax Asses-
sor, and Confederate Veteran.
       Children:
I.   Reuben Lynch Gilliam, b. Nov. 30, 1873, m. Mamie Bell
       (No relation). Mrs. and Mrs. Gilliam reside at 239 Oak
       St., Hot Springs, Arkansas.
II.   Lilas Gilliam, b. 1875, d. 1898.

KILLINGSWORTH of SOUTH CAROLINA

The first one of this family in the southern states was William Killingsworth. He was holding 60 acres in Surry in the Quit Rents of 1704; but does not seem to have resided there long. (Col. Surry).

He made his will in Surry County, Nov. 29, 1709, probated March 7, 1709 (BKS. p. 447) as follows:

"...to son WILLIAM KILLINGSWORTH my old Plantation and Land bounding thereto and a neck of land lying between my two Plantations;....to daughter LUCY GULLEDGE one hog.... to son JOHN KILLINGSWORTH the remaining part of Land, beginning at the Plantation where I now live." Makes wife, Avis, exorx. Wits.: Jno. Cooke, Sarah Bullivant, Mary Underwood. (BK 5, p. 447). His son, William, moved to South Carolina.

After the death of William Killingsworth, his wife, Avis. married John Cook, whose will was probated June 20, 1711. He bequeathed "...to my wife, Avis Cook, what was her former husband's". (BK 6-61)

Avis (Killingsworth) Cook made her will June 9, 1711, probated Aug. 15, 1711. She gave to "...daughter-in-law, Elizabeth Cook, my clothing.....to daughter Lucy Gulledge, clothing ....bequest to sons, William Killingsworth and John Killingsworth. Wits.: John Barker, Joseph Harris, Mary Underwood. (BK 6-75).

The first Killingsworth on record in South Carolina appears to have been William Killingsworth, son of William Killingsworth of Surry, whose will was proved in Charleston June !4, 1762 (Bk. 1760-1767). Two of his sons are named in the will, John and William, and bequests are made to three of his grandchildren: Mary, Priscilla and Jacob, all children of son, William, Jr.

"South Carolina Soldiers and Patriots" compiled by L. Andrea, lists William Killingsworth of Berkley as having served in the Cherokee War under Col. John Chevillette, whose men were mainly from Berkley County. This was William Killingsworth, Sr., who died in 1762. His son, William, Jr., was the father of John, Jesse and Jacob Killingsworth.

The repetition of the names John and Jesse in the family is somewhat confusing. Jacob Killingsworth had a brother Jesse, who was a Revolutionary soldier, and Jacob's eldest child was Jesse. The three brothers are on record in the 1790 Census of Richland County, Camden District. "John Killingsworth had in his family one male over 16, one male under 16, and 4 females. He was a Revolutionary soldier and his family lived near his brother Jacob, in the same neighborhood with Robert Hill,

father of John Hill who married a daughter of Jacob Killingsworth". (Issac Ross and Jean Brown and Allied Families by
Anne Mims Wright, pp. 180 et seq.)

Charleston, S.C. Deed Book ZZ, p. 113, gives this information: William Killingsworth of Amelia Township, Craven County,
(which included what is now Richland) sold to George Dudley on
·Jan. 1, 1760, a tract of 250 acres, and reserves the other half
of the same tract for his son Jacob Killingsworth.

Jacob Killingsworth married Mary Salisbury, daughter of
Pettigrew Salisbury of Richland County. The wife of Pettigrew
Salisbury is unknown, as she is not mentioned in the will, and
probably died prior to 1793 when the will was made. Jacob and
Mary Salisbury Killingsworth were parents of ten children in
1790 according to the Census taken that year. They were married prior to 1770, as their eldest child was born that year.
Their slaves are listed as five. Jesse and his mother administered
on his father's estate in 1798. The estate was unsettled until
1843 when Jesse, the only surviving child at that time, petitioned
the Legislature for a final settlement. The Petition is dated Nov.
4, 1843. (Probate's Box 66; pack 1634).

Green's History of Richland County, South Carolina, p. 99,
gives the Revolutionary services of Jacob Killingsworth thus:
"December II, 1781 - February 21, 1782 as Lieutenant at Orange-
burgh; April 1 - April 30, at Four Holes, and at the Fork of the
Edisto in the regiment of Colonel Taylor. Supplied provisions:
steers, bacon, peas, flour, and sole leather."

A study of Richland County Equity Rolls 242 and 316 together
with the Petition of Jesse for a settlement of the estate, gives a
fairly comprehensive picture of the family of Jacob Killingsworth.
His widow Mary, married a second time to Woodward, evidently
Isom Woodward who figures so prominently in the Killingsworth
affairs at this time. Mary died in October 1827. By this time
daughter Winnifred had died unmarried; daughter Mary Crockett
and her husband had died leaving two orphan children, Mary and
William; son Noel who had married Jane Scott and daughter Sarah
who married John Hill had migrated to Jefferson County, Mississippi and had taken with them Mary and William Crockett, the
orphaned children of their sister Mary Crockett. Son William
had been given power of attorney to act for the Mississippi heirs
in the settlement of the estate. However, the death of son William occurred in 1835, the estate still unsettled. Thus it remained until son Jesse effected the final division in 1843.

Issue of Jacob and Mary Salisbury Killingsworth:
I.   Jesse Killingsworth, b. 1770; d. 1856; married and reared
      a family in Richland County, near Eastover.
II.   Sarah Killingsworth, b. ca. 1772; m. John Hill in Richland
      Co., migrated to Jefferson Co., Miss., ca. 1801, had:
      1. Margaret Allison Hill, b. Jan. 19, 1793, m. Henry H.
         Cheek; issue:
         (1) Sarah Amanda Cheek m. (1) Gardner; (2) Walter;
             had issue.
         (2) Thomas Osborne Cheek m. and had issue.
         (3) Winnifred Hill Cheek m. (1) Robinette; (2) Evans;
             had issue;

(4) Mahala Caroline Cheek m. John Gillespie Brown; had issue.

(5) Margaret Narcisse Cheek m. Robert Miller, had issue.

(6) John Hill Cheek married and lived in Louisiana.

(7) Mary B. Cheek m. Robert Miller; had issue.

(8) Matilda M. Cheek, d.s.p.

(9) William Killingsworth Cheek m. Frances Speed Hill, widow of John Hill, Jr., had issue.

(10) Martha Jane Cheek m. William Strong Flowers, had issue.

(11) Dr. Stephen Hale Cheek, d.s.p.

(12) Susan Hill Cheek m. Dr. Neil Brown, had issue.

(13) Jacob Hill Cheek m. Martha Jenkins; had issue.

2. Jacob Killingsworth Hill, b. Jan. 9, 1795; d. May 17, 1855, m. Rebecca Gibson Sims in 1816; lived in Copiah Co., Miss.; served in War of 1812 as Sergeant in Capt. Twilley's Company, was founder of Pleasant Hill Methodist Church; was a member of the Sons of Temperance; also served with distinction in the State Legislature. Children:

(1) Thomas Brown Sims Hill, died young.

(2) Hannah Elizabeth Ann Hill, m. William Flowers; had issue.

(3) Sarah Ann Hill m. (1) George Dorsey, had Hill Dorsey; (2) Dr. Grant, no issue; (3) Hamden Jordan Mackey and had:
  a. Hamden Jordan Mackey m. Lida Moore.
  b. Elizabeth Ann Mackey m. Dr. Robert Jones.
  c. Mary Rebecca Mackey m. Nathan L. Fulgham.
  d. Clara Frances Mackey m. Robert Burr Mims; had:
    (a) Anne Julia Mims m. William Richard Wright. Their children were: Clara Mims Wright; Anne Robert Wright, Willa Patricia Wright, and Mackey Mims Wright.

(4) Jacob Killingsworth Hill m. Emily Wells; had issue;

(5) Robert A. Hill, died young.

(6) Mary Rebecca Hill, d.s.p.

(7) John Andrew Allison Hill m. Frances Speed, had issue.

(8) Dr. Louis Hobbs Hill m. Nancy Susan Otterson; had issue.

(9) William Thomas Hill, d. young.

III. Mary (Polly) Killingsworth m. William Crockett; both died leaving two young children:

1. William Crockett; reared in home of Noel Killingsworth, m. a DeForest in Iowa and had:
  (1) William Asby Crockett.
  (2) H. Clay Crockett.
  (3) Uncas H. Crockett.

2. Mary Crockett, reared in home of John and Sarah Hill, m. Eli T. Montgomery and had:

> (1) Matilda Montgomery m. (1) Malcolm Cameron, had issue; (2) Sid. Champion; and had issue.
> (2) Dr. Wallace Montgomery, first wife unknown, m. (2) Cora Green.
> (3) William Alexander Montgomery m. Lillian Postel Smith.
> (4) Robert Estel Montgomery m. Jennie Jordan, had issue.
> (5) Talulah Montgomery m. Thomas Lipscomb; had issue.

IV. Margaret Killingsworth, died 1838, m. Ephraim Adams in Richland County and had:
1. Ephraim Adams, Jr.
2. Sarah Adams, m. Joseph Morgan.
3. John Adams.
4. Amanda (Mandy) Adams m. Charles Morgan.
5. Adelia Adams.

V. Mark Killingsworth, died July 29, 1840, m. Nancy Shell of Laurens Co., lived in Abbeville Co., S.C.; is buried at First Creek Baptist Church near Abbeville, S.C.
Children:
1. James Killingsworth; lived in Lavonia, Ga.
2. William Green Killingsworth, b. Feb. 23, 1818, d. May 3, 1873; m. Dec. 24, 1854 Louella Young and had:
> (1) Alice Killingsworth m. a Seawright.
> (2) Selina Killingsworth m. a Young.
> (3) William Killingsworth.
> (4) Fanny Killingsworth m. a Milford.
> (5) Sue Killingsworth.
> (6) Emma Killingsworth, m. a Black.
> (7) Dr. Samuel Killingsworth, b. Jan. 29, 1868, died September 5, 1944; m. Corrie Kay April 11, 1894 and had:
>> a. Grace Killingsworth m. Ashby Turner.
>> b. William Marion Killingsworth m. Eugenia Ruff.
>> c. Mary Elizabeth Killingsworth
>> d. Samuel Fulton Killingsworth
>> e. Martha Florine Killingsworth m. P.A. Smith
>> f. Frederick Kay Killingsworth m. Beatrice Keen
>> g. Robert Blake Killingsworth m. Margaret Mc-Coughrin.
> (8) Corrie Killingsworth.
> (9) Ross Gibson Killingsworth.
3. Sarah Killingsworth m. Sam H. Lockhart.
4. Martha Killingsworth m. Dr. Gibson of Eaton, Ga.
5. Sue Killingsworth m. James W. Black of Abbeville, S.C.

VI. Noel Killingsworth b. 1778, died July 3, 1831, m. Jane Scott of Richland County, S.C.; migrated to Jefferson Co., Miss., about 1801; had:
1. Anon Washington Killingsworth, b. Feb. 18, 1814; died 1882, m. Amelia Brashear; had:
> (1) Uncas B. Killingsworth, died young.
> (2) Katherine N. Killingsworth m. Benizah Ellis; had:

         a. Estelle Ellis.

         b. Scott Killingsworth Ellis.

         c. R. S. Ellis.

     (3) Noel Scott Killingsworth, veteran of Confederate Army.

2. William Killingsworth, died young.
3. Joel Killingsworth, died young.
4. Mary E. Killingsworth, b. August 21, 1817, died Jan. 19, 1847, m. T. J. Grafton; had:

     (1) Sarah E. Grafton m. McClaskey and had issue.

5. Catherine Killingsworth, b. Oct. 23, 1822, died Aug. 25, 1886, m. Richard Scott and had:

     (1) Richard Killingsworth Scott.

     (2) Kate Scott m. W.P. Darden; had issue.

     (3) Jane Ruth Scott, died young.

6. Ananias Killingsworth, b. Dec. 30, 1820, died May 30, 1876, m. Matilda Trimble Dec. 11, 1850; had:

     (1) Anon Ross Killingsworth m. Helen Perrine Ross.

     (2) Roger Trimble Killingsworth m. Jennie Wade; had:

         a. Benjamin Young Killingsworth.

         b. Catherine Dunbar Killingsworth.

         c. Roger Wade Killingsworth.

         d. Matilda Killingsworth.

         e. William Bisland Killingsworth.

     (3) Sally Killingsworth m. Jesse Darden, Jr.; had:

         a. Stella Darden;

         b. Arthur Darden;

         c. Anon Darden;

         d. Jennie Darden;

         e. Martha Darden.

     (4) Jennie Killingsworth m. Seaborn Ross and had:

         a. Frances Alexander Ross.

     (5) Matilda Jane Killingsworth.

     (6) James C. Killingsworth.

     (7) Noel Killingsworth m. Edith Hall; and had: Vivian, Louise and Mathilde Killingsworth.

     (8) William H. Killingsworth.

     (9) Scott Killingsworth m. Mattie Wade.

    (10) Kate Killingsworth m. James Wade.

    (11) Beulah Killingsworth.

    (12) Annapias Killingsworth m. Minnie Wade and had: Nina Rebecca; Minnie Aurelia; Sarah Elizabeth; Anon Ross; Allison Wade; Ellen Idella and Ross Cogan Killingsworth.

    (13) Lula Killingsworth.

    (14) Anita Killingsworth.

    (15) Uncas Killingsworth m. Lola Crosby and had Uncas Killingsworth, Jr.

7. Sarah Jane Killingsworth m. Hamden Jordan Mackey as his 2nd. wife and had:

     (1) Jane Scott Mackey, died young.

     (2) Rosa Ann Mackey m. (1) Lucius Wells, no issue; m. (2) Dr. F. L. Fulgham and had Rose Mackey

and Dr. John Henry Fulgham.

(3) Noel Killingsworth Mackey m. (1) Ophelia Shelby and had: William Hamden; Noel Killingsworth; James Anon; Idaline; Love Shelby and Rosa May Mackey; m. (2) Sally Shelby, sister of first wife, no issue.

VII. Jacob Killingsworth, Jr. (wife unknown) had:
1. Edward Killingsworth.
2. Martha Killingsworth m. Peter Gaffney, had: Charles Jacob; Malvina Mary; Florence Elizabeth; Martha Aramintha and Catherine Estelle Gaffney.

VIII. Anne (Nancy) Killingsworth, born 1775 (1780 Census Record), died March 31, 1838, m. 1805 Green Williams, son of Nathan and Selah Whitehead Williams; had 10 children, only 4 lived to become adults.

1. Joel Eli Williams, born August 13, 1812, died after 1860, m. Mary ------; was active member of Congaree Baptist Church; later transferred to Good Hope where he continued active in church work (Church Records).

2. Sarah Ann Williams, b. March 31, 1816, died December 9, 1873, married October 6, 1835, John Eli Williams, born 1815, died December 12, 1886, son of Eli and Marnea Thompson Williams, and a first cousin to Sarah Ann. They moved to Marion County, Florida, in 1852, near the present town of Ocala. Both were buried at Blue Sink Cemetary near their home.
   Children:
   (1) Eli Green Williams, born March 17, 1839, died February 7, 1862.
   (2) Thomas Edwin Williams, born Sept. 18, 1841, died June 14, 1910, m. Elizabeth A. Seay; had:
      a. Edwin Gustavus Williams, b. July 18, 1865.
      b. Percy E. Williams, b. Jan. 20, 1867.
      c. Jimmy Seay Williams, born Dec. 18, 1871.
   (3) Anne Alice Williams, born Nov. 10, 1843, died January 23, 1923; m. August 3, 1864, Dr. D. A. Vogt and had: Sally Blanch; Lottie Alice; and twins, Ernest and Dora May Vogt.
   (4) John D'Auburn Williams, b. Jan. 14, 1847, died June 16, 1919; m. three times and had issue.
   (5) James Marion Williams, born Sept. 23, 1848, d. Jan. 15, 1887; m. and had issue.
   (6) Josephine Cecile Williams, b. May 22, 1852; d.s.p. October 23, 1930.
   (7) Dora Alberta Williams, b. Sept. 3, 1855, d.s.p. May 16, 1924.
   (8) Carrie Lanetta Williams, b. Aug. 26, 1857, died March 17, 1934; m. March 21, 1883, William Abram Pelot and had:
      a. Sally Evelyn Pelot, b. Feb. 13, 1884, m. Charles Cooper and had: Evelyn Pelot Cooper who m. Caleb Lineberger and had William Carl Lineberger.

      b. John Williams Pelot, b. Feb. 18, 1886, m.
Geraldine Hill and had: Joy Hill Pelot who m.
John R. Mason and had Robin Jeanne and Cyn-
thia Gay Mason.

      c. Marion Edwin Pelot, b. Sept. 27, 1888, d.s.p.
July 25, 1943.

      d. Carrie Josephine Pelot, b. Nov. 3, 1890, m.
Tolar D. Bryan, no issue.

      e. Dora Williams Pelot, b. September 24, 1895,
m. Glenn Robert Ebersole and had:

         (a) Robert Pelot Ebersole, m. Barbara Warren
and had Carrie Gale Ebersole;

         (b) William Glen Ebersole m. Wanda Cowart
and had Glenda Ray Ebersole;

         (c) Daniel Bryan Ebersole m. Hazel Deels;

         (d) Dorothy Ann Ebersole.

      f. Alice Edna Williams Pelot, b. Oct. 1, 1897,
d.s.p. Nov. 25, 1903.

    (9) Jessie Killingsworth Williams b. Oct. 1, 1859, d.
Jan. 4, 1943, m. P.W. Whiteside: had:

      a. James J. Whiteside m. Clarine Williams and
had James J. Whiteside, Jr.

3. Green Killingsworth Williams, b. Dec. 19, 1819, d.
in 1897, m. Frances Bates March 26, 1844; spent his
entire life in the Kingsville and Gadsden section of
Richland County, S.C. and is buried at Good Hope Baptist Church.

    Issue:

    (1) Reginald Williams, b. 1846, Confederate Veteran,
d.s.p.

    (2) John Green Williams, b. May 10, 1851, died Jan.
4, 1926, m. Mary James and had:

      a. Frances (Fanny) Williams m. P.P. Stuckey
and had:

         (a) Edward Green;

         (b) Marion Parrot;

         (c) Mary Elizabeth Stuckey, m. Thomas E.
Freeman and had Mary Elizabeth Freeman.

      b. Sarah Alberta Williams, m. Lawrence Harmon,
no issue.

    (3) Joel Belton Williams born 1854, d. 1932, m. Adel-
ia Hammet and had:

      a. Isabelle Kendall Williams m. Willard H. Wile-
man and had:

         (a) Margaret Wileman, m. Marveen Gordon and
had John and Mary White Gordon;

         (b) Willa Wileman, m. Nicholas Raudozzo and
had Nicholas Raudozzo, Jr.

    (4) William Jesse Williams, b. April 15, 1856, died
April 12, 1921, m. Sarah (Tatty) Howell Reese;
was one of the Red Shirts of Hampton's Brigade
in 1876 uprising; Issue:

      a. Gabriella (Ellie) Augusta Williams, m. Henry

George Smith and had:
- (a) Henry George Smith, Jr., m. Mary Gorman and had Mary Elizabeth Smith;
- (b) Lamar Killingsworth Smith m. Hattie Byrd Brooks and had Lamar K. Smith, Jr.;
- (c) Gabriella Roselma Smith m. T. William Garner and had Stephen Reese Garner;
- (d) Lois Radcliffe Smith m. Robert B. Webster and had: Robert B. Webster, Jr.; Timothy; Susan and Melissa Webster;
- (e) Iris Reese Smith m. Gordon Keith and had Glen Gray and David Blue Keith;
- (f) Reginald Reese Smith;
- (g) Mary Aurelia Smith m. Robert F. Mobbs and had: Robert Fred Mobbs, Jr.; Elizabeth Gabriella, and Melanie Mobbs;

b. Green Killingsworth Williams m. Mary Fleming Bennett and had Green K. Williams, Jr., and Mary Claire Williams.

c. Frances Alberta Williams m. Ellie Givan Shuler March 17, 1924, and had Ellie Givan Shuler, Jr., and Jacob Conner Shuler.

(5) James Bates Williams, b. June 26, 1859, d.s.p. Feb. 11, 1932.

(6) Francis Elkin Williams, b. Jan. 23, 1864, died May 28, 1945, m. Eugenia Gray Jan. 22, 1899 and had:

a. Newland Rivers Williams, b. Feb. 10, 1900, m. Mary Ellen Larson August 31, 1924, and had:
- (a) Alice Evelyn Williams, b. Dec. 18, 1926, m. Russel Clarence Roman May 19, 1946 and had Judith Ellen Roman;
- (b) Roland Francis Williams, b. Feb. 28, 1934.

b. Walters Edward Williams, b. Sept. 9, 1903, m. Emma Louise Huber Oct. 18, 1924, no issue.

c. Francis Elkin Williams, Jr., b. Nov. 8, 1907, d.s.p. Nov. 25, 1930.

4. Nathan David Williams, b. April 12, 1823, d. Jan. 1, 1885, m. Dec. 18, 1852, Catherine Ledington.
   Issue:
   (1) Melvin Ledington Williams, b. July 1, 1853, d. Dec. 8, 1928, m. Frances Clark April 17, 1889.
       Issue:
       a. Maude Eloise Williams m. Jerry Louis Houck and had:
          - (a) Jerry Louis Houck, Jr., m. Lucy Smart, no issue;
          - (b) Jacob Melvin Houck m. Julia Harsanyi and had Jacob Melvin Houck, Jr., and Judy.
          - (c) Anne Houck m. Edwin Wilson, III, and had Edwin Wilson, IV.

       (d) David Williams Houck m. Dora Wells and
         had Phillip and Brenda Sue Houck;
       (e) Elbert Mason Houck.
    b. Florence Eunice Williams m. S. Jackson
      Rain and had: William Jackson; Francis Melvin; and Florence Rain who m. John S. Duke
      and had Jane Duke.
    c. Annie Estelle Williams.
    d. Frances Marion Williams m. Stanley Step
      Beeks and had: Norman; and Eloise Beeks,
      who m. Charles Smith.
    e. Melvin LeRoy Williams, m. Jenette Chewing;
      had:
       (a) Roger Henry Williams, m. Carolyn Ridgill
         and had R. H. Williams, Jr.
       (b) Minnie Frances Williams, m. John Hamer
         McNeill, had Dora, Catherine and Kitty
         Hamer McNeill.
    f. Catherine (Kitty) Williams.
    g. George Frederick Williams, m. Margaret
      Razor and had Michael and Patsy Williams.
(2) Annie Estelle Williams, b. May 27, 1855, died
    young.
(3) Florence Agnes Williams, b. May 5, 1857, d.s.p.
    Feb. 24, 1887. Taught in schools of S.C.
(4) Lula May Williams, b. May 27, 1859, d.s.p.
    June, 1943.
(5) Eva Columbia Williams, b. Mar. 27, 1861, d.
    June 29, 1919, m. William Henry Smith, Dec.
    28, 1888, issue:
    a. Myron Colin Smith m. Sadie McCutchen and
      had Margorie McCutchen Smith who m. Lee
      Frank Berry, Jr., and had Myron Berry.
    b. Catherine (Kitty) Ledingham Smith m. (1) Walker; (2) A. D. Brockett; no issue.
    c. Florrie May Smith m. John Gideon Matthews;
      had:
       (a) James Ladson Matthews, died young;
       (b) Smith Gideon Matthews, m. Julia Sojourner
         and had Edward Chester Matthew, III.
       (c) Richard Smith Matthews;
       (e) Julia Dianne Matthews, died in infancy.
    d. Jacob Ledington Smith m. Edelle Scarborough
      and had Edelle Barrett Smith.
    e. William Harry Smith m. Irma Felder, no issue.
(6) William Colin Williams b. March 10, 1864, died
    Dec. 23, 1943, m. Harriet Ann Smith July 5, 1891
    and had Marie Williams.
(7) Irene Hampton Williams, b. July 20, 1865, d. young.
(8) John Sidney Williams, b. Nov. 9, 1868, d. May 15,
    1921, m. Ida Leslie Gettys March 16, 1903, had:
    a. Nathan David Williams, m. Hazel McCalmont
      and had John David and Marilyn (Lyn) Joan
      Williams.

b. John Sidney Williams, Jr., never married.

c. Catherine (Kate) Williams m. James R. McCaa; had Amelia Catherine (Kaye) and Rebecca Leslie McCaa.

d. Jane Gettys Williams, m. Angus T. Livingston; no issue.

e. Ida Leslie Williams, m. J. Rollings Bell, no issue.

(9) Sarah (Sally) McCollum Williams, b. Nov. 9, 1869 (twin of John Sidney Williams) m. Dec. 18, 1890, William Hampton Shirer and had:

a. William Bernard Shirer, b. Oct. 8, 1891, m. Emmie Stuckey, no issue.

b. Susan Catherine Shirer, b. Jan. 13, 1894, m. James Edward Weeks and had:
   (a) Evelyn Elizabeth Weeks, Baptist Missionary in Georgetown, British Guiana, S.A.;
   (b) James Edward Weeks, Jr., m. Margaret Buff and had Jane Renee, Susanne, James Edward Weeks, III, and Katherine Margaret Weeks;
   (c) Robert Shirer Weeks.

c. Clarence Louise Shirer, b. June 28, 1895, m. Edgar Otho Black and had Mary Louise Black.

d. Ina Evelyn Shirer, b. Feb. 28, 1904.

LITTLEJOHN of SCOTLAND and NORTH CAROLINA

John Littlejohn, born in Stirling, Scotland, married Janet Anderson and had five children:

I. John, born March 30, 1700, m. Jean Robertson (See later)
II. Agnes, b. Aug. 24, 1701, unmarried
III. Janet, born March 26, 1704
IV. Peter, b. 1706, m. Jean Cunningham
V. Alexander, b. 1708

John Littlejohn, son of John and Janet (Anderson) Littlejohn, was born March 30, 1700 and lived in Inverness, Scotland, where he was a grazier. He married Jean Robertson and had seven children:

I. Janet, baptised Oct. 28, 1727, twin of Helen
II. Helen, baptised Oct. 28, 1727, twin of Janet
III. John, baptised Feb. 8, 1729
IV. Jean, baptised Aug. 1731, m. Duncan
V. Alexander, baptised June 1735
VI. William, baptised Feb. 22, 1740, m. Sarah Blount (see later)
VII. James, baptised June 1742

William Littlejohn, son of John and Jean (Robertson) Littlejohn, was born Feb. 22, 1740, at Inverness, Scotland; died March 4, 1817, at Edenton, Chowan County, North Carolina; married Nov. 12, 1771, Sarah Blount, born Feb. 14, 1747, at Edenton, Chowan Co., N.C.; died Oct. 10, 1807, daughter of Joseph Blount. William Littlejohn was shipping merchant and a member of the Protestant Episcopal Church. Sarah Littlejohn was among those Edenton women who refused to accept tea imported through Great Britain on account of the tax (N.C. Roster, p. 570)

Children:

I. Sarah, b. Sept. 25, 1772, unmarried
II. Thomas Blount, b. Dec. 9, 1773, m. Elizabeth Mutter (See later)
III. Jane, b. Feb. 28, 1775
IV. Joseph Blount, b. Oct. 4, 1776, m. 1. Anne Jones, 2. Mrs. Anne Sneed
V. Katherine, b. 1777, unmarried
VI. Anne Blount, b. June 27, 1779, m. John Little
VII. William Alexander, b. May 20, 1781, unmarried
VIII. John Lemuel, b. Nov. 27, 1784, unmarried, died the same year
IX. John Wilson, b. Mar. 12, 1786, m. Elizabeth Blount
X. Helen Frances, b. Mar. 24, 1787, unmarried
XI. Mary Penelope, b. June 6, 1788, unmarried
XII. Elizabeth Margaret, b. Oct. 17, 1789, m. William Jones

XIII. Frances Lennox, b. July 23, 1791, unmarried
XIV. Lemuel Edward, b. April 8, 1797, unmarried

Thomas Blount Littlejohn, son of William Littlejohn and Sarah Blount, was born Dec. 9, 1773, at Edenton, Chowan Co., North Carolina; died Jan. 29, 1854, Oxford, Granville Co., N.C., married Elizabeth Mutter Dec. 6, 1798, died Feb. 19, 1842 at Glenwood, the country home of her daughter in Warren County, N.C. Elizabeth Mutter was the daughter of Thomas Mutter and his wife Elizabeth Moore. (Hathaway 1-269)

Children:

I. Sallie B., b. Sept. 16, 1799, m. Shepherd Kollock
II. Thomas Mutter, b. July 24, 1801, unmarried
III. William, b. Feb. 8, 1803, m. Mrs. Jane Patrick
IV. Elizabeth W., b. Apr. 7, 1805, m. Isaac Jones
V. Margaret Mutter, b. Apr. 17, 1807, m. Roger P. Atkinson
VI. Anne Wilson, m. Benson Jones
VII. Alexander W., b. Feb. 15, 1811, m. Sarah Walker
VIII. John, b. Oct. 12, 1812, unmarried
IX. Joseph, b. July 1, 1814, m. (1) Olivia Bland, (2) Mary Manson
X. James Thompson, b. June 24, 1816, m. (1) Phoebe Dosier, (2) Mrs. S. Meachum, nee Dosier
XI. Lucinda Jane, b. Apr. 12, 1819, m. Alexander Jones (See later)
XII. Frances Blount, b. Jan. 24, 1822, m. George Feild

Lucinda Jane Littlejohn, daughter of Thomas Blount Littlejohn and Elizabeth Mutter, was born April 12, 1819 at Oxford, Granville County, N.C., died March 28, 1896 at Henderson, Vance County, N.C., married April 3, 1839, Granville County, N.C., Alexander Strachan Jones, born Mecklenburg County, Virginia, died Woodley, Warren County, N.C.

Children:

I. Thomas Littlejohn, b. Feb. 4, 1840, m. Pattie Louise Willikins
II. Alice Mutter, b. May 1, 1843; m. William Cheek
III. Alexander S., b. March 1845, m. Belle Daniel
IV. Susan Blackwood, b. Dec. 8, 1846; m. Waller Taylor
V. Sally Kollock, b. 1849, unmarried
VI. Joseph Littlejohn, b. May 1851; m. Anna Taylor
VII. Robert Strachan, 25 years old; unmarried
VIII. Ernest Victor, 33 years old; unmarried
IX. John Tignal, b. Feb. 8, 1848; m. Sallie Williams
X. George Feild, b. Dec. 13, 1856; m. Adelaide Evans Smith (See later)

George Feild Jones, son of Alexander Strachan Jones and Lucinda Jane Littlejohn, was born Dec. 13, 1856, at Woodley, their country home, in Warren County, N.C.; died March 25, 1890, Elberon, Warren County, N.C., married Nov. 21, 1882, Wilmington, New Hanover County, N.C., Adelaide Evans Smith, b. Feb. 12, 1859 at Scotland Neck, Halifax County, N.C., died Sept. 2, 1953 at Warrenton, Warren County, N.C., daughter of George Alexander Smith and Roseella Harris Wiggins. Mr.

Jones was a farmer and a member of the Protestant Episcopal Church. He was educated at John Grahams in Fork Township and Capt. Duggers in Warrenton, N.C.

Children:
I.   Hamilton McRary, b. Aug. 20, 1883; m. Helen Baker
II.   George Herbet, b. Nov. 19, 1884; m. Bessie Fisher Mason
III. Pattie Wiggins, b. March 14, 1886; m. William Henry Dameron

    Children:
1. Mattie Wiggins, b. Jan. 17, 1912; m. Thomas Kenan Smith

    Children:
(1) Thomas Kenan, b. March 22, 1935
(2) Mildred McRary, b. Apr. 23, 1937
2. William Henry, b. Jan. 2, 1914; m. Geraldine Saviers
Children:
(1) William Henry, b. Apr. 25, 1942
(2) Linda Louise, b. Apr. 28, 1947
3. Rosella Wiggins, b. Oct. 12, 1919; m. Charles David Hyatt
IV. Rowe Wiggins, b. Aug. 18, 1887; unmarried; educated at Misses Hawkins School, member of the Protestant Episcopal Church, resides Elberon, Warren Co., N.C.
V.   Ernest, b. Dec. 17, 1888; m. Kathryn Seeler

    Children:
1. Kathryn Wiggins, b. Dec. 22, 1930; m. Douglas More and have a daughter, Sarah Simpson, b. Nov. 19, 1955
2. Mildred Marshall, b. Feb. 10, 1935

LOVELL FAMILY of WESTMORELAND
with
ALLIED FAMILIES of HARRISON and FOOTMAN
by Oliver Harold Carper

The Lovell family traces back to Normandy as early as 1060, and came to England beginning with the Norman Invasion of 1066 with King William I. Robert Lovell, a Peer, is in Norman records as early as 1060 and he left Peerage heirs in England bearing names of Robert, William, John and James down to 1465 (The Complete Peerage, Vol. VII, p. 208). Certainly all the Lovells of Westmoreland used these names, and this apparently indicates a continuation of these ancestral names. The first Robert Lovell came to Virginia prior to Nov. 9, 1635 (Va. land patents, Nugent abstracts), and a Robert Lovell with Patrick Norton patented 1000 acres of land Dec. 2, 1663 on Rappahannock River, a renewal of a Patent dated May 26, 1660. ROBERT LOVELL, the progenitor, or at least the earliest proven, of the Westmoreland Lovells, is first mentioned in existing records Nov. 5, 1666 (Deeds, Patents, etc., p. 329) when he and Elinor, his wife, deeded 150 a land to Daniel Swillivant. He acknowledged the sale in Court but Elinor, his wife, acted through her attorney, John Dinely, "It not being convenient for her to travel." It may be the patentee of 1663 is the same Robert Lovell here mentioned. On July 7, 1670 William Pierce assigned a patent of 500 a on the Potomac River to Robert Lovell, who repatented this land on Nov. 25, 1670 evidently to insure a clearer title (Va. Land Patents). This patent adjoined John Washington on the North and Andrew Monroe to the South, as well as his original holdings. He died ante April 24, 1700, date his Will probated by "his son" Robert Lovell, Jr. the Executor (Orders p. 70). Will Book for that year is among missing documents.

Children, in part, of Robert and Elinor Lovell:

I. Mary Lovell d ante 1703, m. Robert Redman, d. 1704 (W.B. 3, p. 319). One son named Francis Redman d. 1716 without issue. He was devised entire estate by his father except "my old plantation and 160 a belonging to it to Mary Lovell." Francis Redman devised his entire estate to "My beloved kinsman, Robert Lovell." (W.B. 5, p 600)

II. Daughter, who name may have been Elinor Lovell, m. Thomas Beard, 1698 (W.B. 2, p. 158), naming three children - John Beard; Mary Beard, who later m. Nathan Gray, Jr; and Thomas Beard, Jr., dsp 1716, leaving his entire estate "to Cousins Lovell Massey and Mary Lovell." (W.B. 5, p. 602).

III. Daughter, married a Massey, and had issue, a son Lovell Massey, who d. 1764 leaving issue, (W.B. 14, p. 214).

IV. Robert Lovell, Jr. named in Records (Orders 1700 p. 70). See later.

ROBERT LOVELL, Jr., son of Robert and Elinor Lovell, b. ante 1674, d. 1726, m. 1-........Pratt, (may have been Elizabeth), daughter John Pratt, Sr. and wife Mary (Sharpe) Pratt, widow Thomas Sharpe decd, and 2- 1698, Ursula Nicholas (d. ante 1726), widow of Lewis Nicholas, Jr. (1677-1698), son of Lewis Nicholas, Sr. and wife Mary Pope nee Lissen, widow of Nathaniel Pope. Lewis Nicholas, Jr. was Godson of Lawrence Washington, grandfather of our 1st President, from whom he received a legacy of 137 acres land. Lewis Nicholas Jr. devised his entire estate to his wife Ursula Nicholas (1698 W.B. 2, p. 144). Robert Lovell and his wife Ursula Lovell appear as "Exrs Lewis Nicholas decd" (Orders Nov 30, 1699, p. 65a). On May 29, 1706, Robert Lovell proved his rights in Court for the transportation of 11 persons to Colony. (Orders p 25a). On November 20, 1712, the Court appointed him as one of three to make final settlement and distribution of the estate of Capt. Lawrence Washington. (Orders p. 199). He made his Will Jan. 1, 1725/6, and the same was proved Feb. 23, 1726. In it he named all his children then living, and made his son Robert Lovell, Executor. (W.B. 8).

I.   Elizabeth Lovell, m. ......Nicholson (May have been Anthony Nicholson of Whitehaven)

II.   John Lovell, b. 1697, d. 1720, last child of 1st marriage, m. Elizabeth .... The Will of John Pratt, Sr. (W. B. 5, p. 570) devised 400 a to "my grandson John Lovell". He accidentally fell from his horse March 1720 and was killed (Coroner's Inquest report March 20, 1720). They had one child Margaret Lovell m. John Bryan 1736. His widow Elizabeth m. William Harrison, son of George Harrison.

III. MARY LOVELL, b. 1699, d. 1745, 1st child of 2nd marriage, m. ca 1718, Andrew Harrison. (See Harrison under father).

IV. Robert Lovell b. ca 1701, d. post 1769 m. 1- Ann Martin, daughter of Capt. Jacob Martin and wife Sarah Scott, widow of John Scott, and 2- 1743, Sarah Marshall, daughter of John Marshall and his wife Ann (Markham) Marshall. John Marshall was grandfather of Chief Justice John Marshall. Robert left Westmoreland County in 1758, and resided some years in Granville County, N.C. His will, if any, was not found.

Children:

1. Elizabeth Lovell, shown 1744 Spottsylvania County, witness to will.

2. John Lovell, b. 1727, d. 1800 in King George Co. Probably m. twice but there was no issue by 2nd marriage to Ann Weedon 1777. William Lovell, Justice of Fredericksburg, probably was a son of 1st marriage.

3. Robert Lovell m. Elizabeth .... He was an officer in Westmoreland Militia 1754, and later resident of King George County.

4. Jacob Lovell, shown a number of times in Spottsylvania Co. Orders. Died there intestate, and son Daniel

Lovell was Administrator.

5. Daniel Lovell d. post 1777 Pittsylvania County, m. ca. 1765 in King George Co., Elizabeth Riding, widow of Daniel Riding and daughter of Samuel Moon Lovell. They had issue, two known children, Ann Martin Lovell and Samuel Moon Lovell.

6. William Lovell, eldest son of Robert and Sarah (Marshall) Lovell m. in Pittsylvania County April 19, 1774, Mary Dudley. (Pittsylvania Co. Marriages).

7. Sarah Lovell.

8. Mary Ann Lovell.

9. Markham Lovell m. in Pittsylvania Co., a Miss Jones.

V. JAMES LOVELL, b. 1703, d. 1762 Halifax County, N.C. (See later)

VI. Daniel Lovell, dsp ante Jan. 28, 1735 date his Will probated (W.B. 8, p. 254). He devised his entire estate, except two slaves, to his brother James Lovell.

VII. Ursula Lovell m. post 1735 George Riding, and resided King George County. Only two children are known, Elizabeth Riding m. ....Courts, and Daniel Riding m. Elizabeth Moon.

JAMES LOVELL, son of Robert Lovell and his wife Ursula (Nicholas) Lovell, b. ca 1703, d. 1762 Halifax County, N.C., m. ca 1728, wife's name uncertain but apparently a Tyler, whose name was Jane Tyler. He was devised considerable land by his father and was named in four separate Wills as legatee in Westmoreland Co., Va; 1716 his cousin Francis Redman (W.B. 5) 1726 his father; 1735 his brother Daniel Lovell (W.B. 8, p. 254; Joseph Tyler "to my well beloved friend" (W.B. 8, p. 329). He removed to Northampton County, N.C. as evidenced by a deed dated Sept. 13, 1758, in which John Corlew "of Edgecomb County, N.C." deeded to James Lovell "of Westmoreland County" 200 a. "on Roanoke river" opposite Halifax Town (Northampt. D.B. 2, pp. 321-2). He sold this land Feb. 1, 1762. He made his will Dec. 16, 1761, and the same was proven June Court 1762 (Hal W.B. 7, p. 181). He was probably living in Halifax Town then. His children are named in his will and he appointed "Francis Jackson of Prince William County, Va." guardian to the four youngest children. Francis Jackson had married Sally Tyler.

Children:

1. James Lovell, Jr. Exr of his father's Will. In Halifax County as late as July 1767 as evidenced by Court Record James Lovell vs Isaac Jackson and George Norwood.

2. William Lovell d. 1803 m. Mary Harrison - See later.

3. Elizabeth Lovell, probably under 16 when father died. Named with three other younger children as wards of Francis Jackson and returned to Prince William Co.

4. Jane Lovell, ward of Francis Jackson (Id.) May have married a Marlow.

5. Malachi Lovell, ward of Francis Jackson.

6. Ann Lovell, ward of Francis Jackson.

WILLIAM LOVELL, son of James Lovell and wife, who was

probably Jane Tyler, b. ca 1741, d. 1803 m. ca 1764 Mary Harrison, his cousin, d. ante 1803, daughter of Hannah Footman and Lovell Harrison (See Harrison later). After death of his father, William Lovell probably remained in Halifax County with his brother James Lovell, as of May 20, 1769 William Ross "of Edgecomb" sold to William Lovell "of Halifax Co." 315 acres land "in the prong of Marsh Swamp." (Hal D.B. 10, p. 450). A Voucher List shows him as an Indian War Veteran (N.C. Archives). His Will was dated Jan. 15, 1803 and was proved at February Court 1803, and is unique in that it indicates pride of Ancestral Lines, he specifically giving the full names of all his daughters. (W.B. 3, p. 308).

Children:

I. James Lovell m. Patty Parsons Chambliss, daughter of David Chambliss of Halifax County. Went to Davidson County, Tenn. where he was residing in 1813.

II. Jane Tyler Lovell - not married up to 1803.

III. Hannah Footman Harrison Lovell b. 1770, d. 1851, m. 1789 (Anderson's Marriages) to Bennett Dickens - See later.

IV. William Lovell - residing in Halifax County as late as 1813.

V. Polly Lovell m. William Cullom, Jr. and had issue.

VI. John Lovell, received 50 a land under terms of his father's Will.

VII. Jacob Lovell, named in his father's Will.

VIII. Ann Lovell, named in her father's Will. Still unmarried 1803.

IX. Frances Harrison Lovell, called "My youngest daughter" in her father's Will.

HANNAH FOOTMAN HARRISON LOVELL b. 1770, d. 1851, full name as given in father's Will, daughter of William Lovell and his wife Mary (Harrison) Lovell, married 1789, (Anderson's Marriages) Bennett Dickens (1766-1843), son of Hannah and Joseph Dickens. Bennett Dickens, Sr. left Will (Hal W.B. 3, p. 408) naming wife Hannah and all children.

Children:

I. Charles T. Dickens b. 1789-90, d. post 1870 m. Polly Browning, daughter of Margaret (Purnell) and Levy Browning (See Dickens SVF Vol. II).

II. Hester Dickens b. 1792 m. 1817 Julius Hieronymous Zollicoffer. (See SVF Vol. II).

III. Bennett E. Dickens Jr. b. Feb. 3, 1794 d. post 1860 m. his cousin Nancy Dickens, b. June 4, 1804, daughter of James and Martha (Brantly?) Dickens. (See SVF Vol III.)

IV. Malachi Dickens b. ca 1796 d ca 1846 m. 1819, Nancy Dickens, b. 1805 d. 1861, daughter of Samuel Dickens and wife Rebecca (Green) Dickens. Rebecca Green was daughter of Mary and George Green, a Revolutionary Soldier (War Dept. Pension Rec.) and after death of Samuel Dickens she married 1809 Abner Mills.

Children:

1. Margaret Dickens b 1820 m Egbert Lewis, as 2nd wife. (See SVG II)

2. Enoch Dozier Dickens b. 1823 d 1891 m. Frances John Bass. (See SVF II).

3. Rebecca Elizabeth Dickens b 1826 d. 1879-80 m. Jan. 8, 1857 John J. Keeter b. 1825 d. post 1880 son of James Keeter b 1790 and wife Sally Keeter. After death of Rebecca he married Martha (Neville) Ramsey but no issue by this marriage.

Children:

(1) John Long Keeter b. Dec. 25, 1857, d. June 21, 1919, m. Lydia Ann, daughter of William Henry and Sophia Gibson. Issue, four children.

(2) Fletcher Joiner Keeter b. 1860; m. Cora Johnson, daughter of Lovett D. Johnson and his wife Ann M. (Branch) Johnson. They had issue.

(3) Rebecca Jane Alice Keeter b. 1862; d. Feb. 12, 1935; m. her cousin Joseph E. Dickens, son of Balaam Dickens and his 1st wife Margaret Partin. (Children under Father SVF II)

(4) Margaret Ann Keeter was fourth child of John J. Keeter and his wife Rebecca Elizabeth Dickens. Due to printer's error she was omitted in the list of their children given in Southside Virginia Families Vol. II, p. 106. She was born near Darlington, Halifax County, N.C. August 24, 1865 and died Latta, S.C. May 28, 1910. On Jan. 25, 1885 (not Jan. 1st as stated in above book, p. 114) she married her cousin, Robert Patrick Dickens (b. Feb. 7, 1866; d. Jan. 18, 1934), (for his ancestry see Southside Virginia Families, Vol. II). Robert Patrick Dickens and his wife Margaret Ann Keeter had issue, among others, Teresa Hope Dickens who married William Marion Mann, not William Morton Mann, as appears on p. 114 of above mentioned book. For their issue see Southside Virginia Families, Vol. II, pp. 323-4.

For other children Malachi and wife Nancy Dickens see SVF Vol. II, pp. 323-4.

V. Harriett Dickens, daughter Bennett Dickens and wife Hannah Footman Harrison Lovell, m. Guilford Dickens. (See SVF Vol. II).

ANDREW HARRISON of WESTMORELAND COUNTY

by Oliver Harold Carper

The first member of the Harrison Family in Westmoreland was John Harrison who came to the Colony of Virginia ante 1654 with his brother Dr. Jeremiah Harrison and his wife Frances Wingreave. Dr. Jeremiah Harrison settled in York County but did not survive long. In 1654 his widow Frances Harrison patented 1000 a. land in Westmoreland Co. and later married Giles Brent, as his 2nd wife, but had no issue of either marriage. John

Harrison on Sept. 4, 1655 also patented 1000 a in Westmoreland, which patent stated "for want of heirs to sister Mrs. Frances Harrison". They came "of a family widely spread throughout eastern counties of England" that "previous to coming this family had furnished already two emigrants at least who had founded Harrison families in Virginia, Benjamin Harrison x x and Richard Harrison. x x This was doubtless the beginning of their connection in the Northern Neck. x x The Will of John Harrison has not been found but there can be little doubt he was the father of George Harrison who made his will in Westmoreland County Oct. 2, 1713." (Tylers Quarterly V. 6, pp. 203-4)

ANDREW HARRISON b. ante 1685, d. 1730 was not the son of George Harrison. He may have been a brother as the families were closely associated. It seems certain he was a descendant of John Harrison even if not a son. He married 1- ca 1706 Mary Rozier, widow of John Rozier, Jr. decd (Deed of Uses certain negroes to Daniel McCarty May 15, 1715 (Orders p. 267) was made by Andrew Harrison and "Mary, his wife, late Mary Rozier, widow and relict of John Rozier decd), and 2 - married Mary Lovell b 1699 d 1745, daughter of Robert Lovell and his wife Ursula Nicholas Lovell. Considering the times he was appointed by Court to appraise estates he was well known, but he held no public office. His wife Mary Lovell was devised "my old plantation and 160 a that belongs to it" by Robert Redman 1703, her uncle by marriage, and given about 65 a. by her father in 1719 before his death. Andrew Harrison left an estate in King George County, but whether it was an inheritance from his father or not is not known. He died in 1730 prior to Feb. Court when his Will was probated. Mary Harrison, his wife, was named Executrix, and not long afterward married Christopher Edrington, as a 2nd wife. There was one son David Edrington by this union.

Children of Andrew Harrison by each marriage:
I.   Joseph Harrison, son 1st marriage, b ca 1707, m. Peggy .... and resided in King George County and apparently had issue.
II.   Lovell Harrison b. ca 1719, d. post 1760 m. late 1739 or early 1740, Hannah Footman b. 1718, d. 1793, daughter of John Footman, and his 2nd wife Anne Sorrell, widow of John Sorrell, decd. See later.
III.   Ann Harrison d ante 1738 unm. Named Will her grandfather Robert Lovell 1726 and Will Joseph Tyler 1737.
IV.   Andrew Harrison - resided King George Co. and had at least one son Charles Harrison.
V.   Probably named Alexander Harrison and may be the Alexander Harrison living in Sussex County for sometime prior to 1780.

LOVELL HARRISON, b. 1718 d. post 1760, son of Andrew and Mary (Lovell) Harrison, m. Hannah Footman, b. 1718 d. 1793, onl child of John Footman and his 2nd wife Anne Sorrell, widow of John Sorrell, decd. Lovell Harrison was named in 1726 in the Will of his grandfather Robert Lovell (W.B. 8, p. 47), and a petition in Court April 29, 1740 "sets forth his father Andrew Harrison x x personal estate to be equally divided between petitioner, his mother and three other children x x that petitioner's mother, the relict of the said Andrew Harrison intermarryed with Christopher Edrington" and asked for division (Orders p. 44). He and Hannah Harrison, his wife, leased 176 a. "on Machiodock Neck" to Walter Jameison Dec. 25, 1750 for six years, land being tract in "Lease for Lives" to Hannah and her father John Footman 1758 (D.B. p. 266). Lovell Harrison and wife Hannah sold 100 a to Jeremiah Carter (D.B. 11 p. 411 May 11 1752), being land originally purchased by her grandfather John Footman March 25, 1691 (Orders p. 19), and devised Hannah Footman by her father's Will 1739 (W. B. 9, p. 32). Lovell Harrison died intestate but Hannah Footman Harrison died 1793 leaving Will (W.B. 18, p. 295) naming her late husband and all children:

I.   Lovell Harrison. Apparently he was the Lovell Harrison named Godfather to Isham Cain, Albemarle Parish Register April 1775, being then in Sussex County.

II.   Mary Harrison, called "Daughter Mary Lovell" in her mother's will; m. William Lovell - See Later.

III.   Ann Harrison m. Anthony Muse; had issue as her mother mentions "Ann Muse's children" in Will.

IV.   Joseph Harrison, only mention in mother's will.

V.   Harriett Harrison, m. ....Peoples. Alive in 1793.

VI.   Anthony Alexander Harrison, m. 1- as Alexander A. Harrison July 25, 1793 (Wmd Marriages) Alice Nelson; and 2- as Anthony A. Harrison July 16, 1795, Hannah Sanford (Id).

VII. Hannah Harrison, m. Sept. 18, 1792, Benedict Middleton. (Wmd Marriages).

MARY HARRISON, d. ca 1800, in Halifax County, N.C., daughter of Lovell Harrison and his wife Hannah (Footman) Harrison, m. ca 1764, William Lovell, a cousin, son of James Lovell and his wife, who was probably Jane Tyler.

Children: See Lovell under father.

FOOTMAN FAMILY of WESTMORELAND COUNTY

by Oliver Harold Carper

JOHN FOOTMAN, Sr. b. ante 1660, d. 1664, apparently was the son of Henry Footman who had Patent of 300 acres on south side of Acquia River October 1, 1656, which Patent he assigned March 31, 1658 to Samuel Mothershead. (Va. Land Patents). He had been in Westmoreland County as early as 1654 but what became of him the records do not disclose. Existing records, and there are many missing, finds John Footman there well established February 28, 1683 (Orders unindexed p. 280). One of the earlier records of horse racing concerns him and Richard Youell over a race between their respective horses. The dispute was taken to Court and John Footman was awarded "the horse or 1500 lbs. tobacco." (Orders p. 467, January 6, 1686). The case continued in Court records until January 31, 1689 (Orders p. 704) when it was settled. He purchased 100 a. land from John Trammell March 25, 1691

(Orders p. 19) records indicating he had been on leased land previously. He died prior to July 2, 1694, when "Jane Footman, relict of John Footman, decd" secured administration papers. She died post 1697 (Orders p. 255). Her maiden name may have been West.

JOHN FOOTMAN, Jr., b ante 1685, d. November 1739, son of John Footman, Sr. and his wife Jane, who may have been a daughter of John West of Northampton County. He married 3 times; 1- Ca 1703-5 Martha Cox, daughter of Vincent Cox, Sr. and wife Mary (Orders June 20, 1700, p. 64; Orders Jan. 23, 1712, p. 203; Orders June 24, 1724, p. 71a; Orders Mar. 25, 1730, p. 346a); married 2 - 1716 Anne Sorrell, widow of John Sorrell, decd. (W. B. 5, p. 550 John Erwin Apr. 10, 1716; Orders March 26, 1718, p. 341; Orders Feb. 23, 1731 p. 14) and married 3 - Elizabeth Kennon nee Wilder, widow of Richard Kennon (Orders July 26, 1727, p. 176). From February 7, 1705 until his death in 1739 he is continuously in the records, and he held Public office continuously from June 29, 1724 when he was appointed Under Sheriff (Orders p. 176), and was subsequently appointed Acting Sheriff, High Sheriff, Coroner and "Gentleman" Justice, serving many years in latter capacity with such men as Augustine Washington, father of George Washington, on the Judge's bench. He was a very prominent man during this period. He had but one child, and that by his 2nd marriage. His Will was dated October 19, 1739 and was probated November 27, 1739, his daughter Hannah Footman inheriting his landed estate, and his widow the bulk of his personal property. His Will also stipulated if his daughter Hannah Footman died without heirs "of her body" the estate left to her was to go to "my kinsman" John West, of Northampton County.

HANNAH FOOTMAN, b. 1718 d. 1793, daughter of John Footman and his 2nd wife Anne Sorrell, widow of John Sorrell, decd., and the only child of John Footman. She married prior to March 1740, Lovell Harrison, son of Andrew Harrison and his 2nd wife Mary (Lovell) Harrison. She was survivor of "Lease for Lives" to her and her father John Footman in 1738 of 176 acres from Richard Kennon, and she inherited at least 100 a. land plantation purchased 1691 by her grandfather John Footman, Sr. She left a Will dated Nov. 6, 1791 and was probated March 26, 1793 (W. B. 19, p. 295), naming all of their children:

Children under their father - See Harrison.

MACQUENNEY - MCKENNIE

Michael Macquenney was the first of his name in Virginia. The earliest records found of him is that of his will dated April 15, 1686 in which he designates himself as "Michael Makquenney of the Western Branch in Isle of Wight county, planter". He bequeathed to wife Elizabeth "plantation I now live upon" during her life then to his young son" BARNABY. He gave to eldest son JOHN the rest of his land on the northwest side of the Forest Spring Branch provided he settle upon it. Probated Aug. 9, 1686 by Robert Cooper, Jeremiah Exum, John Moore (D.B. 2, p. 254) Other records pertaining to Michael were evidently lost in the burning of Nansemond records.

Elizabeth Mackquenney married secondly Thomas Reeves for on February 10, 1701, Thomas Reeves aged about 62 years deposed that Barnaby Mackquenney's land escheated and was entered upon by his brother John. Elizabeth Reeves, aged 60, also testified to the same. (D.B. 1-1688-1704, p. 339-40) Barnaby Mackquenney was not of age at the time his brother entered the escheat. John Mackenney was granted a patent for 450 acres which lay in Nansemond Oct. 20, 1697. (BK 9, p 98)

John[2] MacKenney, the elder, died about 1710 leaving a son Michael MacKenney who with his wife Rose on April 1710 sold to Richard Exum of Nansemond 200 acres of the said 450 acres of the land granted my father John MacKenney adjoining Jeremiah Exum (Bk 1704-1715 -p 140). (See later)

Barnaby[2] Macquenney on Sept. 10, 1703 and Mary his wife sold to Richard Exum of Isle of Wight all of the land given by my father Michael Mackquenney's will, being part of an escheat Patent granted to his brother John who died before he could execute a deed (I of W D.B. I-340).

Barnaby McKennie received grants in Isle of Wight for 5648 acres for the transportation of 109 persons between 1702 and 1714 which he and his wife sold in 55 deeds executed before they moved to North Carolina. His wife Mary was the widow of Jacob Ricks and the daughter of Judge Jeremiah and Ann Exum. (17 W 60) He moved to what is now Edgecombe county about 1721 settling near Caledonia. He was a Justice of Peace, Judge of the General Court 1727, and member of the Assembly 1735 (Id). His will was dated Aug. 31, 1737.

Children:

I. Barnaby Jr. married Mary, daughter of William Brown, and died in 1736. He gave to daughter PATIENCE McKinnie his dwelling plantation; dau. MARY MCKINNIE 250 acres. If daus. die to Barnaby Lane, son of Joseph Lane; to wife MARY five negroes; to Joseph Lane a plantation; brother Robert McKinnie two mares; to James Howell a tract of land; to Nathaniel Cooper a black mare; to cousin John Lane a horse; Loving wife and Joseph Lane exrs. (Grimes Abstracts)

229

II.   William[3] McKinnie died 1739 before his father Barnaby[2]. In a deed-codicil to his will (Halifax Deed Bk. 1, pp 312-313) Barnaby[2] McKinnie said: "I, Barnaby McKinnie of Edgecombe county by my will bearing date of the 30th day of August (1739) did bequeath unto my son William McKinnie and the heirs of his body lawfully begotten and to their heirs forever a tract of land containing two hundred acres being the plantation whereon my son William then lived who having since departed this life therefor to prevent any objection that may be urged against the descent of the said land as by the bequest in my said will intended know that I, Barnaby McKinnie of Edgecombe County in the province of North Carolina, Esqr. out of natural love and affection which I have and do bear to my grandson Barnaby McKinnie, son and heir-at-law of my son William McKinnie decd and for and in consideration of the sum of five shillings to me in hand paid, do by these presents give grant alien enforce and confirm to him the said land".

Barnaby, only son of William McKinnie, died unmarried in 1761. His will is dated Nov. 9, 1761. Following the preamble, it says "also for preventing Dispute which probably might arise concerning the Distribution of such Estate as it hath pleased God to bestow upon me do hereby****** Give and Bequeath the tract of land and plantation whereon I now Live to my Nephew William Coupland and I also Give and Bequeath to sd William Coupland all my Negro Slaves (Segar and Sarah excepted) also all my other Estate of Every Kind Soever to the sd William****** But if sd William should die before he arrives to Lawful Age then****to his Brother Thomas Coupland and in case that he die before he arrives to Lawful age then the sd Estate To be Divided Between the Sisters, Daughters of Joseph Coupland****". The two slaves undisposed of were to be sold and the proceeds of sale to be used to pay his debts. Nicholas Long and Joel Lane, executors. Witnesses: Sam'l Edwards, John Moore, Thomas Hall (Halifax Will Bk. 1, p. 47)

(Bk. 3, p 28: Will of William Coupland. Dau. Mary Coupland; sister Charlotte Coupland; god-son McKinne Long. Exrs. Nicholas Long of N.C. and Wilkinson Godwin of Va. Wit.: Chas Pasteur, I. Tillery, C. Saunders. Jan. 4, 1782)

William McKinnie had two children: Barnaby, and Mourning who married Joseph Coupland. Barnaby d. unmar.

III.   John[3], d. 1739. John[3] was probably one of the younger sons of Barnaby[2] McKinne. He married before Dec. 30, 1736, when William Parrish's estate was divided between Mary McKinnie, his wife, and Sarah? (Angelina) Parrish, daughter of William Parrish. Angelina Parrish married Barnaby Pope, son of John and Mourning McKinne Pope. John and Mary McKinne had five children:

1. Barnaby, born av. 1738-39. He was of age in 1760 when he made a deed to a tract of land inherited from his father. In that deed he called himself "Barnaby McKinne,

the Younger". Part of the land was granted to Emanuel Rogers, decd., and from him descended to his daughters, Elizabeth and Mary, and by them together with their husbands, John Hubbard and Montford Eelbeck, gentlemen, conveyed by deed 1742.

Barnaby, the younger, made his will March 15,1861; probated June Court 1761; Wife Anne; said wife's son, Isaac Ricks, and her daughter, Mary Ricks; sister Martha McKinne; sister Patience McKinne. Executors wife and Robert Ricks. (Halifax Will Bk. 1, p 31)

After death of Barnaby McKinne, Ann, his wife, married Seth Prior. 1762- Nicholas Long and wife, Mary and others sued Robert Ricks, Seth Prior and his wife, executors of Barnaby McKinne. (Col. Records of N.C., V. 6, p 759)

2. Mary McKinne married Nicholas Long before 1762. She was not mentioned in the will of her brother, Barnaby.

3. Patience McKinne married John Geddy (Gaddy) before 1767, when the land of her deceased brother, Barnaby, was divided among his three sisters.

4. Martha McKinne was still a minor in 1767, when she received through her guardian, Joseph Montfort, one-third of the land of her deceased brother, Barnaby (Division Tripartite, Halifax Bk. 10, p. 28). She married Charles Pasteur.

5. John McKinne, born after his father's death. He evidently died very young as he is not mentioned in any of the numerous guardianship proceedings, nor in his brother's will and in the division of his brother's lands. In 1751, his father, John McKinne of Edgecombe Co., gave negroes to his children, Barnaby, Mary, Patience, and Martha. (Halifax Bk. 4, p. 152)

John[3] McKinne made his will in 1753. Montford Eelbeck was one of the executors, and the will was witnessed by Montford and Mary Eelbeck. In 1757, Montford Eulbeck, Benjamin Hardy and Wm. Richmond were appointed to audit the accounts of Barna Pope, guardian of the orphans of John McKinney.

Mary McKinne, wife of John, made her will in 1754, naming her daughter, Angeliny Pope; sons John and Barnaby; daus. Mary, Patience, and Martha McKinne.

In 1758, Barnaby[4] McKinne, son of William[3] McKinne, was guardian of Barnaby the younger, son of John McKinne.

Of John McKinne's two sons, John died in infancy and Barnaby left no children. This seems to be the end of the male of Barnaby[2] McKinne.

IV. Richard[3], m. Mary Kinchen and died in 1755 without issue. His widow married Blake Baker.

V. Robert[3], m. Martha. On Nov. 10, 1748, he and wife Martha sold land on which they were living to William Speight. In 1762 he was living in Granville County. Unless he left sons it seems no one can claim descent from Barnaby McKinne through the male line.

VI.   Ann, m. William Murphy
VII.   Mourning, m. John Pope (See later)
VIII. Patience, m. Joseph Lane
IX.   Christian, m. William Hurst
X.   Mary Jane, m. John Brown, son of William Brown.

Mourning[3] McKinnie, dau. of Barnaby I, married John Pope who was born in Isle of Wight County, Va., and moved to Bertie, N.C., and later to Edgecombe where he died.

John Pope was a Justice of the Peace for Edgecombe May 16, 1732, Commissioner of the Peace March 6, 1739, Member of the General Assembly from July 22, 1743 until his death. (17C 63)

Children:

I.   Henry Pope m. Tabitha. He made his will in Halifax Oct. 1764 and names eldest son Burrell Pope; sons Willis, John, Wiley and Henry Austin Pope. Exrs. wife Tabitha, John Bradford and Jesse Pope (Bk. 1-144) (For his descendants see 17 C-104)

II.   Jesse Pope died in Georgia in 1818, wife Mary

III.   Lewis Pope, wife Ann

IV.   Winifred Pope died unmarried, will made in Halifax Feb. 7, 1762, proven Sept. 1762 mentions Bros. Jesse & Lewis Pope, cousin Mourning Pope, legacies to Tabitha, Mary and Ann Pope, cousin Willis Pope, Friend John Bradford. Exr. bro. Henry Pope (Bk 1-85)

V.   John Pope

VI.   Barnaby Pope m. Elizabeth Norman and died in Georgia in 1795. His daughter Martha Pope (1765-1805) married Stephen Gibson Sr. in 1784. He was born 1760, died 1838. Their children were: (1) Able, (2) Minor, (3) Stephen Jr. b. 12 Feb. 1800, d. 20 April 1889, m. March 2, 1826 Nancy Wheeler Free, b. Nov. 20, 1805, d. Aug. 16, 1844. (4) John Allen, b. 22 Jan. 1798, d. 14 Nov. 1868, m. 1830 Mary Ann Williams, b. 20 May 1803, d. 24 Dec. 1880. (5) Henry, (6) Nancy m. Andrews, (7) Susannah m. Bacon. Stephen Gibson m. secondly Martha Andrews and had 6 children.

Mary Eliza Gibson, dau. of John Allen Gibson and his wife, Mary Ann Williams, married Captain John Henry Counts, July 11, 1854. She was born Jan. 22, 1831 and died July 25, 1891. He was born May 17, 1826 and died Nov. 12, 1900. They were married at Ocala, Florida. He was Captain of Company H, Marion Hornet's 7th Florida Infantry during the War between the States.

Mary Rebecca Counts, daughter of Captain John Henry Counts was born at Ocala, Florida, Dec. 19, 1856, and married Thomas James Barnes, Aug. 13, 1872 at Ocala.

Children:

I.   LELA LYNWOOD, b. 26 April 1878, m. JOSEPH CLARENCE STONE, of Osceola Milla, Pa., on 27 June 1906 at Trinity Chapel, Washington, D.C.

II.   Thomas Marvin, b. 1880, d. 1887.

III.   Fletcher Counts, b. 6 July 1882, d. (by drowning) 28 Sept. 1938, m. Florence Jean Little 29 July 1908. She was born

15 July 1889.
IV. Margaret Ruth, b. 16 April 1885, m. Earl I. Pearson, also of Ocala, Fla.
V. Albertus, b. 1887, d. 1887
VI. Thomas Henry Grady (known as T.B.), b. 30 September 1890, m. 19 December 1916 Agnes Nolan, b. 29 January 1900.

Mr. John Lynwood Stone, son of Joseph Clarence Stone, was born Aug. 15, 1907 and married Laura Catherine Custer May 12, 1939, born Jan. 2, 1911, died Dec. 10, 1940. Mr. Stone resides at 4626 Butterworth Place, N.W., Washington, D.C. To Mrs. Stone is due credit for furnishing very material information on McKinnie, Exum and Whitehead families.

JOHN MACKQUINNEY
ELDER SON OF MICHAEL AND ELIZABETH MACQUINNEY
by Miss Ray Barnett

John Mackquinney was born between 1660 and 1665. He was dead before 1701 when Elizabeth and Thomas Reeves made affidavits concerning his redemption of his brother Barnaby's land. He was a resident of Nansemond Co., Va., as shown by the escheat patent granted to him in 1697. The name of his wife is unknown. That they were the parents of more than one child is proved by the bond for title from Barnaby Mackquinney to Richard Exum in 1703.

I. Michael Mackquinney, probably the oldest son, was born about 1687; married Rose--------. They were probably residents of Nansemond Co. Their deed, 1710, to Richard Exum says "in Isle of Wight", not "of Isle of Wight." Nothing is known of their children, but some of the unidentified McKinnes of N.C. may be descendants of Michael and Rose.
II. Benjamin McKinnie, was living in Edgecombe Co., N.C., 1720/1, as evidenced by deed from Nath'l Holley and wife conveying 50 acres southside of Morattuck River and south of Michael's Meadows, March 16, 1720/1. Benjamin was of age in 1720/1, and thus was born by 1699, or perhaps several years earlier.

In 1734, Benjamin McKinnie (no doubt son of above Benjamin) "for divers good causes me hereunto moving and in consideration of the sum of 50 pounds paid by my uncle Barnaby McKinnie 50 acres the aforesaid parcel of land being a part of a survey of land made for William Brown and by him lapsed and since is become due to the aforesaid Barnaby McKinnie by virtue of a lapsed patent granted for the whold survey bearing date of 30th of July, 1720, which land was formerly sold by William Brown to Nathaniel Holly to Benjamin McKinnie. Wit.: Isaac Ricks, George Roberson (Edgecombe Co. Bk. 1, p. 32).

In 1743/4 Benjamin McKinnie executed a deed conveying this same 50 acres to Richard McKinnie "for good causes*** land, sold by Benjamin McKinnie to Col. Barnaby McKinne bearing date 1734 but since it was judged that the said Benjamin McKinne was not of age to dispose of the said lands" this deed is to confirm the right of sale of this land to Richard McKinne being part of William Brown's lapsed patent. (Halifax Bk. 5, p. 353)

Col. Barnaby McKinne, called "my uncle Barnaby McKinne" in the deed, was the great-uncle of young Benjamin.

In 1741, Benjamin McKinnie received a grant of 740 acres, Edgecombe Co. (Col. Recs. N.C. Bk. 4, p. 592)

In 1741, Benjamin McKinnie sold to William Kinchen 740 acres in Edgecombe Co., 100 acres of old patent lands purchased of John McKinnie (Halifax Bk. 1, p. 239), and 640 acres to Kanakouary Swamp to Stevens' line and down the swamp to Stevens' corner to red oak in William Foresters' line, the 640 acres granted by patent to Benjamin McKinnie April 2, 1741 (See description of land given by John McKinnie to his cousins William and Mary Brown, and the gift to George Short).

In 1753, Benjamin McKinney was living in Prince Frederick Winyaw Parish, S.C., where his son, Michael, 2 years old, and daughter, Christian, 7 months old, were baptized.

III.   John McKenney. There can be little doubt that he was the son of John and grandson of Michael Mackquinney. He was married and the father of two children, John and Rachel, in 1715- thus born about 1690.

Will of Samuel Payne late of North Carolina***** to loving friend, John McKenney, 22 bbls. of Pitch now in Nansemond, also 22 bbls. pitch lying and to be delivered at the Northwest landing; to John McKenney, son of John, one young horse; to Rachel, daughter of John McKenny, pewter basin to be delivered by my executors in North Carolina; to James and John Caroon 640 acres of land lying by Indian Island and all remainder of estate. James and John Caroon executors. Wit.: Thomas Crocker, Katherine Jones, James Tamrath. Jan. 7, 1715; Apr. 10, 1716. Proven in Coratuck Prec.

It is probable that the John McKenny mentioned in above will was the John McKinnie of early records of Bertie and Edgecombe Precincts, and that these records did n not refer to John, son of Col. Barnaby McKinne. In 1723/ 25 grant to Barnabas McKinne Jr., 180 acres in Bertie Precinct on South side Morratuck River beginning at a gum in John McKinne's corner. The foregoing is the first record of a grant to Barnaby Jr., that I have found. It is generally accepted that Barnaby Jr. was the oldest son of Col. Barnaby, and that John was probably one of the youngest. If that be true, then John was too young to have received a grant in 1723 or 1725. Also, in a number of instances John, son of Col. Barnaby McKinne, is referred to as "John McKinne Jr".

On January 29, 1741/2, Mary McKinnie, probably wife of William McKinnie of Nansemond who held 200 acres in Nansemond in 1704 and who predeceased her, of Edgecombe Co., N.C., made a deed of gift to her three sons: Matthew, William, and Michael, all under 18 years of age. Witnesses were John Crowell and Joseph Lane, indicating a close association between Mary and the family of Barnaby Sr. Mary's husband is unknown, although some McKinne descendants claim he was William, son of Barnaby Sr. North Carolina wills and deeds refute this claim. William McKinne Sr. of Wayne County, N.C. was the son of Mary McKinnie of the above deed of gift.

William McKinne Sr. was born about 1725 in Edgecombe County, N.C.; died 1793, date of his will Jan. 26, 1793, Wayne County, N.C.; married ------Grimes? William McKinne Sr. was appointed 2d Major of the Minute Men of Dobbs Co., N.C. April 22, 1776. Member of N.C. Provincial Congress, from Dobbs Co., which met at Halifax April 4, 1776. 1774-"The first assemblage independent of Royal authority of their representatives in N.C., occurred at Newbern, on Aug. 25, 1784". Member from Dobbs County, William McKinne.

Children:

I. Matthew McKinne, m. ------Smith
II. Barnaby McKinne, son of William Sr. and brother of Richard, was a member of the General Assembly of N.C., from Wayne Co.-In the House of Commons: 1799-1800; in the Senate: 1812-13-14-15. Almost continuous service of father and sons for 51 years.
III. William McKinne Jr., b. Feb. 19, 1749; m. Mary Jernigan (See later)
IV. Richard McKinne, b. 1752; m. Sarah Fellows (See later)
V. Amey McKinne, m. ------Giles
VI. Nancy McKinne, m. --------Goodman
VII. Daughter, m. William Blackman

Richard McKinne, son of William McKinne Sr., was born 1752 in Wayne County, N.C.; died Jan. 27, 1800, in Wayne Co., N.C.; married 172-3 in Wayne Co., N.C., Sarah Fellows, b. 1752 in Wayne Co., N.C., made her will November Court 1837, in Wayne Co., N.C., daughter of Robert Fellows. One Robert Fellows as a member of the Surry Co., Va. Militia received received grants of 1000 acres in Craven and Johnston Cos., N.C. "An Act to establish Warehouses for the inspection of Tobacco in the County of Dobbs 'at Fellows Ferry, on the land of Robert Fellow'." (N.C. Col. Records V. 23, p. 507)

Richard McKinne was Commissioner of Wayne Co., N.C., for the year 1782. He was a member of the General Assembly of N.C., from Wayne Co. - In the House of Commons: 1782-83-86-87-90; In the Senate 1788-89-93-96-97-99. He was among members at the session at Fayetteville, Nov. 21, 1789, who voted to adopt the Federal Constitution, and N.C. entered the Union, the 12th State. Proof of eligibility for DAR membership is found on page 53, Book K, Revolutionary Army Accounts, Comptroller's Accounts, State Dept. of Archives and History, Raleigh, N.C.

Children:

I.   Anny McKinne, b. 1774, m. Joseph Everett

II. Richard McKinne, m. Julia Sasser

III. John McKinne, b. about 1780 (Twin of Barnabas?), m. Olive Fellows (See later)

IV. Barnabas McKinne, b. about 1780 (Twin of John?), m. Chellie McKinne

V. Matthew McKinne, d. unmarried

VI. Robert, m. Zilphia Smith

VII. Sally McKinne

VIII. Polly McKinne

John McKinnie (McKinne), son of Richard McKinne, was born about 1780 in Wayne Co., N.C.; died 1849-50 in Wayne Co., N.C.; married 1810-12 in Sampson Co., N.C., Olive Fellows, born about 1790 in Sampson Co., N.C.; died 1849-50 in DeSoto Co., Miss., daughter of William Fellows and his wife Susannah. Susannah was probably his second wife. She married secondly Josiah Blackman.

William Fellows appointed Captain, Joel Herring Lieutenant, and John Cooper Ensign for ---------County, under command of Brigadier General Ashe at Cape Fear "now in actual service" Tuesday, June 11, 1776 (N.C. Col. Records, V. 10, p. 625) William Fellows appointed recruiting officer for the County of Dobbs, 2nd Sept. 1777. (Ibid. V.22, p. 928). House Journal, 14th April 1778 ---The following were duly elected members of the Commons House of Assembly for the respective Counties and towns, as follows Viz: For Dobbs- William Fellows and Jesse Cobb. (Ibid V. 12, p. 655). William Fellows, William McKinne, Sr. and William McKinne Jr., were among those constituted "Directors and Trustees for designing, building and carrying on the said town (Waynesborough), Jan. 6, 1787.

John McKinne was a Protestant and a farmer and resided in Sampson Co., N.C., Greene Co., Ala., Hardeman Co., Tenn., and DeSoto Co., Miss.

Children:

I.   Dr. William Richard McKinnie, b. 1813; m. Martha Gatewood

II. Elizabeth Coleman McKinnie, b. 1815; m. Stephen Matthews (See later)

III. Dr. John Lebbins T. McKennie, b. 1823; m. sisters (1) Tabitha Smith, (2) Elizabeth Smith

IV. Sarah Ann McKinnie, b. 1827; m. -------Perry

V. Barnabas McKinnie, b. 1830; died unmarried

VI. Austin S. McKinnie, b. 1836; died unmarried

Elizabeth Coleman McKinnie was born about 1790 in Sampson Co., N.C.; died 1865 in Cleveland County (Now Bradley) Ark., married March 9, 1836 in Shelby Co., Tenn., Stephen Matthews, born 1812; died 1869.

Children:

I.   John Isaac Matthews, b. 1837

II. Olive Ann Matthews, b. Mar. 17, 1839; m. as 2nd wife, Nicholas V. Barnett

III. Sarah Elizabeth Matthews, b. Jan. 19, 1841; m. as 3rd

wife, Nicholas V. Barnett

IV. William D. Matthews, b. 1844
V. Martha Matilda Matthews, b. 1845
VI. Stephen R. Matthews, b. 1847
VII. Mary M. Matthews, b. 1849
VIII. Thomas J. Matthews, b. 1852
IX. Lucy B. Matthews, b. 1854
X. Austin Lebbins Matthews, b. 1856
XI. Eudora C. Matthews, b. 1859; m. Thomas Simpson

Olive Ann Matthews, daughter of Stephen Matthews, was born March 17, 1839 in DeSoto Co., Miss.; died Nov. 16, 1862 in Cleveland Co. (now Bradley) Ark., married Jan. 2, 1862, in Cleveland Co., Ark., as his second wife, Nicholas Valentine Barnett, born Feb. 24, 1828, at Mt. Meigs, Montgomery Co., Ala.; died March 7, 1888, Cleveland Co., Ark. Olive Ann Matthews was graduated from Hernando Female Institute, a Presbyterian School, Hernando, DeSoto, Miss., in 1859. The President of the school was Samuel McKinney (not related)

 Child:

I. Sidney O. Barnett, m. Sallie Virginia Rogers, daughter of Dr. Abner Derrell Rogers, a graduate of Philadelphia College of Medicine, 1856, and his wife Mary Jane Davis.
 Children:
 1. Mary Olive Barnett, m. James Nils Swanson
 2. Ray Barnett of Washington, D.C.
 3. Abner Rogers Barnett, m. Tommie Louise Brown
 4. Walter Amis Barnett, m. Julia Frances Berry

William McKinne, Jr. was born in Wayne County, N.C. Feb. 19, 1749. and died there 17 Sept. 1790. In 1770 he married Mary Jernigan, who was born in Wayne County, April 5, 1752 and died there June 4, 1814.

 Children:

I. William McKinne, b. 1771, m. Elizabeth Fulgham. (See later)
II. John McKinne, b. 1771 (twins) m. Elizabeth Pope
III. David McKinne, b. c.r. 1773, m. Mary Wooten.
IV. Mary McKinne
V. Richard McKinne, m. Nancy Cogdell
VI. Alice McKinne, m. Arthur Fulgham
VII. Zilpha McKinne, m. William Fellows
VIII. Michael McKinne, m. Lottie Pope
IX. Nancy McKinne
X. Elizabeth McKinne, m. William Boykin.

William McKinne, son of Mary Jernigan and William McKinne, Jr., was born in Wayne County, N.C. Oct. 29, 1771 and died there Feb. 12, 1842. About 1796 he married Elizabeth Fulgham, the daughter of Winnifred Pierce and Railford Fulgham, who was born in Wayne County, N.C., Sept. 5, 1779 and died there June 13, 1816.

 Children:

I, Barnabas McKinne, b. May 22, 1797
II. William P. McKinne, m. Susan McKinne
III. Railford McKinne, died young

IV. John R. McKinne, b. May 1, 1809, m. Susan Crawford
V. David F. McKinne, b. Aug. 13, 1813, m. Ann E. Whitfield (See later)
VI. Arthur McKinne, m. Harriet Lee
VII. Mary (Polly) McKinne, m. Alexander Hall
VIII. Richard McKinne, b. July 1, 1815, died young
IX. Zilpha McKinne, m. Samuel Woods.

David Fulgham McKinne, son of Elizabeth Fulgham and William McKinne was born in Wayne County, N.C. August 13, 1813, and died there August 30, 1867. On Oct. 15, 1844 he married Ann Eliza, the daughter of Nancy Henry and William Haywood Whitfield, who was born in Lenoir Co., N.C. Oct. 21, 1816 and died at Princeton, N.C. Sept. 22, 1894.

Children:
I. William Haywood McKinne, b. Aug. 23, 1845, died young
II. David Edward McKinne, b. March 3, 1847, m. Sarah Elizabeth Brothers.
III. Alonzo Jerkins McKinne, b. Sept. 15, 1848, died young
IV. Haywood Whitfield McKinne, b.----m. Julia Hooker.
V. Annie Elizabeth Barbara McKinne, b. Dec. 26, 1850, m. William R. Hollowell.
VI. Julia Etta McKinne, b. April 8, 1856, m. S.B. Parker (See later)
VII. William Barnabas McKinne, b. June 4, 1858, died young

Julia Etta McKinne, daughter of Ann Eliza Whitfield and David Fulgham McKinne, was born in Wayne County, N.C. April 8, 1856, and died at New Bern N.C. June 28, 1913. On June 22, 1875, in Wayne County, she married Simmons Baker Parker, who was born at Scotland Neck, N.C., Jan. 19, and died Sept. 7, 1923 at New Ber , N.C.

Children:
I. Harriet E. Parker, b. Apr. 20, 1876, m. L. A. Davis (See later)
II. Irma Waldeen Parker, b. Sept. 18, 1877, died young
III. Mary Etta Parker, b. Feb. 24, 1881, m. Raynor Jones
IV. Elizabeth Anna Parker, b. Sept. 25, 1883, m. George W. Allen.
V. Ina Haywood Parker, b. April 25, 1885, died young.
VI. David McKinne Parker, b. Sept. 25, 1889, m. May Gaskill
VII. Julia Eliza Parker, b. Jan. 3, 1895, m. Eugene L. Cox.
VIII. Emily Wood Parker, b. May 6, 1900, m. Robert V. Rider

Harriet Estell Parker, daughter of Julia Etta McKinne and Simmons Baker Parker was born at La Grange, N.C. April 20, 1876, and died at New Bern, N.C. March 4, 1956. On June 12, 1905, at Raleigh, N.C. she married Leonidas Adolphus Davis, who was born in Craven County, N.C., Dec. 13, 1874, and died at New Bern, N.C., Nov. 26, 1942.

Children:
I. Jefferson C. Davis, b. April 4, 1906, m. Margaret O. Pippen (See later)
II. Julia McKinne Davis, b. Feb. 26, 1910, m. Clifton McCotter.

Jefferson Clark Davis, who now resides at 3941 E. Desmond Lane, Tucson, Arizona, was born April 4, 1906 at New Bern, N.C. On April 6, 1929, at Washington, N.C. he married Margaret Olivia, daughter of Margaret Jane Cromartie and William Joseph Pippen, who was born in Washington, N.C., June 9, 1908.

Mr. Davis was educated at North Carolina State, and University of Hawaii. He is now an Instructor and was previously an engineer. He has lived in North Carolina, Jacksonville, Fla., Baltimore, Md., Honolulu, T.H., Red Bank, N. J., and Tucson, Arizona.

Children:

I.   Jefferson C. Davis, Jr., b. March 20, 1931, m. Sylvia Conally.

WHITEHEAD of ISLE of WIGHT

ARTHUR WHITEHEAD[1] was probably born in England about 1625, and came to Virginia sometime before 1643. He died about 1655, presumably in Isle of Wight County. His place of birth in England is not known at this time.

On 22 March 1643, he was listed as one of the Head Rights of Obedience Robins, who on that day received a patent for 450 acres in Northampton County, Virginia, bounded by a former devisement of the said Robins for the transportation of nine persons: John Coleman, Henry Edwards, ARTHUR WHITEHEAD[1], Nicholas Every, John Ellis, Henry Baston, Stephen Horse (probably Horsefield), Thomas Chapman, and John Carter. Of these it is interesting to note that all but two of the family names are subsequently found in the records of Isle of Wight County, which supports the conclusion that ARTHUR WHITEHEAD[1] settled there. (C.P. 225)

The name of his first wife is not known, but they were probably not long married at the time of her death, as only one child, a son ARTHUR[2], is known to have resulted.

ARTHUR[1] then married a Katherine, whose last name is also not known. They had no children, and ARTHUR[1] died about 1655.

In 1670, William Ruffin assigned 200 acres of land to Katherine Thornton, with reversion to her two children, ARTHUR[2] WHITEHEAD and Rebecca Thornton. Three facts indicate that Katherine was not his daughter. First, the year of her birth is given as 1634, the year before William Ruffin arrived in Virginia from England, as a boy of 18. Second, he does not designate her as his daughter in this land assignment. Third, his son Robert Ruffin "of the County of Surry", on 21 January 1675/76, in a deed to Thomas Giles of Nansemond County, speaks of "my plantation on which my decd. father William Ruffin of Isle of Wight lived, except 200 acres which my decd. father made over to Katherine as his sister. Some close relationship evidently existed, but what this was is not known. (V.H.G. 262-263)

On 11 August 1673, ARTHUR WHITEHEAD[2], in consideration of affection for his sister Rebecca Horsefield, then wife to Stephen Horsefield, gave her some cows. Possibly this was his wedding present to his half sister. At any rate, it does show that Rebecca Thornton was born about 1655, assuming her to have been about 18 at the time of her marriage to Stephen Horsefield. This would further indicate that Katherine married her second husband no later than 1655 and possibly earlier, so that ARTHUR[1] must have died before that year, and, of course, his son ARTHUR[2] also was born before then. (17C. 565)

Sometime between 1676 and 1687, the year in which Katherine died, her second husband died, and she married for the third time. Her third husband's name was Bathe (Bythesea), and he also predeceased her. On 11 October 1687, the nuncupative will of Katherine Bathe was recorded in Isle of Wight County, by which she left legacies to her son-in-law Stephen Horsefield, his wife and children; and to son ARTHUR WHITEHEAD[2], "whom she declared was unnatural to her", thus showing him to have been her step-son by her first marriage to ARTHUR WHITE-HEAD[1]. This Stephen Horsefield was undoubtedly the son of Stephen Horse (field) who was one of the emigrants with the first ARTHUR WHITEHEAD[1], listed with the head rights of the Obedience Robins patent in 1643, above mentioned.

Child:

I.   ARTHUR[2], b. about 1650; d. 1710/11; m. MARY GODWIN[4], the dau. of WILLIAM GODWIN[3] of Isle of Wight County (See later).

ARTHUR WHITEHEAD[2] was born about 1650 in Isle of Wight County, Virginia, and died there about 1710. He married MARY GODWIN[4], the daughter of WILLIAM GODWIN[3]. (G.B. 2-52; W. & D. Bk. 2-528; C.-M-35)

The earliest presently known record of ARTHUR WHITE-HEAD[2] occurs 11 August 1673, when he gave some cows to his half-sister Rebecca Thornton, probably as a wedding present after her marriage to Stephen Horsefield. On 9 February 1687/8, he presented the inventory for the estate of Christopher Wade. Captain Thomas Godwin was one of the creditors of this estate. About 1696, William Strickland and his brother Mathew sold 200 acres of land to ARTHUR WHITEHEAD[2], and this deed was attested by BARNABY MACQUINNEY[2], Jno. (X) Barrett, and John Worrell. Three years later, on 1 February 1699, William Strickland and his wife Oliffe sold another 150 acres to ARTHUR WHITEHEAD[2] at George Pierce's line, as attested by John Giles, John Chapman and Andrew Woodley. Sometime in 1704, he appraised the estate of John Cooke, along with George Pierce, William Johnson and John Bardin. The following year, on 9 April 1705, with William Johnson and Henry Pope, he was one of the appraisers of the estate of George Pierce. The last recorded reference to ARTHUR[2] occurs 30 March 1721, ten years after his death, when Richard Braswell patented 365 acres in Urah Meadows in Chowan County, N.C., on ARTHUR WHITEHEAD's[2] line and John Cotton's indicating that he had purchased lands in North Carolina before his death. No further records are found, either of himself or of his widow, but further study of the land records of Isle of Wight County might be fruitful.

In his will he made bequests to his son WILLIAM[3], and wife MARY[4], the latter being named executrix. Philip Rayford, Philip Pierce, and Thomas Boone are named as witnesses, and the will is dated 11 January 1710/11, but no date is given for its recording. (W. & D. Bk. 2-528; C-1-72-73)

Child:

I.   WILLIAM[3], b. about 1672; d. after 1711.

WILLIAM WHITEHEAD[3] was born in Isle of Wight County, Virginia, about 1672. The date of his death is uncertain, but it was after 1711, since he was mentioned in his father's will as one of the legatees in 1710/11.

No records of WILLIAM[3] or his wife or widow have been discovered after 1711, as of this writing. It is certain that he married and had at least three and possibly four sons. As early as 1723, the estate of William West was settled by ARTHUR WHITEHEAD[4] in Isle of Wight County. In 1726 Barnaby Thomas, the son of William Thomas of Isle of Wight, bought 250 acres of land from Lazarus Whitehead. Also an inventory was returned for the estate of Robert Whitehead of Surry County, Virginia, in 1731. It seems positive that ARTHUR[4] and Lazarus were sons of WILLIAM[3], and probable that Robert was also, for no records of any earlier Whiteheads in this area exist than those already given. The names of the first two, and those of their later descendants, further confirm their being the sons of WILLIAM[3]. The existence of another son is clear in the will of ARTHUR WHITEHEAD[4], dated 12 March 1744, in Southampton County, Virginia, wherein he mentions his brother William as one of the executors. This brother and another brother Lazarus were witnesses to this will.

Children:

I. ARTHUR[4], b. about 1693; d. 1750/51; m. (1) ISABELLA[2] PURCELL, dau. of ARTHUR PURCELL[1] and his wife MARY; 2. ANN COOK (See later)
II. Lazarus.
III. Robert
IV. William

ARTHUR WHITEHEAD SR.[4] was born about 1693, probably in Isle of Wight County, Virginia. He died at his plantation in Southampton County, Virginia, in 1750/51, as indicated by his will, probated there at that time.

ARTHUR[4] first married ISABELLA PURCELL[2], the daughter of ARTHUR PURCELL[1] and his wife MARY of Isle of Wight County. After her death he married Ann Cook, the daughter of Reuben and Hannah Cook, also of Isle of Wight County. She is not named in his will, dated 12 March 1744, and recorded 10 January 1750/51. On 9 July 1752, however, it is recorded that Ann Whitehead's dower was paid, signed by ARTHUR's[4] son Lewis, so she evidently married him between 1744 and 1750. In all probability, all of the children named in ARTHUR'S[4] will were by his first wife ISABELLA[2].

The first record of ARTHUR WHITEHEAD[4] occurs on 21 April 1717, when his first wife's father, ARTHUR PURCELL[1], left a legacy to "daughter ISABELLA[2], the wife of ARTHUR WHITEHEAD[4]". This will was not recorded until 27 May 1729. On 29 October 1723, when he settled the estate of William West, he was about 30 years of age. ARTHUR[4] appraised the estate of Edward Powers Sr. along with Samuel Brown and John Vasser on 28 July 1729. The records show that in February 1736 ARTHUR[4] was one of three appraisers of the estate of Robert Vick, and in August of the same year he, John Pope Jr., and Thomas Davis appraised the estate of John Vasser Jr. Again, in July of 1737, ARTHUR WHITEHEAD[4], John Pope, and Richard Vick were appraisers of the estate of William Worrell.

ARTHUR WHITEHEAD SR, [4] was one of the witnesses to the will of his son ARTHUR JR. [5] on 6 January 1748. Also witnessing this will were his son-in-law Joseph Cobb, Jr., who married his daughter Catrin and his daughter-in-law Mary (Watkins) who married his son Lewis. The last recorded action of ARTHUR [4] occurred in March 1748, two years before his death, when he, Chaplin Williams (a son of CAPTAIN THOMAS WILLIAMS [3]), and John Edwards appraised the estate of John Edwards.

ARTHUR WHITEHEAD [4] made his own will on 12 March 1744, and it was recorded 10 January 1750/51. In it he names his eldest son ARTHUR [5], who received land adjoining William Turner; grandson Arthur Whitehead; son Lewis, who was left land bought of William Powers and land on the Pottycassey Creek in Northampton County, North Carolina, south of the Meherring River; son Nathan, who received land on Fishing Creek in Carolina; grandson Benjamin Whitehead; daughter Catrin Cobb; grandson Jacob Vick; daughter Mary; and daughter Ann, who was left a plantation and negro Toney, and a feather bed. Executors names were brother William Whitehead, Capt. Thomas Jarrell, and Mrs. James Washington. The witnesses to this will were his brothers William and Lazarus Whitehead, and William Bock.

Several, if not all, of his family were Quakers, and attended the Pagan Creek Monthly Meeting in Isle of Wight County, as evidenced by the fact that it is recorded in the minute book of that meeting for 20 January 1745/6 that ARTHUR'S [4] son Lewis Whitehead was at liberty to marry Mary Watkins. Again, at the 15th August 1747 meeting, it is recorded that ARTHUR'S [4] daughter Mary Whitehead was at liberty to marry Benjamin Denson.

Children:

I. ARTHUR JR. [5], b. about 1715, or earlier; d. 1749; m. PATIENCE ------.

II. Lewis, b. about 1717; d. 1759; m. Mary Watkins in 1746; had children: 1. Isabel, m. James Allen Bridger; 2. Mary, m. Daniel Mills; 3. Elizabeth; 4. Patty; 5. John; 6. an unnamed son.

III. Nathan, b. about 1719; m. Mary Davis, sister of John, Martha and Judah Davis, and of Alice Bryant. He married (2) Rachael ------. (See later)

IV. Patience, b. about 1721; m. a Vick, had son Jacob.

V. Catrin, b. about 1724; m. Joseph Cobb Jr., son of Joseph Cobb Sr., and his wife Susannah. They had children: 1. William, m. his cousin Barsheba Whitehead in Watauga District of East Tennessee; 2. Mary, m. Henry Massengill of Watauga.

VI. Mary, b. about 1727; m. Benjamin Denson in 1747.

VII. Ann, b. about 1730; m. (1) Jesse Williams, the son of Benjamin Williams and Nichola Fourre; (2) James Fillyaw of Onslow County, N.C. Jesse Williams was the great grandson of JOHN WILLIAMS [1]. They moved to Onslow County, N.C., and had children: 1. Sarah; 2. Hester, b. about 1753, m. before 1778 to Daniel Humphrey, b. 1750, d. 1804; 3. Lot; 4. Hannah; 5. Senea; 6. Polly; 7. Jesse; and 8. Uz. Lot, Hannah, Jesse and Uz were all minors in 1780, and Senea and Polly were born after 1773

and before 1778. The probability that Ann Whitehead m. Jesse
Williams is supported by the fact that her daughter Hester
(Williams) Humphrey named one of her sons Whitehead
Humphrey.

ARTHUR WHITEHEAD JR.[5] was born about 1715 in Isle of
Wight County, Virginia, and died in 1749 at his plantation in
Nottoway Parish in the same county.

His wife's name was PATIENCE, but her family name is
not known. After his death, she married Thomas Jones, as indicated by the fact that her son Lewis Whitehead, PATIENCE
Jones and Thomas Jones signed the inventory for the estate of
ARTHUR WHITEHEAD JR.[5], and also signed his estate account,
which was recorded 7 February 1750.

ARTHUR JR.[5] was left land adjoining William Turner, by
the will of his father ARTHUR WHITEHEAD SR.[4], dated 12
March 1744. Since he predeceased his father about one year,
this land presumably went to the heirs of ARTHUR[5] when his
father's estate was divided.

ARTHUR WHITEHEAD JR.[5] made his will 6 January 1748,
and it was recorded 13 April 1749. He left land on Blunt's
Swamp to his son Arthur, and other legacies to his brother,
Lewis Whitehead, sons Lazarus, William, and Jesse, and daughters Edith and SEALLAH[6], and wife PATIENCE. His wife and
brother Lewis Whitehead were named executors. His father
ARTHUR WHITEHEAD SR.[4], his aunt Catrin's husband Joseph
Cobb Jr., and his brother Lewis's wife Mary Whitehead were the
witnesses to this will.

Children:

I. Arthur, b. about 1737; d. 1758, unmarried.
II. Lazarus, d. 1775; m. Elizabeth ------, and had; 1. Ar-
thur; 2. Jesse, m. Esther Marshall 16 January 1787;
3. Molly; 4. John, m. his cousin Katherine Whitehead;
and 5. Salley.
III. William m. and had dau. Katherine, who m. her first
cousin John Whitehead, son of Lazarus Whitehead.
IV. Jesse.
V. Edith, m. Thomas Boone.
VI. SELAH[6], b. about 1745; d. 1818; m. 1. NATHAN WIL-
LIAMS[5] of Northampton County, N.C., and moved to
Richland District, S.C., where she died. Had children
by 1st husband: 1. Joel; 2. ELY[6]; 3. Green; and 4. another son whose name is unknown. She m. 2. John Bran-
ham between 1785 and 1788, and had a son Richard, another son, and a daughter.

Nathan Whitehead, son of Isabella (Purcell) and Arthur[4]
Whitehead, died in Nash County, North Carolina in 1779. He
married Rachael ------ and the following children: 1. Nathan,
m. Feb. 27, 1805, Sarah, dau. William Boddie. She m. (2)
Elisha Lott; 2. Thomas who married Elizabeth Culpepper; 3.
Benjamin; 4. Rhoda, m. ----Nicholson; 5. Isabel, m. Bell;
6. Chloe, m. Erasmus Culpepper (see later); 7. Mary, m.
------ Sandiford; 8. Henry; 9. Mathew.

Chloe Whitehead, daughter of Nathan and Rachel Whitehead,
married August 17, 1765, Erasmus Culpepper, born probably

in Edgecombe County, North Carolina, died 1783, Nash County, North Carolina. They had five children: 1. Mathew; 2. Osborne; 3. Nathan, m. Frances Gardner (see later); 4. Sampson; and 5. Rosemond.

Gardner Culpepper was born Dec. 11, 1810, in Warren Co., Georgia; died May 24, 1868, Thomas County, Georgia; married Jan. 1, 1837, Warren County, Georgia, Carolina Jones, b. April 28, 1815, Georgia, died Nov. 18, 1885, Boston, Thomas County, Georgia, the daughter of Henry Jones and his wife, Nancy Stewart.

Children:

I. Mary Culpepper, b. Feb. 20, 1848
II. John Gardner Culpepper, b. 1843
III. Amanda E. Culpepper, b. March 9, 1840, m. Mitchell B. Parramore.
IV. William Culpepper, b. Feb. 14, 1845, m. Jane Turner
V. Sterling Gardner Culpepper, b. March 11, 1851, m. Susan Elizabeth Foy (See later)
VI. James Thomas Culpepper, b. Feb. 20, 1855, m. Bamah Reid.

Sterling Gardner Culpepper, born March 11, 1851, at Boston, Thomas County, Ga., died Nov. 21, 1907, Dallas, Texas, married Nov. 21, 1878, Boston, Thomas County, Ga., Susan Elizabeth Foy, born June 25, 1848, Boston, Thomas County, Ga., died June 5, 1887 Boston, Thomas County, Ga., daughter of James M. Foy and Mary Frances Parramore.

Children:

I. Mary Foy Culpepper, b. Dec. 1, 1880, m. R. S. Waldron (See later)
II. Susie C. Culpepper, b. Dec. 17, 1881
III. John Gardner Culpepper, b. April 20, 1883
IV. Ben Hill Culpepper, b. Sept. 1, 1885
V. Ruth Culpepper, b. Jan. 6, 1887

Mary Foy Culpepper, daughter of Sterling Gardner Culpepper and Susan Elizabeth Foy, was born Dec. 1, 1880, at Boston, Thomas County, Ga., died Nov. 20, 1949, St. Louis, Mo., married Jan. 10, 1898, White Springs, Hamilton Co., Fla., Roman Simeon Waldron, born May 11, 1871, Hamilton County, Fla., died March 24, 1928, St. Louis, Mo.

Children:

I. Ruth Allison Waldron, b. Oct. 24, 1898; m. Adolph B. Hill Jr. (See later)
II. Mary Elizabeth Waldron, b. Oct. 10, 1899; m. Geo. Lester Schaberg.
III. Roman Simeon Waldron Jr., b. Jan. 3, 1909, died unmarried
IV. Foy Culpepper Waldron, b. Jan. 3, 1909, died unmar.

Ruth Allison Waldron, born Oct. 24, 1898, at Houston, Harris County, Texas, daughter of Roman Simeon Waldron and Mary Foy Culpepper, married July 2, 1925, at St. Louis, Mo. Adolph Burge Hill Jr., born Nov. 30, 1886, Nashville, Tenn., son of Adolph Burge Hill Sr. and Julia Morgan Hicks. Mr. Hill is an Episcopalian and was educated at Washington University. They reside at 4925 Pershing St., St. Louis 8, Mo.

RUFFIN and DE LOACH of SURRY, VIRGINIA, NORTH CAROLINA and MISSISSIPPI

(Continued from page 264, Virginia Historical Genealogies)

William[4] Ruffin (ca 1708-1781), son of William[3] Ruffin and his wife, Faith Gray, daughter of William Gray, (For Gray see V. H. G. -309) married about 1742. The name of his wife is unknown. She died prior to the date of his will. He was born in Bertie County, North Carolina in that section which in the year 1741 was made into Northampton Co.

On January 12, 1773 he bought from Shadrack Stevenson of Edgecombe County, N.C., for ℔ 100 of Proclamation money, 100 acres of land in Northampton on south side of Bridger's Creek at Cashy road, said land given by Charles Stevenson.

William Ruffin's will was dated March 1, 1799, probated November term 1781. His children mentioned in the will were: I. William; II. Richard married Avarilla De Loach, sister of William De Loach; III. Purity, b. 1746, m. William De Loach (See later); IV. Faith, m. ------ Pender.

William DeLoach married in 1763 Purity Ruffin, daughter of William Ruffin of Northampton County, North Carolina, as shown by joint deed given by William DeLoach and his wife Purity; also by will of William Ruffin and by will of her brother, Richard Ruffin of Wayne Co., N.C. William DeLoach was father of Ruffin DeLoach, as shown by Power-of-Attorney given by William DeLoach in 1792 to "my son" Ruffin DeLoach, on record at Tarboro, Edgecombe County, North Carolina. He moved from Edgecombe Co., N.C., to Sumner Co., Tenn., and from thence to Logan Co., Ky.

William DeLoach and Purity Ruffin DeLoach were the parents of:
I.   Ruffin DeLoach (See later)
II.   William DeLoach
III.   Samuel[6] DeLoach, d. 1791-92; m. Elizabeth Hopper and had:
        1. Mary DeLoach m. William Sneed and had a daughter, Mary DeLoach Sneed who married her cousin, George Sneed.
IV.   Thomas DeLoach
V.   Mary Deloach, b. Aug. 9, 1777; d. July 9, 1837, Ky.; m. ca 1795/9, John Sutton, b. Sept. 15, 1772; d. June 21, 1826, had
        William DeLoach Sutton (1803-1875) m. 1839 Eliza Molle McReynolds (1803-1873) had
        Eliza Williston Sutton (1845-1900) m. Geo. Strother

Browning (1834-1910) had
George Francis Browning (1881-   ) m. Blanche David-
son, had
George Francis Browning Jr., (1914) had
Cynthia
Brenda
VI.   Sarah DeLoach m. Glidewell Killebrew
VII.   Celia, m. Isaac Pennington.

Ruffin DeLoach married Abba Mercer Oct. 1783, daughter
of John Mercer of Norfolk County, Virginia, and Mary Gay,
daughter of Henry Gay of Edgecombe County, N.C. Ruffin De-
Loach moved from Edgecombe County, N.C., and settled in
Sumner Co., Tenn., and from there he and his family floated
down the Mississippi River on a "Kentucky Boat", in the same
caravan as Admiral Farragut's father and his family, and
landed at Ft. Adams, Wilkinson County, Mississippi, where
his will and that of his wife, Aba Mercer, are on record at
Woodville, Wilkinson County, Mississippi. Ruffin DeLoach and
his family moved from Ft. Adams and settled at Pinckneyville,
Mississippi, on the plantation called "Meteraire". John Mercer
was a Lieutenant in the Revolutionary War.

Ruffin and Abba DeLoach were the parents of:
I.   John Mercer DeLoach, known as Captain Jack DeLoach
II.   William Ruffin DeLoach, who fought in War of 1812 and
died shortly thereafter of wounds sustained in the war.
III.   Jesse DeLoach
IV.   Elizabeth DeLoach (See later)
V.   Olivia DeLoach who m. John McElrath in Tennessee in
1808

Elizabeth DeLoach married Dr. James Orr and moved with
her father, Ruffin DeLoach to Wilkinson County, Mississippi.
Dr. James Orr enlisted in the War of 1812 as a private Sept.
24, 1812, was promoted to Surgeon's Mate and served throughout the war (Report Adjutant General's Office)

Elizabeth DeLoach and James Orr were the parents of:
I.   Evelina DeLoach Orr (See later)
II.   Mary Orr who m. -------Trimley
III.   Ruffin H. Orr
IV.   Wright B. Orr
V.   John Orr who died in infancy

Evelina (Evelyn) DeLoach Orr, born about 1810, and died
March 7, 1875, married John McNulty from near Philadelphia,
Pennsylvania, on March 29, 1827. They lived and died at Ft.
Adams, Wilkinson County, Mississippi.

Evelina (Evelyn) DeLoach Orr and John McNulty were
the parents of:
I.   Thomas, who died in infancy
II.   Mary Ann, who died at school at Pascagoula, Mississippi,
age 17
III.   Elizabeth Ellen McNulty who married Benjamin Rowe of
West Feliciana Parish, Louisiana (See later)
IV.   John Wall McNulty who died during the Civil War - was
killed in action. He married Augusta Pressley of Louisi-

ana. Children by this union were:
1. Ida Augusta who died when a child
2. Mary Evelyn who died in infancy.

Elizabeth Ellen McNulty, born 1835 and died in March 1855, married Benjamin Rowe on March 27, 1851; they lived on Rose Hill Plantation, Wilkinson County, Miss. Elizabeth Ellen McNulty and Benjamin Rowe were the parents of:

I.   A son who died in infancy
II.   Ella Evelyn (Unmarried), born in 1853 and died in 1941
III.   Sarah Elizabeth Rowe married Darling Babers who came from South Carolina as a boy with his father, John Babers, and settled in Bienville Parish, Louisiana. After the Civil War, Darling Babers settled in Ft. Adams, Mississippi, as a planter.

Sarah Elizabeth Rowe, born April 1855, died 1927, married October 11, 1876, Darling Babers. Darling Babers served in the Civil War, first under General Stonewall Jackson in the Valley Campaign, and later under General Lee at the Battle of Gettysburg, was taken prisoner and sent to Fort Delaware.

Sarah Elizabeth Rowe and Darling Babers were the parents of

I.   Elwyn, died in infancy
II.   Evelyn DeLoach McNulty, born June 21, 1879, died in March 1923, married George L. Roger
III.   Bertram Ferman Babers, born September 1880 (See later)
IV.   Edith Alpha Babers, born November 2, 1881, married James Charles St. Germain
     Children:
     1. Elise Ludivine, single
     2. Aimee Mercer St. Germain, married Louis Broussard
     3. Edith Alpha St. Germain
V.   Lenore leBaron Babers, born Oct. 20, 1883, married James Edward O'Donnell (See later)
VI.   Sarah Elise Babers, born Jan. 2, 1890, m. Harold Beresford White, and had one child: Harold Beresford White

Bertram Ferman Babers, son of Elizabeth (Rowe) and Darling Babers, married Lucile Walsh Jackson, December 23, 1903.

     Children:
I.   Vincent Darling Babers, b. Oct. 26, 1904, died young
II.   Bertram Ferman Babers II, b. June 14, 1906, m. Aug. 24, 1929, Vida Pelayo.
     Children:
     1. Bertram Ferman Babers III
     2. Sharon Miskell Babers
     3. Eldrige
     4. Horatio Jackson
III.   Hannah Eldredge Babers, b. May 2, 1908, Rosemound Plantation, West Feliciana Parish, La., m. Dec. 23, 1929, St. Francisville, West Feliciana Parish, La., Montrose Hamilton Barrow, b. Feb. 6, 1905, St. Francisville, La., son of Ruffin Bennett and Eliza Amanda (Hamilton) Barrow. Mr. Barrow was educated at the University of Tulsa and the Colorado School of Mines. He is District Manager of the Foster Wheeler Corporation, in Houston,

Texas. He belongs to the Protestant Episcopal Church. Mrs. Barrow is a member of the United Daughters of the Confederacy, Daughters of the American Revolution and the Colonial Dames. They reside at 901 Kirby Drive, Houston, Texas.

Children:

1. William Ruffin Barrow, born Oct. 3, 1942
2. Mary Anne Barrow, born Nov. 15, 1948

Lenore Babers, daughter of Elizabeth (Rowe) and Darling Babers, was born Oct. 20, 1883, at Fort Adams, Wilkinson Co., Miss., married July 7, 1916, at Des Plaines, Cook Co., Ill., James Edward O'Donnell, born July 16, 1883, Chicago, Cook Co., Ill. Mrs. O'Donnell was educated at Sacred Heart College, Newcomb College, Tulane College, New Orleans, La. They reside at Woodville, Miss; address P.O. Box 462.

NORWOOD of NORTH CAROLINA

(Continued from page 334, S.V.G. 11)

Nathaniel Norwood, originally of Northampton County, North Carolina, but later of Granville County, N.C., was the son of George Norwood of Northampton, who died in 1749.

Nathaniel Norwood, Benjamin Norwood, his son and Joseph Aiken, (Benjamin's wife's father) all signed the Oath of Allegiance to the Colony of North Carolina, May 2, 1778. This was an act passed at New Bern, N.C. 15 Nov. 1777. (Col. Rec. Bk, 22 p. 175) Every man of Island Creek District, where they lived, took this oath.

Nathaniel Norwood made his will in Granville County on Sept. 2, 1779; same probated in February Court, 1784. (W.Bk.1 p. 385) In his will, he names his wife MARY and the following children: WILLIAM, dsp. JOHN, GILLIAM, JORDAN, BENJAMIN (See later), PENELOPE GLOVER, SUSANNE GLOVER, GEORGE (see p. 333 S.V.F. 11) NATHANIEL, SARAH PAROTT.

Benjamin Norwood, son of Nathaniel, died in Granville Co. in 1847. On April 8, 1782 he married Mary Aiken, daughter of Joseph Aiken of Mecklenburg Co., Va.; later of Granville Co. N.C., and his wife Mary.

. Benjamin Norwood's will is in Book 17, p. 133. In it he mentions children: JOHN, BENJAMIN, JR. m. Catherine Norwood; MARGARET, m. Thomas B. Barnett; NANCY, m. Wesley Pitchford; JOSEPH A., m. Letty Royster; WILLIAM A., m. Rebecca Thomas; MARY, m. Mr. Jenkins.

William Norwood, son of Benjamin, died in Granville Co. about 1839. On Nov. 9, 1807 he married Rebecca Thomas, who died about 1873. They had the following children: NATHANIEL MACON, b. Aug. 26, 1812, m. 1st. Martha H. Barnett; PHILLIP T.; EMILY; LEONARD H.; JAMES S.; WILLIAM S., b. 1831; GEORGE WASHINGTON (see later), b. 1821 m. (1st) Sarah Jane Walker; (2nd.) Betty Lawson; EDWARD?

George Washington Norwood, son of William, was born in Granville Co., N.C. 1821 (1850 Census) and died in Winston-Salem, N.C. in 1878. On Nov. 8, 1847, he married in Person Co., Jane Walker, who was born in 1831 (Census 1850) and died in Person Co. about 1869. She was the daughter of Byrd Walker. Later he married Bettie Lawson, daughter of Jane Bailey and David Lawson.

The children of George W. Norwood and wife Jane Walker were: WILLIAM P., b. Nov. 22, 1848, m. Frances Northam; TOMESINA SUE, b. June 13, SARAH JANE, May 30, 1852, d. 1853; GEORGE THOMAS (see later), b. April 23, 1854, m. Jennie Lawson; DETRON, dsp.; SIDNEY b. Nov. 8, 1859, m.

Laura V. Chambler; CHARLES Q. b. March 7, 1864, m. Pattie Wyatt Jeffress; MOLLY ELFREDA, b. Nov. 27, 1865, m. Wm. King Ballow. His second wife, Bettie Lawson, had two children: Kate, died young, and JOHN DAVID NORWOOD.

George Thomas Norwood, son of George and his wife Jane Walker, was born in Granville Co. N.C. April 23, 1854, and died Sept. 10, 1916 at South Boston, Halifax Co., Va. On Nov. 23, 1887, at Harmony, Halifax Co., Va. m. Jennie Lawson, who was born there Mar. 26, 1856 and died in South Boston, March 23, 1935. She was the daughter of Jane Bailey and David Lawson. George Thomas had the following children: GEORGE V,, b. Oct. 26, 1888, and RUTH. b. Aug. 26, 1892, both died in infancy; JANE LAWSON. b. Oct. 9, 1894, m. Victor V. Shepherd, HELEN (see later), b. Oct. 23, 1896, m. Edward Hamlin; MARY. b. July 12, 1898, dsp. 1934.

Helen Norwood Hamlin of 568 Main Street, South Boston, Va., was born there Oct. 23, 1896 and there on Oct. 30, 1923 she married Edward Reamey Hamlin, who was born Nov. 19, 1889 in Danville, Va., the son of Sarah Arney and Frank Mallory Hamlin. No children.

NORWOODS of SOUTH CAROLINA

(Continued from V.H.G. p. 334)

Edward Norwood, son of Lydia and William Norwood, b. 1662-3; (first appears as a tithable 1679) married prior to July 6, 1680, Naomi, daughter of Richard Smith of Charles City County (Surry Order Bk. 1, pp. 306, 312) and moved to Chowan County, N.C., prior to Jan. 11, 1685, when the birth of Jane, daughter of Edward and Naomi Norwood is recorded in the Parish Register. (Hathaway, III, p. 215) No further records concerning Edward Norwood have been furnished. He is said to have had a son, John, who was the father of Theophilus Norwood of South Carolina.

Theophilus Norwood was a "son-in-law" of William Johnson who made his will Nov. 5, 1726, probated March 5, 1727-28. (Grimes, p. 189) William Johnson gave land to sons Thomas, John, Stephen and Ezekiel Johnson and mentions his son-in-law THEOPHILUS NORWOOD; wife and executrix was Sarah Johnson. Wits.: Enoch Ward, Richard Canady and John Sampson.

"Son-in-law" usually meant "step-son" and since Mr. Johnson did not mention any daughters it is probable that he married Theophilus' mother. William may have been the son of John Johnson of Albemarle County who made his will there in 1694. (Id. 188)

Theophilus Norwood petitioned for a patent for 640 acres in Carteret County Sept. 13, 1737 and received a land grant in Cravens County, adjoining Carteret in 1746. (Col. Rec. IV, p. 803)

There were other Norwoods living in Craven who were probably related to Theophilus; for a William Norwood made his will in Craven, Dec. 30, 1747, probated March 25, 1746. He evidently died unmarried for he mentions sister MARY LANE; niece Mary Raben; brother THOMAS NORWOOD, nephew JOHN NORWOOD; executors Walter Lane and Barnabas Russell.

A Mary Lane and an ELIZABETH NORWOOD witnessed the will of Penelope Dept in 1732. (Id. p. 97)

Thomas Norwood, evidently brother of the above William Norwood, had his will probated in Craven, March 24, 1758. He leaves his son WILLIAM one shilling; mentions "other children" but not by name; executrix, wife Frances. Wits: Henry Ince and SISSELY NORWOOD. (Grimes 270; Hathaway I, 357)

Theophilus Norwood moved to the Darlington District in South Carolina about 1750. Deeds to his property in Craven may show when he moved. No evidence from the Darlington County records concerning him is supplied. Inasmuch as he appears to have been over 21 when he was mentioned in William Johnson's will made in 1726, he was probably born between 1701 and 1705. The date of his death is not known. He seems to have been too old to be the father of the children shown below. A generation seems missing. It is stated by descendants that these three children were sons of a Theophilus Norwood who served in the Revolution.

A younger Theophilus Norwood, said to have been born in Orange County, Va., in 1725, but who was probably the son of the elder Theophilus who was a grown man in 1725.

Theophilus, the younger, born 1725?, married Eliza St. George. He served in the Revolution. A warrant was issued as follows:

"No. 327. Issued the 27th of May 1785 to Mr. Theophilus Norwood for fifty Liv. O. (eight pounds 14/31/4 stlg. for Military duty before and since the reduction of Charleston, also for a Horse lost in service. Pr. acct. audited-principal Ł 58, 14, 31/4 annual Interest Ł 4, 2, 2". (No. 327 Lib. 0)

The date of his death is not given. There may be some confusion in separating his Revolutionary War records from that of his son Theophilus Jr.

Children:

I.   John, b. 1751 at Society Hill, S.C., died 1826 at Darlington, S.C.; m. Martha Warren, daughter of Martha (DuBose) and Jesse Warren. He served as a Captain in Marion's Brigade during the Revolution. (Marion's Men, by W. W. Boddie, p. 18) In the Census of 1790, as "Captain John Norwood" he was residing in Abbeville County, head of a family consisting of himself, 1 son over 16, 4 sons under 16, wife and 1 daughter. Their children were:
1. John Norwood
2. Elias Norwood
3. Alexander Norwood
4. Joseph Norwood, b. July 16, 1792; d. 1871; m. Oct. 16, 1823, Sarah Ann McIntosh of Society Hill, S.C., born June 9, 1802; d. 1872. Children:
   (1) James Hart Norwood, m. Virginia, dau. of Jesse Tyson
   (2) John Elias Norwood
   (3) Mary Ann Norwood
   (4) George Alexander Norwood, b. Oct. 23, 1831 at Hartsville, S.C.; d. 1809; m. Mary Louise Wilkins, March 28, 1858; d. 1913. They had eight children: Mary King; Sarah McIntosh; George Alexander; John Wilkins; Louise; Samuel Wilkins; Joseph Jr; and Anne Norwood
   (5) Jesse Warren Norwood
   (6) William Thomas Norwood, b. 1846; d. 1909; m. 1869, Mary E. Feaster, b. 1850; d. 1906
5. Jesse Warren Norwood
6. Margaret Norwood, b. 1776; d. 1851; m. Albert Fort,

b. 1758; d. 1841
7. Martha Norwood
8. Mary Norwood
II.   Samuel, b. 1757; m. Martha Waddell? (See later)
III.   Zacharias, b. 1766; m. Elizabeth Du Bose, daughter of
Isaac Du Bose, and granddaughter of John Du Bose of
Darlington County, S.C. Zacharias was living in Darling-
ton County in 1790, with 1 son over 16, 2 sons under 16,
and a daughter. One of his sons, LORENZO DOW NOR-
WOOD, b. Dec. 11, 1806; d. 1880; m. Katherine Ann Mc-
Laughlin, b. 1813; d. 1895. They were the grandparents
of Mrs. Ann Norwood Cooper of Perry, Ga. Another son
was McAnasses Norwood, b. 1794; d. 1846; m. as his
second wife Annie Louise Cook, b. 1802; d. 1861.
IV.   Theophilus, Jr. seems to have served in Virginia in the
Revolutionary War with his brother Samuel in Captain
Purvis' company of the Regiment of Rangers commanded
by Colonel William Thompson. Their record is as follows:
South Carolina Historical & Genealogy Magazine Vol.
II P 185
A general return of Col. Thompson Regiment
of Rangers.
Samuel Norwood - 10 July 1775 - 22 years
Virginia - 5' 9". Pay 46.13: (4)
Theophilus Norwood - 19 July 1775 - 20 years
Virginia - 5' 10" - Pay 40:13 (4)
South Carolina Historical & Genealogy Magazine
Vol I Page 301
Pay bill of Capt. Purvis Company in the
Regiment of Rangers, commanded by William
Thompson, Esq., up to 22nd September 1775.
Samuel Norwood, Jr., 1 month
Theophilus Norwood, 1 month
South Carolina Historical & Genealogy Magazine
Vol V P 55
Record of payments of the South Carolina Line-
Payroll of Capt. George Liddell's Company for
August, September, October 1779.
Private Theophilus Norwood
South Carolina Historical & Genealogy Magazine Vol.
VII - P 222 - Bounty Grants to Revolutionary Soldiers-
records in the office of the Secretary of State (N.B.-
probably now in the Historical Commission on Colonial
South Carolina)
John Norwood - Heir-in-law of David Norwood
P 59
Samuel Norwood - p. 222
Theophilus Norwood - p. 402
Theophilus Jr. Made his will in Abbeville, S.C. April 13,
1787, probated July 9, 1790 (Box 70, Package 1721) as
follows:
I Do Constitute and ordain John Middleton and Samuel
Porter Lawful Executors First I Will and bequeath unto

Elener my beloved Wife all my moveable affects. Also I
will and Bequeath al my Lands and tenements unto my
three beloved sons, viz; Samuel Norwood and John Middleton Norwood Richard Norwood and Debts own to me
And all Debts that I am in are to be paid out of the above
named three boys I have of the Estate and do here by Dis-
anul all and every former will and testaments Ratifying
and confirming this and no other to be my will and testament in witness whereof I set my hand and seal this thir-
teenth day April one seven hundred Eighty seven Signed
Seled and acknowledged before us witness

Samuel Norwood   Theophilus Norwood
John Middleton

Samuel Norwood, son of Theophilus and his wife Eliza St.
George, was born in the Darlington District, S.C., married
Martha Waddell and died in Mississippi. He served as a private
in Capt. John Norwood's company in Marion's Brigade, South
Carolina Line (D.A.R. 110, p 245)

Books L - N P 3 - 4 No. 596 Lib. W.
Issued 16 April 1785 to Mr. Samuel Norwood for
two pounds 101 Sterling; 25 days duty in the
militia. Account audited. Principal Ⴠ 2.10
Interest 5/6

Books O & O - Page 261 - No. 326. Lib. O
Issued the 27th of May 1787 for Mr. Samuel
Norwood, June for 24, twenty-four pounds -
1 4/3 - 1/4. Service for militia before and
since the Reduction of Charleston. Account
audited.

Principal Ⴠ 1, 14, 7

It will be noted that a Samuel Norwood Jr. served one month.
He cannot be identified unless he is an unknown son of Samuel
Senior.

Children:
I.   Elias Norwood, b. Dec. 24, 1788; m. Catherine Chand-
       ler (See later)
II.   John Norwood
III.   Abel Norwood

Elias Norwood, son of Martha Waddell and Samuel Norwood,
was born Dec. 24, 1788 in Amite County, Miss., and died May
22, 1848, at Norwood, E. Feliciana Parish, Louisiana, where
in Dec. 1815 he had married Catherine Chandler, who was born
in 1797 and died June 11, 1875. Their children were: Abel John,
1818-1896 (see later); Martha, dsp; Isiah; Mary Eleanor, m.
Dr. Louis Perkins; Joseph; Samuel.

Abel John Norwood, son of Catherine (Chandler) and Elias
Norwood, was born May 15, 1818 at Norwood, E. Feliciana
Parish, Louisiana, and died there Sept. 3, 1896. He married
(1) Miss Stanley and had Joseph and Kate Emily Norwood; m.
(2) Cecelia Nettles and had Abel John Alexander Norwood. In
April of 1850, at the home of H.P. Street, in Amite County,
Mississippi, he married thirdly Amanda Carolina Buckholdts,
who was born June 9, 1832 in Amite and died May 27, 1861 at

Norwood, La. She was the daughter of Victoria Carolina Batch-
elor and Abel H. Buckholdts.

Children of Amanda C. and Abel John Norwood:

I.   Ella Victoria Norwood, b. 1851; m. D. W. Pipes
II. Mary Amanda Norwood, b. Oct. 15, 1853; m. Thomas
     Barton Lyons (See later)
III. Duncan Isiah Norwood, b. 1855; m. Ellen Gayden
IV. Julia Norwood, b. 1857, m. John A. Redhead
V.   Abel John Norwood, Jr., b. 1860; m. (1) Ella Smith;
     (2) Evelyn Jones.

Mary Amanda Norwood, the daughter of Amanda C. and
Abel John Norwood, was born at Norwood, E. Feliciana Parish,
Louisiana, Oct. 15, 1853, and died July 11, 1927 at Charlottesville, Va. On July 13, 1872 at Clinton, La., she married Thomas Barton Lyons, who was born in Clinton Nov. 17, 1838, and
died June 1, 1909 at Charlottesville, Va.

Children, not in order of birth:

I.   Mary Norwood Lyons, b. June 1, 1873; m. John Wood
      Fishburne
II.   Carolina Barton Lyons, b. Dec. 18, 1877, m. Arthur B.
      Harris
III. Margaret Lyons, b. Jan. 20, 1883; died in infancy
IV.   Eleanor Lyons, b. June 11, 1876; m. Lee Carrington
      Bradley (See later)
V.   Lavilla Balknap Lyons, b. Sept. 12, 1881; m. Langdon
      Lea.
VI.   Thomas Barton Lyons, Jr., b. Aug. 4, 1885; m. Mary
      Casey
VII. Katherine Lyons, b. March 23, 1891; m. Walter Myers

Eleanor Lyons Bradley of 640 Idlewild Circle, Birmingham,
5, Alabama, daughter of Mary Amanda Norwood and Thomas
Barton Lyons, was born at Clinton, La., June 11, 1876, and
married June 24, 1896, at Charlottesville, Va., Lee Carrington
Bradley, who was born at Elyton, Ala., Nov. 12, 1871, and
died May 31, 1942 at Birmingham, Ala. He was the son of Sarah
Jane Gurley and Richard Carrington Bradley, and was a noted
lawyer of Alabama.

Children:

I.   Lee Carrington Bradley, Jr., b. Sept. 27, 1897; m.
     Mary Allen Northington
II. Thomas Lyons Bradley, b. Jan. 20, 1899, d. Dec. 17, 1920

Zacheriah Norwood, who made the following will, has not
been identified and connected but he is evidently one of the family. (It is regretted that more complete information could not
be ascertained concerning this South Carolina family).

Will of ZECHERIAH NORWOOD
CHARLESTON COUNTY COURTHOUSE

VOLUME NO. 43 Pg. No. 664 Box 20 No. 8

State of South Carolina---I, Zecheriah Norwood late of St.
John's Berkeley in State, do say that the Tract of land on Lynche's
Creek in Darlington District which formerly belonged to my father
and in the division of his lands was allotted to my BROTHER
JOHN after whose death I purchased it, which said tract of land

adjoins another tract which was allotted to my BROTHER JAMES
now resising in Mississippi, the said two tracts together lying
between lands of Bird and Daniels and being now in the pofsefsion
of Edward Smith I will and direct shall be sold by my Executors
and the money arising from the sale thereof appropriated to the
use of the three younger children of my late BROTHER THEO-
PHILUS absolutely and forever. I give and bequeath my servant
Dinah and her three younger children namely, Nany, Maria and
James to Philip I. Porcher with the fullest confidence that they
will be protected and treated kindly. I give and bequeath my
watch to my daughter Catherine. All the Rest, Residue and remainder of my Estate Real and personal, whatsoever and where-
soever, I give, devise and bequeath to my children ELIZABETH,
MARY, CATHERINE, THOMAS, and THEOPHILUS, absolutely
and forever, to be equally divided among them share and share
alike, and will is that the share of my daughter ELIZABETH
shall be to and for her sole and separate use, not subject to the
debts contracts or control of her husband Daniel Kelly. I nom-
inate and appoint my friends Alexander Mazyck and Philip I.
Porcher Executors of this my Will, Aug. 22, 1843.

This will and that of Theophilus Norwood, also many Bible
records herein, were kindly furnished by Mrs. Lee Carrington
Bradley, Sr.

DRAKE of ISLE of WIGHT and NORTH CAROLINA

The celebrated Sir Francis Drake did not have any sons, but he had several nephews, and it may be that this family descended from one of these nephews (D N B).

The first of the name in Isle of Wight was James Drake, who was a headright of Robert Eley who patented 600 acres in Isle of Wight Sept. 17, 1639, for the transportation of 11 persons. (17C. p. 517) (C. P. 114)

James Drake witnessed a deed in Isle of Wight in 1644. (17C. p. 517) Nothing further is known of him as he probably moved to Nansemond, where the records were destroyed.

John Drake first appears in the records on April 10, 1703, when he begged pardon in court from William West. (17C. 649) He may have been the son or a relation of a John Drake "late of the County; decd."" who patented 100 acres and deserted it and a patent was granted to William Fowler, 21 Oct. 1690. (Id. 646) This patent for 100 acres had been taken out by Drake in 1682 (P. B. 7-182).

Samuel Browne, in his will made in 1739, gave a legacy to daughter Mary, wife of John Drake, and to his grandsons Jesse Drake and Samuel Nicholas Drake. (C-2, 98)

John Drake in 1739 witnessed the will of John Vasser.

In 1722 Thomas Drake, John Drake, Nicholas Williams, John Drake, Jr. and Richard Drake signed a petition. (Calender of State Papers, Colonial, Vol. 1, p. 204) On May 28, 1733, Thomas Drake, Jr., witnessed the will of John Johnson. (C-2-65).

Mary Boddie, third wife of William Boddie, in her will made in 1727 gave her son-in-law, Thomas Drake, her whole estate. Her first husband was Owen Griffin, second Robert Edwards, third, William Boddie. Thomas Drake had married her daughter, Ann Griffin, daughter of Owen. Thomas Drake made his will in Southampton, Oct. 3, 1758. He mentions wife, Anne, sons JOHN, 'THOMAS, WILLIAM, and LAZARUS; daughter MARY, wife of William Williams; wits.: Benj. Williams, Jacob Williams, Albritten Drake. (C. p. 25.)

John Drake made his will in Southampton, Mar. 15, 1753, mentions eldest daughter MARY; daughters ANN and CATHERINE PULLY: sons: JOSHUA, THOMAS, BARNABY and TIMOTHY. (C. p. 12)

John and Thomas Drake, above mentioned, and Richard Drake are said to have been brothers. Richard Drake and Thomas Drake patented land in Isle of Wight in 1713. The land of the Drakes fell in Southampton when it was cut off from Isle of Wight in 1748.

Richard Drake made his will in Southampton County Feb. 28, 1759, probated May 13, 1759. (C. p.29) He and his wife Margaret had a large family of seven sons and four daughters.

258

The sons were: FRANCIS, MATTHEW, NATHANIEL, TRISTRAM, WILLIAM, BRITTEN, RICHARD, JR., and EDMOND; daughters: ELIZABETH, MARTHA. who married Jacob Williams (See later).

Jacob Williams was born about 1711 and resided in Southampton County, Va. He married about 1735 MARTHA DRAKE, daughter of MARGARET and RICHARD DRAKE. Children born to his union in Southampton Co., Va.: JOHN, b. 1736, m. Mrs. FRANCES SLATTER (nee Bustin) of Halifax Co. in 1767, and was a major in the Revolutionary War. (Revolutionary Army Accounts, Vol. 12, Sect. of State of N.C.) His will was made 11 Sept. 1794, probated 1795.

Children born in Halifax County, N.C.

I.   MARY ANN WILLIAMS, b. about 1768, m. (1) William Battle, (2) William Arrington.
II.   ELIZABETH WILLIAMS, b. about 1770, m. Shed Flewellen, of Nash Co., N.C., and later moved to Warren County, Georgia, where she died in 1844, leaving a large estate.
III.   SALLIE WILLIAMS, b. 12 Dec. 1772, m. Thomas Turner Persons.
IV.   NICHOLAS WILLIAMS, b. 1774, m. Miss Baker, of Warren Co., Ga., died without issue.
V.   FRANCES WILLIAMS, b. 1776, m. JOHN HODGES DRAKE of Nash Co., N.C. (See later)
VI.   MARTHA WILLIAMS, m. Noel Pitts.
VII.   LUCY WILLIAMS, b. 15 March 1782, m. George Boddie as his second wife.
VIII.   REBECCA WILLIAMS (Twins), b. 15 March 1782, m. Alexander Sorsby.

John Drake who seems to have been the father of James Drake of Bertie Co., N.C. married Jemima, sister of Thomas Parnell of Isle of Wight. In his will, probated June 9, 1688, Thomas Parnell mentions his sister, Jemima Drake, and gives JOHN DRAKE "my coat of Camel hair."" They probably moved to Nansemond, where the records are destroyed. He is said to have died before 1690. (ante)

A John Drake, probably his son, made his will in Bertie, Jan. 5, 1728, same probated May Court, 1729. He gave son JAMES DRAKE "my Manor Plantation; mentions wife Sarah; and appoints JAMES BRYANT his "father-in-law"" executor. (Grimes, 102) The designation "father-in-law"" in those days could be interpreted two ways. that either he had married Bryant's daughter or Bryant had married his mother.

What creates a genealogical puzzle that is difficult to analyze is that William Bridgers of Bertie made his will March 11, 1728-29, same probated Nov. 1729. He mentions several children, calls Benjamin Bridgers and WILLIAM BRYANT, brothers and names JOHN DEW "his father" executor. His wife was SARAH who later re-married, made her will as SARAH COTTEN, naming the same Bridgers children mentioned in her first husband's will and her additional Cotton children (Grimes 47-84). It seems that William Bridger's wife SARAH was a daughter of JOHN DEW and his wife, said to be Susannah Shearer. "Brother" William Bryant is said to have married Patience Dew, sister of William's wife Sarah. This would make them "brothers-in-law."

However, JAMES BRYANT in his will probated March 11, 1731, names his sons: WILLIAM BRYANT, JOHN DEW, RICHARD BRASWELL, JAMES BRYANT, THOMAS BRYANT and Matthew Telar. Exrs.: JOHN DEW and JAMES BRYANT; wit., AARON DRAKE.

WILLIAM BRYANT is said to have married Patience Dew, sister of Sarah, wife of William Bridgers who called "William Bryant" his brother. James Bryant's wife, not named in his will was "Sarah". On June 23, 1715, they assigned a patent to William Braswell. She gave JOHN DEW a power of attorney to relinquish her dower rights. (Hathaway 28) Why did James Bryant call John Dew a "Son" which would seem that Bryant had married John Dew's mother; and here a John Dew is given a power of attorney by James Bryant's wife, which often indicates a relationship. Now John Drake had a wife named Sarah, also he called James Bryant his "father-in-law". Did John Drake marry a daughter of James Bryant or a daughter of James Bryant's wife? In Wheeler's History of North Carolina, page 275, Wheeler states that James Drake and Benjamin Bridgers were "half-brothers". This can only mean that John Drake's wife Sarah re-married Benjamin Bridger's father, Benjamin, who had a wife named "Sarah" before 1740 when they made a deed.

JAMES DRAKE
by Martha Drake Avent

James Drake of Wheeler's History fame was born in 1726, died about 1791. He married twice, first to Sophia Valentine, by whom there were nine children, three sons: ALBRITTON, JAMES, SILAS; and five daughters. His second marriage was to Mrs. Hartwell Hodges Davis, daughter of Benjamin Hodges and his wife Constance Goodrich (for her ancestry see S.V.F. -1-218) of Isle of Wight, later Southampton. She was the widow of Thomas Davis of Isle of Wight. By this marriage there were two sons: JOHN HODGES DRAKE (See later), and BENJAMIN DRAKE.

Wheeler in his History says: "During the Revolution, about 1778, Captain Beard attacked the house of JAMES DRAKE, Esq. of Nash County, N.C. with a band of Tories. There was no one in the house but Mr. Drake, his son ALBRITTON then about seventeen years of age, and Benjamin Bridgers his half brother, Nathaniel Nichols, Henry Massenger and Robert Pilland.

"Albritton, who was one of a corps of light horse and had been on active duty, scouring the country for these very men, ran out and fired. The Tories then surrounded the house and ordered a surrender. Old Mr. Drake seized a gun and advanced on the foe. The Tories, headed by Beard, sword in hand, rushed into the house; Beard was met by young Albritton Drake with a cutlass, but at the first blow, young Drake's cutlass struck the joist above his head and broke off at the hilt. The old man then joined in the melee, with his gun clubbed, but was soon cut down by the sword of Beard, and was so seriously wounded that he was a gore of blood.

"Seeing her husband cut down, old Mrs. Drake rushed in, not with a weapon, but a "jug of old Nash" even to this day celebrated for its excellent flavor. Her entreaties, and the more potent influence of the liquor produced a parley. She plied them so liberally with the brandy that peace was restored. Beard had been an aspirant for the hand of her daughter.

During this time Captain Peter Goodwin with a troop of horse, galloped up. Albritton Drake threw up his hat and gave a loud Halloo; Goodwin made a furious attack and Beard and his men made a precipitate retreat. He was encountered by Bridgers, who was near; Bridgers gun missed fire, and Beard used his sword, but was knocked down by Bridgers, who thought he had killed Beard, and went to the house and informed them that he had killed Beard. They all went out to see his dead body, but Beard had recovered so as to sit up. He was then taken into custody.

A Negro man, Simon, who had a wife at Drake's, caught another one of the band named Porch. There were taken to Col. Seawell in Franklin County. They were there tried by Court Martial and both forthwith hung. Such was the end of Captain Beard.

Mr. Drake died in 1790 in the 65 year of his age.

His brave son Albritton, married and then settled in Robeson County, N.C. where his son John lived; then moved to Kentucky. He raised a large family. (See later) His son Col. JAMES P. DRAKE, commanded an Indiana Regiment in the war with Mexico. He died at 80 years of age.

Dr. John Hodges Drake, son of James Drake, was born July 29, 1767, in Nash County, N.C., died in Auburn, Ala., Dec. 11, 1859; married about 1835, Miss Frances Williams, daughter of Major John Williams of the Revolution who married Mrs. Bustin of Halifax Co., N.C. May 1794. She was born in 1776 in Halifax Co., and died Feb. 1840. (Revolutionary Army Accts., Vol. 12, Sec. of State of N.C.) Their children were:

I. Martha Joanna Williams Drake, b. Dec. 26, 1795, m. John Arrington, Jan. 28, 1812. (See later)
II. Nicholas John Drake, b. July 10, 1798, m. Elizabeth Armstrong Oct. 21, 1828.
III. John Hodges Drake, Jr., b. Jan. 19, 1801, m. Mary R. Williams, May 27, 1828.
IV. Frances Maria Drake, b. Oct.29, 1803, m. Thomas Flewellen.
V. Eliza Hodges Drake, b. Dec. 21, 1805.
VI. Hartwell Caroline Drake, b. Jan. 20, 1808, m. Robert Williams.
VII. Louisa Ann Drake, b. Feb. 21, 1811, m. Jas. F. White, July 17, 1839.
VIII. John Calvin Drake, b. April 3, 1814, d. 1898, m. Mary Flewellen April 3, 1839.
IX. John George Franklin Drake, b. Dec. 1816, d. 1886, m.

Mary Ann Harrison. (See later)
X.   John William Wallace Drake, b. March 25, 1819, d. Oct. 1866, Auburn, Ala., m. Vanlencia Mitchell.

Dr. John George Franklin Drake, born Dec. 3, 1816, died Dec. 19, 1886, married Mary Ann Harrison, daughter of Mr. John (Jack) Harrison, Oct. 24, 1843. She was born July 24, 1824, and died Feb. 20, 1897. Their children were:

I.   John William Wallace Drake, b. Aug. 12, 1846. He was a Junior Reserve in the Confederate Army, and contracted Typhoid fever in Camp and died at home, Aug. 26, 1864. (Roster of Nash Co.-Capt. J. Thorpe)

II.   Olivanza W. Drake, b. Feb. 22, 1849, d. Oct. 22, 1937; m. (1) Thomas Cooper, one child, Mary Elizabeth; m. (2) William A. Williams, Children: Daisy Primrose, Mary Franklin and Roberta.

III.   Mary Louisa Drake, b. March 23, 1851, d. April 10, 1927, m. James Thomas Daniel Avent, Dec. 3, 1879. Children: CAROLINA LOUISA AVENT, KATHERINE BELL AVENT, MATTIE DRAKE AVENT, JAMES FRANKLIN AVENT, THOMAS ALVAH AVENT, JACOB BATTLE AVENT.

IV.   George Douglas Drake, b. May 28, 1855, d. Aug. 16, 1897, m. Rebecca Clark.

V.   Frances Caroline Drake, b. Sept. 24, 1857, d. Jan. 22, 1935, m. James Cooley. Children: Gideon Frank Cooley, b. 'Feb. 2, 1879; Roger Douglas Cooley, b. March 13, 1881; Wallace Drake Cooley, b. March 10, 1883; Ethel Primrose Cooley, b. June 30, 1885; Hattie Lee Cooley, b. Dec. 5, 1888; Gladys Harrison Cooley, b. Feb. 1, 1893; Mary Lillian Cooley, b. Sept. 23, 1895.

VI.   Belle Harrison Drake, b. Nov. 22, 1860, m. John S. Terry. Children: Annie Hodges Terry, Carolotta Belle Terry, Dulcie Terry, Johnny Belle Terry.

VII.   Jeff Davis Drake (female), b. Oct. 16, 1863, m. James B. Cooper. Children: James Thomas Cooper, b. 1891; Mitchell Drake Cooper; George Arrington Cooper, b. 1898; Alvah Davis Cooper, b. 1900; Mary Louise Cooper, b. 1907.

VIII.   Lillie Hodges Drake, b. Aug. 20, 1865; m. John B. Pearce. No children.

(Miss Mattie Avent notes; copied from old family records, Aug. 1931, were kindly furnished)

Martha Joanna Williams Drake, born Dec. 26, 1795, married Jan. 26, 1812, John D. Arrington, son of General William Arrington and his first wife, Anne Jackson. Their children were: I. Nicholas; II. Belle, who married Douglas A. Lindley of San Francisco; III. Helen, married Mr. Shipley and moved to California; IV. Martha; V. Maria Louisa; VI. Louisa Caroline both drowned as young ladies when their boat overturned in Pearl River near Montechello, Miss.; VII. John Hodge, born Aug. 5, 1818 (See later); VIII. Algernon Sidney, born Sept. 1, 1814; IX. Elizabeth, married M.E. Quint and moved to California; X. Amanda Malvina, born Dec. 5, 1825, married (1) Charles Henry Fox, (2) William J. Smith (See later).

Amanda Malvina Arrington, daughter of Joanna W. Drake

and John D. Arrington was born Dec. 5, 1825; died Sept. 6, 1892. At Montecello, Miss., in 1841 she married Charles Henry Fox, who was buried in the Fox graveyard in Lawrence Co., Miss. Their children were: George Hill; Cornelia Ann; Robert N.; Charles L.; Sam; Ida; Mattie; and George Fox.

At Monticello, Miss., in 1864, Amanda Malvina Arrington Fox married William J. Smith, who joined the Confederate Army in 1861 at Little Rock, Ark., and served with Company G, 11th Infantry. He was captured and held prisoner at Johnson Island. They had one daughter, Rosa Bell, born Aug. 28, 1865, in Lawrence Co., Miss., and died Feb. 11, 1936 and is buried in the Calvary Baptist Church Cemetary at Silver Creek, Miss. (See Later)

Rosa Bell Smith first married Thomas Jefferson Bankston, who is buried on the plantation near White Sand, Jefferson Davis County, Miss. They had two children, Grover Cleveland and Varina Estelle Bankston. Rosa Bell Smith Bankston, in 1890, married secondly, Joseph George. They lived for many years at White Sand but later moved to Silver Creek, Mississippi.

The children of Rosa Bell Smith and Joseph George are:
1. Minnie Malvina George
2. William Sam George, World War I Veteran, received French decoration for bravery Croix de Guerre.
3. Monroe George (deceased 36) World War I Veteran. His Registration Certificate 39-ASU SN RF C 1300-535 - Joined Navy June 5, 1917.
4. French George, World War I Navy Veteran, World War II Veteran (Army)
5. L. F. George
6. Willie Brown George
7. Lena George, m. Dr. Frank Turner White (See later)
8. Mamie George, died of burns at 7 years.
9. Jennevieve Lucy George
10. James George

Lena George married Dr. Frank Turner White May 6, 1929, at the First Methodist Church, Birmingham, Alabama. Lena George attended the Mississippi Woman's College at Hattiesburg, Mississippi and traveled widely throughout the United States, Mexico, Canada, and Europe. At present (1956) she is President of the Dental Auxiliary to the Third District Dental Society and State of Tennessee President-elect. Dr. Frank Turner White served with the U.S. Nathonal Guard on the Mexican Border 1915-16. In 1917 he was recalled into World War I service where he served as Sergeant with Co. B, 117th Infantry, 30th Division. He served with American Expeditionary Forces on the Somme Front October 8, 1918 - Estress Area - Belgium from July to September 15, 1918. He received wounds in left leg incurred in France. Received Honorable Discharge from Army at Fort McPherson, Georgia, September 15, 1919 - Service Number 1309613. He is a graduate of Vanderbilt University, Class 1924.

Children of Lena George and Dr. Frank Turner White:
1. Jenny Jo White, born Sept. 11, 1930, Twin
2. Sally Ann White, born Sept. 11, 1930, Twin

Jenny Jo White married Stahle Linn, Jr., December 12, 1953.
Jenny Jo is a graduate of Randolph Macon Woman's College,
Lynchburg, Virginia 1952 and worked on her Master's degree
at University of North Carolina. She has traveled widely through-
out the United States, Mexico, Canada, and Europe. Stahle Linn,
Jr. has a graduate Bachelor of Arts Degree of University of North
Carolina and a Law Degree from the University of North Carolina.

Sally Ann White married Charles Steele Baird, June 17, 1953.
Sally Ann attended Randolph Macon Woman's College, Lynchburg, Virginia for two years and transferred to Vanderbilt University, Nashville, Tennessee, where she graduated 1952. She
also held a Teacher's Certificate from Peabody College in Nashville. She has traveled widely throughout the United States,
Mexico, Canada, and Europe. Charles Steel Baird graduated from
Vanderbilt University in 1952. Had one year of law at the University of Virginia. Served three years in the Navy and at the present (1956) is a 3rd year law student at the University of Virginia.
    Children of Sally Ann and Charles Steele Baird are:
    1. Melissa Dubois Baird, born October 17, 1954, at Nor-
        folk General Hospital, Norfolk, Virginia.

    Dr. John Hodge Arrington I, the son of Martha Joanna Wil-
liams Drake and John D. Arrington, was born in Nash County,
N.C., Aug. 5, 1818, and died in Lawrence County, Miss., June
1863. On Jan. 21, 1845 in Lawrence Co., he married Patience
Anna Serena Hunt Fox, who was born Dec. 26, 1827, in Lawrence Co., and died there Mar. 12, 1911. She was the daughter
of Patience Anderson Jeffries Hunt, who was born Nov. 9, 1789,
and died April 16, 1851, and Arthur Fox, who was born Aug. 19,
1788 and died Jan. 9, 1852, the son of Elizabeth Hunt, born Oct.
18, 1750 and died July 6, 1843, and Jacob Fox, Revolutionary
Soldier, who was born 1745 and died 1807.

    Dr. Arrington was educated in New Orleans, La., and lived
and practiced in Lawrence County, Miss.

    Children: Elizabeth Lark, d., cr. 1870; m. Dr. T. A. Young-
blood; Lelia; Lucy, both died as young ladies; A. Sidney, d. at
2 years; John Hodge, b. Oct. 8, 1863; d. Aug. 26, 1946; m. Nancy Jane Johnston. (See later)

    John Hodge Arrington II, son of Patience A.S. Hunt and Dr.
John Hodge Arrington, was born in Lawrence Co., Miss., Oct.
8, 1863 and died at Monticello, Miss., Aug. 28, 1946. On Mar.
4, 1894, he married Nancy Jane Johnston, who was born Jan. 10,
1894 and died Nov. 25, 1912; the daughter of Susan Eaton and
George Washington Johnston. Mr. Arrington was educated at the
University of Mississippi and held Bachelor of Philosophy and
Bachelor of Laws degrees. He lived and practiced law at Monti-
cello, Miss.
    Children:
I.   Anna Lee Arrington, b. Dec. 2, 1894; m. Aug. 8, 1920
      Theodore Bulkley Ford, Jr., son of Minerva Foxworth,
      born Aug. 15, 1860, and married Feb. 26, 1879, Dr.
      Theodore Bulkley Ford, who was born Dec. 6, 1848. They
      have one son:

Theodore Bulkley Ford III, born June 28, 1923; married Mary Lou Cabral, born November 20, 1928. They have three children: Shelly Ann Ford, born August 20, 1953; Theodore Bulkley Ford IV., born January 11, 1955; Fox Arrington Ford, born September 29, 1956.

II. Richard Olney Arrington, State Supreme Court Judge, b. Jan. 21, 1897; enlisted in Navy, World War I, in April, 1917; m. Ethel Ramsey on Dec. 15, 1926. They have three children: Richard Olney Arrington, Jr. (atty), b. Jan. 3, 1928; Myron Lamar Arrington, b. Sept. 16, 1930; Nancy Ann Arrington, b. March 4, 1933.

III. Jo. Drake Arrington, b. March 14, 1899; m. Mable Smith. (See later)

IV. Dr. George Lamar Arrington, b. Sept. 16, 1901; m. Oct. 6, 1933, Mary Wilbourne. They have two children: Mary, b. Aug. 1935; George Lamar Arrington, Jr., b. July 1937.

V. Susanna Eaton Arrington, b. Nov. 19, 1904.

VI. Dr. John Hodge Arrington, III., b. April 17, 1907; in World War II he served in the Air Force, discharged as Captain. Sept. 30, 1937 he married Madeline Shafer. They have three children: Madeline Ann, b. Aug. 15, 1938; John Hodge, IV; Nancy.

VII. Arthur Fox Arrington, b. Aug. 21, 1909; served in Air Force, World War II; m. Aileen Sims. No children.

VIII. Helen Quint Arrington, b. Dec. 10, 1911; m. Feb. 18, 1934, Riley E. Davis. They have a son, Riley Arrington Davis, b. Nov. 12, 1936.

Jo Drake Arrington, whose present address is P.O. Box 35, Gulfport, Miss., is the son of Nancy Jane Johnston and John Hodge Arrington II. He was born at Monticello, Miss., March 14, 1899 and enlisted in the Navy, in World War I, the day after war was declared, April 7, 1917. On August 16, 1927, at Moss Point, Miss., he married Miss Mable M. Smith, who was born there Oct. 17, 1897, the daughter of Ella B. Brooks and Arthur H. Smith. Mr. Arrington is a lawyer, and was educated at the University of Mississippi, Harvard University, and holds a B.A. degree from the Catholic University of America in Washington, D.C. and an LL.B. from Cumberland University, Lebanon, Tenn.

Albrittain Drake, son of Sophia (Valentine) and James Drake of Nash Co., N.C., was living in Robeson County in 1790. According to the U.S. Census of that year he was head of a family consisting of himself, one son under 16 years of age and a wife and one daughter. He was born 1755 in Nash Co., N.C.; died Nov. 14, 1835, Muhlenberg Co., Ky.; married April 10, 1785, Nash Co., N.C., Ruth Collins, born Nov. 12, 1765, Nash Co., N.C.; died March 4, 1847, Muhlenberg Co., Ky., daughter of Michael Collins. He was a planter and a member of the Methodist Church.

John Drake, born in Robeson Co., N.C., May 26, 1786; died April 28, 1863, was his only son. John Drake married first Feb. 18, 1806, Elizabeth Alford, born Nov. 15, 1789, died

Sept. 9, 1823. His second wife was Margaret McLauchlan by whom he had one daughter, Elizabeth Margaret, born May 6, 1829.

Elizabeth Alford was a daughter of Clarkey (McTyer) and Sion Alford who is said to have been a Soldier of the Revolution. Sion Alford was the son of Jacob Alford who was born in New Kent County, Va., Dec. 12, 1738, the son of Susannah and Lodwick Alford. (Parish Register and Vestry Book) Jacob died in Robeson County in 1794. leaving his property by will to his second wife, Mary, and children, Warren, Elias, SION, James, Mary, Wiley and Charity.

Children of Elizabeth (Alford) and John Drake:

I. Martha Susan, b. 10-17-1808; m. John Drake:
II. Ruth Collins, b. 11-3-1810; m. David D. Salmon (See later)
III. Zacharia Alford, b. 3-5-1810; m. (1) Sophia Alford, (2) Charity Hedgpath
IV. Pamelia Ann, b. 4-9-1815; m. Wm. C. McNeill
V. Clarkie Sophia, b. 5-11-1817; m. Malcolm Purcell
VI. James Perry, b. 10-27-1820; m. Orpha Williams
VII. Albrittian John, b. 10-9-1822; m. Carrie McRae

Ruth Collins Drake, daughter of John and Elizabeth (Alford) Drake, was born Nov. 3, 1810, in South Carolina; died July 31, 1886 in Mississippi; married Jan. 13, 1831 Robeson County, North Carolina, David Douglas Salmon, born Aug. 22, 1805 in Marion County, South Carolina; died July 5, 1870, Tate County, Miss., son of Samuel and Joannah (Likens) Salmon. Joannah was born Oct. 15, 1785. Samuel Salmon was born April 1, 1781, son of Ludlow Salmon of New Jersey.

Children:

I. Elizabeth Ann Salmon, m. 11-18-1852 Archibald McCormick.
II. Joan Salmon, m. 11-17-1859, J. B. McColl
III. Henrietta Salmon, m. 4-25-1869, Preston McKellar (See later)
IV. William D. Salmon, m. 6-9-1868, Mary J. Pamplin
V. Joseph Miller Salmon, b. Feb. 19, 1837; m. Dolly Annie W. Williams (See later)
VI. ʾDavid Douglas Salmon, m. 10-12-1873 Sophie Alma Hawkins.
VII. Eliza J. Salmon, m. 12-28-1875 Robert Pifer
VIII. Frances Romaline Salmon, m. 1870 Silas Ammons
IX. Novella Drake Salmon, m. 12-10-1873 W. T. Gunter
X. Harriet M. Salmon, b. Dec. 10, 1852; unmarried

Joseph Miller Salmon was born Feb. 19, 1837, Marion County, South Carolina; died Aug. 11, 1910, Senatobia, Tate County, Miss.; married April 21, 1870, Senatobia, Miss., Dolly Annie Wells Williams, born March 2, 1848, Senatobia, Miss.; died June 23, 1915, Senatobia, Miss., daughter of Emry and Sylvester Jane (Gunter) Williams. He was a planter and a member of the Methodist Church.

Children:

I. Lena Jane Salmon, b. Jan. 30, 1871; m. Berry Boswell Brooks Sr. (See later)

II.   Thomas Emry Salmon, b. Aug. 28, 1872; m. Estelle
       Scott.
III.   Sallie Ruth Salmon, b. Sept. 27, 1875
IV.   Joe Campbell Salmon, b. Aug. 4, 1876; m. Malinda Jane
       Burford
V.   Edker Clifton Salmon, b. Sept. 16, 1878
VI.   Sadie Mabel Salmon, b. Nov. 14, 1883 (Twin)
VII.   Annie Maud Salmon, b. Nov. 14, 1883 (Twin)
VIII. Essie French Salmon, b. Aug. 19, 1885; m. Claude Davis
       Lena Jane Salmon was born Jan. 30, 1871 in Tate Co., Miss.,
died July 4, 1954, Memphis, Shelby Co., Tenn.; married May
17, 1898, Senatobia, Tate Co., Miss., Berry Boswell Brooks
Sr., born July 21, 1860, Independence, Tate Co., Miss.; died
Dec. 16, 1936, Brickeys, Lee Co., Ark. Mr. Brooks was a
planter and a member of the Methodist Church.
       Children:
I.   Everett Hope Brooks, b. Oct. 16, 1899, Senatobia, Miss.,
       m. Jan. 30, 1924, Memphis, Tenn., Evelyn Fay Halley,
       b. Aug. 23, 1904, Phillips Co., Ark.
       Children:
       1. Everett Hope Brooks Jr., b. May 16, 1926, Memphis,
          Tenn.
       2. Bettye Jane Brooks, b. Sept. 24, 1928, Memphis, Tenn.,
          m. Dec. 30, 1948, William Shaw Bennett, Memphis,
          Tenn.
II.   Berry Boswell Brooks, b. Feb. 2, 1902, Senatobia, Miss.,
       m. Apr. 27, 1929, Blytheville, Ark., Virginia Feild
       Walton, b. Aug. 6, 1904, Jonesboro, Craighead Co.,
       Ark., daughter of Allan Walton and Virginia (Warren)
       Feild who m. Oct. 21, 1903. Mr. Brooks was educated
       at Washington and Lee University; is a Cotton Merchant,
       Planter and Explorer and a member of the Methodist
       Church. Mr. and Mrs. Brooks reside at Epping Forest
       Manor, 3661 James Road, Memphis, Tenn. They have
       one daughter, Virginia Walton Brooks, b. June 4, 1933,
       who accompanied her parents on their Big Game Hunting
       and Photographic Expedition in 1947 and 1949. When four-
       teen years old she shot a charging elephant, becoming the
       youngest person in the world to ever do that. She assisted
       her parents in collecting specimens for the Berry Brooks
       African Hall and Wing of the Memphis Museum of Natural
       History, which they donated to the city.
       Henrietta Salmon, daughter of David Douglas and Ruth Col-
lins (Drake) Salmon, was born June 18, 1845, in South Carolina; died Dec. 15, 1919, at Senatobia, Miss.; married Apr.
25, 1869, at Senatobia, Miss., Preston McKellar, a Confederate Soldier, born May 6, 1848, in Marion County, South Carolina; died Feb. 5, 1922, at Senatobia, Miss.
       Children:
I.   Robert Lee, b. 1869 (See later)
II.   Zienliaker, b. 1872
III.   John Douglas, b. 1874
IV.   Elizabeth Jane, b. 1875

V.   Peter Salmon, b. 1877
VI.   Snow Etta, b. 1880; m. L. E. Pierce
VII. Joe A., b. 1882
VIII. James Cleveland, b. 1884
IX.   Ruth Hoyt, b. 1886

Robert Lee McKellar, son of Preston and Henrietta (Salmon) McKellar, was born Nov. 24, 1869, at Senatobia, Miss.; died Aug. 27, 1949, at San Diego, California; married Oct. 17, 1896, at Dallas, Texas, Mattie Laura Smith, born Sept. 2, 1874; Emery, Texas; died March 5, 1948, San Diego, Calif.; daughter of William Henry and Mary Ann (Bobbett) Smith. Mr. McKellar was a Real Estate Broker and a member of the Presbyterian Church.

Child: (Had other children)
I.   Earle Preston, b. Oct. 8, 1897; m. Madge Marie Hale.

Earle Preston McKellar was born Oct. 8, 1897, in Dallas, Texas, and married Dec. 2, 1919, in Coronada, San Diego County, Calif., Madge Marie Hale, born Sept. 1, in Gypsum, Saline Co., Kansas, daughter of Samuel Hale and Jessie Arminda (Shallenbarger) Hale. Mr. McKellar was educated at the Mass. Institute of Technology. He served as an aviator for the United States Navy as an officer for twenty-one years. He served in both World Wars. He is physically retired. He is a member of the Protestant Episcopal Church. They reside at 3407 Albatross St., San Diego.

Children:
I.   Robert Hale, b. March 2, 1922, d. April 22, 1922.
II.   Earle Preston Jr., b. July 5, 1923; m. July 23, 1943,
      Virginia Mae Gates.
      Children:
      1. Robert Earle, b. Aug. 7, 1945, Oakland, Calif., d.
         Feb. 23, 1950
      2. Margaret Joyce, b. June 11, 1944
      3. Gerald Eugene, adopted in 1955
      Earle Jr. enlisted in 1941 in the US Navy in aviation. At
      present is stationed in Guam.
III. William Hale, b. Nov. 29, 1925; m. Feb. 14, 1956 Mildred
      Eleanor Grenfall and has one son, Edward Earle, b.
      Dec. 9, 1957 in Redding, Calif. William Hale was also
      in the US Navy during the Second World War, being physically retired.

HOLLAND of NANSEMOND

The Hollands are a distinguished family in England. They were Earls of Kent in Feudal times (see chart in V.H.G.-340) and they are still in the House of Lords. At present time a Holland is Viscount Knutsford, and another one Baron Rotherham. They were also a well known gentry family of Lancanshire from whom this Virginia family may be descended.

The first of the name in Virginia was a Gabriel Holland. He and Richard Holland were killed by the Indians in a massacre at Berkeley Hundred in 1621. (Rec. of Va. Co. Vol. III p. 396)

Sergeant Gabriel Holland was living at Jamestown at the time of the massacre of 1622. His wife Mary was granted a patent of 12 acres "On the Island of James City", August 14, 1624. (C.P. 8) They appear in the records of the General Court up to about 1627, but disappeared after that. The James City County records are destroyed.

John[1] Holland of Nansemond is the first ancestor of this present Holland family. He was a headright of Lt. Col. Blake and Edward Isom who patented 2500 acres in Nansemond, Feb. 20, 1664, for the transportation of 60 persons, among whom was John Holland. (C.P. 444)

On April 20, 1682, John[1] Holland patented 760 acres in the Upper Parish of Nansemond at the miles end of Walter Bagley; and on April 16, 1683, he patented 200 acres in the same parish at a place called Kinsale. Another patent was granted him April 20, 1694, for 500 acres on the east side of the Cape. A Henry Holland also patented 427 acres Oct. 29, 1696, on back swamp of Summerton Creek.

The date of death of John[1] Holland is not shown; but from circumstantial evidence it appears that he had four sons: HENRY, JAMES, JOSEPH, and JOHN HOLLAND, JR. (The deeds mentioned below are all from Isle of Wight records.)

I.   Henry[2] Holland, on Jan. 24, 1717, deeded 23 acres adjacent his and James Holland's lands. This land was evidently part of his patent dated Jan. 24, 1717, for 205 acres in Nansemond adjacent his land and James Hollands land, consideration, 25 shillings. (P.B.10-358) In June, 1733, he deeded land adjacent to John Holland, Senior, John Winborn, Jr., Ann Ballard and his own land. James Holland, on the same date, patented 295 acres in Nansemond, adjacent Henry Holland's land. (P.B.-358) It appears here that James and Henry Holland were re-patenting the 500 acres of their father; granted in 1694. In August, 1736, Henry Holland deeded 146 acres lying between Henry Hedgepath and James Holland on Coronah Swamp. Also in 1733, as Henry Holland of Nansemond County he sold land to Thomas Vaughan on East side of Chowan River in North

Carolina. This deed was witnessed by Joseph Holland. (Hathaway 11-444) On Aug. 4, 1733, John Vaughan of Nansemond sold 150 acres on south side of Chowan River. The witnesses were: Henry Holland, James Holland, Jo. Holland.

In Bertie Co., a Joseph Holland is mentioned as guardian of Frederick Holland, son of Henry Holland. A Frederick Holland, born about 1790, appears in the 1820 records of Nansemond County. A Joseph Holland made his will in Bertie Co., N.C. in 1791. He mentions son Joel Holland; wife Mary; dau. Sarah Tomas; gr.dau. Sarah Holland. We are unable to correctly place him.

Henry[2] Holland's children appear to be:

(1) Joseph[5] Holland of Kingsale Swamp, which lay in both Nansemond and Isle of Wight (See later)

(2) Henry Holland, Jr. His children seem to have been:
((A) Henry[4]; (B) Robert; and (C) Job[4]. This Job Holland made his will Aug. 30, 1789, probated Feb. 3, 1790 in Isle of Wight. He mentions sons: Job[5]; Meredith; Elijah; dau. Bathsheba Watson; daus. Betsy; and Polly; wife Mary. The witnesses were: Thomas Daughtry, Uriah Vaughan and Aaron Holland. (C.3-143)

(3) Robert Holland, who made his will in Isle of Wight in 1797. He mentions wife Patience; son James; daus. Sally Davis, Betsy Randolph, Milly Hancock; and to Everett, son of my son Everett, slaves to be divided between Charles, Everett and Nancy Holland; grandson Robert Marshall; son James Holland. (C-I-III-195) (See later)

(4) A James[3] Holland, in 1756, in Isle of Wight, sold 426 acres adjacent John Holland, Sr., John Winburn, William Holland, and Henry Holland, Jr. He appears to be deeding Henry Holland's patent of 1696, and may have been his son. In 1763 he also sold 230 acres, part of a patent to Henry Holland.

Joseph[3] Holland, was son of Henry[2] Holland as proven by a deed of 1751. (See later) Henry had sold land near the head of Coronah Swamp (ante) and on Sept. 12, 1736, John[4] Holland, son of Joseph[3] Holland, sold 96 acres on line of Joseph Holland near Coronah Swamp.

On Jan. 12, 1744, Thomas Sanders of Newport Parish, Isle of Wight, sold Joseph Holland, for Ł 35,235 acres in Isle of Wight between the main Kingsale Swamp and Queen's Grave Swamp, beginning at a marked oak between the line of John Winburn and said Thomas Sanders, being part of a patent of 1650 acres granted to Johnathan Robinson, Richard Thomas and John Sanders April 23, 1681. John Sanders devised his part to four of his sons, and by several conveyances, Thomas Sanders was seized and possessed of the 235 acres. Witnesses: John Winburn, James Uzell, JOSEPH HOLLAND, JR.

Joseph Holland bought 150 acres of William Murfee, March 26, 1745, of Upper Parish of Nansemond, said land lying in Lower Parish of Isle of Wight, adjacent to George Keen and

William Sanders, part of a patent granted April 23, 1681 to (same three persons mentioned above) and the aforesaid John Sanders by his last will and testament devised this part to two sons, William and Richard Sanders, and same came to the hands of John Sanders son of the aforesaid Richard Sanders and grandson to the aforesaid John Sanders, and by the death of John Sanders became an inheritance of his brother, Robert Sanders who sold same to Thomas Sanders by deed bearing date April 13, 1733 and Thomas Sanders sold to William Murfee Sept. 27, 1737, who now sells to Joseph Holland. Wits.: Phillip Cremer, James Uzzell, Henry Holland.

On May 1, 1751, John Winburn of Nansemond sold to JOSEPH HOLLAND son of HENRY HOLLAND, deceased, with consent of his wife Phoebe, 75 acres on SOUTH SIDE of KINGSALE SWAMP, being part of a patent to Jonathan Robinson etc., dated April 23, 1681, and by conveyance came to John Winburn's wife from her grandmother, PHOEBE KIRL in 1706. Witnesses: Henry Holland, Robert Holland, Job Holland.

Joseph[3] Holland's sons, from the above deeds and witnesses, were John Holland and Joseph[4] Holland, Jr., who was a grown man in 1744. (See later)

Joseph[4] Holland evidently Joseph Holland, Jr., of 1744, witnessed the will of Isobel Johnson (C. III-69) on August 15, 1773. Also on Feb. 26, 1782, he was mentioned in the will of Henry Johnson, Sr., who names sons Aaron and William and gave son Henry land adjoining Mason Johnson and JOSEPH HOLLAND. The witnesses were: John Darden, Barnaby Holland and Benjamin Holland. The last two named were securities. (C. III-109).

This Joseph Holland is said to have been known as Joseph Holland "of Spivey" or Joseph Spivey Holland. He is said to have died without a will in Isle of Wight in 1799. His known sons were Lewis Conner Holland and Lawson S. Holland, who moved to Georgia. Captain Joseph Holland "of Kingsale" in Nansemond seems to have been his son. (See later)

Captain Joseph Holland "of Kingsale" is the way his name appears on Tax records of Nansemond and Isle of Wight Counties, Va., from about 1790. His widow Elizabeth Holland of "Jasper County, Ga.", as "Widow of a Revolutionary Soldier" received the Coweta Co. lands in a land drawing in Georgia. Doubtless, he was a Capt. of Nansemond Militia after the Revolution. Though his will was destroyed (with the Nansemond records) it is referred to in the tax records as leaving lands to his sons Washington and Randolph; also he had earlier given land to Joseph J. - they received their land when they became of age.

Captain Joseph Holland of Kingsale died about 1804-05. (Nansemond Tax Records) His wife was Elizabeth Ann Odem, who died after 1835 in Georgia. She may be perhaps the daughter of Richard Odem who died 1789 in Anson County, N.C., and whose wife was also "Elizabeth Anne."

Children:

I. Joseph John Holland, b. cir. 1784, m. Nancy Parker. (See later)

II.   Randolph Stott Holland, b. cir. 1796; either d. cir. 1815 or is the Randolph Holland later in Putnam Co., Ga.

III.   Charlotte Elizabeth Holland, m. Jonas (or Lemuel) Lawrence.

IV.   George Washington Holland, b. July 1795, m. Mary Ann Griffin. (See later)

V.   Jonas Herman, b. 1800, m. (1) Ann Hines, (2) Mary Ida Scott, (3) Eunice White.

It is possible that the following are also his children: Isaac O. Holland; Hilliard B. Holland; Gertrude Holland, m. ----- Fitzpatrick; Virginia Holland; Mary Holland, m. Moses Gresham.

George Washington Holland, (called "Washington"), born at Holland, Nansemond County, Virginia, July 1795, was the son of Elizabeth Ann Odem and Capt. Joseph Holland of Kingsale. He died after 1840 in Georgia. He married in Nansemond County, Virginia, Jan. 26, 1816, Mary Ann Griffin, born May 4, 1799, and died at Monticello, Jasper Co., Georgia, May 8, 1840.

George Washington Holland served through the War of 1812 from Nansemond County, Virginia. Letters to him addressed to "Major George Washington Holland" around 1840 were sent from Virginia to Monticello, Georgia before stamps were used. In 1817 he sold the land left him by his father and moved to Ga.

Children:

I.   Richard O. Holland, b. Jan. 18, 1818, d. an infant.

II.   Dr. Joseph Alfred Holland, b. Aug. 29, 1820, m. Sarah A. Flewellen.

III.   Charlotte Elizabeth Holland, b. Sept. 31, 1822, m. Hugh Parks Fitzpatrick.

IV.   George W. Holland, Jr., b. Aug. 30, 1824, m. Elizabeth Reese. (See later)

V.   Virginia L. Holland, b. Sept. 24, 1828, died in infancy.

VI.   Lucius Henry Holland, b. Oct. 11, 1830, d. in infancy.

VII.   Mary Ann Holland, b. May 6, 1840, m. Dr. Hardy Smith.

George Washington Holland, son of Mary Ann Griffin and George Washington Holland, was born at Monticello, Ga. Aug. 30, 1824, and died at Bremond, Robertson Co., Texas, May 26, 1904. On June 17, 1845, at Monticello, Ga. he married the daughter of Cutbert Reese and Tabitha Clark, Elizabeth Sarah, born Feb. 22, 1826 at Hillsboro, Ga. and died April 2, 1886, in Bremond, Texas.

George Washington Holland, Jr., was educated at the University of Georgia. Before the Civil War he farmed a large plantation in Alabama, later he taught English in the Tuskeegee Institute (now a school for negroes), then moved to Calvert, Texas, in 1868.

Children:

I.   George Cuthbert Holland, b. April 8, 1846, m. Mary A. Davis, d. Aug. 30, 1869.

II.   Joseph Alfred Holland, b. March 27, 1848, m. Susan J. A. Youngblood (See later).

III.   Hugh P.K. Holland, b. April 10, 1852, m. (1) Mary Da-Davis, (2) Mary Curlee.

IV.   William Walter Holland, b. July 30, 1854, m. (1) Lucy
        Taylor, (2) Beulah McWhorter.

Judge Joseph Alfred Holland, son of Elizabeth Reese and
George Washington Holland, Jr., was born at Monticello, Ga.,
March 27, 1848, and died at Houston, Texas, August 16, 1937.
On March 5, 1867, at China Grove, Pike County, Alabama, he
married Susan Jane Augusta, the daughter of Tinzy Terrell
Townsend and Dr. Oliver Youngblood, who was born in China
Grove, Alabama, Dec. 9, 1847 and died in Houston, Texas,
Sept. 10, 1931.

Judge Holland was educated at Tuskeegee Institute in Alabama, practiced law in Orange and in Amarillo, Texas; was
District Judge at Marlin and Fort Worth, Texas; District Attorney in Fort Worth.

Children:

I.   George Embrey Holland, b. Nov. 24, 1868, m. Edwena
        (Winnie) Buell.
II.   Ihna Imola Holland, b. Feb. 2, 1872, m. John Wiley
        Link. (See later)
III.   Willie Pearle Holland, b. Dec. 24, 1873, m. James
        Portwood.
IV.   Ida Novella Holland, b. Nov. 20, 1876, m. (1) Henry B.
        Jackson, (2) A. W. Voorhees.
V.   Joseph Alfred Holland, Jr., b. Oct. 4, 1879, m. Grace
        Van Valkenburg.

Ihna Imola Holland, daughter of Susan Jane Augusta Youngblood and Judge Joseph Alfred Holland, was born Feb. 2, 1872,
at Bremond, Texas, and is now living at 819 Lovett Blvd., Houston, Texas. On October 21, 1891, at Amarillo, Texas, she
married John Wiley Link, son of Emmaline Henry and David
Lowman Link, who was born in Gallatin, Tenn., and died at
Houston, Texas, March 18, 1933.

Ihna Holland was educated at Baylor University, Waco, Tex.,
J. W. Link was educated at Vanderbilt University, Nashville
Law School, and Baylor. He was a lumberman and an attorney,
and Mayor of Orange, Texas. He was also President of Miller-
Link Lumber Co.; Vice-president of the Kirby Lumber Co.; of
Tex.-La. Lumbermans Assn.; of Link Oil Co.; of Houston Land
Corp.; of the Dr. Pepper Co.

Mrs. Link is residing at 819 Lovett Blvd., Houston, Texas.

Children:

I.   Emma Augusta Link, b. Nov. 26, 1892, d. Sept. 29, 1898.
II.   Ura Aetrone Link, b. Aug. 12, 1894, m. Wm. R. Eck-
        hardt, Jr. (See later)
III.   Ihna Imola Link, b. Dec. 6, 1896, m. Elwyn Carroll.
IV.   Dora Link, b. Feb. 4, 1898, m. Chas. Wells Shartle, Jr.
V.   John Wiley Link, Jr. b. July 5, 1903, m. Helen Wicks.
VI.   George Harold Link, b. April 17, 1906, m. Marcita Drouet.

Mrs. Ura Link Eckhardt, whose present address is 4522
Willow Bend Blvd., Bellaire, Texas, the daughter of Ihna Imola
Holland and John Wiley Link, was born in Amarillo, Texas,
Aug. 12, 1894. In Houston, Texas, Oct. 21, 1914, she married
William Rudolf Eckhardt, Jr., the son of Iris Dee Kent and Dr.

274

William Rudolf Eckhardt, who was born in Houston, Dec. 3, 1892.

Mrs. Eckhardt was educated at Mount Vernon Seminary, Washington, D.C., and Newcomb College in New Orleans, La. Mr. Eckhardt was educated at Texas A & M College. He was Manager of Beaumont Ship Bldg. & DryDock Co. during World War I. He is now manager of the Polar Wave Ice Co.; and the Ice Skating Rink at Bellaire, Texas. Mrs. Eckhardt, after a careful research, kindly furnished most of the information used in this chapter.

Children:

I.   William Rudolf Eckhardt, III, b. Dec. 14, 1915; m. Elra May Hodges.
II. John Link Eckhardt, b. April 30, 1921; m. (1) Gertrude Robertson, (2) Carolyn Dorothea Holl.
III. Byron Kent Eckhardt, b. April 27, 1925, m. Irene Watkins.
IV. Gloria Joyce Eckhardt, b. Aug. 8, 1929, m. Julian Clay Chalon.

Lewis Conner Holland, son of Joseph Holland of Spivey, or Joseph Spivey Holland as he was sometimes called, was born in Suffolk, Nansemond County, Virginia, where in 1809 he married Elizabeth Washington.

Children:

I.   Frances A. Holland, m. Lemuel Laurence.
II. Joseph Lawson, b. 1811, m. Jane Jordan.
III. Kathrene Elizabeth Holland, b. 1812.
IV. Ellen A. Holland, b. 1813, m. (1) Bryant, (2) Alexander Duncan, (3) Durham, (4) Wilson.
V.   Lavinia W. Holland, b. 1815, m. Col. Burwell Jordan.
VI. Clotilda J. Holland, b. 1818, m. Henry H. Herrington. (See later)
VII. William Perryn Holland, b. 1820.

Clotilda Jane Holland, daughter of Catherine Elizabeth (Washington) and Lewis Conner Holland, was born in 1820 in Suffolk, Va. In 1842, at Smithville, Ga., she married Henry Harrison Herrington, who died in 1864 at Mineral Wells, Tex. Clotilda Holland Herrington died at Montgomery, Texas, in 1863. Mr. Herrington was a Cotton Mill owner.

Children:

I.   Eudocia Jane Herrington, b. April 13, 1843, m. Wm. W. Arnett. (See later)
II. Ellen Amamda Herrington, b. Feb. 10, 1847.
III. William Perrian Herrington, b. Nov. 5, 1849.
IV. Blackshire Herrington, b. June 5, 1851.
V.   Lavinia Washington Herrington, b. May 12, 1855.
VI. John Lawson Herrington, b. Sept. 16, 1858.

Eudocia Herrington, daughter of Clotilda Jane Holland and Henry Harrison Herrington, was born at Smithville, Georgia, April 13, 1843, and died in Uvalde, Texas, on June 11, 1925. On Feb. 23, 1874, at Salado, Texas, she married William Washington Arnett, who was born Jan. 1, 1823, at Tuscumbia, Ala., and died at Brackett, Texas, Dec. 23, 1892.

Children:

I.   Calvin Curlee Arnett, b. July 8, 1875, m. Eliza Knowlton.
II.   William Washington Arnett, b. Feb. 22, 1877.
III.   Minnie B. Arnett, b. Feb. 22, 1879, m. Thomas M. Mi-
       lam. (See later)
IV.   Georgie A. Arnett, b. July 9, 1882, m. Sudie Allen.
V.   Bertie Stover Arnett, b. Jan. 24, 1888.

Minnie Bruce Arnett Milam, whose present address is Box 533, Ft. Stockton, Texas, who was born Feb. 22, 1879 at Brackett, Texas, was the daughter of Eudecia Herrington and William Washington Arnett. On Aug. 24, 1897, at Rock Springs, Texas, she married Thomas Monroe Milam, who was born at Enloe, Texas, June 22, 1875, and died at Ft. Stockton, Texas, June 8, 1942. He was the son of James LaFayette Milam.

Children:

I.   Jeanette Milam, b. Aug. 28, 1904, m. Lucian Thomas
      Jones.
II.   Lenore Milam, b. Oct. 8, 1910, m. Tom Richard Kenzie.
III.   Mary Milam, b. Sept. 10, 1917, m. Fred William Bogardus.
IV.   Benjamin Wilson Milam, b. Jan. 5, 1919, m. Helen Barlow.

Robert[3] Holland, son of Henry[2] Holland, married Patience (Everett?) He appears in tax lists 1782 as father of James; and in Census of 1782. In his will dated February 5, 1797, proved February 5, 1799, he mentions wife Patience, sons Everett and James; daughters Sally Davis, Betsy Randolph and Milly Hancock; Everett Holland, "son of my son Everett", grandson Robert Marshall, Charles, Everett and Nancy Holland. His grandson, Everett Holland, was presumably of age, since he is mentioned by name in the will, and no record of appointment of a guardian appears. Robert Holland had other grandchildren - his three daughters were all married. He was therefore not a young man when he made his will - probably about 70 years old, born 1715-1725. He resigned as a captain of Militia during the Revolutionary War. This indicates that he had reached or was approaching the age limit (60-65). Older men always served in the militia. Robert Holland was a vestryman of the Brick Church as early as 1777. The Vestry was composed of older men, and he was probably of mature years at that time, perhaps 55 or 60 years of age. (Tax lists - Isle of Wight County; Wills of Isle of Wight County, Book 2, p. 183; Boddie's Isle of Wight County, 179, 186, 190.)

James Holland, father of Hardy Darden Holland, appears in Tax Lists 1782 as James Holland, son of Robert. James Holland married Alice Darden. Both Robert and James Holland appear in the 1782 Census as heads of families. (James Holland, born 1770, married 1790 Polly Harris could not have been son of Robert as he would have been only 12 years old in 1782). James Holland, son of Robert, was of age in 1782. Since he was married to Alice Darden before 1773 he was probably born about 1750. His wife, Alice Holland, was the daughter of Hardy Darden who signed his will Oct. 2, 1773, in which he mentions daughter Alice Holland. Even allowing for early marriages of these times, she was born not later than 1758, probably earlier.

The estate of James Holland who married Alice Darden was appraised February, 1801, signed by James Holland, Wiley Langford and George Clements.

Hardy[5] Darden Holland, son of Alice (Darden) and James Holland, was the great-great-grandfather of Mr. James G. W. MacClamroch of Greensboro, N.C. A complete account of Mr. MacClamroch's descent from his above great[2] grandfather appears in the Darden chapter on pages 92 and 93 of "Southside Virginia Families", Vol. 1. To him should be given credit for kindly obtaining much of the information used in preparing the Darden and Holland chapters.

A William Holland who lived on a plantation adjoining John, Sr., Henry Holland, Jr. and James Holland as shown in James Holland's deed of 1756 heretofore mentioned was certainly of this family, but the records do not show who was his father. His mother was Mary, daughter of William Daughtry, Sr., who made his will Dec. 24, 1751, and mentioned therein his daughter Mary Holland and his grandson William Holland. (W.B.-5-436; C-11-160) One of the witnesses to the will was Charles Darden.

William Holland, as William Holland, Sr., made his will Feb. 5, 1785, and mentions sons: MILES, BENJAMIN, ELISHA, ABRAHAM, and WILLIAM. Will was probated Oct. 5, 1786. Wits.: Benjamin Holland, Barbary Holland, Charles Darden.

Benjamin Holland, son of above William, witnessed the will of Henry Johnson, Sr., together with Barnaby Holland, Feb. 26, 1782. He and Barnaby were surities. (C-108) Benjamin made his will Dec. 16, 1799, probated July 7, 1800. He mentions daughters: ANN CARR, ELIZABETH DARDEN, PATIENCE JOHNSON; son, JACOB; and gives a legacy to Elenah Holland. Son BENJAMIN executor; Wits.: Mills Butler, Mills Holland, Aaron Holland. Surity, Mills Darden.

Joseph[5] Holland, son of Ann (Odom) and Capt. Joseph Holland, "of Kingsale", married Nancy Parker. He made his will Oct. 12, 1826, probated in Isle of Wight Jan. 1, 1827. He names sons: WILLIS H.; JOSEPH J.; JOHN MONRO; SAMUEL HAWKES; JAMES WASHINGTON; daus.: JULY; NANCY; SUSANNA: LUCY LEVINA: EMELINAH VIRGINIA; GEORGIANA and ANN MATILDA NORFLEET. (Vol. 17-420)

An Elijah Holland on June 2, 1758, patented 400 acres in U.P. of Nansemond, adjoining Thomas Godwin, himself, John Bartley and Joseph Goodwin, granted to Michael Gill, Feb. 11, 1664, the title of which has since vested in said Elijah Holland.

Job[5] Holland, son of Job[4] Holland, and grandson of Henry[3] Holland, lived in Nansemond and died there Jan. 8, 1829. His children were: Zechariah, born 1797, married Matilda Ann Howell (See later); Elizabeth, born 1800, married James Barnes; Mary, married Isaac Lee.

Zechariah Holland, son of Job Holland, was born in Nansemond in 1797 and died there August 6, 1826. In 1817 he married Matilda Ann Howell, who was born Sept. 19, 1799, in Nansemond, and died there March 22, 1877. She was the daughter of Anne Phillips and Edward Howell, Jr. (1750-1817), who had been a Corporal in Capt. Goodman's Co., N.C. Regiment in Revolution. A notation says he was "sick at Valley Forge". Zachariah Holland was a Sergeant in Capt. Jeremiah's Rawles Company, 50th. Regiment, in the War of 1812.

Children:
I. Robert H. Holland, b. Oct. 16, 1819, m. (1) Elizabeth Everett (2) Margarett O'Beery. (See later)
II. Elizabeth Anne Holland, m. Albert K. Rawles.
III. Zachery Everett Holland, b. 1821, m. Ann Scott Pretlow.
IV. Dixon Howell Holland, m. Eliza Sumner.

Robert Howell Holland, son of Matilda Ann Howell and Zechariah Holland, was born in Nansemond, Oct. 16, 1819, and died at Holland, Va., Nov. 9, 1908. He was a Minister of the Southern Christian Church. In 1849, in Nansemond, he married first, Elizabeth Lee Everett, and second Margarette O'Beery, who was born in Nansemond, the daughter of Martha Battle and John O'Beery, and died in Holland, Va., July 20, 1902.

Children:
I. Eugenia M. Holland, b. July 27, 1850, m. Benj. G. Porter. (See later)
II. Augustina Holland, b. 1851, m. Joseph B. Johnson.
III. Robert W. Holland, m. Addie Roberts.
IV. Job Holland, b. 1861, m. Nannie Jones.
V. Jessie Holland, b. 1865, m. Isaac Luke.

Eugenia Marina Holland, the daughter of Margarette O'Berry and the Rev. Robert Howell Holland, was born in Holland, Va., July 27, 1850; and died at Norfolk, Va., Aug. 12, 1911. She was graduated from Murfresboro N.C. College, and on Dec. 15, 1875, at Holland, Va., she married Benjamin Godwin Porter, born Nov. 20, 1843, near Holland, Va., and died at Norfolk, Va., March 9, 1916. Mr. Porter had been a Lieutenant in Company K, 41 Virginia Infantry at Appomatox.

Children:
I. Robert Holland Porter, m. Florence Lyon.
II. Benj. G. Porter, b. Feb. 6, 1881, m. Minnie Stone. (See later)
III. Margaret E. Porter, b. Nov. 12, 1885, died as an infant.
IV. Lillian Porter, b. Oct. 19, 1883.

Benjamin Guy Porter, who was born February 6, 1881, at Holland, Virginia, the son of Eugenia Marina Holland and Benjamin Godwin Porter, on October 11, 1905, at Norfolk, Virginia, married Minnie Estelle Stone, who was born at Creeds, Virginia, January 20, 1884, the daughter of Jacamine Batten and John Thomas Stone, and died at Norfolk, Virginia, August 3, 1948.

Mr. Porter was a merchant and hotel owner. He graduated at Elon College, and lived in Holland, Va., and Elon, N.C.

Children:
I. Elizabeth L. Porter, b. Dec. 29, 1907, m. Jas. L. Bennett. (See later)
II. Helen Stone Porter, b. Aug. 10, 1910, m. Walker F. Martin.

Elizabeth Leigh Porter Bennett, whose present address is 104 Laurel Lane, Virginia Beach, Va., was born at Norfolk,

Virginia, December 29, 1907, the daughter of Minnie Estelle
Stone and Benjamin G. Porter. On June 12, 1937, at Virginia
Beach, she married James Lawrence Bennett, who was born at
Brooklyn, N. Y. Mrs. Bennett holds an A. B. from Hollins
College, and an M. A. from Columbia University. Her children
are:

I.   James Lawrence Bennett, Jr., b. Feb. 14, 1939
II.   Robert Holland Bennett, b. March 9, 1941
III. Anne Randolph Bennett, b. March 1, 1945.

Thomas Holland, a Revolutionary Soldier, probably born in
Nansemond County, Va., married a Miss Rickman and died in
Greene County, Georgia in 1828. Their children were: Thomas;
James; Robert; Benjamin; Harrison, b. Oct. 24, 1779, m. Eliza-
beth Ramland; John Rickman, b. May 8, 1786, m. Elizabeth
Walker (See later); William A., b. Nov. 11, 1791, m. Phetna
McBee; Elizabeth, m. William Hammand; Sarah, m. Samuel
H. Nelms; Nancy, m. James Goodwin.

John Rickman Holland, son of ------ Rickman and Thomas
Holland was born in Virginia, May 8, 1786, and died in Dublin,
Texas, Nov. 10, 1863. On Jan. 16, 1812 in Putnam County,
Ga., he married Elizabeth Walker, who was born in 1794 and
died July 4, 1861, at Menlo, Ga.

    Children:
I.   Thomas Walker, b. Feb. 14, 1813, m. (1) Mary Good-
      win, (2) ------Hightower.
II.   William A., b. July 18, 1814, m. Amanda Nelms.
III. Mary Burns, b. Sept. 26, 1816, m. Thomas T. Bell.
IV.   Nancy Ann, b. Nov. 1817, m. Henry Lyda Jackson (See
      later).
V.   Sarah Jane, b March 24, 1819, m. Alexander Dobkins.
VI.   John Benjamin, b. June 19, 1821, m. Mary Ann Covington.
VII. Martha Elizabeth, b. 1823, m. Moses Holland.
VIII. Samuel Eley, b. Dec. 6, 1826, m. (1) Mary Scott, (2)
      Clara A. Thomas, (3) S. McCarthy.
IX.   Simresda Catherine, b. Aug. 24, 1828, m. Wm. B. Cov-
      ington.

Nancy Ann Holland, daughter of Elizabeth Walker and John
R. Holland, was born in Putnam County, Ga., 1817, and died at
Ft. Gates, Texas, June 11, 1859. On Oct. 13, 1835 she mar-
ried Henry Lyda Jackson, who was born in Buncombe County,
N. C., Aug. 11, 1810, and died Dec. 22, 1880, at Auburn, Tex.

    Children:
I.   John Holland L. Jackson, b. Oct. 23, 1836, m. Susan
      Louise Presley.
II.   Andrew D. Jackson, b. July 21, 1838, dsp.
III. Benjamin F. Jackson, b. Aug. 19, 1840, m. Eady E.
      Swofford. (See later)
IV.   Thomas Benton Jackson, b. Nov. 30, 1842, m. Mary
      Susan F. Burnett.
V.   Elizabeth Ann Jackson, b. Nov. 25, 1844, m. Edward
      Fullerton.
VI.   Henry Basil Jackson, b. Dec. 25, 1846, m. Frances
      Elizabeth Anderson.

VII.   Martha Ann Walker Jackson, b. Apr. 14, 1849, m. John F. Campbell.

VIII. Rebecca Smith Jackson, b. Nov. 9, 1850, m. Richard Jones.

IX.   Joseph P. Jackson, b. Sept. 8, 1852, dsp.

Benjamin Franklin Jackson, the son of Nancy Ann Holland and Henry L. Jackson, was born near Rome, Ga., Aug. 19, 1840, and died at San Antonio, Texas, Jan. 22, 1912. On Mar. 8, 1866, at May Pearl, Ellis Co., Texas, he married Eady Elvena Swofford, the daughter of Eady Prewett of North Carolina and John Hoyle Swofford, was born in Cleveland County, N.C., July 9, 1848, and died Oct. 28, 1934, at Coppers Cove, Texas.

Children:

I.   Esther Delcena Jackson, b. Dec. 27, 1869, m. J.W. Davis. (See later)

II.   Wycliffe Greene Jackson, b. Feb. 3, 1873, m. Alice Breeze.

III.   Benjamin Jay Jackson, b. Sept. 18, 1874, m. Ellyn Pennington.

IV.   Ewell S. Jackson, b. Sept. 23, 1876, m. Martha Sault.

V.   Lettie Rhoda Jackson, b. Jan. 5, 1879, m. Russell L. Raines.

VI.   Amy Judson Jackson, b. Jan. 11, 1881, m. Wm. Reed Graham.

VII.   Iva Pearle Jackson, b. Apr. 1, 1882, m. Sidney Albert Turner.

VIII. Luke Benjamin Jackson, b. Aug. 29, 1884, m. Rose Wauford.

IX.   Jennie Elvena Jackson, b. Aug. 18, 1887, m. John Edwards.

X.   Ruth Winifred Jackson, b. Sept. 30, 1891, m. Charles Angus Morse.

Esther Delcena Jackson, the daughter of Eady Elvena Swofford and Benjamin Franklin Jackson, was born at May Pearl, Ellis Co., Texas, Dec. 27, 1869. On Jan. 16, 1889, at Auburn, Texas, she married Joseph Wilson Davis, who was born in Alabama, Jan. 5, 1864, and died at Lometa, Lampasas Co., Texas, June 5, 1941.

Children:

I.   Alta Elvena Davis, b. Nov. 30, 1889, m. Eliza Elmo Cass.

II.   John Benjamin Davis, b. Dec. 13, 1892, m. Maud Herring.

III.   Bertha Marian Davis, b. June 25, 1894, m. Harry Lester Pearce.

IV.   Edith Pearl Davis, b. Sept. 11, 1897, m. George M. McCall. (See later)

V.   Ora Esther Davis, b. Sept. 25, 1899, dsp Jan. 16, 1932.

VI.   Lettie Judson Davis, b. Feb. 9, 1901, m. Olen Harvey Smith.

VII.   Samuel Brice Davis, b. Aug. 18, 1903, m. Mary Virginia Carver.

VIII. Joseph Ray Davis, b. Jan. 27, 1905, unmarried.

Edith Pearl Davis, the daughter of Esther Delcena Jackson and J.W. Davis, was born Sept. 11, 1897, at Pidcoke, Texas. On June 6, 1920, at Lometa, Tex., she married George Montgomery McCall, the son of Margaret Kezia Overstreet and Walter Andrass McCall, who was born at Grove, Bell Co., Texas, Sept. 24, 1889. He farmed in Llano County, Texas, and they now reside at 1211 N. 4th Street, Temple, Texas.

Children:

I.   Esther Margaret McCall, b. Sept. 15, 1921, m. Wm. Edwin Milner.

II.   Edith Carol McCall, b. April 9, 1923, m. Howel Webster Woodfin.

III. Norma Jean McCall, b. Feb. 28, 1925, m. Joseph F. Dennis.

James[2] Holland, second son of John[1] Holland, re-patented part of his father's grant of 1694 for 500 acres as heretofore shown. In 1722 he sold 345 acres adjacent land of John and Henry Holland. Isle of Wight deed. It is difficult to determine whom were his children.

John[2] Holland, son of John[1] Holland, was probably the John Holland, Sr., who whitnessed deeds in 1733 and 1756. (ante)

Joseph[2] Holland held 100 acres in Nansemond in 1704. He was also probably a son of John[1] Holland.

The above three persons were evidently the ancestors of the numerous Holland family of Nansemond.

Heads of Families, Virginia, 1784. Nansemond County.		Roster of soldiers from North Carolina in the American Revolution
Heads of families.		
Capt. Sumner's, Holland's & Darden's Companies of Militia, List of Elisha Darden. White Souls.		Holland, Bazel.
		Holland, Beason.
		Holland, Charles.
Holland, James (of Ro)	6.	Holland, Daniel.
Holland, Jesse	4.	Holland, Fred'k.
Holland, William	5.	Holland, Henry.
Holland, Joseph	6.	Holland, Isaac, Jr.
Holland, Henry (of Jno)	9.	Holland, James
Holland, James (of Danl)	3.	Holland, Jeremiah.
Holland, John (of Sole)	1.	Holland, Joseph.
Holland, Solomon	6.	Holland, Josiah.
Holland, Jobe	2.	Holland, Matthew.
Holland, James (of Jas)	6.	Holland, Reason.
Holland, Elisha	2.	Holland, Spear.
Holland, Henry (of Dn.)	4.	Holland, Spier.
Holland, Titus	2.	Holland, William.
Holland, Henry (of Jos.)	4.	
Holland, James (of Jos.)	5.	
Holland, Jno. (of Moses)	5.	
Holland, Absalom	7.	
Holland, Benja.	5.	
Holland, Joshua	7.	
Holland, Joseph (of Jos.)	7.	
Holland, Danl.	4.	
Holland, Thomas	6.	
Holland, Brittain	1.	
Holland, Henry, Sr.	7.	
Holland, David	5.	

SORRELL of ENGLAND and VIRGINIA

Copied from Visitations of Essex 1634;

Harleain Society Volume 13, pages 490-491.

William Sorrell
of High Easter in Co.
Essex.

Thomas Sorrell
of High Easter

Robert Sorrell
of High Easter

Clement, who
remarried
Thomas Wiseman.

John Sorrell
of Much
Waltham, Essex

Alice, da.
of Tendring.

Thomas Sorrell
of High Easter

Robert Sorrell
of Much
Waltham

Margery, da. of
John Tarling
of Essex.

John Sorrell
of Stebbing
Parsonage, Essex
Clerk of the
Assizes.

Margery, widow of
Robt. Bernard, da
of Robert Sorrell
of Waltham

[1]John
Sorrell
DSP
Aug. 26,
1626

[2]Robert
Sorrell
of
Writtle

Mary, da.
Thos.
Everard, of
Waltham
Magna.

Thomas Sorrell
of Stebing
(living 1634)

Susan, da. of
John Coley of
Colchester.

John Sorrell

Thomas
Sorrell

William
Sorrell

3 daus.

[1] Thomas
Sorrell

[2]John
Sorrell

Mary, da. of
Thos. Aylett
of Coggshall
Essex. d. May 26,
1652, aged 46.

Anne
Sorrell

Mary
Sorrell
m
Wm. Coniers
of Chelmsford

Mary
Sorrell
m.
Nicholas
Coniers of
Mount
Wessing

Mary
Sorrell, only
dau. aged 5
1634.

Susan Sorrell
b. 1591

John Litle, b.
1578 at
Hawstead

3ROBERT SORRELL
of Virginia

SORRELL - entries in a transcript of the parish registers
of Great Dunmow, Essex. Marriages 1558-1800. Following was
furnished by Mrs. W. T. Fowler of Lexington, Ky., who visited
in Essex.

1599, April 23, John Sorrell and Marie Paules (High Easter)
1567, June 28, John Sorrell and Tomazine Bankes.
1577, Sept. 8, Gregory Cooke and Margery Sorrell.
1605, Nov. 21, Andrew Earle and Margery Sorrell.
1611, Oct. 7, Constantine Livermer and Agnes Sorrell.
1626, July 17, Richard Clark and Susan Sorrell.
1643, Nov. 22, Robert Sorrell and Rebecca Woodward.
1788, Jan. 1, Richard Sorrell (Aythorp Roding) and Anne
Bernard, Lic.

WOODWARD, Parish Registers Great Dunmow, Essex,
1558-1800

1615, Nov. 13, John Woodward and Alice Garrold.
1617, Sept. 25, Thomas Bush and Margaret Woodward.
1619, June 3, Nathaniel Staines and Priscilla Woodward (Stanes)
1621, Jan. 28, John Joy and Helena Woodward.
1629, Nov. 30, John Sturton and Helen Woodward
1636, June 6, Christopher Tyffin and Jane Woodward.
1643, Nov. 22, Robert Sorrell and Rebecca Woodward
1645, Apr. 8, Daniel Fuller and Alice Woodward
1648, Oct. 18, John Preene and Sarah Woodward
1649, May 14, William Twinnow and Ellen Woodward.

A John, Robert and Richard Sorel registered at Oxford University between 1273 and 1300. They may have been students from France. A search of the English Calender of State Papers should reveal how long the family resided in England before the time of the first William Sorrell in the Visitations.

A William Sorrell of England in his will provided for his burial in Boulogne, France. The will gives no family data except that he leaves his lands and affairs in the keeping of a brother, John Sorrell. It seems that a part of his estate was located in that part of Essex which is now London. The will is said to have been in French or Latin. A copy was not furnished and date not given. The Sorrells were traditionally Hugenots.

Morant, in his "History of Essex" (1760) says that Bartholomew Brock of the Manor of Frier's Hall, on Sept. 7, 1601, conveyed the Rectory of Stebbing to John and Thomas Sorrell. (p. 415) He also states that John Hawkins of Hide Hall "sold that estate about 1650 to John Sorrell, gent. That family were then Lessees of their parish (Much Waltham) and had also the parsonage of Stebbing." (Vol. 1, p. 85) "John Sorrell, father as we suppose of the John above mentioned, died August 12, 1626". (Morant). (From the chart this John appears to be the uncle of John Sorrell, above mentioned and the eldest son of Robert Sorrell of Much Waltham. According to the chart he died single and his brother Robert would be his heir.)

Morant further states that "John Sorrell, purchaser of 'Hide Hall' married Mary, daughter of Thomas Aylett of Coggshall, who died May 26, 1652, in the 46th year of her age. (Epitaph in church)" Their son and heir, John Sorrell of "Hide Hall" and Waltham Parsonage married Sarah, daughter of Richard Hale of Beckhampton in Kent, gent. Two sons died young. Arms, Gules 2 Lions Passent ermine." (Vol. 1, p. 85)

Robert Sorrell, father of the Robert Sorrell of Virginia, married Mary, daughter of Thomas Everard of Waltham Magna. The Everard family held the Manor of Langleys in Essex; and Morant in stating how they acquired it says, "John Slixton of Hornden, Sr., and John his son did on June 26, 1529, convey their moiety of the Manor of Langleys to Richard Everard. The other moiety was in the Cornish family, ancient inhabitants of this parish where John Cornish lived in 1398 and held lands called "Adgores" of Waltham Hall. He is said to be then in the service of the Lady of Waltham Bury Manor. They continued here till the reign of Edward VI. Jan. 7, 1515, John, son and heir of John Cornish, son and heir of Thomas Cornish of this place and Iodena his wife conveyed their part of this manor to Thomas Everard of Great Waltham who had married their daughter and heir named Joan or Mary. (Id. 87) Arms of Cornish: Sable a chevron battilie, or, between 3 roses, argent.

Robert Sorrell, son of Robert Sorrell of Writtle, Essex, and his wife Mary, daughter of Thomas Everard of Waltham Magna, married Rebecca Woodward, of Great Dunmow, Essex, on Nov. 22, 1643 (Register). Robert patented 800 acres in James City County, Va., on April 10, 1651, "Being an island within Warrany Cr. bounded S. by E. towards land of Edward Cole, N towards Joyner's Neck, S towards the mouth of said creek and E. towards the land of Bennett Freeman for the transportation of two persons. "Vid County Court Booke." (C.P. 212) The County records have been destroyed, but the two persons may have been himself and wife Rebecca.

A Robert and John Sorrell were headrights of Thomas Wright of Lower Norfolk who patented land there in 1647. Francis Fleetwood used three of Thomas Wright's headrights for patenting land in lower Norfolk in 1652, including Robert and John Sorrell. (C. P. 166, 274) These traded headrights may have been those of Robert and his young son, John Sorrell, who were returning from England.

The Wright family may have been related to the Sorrells, for Thomas Wright who made his will in Norfolk Co., in 1654 had a grandson, John Wright, who disappears from the county records of Norfolk, and may have been the John Wright who in 1713 gave a heifer to Anna, daughter of Thomas and Elizabeth Sorrell. (McIntosh 15-120; Fothergill 53)

Robert[1] Sorrell patented 700 acres of land in James City, Nov. 20, 1653, "on the Southermost Branch of Warrancy Creek next to Henry Soanes" (C.P. 240)

In 1657 Robert Sorrell purchased William Davis, a servant, from Col. Thomas Swann, for 2,000 pounds of live pork. In referring to Davis' freedom he said: "William, if thou wilt be ruled by me, I will prescribe one to thee that will plead thy cause and ask thee nothing," and withal nominated Mr. Morryson. (Surry, Vol. 1, -117) Robert Sorrell of Chiakhominy in James City County sold to Martin Collins of York County 497 acres purchased of John Hommwood, who purchased it of John Hamlett who acquired it of Richard Hamlett who patented it. (York, Vol. 4, 338) He was one of Berkeley's adherents and fell "in his Majesty's ser-

284

vice before James City." This was in Bacon's siege of Jamestown. The General Court ordered Feb. 20, 1682, that "Rebecca
Sorrell, the widow of Captain Robet Sorrell, who was lately
killed in his Majesty's service, and his estate since plundered
and taken away by the Rebells, be allowed out of the public levy
40,000 lbs. tbco. and what of her goods can be found returned
to her." (J.B. 1682)

The only known child of ROBERT[1] and REBECCA SORRELL
was JOHN[2] SORRELL mentioned in the will of John's son THOM-
AS[3] SORRELL, dated January 12, 1725. Thomas bequeathed to
his son JAMES[4] SORRELL "the land in James City County which
my honored father JOHN[2] SORRELL devised to me." (See later)

WILLIAM SORRELL of Elizabeth City may have been another
son. Inventory of his estate signed by Sarah Sorrell was filed
there Dec. 18, 1689. Division of the estate gives a part to Sarah
Sorrell, widow; to John Sorrell at Mr. Needhams; to George
Sorrell at Edward Lattimores; to Elizabeth Sorrell at Mr. John-
sons; to William and Thomas Sorrell at John Naylor's. John
Naylor and Edward Lattymore ordered to return an account of
the estates of the orphans of William Sorrell. Sept. 11, 1693.
(O.B. 1689-1699, p. 9-119-124-129.) John Naylor, in his will
dated Sept. 29, 1694, probated Oct. 10, 1694, gives a legacy
to Thomas and William Sorrell.

EDWARD SORRELL of James City Co., who on June 10,
1703, with his wife ALICE, "executrix of the will of Benjamin
Goodrich, gent. late of said county, decd." made a deed to land
in James City adjoining Mr. Sorrell and Mr. Hamlette.

John[2] Sorrell, son of Robert[1], may have married a daughter
of the Reverend James Breechin who in his will dated Oct. 21,
1721, probated April 6, 1722, mentions late wife Anna, sons
William and James, daughters Anna and Jane. (Other legatees)
and "...to JAMES and ANN SORRELL 1 hogshead of tobacco
each; to Kinsman THOMAS SORRELL, a mourning ring." (Fother-
gill-77)

Thomas[3] Sorrell, in his will made in 1725, desired to be
buried by his dear mother, which indicated his mother was dead.
Thomas[3] Sorrell moved to Westmoreland where he was Clerk of
the Court from Dec. 20, 1715 to Oct. 1726. He married Elizabeth, daughter of Daniel Ocanny of Westmoreland, who in his
will dated and probated 1716 mentions his "son-in-law Thomas
Sorrell" and also his Crabbe grandchildren (Fothergill, p. 61).
Osman Crabbe, son-in-law of Daniel Ocanny, died in 1713 and in
his will appointed his "brother-in-law Thomas Sorrell" trustee.
(Id. 69)

Osman Crabb was a son of Temperance Gerard, dau. of Dr.
Thomas Gerard, who married (1) Daniel Hutt; (2) Osman Crabbe;
(3) Benjamin Blanchflower. Temperance's sister Anne Gerard
married (1) Walter Brodhurst; (2) ------ Brett; (3) Col. John
Washington. (Tyler's Q., Jan. 1923) Osman Crabbe, Jr., Married Sarah Occany, who later married (2) unknown; (3) ------
Dunbar. Thomas Sorrell was executor of Osman Crabb's will.

Thomas Sorrell's will, dated Oct. 8, 1725, and proved Feb.
22, 1726, as follows: "...to son James all the land I live on; all

my lands at the head of Nominy where I formerly lived to my son John, and also to him the lands devised to me by my father-in-law Daniel Occany; to my son James the land in James City County which my honored father, John Sorrell, devised to me and also 1/3 of my mill. 2/3 of my mill to my son John. To my nephew Thomas Sorrell the land where James Holloway now lives, on condition that my nephew quit claim title to the land adjoining my dwelling seat which he hath promised.

I have purchased the land in James City County devised to my brother John Sorrell, dec'd...... to my loving consort all her wearing apparel, rings, etc., horse saddle, and furniture, the use of three slaves and all my other estate during my childrens minority, she clothing and educating them. All the rest of my estate equally between wife and children. To son John two negroes and to son James, after his mothers death, those given to her. To my aforesaid nephew and his sisters, Elizabeth and Frances a mourning ring apiece and a prayer book to each. (Motto on rings, "Memento Mori") bequests to daughters Ann and Winifred. Son James to be an assistance to his mother in teaching his little sisters, which I charge upon my blessing do." The will appointed Loving consort, Elizabeth, Capt. George Turbeville and Wm. Sherman as executrix and executors.

Mr. T. P. Hughes, Jr., in his letter of Jan. 21, 1957, kindly points to the fact that the court records, dated Feb. 25, 1726, show that George Turbeville and William Sherman, THE SURVIVING EXECUTORS, are to administer the will. This proves that Elizabeth died sometime between the date of the will, Feb. 22, 1725, and the date of a codicil made to the will on Jan. 12, 1726. This codicil did not mention his wife, "Elizabeth" but provided "that son James was to give John 5000 lbs. tbco., and to each of his sisters 1000 lbs. tbco. when each of them shall attain their respective ages or Day of Marriage, and if he (James) refuses to comply then land and plantations revert to John."

Mrs. Fowler, after much research, arrived at the conclusion that the name "Occany" derived from the O'CAHANE tribe in Northern Ireland.

Children of Elizabeth (Ocanny) and Thomas Sorrell:

I.   James.
II.   John, m. Judith Heath, who made her will, Feb. 6, 1786, probated Feb. 28, 1786. Her legatees were son THOMAS 40 sh.; son JAMES rest of estate, lands and negroes. (Fothergill-184)
III. Lettice, m. Ambrose Callis. "On Feb. 25, 1730, Ambrose Callis, who intermarried with Lettice, one of the daughters and legatees of Thomas Sorrell, late of the county decd.; not only the said Callis signed in right of his wife, but that all other said children of said decedent may know the rationable parts of their said father's estate." (Id. O.B. 1721-31-p.356) Ambrose Callis died in 1737 and Lettice then married John Wilcocks, who died intestate in Frederick County, 1748. (W.B. 1, p. 176) She had two Wilcocks daughters, one married John Reed and the other William Warren. They moved to Danville, Ky. Lettice married

thirdly, Charles Buck and had two sons, Charles and Thomas Buck. One moved to Woodford Co., Ky., and the other lived near Front Royal, Va. Charles Buck, Sr., made his will in Shenandoah Co., Va., in 1770. His wife survived him.

IV.   Elizabeth, daughter of Thomas and Elizabeth Sorrell, was' mentioned as a godchild in will of John Erwin, dated April 10, 1716, and given two years schooling. (Id.-57) She married Chandler Aubrey, for on May 27, 1740, Chandler Aubrey, "lately intermarried with Elizabeth Sorrell, one of the daughters and legatees of Thomas Sorrell, gent. decd." signed for his wife's part of the estate. (O.B. 1739-43, p. 52, Westmoreland.)

V.   Sarah, m. Francis Atwell for on Dec. 28, 1736, "Francis Atwell, who lately intermarried with Sarah Sorrell, one of the daughters of Thomas Sorrell, gent. decd.", was granted an order for his part of his wife's estate.

VI.   Winifred.

VII.   Ann, m. Samuel Earle. (See later)

John[3] Sorrell (John[2], Robert[1]) brother of Thomas[3] and mentioned in Thomas' will 1726 as "deceased", married "Anne", last name unknown. John Erwin in his will of 1726 mentions his goddaughter "Frances" daughter of John and Anne Sorrell (Fothergill-57); and Thomas Sorrell, in his above will, mentions his nephew, Thomas Sorrell, and his sisters Frances and Elizabeth.

John Erwin's will, dated April 10, 1716, was as follows: ...Godchildren, John, son of George and Ann Sorrell; Frances, dau. of John Sorrell and his late wife Anne; Jemimah, dau. of John and Hannah Aubrey; John son of John and Frances Aubrey; John son of Chas. and Temperance Lucas; Elizabeth, dau. of Thos. and Elizabeth Sorrell, (md. Chandler Aubrey); all to have 2 years schooling each; to Wm. Clark, my overseer; friends John Aubrey and Thomas Sorrell, executors. (Fothergill-57)

Children of Anne and John Sorrell:

I.   Elizabeth.

II.   Thomas, who with his wife, Martha, deeded John Tuberville, Dec. 24, 1772, 186 acres (except family burying ground) on the north side of Nominy mill pond and south side of John A. Washington's mill pond, adjoining land purchased of Mr. John Bushrod from John Sorrell, the said land being inherited by the said Thomas from his father, the said John Sorrell.

III.   Frances.

Ann Sorrell, daughter of Elizabeth (O'Canny) and Thomas Sorrell, married 1726 Samuel[3] Earle, son of Phillis and Samuel[2] Earle of Westmoreland County. Samuel Earle was born in Westmoreland in 1692 and died in 1771 in Frederick County, Va. He was educated at the College of William and Mary and was a member of the House of Burgesses, 1743-44. (B.J. VI-p.83) He was also High Sheriff of Frederick County; Church Warden of the parish in 1751; Major of Col. George William Fairfax's Colonial Regiment and Justice of the County Court. Anna Sorrell Earle died in 1748 and is buried in what is now Warren County near "Greenway Court."

Inscription on Tomb of Anna Sorrell Earle.
Here Lies the Body
of Anna the wife of
Samuel Earle of this County
who departed this Life the 30
day of December A Domini 1748
in the 41 year of Her Age.
She was a Religious, Devout & Godly
Woman, a Loving & Virtuous Wife
and Indulgent Mother, a liberal Mistress
a kind Neighbor, a true Pattern of Goodness
an example to all Her Followers
and by all much Lamented.
I pray to God His Blessing send
All Mortals to make such an End.

Children:

I. Daughter (name unknown) b. cr. 1728, m. Col. Charles Buck.
II. Samuel Earle, b. 1727, m. Miss Perkins.
III. Judge Baylis Earle, b. 1734, m. Mary Prince. (See later)
IV. Col. John Earle, b. June 5, 1737; m. (1) Thomasine Prince, (2) Rebecca Wood. (See p. 366, S.V.F., Vol. 2 for his descendants.
V. Rachel Earle, b. cr. 1740, m. George Neville, Jr.
VI. Hannah Earle, b. cr. 1742, m. Samuel Wilcox?
VII. Lettice Earle, b. cr. 1748; m. Col. John Neville.

Judge Baylis Earle, the son of Anna (Sorrell) and Samuel Earle, was born in Virginia in 1734 and died at Spartanburg, S.C. Jan. 6, 1823. On April 16, 1757, in Frederick County, Va. he married Mary Prince, born in 1744 and died at Spartanburg, S.C. in 1807. She was the daughter of Sarah (Berry) and John Prince. Judge Earle was a Lt. Col. in the Virginia Militia in 1767 (Cartmell) and served in the Revolution.

Children:

I. Sally Earle, b. Jan. 4, 1759; m. (1) Edward Hampton, (2) Chas. Littleton.
II. Samuel Earle, b. Nov. 30, 1760, m. Harriet Harrison.
III. Jack Earle, b. 1762, dsp.
IV. Anna Earle, b. Dec. 24, 1764; m. Ephriam Reese.
V. John Earle, b. Sept. 18, 1776; m. Nancy H. Burns. (See later)
VI. Bayliss Earle, Jr., b. Sept. 11, 1768; m. Anna Mosely Hewlett.
VII. Damaris Earle, b. Jan. 11, 1771; m. Michael Dillingham.
VIII. Rhoda Earle, b. May 25, 1773; m. Benjamin Clark.
IX. Miriam Earle, b. Nov. 4, 1775; m. John William Gowen.
X. Thomas Prince Earle, b. Sept. 16, 1778; m. Mary Stallard.
XI. Edward Hamton Earle, b. Oct. 15, 1789, m. Susan Davis.
XII. Theron Earle, b. March 13, 1783; m. Hannah Miller.
XIII. Asphasia Earle, b. Feb. 21, 1785; m. Mary Montague.
XIV. Providence Earle, b. July 10, 1788; m. John Lucas

John Earle, son of Mary Prince and Judge Baylis Earle,

was born in Frederick County, Va., Sept. 18, 1776 and died
before 1820 on the Wilderness Road between Mississippi and
South Carolina. Before 1790, at Greenville, S.C., he married
Nancy Holland Burns, the daughter of Elizabeth Holbrook and
Joseph Burns, who was born Dec. 4, 1773, in Frederick County,
Va., and died at Pontotoc, Miss., Aug. 8, 1848. John Earle
lived in Virginia, South Carolina, Kentucky, and Mississippi,
and served in the War of 1812 from Mulenburgh, Ky.

Children:

I.   Samuel Earle, m. Polly Clark.
II.   Harriet Earle, m. John Cravens.
III. Ezias W. Earle, b. Feb. 4, 1800; m. (1) Rebecca Clark;
(2) Sally Clark; (3) Isabella Herndon; (4) Elizabeth Mont-
gomery. (See later)
IV. Messenia Earle, m. William Davis.
V.   Ezais Earle, m. Louisa Hamilton.
VI. Benjamin Clark Earle, b. April 1818, m. Elizabeth Lucas.

Ezias W. Earle, son of Nancy Holland Burns and John Earle,
was born at Greenville, S.C., Feb. 4, 1800, and died March
5, 1877, at Charlestown, Ky., he was married four times and
had children by the first three wives. His first wife, Rebecca,
born cr. 1800, had one son, James Earle, who died in 1818.

Children of second wife; Sally H. Clark, b. Mar.13,1794:

II.   Pickens Pulaski Earle, b. Jan. 28, 1820; d. 1823.
III. Rebecca W. Earle, b. August 15, 1821, d. 1823.
IV. Rhoda Ann Earle, b. Dec. 31, 1822, m. Edward T. Wil-
liams.
V.   Baylis Pinckney Earle, b. Oct. 28, 1824; d. 1825.
VI. Talitha Cumi Earle, b. Sept. 13, 1827; m. Dr. P.J.Bailey.
VII. John Leland Earle, b. April 16, 1830; m. Mary Dobyns.
VIII. Martha Henrietta Earle, b. Jan. 12, 1834; m. John Bled-
soe Laffoon.
IX. Amarylis Bomar Earle, b. Oct. 13, 1837; m. (1) Peyton
Nance; (2) Joe Hunter.
X.   Thomas Buck Earle, b. Dec. 2, 1841; m. (1) Mary King;
(2) Elizabeth Cargyle.
Children of third wife, Isabella Herndon, b. July 9, 1802
in Ky., d. 1860 in Mo.
XI. George Robert Earle, b. May 24, 1843; killed C.S.A.
Dec. 2, 1862.
XII. Benjamin P. Earle, b. April 22, 1846; m. Mary Ann
Roberts. (See later)

Dr. Benjamin Prince Earle, son of Isabella Herndon and
Ezias Earle, was born in Robinson County, Tenn., April 2, 1848,
and died in Charlestown, Ky., April 30, 1918. On April 22, 1875,
at Charlestown, Ky., he married Mary Ann Roberts, daughter
of Nancy Jane Jones and Thomas Lynch Roberts, who was born
in Charleston, Nov. 27, 1857, and died there March 25, 1918.
Dr. Earle was educated at the University of Louisville and the
Hospital College.

Children:

I.   Ila Earle, b. April 2, 1876; m. William T. Fowler. (See
later)

II.   Lulu Earle, b. Oct. 26, 1877; m. Ambrose Claude King.
III.   Ezias Roberts Earle, b. March 10, 1880; m. Elise Wright.
IV.   Georgia Isabelle Earle, b. March 8, 1883, d.s.p.
V.   Irbie Benjamin Earle, b. July 27, 1885; m. Frances Mc-
        Kenna.
VI.   Dora Earle, b. March 5, 1888, dsp.
VII.   Thomas Evans Earle, b. March 9, 1890; m. Elinor South-
        gate.
VIII.   Dudley Herndon Earle, b. Sept. 3, 1892; m. Adelaide
        Morgan.
IX.   Amma Nell Earle, b. June 12, 1897; m. Alfred Vernon
        Hall.

Ila Earle, daughter of Mary Ann Roberts and Dr. Benjamin
P. Earle, was born in Charleston, Ky., April 2, 1876, and was
married there on July 8, 1896 to William Thomas Fowler, the
son of Mary Catherine Eison and Daniel Ephriam Fowler. He
was born in Caldwell County, Ky., Oct. 2, 1873, and died at
Lexington, Ky., July 30, 1942. Mr. Fowler was a lawyer and was
educated at Prof. H.H. Boring's Private School in Lexington
and South Kentucky College at Hopkinsville, Ky. Mrs. Fowler
now resides at 215 S. Ashland Avenue, Lexington, Ky.
        Children:
I.   William Earle Fowler, b. Sept. 12, 1897; m. Reba Brown-
        field.
II.   Robert Herndon Fowler, b. Nov. 23, 1898; d. 1899.
III.   George Leonard Fowler, b. Sept. 20, 1900; m. Alice Bur-
        rell.
IV.   William Thomas Fowler, Jr., b. Oct. 9, 1906; m. Mar-
        guerite Madigan.
V.   Daniel Eison Fowler, b. Nov. 20, 1908; m. Louisa Bickel.
VI.   Mary Prince Fowler, b. July 20, 1911; m. A.V. McKenna.
VII.   Benjamin Baylis Fowler, b. Mar. 9, 1916; m. Eleanor
        Randolph.

See Pedigree page 233 V.H.G. for further line of descent to
the Mildmay family. Also to Sorrell chart, ante, taken from
Visitations of Essex, which also connects with the Everard
family. The Mildmay connection with Everard is verified by
Everard pedigree in the Visitation of Essex (Harleian Society,
Vol. 13, p. 193) This shows that Thomas Everard's daughter
Mary married Walter Mildmay of Writtle in Essex. This agrees
with the pedigree of Mildmay which shows that Walter Mildmay
of Writtle , living in 1483, married a daughter of Thomas Everard of Much Waltham (Harleian Society, Vol. 13, p. 290)

Unfortunately, while the Sorrell pedigree, (ante) shows that
Robert Sorrell of Writtle married Mary, daughter of Thomas
Everard of Waltham Magna, there is no confirmation of this in
any of the Everard pedigrees shown in the Essex Visitations.

Since Walter Mildmay, above, was living in Writtle in 1483,
it seems from the Sorrell chart that Mary Everard, wife of
Robert Sorrell, was of a later date, probably a grandaughter of
the Thomas Everard of 1483. On May 16, 1482, Thomas Everard
sold part of the Manor of Langleys, which confirmed her living
at the time of the above date. (Morant 2-86)

It is suggested that the parish registered records of births
and deaths of the Sorrells of Great Dunmow and Waltham Magna,
which are deposited in Chelmsford, be searched. Also the wills
and administrations of this family in P.C.C. and Essex courts
be obtained. Insufficient time did not allow for this search to be
undertaken.

There is a minor mistake in the Mildmay chart, page 233
V.H.G. Sir Thomas Mildmay should be plain "Thomas Mildmay"
and he died in 1547 leaving a will, and not in 1566. It was his
son, "Sir Thomas Mildmay" who died in 1566.

(Continued from Thweatt Family ante)

Thomas Thweatt, who was born April 28, 1782, in Virginia and died there Sept. 21, 1845; married Sallie, the daughter of James Thweatt.
Children:
I.   Lucy Osborne Thweatt, m. Agricola Feild.
II. Archibald Thweatt, m. Sarah Fitzgerald. (See later)
III. Susan Field Thweatt, m. Dr. Fitzgerald.
IV. Sallie Green Thweatt, m. Francis Fitgerald Jones.
Archibald Thweatt, who was born in Virginia Jan. 1810 and died there Aug. 23, 1876, m. Sarah Katherine, daughter of Francis Fitzgerald, who was born in Virginia May, 1814, and died there Aug. 18, 1889.
Children:
I.   Francis Fitzgerald Thweatt, b. 8/28/1837; m. Bettie Baird.
II.   Thomas Fitzgerald Thweatt, b. 3/13/1839; d. 8/20/1876.
III. Archibald Thweatt, b. 9/7/1840; d. 8/27/1878.
IV.   Richard Noble Thweatt, b. 2/7/1842, m. Bettie Green. (See later)
V.   Louisa Jones Thweatt, 8/29/1843; m. A. Theo Powell.
VI.   Sarah Green Thweatt, b. 8/3/1845; d. 8/30/1870.
VII. George Charles Thweatt, b. 4/3/1847; d. 4/2/1872.
VIII. Mary Thweatt, b. 12/11/1849; d. 4/14/1916.
IX.   Frances Thweatt, b. 12/23/1850; m. Chas. H. Zehmer.
X.   John Thweatt, b. 7/28/1853, m. Cora Fox.
XI.   Lucy Katherine Thweatt, b. 10/26/1857, m. Thos. C. Bourdon.
Richard Noble Thweatt, who was born at Dinwoodie, Virginia, 2/7/1842; and died 9/12/1878 at Memphis, Tenn., married 12/22/1869 Bettie Green, who died about 1880. He was educated at Hampden Sydney College, and was a High School Principal.
Children:
I.   Archibald Thweatt, b. 1867.
II.   Willis Thweatt, b. 1871.
III. Richmond Fitzgerald Thweatt, b. 1875, m. Mary Vance. (See later)
Richmond Fitzgerald Thweatt, who was born March 23, 1875 at Memphis, Tenn., and died Oct. 9, 1928 at Chickasha, Okla.; on April 24, 1899, at Humboldt, Tenn., married Mary E., the daughter of Emma James and John David Vance, who was born at Gibson, Tenn., Aug. 27, 1876. Mr. Thweatt was a teacher and Newspaper Editor.

Children:

I.   Vance Thweatt, d. 1912.

II.   Bate Thweatt, d. 1907.

III.   Dorothy Thweatt, b. 1907, m. Bennett M. Bond.

IV.   Richmond F. Thweatt, Jr., b. 1912, m. Viola Mills.

V.   Virginia Thweatt, b. 1915; m. (1) H. J. Brownson; m. (2) Lynn O'Neal.

VI.   C. Harold Thweatt, b. 1910; m. Frances Phelps.

C. Harold Thweatt, who resides at 221 Northwest St., Oklahoma City, Okla., was born at Chickasha, Oklahoma, June 7, 1910; and married Oct. 19, 1946, Frances, the daughter of Carrie Warren and Charles H. Phelps, who was born in Oklahoma City March 21, 1915. Mr. Thweatt is a lawyer, and was educated at the University of Oklahoma.

Children:

I.   John Vance Thweatt, b. 8/22/1948.

II.   Richard Russell Thweatt, b. 12/2/1950.

HARRIS of CHARLES CITY and ISLE of WIGHT COUNTIES
VIRGINIA

John Harris, born 1588-9, founder of his family was an Incorporator of the Third Charter of the Virginia Company of London and subscribed Ł 37, 10 s. (Brown's Genesis) He was residing in Charles City County, Va., at West and Shirley Hundred on the 16th of February, 1623, with his wife Dorothy and two infants, and near him was Thomas Harris, residing at the Neck of Land in the same county. (Cal. S. P. Colonial, Vol. 1675-76, pp. 64-65.)

In the census taken the 24th of February, 1624-25, John Harris does not show in the census because he was then in England, but Thomas Harris, probably his brother, age 38, and his family were still residing in Charles City County. (Alexander Brown)

We know that John Harris was then in England because the Parish Registers of St. Dunston in the East of Stepney, London, show that on May 1, 1624 "John, sonne of John Harris of Virginia, gent. and Dorothy his wife, borne in the House of Edward Lymbry of Lyme House, mariner, the same day baptized." (New Eng. Gene. Reg. Vol. 46, p. 146-148) He may have returned to England to claim a legacy of Ł 400 given him by his brother William, who died in 1622. The designation of "gentleman" in the Parish Register in 1624 would indicate that he was entitled to a court of arms. All these circumstances tend to show that he was very probably the fourth son of Sir William Harris of Crixe, Essex.

That John Harris was a Member of the Virginia Company is proven by the fact that while he was in London, Sir Peter Courteen wrote him from Holland about some of the Virginia Company's business. (Cal. S. P. Col. Series, Vol. 1675-76.)

"July 4, 1624, Sir Peter Courteen to John Harris. About the sale of Va. tbco. Thanks him for his pains taken in the Va. Business. Tobacco of Va. will now yield no price, the markets are overlaid"." Memo. July 10, 1624. I wrote to Sir Peter to remit to me here in safety".

"June 17, 1625. Sir Peter Courteen to John Harris. Desires him to procure patent upon some of the Company's name, John Powell to have leave to sail and bring victuals unto the Plantation of Va. which would be to the company's profit." "Memo. answered June 26, that the Virginia Company was moved but could not prevail in regard they are afraid he should go to the West Indies."

He returned to Virginia and was residing in the corporation of Charles City in 1626, where he had 200 acres planted. (Hot. Imm. p. 268) This was the same John Harris because the records show that he had a wife and daughter, both named Dorothy. (Va. Mag. Vol. 25, p. 343) He was a Burgess for Shirley Hundred Main, 1527-30. (Burgess Journals)

John Harris died in Charles City County before Oct. 14, 1638, for on that date Francis Derrick makes a bill of sale to Richard Johnson as follows: "Whereas John Baker and Dorothy his wife, daughter of the late deceased Serjeant John Harris, have by order of Court at Henrico the 27th day of August last, surrendered unto mee, Captain Francis Derrick all right and title which they claim under the dividend of land belonging to the late deceased George Calcott, which was given to the said Dorothy by the last will and testament of the said Calcott as by the surrender in the said court and by the patent and will recorded at James Cittie, etc. (C.P. p. 113)

Dorothy Harris must have married John Baker very young, for she must not have been 18 years old Nov. 20, 1637 when John Baker received a grant of land in Charles City County: "150 acres E. upon Causon's field Cr. N. upon Appamattock Riv., towards the Citty Cr. W. into the main woods & S. up along the Cittie Cr. 50 due in right of his first wife, Pericilla Palmer, 50 acres by deed of gift from his Mother-in-Law Jone Palmer 2 Jan. 1633; & 550 acs. due for his own per. adv. of his late wife Alice, of his wife Dorothy & for transporting 8 persons (ibid. p. 75) It is not known when John Baker died, but he had died before March 10, 1655, for on that date Captain Daniel Luellin received a grant of land in Charles City County "... 270 acres on the head of Sherly Hundred, commonly known by the name of rich Levell.... & S. upon land lately belonging to Sarjant John Harris,.... 270 acs. by pat. dated 26 Oct. 1650; 200 acs. by patent 11 July 1663, 63 acs. purchased of Dorothy Baker, the relict of John Baker, etc. All of which several parcels were ordered to be included in one patent." (ibid. p. 317.) It does not state when Dorothy, the relict of John Baker sold him this land. At this time John Bond owned land in Charles City County. On April 18, 1653, Thomas Cole received a grant of land in Charles City Co. on North side of Ward's Creek, "and on Cross Creek which divides same from John Francis, opposite against John Redishe's land and S.S.W. on Capt. Bond's land". (ibid. p. 314) Dorothy Harris Baker seems to have married Capt. John Bond about this time or a little later. John Bond was born in 1619, for on Aug. 9, 1664 he made a deposition in Isle of Wight County and gave his age as 45. (17C.p.536)

Children of John[1] Harris and wife Dorothy:

I.   Thomas[2] Harris, from all indications, is the child Harris mentions in 1623, born about 1614. married Alice (West?), and died in Isle of Wight County in 1672. (See later)

II.   Dorothy[2] Harris, born 1619. married John Baker and 2nd. Captain John Bond and moved to Isle of Wight. (for Bond children see later). From the records in Isle of Wight

she appears to have been the sister of Thomas Harris.
John Bond sold Thomas Harris a corn mill at the head of
Pagan Creek, Jan. 18, 1663. Wits.: Henry King, Alexander Phillips. Thomas Harris and Alice, his wife, sold
to Major John Bond 190 acres in Isle of Wight comprised
in two patents - land at head of Pagan Creek, one in name
of John Vaser for 150 acres dated Nov. 18, 1635, the
other for 40 acres in the name of Thomas Harris, Aug.
14, 1652. Oct. 20, 1664. Wits.: Henry King, Alice (X)
Phillips. (17C. p. 539) On July 29, 1650 John Bond was
granted land, 670 acres on North side of Rappa. River
in Corotoman River, for transportation of 15 people. (C.
P. 471) On Oct. 14, 1665, John Meredith patented 600
acres..."part of 760 acres granted Major John Bond,
July 29, 1650". (C.P. 530) On Feb. 21, 1663, Nicholas
Cobb was granted 202 acres in Isle of Wight, joining Nicholas Smith and Major John Bond. (C.P. 512)

Evidence of the relationship between Dorothy Bond
and Thomas Harris is the relation of both families to
Richard Sharpe. John Bond left property to Richard Sharpe
in his will, and Dorothy Bond in her will written July 10,
1684 and probated Oct. 9, 1684, made Richard Sharpe
trustee, and also provided that her grandson, William
Watson was to live with Richard Sharpe. (Isle of Wight
Will and Deed Bk. 1, pp. 62 & 239) Thomas Harris, son
of Thomas and Alice, left his daughter, Ann, in care of
Richard and Ann Sharpe.

Captain John Bond was promoted to be a Major of the
Isle of Wight Militia and also served in the House until
1660, with the exception of 1656 when he was sheriff. "In
1656, Major John Bond sheriff of Isle of Wight complains
that the county has been overrated in the list of tithables
by thirty-eight persons amounting to 1,292 pounds of tobacco." (17 V.M. p. 130) Major John Bond was a dissen-
ter of some sort as the Assembly in 1659 expelled him
from his office as Justice in Isle of Wight for his "Schis-
matical tendencies". (17 C. p. 101)

Major John Bond made his will Jan. 6, 1668, probated
3 May, 1669. Leaves son William Bond land where I now
live; son John Bond another tract; dau. Frances Bond,
furniture, etc., wife Dorothy exrtx. Friends Capt. Francis England, Arthur Smith, and Richard Sharpe, overseers,
John Bennett, Thomas, Wm. Cook, Jr.

Dorothy Bond's will was dated 10 July, 1684, probated
Oct. 9, 1684. She left to son, John Bond household goods;
to grandson William Watson a colt; remainder of estate to
be divided between sons William and John Bond and my
grandson, William Watson, Watson to go to Richard Sharpe
and remain until of age, if Sharpe dies to go to two uncles.
Sharpe to give him 2 years schooling. Richard Sharpe and
Geo. Bell, exrs.

Children of Dorothy Bond and John Bond:
1. William Bond.

2. John Bond, m. ------ Bell, sister of John Bell. (ibid
   p. 274) John Bond, in his will of 15 Feb. 1687, probated
   April 9, 1688, leaves to William Manyard 3 cows; to
   to William Watson a bequest, if he die to go to son John
   Bond; to son John Bond all land and property; to John
   Harmon all of wife's clothing. John Bell, my wife's
   brother to be exr. John Bell to live on plantation with
   "my two children, my wife's and my own" and bring
   them up with the estate to learning. If son John die
   without issue, to Will Watson and William Manyard
   John Portis, Reuben Gladhill, Thomas Bowill.

3. Frances Bond, m. John Watson. Children, John Watson; Mary Watson; William Watson mentioned in above
   wills.

III.   John[2] Harris, son of John[1] and Dorothy Harris, born in
       London, May 1, 1624, was living in Charles City County
       in 1664 (Chas. City Rec. 1664-1665, p. 487.) THOMAS
       HARRIS of London and GEORGE HARRIS in Charles City
       County were probably sons of John[2] Harris (John[1]).
       GEORGE[3] HARRIS married Sarah ------; and died in
       Charles City County 1663. "Power of Attorney, 4 Oct.
       1663, Sarah Harris, Administrater of George Harris, de-
       ceased, to Thomas Grendon to collect debts" signed Sarah
       Harris; test. James Minge. (Fleet 13, p. 94) SARAH the
       widow of George Harris, married 2nd. Thomas Stegge,
       Jr., (son of Thomas Stegge who died in 1651) a member
       of the Council 1664, Auditor General, 1664-1670, was a
       brother of Grace Stegge who married John Byrd, father of
       William Byrd, the first of Westover. (V.M. 1, 441) The
       will of Colonel Stegge, Jr.: "Thomas Stegge of the County
       of Henrico, Esqr., in Virginia, 31 of March, 1670: First
       I give and bequeath to my beloved wife for Ornaments for
       her person as a token of my loving remembrance for the
       affection and tender care of me in Sickness and health, all
       her wearing Apparel for her body Whether Silk, Woolen
       or Linnen and all the Rings, Jewels and Bracelets which
       she hath, as also the complete half & moiety of all the
       Plates & all the ready Money in the House, and more, one
       mare named Hocke & her increase from this Time, and
       more one Indian Girl.... to her Executors or Assigns
       for ever. And if she resolve to go for England, my Will
       is that she may have full power to accomodate herself with
       bedding, Provisions & other Necessarys for her Voiage
       without the Contradiction of any person whatsoever, and
       further She's hereby given full power to bestow upon her
       Friends at her departure the Value of 20 lbs. Sterling....
       the sum of one Thousand two hundred Pounds of Good
       Currant Money of England for the more certain sure and
       quicker Payment of which Sum of Twelve Hundred Pounds
       to my said wife or her Assigns. I do hereby order & de-
       sire Mr. Thomas Grendon of London to pay unto my said
       Wife or her order as soon as conveniently. She may after
       his advice received all such Sum or Sums of Money as

are due belonging appertaining in his hands or Custody. etc., etc."

Sarah, the widow of George Harris, married 2ndly, Thomas Stegge, Jr., and as her 3rd Husband, Thomas Grendon. That she married a fourth time is shown by the two following letters written by William Byrd. The first dated Virginia, March 20, 1685, to Perry and Lane, London, says: "Mr. Brain (who hath married Mrs. Grendon) pretends great matters though I cannot conceive what encouragement they have found this year, coming into the Country in Sept. with 30 servants and 1200 pounds worth of Goods". and again on March 31, 1685 "to Father Horsmandon".....All our friends here are in health but poor Coz. Grendon, who dyed at Sea the 10th. Oct. last, and my Aunt was marryed again in about the latter end of Jan'ry to one Mr. Edward Brain, a Stranger to all here but pretends to be worth money, if not the Old Woman may herself.....Capt. Randolph and Myself are Exrs. for the Estate in Virginia, and they are now about to Sue us for the 1500 lbs. Jointure Mr. Grendon made her". (12 V. 405)

Elizabeth, widow of Thomas Stegge, and mother of Thomas Stegge, Jr., married after the death of her first husband, Thomas Grendon, and they were the parents of the Thomas Grendon who became the third husband of the muchly married Sarah above. (V.-1-441) (From "William Byrd Title Book", the Va. Mag. Vol. XLVIII, pp. 31 & 52)

Also from "Wm. Byrd Title Book" (Va. Mag. 50, p. 260): Deed of Lease & release Nov. 26, 1674-Nov. 27, 1674 of Thomas Harris, Cit. & Merchant of London to Thomas Grendon, Jr., of Westover Parish, Chas. City Co., Va. Conveying all that portion of Cawsey's Care in Chas. City Co., Va., containing 1200 acres late in possession of Walter Aston son to Lt. Col. Aston, all which said land & premises except about 300 acres, said Aston devised by will dated February 1666/67 to George Harris of Westover in Virginia, merchant lately deceased; and the other 300 acres was sold by Walter Aston, Jr. in his lifetime, viz. 200 acres to William Edwards and 100 to Mrs. Hannah Hill and afterwards purchased by said George Harris in his lifetime. The lands are bounded south by land of Mary Clerk, alias Shipley, now or late in tenue of Richard Shute; Southwest and west on Aston's Creek and the heads of Shirley Hundred; north and northwest on the lands of Daniel Luellin and the main woods; north east and east on Kimmedys Creek and lands late of Hardaway; which said lands said George Harris died seized and are since descended to his brother Thomas Harris, party hereto, as heir to said George Harris, together with all other lands and hereditaments whatsoever whereof the said George Harris died seized in Virginia.

The conveyance named in these deeds was a general release properly executed to the said Thomas Harris by

Thomas Grendon, Sr., (by power of attorney for Thomas Grendon, Jr. and Sarah, his wife, late wife of George Harris) releasing said Thomas Harris from all action, accounts of Thomas Grendon, Jr., and Sarah, his wife such as Administrators, with will annexed of George Harris or otherwise and also in consideration of 35 pounds lawful money of England. Signed THOMAS HARRIS. Wits.: Simon Simons, Thomas Gower, John Ludwell, Samuel Wilson, Thomas Grendon, Sr., Bartholomew Clements, Gower Ludwell. Proved in Court (General Court?) June 1675 by Capt. Bartholomew Clements that this is the writing by deed of Thomas Harris. Teste: Henry Hartwell, Clerk.

George Harris, brother of the above Thomas Harris, was also a merchant in Charles City County. (Fleet 13, 94-95) George does not appear in the records until about 1664. The land given to George Harris by Walter Aston, Jr., joined the Aston's and Hardaway's and it appears that the Hardaways may be related to the Harrises.

In 1678 administration of the estate of a Thomas Harris, decd., was granted JOHN ECHOLS and JOHN HARDAWAY, jointly, both of the Parish of Westover. Security, Samuel Phillips. Appraiser JOHN TURNER (O.B. 1677-79, p. 184) In 1678, John Hardaway and John Echols appeared in court in behalf of the orphans of Thomas Harris, showing that John Bland stands indebted to them for 400 lbs. tobacco; which payment Madam Sara Bland confirms payment to Major John Stith, guardian of said orphans.

It appears that John Echols and John Hardaway may have married into that family, on account of the given names being similar to the Harris family names. John Hardaway either married Frances Baker, daughter of Dorothy Harris and John Baker, or Frances Harris, an orphan of Thomas Harris.

The children of Frances and John[2] Hardaway were:
1. Dorothy Hardaway, m. Henry Hatcher of Henrico.
2. Edith Hardaway, m. (1) Henry Tyler of York; (2) Pierce of York.
3. John[3] Hardaway, Jr.
4. Sarah
5. Thomas, m. Jane Smith.

IV. Robert[2] Harris in Isle of Wight and Surry Counties may have been a son of Dorothy and John[1] Harris, born after their son John. His son Robert[3] gave mark of his cattle in Isle of Wight on Oct. 8, 1673. (17C. p. 533) Anthony Spilltimber of Surry commenced suit against John Jennings before the Hon. Gov. and Council of State at a General Court at James City in Sept. 1665, in right of Mary his wife and daughter of Robert Harris of Isle of Wight, deceased, and sister unto Martha, daughter of said Harris and late wife to John Jennings, concerning his right to 250 acres of land held by said Jennings Etc., (ibid. p.

551) "Matthew Swan, the ringleader against high taxes...
in 1675 married Mrs. Mary Spiltimber, widow of Anthony
Spiltimber and daughter of Robert Harris...etc. (Col.
Surry, p. 106)

Children of Robert Harris and his wife ------:
1. Robert Harris.
2. Mary Harris, m. (1) Anthony Spiltimber; (2) Matthew
Swan.
3. Martha Harris, m. John Jennings.
(There may have been other children).

Thomas[2] Harris has been placed as the "child Harris", oldest child of John and Dorothy Harris, because of his close connection with Major John Bond and his wife Dorothy who was
doubtless Dorothy Harris. The ages also agree. Thomas Harris
and Dorothy Bond each named their first child John; they appear
to have moved to Isle of Wight about the same time. In 1640,
Thomas Stegg, Merchant, was granted 1,000 acres in Charles
City County, 200 acres of this was formerly granted to Thomas
Wheeler and, later, assigned to Patrick Kannaday, Mariner, by
James Turner and Thomas Harris, assignees and attorneys of
said Wheeler, and by Kannaday to Stegg. Due to order of court
dated Oct. 15, 1640. (C. & P. - 118) Thomas Harris' oldest
grandson, Edward, married Mary Turner, granddaughter of
James Turner of Isle of Wight. When Thomas Harris moved to
Isle of Wight he appears to have left his second son, Thomas,
in Charles City, probably with his grandmother, or uncle. His
oldest son, John, was mentioned in the Isle of Wight records
many times but there was no mention of Thomas until his father
made his will in 1672. In 1664 John, son of John and Dorothy
Harris, and Thomas, exactly right age to have been son of
Thomas and Alice Harris, were in Charles City County. "The
deposition of John Harris, aged 37 years or thereabouts, sworn
and examined this 25 of July 1664 (born 1627), "The deposition
of Thomas Harris, aged 28 years, or thereabouts, sworne and
examined this 25 of July, 1664 (born 1636). (O.B. 1664-1665,
pp. 487, 488). "We underwritten being summoned and sworne for
jurymen to sitt on and view the Corps of George Bollington etc.
Friende Bollington was brought to an untimely end by and acci-
dental fall from an horse 25 d. of S'ber 1664. John Stitch, Rich.
Parker, John Harris, Thomas Harris, p. 21". (ibid, p. 519).
"Thomas Harris three dayes prest to carry Ires ? to the Governor. .0030, p.16" (Ibid p. 511). Before finding the above records Thomas[3] Harris Jr. was placed as born ca. 1636.

Thomas[2] Harris was born ca. 1614 and married Alice West
(?) about 1634. She married, secondly, John Sojourner. Thomas
Harris appears to have been in Charles City County in 1640 and
moved to Isle of Wight after 1650. He received a grant of 40 acres
in Isle of Wight Aug. 14, 1652, at the head of one of the branches
of Pagan Creek, bounded with his own land on the northeast,
Francis Smith on the southwest, Thomas Pritchard on the Southeast, and John Davis on the Northwest: for transferring Peter
Bell. (C. & P. p. 278)

On March 2, 1658, Thomas Harris received 1,000 acres

in Isle of Wight upon a swamp running into the wester.. branch
of Nansemond River, including two Indian fields, for transporting 20 persons, names given but not his own name in the list,
nor any one a member of his family (Ibid, p. 386). This patent
was renewed March 18, 1662 (Ibid, p. 386). On the same day the
above patent was renewed, March 18, 1662, he received 600
acres in Lancaster County, bounding northeast upon a branch
of Corotoman River and upon land of one Hawkes, southeast upon land of Wm. Thatcher, etc. This land was granted to Gervase
Dodson June 4, 1655, and sold, by him, to said Thomas Harris, for 4800 lbs. of tobacco, and cask. Gervase Dodson appointed Francis Hobbs attorney to acknowledge sale. (Ibid, p.
436 & 17th Cen. Isle of Wight, p. 522). In his will 1672 Thomas
Harris left this land in Lancaster County to his oldest son,
John Harris.

John Bond had received a grant on Corotoman River, in Lancaster County, before Thomas Harris bought this land from Gervase Dodson. Both John Bond and Thomas Harris bought land in
Isle of Wight from Francis Hobbs. After the death of Thomas
Harris, on July 22, 1678, "Joseph Bridger, Esq. sells to John
Harris and Thomas Harris, a tract of land formerly sold Thomas Harris, their father, by Capt. Francis Hobbs and his wife,
formerly belonged to Nathan Floyd and to Bridger by escheat -
land in Upper Parish". (17C. p. 581) Joseph Bridger made his
will Aug. 3, 1683, and left to his son William "land granted me
by escheat of 850 acres formerly belonging to Nathan Floyd,
except what is disposed of by me to Francis Hobbs, Mrs. Dor-
othy Bond, and William Blunt" etc. (Will & Deed Bk. 2, p. 250).
"The new members of the House who represented this county in
1653-54 were Daniel Boucher, Francis Hobbs, and Capt. John
Bond". Daniel Boucher made his will Dec. 4, 1667, probated
May 1, 1668. He bequeathed legacies to kinsman Robert Boucher,
Hodges Council, and William and Mary, children of William Hunt."
Mary Hunt married 1st. Robert Edwards and her daughter, Judith
Edwards married Thomas Harris, grandson of Thomas Harris.
Francis Hobbs' daughter, Margaret Hobbs, married John Har-
ris, oldest son of Thomas and Alice Harris. Francis Hobbs wit-
nessed Thomas Harris' will in 1672, and Thomas Harris Jr. wit-
nessed Francis Hobbs' will in 1687. This was Francis Hobbs,
Jr. It is not known when Francis Sen. died.

On Jan. 13, 1663, John Bond sold to Thomas Harris a corn
mill at the head of Pagan Creek. Wit: Henry King, Alex. Phillips
(17th Cen. I. of W. p. 549). Thomas Harris and Alice, his wife,
sell to Major John Bond 190 acres of land comprised in two patents, land at head of Pagan Creek, one in name of John Vaser
for 150 acres dated Nov. 18, 1635, the other for 40 acres in the
name of Thomas Harris Aug. 14, 1652. Deed dated Oct. 20,
1664. Teste. Henry King, Alice X. Phillips (Ibid, p. 539). Thomas Harris sells his mill to Giles Driver Nov. 1, 1667. His wife
Alice also signs. Wit. John Bond, John Hardy. (Ibid, p. 550).
On Feb. 9, 1665/6, Thomas Harris and John Munger were sureties for Mary Davis, Administrator of the estate of Samuel Griffin. (Admm. p. 12). He gave power of attorney to his wife, Alice

Harris, on May 6, 1668. Wit. John Harris (his eldest son), and John Flower (17 C. p. 551). On Sept. 25, 1669, Thomas Harris and Wm. Bressie were sureties for William Yarrett (Admns.- p. 21). On March 2, 1669, he and John Newman were sureties for Lucy Ogborne to settle her husband Symond Ogborne's estate. (Ibid, p. 23). On Oct. 20, 1670 he and John Portis were sureties for Elizabeth Bragg to administer on her husband James Bragg's estate. (Ibid, p. 26). The inventory of the estate of Robert Collier was "presented by Mr. Thomas Harris", recorded Sept. 9, 1670 (Will & Deed Bk. 2, p. 90). The appraisal of the estate of Robert Colier was made Dec. 15, 1670, by Henry Plumpton, James Collins, John Porter, was presented by Richard Sharpe and John Watson. It was recorded Jan. 9, 1670 (Ibid, p. 94). John Bond died before this, and John Watson was son-in-law of John and Dorothy Bond. Evidently Robert Collier was closely connected with Thomas Harris, Richard Sharpe's family, and that of John and Dorothy Bond. Dorothy Bond must have been sister of Thomas Harris and Richard Sharpe married Ann, daughter of Thomas and Alice Harris. John Bond willed property to Richard Sharpe in his will in 1668. Dorothy Bond, in her will dated July 10, 1684, willed that her grandson, William Watson, live with Richard Sharpe, who was trustee of her estate. Thomas Harris Jr. in 1687 willed that his daughter, Ann, was to live with Mrs. Ann Sharpe, and Richard Sharpe, in his will, Jan. 15, 1699, bequeathed to Ann Harris and she was the first one mentioned in his will.

    Thomas Harris made his will in Isle of Wight March 30,1672, recorded June 10, 1672 (W. & D. Bk. p. 111, Bk. 2). He left his eldest son, John Harris, his land in Lancaster County, to sons, John and Thomas, the "land which I now live upon" to be equally divided and requested that each to live upon it. He left to daughter Mary "to be given to her on her wedding day" a silver tankard, a feather bed and furniture, a brass kettle of 16 gallons, 3 qts., three pewter dishes, three plates, six spoons, a cow and calf and two heifers. To "rest of my children"; wife Alice Harris, "whole and sole executrix". He did not mention his daughter Ann, who married Richard Sharpe. She was probably given, the same he gave Mary, when she married. His "loving friends, Major Nicholas Hill and John Jennings to be overseers to this my last Will and Testament". It was witnessed by Francis Hobbs and Lewis Rogers.

    Children of Thomas and Alice Harris: (Other children not mentioned)

I.   John[3] Harris, born about 1636, died in Isle of Wight 1713, married first Margaret Hobbs, daughter of Francis Hobbs, and sister of Francis Hobbs, Jr. Francis Hobbs made his will March 4, 1687, and left Alice Davis; cousin John Davis; cousin Margaret Harris, the daughter of John Harris, and brother John Harris was made executor.(Will & Deed Bk. 2, p. 280). Margaret Harris, wife of John Harris, died Nov. 16, 1687. He married, second, Elizabeth Church. He was over forty years old before his first marriage. After his second marriage he joined with the Quakers and became a very devout member. His family record is found among the Quaker Records of Nansemond County. He married Elizabeth Church "13th day of ye fourth month in ye year 1689".

Children of John Harris and his first wife, Margaret Hobbs:

1. Margaret Harris, b. June 13, 1682
2. Alice Harris, b. June 17, 1685
   Children by his second wife, Elizabeth Church
3. Elizabeth Harris, b. March 15, 1692
4. Isabella Harris, b. April 17, 1695
5. Susannah Harris, b. Nov. 19, 1699
6. Anne Harris, b. Nov. 18, 1702
7. Mary Harris, b. May 12, 1706
8. Martha Harris (Not in Quaker Records, but mentioned in her father's will)
9. Ruth Harris, "daughter of John Harris, died ye 11th of ye 4th Month 1679"

II. Thomas[3] Harris, appears to have married Ann ------ (See later)

III. Ann[3] Harris, married Richard Sharpe, not mentioned in his will probably because he had given her a dowry when she married. Richard Sharpe made his will Jan. 1699, recorded April 9, 1700 (W. & D. Bk. 2, p. 422), and bequeathed to Ann Harris, daughter of his wife's brother, Thomas Harris. His wife predeceased him.

IV. Mary[3] Harris
Other children not mentioned by name in father's will.

V. Edward[3] Harris, m. Martha Hardy (?) See later
Thomas[3] Harris (Thomas[2], John[1]) was born circa 1636 and died in Isle of Wight County 1688. He married Ann about 1661. She predeceased him and her family name is unknown. She had a daughter named Ann, and each of her children had a daughter named Ann. John Harris, uncle of Thomas and closely associated with him in Charles City Co., received a land grant of 500 acres in Lancaster County on Jan. 11, 1661 for transporting ten persons. The first on the list of his headrights was Ann Harris (C. &P. p. 396). She may have been the wife of Thomas. On account of the relationship between Ann's family and the Turners she may be the Ann Harris who made the following petition in Charles City County:

"James Mason lately dying intestate, Col. Edward Hill, High Sheriff to take possession of all personal estate xx Math Tyler and Edward Lowe xxx rightly to Mary, the dau. of Mary Gilly, the late wife of the deceased Mason. Petition of ANN HARRIS shows that a proportion was given by the mother of two orphan girls upon her death bed   The other one by the name of DOROTHY TURNER was the late wife of James Mason (O.B. 1677-79, p. 382) Richard Lygon v. James Mason estate Ed Gilly Jr., claimant in right of his wife Mary given by her father Roger Williams by record appears V. James Mason's estate" (O.B. 1677-79, p. 415) Richard Lygon was a son of Colonel Thomas Lygon and his wife Mary Harris, daughter of Thomas[1] Harris of Henrico.

Thomas[3] appears not to have moved to Isle of Wight until
after his father's death in 1672. His father bequeathed him one-
half of the land on which he lived and requested he live upon it,
and, also, 280 acres which he bought of "the Indian town". Thomas Harris witnessed a deed of William Boddie's April 1, 1677.
He bought 150 acres of land, in Isle of Wight, from Philip and
Sarah Raiford March 4, 1687 (17th C.-p.596). It is interesting to
no e that James Harris, a grandson of Thomas, in Granville
Co., N.C. on Jan. 3, 1753, sold land in Southampton Co., Va.,
that was granted to Philip Raiford. Thomas Harris received a
grant in Isle of Wight of 183 acres in 1685 (Bk. 7, p. 441). Edward Harris, another grandson of Thomas, on June 10, 1746,
sold to John and Daniel Batten 240 acres in Isle of Wight that
was granted to Thomas Harris April 27, 1686 (Deed Bk. 7, p.
326). Thomas Harris witnessed Francis Hobbs' will March 4,
1687, and made his own will March 14, 1687. It was recorded
Oct. 7, 1688 (Will Bk. 2-Part 2, p. 285). He was "sick and
weak" and it was signed with his mark. Edward, his eldest son,
was married, but appeared to be living with his father. He said
in his will Robert Harris was to live with John Fulgham three
years, his son George was to live with John Turner four years,
Martin to remain with his brother, Edward Harris, six years,
son William to live with Bridgman Joyner seven years, daughter Ann to live with Mrs. Ann Sharpe seven years if Mrs. Sharpe
shall live so long, Edward, executor, overseers Mr. John Fulgham and Mr. John Turner. He left to dau., Jane Jones.

Children of Thomas[3] Harris and Ann Harris:

I.   Edward[4] Harris, born about 1663, married Mary Turner,
        daughter of John and ----- (Tomlin) Turner about 1685.
        (See later)

II.   John[4] Harris, born 1665, was living in Isle of Wight in 1711,
        for on March 26, 1711, there was an agreement between
        John and Thomas Harris to divide the land they owned
        jointly - 350 acres to divide - given by patent April 30,
        1685, at the head of Lawn's Creek, and Thomas "not only
        willing to maintain and preserve the brotherly love" be-
        tween them that now is but ever hereafter to themselves and
        posterity to prevent all lawsuits between them and their
        heirs according to the wish of their father expressed etc.
        250 acres of the tract formerly belonged to their father,
        the other surveyed and taken up by said John and Thomas
        and joined. The land on south to belong to Thomas except
        the rents due from Thomas Davis and wife, which is to be
        divided. (D.Bk.2, p. 181 & 182). John appears to have
        moved from Isle of Wight, and is probably the same John
        Harris who was granted land in North Carolina in 1720 at
        mouth of Cypress branch below Edenton, on the sound.
        (Ray- "Old Albemarle" p. 593). They stated their property
        was in Upper Parish of Isle of Wight.

III.   Thomas[4] Harris was born in 1667, for he made a deposi-
        tion in 1692 that he was then 25 years old. (D.Bk. 1, p.
        52). He married Judith Edwards, daughter of Robert Ed-
        wards and his wife, Mary Hunt Edwards. Judith's mother

married, second, Owen Griffen, and third, William Boddie. Proof of his marriage to Judith Edwards is as follows: On Dec. 7, 1758, Mary Harris deeds all her interest in some land to Robert Tynes, "It being the same land that John Saunders purchased of James Bragg, which said land was formerly property of Robert Edwards who died intestate leaving three daughters to whom the said land descended, one of which said daughters intermarried with Thomas Harris and departed this life leaving issue, Benjamin Harris, her son and heir at law, who also departed this life leaving issue the said Mary Harris, party of these presents, his daughter and heir who inherited one third part of this land". Wit. Joseph Bridger, Brewer Godwin, Bartholomew Lightfoot (D. Bk. 10, p. 31 & 32). In 1702 the magistrates and militia of Isle of Wight prepared an address of loyalty to Queen Anne. They stated that they "resented the attempt made upon our Religion, Laws, and Liberty by the late unaccountable action of the French King in owning and declaring the pretended Prince of Wales to be the King of England". This address was signed by the Militia Officers of the county. "Lieutenant Thomas Harris" was one of the names signed. (17C. p. 169). Thomas witnessed his uncle, John Harris' second marriage, to Elizabeth Church. His wife, Judith Harris, witnessed John Harris' will in 1712. Thomas Harris died early in 1712. His estate was appraised by R. Proctor, John Harrison, Philip Wheadon, James Wilson, and was signed by Judith Harris, March 23, 1712. (Will & Deed Bk. 2, p. 556). After his death his widow, Judith Harris, married ------ Clark. Her mother, Mary Boddie, in her will written Jan. 17, 1727, left to daughter, Judith Clark. (Bk. 3, p. 299).

Children of Thomas[4] Harris and Judith Edwards:

1. Thomas Harris, married Hannah ------ and died in 1730. His will was written Dec. 23, 1729, recorded March 23, 1730. (Bk. 3, p. 199)

   Children:

   A. Joshua Harris died in Southampton Co., Va. His estate recorded June 14, 1770. (Bk. 2, p. 324)

   B. Mary Harris

   C. Thomas Harris, born 1729, m. Sarah Lane, dau. of Richard Lane. Moved to Granville Co., N.C., (later Bute & Warren). Jan. 27, 1735 he deeds to Joshua Harris of Southampton Co., Va. "land granted Thomas Harris the elder, pat. dated Mar. 24, 1725; given to Thomas Harris by last will of Thomas Harris Dec. 25, 1729" (Southampton Co., Bk. I, p. 466) He died in Bute Co., N.C. 1770 (Warren Co. Bk. A, p. 136)

      Children:

      a. West Harris
      b. Elizabeth Harris
      c. Solomon Harris

2. Henry Harris, mentioned as brother in Thomas Harris' will in 1729, married Mary Drew, granddaughter of Edward Drew. (Southampton Co., Va., Bk. I, p. 8) See later.

3. Benjamin Harris, married and had a daughter Mary.

IV. Jane[4] Harris, eldest daughter of Thomas and Ann, married ------ Jones, before her father made his will. John Sturdy made his will in Isle of Wight April 14, 1702 and bequeathed to Jane Jones for "her care in looking after me in ye time of my affliction" etc. "to god-daughter, Sarah Jones". John Barrett, William Harris and Mildred Harris witnessed his will. (Will & Deed Bk. 2, p. 444).

Known children of Jane Harris and her husband, ----- Jones:

1. Joseph Jones, was one of the executors of his uncle, Martin Harris' will.

2. J. William Jones, was one of the executors of Martin Harris' will.

3. Sarah Jones, mentioned in John Sturdy's will.

There may have been other children.

V. Robert[4] Harris, son of Thomas and Ann Harris, was born circa 1674, died in Isle of Wight 1740. (Wills & Accounts-1733-1745, Vol. 4, p. 266) His father, in his will, desired him to live with John Fulgham for three years. He appears to have married Ann Fulgham, daughter of Michael Fulgham. (See later)

VI. George[4] Harris, son of Thomas and Ann Harris, born circa 1676. He made his will in Isle of Wight Dec. 15, 1719, recorded Aug. 22, 1720. ("The Great Book"-Bk. 2, p. 47) He married Martha ------. Martin Harris, Daniel Doyle, & John Bowen witnessed his will.

Children of George and Martha Harris:

1. George Harris, m. Elizabeth Hayes (D.Bk. 7, p.231) Sept. 7, 1766, Robert Hayes deeded to Charles, s. of Elizabeth Harris. (W.Bk.8, p.76)

2. Robert Harris, married Jane------.

3. Elizabeth Harris; 4. Sarah Harris; 5. Joseph Harris and 6. William Harris.

VII. Martin[4] Harris, son of Thomas and Ann Harris, under his father's will was to live with his brother, Edward Harris, for six years. He witnessed his brother George's will in 1719. His property fell in Southampton when it was formed from Isle of Wight. He did not marry. He made his will in Southampton Co. Feb. 1, 1747, recorded April 12, 1750. He left to James Harris, son of Edward; Mathew Harris, son of Robert; John Harris, son of Robert Harris; William Harris, son of George Harris; James Harris, son of Robert Harris. Executor, John Dunkley, Joseph Jones, J. William Jones. Witnesses: Catherine Dunkley, Joseph Mounger. At end of will was - "memorandum - it is my desire that James Harris on my giving him my land to make over to his brother Mathew Harris his part of the land given him by his father,

Robert Harris". (Southampton Co. Will Bk. 1, p. 10)

VIII. William[4] Harris, son of Thomas and Ann Harris, married Rebecca ------. He died in Isle of Wight in 1740. His estate was appraised by John Bowin, John Dawson, and Nicholas Williams (Will Bk. 4, p. 308) His family is not traced.

IX. Ann Harris, youngest daughter of Thomas and Ann Harris, was left by father to live with Mrs. Ann Sharpe. Richard Sharpe left to her in his will (Will Bk. 2, p. 422).

Edward[4] Harris, son of Thomas and Ann Harris and grandson of Thomas and Alice Harris, was born about 1660, and married Mary Turner, daughter of John Turner, about 1685. He made his will in Isle of Wight Co., Va., April 27, 1733, probated March 25, 1734, witnessed by Thomas Atkinson and John Harris. He stated he was from Upper Parish in Isle of Wight. He left to son Edward, "land adjoining John Johnson and John Turner, being land which was granted to my father, Thomas Harris; son Jacob, land on the Flatt Swamp of the Meherrin River; sons Nathan and West Harris, the land granted me on the north side of Warwick Branch; son Daniel, daughter Ann; daughter Martha Williamson; son James; wife Mary. Executor, son Nathan Harris. (Isle of Wight, Will Bk. 3, p.391)

His son, Nathan[5] Harris, moved to Brunswick Co., Va., and has been confused with another family of Harris. He married in 1737 Catherine Walton, daughter of Col. George Walton of Brunswick Co. "They had 14 children, first child born 1739 married Rebecca Lanier of Va. in 1760, daughter of Sampson Lanier and Elizabeth Chamberlain (Sampson 3rd child of Thomas Lanier and Elizabeth Washington)". "Thomas, son of Louis Lanier of Bordeaux, France".?(C.S. 71 Harris. N. 315 Va. State Library, Richmond, Va.)

In 1737 there is a deed of gift from George Walton to his daughter, Catherine, wife of Nathan Harris, proved by oaths of Richard Ledbetter, Henry Ledbetter & Wm. Sims; also a deed of George Walton to daughter Mary, wife of Richard Ledbetter (Brunswick Co. O.B. 2, p. 50)

When Greensville County was formed from part of Brunswick, Nathan and Catherine Harris' land fell in it. On July 28, 1788, there is a deed from Nathan Harris of Co. of Greensville, Va., & Katherine Harris, his wife, to Hubbard Harris, 272 acres for natural love etc. that was given to said Katherine by her father, Capt. George Walton (Greensville Bk. I, p.227).

Nathan Harris made his will in Greensville Co. April 30, 1793 as follows-- Sons, Nathan, Walton (See later), Howell, Isaac; grandchildren, Elizabeth Hoard, Harris Colman, Catherine Coleman, Polly Hargrove & John Coleman; daughters, Jane Williams, Elizabeth Allen; daughter Anna and John Patrick; son Hubbard Harris; grandson, Thomas Camp Harris, grandsons (orphans of David Harris), Peter and John Harris. Executors: Howell Harris, Hubbard Harris & Wm. Vaughn Esq. of Brunswick Co. (Will Bk. I, p. 238)

There is an inventory and appraisement of the personal estate of Catherine Harris, deceased, June 20, 1812 (Will Bk. 2, p. 285).

Rebecca Harris made her will in Greensville Co., Jan. 11, 1816 and left to two daughters, Sally Vaughn & Rebecca White & to son, William Harris. Witness: Herbert H. Harris, Asa B. Harris.

Daniel[5] Harris (Edward[4], Thomas[3], Thomas[2]) was born about 1695 in Isle of Wight Co., Va. son of Edward[4] and Mary Turner Harris. He married Jane Jordan from Surry Co., the younger daughter of George and Mary Jordan. George Jordan made his will in Surry May 18, 1718, probated Aug. 20, 1718 (Bk. 7, p. 145). He mentioned sons, George, Arthur, Thomas, James, River, and Charles, and daughters, Mary Anderson and Elizabeth Baley, and said Wife Mary "to maintain my three youngest children". Daniel Harris and Jane Jordan were married about 1725, and moved with Jane's two brothers to North Carolina. Arthur Jordan settled in Northampton Co., N.C., and George Jordan in Granville Co. On Dec. 8, 1743, Benj. Blunt of Isle of Wight deeded to Daniel Harris of Edgecombe Co. 290 acres in Edgecombe on north side of Fishing Creek for 30 pounds (Halifax Co. Bk. 5, p. 335). In 1754 William Bobbitt of Orange Co. sells Daniel Harris of Granville Co. 150 acres in Granville on south side of Little Fishing Creek (Granville Co. Bk. B, p. 453). He received a grant from Lord Granville on March 6, 1760, and another on March the eleventh for 185 acres (Ibid, p. 148). Daniel owned land joining his brother, West Harris, and their oldest brother, Nathan Harris, lived in Brunswick Co., Va., just across the Roanoke River from Daniel and West. There is a deed dated Sept. 12, 1750 between Daniel Harris and West Harris of Granville Co., N.C. and Nathan Harris of Brunswick Co., Va., selling to Robert Murry of Middlesex Co., Va., for 80 pounds, two tracts of land in Southampton Co., Va., left them by their father, Edward Harris, on the south side of Wareck Branch, one tract of 280 acres being given to Daniel Harris by Edward Harris, his father's will bearing date of 27th day of April 1753 and granted to said Edward Harris in 1713; the other tract of 250 acres being left to be divided between Nathan Harris and West Harris (Southampton Bk. 1, p. 84).

Daniel Harris was Captain of the Militia of Granville Co. in 1754. "In Capt. Daniel Harris' Company - 185 men". Five of his first cousins were mentioned as being in his company, Michael Harris, Charles Harris, Robert Harris, James Harris and Joseph Harris. (N.C. R. Vol. XII., p. 369, 374, & Vol. V., p. 592)

Capt. Daniel Harris died intestate in Bute County in 1765 and his wife, Jane Harris was administratrix (Warren Co. Wills - C.R. 15.008, Historical Commission). Jane Harris made her will Dec. 6, 1769 (Warren Co. Will Bk. 1, p. 125). On 9th day of May 1770 an inventory of Jane Harris' estate was presented to Court. Her oldest son, Jordan Harris, was administrator.

Children of Capt. Daniel Harris and his wife Jane Jordan:

I.   Jordan Harris, with his brother, Drury, moved to Georgia.
II.   Mary[6] Harris, born ca. 1740, married Nathaniel Nicholson (See later)
III. Sterling Harris resided in Franklin Co., N.C.

IV.   Sarah Harris, married Sampson Munger
V.   Edward Harris
VI.   Daniel Harris resided in Franklin Co.
VII. Drury Harris moved to Georgia in 1816
VIII. Tabitha Harris married James Walker after 1769
IX.   Britain Harris was member of the General Assembly from Franklin Co., also the House of Commons 1788-97, 1799, 1803-1804

Mary[6] Harris (Daniel[5], Edward[4], Thomas[3], Thomas[2]), oldest daughter of Capt. Daniel Harris and his wife, Jane Jordan, born about 1735, married Nathaniel C. Nicholson about 1760. Nathaniel Nicholson was oldest son of James Nicholson and his wife, Anne Davis, who moved from Surry, Va., about 1752. Both James and his son, Nathaniel, were in the Granville County Militia in 1754. Anne Davis was the daughter of James Davis and his wife, Elizabeth Warren, who was the granddaughter of Thomas Warren who built the famous Warren House. Nathaniel Nicholson died before his father's death. He made his will April 21, 1789, in Warren Co., N.C., probated August Court 1790 (Will Bk. V., p. 172). Mary Harris Nicholson died in 1816. She was executrix of his estate with her son, Brittain Nicholson as executor. On Jan. 8, 1816, Nathaniel and Mary Nicholson's youngest son, with his uncles, is selling land in Franklin Co., to another uncle: Jordan Harris of State of Georgia, County of Green, Jacky J. Nicholson of North Carolina, County of Warren, Sterling Harris of North Carolina, County of Franklin, Drury Harris of Georgia, Daniel Harris of North Carolina, County of Franklin, James Walker and Tabitha Walker of N.C., County of Warren - Parties of the first part - and Herbert H. Harris of N.C., County of Franklin, party of the second part, for land in Franklin County that had belonged to Capt. Daniel Harris. (Franklin Co. Bk. 17, p. 278).

    Children of Nathaniel Nicholson and his wife, Mary Harris:
I.   Harris Nicholson, moved to Sussex County, Va., when quite young
II.   Britton Nicholson, m. Mollie Harris in Warren Co., Apr. 18, 1794, daughter of Michael and Susanna Harris
III.   Alahjar Nicholson
IV.   Urbane Nicholson, married ------ (Mary). He died in Warren Co. 1811.
V.   Lucy Nicholson, married ------- Coleman
VI.   Polly Nicholson
VII. Nancy Davis Nicholson, married Henry Harris in Warren County
VIII. John[7] Jordan Nicholson, born 1775, died in Warren Co. in 1870 at age of 95 years. He was the youngest son of Nathaniel and Mary Harris Nicholson. His family all called him "Jacky John", but, when he was older he signed his name, John J. Nicholson, and when he was old, most every one called him "Uncle Jack". He was a volunteer in the War of 1812, and was stationed at Norfolk, Va. He was under the command of Col. Laughter who was also from Warren County. He did not marry until he was forty-one years old. He married Sallie Rivers Shearin Jan. 23, 1816.

She was only daughter of Gardner Shearin and his wife, Judith Williams. He made his will in Warren County, Feb. 1, 1861, probated 1870. Warren County Bk. 51, p. 24).
Children:
1. Alexander Nicholson, b. Nov. 11, 1816
2. Elizabeth Maria Nicholson, b. April 7, 1819, m. John B. Newsom Nov. 26, 1836
3. Adkin Nicholson, b. Jan. 3, 1822, m. Mary Jane Harris, daughter of James Young Harris and his wife, Nancy Brown, Dec. 11, 1851
4. Nathaniel Nicholson, b. Feb. 20, 1824, m. 1st Amarilla Shearin; 2nd. Jane Pope
5. Mary Ann Nicholson, b. Dec. 7, 1825, died young
6. Sarah[8] Rivers Nicholson, b. July 2, 1829 (See later)
7. John Hyrum Nicholson, b. June 5, 1832, m. Bettie Shearin and resided at the old Nicholson home in Warren County.

Sarah[8] Rivers Nicholson, born July 2, 1829, daughter of John Jordan Nicholson and his wife, Sallie Rivers Shearin, married John Charles Myrick November 19, 1852. They moved to Halifax County and bought a farm one mile from Littleton where they resided until their deaths.
Children:
I.   Thomas W. Myrick, born Aug. 29, 1853, married Dora Freeman Nov. 17, 1875
II.   John Jesse[9] Myrick, born August 25, 1855, married Emma Brown Harris from Macon, Warren County, N.C., October 15, 1879 (See later)
III. William Henry Myrick, born August 13, 1859, married Lucy Lee King Feb. 9, 1887
IV.   Robert W. Myrick, born May 18, 1862; moved to Texas and died unmarried
V.   Fletcher H. Myrick, born October 19, 1866; died unmarried at the home of his nephew, Walter B. Myrick

Emma Brown Harris, daughter of James Henry Harris and his first wife, Sarah Noel Egerton (b. Apr. 24, 1834; d. Feb. 22, 1859) was an only child by his first wife. She was born Sept. 10, 1856, died in Littleton, N.C., July 7, 1927. She married John Jesse[9] Myrick October 15, 1879. He was a merchant in Littleton until his death September 15, 1930. He and his wife were active members of the Methodist Church in Littleton and he was a Steward in the church for many years. He was also active in politics and was County Commissioner for Warren County for about twenty-five years.
Children of John J. Myrick and his wife, Emma Brown Harris:
I.   Walter Blair Myrick, b. July 25, 1880; d. Nov. 9, 1953! m. Eva Glasgow Feb. 6, 1924. He was in business with his father in Littleton for a number of years, and later, worked with Roses 5-10-25 Ct. Stores in Henderson, N.C.
Children:
1. James Egerton Myrick, U.S. Navy; Grad. U.S. Naval Academy, m. Eleanor Hayes of Elkin, N.C. June 18, 1949. They have three children.

      2. Alice Blair Myrick, m. John James June 4, 1947. He
      is an attorney-at-law of Weldon, N.C.

II.   Sarah Myrick, b. Feb. 2, 1882, received her education at
      Littleton Female College, and specialized in art; m. Romu-
      lus B. Parker (Rom) Oct. 18, 1916. He died Aug. 1, 1939
      Children:
      1. Romulus B. Parker Jr., m. Mary Sue Edmondson June
         29, 1945. He is an attorney-at-law at Enfield, N.C.
      2. Walter Myrick Parker, is unmarried and resides with
         his mother in Engield, N.C. He is interested in look-
         ing after the family property and is in the insurance
         business.

III.   Jesse Clarence Myrick, graduated from State College,
      Raleigh, N.C. in Electric Engineering. He was born May
      29, 1885, m. Mary Stuart Egerton of Louisburg, N.C.,
      Jan. 1, 1917. He worked in Panama during the construc-
      tion of the Canal, and later was Superintendent of the Pa-
      cific Locks in Panama. He is now retired and they reside
      in Raleigh, N.C. Have no issue.

IV.   Emma Nelson Myrick, b. Feb. 17, 1888, grauduated from
      Littleton Female College, and taught school for a few
      years. She married Paul Howard Rose Sept. 13, 1911;
      founder of the chain of Rose's 5-10-25¢ Stores. He died
      Jan. 1954. He was a distinguished business and civic
      leader in the Carolinas and Virginia. She resides in Hen-
      derson, N.C., and Virginia Beach, Va.
      Children:
      1. Virginia Rose, died young
      2. Jessie Myrick Rose, m. Lucius H. Harvin II, March
         8, 1938. He is Vice-president of the Rose Chain of
         stores.
      3. Alice Warrick Rose, m. William J. Vaughn Sept. 12,
         1946. He is President of the P.H.R. Cradle Shops
         Corporation. They reside at Virginia Beach, Va.
      4. Emma Thomas Rose, m. John T. Church, Dec. 31,
         1944. He is Vice-president of the Rose Chain of Stores.

V.   Alice Henry Myrick, b. Dec. 17, 1890; m. Howard Brown-
      ing April 8, 1914. He was a Druggist in Littleton, N.C.
      Children:
      1. John Ray Browning, m. Margaret Turner Sept. 24,
         1938. He graduated from Cooper's Union Art School
         in New York. He is now Advertising Manager for the
         P.H.R. Center in Norfolk, Va.
      2. Walter Clarence Browning, m. Lucille White, Jan.
         15, 1949. He is with the U.S. Dept. of Revenue, Rocky
         Mount, N.C.

VI.   Lula Rhodes Myrick, died young

VII. Carrie Winifred Myrick, b. Jan. 13, 1898, is unmarried;
      has retired from teaching, and now resided in Littleton,
      North Carolina

    West Harris, the son of Edward and brother of Nathan, was
born in Isle of Wight County of Virginia, then moved to North
Carolina before the Revolutionary War and settled in Montgom-

ery County. He was a Major in the Revolutionary War at the age of 69 years old. After Peace he represented his fellow Citizens in the General Assembly of the State (N. C. Troops Cont. Line) He died in Salisbury, N. C. His tombstone states: "West Harris born August 13, 1716, and died May 14, 1795, aged 79 years, 9 months and 10 days". Father of six sons named in order of ages: Isham (1741); Turner; Dred (Ethelred); Rowland (1754); West (1756); m. Edith Ledbetter, see later; Arthur (1758); in 1740 he married Mary Turner. His daughters were: Elizabeth; Pricilla; Pattie; Mary (1760); Patience.

West Harris, Jr., son of Mary Turner and West Harris, was born in 1756, died Montgomery County (Wheeler's Historical Sketches of N. C.) Colonel West Harris, son of West Harris - the first and Grandson of Edward Harris, was Member of General Assembly 1797-1799 and 1801-1802 from Montgomery County.

West Harris, Jr., entered the North Carolina Line of the Continental Army as a Lieutenant and notwithstanding his youth, by patriotism, zeal and intrepidity he was advanced before the end of the war to the Rank of Colonel. Notice of his death was published in the "Western Carolinian" August 7, 1826 died at his residence in Montgomery County (at the Gold mines in Bearden Creek of which he was proprietor) North Carolina Troops in the Continental Line" a register of Officers with dates of Commissions made up under direction of the Secretary of State with dates from records in his office Oct. 1884. (Entered 9th Regiment of N. C. Troops in the Continental line - West Harris November 28th 1776, Roster p. 37).

Children of West Harris and Edith Ledbetter: Green; Allen; West; Henry; Absolm; Pinkney; Edity; (1798); Rowland, born 1803 married Jennet Turner.

Rowland Harris, who was born in 1803 in Montgomery Co., was the son of Edith Ledbetter and Col. West Harris, Jr., married Jennet Turner who was also born in 1803 in Montgomery County, N.C. Children were: Elisha, b. Nov. 2, 1828, m. Patience Poole. (See Later); William Harris, b. 1831; Elizabeth, b. 1836; L. T. Harris, b. 1838; Martin, b. 1840; Brittian, b. 1841; Rebecca, b. 1845; T. Preston, b. 1847; Thomas, b. 1851; Claiborne, b. 1853; Rowland B., b. 1856

Elisha Harris, the son of Jennet Turner and Rowland Harris was born in Montgomery Co., N.C., Nov. 2, 1828, and died at Fayettesville, N.C., April 28, 1880. On April 10, 1852, he married Patience, the daughter of Susan and David Poole, who was born in Troy, June 5, 1833, and died at Fayetteville, March 19, 1897. Children: I. Thomas W. Harris, b. Sept. 9, 1853; m. Sara Frances Haywood (see later); II. Sarah A. Harris, b. 1855; III. David Frank Harris, b. 1858; IV. George Washington Harris, b. 1860, m. Lucinda Poole; V. John W. Harris, b. 1862; VI. James D. Harris, b. 1863; VII. Calvin Harris, born 1864; VIII. Jane Harris, born 1865; IX. Mary Harris, b. 1866.

Thomas Wiley Harris who was born Sept. 9, 1853, near

Troy, N.C., the son of Patience Poole and Elisha Harris, died Sept. 17, 1882 at Little Rock, Ark. On Sept. 9, 1873 at Fayetteville, N.C. he married Sara Frances, the daughter of Cecil Susan Green and Moses Haywood, who was born at Troy, N.C. May 14, 1854 and died at Fayetteville, N.C. June 17, 1883.

Children:

I.   Dora Harris, b. May 14, 1875, m. (1) Hooper Averitt; m. (2) Tom Jones.
II.   David A. Harris, b. Jan. 25, 1877.
III. Viola Jane Harris, b. April 30, 1879, m. John A. Johnson. (See later)
IV. Keeney E. Harris, b. Dec. 2, 1881, m. Margaret Pierce.

Viola Jane Harris, daughter of Sarah Frances Haywood and Thomas Wiley Harris, was born April 30, 1879, at Fayetteville, N.C. On July 11, 1894, at Jackson Springs, N.C. she married John Abraham Johnson, who was born July 16, 1866, at Cameron, N.C., and died there July 2, 1938.

Children:

I.   Herman Wiley Johnson, b. Oct. 14, 1900, m. Mary Ann Cameron.
II.   Cleoplas Edward Johnson, died young.
III. Aldon Franklin Johnson, b. Oct. 17, 1905, m. Lucille Thompson.
IV. Alma Frances Johnson, b. Oct. 17, 1905, m. Claude Seawell.
V.   Verna Mae Johnson, b. Aug. 31, m. John Frank Minnick.
VI. Eunice M. Johnson, b. Oct. 6, 1910, m. Wm. Henry Hessick, Jr. (See later)
VII. John Rossewelt Johnson, b. June 20, 1912, m. Lucy White.

Eunice Marguritte Johnson, daughter of Viola Jane Harris and John Abraham Johnson, was born at Cameron, N.C., Oct. 6, 1910. On August 18, 1934, at Washington, D.C., she married William Henry Hessick, Jr. Their present address is 5250 Woodlawn Avenue, Kenwood, Washington 15, D.C.

Eunice Johnson went to a small college in North Carolina and in 1931 went to Washington, D.C.. to study law at the then National University, where she met William Henry Hessick, Jr They were married in 1934 while still in Law School. They both received an LLB degree at what is now George Washington University. Eunice Johnson Hessick was admitted to the District of Columbia Bar, Supreme Court of the District of Columbia, in November, 1939. She gave her services to the Legal Aid Bureau as an attorney during the war. Her husband is now a business executive.

Children:

I.   Sydney May Hessick, b. Feb. 14, 1936.
II.   William Henry Hessick, III, b. Feb. 29, 1940.
III. Frederick Andrew Hessick, II, b. July 14, 1947.

Walton Harris, son of Catherine and Nathan Harris, was born in Brunswick County, Virginia, Dec. 16, 1744, and died in Wilkes County, Georgia. In 1760 he married Rebecca, daughter of Elizabeth Chamberlain and Sampson Lanier; she was born about 1744. Walton Harris was a Captain in the Revolutionary War. (Smith's History of Georgia, p. 160). Their children were: Buckner; Sampson; Joel; Augustine; Edwin; Nathan; Simeon; Walton; Elizabeth; Littleton; Jeptha Vinning, b. April 27, 1782, m. Sarah Hunt. (See later).

Jeptha Vinning Harris, son of Rebecca Lanier and Capt. Walton Harris, was born April 27, 1782, in Wilkes County, Georgia, and died near Marietta, Ga., in 1856. On October 11, 1804, he married Sarah, the daughter of Nancy Martin Carter and Dr. Richardson Hunt, who was a Major in the Revolutionary War. Sarah was born June 15, 1789, and died at Madison, Ga. Jeptha V. Harris was educated at the University of Georgia. He was a lawyer and General of Georgia State Militia. Their children were: James Walton, b. Aug. 1, 1805, m. Martha Watkins, (See Later); William Littleton, b. July 6, 1807; George Hunt; Ann R.; Sarah E.; Jeptha Vinning; Eligah Willis; Rebecca Lanier; Mary Louisa; Eugene Upson; Susan J.; Laura Tallulah.

James Walton Harris, son of Sarah Hunt and Jeptha Vinning Harris, was born in Elbert County, Georgia, Aug. 1, 1805 and died in Columbus, Miss., Nov. 16, 1887. In Elbert County, Georgia, he married Martha, daughter of Susan Daniel and John Watkins, (said to be a Revolutionary Soldier). Martha was born at Lexington, Ga. Sept. 13, 1807, and died at New Orleans Oct. 25, 1898. James Walton Harris was a lawyer, graduated from University of Georgia and lived in Columbus, Miss.

Children:

I.   Susan Ann Harris.
II.   Sarah W. Harris, m. June 13, 1833, m. Thos. B. Bailey. (See later)
III.   Martha Eliza Harris, m. Joel M. Acker.
IV.   Lucy Ann Harris, m. Capt. W. Winston.
V.   William Henry Harris.
VI.   Dr. Jeptha Vinning Harris, m. Mary Perkins.
VII.   Mary Elizabeth Harris, m. Dr. Augustine Lanier.
VIII. James Walton Harris, m. Gertrude Garrard.

Sarah Watkins Harris, the daughter of Martha Watkins and James Walton Harris, was born in Elbert County, Georgia, June 13, 1833, and died at Columbus, Miss. June 12, 1885. On Nov. 11, 1856, at Columbus, she married Thomas Brownrigg Bailey, who was born at Ashville, North Caro., April 15, 1825 and died at Columbus, Miss., March 13, 1883. Mr. Bailey served with the North Carolina troops throughout the War between the States. He was a teacher by profession; graduated from the University of North Carolina, and taught in Georgia, North Carolina, and Mississippi.

Children:

I.   Martha Harris Bailey, b. Aug. 31, 1857.
II.   Sarah E. Bailey, b. Oct. 25, 1858, m. Thos. Wm. Hardy. (See later)
III.   Lucy Winston Bailey, b. Nov. 30, 1867, m. Robert Baskerville Hardy.

Sarah Elizabeth Bailey, daughter of Sarah Watkins Harris

and Thomas Brownrigg Bailey, was born at Columbus, Miss.,
Oct. 25, 1858, and died there Jan. 29, 1936. On June 30, 1881
at Columbus, she married Thomas William Hardy, who was
born in Lunenburg County, Virginia, Nov. 26, 1849, and died
at Columbus, Dec. 3, 1917.

Children:

I.   Martha Ann Hardy, b. Aug. 1, 1882.

II.   Thomas Bailey Hardy, b. Mar. 7, 1884, m. Mary Ita
Sherman.

III.   Lucile B. Hardy, b. Apr. 13, 1888, m. Orman L. Kimbrough. (See later)

IV.   Lunore Hardy, b. Mar. 28, 1891, m. Thomas Carlton
Billups.

V.   James Harris Hardy, b. Dec. 6, 1894, m. (1) Bessie
Hall; (2) Ruth Maxwell.

Lucile Bridgeforth Hardy, daughter of Sarah Elizabeth
Bailey and Thomas William Hardy, was born at Columbus,
Miss., April 13, 1888, where on Nov. 10, 1908, she married
Orman Lanier Kimbrough, who was born at Greenwood, Miss.,
Oct. 20, 1884 and died there Sept. 27, 1949. Mr. Kimbrough
was a lawyer, a graduate of K.M.I. and the University of Mis-
sissippi.

Children:

I.   Orman L. Kimbrough, Jr., b. Dec. 17, 1910, m. Ellen
Norfleet Moore.

II.   Sarah Bailey Kimbrough, b. Aug. 7, 1912, m. Richard
Cunliffe McBee, Jr.

III.   Lucile Southworth Kimbrough, b. Dec. 23, 1914, m. Ray-
mond Eugene Himes.

IV.   Lenore H. Kimbrough, b. Feb. 7, 1918, m. Geo. H. Mc-
Lean, Jr. (See later)

V.   Mary Hunter Kimbrough, b. July 18, 1921, m. Hilliard
Megee Harper.

Lenore Hardy Kimbrough, daughter of Lucille Bridgeworth
(Hardy) and Orman Lanier Kimbrough, was born at Greenwood,
Miss., Feb. 7, 1918; and there, on Nov. 22, 1940, she married
George Hite McLean, son of Helen Ruth Hite and Lee Davidson
McLean, who was born at Winona, Miss., April 3, 1917. Mr.
McLean is a lawyer, a graduate of the University of Mississippi;
he served as a Lieutenant on overseas duty in World War II.
They now live at 405 East Adams, Greenwood, Miss.

Children:

I.   Lenore Kimbrough McLean, b. Feb. 16, 1942

II.   George Hite McLean, Jr., b. Feb. 26, 1944

Edward[3] Harris was a son of Edward[2] Harris and wife Alice,
although not named in Edward's will. He was one of the "other
children" left to the benevolence of Edward's wife. This seems
proven by a deed from John Harris of Isle of Wight, son and
heir of EDWARD HARRIS, decd., to Capt. David Fox for 600
acres patented by Thomas Harris, decd., Mar. 18, 1662 and
Jan. 13, 1674. John Harris, son and heir of Thomas Harris
of Isle of Wight gave Nicholas George a power of attorney to
represent him Dec. 17, 1674. (Lancaster D.B. 1666-82, p.
207, 208; Duval II, p. 59)

Edward[3] Harris died intestate in Isle of Wight. Inventory
worth 9685 lbs. Tbco. was filed by George Hardy, June 9,1677;
appraised by Edward Bechinoe, et. al. Martha Harris, late
wife of Edward Harris, was deceased April 4, 1676. George
Hardy presented an inventory of her estate in ORPHANS COURT
May 1677. The orphans are not named but they and their descendants can be distinguished by the name "Hardy", probably
Martha's name, among their children.

Edward[4] Harris, who had a son named "Hardy" was probably a son of Edward[3] Harris, above. He married Mary Thorpe,
daughter of Timothy Thorpe. (C-M-25; Southampton W.B. 1-
p. 37) She afterwards married Owen Myrick. (Southampton
W.B. 1, p. 37; C-M-36)

Timothy Thorpe made his will in Southampton, legatees as
follows: daughter Margaret, wife of James Bruce; daughter
Mary, wife of Owen Mirick; granddaughter Mary Harris; granddaughter Ann Harris; granddaughter Mary Barham; son John;
son Timothy; son Joseph; daughter Olive Atkinson. Exrs.; John
and Timothy Thorpe; dated Dec. 2, 1750, recorded March 14,
1750/1. Wits.: Edward Harris, Francis Hilliard, Thomas Am-
mon.

Edward[4] Harris made his will Aug. 26, 1739; probated Sept.
22, 1740, as follows: "...to son EDWARD 240 and 140 acres.
to son LEWIS HARRIS land purchased of John Dortch.... To sons
JOEL and AMOS HARRIS 520 acres equally divided, and appts.
Owin Myrick and Timothy Thorpe to divided same...to son HAR-
DY HARRIS the plantation where I live...Negroes to sons when 21,
and daus. MARY and ANN HARRIS. Wife and son Edward Exrs.;
Nathaniel Ridley, Timothy Thorpe. (W.B. 4, I of W. p. 293)

John[4] Harris, son of Edward[3] Harris and wife Martha Hardy(?)
made his will 1st. day of 12th. month 1712; (Quaker); probated
May 25, 1713, as follows: "...to three daus. ISABELL; ALICE;
ELIZABETH, 300 acres formerly given me by Hugh Campbell;
...to Lawrence Brown, when he is free; . . . to wife Mary; at
wife's death her land to 4 daus., SUSAN; ANNE; MARY; MARTHA;
wife exrx.; Mathew Jordan and John Scott, overseers. Wits:
Judith Harris, Wm. Story, Matthew Jordan.
Children:

I.   Isabella, m. Nicholas Fulgham. (C-M-20; W.B. 4, p. 142)
II.   Alice, m. Thomas Fiveash. (C.M. 20; W & D B.2.,p.559)
III.   Elizabeth; IV. Susan; V. Anne; VI. Mary; VII. Martha.

Henry[5] Harris, son of Judith (Edwards) and Thomas[4] Harris,
married Mary Drew, granddaughter of Edward Drew. Henry, together with Jacob Harris and John Person appraised the estate
of Richard Thomas, Nov. 9, 1752. In 1754, not recorded until
1758, Henry Harris, Wm. Person and Jacob Harris appraised
the estate of John Scott. On Oct. 12, 1754 Henry Harris and
Edward Harris appraised the estate of Henry Person. Appraisal
presented by Mary Person, widow. There appears to have been
some relationship between Henry and the Person family.

Henry died intestate. Inventory of his estate was presented
in Southampton in 1755. (Torrence Wills, p. 197). His children
are unknown, but Henry[6] Harris, shown hereafter seems to be

his son, and the "brothers" mentioned in Henry[6]'s will in 1791 may be the children of Henry[5] Harris.

Henry[6] Harris, and Mary Harris his wife, Aug. 7, 1772, deeded Nathaniel Harris land lying in Parish of St. Luke's, south side of Flatt Swamp, 280 acres patented by HENRY HARRIS in 1727. (BK 4-471) This patent of 45 years previously is presumed to be that of his father, Henry[5] Harris. Henry[6] Harris appears often in the records of Southampton until his death there in 1791. He bequeathed his whole estate to his daughter NANCY if she lived to be 21; otherwise whole estate to go to..."the children of my brothers, Benjamin, Hardy, Abraham and Meschalind.

Benjamin[6] Harris, seemingly the brother Benjamin above, was undoubtedly a descendant of this branch of the Harris family for in his will shown below he had a grandson named "WEST" and a son named "HARDY". The first one being the family name of the wife of Thomas[2] Harris, and the second one the probable wife of Edward[3] Harris. Benjamin married Faithy Smith, daughter of Jane and Lawrence Smith. Lawrence and Jane were married before July 16, 1722, when they sold to Wm. Bynum land in Surry which Lawrence had bought Oct. 1717 from Wm. Ham of Lawnes Creek Parish, Surry. (Vol. 1715-50, pp. 316-409--11) Jane may have been the daughter of Francis Riggan (Regan) who in his will dated March 19, 1725/6 in Surry, named wife Jane, daughters Elizabeth, Jane Mary, and Faith.

Lawrence Smith was the son of Nicholas Smith and Elizabeth, daughter of John Flood, Jr. (See Nicholas Smith family, page 371, S.V.F., Vol. I) (See Flood Family V.H.G. p. 303) John Flood, Jr. was the son of Colonel John Flood who served in the House of Burgesses for nearly 22 years. John Flood, Jr. made a deposition in 1652 stating that he was 30 years of age or thereabouts; born in 1622, he died in 1672. (Surry 1652-1670, p. 18) He had at least three children: Elizabeth Smith, Jane Lane, and John Flood, III. On 29th day of the 9th month 1672, John Smith, who married the relict of Luke Mizell, which said Mizell was security for Hezekiah Bunnell, for the estate of John Flood's orphans, petitioned the court (Id. 1671-1684/5 p. 106) Jan. 7, 1672/3 Hezekiah Bunnell presents the surieties for John Flood's estate....John Flood acknowledged to have received from Hezekiah Brunnell, one cow, etc., it being the whole of what estate the above said Brunnell had by order of court belonging to me after decease of my father.

Benjamin Harris made his will July 7, 1771, probated in Southampton County on April 10, 1774, as follows: legacy to son Benjamin with reversion of bequest to grandson West Harris and to his next youngest brother; son Absalom; son Hardy, a tract bought of John Person, with reversion of bequest to son Michael, the said son to have also the land bought of Jesse Boykin; wife Fathey Harris. My estate is to be divided by my friends, Joseph Smith, William Blunt and John Blunt; daughter Mary; son Absalom. Exs.: wife and son Absalom Harris. Wits.: William Blunt, Joseph Smith, Will Harris. By this will his children were: ABSALOM, m. (1) Elizabeth Tarver, (2) Clara Jeter (See later); BENJAMIN; HARDY; MICHAEL; and MARY.

Absalom Harris, son of Faithy and Benjamin Harris, was born at Southampton, Va., May 27, 1752, and died in Hancock County, Georgia, Nov. 9, 1824. In Southampton he married Dec. 21, 1774, Elizabeth, the widow Jordan, and daughter of Andrew Tarver (will, Northampton Co., N.C. March 1780), who died between 1783 and 1784 in Greenville County, Va. Later Absalom married Clara Jeter.

Children of Elizabeth and Absalom Harris:

I. Benjamin Harris, b. Dec. 7, 1775, m. Mary Rosser.
II. Rebecca Harris, b. March 28, 1777, m. (1) Joel Reese, (2) Joseph Turner
III. Elizabeth Harris, b. Feb. 15, 1779, m. Wiley R. Blount.
IV. Henry Harris, b. May 15, 1781, m. (1) Mary E. Harris, (2) Mary Sasnett (See later).
V. Dorothy, b. Jan. 7, 1783, m. (1) Joseph Chappell, (2) Bernard Young.

Children of Clara Jeter and Absalom Harris:

VI. Edmund Smith Harris, b. Oct. 10, 1786, m. (1) Frances Hall, (2) Mary Hamilton.
VII. Jane Jeter Harris, b. Dec. 30, 1788, m. Chappel Sledge.
VIII. Brittain Dawson Harris, b. Nov. 22, 1794, m. (1) Jane Sanders (2) R. Kirk.
IX. John Griffin Harris, b. June 16, 1797, m. Elizabeth Sanders.

Henry Harris, son of Elizabeth and Absalom Harris, was born May 15, 1781 in Greensville County, Va., and died Dec. 24, 1858 at Greenville, Meriwether Co., Georgia. On Jan. 1, 1807, in Hancock County, Georgia, he married Mary Elizabeth, the daughter of Nancy Evans and Samuel Harris, who was born in Hancock County, Ga., Feb. 18, 1792, and died there Sept. 6, 1817. On Oct. 14, 1818 he married secondly Mary Sasnett, who was born Dec. 8, 1795, and died Feb. 19, 1861.

Children of Mary Elizabeth and Henry Harris:

I. Nancy Harris, b. Nov. 2, 1807, m. John Slaton.
II. Elizabeth Harris, b. Aug. 24, 1809, m. Dixon Hall.
III. Clara W. Harris, b. July 1, 1811, died young
IV. Benjamin T. Harris, b. March 18, 1813, m. Judith A.P. Sasnett (See later).
V. Samuel Wiley Harris, b. May 18, 1815, m. Ann Jackson.
VI. Mary Ann Harris, b. May 29, 1817, m. Richard Phillip Sasnett.

Children of Mary Sasnett and Henry Harris:

VII. Absalom Harris, b. March 10, 1821, died young.
VIII. Sarah Ann Harris, b. Dec. 9, 1823, died young.
IX. Henry R. Harris, b. Feb. 2, 1828, m. Eliza Ann Gresham.
X. William Terrell Harris, b. Nov. 12, 1829, m. Leonora Chambers.

Benjamin Tarpley Harris, son of Mary Elizabeth and Henry Harris, was born in Hancock County, Georgia, March 18, 1813, and died at Sparta, Ga., Feb. 26, 1872. On Oct. 20, 1831, at Sparta, he married Judith Ann Parker, the daughter of Rhoda Henderson, Turner and Joseph Richard Sasnett, who was born in Hancock County, Ga., Jan. 20, 1817, and died at Sparta, Ga., Dec. 23, 1881.

318

Children:
I. Mary Jane Rebecca Harris, b. Nov. 11, 1832, m. Benj. H. Bigham.
II. Louisa Elizabeth Harris, b. Dec. 31, 1844, m. Lavoisier L. Lamar.
III. Ketura Sasnett Harris, b. Aug. 17, 1836, died young.
IV. Josephine Beaufort Harris, b. Nov. 4, 1838, m. Lucius M. McGehee.
V. Henry Harris, b. Oct. 20, 1841, m. Susan A. Williams (See later)
VI. Clara Claudia Harris, b. Sept. 8, 1847, m. David Dickson
VII. Sally Sasnett Harris, b. May 22, 1860, m. Wm. H. Bone, died April 21, 1881.

Henry Harris, son of Judith Ann Parker Sasnett and Benjamin Harris, was born at Sparta, Ga., Oct. 21, 1841, and died there July 29, 1909. On Dec. 21, 1875, at Sparta, he married Susan Amelia, daughter of Martha Jane (Patillo) and Elijah Williams, who was born in Houston County, Ga., June 22, 1849, and died at College Park, Ga., Jan. 20, 1923.

Mr. Harris was educated at Mt. Zion Academy, Hancock Co., Ga; at Emery College, Oxford, Ga.; and graduated 1861 at the newly named Alabama Polytechnical Institute, Auburn, Ala.

Children:
I. Louisa Harris, b. Apr. 1, 1877, m. (as second wife) Lemuel M. Park. (See later)
II. Benjamin Tarpley Harris, b. April 6, 1879, died in childhood.
III. Martha Harris, b. Oct. 12, 1882, unmarried, kindly furnished this data on the Benjamin Harris line.
IV. Charles Henry Harris, b. Sept. 28, 1884.
V. Emory Harris, b. Jan. 1, 1888, died in childhood.

Louisa Harris Park, daughter of Judith Ann Parker Sasnett and Henry Harris, was born at Sparta, Ga., April 1, 1877 and died in Atlanta, Ga., Oct. 19, 1947. On July 15, 1894, at Atlanta, she married as his second wife, Lemuel Madison Park, son of Sarah Truly Robertson, b. March 19, 1805, died Oct. 28, 1882, m. Oct. 25, 1827 John Park, b. Jan. 24, 1800, Jackson Co., Ga., died Sept. 8, 1849, at Greenville, Ga. Lemuel Madison Park was born at Greenville, Ga., Nov. 16, 1846, and died at Atlanta, Nov. 19, 1916.

Mrs. Park was educated at La Grange Female College, La Grange, Ga., and lived at La Grange and Atlanta, Georgia.

Children:
I. Harold Harris Park, b. La Grange, Ga., Jan. 29, 1897, m. Eilee Maloney. Enlisted in World War I, Aug 28, 1918. Assigned Co. M. and Inf. Replacement Reg., Camp Gordon, Ga. Appointed Corporal Nov. 1, 1918, later transferred to 4th Co. 1st. Convalescent Battallion, Gordon, Ga., from which discharged Mar. 6, 1919.
Children: Mary Louise Park; Arthur Joseph Park, who enlisted in U.S. Air Force Reserves National Guard in 1948; activated 1950; and separated June 21, 1952, after

serving 53th. Wing, 137th. Fighter Bomber Squadron.

II. Arthur Harris Park, b. La Grange, Ga. Feb. 13, 1899, m. Rebecca Leland. Enlisted in World War I, June 5, 1918. Trained at Plattsburg, N.Y. and at 19 was commissioned 2nd. Lieutenant, Sept. 16, 1918. Discharged Dec. 22, 1918. After the War he was a charter member of the Governor's Horse Guards; Commissioned 2nd. Lieutenant Cavalry Reserve, Nov. 1923; 1st. Lieutenant, C.R. Oct. 1926; further advanced to Captain and Major. Called into active service 1940 for a year of administrative duties at Camp Clayborn, La. Recalled in May 1942, served 31 months commanding 603rd., and 650th. Tank Destroyer Artillery Battallions and 425th. Armored Field Artillery. Graduate of advanced course of Cavalry School Acting Hq. Commandant 37th. Army Corps; separated March, 1945. Child: Leland Madison Park.

III. Madison Lemuel Park, b. College Park, Dec. 6, 1902, d.s.p. July 1, 1922.

Harris Line from Charles Harris

Charles Harris (Robert, Thomas, Thomas) was son of Robert Harris and his wife Ann Fulgham. He was born in Isle of Wight County, Va., about 1722, moved with his brothers to Granville County, N.C. before 1750, the part of Granville that became Bute County in 1764, and Warren, in 1779. He married Rachel Egerton (b. June 9, 1732, d. 1823) in 1749. She was oldest daughter of John Egerton and Elizabeth (Nicholson) Egerton. He died in Warren County in 1791. There was a division of the estate of negroes belonging to Charles Harris, deceased that year. (Warren Co. Accounts of Estates - C.R. 100.024) Rachel Harris made her will in Warren County September 8, 1818, and it was probated at February Court 1823. (Warren Co. Wills-C.R.100.043. p.88). She lived to be ninety one years old.

Children of Charles Harris and his wife Rachel Egerton:

I. Fredrick Harris, born March 25, 1750
II. Sally Harris, b. Feb. 9, 1752, m. James Maeler Jan. 3, 1778.
III. Elizabeth Harris, m. Randolph Bobbitt
IV. Patience Harris, m. John Bobbitt Jan. 16, 1789 (See later)
V. Nancy Harris, m. her first cousin John Judkins Egerton, on Aug. 21, 1798, son of James and Martha (Judkins) Egerton
VI. Charity Harris, m. ------- Cockley.
VII. Priscillah Harris, m. Lenn Kinball
VIII. Bedford Harris, m. Priscilla Lancaster in 1811.
IX. Simon Harris
X. Wilmot Egerton Harris, b. Nov. 13, 1769, m. Coley Morris Jan. 1, 1799.
XI. Cherry Harris, m. William Calclough.

Patience Harris, daughter of Charles Harris and his wife,

Rachel Egerton, born about 1765, married John Bobbitt Jan. 16, 1789.

Children:

I.   Rachel Egerton Bobbitt, born 1800, died 1882, married Jesse Myrick (b. Sept. 7, 1796, d. 1845), son of Charles Myrick and his wife Martha Ray, April 2, 1821.
John Bobbitt and his wife Patience probably had other children.

Children of Jesse Myrick and his wife Rachel E. Bobbitt:

1. Benjamin Myrick, m. Elizabeth Pearson Dec. 24, 1841. Moved to Yellow Bush Co., Tenn.
2. John Charles Myrick, m. Sarah Rivers Nicholson. (See later)
3. Finetta Myrick, m. Thomas P. Gardner March 8, 1848.
4. Lafayette Myrick moved to Tenn. soon after Civil War.
5. Alexander Myrick, died in service in Civil War
6. George Myrick m. Harriet Clements
7. Jesse Myrick killed in Civil War
8. Fletcher Myrick, killed in Civil War
9. Hardy Myrick died while in Civil War
10. Louisa Myrick, m. Capt. John Collins.
11. Robert A. Myrick m. Sallie H. Beckham Jan. 15, 1867.

John Charles Myrick, b. 1825, m. Sallie H. Beckham Jan. 15, 1867. Their son, John Jesse Myrick, m. Emma Brown Harris, mother of Mrs. Romulus B. Parker, Sr.

EXUM of VIRGINIA and NORTH CAROLINA

Richard and Thomas Exum are the ancestors of this well-known and widely spread Southern family. They were probably brothers. The name is also spelled Exam, Exom, Exium in the records. It may have been derived from "Axholm" but there is a tradition in the family that they came from a town named "Exham" in England.

Richard Axom and Thomas Godwin received two grants of land situated on the southside of the Rappannock River on May 22, 1650, now in Essex County, from Sir William Berkeley, Gov. of Virginia. The first one was for 550 acres "beginning at a point called 'Troublesome Point' and running S.S.E. for 320 poles by the main river side and for a breadth of 273 poles unto a marked post standing by the side of a brook called "Axum's Brook", etc. For the transportation of 11 persons among whom were Richard Axom and Sarah Tomblin. (C.P. 197) (P.B. 2-244, 245).

The second patent was for 1000 acres situated on the S. side of Rappa. River in Brecknerk Bay adjoining on and below land of John Landman for the transportation of 20 persons among whom were Thomas Godwin, once, and Sara Tomblin, twice (Id).

Inasmuch as the first grant was for land running down to "Axum's Brook", it is evident that the Axum family was located there prior to the issuance of the grant. We find in a Norfolk County court record dated Jan. 30, 1646, that "John Nansel came into this country with Richard Exam by indenture for three years" (Bk. B-24).

Richard Exum died on his plantation on the Rappahannock River before Oct. 28, 1668, for on the 28th of the 7th month, 1668, Thomas Godwin deeded one half of their joint patent for 1000 acres held by himself and Richard Exum, deceased, to Richard's widow and orphans.

Rappahannock County was divided into Richmond and Essex Counties. Essex was the county south of the river where the Exum and Godwin lands were located. In the Essex records this old assignment or deed of land made in 1668 by Thomas Godwin was as follows: (abstract) "Thomas Godwin send greetings, whereas Sir William Berkeley did grant a patent of 1000 acres on the south side of Rapp'k River unto Richard Exum, dec'd. and me, the said Thomas Godwin, bearing date of May 22, 1650, Now Know Ye that after the s'd Richard Exum, deceased, his widow in behalf of HIS CHILDREN THE ORPHANS to whom the said Exum did give his s'd part of the land, did with my consent make choice of the upper or Westward side of the 1000 acres, and I chose the lower or Eastward side (it being equally divided). I do hereby assign and make over all my right to said land unto Robert Tomlyn (Essex D.B. 3-523).

The two known children of Richard Exum were THOMAS and JEREMIAH EXUM as will appear later. Thomas Godwin moved to Nansemond County where he had patented land in 1652. He was soon followed by the Exums.

That Thomas and Jeremiah were sons of Richard Axom or Exum is proven by a deed shown in "Essex Land Trials, 1711-1716, pp. 44, 48" wherein a law suit, a deed made May 8, 1685 by Jeremiah and Thomas Exum, sons of Richard Exum, to a Mrs. Gouldman of the land inherited from their father was recorded.

On March 24, 1676/7 in Nansemond County Thomas Exum witnessed the will of Thomas Godwin, the joint patentee with his father in 1650. In turn Thomas Godwin Jr. and Mary Godwin witnessed the will of Jeremiah Exum in Isle of Wight Sept. 3, 1712. It appears that there must have been some relationship between the Exums and Godwins because they were associated together in land transactions and witnessed one another's deeds and wills.

Thomas Exum, brother of Jeremiah, appears to have lived either in Nansemond or near the border line between that county and Isle of Wight. On Feb. 6, 1667, he patented 179 acres in Isle of Wight and Nansemond. Thomas Exum and Sarah, his wife, of Isle of Wight County on May 29, 1678, sold to John Ison a parcel of land in the Parish of Chuckatuck containing 179 acres by patent bearing date of Feb. 6, 1667. Wits. Joseph Moody, Thomas Godwin (I. of W. BK 1662-1715, p. 378). Thomas Exum and Edmund Godwin (son of Thomas) were witnesses to a deed of Henry Reeves of Rapahannock to Thomas Godwin of Chuckatuck of 400 acres of land, part of a patent of 600 acres formerly granted Godfrey Hunt and by him conveyed to his deceased father Henry Reeves on south side of Chuckatuck Creek called "Beaver Dam" (170-600).

Thomas Exum was a Justice of the County Court in Isle of Wight in 1692 (So. Hist. Assn. VI-306). He probably died in Nansemond where the records are destroyed as there is no further record of him in Isle of Wight.

Jeremiah[2] Exum, son of Richard[1] Exum of Rappahannock appears to have settled in Isle of Wight before Feb. 17, 1675, for on that date he and Colonel Thomas Godwin were sureties on the bond of Elizabeth Webb, executrix of James Webb's, deceased. (Admn. & probates, p. 39) (C-1-103). Elizabeth Webb appointer her father, Col. Thomas Godwin, her attorney. She married secondly Joseph Woory, nephew of Sir John Yeamans, Governor of Carolina. Joseph Woory died in 1694 and she then married Samuel Bridger who died in 1713 and gave James Webb Jr. a legacy of 20 sh. (17C 427). Elizabeth Bridger, who survived three husbands, made her will in 1718 and gave legacies to granddaughters, Elizabeth and Martha Norsworthy. Her daughter, Elizabeth Webb, was the first wife of George Norsworthy. George married secondly Christian, daughter of Jeremiah Exum. (17C-462). James Webb Jr. was a Captain of Militia in 1700 and died in 1720 leaving sons, Giles and Richard Webb.

On March 10, 1678, Jeremiah Exum was one of the appraisers of the estate of Nathaniel Powell (BK A-172). Also on April 15,

1686, he witnessed the will of Michael McKinnie (Id-254). On Oct. 23, 1689, he and Robert Lawrence and others presented an account of the estate of THOMAS CULLEN (Id-298). Thomas Cullen died intestate and on Oct. 20, 1689, administration was requested by Robert Lawrence, Robert Cooper, and Thomas Sykes (C -1-113) George Green, who had married Jeremiah's daughter, Anne Exum, made Jeremiah and his son, Richard Exum, executors of his will Oct. 8, 1705 (Id-475). Jeremiah Exum was an Associate Justice of the Isle of Wight County Court in 1680-93-94 (17C 1704-5).

Jeremiah Exum and wife, Ann, of Isle of Wight, sold to FRANCIS BRANCH (conveyed by Thomas Luton of N. C. as their attorney) on Jan. 6, 1707/8, 138 acres at the mouth of Mattacommack Creek, bounded on the South East side by land of Nicholas Crisp and on the North West by land of Nathl. Chevin, as may appear by an assignment of Dower from Thomas Cullen of Dover May 23, 1687. Power of Atty. dated Jan. 6, 1707/8. Test Nathaniel Chevin. (Hathaway 1-94) (Book W. Edenton).

It is difficult to understand why Thomas Cullen should make an assignment of DOWER to Jeremiah and wife, Ann. Is "dower" wrongfully interpreted for the word "Dover"? If not, whose dower did Thomas Cullen assign?

Francis Branch and Ann, his wife, on July 15, 1712, deeded the above 138 acres of land "at the mouth of Mattacommack Cr., bounded southeast by lands of Nicholas Crisp, which were formerly the lands of Joseph Gilbert, and northwest by lands formerly John Porter and lately occupied by said Crisp as per deed of Thomas Cullen of Dover, dated May 23, 1678. Wits. Thos. Luton, Henry Bonner (Hathaway- 98).

Capt. Thomas Cullen was a member of the Council and General Court of Governor Peter Carteret which met July 15, 1670 (Id. 135). There is no record of his death in North Carolina. Was the Thomas Cullen who died in Isle of Wight in 1689 the Captain or his son?

Jeremiah is said to have married a daughter of John Lawrence. This is supported by a deed made by Richard Exum and Robert Lawrence under power of attorney from Robert Lawrence Sr. and Jane, his wife. Jeremiah Exum and wife, Ann, Henry Sanders and Richard Taylor to give them authority as their agent to sell "Black Rock" containing 300 acres formerly possessed by John Lawrence Sr. (Hathaway Vol. 1, p. 90). There does not seem to be an exact copy of said deed for in the copy we have, taken from Edenton Book "W", p. 58) the name of Jeremiah and Ann Exum does not appear.

Robert Lawrence Jr. and Richard Exum, under the power of atty. conveyed this land to Col. Thomas Pollack. John Thomas of Nansemond, in right of Mary his wife, daughter of John Lawrence, made a separate deed of his wife's share of the property given by his will dated Jan. 22, 1696 to his daughter, Elizabeth Lawrence, who dying unmarried gave said property to her sister Priscilla (See deed 17C-494). Up to time of going to press this problem has not been solved.

Jeremiah Exum made his will Sept. 13, 1712, probated Mar.

1720. He gave legacies to daus. Elizabeth and Mourning; to dau. Christian land bought of James Collins; to gr.dau. Catherine Scott a negro; to my COUSIN JANE EXUM a cow and calf; to wife plantation where I now live and at her death to daus. Elizabeth and Mourning; personalty including negros to daus. Sarah, Mary, Eliz., Jane, Mourning and Christian. Wits. John Gibbs; Thomas Godwin Jr.; Mary Godwin (G.B. 21)

"Cousin Jane Exum" was the widow of William Exum of Isle of Wight who died in 1700 (See later). "Cousin" in those days usually meant "niece" or "nephew" but it was sometimes loosely used.

Ann Exum, wife of Jeremiah, made her will Feb. 3, 1726/27; pro. Mar. 27, 1727. She gave legacies as follows: to gr. dau. Katherine Godwin a gold ring; to gr.sons, Jeremiah Lawrence and Exum Scott 30 sh. apiece; to gr.son Richard Exum Outland my silver beaker and small chest; to gr.dau. Ann Murphy a negro; remainder to be divided among 5 daus. Mary McKinney, Eliz. Exum, Jane Outland, Mourning Scott, and Christian Norsworthy and a sixth part to children of my decd. dau. Sarah. Son-in-law William Scott, Exr. (W.B. 3-19).

Their children were:
I.   Captain Richard Exum, died unmarried
II.   Mary, m. (1) Oct. 14, 1699 Jacob Ricks, son of Jacob and Katherine Ricks; m. (2) Col. Barnaby McKennie (See later).
III.   Ann Exum, m. George Green and predeceased her parents dying without issue.
IV.   Elizabeth, died unmarried
V.   Jane, m. Richard Outland
VI.   Mourning, m. William Scott
VII.   Christian, m. as his second wife, Col. George Norsworthy.
VIII. Sarah, m. Robert Lawrence Jr.

Thomas Exum, very probably a brother of Richard Exum, together with Thomas Wright bought land from John and Margaret Paine in Rappahannock County Nov. 10, 1656 (Vol. 1-146). On Jan. 1, 1660 for 6000 lbs. of Tobacco Thomas Exum and wife, Ann, deeded to Capt. John Weir all of his right to certain lands conveyed Nov. 10, 1656 to Thomas Exum and Thomas Wright by John Paine and wife, Margaret, which they had acquired from Francis Hobbs (Id-147). This land consisting of 1000 acres on N. side of Rappa. River had been patented by Francis Hobbs, Aug. 20, 1650 (C.P. 196). On Nov. 15, 1653, John Payne patented 940 acres "lying upon the N. side of Pepetick Creek and a creek at the foot of certain white cliffs" which said land had been formerly granted to Francis Hobbs Aug. 20, 1650 and assigned to said Payne. (C.P. 251).

Thomas Wright was a neighbor of Payne for on Nov. 25, 1657 he patented 298 acres on N. side of Rappa. River and on the West side of PEPTICK Creek (C.P. 364). John Payne also patented another tract of 653 acres on N. Side of Rappa. River "beginning at Miles end of land purchased of Francis Hobbs" (C.P. 364).

This is the only record of Thomas Exum and wife, Ann,

found at present time. It seems that he had a son William Exum who first appears on the scene March 24, 1663, when Walter Bunce conveys a servant to William Exum. Wits: ----- Sayer, ------ Budge (Rap. 1-367). In January 1667, Thomas Duke Jr. gives power to William Exum to receive cattle which belonged to his wife, Margaret. (Id Vol. II-136) One wonders if Margaret, his wife, was Margaret formerly the wife of John Payne.

William Exum appears soon afterwards in Isle of Wight County where on Oct. 9, 1667, he served on a coroner's jury which found that Edward Burgess died a natural death. On April 9, 1671, he witnessed a power of attorney made by Wm. Bressie.

Francis Hobbs, after selling his patent of 1000 acres on the Rappahannock to John Payne in 1653 (who sold part of the said Tract to Thomas Exum) preceded William Exum to Isle of Wight County where he was known as Captain Francis Hobbs and represented Isle of Wight County in the House of Burgesses 1653-54 (17C 100). In fact he probably never lived on the Rappahannock but was only engaged in a land speculation for on Jan. 18, 1647, he sold to John Payne a plantation that he enjoyed by lease on the Nansemond River (17C 515).

William^2 Exum on April 29, 1679, "planter of the Upper Parish of Isle of Wight" bought 300 acres from John and Mary Davis on the Main Swamp in Isle of Wight (17C 450). John Payne was a nephew of Captain Francis Hobbs and was given a legacy in the Captain's will probated in 1688 (C-1-41).

On the 9th day of the 9th month 1693 William Exum received a patent for the transportation of nine persons among whom were himself, Jane his wife, Francis his son, and Samuel Browne (BK. 1688-1704-p.8). This must have been for he had been in Virginia for some time. He and his wife Jane purchased the headrights of Richard Holeman for 1230 acres April 1, 1702 (Bk. F-449).

(For more about William Exum and the Exum family see pages 450-458, 17th Century Isle of Wight).

William^2 Exum made his death bed will Dec. 3, 1700, probated Feb. 10, 1701.

Children:

I. Francis, m. Mary -----, who made her will in 1749, probated 1752 (Bk. 5, p. 451). Her legatees were son FRANCIS, dau. ELIZABETH SMITH, daus. OLIVE and ANN WILLIAMSON, dau. Mary Exum Extx. (C II 161).

Francis, her only son, made his will in Southampton April 30, 1753, probated Sept. 15, 1753. His legatees were friend Simon Turner land in Brunswick County, sister ELIZABETH SMITH, nephew EXUM WILLIAMSON, sister ANN WILLIAMSON, sister OLIVE WILLIAMSON, sister MARY JORDAN land in Isle of Wight where she lives. Wits. Joshua Cloud, John Person, John Mundell.

II. William^3 Exum, m. Susannah (See later).

III. Deborah, m. Edward Jones.

William^3 Exum was born in Virginia as he was not among the headrights of his father as was his brother Francis. His widow was Susan or Susannah last name unknown. The Quit Rent

rolls show he held 1400 acres in 1704 in Isle of Wight County.
He made his will April 25, 1720, probated August 22, 1720
(Great Bk. 51).

Children:

I. John[4], m. Elizabeth (See later)
II. William[4], m. Patience Purcell (See later)
III. Joseph, m. Mrs. Elizabeth Jones, widow of Joseph Jones
and dau. of William Kinchen (See later)
IV. Robert, made his will in Southampton County (Bk. 5-469)
V. Ann, m. ------ Williamson and made her will March 14,
1752, probated Feb. 1, 1753, and mentioned the following legatees: sister Sarah Exum, brothers John, William
and Joseph Exum; Cousins Ann Westray, Susannah Atkinson, to Eliza Exum. Exrs. friend Thomas Exum and brother John Exum. (W.B. 6-32; C II 164)
VI. Sarah

John[4] Exum, son of William and Susan Exum, as son and
heir of his father William Exum, joined in a deed with his mother
Susan who released her dower rights (G.B.-382). He moved to
Edgecombe County, N.C., for on Nov. 20, 1752, as "John Exum
of Edgecombe County" he deeded Benjamin Exum 320 acres in
Southampton. He made his will in Edgecombe Jan. 23, 1775,
probated April 1775 (W.B. A-236) (Abstract of Edgecombe Wills,
p. 123, by Williams and Griffin)

Will of John Exum. Jan. 23, 1775. Apr. Ct. 1775.
Son: BENJAMIN, 1/7 of slaves, plantation whereon I live,
purchased of THOMAS BROWN & JOHN BROWN on Swift Creek;
gr.son: BENJAMIN, plantation purchased from JAMES CARTER,
lands purchased from JAMES SPIER, and tract joining CHARLES
PORTER, WILLIAM GEORGE, on Hugh's Marsh, adjoining JOHN
MIALS and WILLIAM KINCHEN; son: BARNEBY, Ƚ 20 Va. Cur-
rency; dau: SARAH MIALS, wife of THOMAS MIALS, 10s; son:
(dec'd) THOMAS - MARY EXUM, widow of son THOMAS, 1/6 of
remainder of estate to be divided between her and her chil. Son
and Exr. ETHELRED; remainder estate divided between son
ETHELRED, gr.son BENJAMIN and daus: SARAH PHILIPS,
MARTHA JOHNSON and ELIZABETH WILLIAMS. Gr. son:
BENJAMIN to pay to his sisters Ƚ 5 cash .... TABITHA EXUM,
MARTHA EXUM Ƚ 5. Exr: son-in-law, JAMES WILLIAMS. Wit:
WILLIAM KINCHEN, ETHELRED PHILIPS, SARAH KINCHEN,
REBRKAH POPE.

Benjamin[5] Exum, eldest son of John Exum, married Martha,
last name unknown. He had an active part in the Revolution. On
Oct. 18, 1775 he was certified as a Lieutenant of the Second
Company of Minutemen (N.C. Col. Rec. Vol. 10, p. 284). On
Nov. 12, 1776, he represented Dobbs County in the First Constitutional Convention of N.C. and signed the Constitution (Id.
10-914). He represented Dobbs County in the Senate Jan. 19,
1779 (Id. 13-532). Wayne County was cut off from Dobbs and
he was made Colonel of the Wayne County militia. He commanded
this regiment in person in the field at the disastrous Battle of
Camden where the regiment suffered heavy losses. This was on
Aug. 16, and 17, 1780 (Vol. 14-423; Vol. 15- 169, 406). On Sept.

3, 1780, his regiment was at Ramsey Mills (Id. 15-174). In 1781 he commanded the Second Regiment of N.C. Militia (Id. 16-1057). His date of death is not known as no will or administration of his estate has been found. His known children were: (1) BENJAMIN; (2) WILLIAM; and (3) MATTHEW; to whom their father deeded land in 1788 (D.B. 4-145) (4) MARTHA; (5) TABITHA who married Benjamin Smith of Wayne County whose daughter Sarah Smith married Bennett Boddie (17 C-45).

William Exum, son of Colonel Benjamin. In an old Bible of the Exum family now owned by -------------- are the following entries:

William Exum, son of Benjamin and Martha his wife, born Oct. 4, 1770

William Exum married to Nancy Moring July 1796. She died Aug. 8, 1805.

William Exum married to Winifred Howe April 3, 1807. She died March 10, 1829.

William Exum married to Abscela Atkinson April 15, 1830.

From here the Bible skips to the children of JESSE EXUM and his wife AMY JORDAN, the birth of whose children is shown as follows:

1 Benjamin Exum born Oct. 25, 1811, m. Sarah Westbrook
2 James Ethelred Exum, born May 2, 1813, m. Martha Sugg (See later)
3 Charlotte Exum, born -- 25, 1814, No descendants.

Since Jesse's oldest child was born in 1811 and William Exum was first married in 1796, Jesse could not have been a son of William. Therefore it seems Jesse was a son of Colonel Benjamin Exum's oldest child, BENJAMIN, who was mentioned in the will of his grandfather John Exum in 1775.

James Ethelred Exum, born May 2, 1813, Greene County, N.C.; married May 14, 1835, Snow Hill, Green County, N.C., Marinda Aldridge Sugg, born Greene County, N.C.; died Feb. 22, 1853, Greene County, N.C., dau. of Josiah Sugg and Elizabeth Aldridge.

Children:

I.   Elizabeth Exum, b. Oct. 26, 1838; m. R. W. Pridgen. No descendants
II.   Amy Jordan Exum, b. March 11, 1841, m. G.F.M. Dail (See later)
III.   Emily, b. Oct. 2, 1842; No descendants
IV.   Anneliza, b. Oct. 26, 1844, died unmarried
V.   Martha, b. Oct. 29, 1846, twin of Penina, died
VI.   Penina, b. Oct. 29, 1846, twin of Martha, m. ----- Hughes.
VIII   Josiah, b. Aug. 20, 1848, m. Martha Sugg
VIII.   John Albert, b. Nov. 9, 1850
IX.   Benjamin Franklin, b. May 4, 1852; unmarried

Amy Jordan Exum, born March 11, 1841, Greene County, N.C.; died April 27, 1923, New Bern, Craven Co., N.C.; married May 25, 1859, Snow Hill, Greene County, N.C., Geo. Francis Marion Dail, born Feb. 20, 1833, Wayne Co., N.C., died April 16, 1893, New Bern, Craven Co., N.C., son of William Dail.

Children:
I.   William J. Dail, b. Feb. 21, 1860; d. 1862
II.   Laura Vance Dail, b. Aug. 12, 1862; m. William Roberts Guion
III.   Albert H. Dail, b. Sept. 27, 1864; d. 1871
IV.   George W. Dail, b. Oct. 8, 1867; d. 1870
V.   Hattie L. Dail, b. Nov. 27, 1869; m. Roscoe Nunn
VI.   George Deaver Dail, b. Oct. 17, 1872, unmarried, d. about 1936.
VII.   Rosa Amy Dail, b. Feb. 7, 1875; unmarried
VIII. Lena Marinda Dail, b. Nov. 29, 1877; m. Milton Wood Warren (See later)
IX.   Jennie V. Dail, b. July 19, 1881; d. Sept. 30, 1886

Lena Marinda Dail was born Nov. 29, 1877, New Bern, Craven Co., N.C.; married Oct. 16, 1902, Snow Hill, Green Co., N.C., Milton Wood Warren, born June 18, 1875, Green Co., N.C.; died Oct. 18, 1935, Raleigh, Wake Co., N.C.

Children:
I.   Elsie Warren, b. July 25, 1903; m. Hal T. Macon (See later)
II.   George Francis Warren, b. Aug. 30, 1905; m. (1) Mary MacRue, (2) Elizabeth Best
III.   Amy Warren, b. Feb. 16, 1910; m. Walter Ra

Elsie Warren was born July 25, 1903, Snow Hill, Green Co., N.C.; married April 28, 1928, Snow Hill, Greene Co., N.C., Hal Thomas Macon, born July 26, 1899, Warrenton, Warren Co., N.C.; died Dec. 3, 1942, Raleigh, Wake Co., N.C., son of Hal Thomas Macon and Kate Shelton Thomas. Hal Thomas was graduated from Graham School in Warrenton, N.C., and N.C. State College. He was a civil engineer, chief right of way engineer for N.C. Highway Comm. He served a short time in World War I.

Children:
I.   Elsie Dail Macon, b. June 13, 1931
II.   Mary Lou Macon, b. Dec. 27, 1936

William[4] Exum (William[3], William[2]) married Patience, daughter of Arthur Purcell and mentioned as his daughter in his will July 1745 (Bk. 5-3). William Exum's land fell in Southampton where he made his will Oct. 17, 1756, probated Jan. 13, 1757 (Bk. 1-210; C - Wills p. 21). His legatees were wife Patience and to her and ten children, JOSEPH, BARNABY, WILLIAM, MOSES, MICHEL, ELIZAH, MARY, ARTHUR (See later), SARAH and PARNELL ROBERT PURCELL EXUM. Exr. son William. Wits: Joseph Gray, Martha Purcell. Patience, wife of William Exum, died before April 1775 when her estate was appraised (W.B. 3-128).

Arthur[5] Exum, son of William and Patience Exum, married October 1769 Mary, daughter of Stephen and Lucy Simmons. This is proven by a suit pertaining to the division of Stephen Simmons estate in Southampton (O.B. 5-199) (C.M. 19). He married secondly about the close of the American Revolution, Elizabeth ------, last name unknown, probably in Northampton Co., N.C., where during the war he procured supplies for the N.C.

troops (Unpublished N.C. Rev. Accts, Book VI, 50-4, Book VI, 91-3, Book IX 111-2). His wife Elizabeth died before Sept. 12, 1805, for on that date he married thirdly, Sarah Davidson in Sumner County, Tenn. (W.B. 1-22). She died in Davidson County about 1820 (Settlement of Exum estates).

Arthur Exum and family moved to Northampton Co., N.C., about 1780 where he was buying supplies for the army. After the war he moved back to Southampton before Jan. 1, 1785, for the gravestone of his daughter, Sarah Exum Reynolds in Jacinto Cemetery, Alcorn County, Miss., shows that she was born in Southampton Co. on that date.

On Feb. 16, 1797 he and his children sold their lands and removed to Sumner Co., Tenn., where he bought 125 acres from John Walker (Indent 25, Oct. 1814, registered Aug. 9, 1815). He died in June or July 1810, his third wife as previously stated died about 1830.

Children by 1st wife, Mary Simmons:

I. Joseph, b. c-1770-1, over 45 in 1829 U.S. Census, Sumner Co., Tenn., in which he, two sons, two daughters, and wife are listed. As Joseph is first of the children to sign deed in Southampton Co., Va., Feb. 17, 1797, he was apparently the eldest surviving child of this 1st. marriage.

II. William, b. c-1772-3, over 45 in 1820 U.S. Census, Sumner Co., Tenn., in which he, 3 daughters, and wife are listed. He was 2nd child to sign deed with father in Southampton Co., Va., Feb. 17, 1797.

III. Elizabeth, b. c-1774-5; m. Adonijah Edwards. She was over 45 in 1820 U.S. Census for Dixon Co., Tenn., in which she, her husband, 3 sons and 1 daughter are listed. She was the third child listed as signing deed with her father in Southampton Co., Va., Feb. 18, 1797.

Children by the 2nd wife, Elizabeth --------;

IV. Mary (Polly), b. c-1782-3; m. (date unknown) William Reynolds. His age is given as 60-70 in 1840 U.S. Census for McNairy Co., Tenn. The same gives Mary's age, seemingly about 10 years short (40-50 is about 10 years too young. She, her husband, two sons (15-20) are listed in this census.

V. John, b. July 4, 1784, in Southampton Co., Va.; d. June 26, 1858, Madison Co., Tenn. (Gravestone and family records); m. March 26, 1814, Martha (Patsy) Hannah, Davidson Co., Tenn. (Marriage Bk. 1, p. 149). They had eight children: 1. Liza, m. a Garland; 2. Minerva, m. a Coz; 3. Rebecca A., m. a Cathey; 4. Martha, m. a Newton; 5. Robert; 6. Felix; 7. John; 8. Joseph.

VI. Sarah, b. Jan. 1, 1785, in Southampton Co., Va. (Gravestone in Jacinto Cemetery in Alcorn Co., Miss.); d. Oct. 15, 1862; m. Josiah Reynolds - c-1806-7 (See later).

VII. Martha, b. Feb. 1, 1787, in Southampton Co., Va.; m. Mabry Walton (See later).

VIII. Rebecca, b. c-1789-1800 (U.S. Census 1830, Davidson Co., Tenn., gives her age 30-40 years; d. probably in Mc-

Nairy Co., Tenn.; m. Nov. 10, 1818, John T. Scott, Davidson Co., Tenn. (Mar. Bk. 1, p. 201); is listed in 1830 census with husband, 2 sons and 3 daughters.

IX. Margaret, b. c-1789-1800. U.S. Census 1840 McNairy Co., Tenn., gives her age 40-50; d. in McNairy Co., Tenn., or Old Tishomingo, now Alcorn Co., Miss.; m. Abner Champion. Census gives his age as 30-40, obviously 10 years too low. Listed in said Census are herself, husband, 4 sons and 2 daughters.

X. Robert, b. July 25, 1798, Sumner Co., Tenn.; d. Dec. 24, 1851, Madison Co., Tenn. (Bible Record), m. Davidson Co., Tenn., Sept. 29, 1823, Eliza, sister of Martha (Patsy) Hannah, who m. his brother John Exum above, b. July 7, 1808, d. Aug. 17, 1877, Madison Co., Tenn. (Bible Records of son, Martin Van Buren Exum, decd.) Children:

1. John F., b. 1/20/1825; d. 1889; m. Nancie Chatham.
2. George Washington T., b. 2/27/1827; d. 1/2/1899; m. (1) Margaret Carolina Watson, 12/13/1854; m. (2) Josephine Langford.
3. James, m. b. 7/9 (or 6, not clear) 1829; d. 5/3/1899; m. Ann Jones.
4. M. E., b. 12/22/1832; died young
5. Joseph W., b. June or Jan.? 12, 1834. Never married; died a prisoner of war at Rock Island, Ill., 12/23/1863
6. Louisa, b. 2/28/1836, never married; d. Jan. 18, 1908.
7. Samuel H., b. 2/28/1828. Never married; d. Feb. 1862 in Civil War.
8. Martin Van Buren, b. 12/25/1839; d. 12/24/1918; m. 12/7/1875, Sarah Moore.
9. Robert Exum, Jr., b. 2/5/1842
10. William Exum, b. 3/1/1844
11. Rebecca Ann, b. Sept. 5, 1847; d. 1/25/1852. Above taken from Bible and other records of Martin Van Buren Exum, dec'd.

XI. Arthur, Jr., b. c-1806, Listed 10-16 in 1820 Census for Davidson Co., Tenn.; m. 12/16/1839, Catherin Taylor, Davidson Co., Tenn.

XII. Patience, b. c-1807. 10-16 in 1820 Census for Davidson Co., Tenn.; d. probably in McNairy Co., Tenn.; m. 1/20/1822, Moses Patterson, Davidson Co., Tenn. (Mar. Bk. 1, p. 253) His age is listed as 40-50 in 1840 Census for Davidson county, Tenn. Listed in 1840 census herself, husband and 1 daughter and 1 female 60-70 probably mother of Patterson. (Certainly not Sarah Davidson Exum, mother of Patience, as she was deceased by early 1830's.)

XIII. Dr. Elijah S., b. 1810 in Davidson Co., Tenn; d. in Cheatham Co., which had been erected in 1856, mainly from Davidson Co., Tenn. He m. (1) July 15, 1835 Sallie Carter, b. 1820; d. 1848 (at birth of only child, William C. Exum, b. May 6, 1848). Elijah m. (2) Elizabeth (Goodspeeds History of Tenn. & Tipton Co., p. 894) Usery, by whom he had two children: Sallie Bettie (Elizabeth) Exum

and Elijah Robert, b. 1855, d. 1907. Sally m. 6/20/1869
Jake H. Judd, Cheatham Co., Tenn., who died in 1949.
Sally is still living. I visited her home May 5, 1955. This
information was kindly furnished by Mr. Roy Watterson
Black, Sr.

Sarah[6] Exum, daughter of Arthur[5] Exum and his 2nd wife,
Elizabeth, who was born Jan. 1, 1785, Southampton Co., Va.;
died Oct. 15, 1862, Jacinto, Tishomingo Co., Miss.; married
probably Sumner Co., Tenn., 1806/7 Josiah Reynolds, b. 1769,
N.C., died 1833, Smith Co., Tenn., son of John Reynolds and
Martha Gay.

Children:

I.   Bluford Reynolds, b. 1808; m. (1) ---------; (2) Sarah
        -------.
II.   Guilford Reynolds, b. June 2, 1810; never married
III.   Mark Reynolds, b. 1812; died young
IV.   Clinton Burke Reynolds, b. Nov. 16, 1813; m. Elizabeth
        J. Robinson (See later)
V.   Lucinda Reynolds b. 1816, m. (1) Isom Herod; (2) Abra-
        ham Ford.
VI.   Arthur Exum Reynolds, b. Nov. 29, 1817; m. Minerva Driver
VII.   Sarah Louisa Reynolds, b. March 18, 1820; m. (1) Alex-
        ander Robinson; (2) James Hollandsworth
VIII.   Josiah John Reynolds, b. July 21, 1823; m. Nancy Louisa
        Smith

Clinton Burke Reynolds was born Nov. 16, 1813, in Smith
Co., Tenn.; died Sept. 27, 1857, Drew Co., Ark.; married
May 30, 1833, Smith Co., Tenn., Elizabeth Johns Robinson,
born Sept. 14, 1814, Smith Co., Tenn., died July 17, 1879,
Jacinte, Prentiss Co., Miss., daughter of Stephen Robinson
and Martha Meador.

Children:

I.   Lafayette Pitt Reynolds, b. March 6, 1834; m. Emma
        James Petty (See later)
II.   Guilford C. Reynolds, b. May 15, 1836; m. Mary Cowan
III.   Sarah Louisa Reynolds, b. Jan. 10, 1839; m. James H.
        Sherring
IV.   Lucinda Minerva Reynolds, b. April 2, 1841; m. William
        H. Miller
V.   Arthur Meador Reynolds, b. Jan. 29, 1843; m. (1) Eliza-
        beth Cole; (2) Sue B. Houston
VI.   Luther James Reynolds, b. July 24, 1845
VII.   Bluford Clinton Reynolds, b. Jan. 18, 1848; m. Amelia
        Moore.
VIII.   Josiah Clinton Reynolds, b. Sept. 21, 1850, m. Josephine
        Chastain
IX.   Martha Frances Reynolds, b. May 29, 1853; unmarried
X.   John Exum Reynolds, b. Oct. 19, 1856; m. Mary Robin-
        son.

Lafayette Pitt Reynolds was born March 6, 1834, Smith Co.,
Tenn.; died July 31, 1911, Booneville, Prentiss Co., Miss.;
married Jan. 2, 1862, Rienzi, Tishomingo Co., Miss., Emma
James Petty, born Sept. 22, 1833, near Pittsboro, Chatham

Co., N.C., died Nov. 21, 1907, Booneville, Prentiss Co.,
Miss., daughter of John Tapley Petty and Maria James Neal.
Mr. Reynolds was a lawyer and served as 1st Lt., Company A,
2nd. Miss. Regiment.
Children:
I.   Mary Jessie Reynolds, b. April 5, 1863; never married
II.   Martha Julia Reynolds, b. April 13, 1865, never married
III.   Henry Davenport Reynolds, b. Aug. 3, 1867; m. (1) Sarah
        A. Jobe, (2) Lillian Glass
IV.   Junius Wesley Reynolds, b. July 19, 1871; m. Nancy Bell
        Jobe
V.   John Burke Reynolds, b. Oct. 10, 1872; m. Elizabeth
        Privett

    Henry Davenport Reynolds was born Aug. 3, 1867, in Jacinto,
Tishomingo Co., Miss.; died Dec. 20, 1936, Livingston, Polk
Co., Texas; married May 12, 1889, Rienzi, Alcorn Co., Miss.,
(1) Sarah Arabella Jobe, born Oct. 8, 1866, Jacinto, Tishomingo
Co., Miss.; died May 10, 1928, Houston, Harris Co., Texas,
daughter of William Franklin Jobe and Milbury Jane Walker. Mr.
Reynolds married (2) Lillian Glass.
        Children:
I.   William Lafayette Reynolds, b. Aug. 18, 1892; m. Marguer-
        ite Hill
II.   James Boone Reynolds, b. May 5, 1894; unmarried
III.   Zilpah Reynolds, b. March 6, 1897; m. Robert C. Gibson
IV.   Patrick Henry Reynolds, b. Feb. 6, 1899; died young
V.   Katherine Bell Reynolds, b. May 1, 1901; has a B.A. de-
        gree from the University of Texas and lives at 4211 Caro-
        lina, Houston 4, Texas
VI.   Bess Jobe Reynolds, b. Sept. 7, 1905
        Children by 2nd marriage:
VII.   H. D. Reynolds, b. 1921; m. Mary Dean Grimes
VIII.   Lillian Reynolds, b. Sept. 24, 1929, unmarried.

    Martha[6] Exum, daughter of Arthur[5] Exum and his second wife,
Elizabeth, was b. Feb. 1, 1787, Southampton Co., Va., d. May 16, 1689
Grey's Cr., Hardeman Co., Tenn., m. Feb. 23, 1809, Goose Creek,
Sumner Co., Tenn., Mabry Walton, b. Oct. 7, 1785, Greenville Co.,
Va., d. July 16, 1851, Grays Creek, Hardeman Co., Tenn. Mr. Wal-
ton was a farmer and landowner. Children:
I.   John Ingram Walton, b. July 4, 1810, m. Elizabeth, dau.
        of John C. Teague (See later)
II.   Elizabeth Tarver Walton, b. Jan. 23, 1812; never married
III.   William Walton, b. Jan. 17, 1814; to Arkansas
IV.   Drewry (Drury) Douglas Walton, b. Feb. 15, 1816; d. s. p.
V.   Robert Harris Walton, b. April 7, 1818, m. Sarah (Ram-
        sey) Kearney (a widow)
VI.   James Monroe Walton, b. June 18, 1820; m. Margaret
        Catherine Teague
VII.   Albert Gallatin Walton, b. Nov. 20, 1822; died young, un-
        married.
VIII.   Joseph Gray Walton Sr., b. June 21, 1825; m. Elizabeth
        •Jane Flynn
IX.   Andrew Jackson Walton, b. March 25, 1828; m. Nancy C.

(Marsh) Smith, widow

X.   Americus Exum Walton, b. May 22, 1830; died aged 8 years, 9 months

John Ingram Walton was born July 4, 1810, Goose Creek, Sumner Co., Tenn.; died 1877, Toone, Hardeman Co., Tenn.; married Dec. 27, 1838, Clover Creek, Hardeman Co., Tenn., Elizabeth Teague, born 1814, N.C.?; died Sept. 15, 1902, Toone, Hardeman Co., Tenn. Mr. Walton was a farmer and landowner.

Children:

I.   Martha Ann Walton, b. Oct. 10, 1839; m. James W. Maroney

II.   Mary Frances Walton, b. Oct. 18, 1840; m. Jesse T. Gibson.

III.   Wesley Monroe Walton, b. Aug. 4, 1842; died aged 4 years

IV.   George Day Walton, b. Aug. 22, 1843; died aged 3 years

V.   Thomas Jefferson Walton, b. Dec. 21, 1845; m. Callie Parker

VI.   Joseph Gray Walton, b. June 6, 1847; m. (1) Henriette Barham, (2) Temperance Ann Ruffin (See later)

Joseph Gray Walton was born June 27, 1847, Bolivar, Hardeman Co., Tenn.; died March 23, 1904, Toone, Hardeman Co., Tenn.; married (1) Jan. 4, 1872, Bolivar, Hardeman Co., Tenn., Henrietta Barham, born Cloverport, Hardeman Co., Tenn.; died Oct. 7?, 1876, Toone, Hardeman county, Tenn. Mr. Walton married (2) Temperance Ann Ruffin.

Children by first wife.

I.   Dolly (Dorothea) Walton, b. Sept. 28, 1872; m. Frederick Pearl Brown

II.   Sarah Frances Walton, b. Dec. 16, 1873, m. James Hardy Black (See later)

III.   Helen Parthenia Walton, b. Sept. 4, 1876; m. Wm. Roberts

Children by second wife:

IV.   William Drake Walton, b. Dec. 29, 1883; m. Maggie Lambert

V.   Tilman Eugene Walton, b. March 14, 1889; m. (1) Elizabeth Robinson, (2) Birdie Cearley

VI.   Ella Mae Walton, b. May 6, 1894; m. Russell Patrick

Sarah Frances Walton, was born Dec. 16, 1873, Toone, Hardeman Co., Tenn.; died Jan. 1, 1945, Bolivar, Hardeman Co., Tenn.; married Feb. 27, 1895, Roone, Hardeman Co., Tenn., James Hardy Black

Children:

I.   Roy Watterson Black Sr., b. March 3, 1896; m. Katherine E. Vincent (See later)

II.   Homer Walton Black, b. Sept. 19, 1898; m. Fanny Hughes Robinson

III.   Roscoe Hardy Black, b. Sept. 22, 1900; m. Novie Garrett

IV.   Ira Wood Black, b. Oct. 9, 1905; m. Lillie Mai Reid

V.   Orien Francis Black, b. Feb. 17, 1908; m. Emodeen Brumblow

VI.   Ethel Maryann Black, b. Oct. 11, 1910; m. Estil Jason Kirksey

VII.   Sarah Gretchen Black, b. March 20, 1915; m. Clyde Glasscock

Roy Watterson Black, of Bolivar, Tennessee, was born Mar. 3, 1896, Toone, Hardeman Co., Tenn.; married Nov. 10, 1921, Bolivar, Hardeman Co., Tenn., Katherine Eugenia Vincent, born July 21, 1897, Middleburg, Hardeman Co., Tenn., daughter of Joseph Hiram Vincent and Helen Eugenia Whitton.

Mr. Black is a retail merchant and part time genealogist. He was in the Kaiser Wilhelm (1st World) War (ASN.2691783) 5/6/1918 to 3/14/1919. Sgt. Instructor in Signal School in U.S. Alderman, Bolivar, Tenn., Jan. 1929-July 1937; Mayor July 1937 to Jan. 1945. Past Pres. Cumb. Presbyterian Educational Endowment Com. Past Com. American Legion, Member Tenn. Hist. Com. Exec. Committee, Member Virginia Hist. Soc., Member Soc. of Genealogists, London.

Children:

I. Howard Vincent Black, Vet. 2nd World War. ASN-14-121,880 b. Oct. 6, 1922
II. Joseph Amos Black, Vet. 2nd World War, ASN-14,205,050, b. Oct. 21, 1926, m. Mary Will Conley
III. Katherine Black, b. Sept. 8, 1934; m. James Norris Bush.
IV. Roy Watterson Black Jr., Vet. Korean Conflict. ASN-AF-25274663, b. March 4, 1936

Joseph Exum, son of William and Susannah Exum, married Elizabeth Kinchen Jones, daughter of William and Elizabeth Ruffin Kinchen, and the widow of Joseph Jones, who died Dec. 5, 1726. She married Joseph Exum prior to 1730. She and her husband moved to North Carolina in 1749. Joseph Exum died about 1770.

Colonel Kinchen Exum, son of Joseph and Elizabeth Kinchen Exum, was born in Virginia. His wife is unknown.

Kinchen Exum, who died near Camden, S.C., in 1819, was the son of Col. Kinchen Exum of North Carolina. He married Margaret Williams, the daughter of James and Dicey ---- Williams, about 1805. Mrs. Margaret Exum married secondly, David Perkins and died in 1840. Their Exum sons were listed in the following order by Mary Ellen Exum (1876-1936):

I. Benjamin Exum, b. 1807, moved to Clark County, Kentucky. (See later)
II. Joseph W. Exum, died in Yazoo County, Mississippi
III. William Exum, died in East Carroll Parish, Louisiana.
IV. James Exum, no information.
V. Edward Exum (1813-57) died in Yazoo County, Mississippi (See later)
VI. Kinchen Exum (1816-67) died in Yazoo County, Mississippi.

Benjamin Exum, born in 1807, eldest son of Kinchen and Margaret Williams Exum, moved to Clark County, Ky., and married Emily Hieronymous, the daughter of Benjamin Hieronymous and his wife, Mary Bush, daughter of Captain William Bush, who came to Boonesboro, Ky., in the company of settlers led by Daniel Boone.

Children:

I. Margaret Lynch Exum, b. 1837; d. April 21, 1927 at the age of 90 and is buried in the Exum lot at Frankfort, Ky.
II. Ann Minerva Exum, m. Cassius Merrill. No children.

III.   Edwin Browning Exum, accidentally fell out of a hotel window while trying to open it and was killed.

IV.   Robert Boggs Exum, Confederate Soldier, m. Bessie Lawrence of Frankfort, Ky. They had one child, Lawrence Exum, who married Lillie Ambrose of Lawrenceville, Ga., and died without issue.

V.   James Kinchen Exum, b. March 8, 1841, Confederate Soldier, was mortally wounded at the Battle of Shiloh and died April 16, 1862.

VI.   Charles Frances Exum, b. Feb. 8, 1851, m. Kathrene Martin Moore, Oct. 28, 1884, daughter of Thomas and Maria Bright Moore of Winchester, Ky. Charles studied law at the University of Virginia. He was a member of the Episcopal Church and a brilliant lawyer. He died Sept. 19, 1942 and is buried beside his wife who died Jan. 16, 1920. Their children were: Thomas Moore Exum b. Aug. 16, 1885 and Margaret Bright Exum, b. Dec. 25, 1889.

Edward Exum, b. April 16, 1813, d. Dec. 20, 1857, 5th son of Kinchen and Margaret Williams Exum, married in 1846 Mary Ann Day born May 15, 1831, d. Aug. 24, 1892, the daughter of Robert and Nancy Mathia Day. He owned a large plantation in Yazoo County, Miss. He and his wife were buried in the Day cemetery.

Children:

I.   Kinchen William Exum, b. April 30, 1848, m. 1875, Susan Virginia Ledbetter, eldest daughter of Richard and Martha Ann Hendricks Ledbetter, and granddaughter of John Middleton Hendricks and his wife Susan Bull.

Children:

1. Mary Ellen Exum, b. July 29, 1876; d. Sept. 13, 1939.
2. Her twin sister, died at birth.
3. Anne Exum, died in infancy.
4. Nannie Day Exum, b. June 27, 1880; m. David Wendell Priestly and lives at Clayton, New Mexico.
5. Richard Ledbetter Exum, b. June 4, 1882, m. Dec. 26, 1926, Lena Melissa Dixon, b. Nov. 18, 1904, daughter of William and Lilly Tucker Dixon of Vaughn, Miss. Mr. Exum attended Mississippi Agricultural and Mechanical College at Starksville, Miss., and owned a large farm in Yazoo County. Children: Lena, b. Nov. 30, 1927; Lilly, b. Nov. 8, 1928; Sue Virginia, b. Dec. 19, 1929; Mary Ellen, b. Jan. 26, 1933; Richard Ledbetter Exum, a girl died in infancy and is buried beside her father in Blackjack Cemetery
6. Sue Virginia Exum
7. Kinchen William Exum.

II.   Wirt Exum, d.s.p.

III.   Robert D. Exum

CHARLEMAGNE LINEAGE OF JAMES G. W. MacCLANROCH
BACK THRU HIS IMMIGRANT ANCESTOR, THOMAS WARREN
OF SMITH'S FORT PLANTATION, SURRY COUNT, VIRGINIA,
AS WORKED OUT BY HIS (JGWM'C) "WARREN LINE" COUSIN,
LUNDIE W. BARLOW. (MR. MacCLANROCH HAS ANOTHER
MATERNAL LINE BACK TO CHARLEMAGNE - THRU HIS
IMMIGRANT ANCESTOR, CAPTAIN CHARLES BARHAM OF
SURRY COUNTY, VIRGINIA.)

Charlemagne, Emperor of the West, died 814, married Hilde-
garde, daughter of Count Gerold:

Louis, Emperor of the West, died 840, married Judith, daughter
of Welf, Duke of Bavaria:

Charles, Emperor of the West, died 877, married Ermentrude,
daughter of Odo, Count of Orleans:

Louis, Emperor of the West, died 879, married Adelaide:

Charles, King of France, died 929, married Eadgifu, daughter
of Edward, son of Alfred the Great, King of England:

Louis, King of France, died 954, married Gerberga, daughter
of Henry, Emperor of Germany:

Charles, Duke of Lower Lorraine, died circa 994, married
Bonne, daughter of Godfrey, Count of Verdun and Ardennes:

Gerberga of Lorraine, married Lambert, Count of Louvain,
died 1015, of the lineage of Charlemagne:

Maud of Louvain, married Eustace, Count of Boulogne, died
circa 1049;

Lambert, Count of Lens, died 1054, married Adelaide, daughter of Robert, Duke of Normandy, of the lineage of Charlemagne:

Judith of Lens, married Waltheof, Earl of Huntingdon and North-
umberland, died 1076:

Maud of Huntingdon, married, secondly, David, King of Scotland,
died 1154, of the lineage of Alfred the Great; married first
Simon de St. Liz, Earl of Huntington (See Chart A)

Henry, Earl of Huntingdon, died 1152, married Ada, daughter
of William de Warenne, Earl of Surrey, of the lineage of Charlemagne, and of Hugh Capet, King of France:

David, Earl of Huntingdon, died 1219, married Maud, daughter
of Hugh, Earl of Chester, of the lineage of Charlemagne, of
Alfred the Great, and William the Conqueror, King of England:
(See also Aston Chart, page 276 V.H.G. with correction on
page x, S.V.F., Vol. 2)

Ada of Huntingdon, married Sir Henry de Hastings of Ashill, died 1250, of the lineage of Charlemagne:

Hillaria de Hastings, married Sir William de Harcourt of Stanton Harcourt, died 1271, of the lineage of Charlemagne and of Alfred the Great:

Sir Richard de Harcourt, of Stanton Harcourt, died 1283, married Margaret, daughter of John, Lord Beke of Eresby:

Sir John de Harcourt of Stanton Harcourt, died 1330, married Ellen, daughter of Sir Eudo la Zouche of Haryngworth, of the lineage of Charlemagne, of Alfred the Great, of Brian Boru, King of Ireland, and of Llewellyn, Prince of North Wales:

Matilda de Harcourt, married Henry Crispe of Standlake, Esquire, died after 1387:

John Crispe, of Kingston, Esquire, died after 1404, married Anne, daughter of William Phettiplace of Kingsey, Esquire:

Henry Crispe of Cobcote, Esquire, died circa 1426, married Joan, daughter of Nicholas Dyer, of Rotherfield, Esquire:

John Crispe of Whitstable, Esquire, died 1475, married Joan, daughter of John Sevenoaks of Sevenoaks, Esquire.

John Crispe of Canterbury, Esquire, died circa 1503, married Agnes, daughter of John Queke of Quex-in-Thanet, Esquire:

John Crispe of Quex-in-Thanet, Esquire, died circa 1534, married Avice, daughter of Thomas Denne of Kingston, Esquire:

Margaret Crispe, married John Crayford (Crafford) of Great Mongham, Esquire, died circa 1535:

Edward Crayford (Crafford) of Great Mongham, Esquire, died 1558, married Mary, daughter of Henry Atsea of Herne, Esquire:

Sir William Crayford (Crafford) of Great Mongham, died 1623, married Anne, daughter of John Norton of London, Esquire:

Anne Crayford (Crafford), married John Warren of Ripple, Esquire, died 1612:

William Warren of Ripple, Esquire, died 1631, married Catherine, daughter of Thomas Gookin of Ripple Court, Esquire:

Thomas Warren of Surry, Virginia, Esquire, died 1670, married 3rd Jane (? Allen):

Allen Warren of Surry, Esquire, married Elizabeth, daughter of John Clements of Surry, Esquire:

Allen Warren II of Surry, Esquire, died 1733, married Anne, daughter of Robert Hart of Surry, Esquire:

Allen Warren III of Surry, Esquire, died circa 1780, married Mary Phillips:

Jesse Warren of Surry, Esquire, died 1794, married Martha:

Jesse Phillips Warren of Surry, Esquire, died 1829, married Sarah Caroline Bell:

338

Lucy Caroline Warren, married William Major West of Surry, Esquire, died 1866:

Samuel Edwin West of Surry, Esquire, married Oceana Winifred, daughter of William Gray Gwaltney of Isle of Wight, Virginia, Esquire:

James Gwaltney Westwarren MacClamroch of Greensboro, Esquire:

Drawn by Lundie W. Barlow

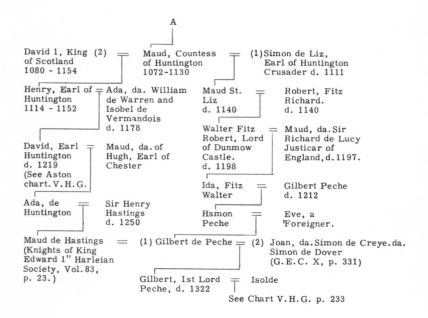

Also in the same chart, Gilbert, first Lord Peche, was not a son of his father's first wife, Maud de Hastings, but was the eldest son of his second wife, Joan, dau. of Simon De Creye and widow of Richard de Dover, Lord of Chilham, Kent. (Inq. P.M. Vol. VI. No. 353. See The Complete Peerage by G. E. Cockayne, Vol. X, p. 336, note "b".) In the pedigree heretofore published by the Harleian Society, it was supposed that the eldest son of Gilbert Peche, d. 1291, had succeeded to his estates, but his eldest son, the son of Maude de Hastings, was disinherited in favor of his eldest son by second wife. This eldest son by second wife who became 1st. Lord Peche had two sons, Gilbert, 2nd. Lord, and Simon, later Sir Simon Peche. (Id. 337 note "e".)

Accordingly a change should be made in the pedigree on page 233, V.H.G. as shown in the new pedigree, above.

BODDIE

An extensive account of this family appears, with citations of authorities, in "Seventeenth Century Isle of Wight". For the purpose of brevity an account appearing in Burke's "Landed Gentry" 1939-40 is repeated. Two new generations have arrived on the scene since "Boddie and Allied Families" was written in' 1918.

BURKE'S LANDED GENTRY 1939 - page 2569

LINEAGE, WILLIAM BODDIE, Captain in the Navy of Henry VIII, sometime stationed at Portsmouth, had two sons.
- I. William, Merchant Tailor of London, d. 1557 leaving two sons,
    - 1. John, of Rayleigh, Essex, d. 1580
    - 2. William, Merchant Tailor of London.
- II. John, of whom presently,

The younger son,
John Boddie, appointed in command of the North Fleet against the enemies of Ireland, 1580, Captain at the Defeat of the Armada, 1588, received augmentation of his Armes from the Queen for his services, 16 July 1589, of two ragged staves with a coronet in a canton, in charge of the Navy Yard at Portsmouth after the defeat of the Armada. He m. Thomasine, dau. of John Mildmay of Cretingham, third son of Sir Thomas Mildmay, Knt., of Chelmsford Co. Essex (see Burke's Peerage, Mildmay, Bar), and was bur. at St. Olaves, Hart Street, London, 22 May 1591. He had issue,
- 1. Anthony, Merchant Tailor of London, m. Alice Twynes.
- 2. Thomas, of whom presently,
- 1. Christian, m. Thomas Parker of Cambridge
- 2. Katherine, d. unm.,

The younger son,
Thomas Boddie, recorded his Arms impaling Mildmay in the Visitation of the Heralds to Essex (see below), m. his first cousin, Mary, dau. of Thomas Mildmay of Framlingham, Suffolk and was bur. at Fryerling, Essex 28 April 1627. He had issue two sons and a dau.
- 1. John, of whom presently,
- 2. Robert, b. 1616 emigrated to America in 1635 with his brother-in-law Richard Heaward, and settled in Virginia.
- 1. Anne, m. Richard Heaward of Hornchurch.

The elder son,
John Boddie of London and Ingatestone, Essex, m. Mary (who m. 2ndly at St. Botolph's, Aldgate, London, 17 May 1641,

John Wallhead, of Ingatestone). John Boddie was bur. at Fryering, Essex 11 Aug. 1640, and left with other issue, a son,

William Boddie, emigrated with his first wife, Anne, and his dau. Mary (who m. John Browne) to Isle of Wight Co. Va. in 1661, where he received a grant of 6,700 acres for taking with him 67 servants. He was bapt. 1633; m. 2ndly, 1683, Elizabeth, by whom he had issue,

I.　　John Boddie, of whom presently.
II.　　Elizabeth Boddie, m. Alexander Matthews.

He m. 3rdly, Mrs. Mary Griffin, and d. 1717. His son by his second marriage,

John Boddie, b. 1685; m. Elizabeth, daughter of William Thomas and his wife Elizabeth Hill, who was the daughter of Col. Nicholas Hill, Member of House of Burgesses (1663-1666) and Silvestra Bennett, daughter of Edward Bennett, Burgess from his plantation, "Bennetts Welcome" 1628. (Adventures of Purse and Person, p. 89.) Elizabeth (Thomas) Boddie m. 2ndly., John Dawson, Colonel of Northampton Regt., Associate Justice of the Supreme Court of North Carolina. John Boddie d. Mar. 1720, leaving issue:

I.　　William, of whom presently.
II.　　John, m. Elizabeth Jeffries and removed to South Caro-
lin　　lina, where he became the ancestor of that branch of the
　　　　family.

William Boddie, removed to North Carolina in 1734, a Lieutenant in Northampton Foot in Spanish War 1748, and French and Indian War 1754-55, b. 1712; m. Mary, daughter of Capt. William Bennett, of the Roanoke Company in the Spanish War.

　　　　His children were:
I.　　Nathan, b. Feb. 22, 1732, m. Chloe Crudup. (See later)
II.　　Temperance, m. Solomon Williams. (See later)
III.　　Elijah, d. unm. Oct. 1761 leaving a will.
IV.　　Willis, m. Catharine Barnes.
V.　　William, b. May 10, 1749, m. Martha Jones, of Halifax.
　　　　(See later)

Nathaniel Boddie of Rose Hill, Nash County, North Carolina, Delegate to the State Convention at Halifax, which declared for Independence, 4 July, 1776, Member House of Commons 1777, Member Senate 1778-81, b. Feb. 22, 1732; m. June 1762, Chloe, daughter of John Crudup, and died Dec. 7, 1797, leaving issue:

I.　　Bennett, of whom below.
II.　　Elijah, b. 1763; m. Elizabeth Taylor.
III.　　George, b. Nov. 19, 1769; m. (1) Susanna Parham Hill,
　　　　(2) Lucy Williams (See later).
I.　　Temperance, b. 1767, m. Colonel Jeremiah Perry.
II.　　Mary, b. 1771; m. Joshua Perry (See later)
III.　　Elizabeth, b. April 10, 1776; m. Capt. John Perry.
IV.　　Mourning, b. Feb. 25, 1778; m. Major James Hilliard
　　　　(See Hilliard Family, S.V.F., Vol. II)

Temperance Boddie, daughter of Mary Bennett and William Boddie, married Capt. Solomon Williams, who died in Warren County, N.C. July 28, 1794. He was a son of Samuel Williams who died in Edgecombe County 1754. A Solomon Williams served for $2\frac{1}{2}$ years in Donoho's Company, 6th Regiment, Continental Line. (N.C. Roster, pp. 90, 565)

Children:

I.   Henry G. Williams, b. May 24, 1765, m. Lucy B. Tunstall (See later).

II.   William Williams, m. (1) Ruina Webb; (2) Elizabeth Kearney.

III.   Samuel Williams, m. (1) Mary Persons, (2) Mary Eaton.

IV.   Elizabeth Williams m. Gen. William Williams (her first cousin)

V.   Temperance Boddie Williams, m. George Tunstall.

Henry Guston Williams, son of Temperance Boddie and Capt. Soloman Williams, was born May 24, 1763, at Gunston Hall in Warren County, N.C. On Aug. 15, 1793, he married Lucy Barker, daughter of Elizabeth (Betsy) Barker and William Tunstall, who was born in Pittsylvania or Henry Co., Va. May 20, 1775, and died at Buxton Place, Warren Co., N.C., March 15, 1857.

Children:

I.   Dr. Soloman Williams, b. Aug. 23, 1794, m. Caroline M. Alston.

II.   William Tunstall Williams, b. July 25, 1796, d.s.p.

III.   Lucy Barker Williams, b. Nov. 30, 1798, m. Elijah Boddie Perry.

IV.   Elizabeth B. Williams, b. Feb. 4, 1800, m. Samuel Perry.

V.   Henry Guston Williams, b. April 22, 1802, m. Elizabeth Nicholls Arrington

VI.   Mary Temperance Williams, b. July 2, 1804, m. S. H. Gee.

VII. Marina Caroline Williams, b. July 16, 1806, m. Mark Harwell Petway.

VIII. Harriet Rowena Williams, b. Feb. 5, 1809, m. Dr. Landon Clanton.

IX.   John B. Williams, b. July 26, 1815, m. Mary T. Hilliard (See later)

X.   Martha Louisa Williams, b. Feb. 22, 1811, m. Charles James Gee.

XI.   Samuel Tunstall Williams, b. April 22, 18--, d.s.p.

John Buxton Williams, the son of Lucy Barker Tunstall and Henry Guston Williams, was born July 25, 1815, in Warren Co., N.C., and died at Buxton Place, Warren Co., N.C. He married his cousin Mary Temperance Hilliard, the daughter of Mourning Boddie (daughter of Nathaniel Boddie of Rose Hill, Nash Co., N.C.) and James Hilliard (b. Oct. 30, 1868) who was born at Hilliardstown, Nash County, N.C., Nov. 16, 1816.

Children:

I.   James Hilliard Williams, b. Oct. 7, 1835, m. Susan Elizabeth Lyon.

II.   Lucy Tunstall Williams, d.s.p.

III.   Henry Guston Williams, b.---, killed at Malvern Hills, Va.

IV.   Dr. John Buxton Williams, m. Carrie Peters.

V.   Soloman Buxton Williams, b. Aug. 22, 1846, m. Eve Thornton

VI. Tempie Hilliard Williams, b. Dec. 7, 1848, m. John Alexander Dameron.

VII. Jonas Carr Williams, b. Dec. 24, 1850, m. Martha C. Jones (See later)

VIII. Romeo M. Williams, d. s. p.

IX. Dr. Thomas Barker Williams, b. Aug. 9, 1855, m. Lucy Thweatt Jerman.

C. Dr. Buxton Boddie Williams, b. March 18, 1858, m. Martha Edward Alston.

  Jonas Carr Williams, son of Mary Temperance Hilliard and John B. Williams, was born at "Sunny Hill Farm", Warren Co., N.C., and died at "Shady Hill", Warren Co., N.C. On Dec. 27, 1871, he married Martha (Pattie) Clark Jones, daughter of Lucy Barker Pettway and Joseph Speed Jones, who died July 4, 1889, at "Shady Hill", Warren Co., N.C.

  Children:

I. Eva Thornton Williams, b. Oct. 3, 1872, m. C. D. Tharrington.

II. Joseph Speed Williams, b. March 10, 1874, m. Hattie Hill.

III. Lucy Pettway Williams, b. Dec. 25, 1876, d. s. p.

IV. John Buxton Williams, b. Jan. 12, 1878, m. Maria Williams.

V. Mary Ann Williams, b. 1880, m. B. G. Tharrington.

VI. Tempie Dameron, b. June 30, 1882, m. Geo. D. Wheelen.

VII. Marina Cook Williams, b. Sept. 24, 1883, m. E. S. Paddison.

VIII. Mark Pettway Jones Williams, b. Oct. 7, 1885, m. Edna Draughan

IX. Frank Graham Williams, b. Dec. 26, 1886; m. Fanny G. Cook. (See later)

X. Martha (Pattie) Jones Williams, b. May 6, 1889, d. s. p.

  Frank Graham Williams, son of Martha (Pattie) Clark Jones and Jonas Carr Williams, was born at "Shady Hill", Warren Co., N.C., Dec. 29, 1886, and on June 11, 1913, in Atlanta, Ga., he married Fannie Grier, the daughter of Frances Grier and Joseph Samuel Cook, who was born in Atlanta, Ga., June 29, 1890. They now reside at 3695 Peachtree Road, Atlanta, Ga. He is Chairman of the Board of the F. Graham Williams Co., Atlanta, Ga.

  Children:

I. Virginia Alston Williams, b. Jan. 12, 1924, m. Russell B. De Coudres, Jr.

  Children:

  1. Barbara Virginia De Coudres, b. Jan. 1, 1945.

  2. Frank Graham De Coudres, b. April 8, 1948.

  3. Suzanne De Coudres, b. Nov. 18, 1952.

  4. Russell B. De Coudres, III, b. Jan. 13, 1955.

  Copy of a letter from Solomon Buxton Williams to John T. Boddie.

Warrenton, N.C.

--------- 1895

Mr. Jno T. Boddie,

  I am sorry to find most of my records are destroyed......
moves...and the old papers were put away, and the rats have

destroyed about all I had. My mother made many notes of interest which I find are destroyed also.

The old paper sent is a sample of many that are gone. It seems as if William Bennett, by a former marriage to Mary Hardy, had a daughter who married William Boddie, named Mary (also Grace, Nancy and William). These three daughters were called "the three Graces". Jas. Carey was a very wealthy Tory. He took a survey of Cuba, a very good one, which I have. I had an uncle Jas. Carey Hilliard, named for him. He died without issue & there are several millions in Bank of England &, &c.

My mother said William Boddie married Mary Bennett; but that memorandum is eaten up; also I had an uncle named Bennett, you see that name all along.

John Crudup married Mourning Dickson, Nathan Boddie married Chloe Crudup. My mother made no record of where Wm. Boddie was born, don't think she knew but often heard her laugh at what your grandfather Geo. would say..... "that if whe went back too far she'd come to a "London Tailor".

William Boddie's mother was a Bennett. You see the children were double Bennetts. (His grandmother was a daughter of Silvestra Bennett).

I will see my sister Mrs. Tempe Dameron next Saturday & see some of the old records then. My engagements are such that I can't see before that time. Sorry I cant send my mother's records. She was Tempe Hilliard.

Your friend & kin,
S.B. Williams.

The old papers were the Bennett Bible records shown on page 86 of Boddie and Allied Families.

Mary Boddie, daughter of Chloe Crudup and Nathan Boddie was born March 24, 1771, in North Carolina, and married Joshua Perry, of Franklin County, North Carolina, who died there June 7, 1809.

Children:

I. Elijah Boddie Perry, m. Lucy Barker Williams.
II. Green Perry, m. Mary Johnson.
III. Temperance Boddie Perry m. William Rosser Hinton.
IV. Ann Perry m. Charles Lewis Hinton.
V. Mary Eliza Perry, b. 1809, m. Leonard Henderson Seawell. (See later).
VI. Major Samuel Perry, b. Feb. 15, 1795, m. Elizabeth B. Williams.

Mary Eliza Perry, daughter of Mary Boddie and Joshua Perry, was born in 1809 at Louisburgh, Franklin Co., N.C. and died at Marion, Ala., in 1896. At Raleigh, N.C., on Sept. 4, 1827, she married Dr. Leonard Henderson Seawell, the son of Leonard Grizelle Hinton (daughter of Pheribe Smith and John Hinton) and Judge Henry Seawell, of the Supreme Court of North Carolina, and son of Martha Macon and Joseph James Seawell. Dr. Seawell was born at Raleigh, N.C., Nov. 30, 1805, and died at Marion, Ala., Nov. 22, 1858. He was educated at the College of North Carolina, Brighton College, Bingham College, and Jefferson Medical College.

Children:

I. Mary Indiana Seawell, b. Dec. 3, 1828, m. Col. R. T. Jones (See later)
II. Henry Green Seawell, d.s.p.
III. Joseph James Seawell, b. Nov. 1831, m. Ann Eliza Seawell, (Cousin)
IV. Nancy Perry Seawell, died young.
V. Frances Rush Seawell, m. William Augustus Jones.
VI. Leonard Henderson Seawell, Jr., b. April 12, 1938, m. Eliza A. Foster.
VII. Martha Macon Seawell, b. Jan. 2, 1840, m. Samuel Wilson McKerall.
VIII. Charles Hinton Seawell, b. March 18, 1844, m. Loudie Ravasies.
IX. Margaret Seawell, b. Feb. 4, 1847, d.s.p.
X. Richard Bullock Seawell, m. Mary Perry

Mary Indiana Seawell, daughter of Mary Eliza Perry and Dr. L.H. Seawell, was born at Raleigh, N.C., Dec. 3, 1828, and died Feb. 18, 1905 at Selma, Ala. On Sept. 30, 1847, at Marion, Ala., she married Col. Robert Tingnal Jones, C.S.A., the son of Judith Bailey Hall and James Beverly Jones, who was born Oct. 8, 1815, in Mecklenburg County, Virginia, and was killed at the Battle of Seven Pines, in Virginia. (Judith Bailey Hall was the daughter of Dr. Robert Hall of Halifax County, N.C., who married James Beverly Jones, son of Tingnal Jones, Jr., and grandson of Major Harwood Jones of Warwick Co., Va.) Col. Jones graduated at U.S. Military Academy.

Children of Mary Seawell and Col. R. T. Jones

I. James Beverly Jones, b. Oct. 11, 1848, d.s.p.
II. Leonard Seawell Jones, b. Feb. 6, 1850, m. Claudia C. Howze. (See later)
III. Mary Frances Jones, b. Feb. 12, 1851, d.s.p.
IV. Robert Tignal Jones, b. May 17, 1852, d. Aug. 15, 1853.
V. Martha Anderson Jones, b. June 8, 1953, d.s.p.
VI. Tingnal Jones, b. Sept. 25, 1854, d. Aug. 31, 1855.
VII. John Jones, b. Jan. 19, 1856, d. July 31, 1857.
VIII. Edward Henry Jones, b. Jan. 15, 1859, d.s.p.
IX. Roberta Anna Jones, b. Apr. 25, 1861, d. Nov. 19, 1865.

Leonard Seawell Jones, son of Mary Indiana Seawell and Col. Robert Tingnal Jones, was born at Marion, Ala., Feb. 2, 1850, and died at Selma, Ala., Nov. 6, 1898. On Jan. 25, 1877, at Marion, Ala., he married Claudia Clayton Howze, the daughter of Claudia Caroline Clayton (daughter of Hon. Augustin Smith Clayton, U.S. Rep. from Georgia) and Capt. John Howze, son of Henry Yarborough Howze. Mrs. Jones was born at Marion, Ala., Sept. 21, 1855, and died at Selma, Ala., Feb. 7, 1940.

Children:

I. Mary Indiana (Inda) Jones, b. Dec. 9, 1877, m. Lester Carman Griffith.
II. Henry Howze Jones, b. Jan. 9, 1880, unmarried.
III. Mabel Clayton Jones, b. Feb. 19, 1888, m. Ralph Dudley Nicholson.

IV.   Robert Tingnal Jones, m. Mary Martin Milhous. (See later)
     Robert Tingnal Jones, son of Claudia Clayton Howze and Leonard Seawell Jones, was born at Marion, Ala., Aug. 23, 1890, and died at Selma, Ala., Nov. 23, 1954. On Oct. 14, 1914, at Selma, Ala., he married Mary Martin Milhous, the daughter of Harriet Shields Martin (daughter of Atlas Jones Martin) and Philip M. Milhous (son of Franklin Lemuel Milhous) who was born in Selma, Ala., Feb. 23, 1892.
     Mr. Jones was educated at the Alabama Polytechnic Institute and the University of Alabama. He was a farmer and a Gulf Oil distributor.
        Children:
I.   Hallie M. Jones, m. B.M. Miller Childers. (See later)
II.   Leonard Seawell Jones, b. Feb. 1918, m. Mary Drue Berry.
     Hallie Milhous Jones, daughter of Mary Martin Milhous and Robert Tingnal Jones, was born at Selma, Ala., June 20, 1928, and married there Jan. 28, 1950, Benjamin Meek Miller Childers, son of Margaret Otis Miller (daughter of Gov. B. M. Miller of Alabama) and Erasmus Roy Childers (son of Osborn Franklin Childers, Sr.) who was born at Selma, Ala., Oct. 1, 1926.
     Mr. Childers is an Attorney at Law, and was educated at the University of Alabama. Mr. and Mrs. Childers now reside at 500 Union Street, Selma, Ala.
        Children:
I.   Caroline Pinson Childers, b. Nov. 2, 1951.
II.   Robert Tingnal Jones Childers, b. Oct. 14, 1954.
     George Boddie, youngest son of Nathan, inherited "Rose Hill" Nash County, N.C., from his father. He married first, May 7, 1790, Susan Parham Hill, daughter of Rebecca (Parham) and Thomas Hill Jr., born in 1760, died Sept. 15, 1798. Thomas Hill, Jr., was the son of Thomas Hill and wife Tabitha, shown on page 168 of S.V.F., Vol. 2.
     In March, 1798, George Boddie was appointed guardian of Polly and Temperance Hill, orphans of Thomas Hill in Franklin County. His sureties were John Foster, Thomas Hill, John Powers. Rebecca Hill, widow of Thomas Hill, Jr., made her will in Franklin County, N.C., Aug. 25, 1820, as follows: I give to my three living children and Thomas H. Boddie, to wit, William Johnson, Rebecca Foster, Mary Goodloe, Thomas Boddie, all my property to be divided between them." Exrs.: David S. Goodloe and William Johnson. Wits.: Elijah B. Perry, Leachy Johnson. (W.B. G-p.9) Her first husband was Shugan Johnson, by whom she had William Johnson and James Johnson. Her Hill children were: 1. Susan Parham Hill, m. George Boddie; 2. Thomas Hill III; 3. Rebecca Hill, m. John Foster; 4. Martha Williamson Hill, b. Sept. 11, 1778, m. Nathaniel Green Macon; 5. Mary (Polly) Hill, m. David S. Goodloe; 6. Temperance Hill, m. Robert Mebane.
     George Boddie, born Nov. 19, 1769, died Dec. 12, 1842, represented Nash in the House of Commons in 1800, 1801, 1812, and in the Senate 1813-1814. He married secondly, Lucy, daughter of Major John Williams of Halifax, who served as a regimental commissary during the Revolution. (Rev. Accts. Vol. 12)

Children of first wife:
I. Rebecca, b. Feb. 7, 1791, m. James Peters. (See later)
II. Chloe, b. Dec. 24, 1792, m. John Drake.
III. Nathan, b. Oct. 17, 1795, m. Mary Thomas Smith.
IV. Thomas Hill, b. Nov. 12, 1797, m. Clarissa Lanier. (See Lanier, S.V.F., I, p. 309)
V. Mary, b. Feb. 22, 1802, m. Josiah Crudup.
VI. Elizabeth, b. Jan. 9, 1804, died in infancy.
VII. Catherine, b. Aug. 9, 1805, m. (1) Marmaduke Bell; (2) Malcom McNeill.
VIII. George, b. May 6, 1807, m. Mrs. Louise (Clark) Forbes.
IX. Louisa, b. Feb. 1809, m. Bartholmew F. Moore and died without issue.
X. John Williams, b. Nov. 30, 1810, d.s.p. 1864 in Hinds Co., Miss. (See later)
XI. Elijah, b. Aug. 17, 1812, d.s.p. Sept. 17, 1812, in Jackson, Miss. He wrote a short history of the family in 1840.
XII. William Bennett, b. June 17, 1814, m. Eliza Ann Alston.
XIII. Lucy Williams, b. Apr. 29, 1816, m. Bartholomew F. Moore, Atty. Genl. of N.C.
XIV. Van Rensalaer, b. Apr. 15, 1818, m. Caroline M. Perry.
XV. Temperance Ann, b. Apr. 14, 1820, m. John G. Yancey.
XVI. Willie Perry, b. July 22, 1822, m. Martha Rivers McNeill.
XVII. Nicholas Williams, b. Aug. 25, 1825, m. Louisiana Crudup Boddie. (See later)

Nicholas Williams Boddie, youngest of seventeen children inherited "Rose Hill" from his father, George Boddie, who married secondly Lucy Williams. He was born at Rose Hill, Nash County, N.C., Aug. 25, 1825, and died there June 22, 1894. On Dec. 5, 1850, in Troup County, Georgia, he married his first cousin, Louisiana Crudup Boddie, the daughter of Elizabeth Battle and Nathan Van Boddie, (the son of Bennett Boddie) who was born in Troup Co., Ga., May 9, 1826, and died at "Rose Hill", Sept. 12, 1901.
        Children:
I. Lucy Williams Boddie, b. Oct. 9, 1851, d.s.p.
II. Nathan Van Boddie, b. Jan. 10, 1854, d.s.p.
III. George Van Boddie, b. July 26, 1855, d.s.p.
IV. Nathan Van Boddie, b. July 26, 1855, d.s.p. (twins)
V. Nicholas John Williams Boddie, b. May 13, 1857, d.s.p.
VI. Elijah Hilliard Boddie, b. April 12, 1859, d.s.p.
VII. Bennett V. R. Boddie, b. April 21, 1861, d.s.p.
VIII. Louisiana Crudup Boddie, b. April 3, 1863, m. Bennett Boyd Bunn (See later)
IX. Elizabeth Van Boddie, b. Dec. 4, 1864, d.s.p.
X. Thomas Alfred Boddie, b. Aug. 29, 1866, d.s.p.

Louisiana (Anna) Crudup Boddie, daughter of Louisiana Boddie and Nicholas Williams Boddie, was born at Rose Hill, Nash Co., N.C., April 3, 1888, and is living at Pine Forest Rest, Potecasi, N.C. On Sept. 19, 1888, at Rose Hill, she married Bennett Boyd Bunn, the son of Sarah Sims and William Bennett Bunn, who was born in Nash County, N.C., Feb. 5, 1847, and died at Rocky Mount, N.C., March 20, 1895.

Children:

I. Bennett Bunn, b. July 31, 1889, d. in infancy.
II. Nicholas Boddie Bunn, b. July 31, 1889 (twin) m. Lucy V. Mayo. (See later)
III. Peter Hines Bunn, b. 1890, d. 1892.
IV. Peter Hines Bunn, b. April 19, 1893, m. Mary Sills.
V. Lucy Bennett Bunn, b. March 17, 1893, d. s. p. Dec. 1, 1943.

Nicholas Boddie Bunn, who on July 7, 1914, had his name changed to Nicholas Bunn Boddie by the Superior Court of Nash County, was the son of Louisiana Crudup Boddie and Bennett Boyd Bunn. Nicholas Boddie Bunn stated that he desired to have his name changed on account of the fact that his grandfather Boddie bore the name of "Nicholas Boddie", and all of his male predecessors having died in the past, there is no one in his family to bear the name of Boddie. It will be noted that Nicholas' mother was the only survivor of ten children. He was born July 31, 1889, at Rocky Mount, N.C., and died there Nov. 5, 1951. On Oct. 23, 1924, he married Lucy Valeria, the daughter of Annie Blount Bryant and Columbus Washington Mayo. She was born April 4, 1898 in Edgecombe Co., N.C. She was taken to "Rose Hill" as a bride, and died at Rocky Mount, N.C. Oct. 4, 1954.

Children:

I. Nicholas Bunn Boddie, b. July 8, 1927, m. Betsy A. Bunting. (See later)
II. Benjamin Mayo Boddie, b. Dec. 6, 1929, m. Jean Carolyn Cockrell (See later)
III. Lucy Ann Boddie, b. Sept. 5, 1931, m. Oct. 11, 1955, Joseph Beaman Brewer.

Nicholas Bunn Boddie II, whose present address is 405 N. Parker Street, Rocky Mount, N.C., was born at "Rose Hill", Nash County, N.C., July 8, 1927. On Oct. 4, 1952, at Wilson, N.C., he married Betsy Anne, daughter of Violet Huntington Taylor and Tom George Bunting, who was born at Nashville, N.C., April 30, 1924.

Mr. Boddie was educated at the University of North Carolina and now operates a hotel at Virginia Beach, Va.

Children:

I. Betsy Bryan Boddie, b. Oct. 7, 1953
II. Anne Holt Boddie, b. May 20, 1955

Benjamin Mayo Boddie of 800 Hill Street, Rocky Mount, N.C., was born at "Rose Hill", Nash Co., N.C., Dec. 6, 1929. On Dec. 31, 1950 at Rocky Mount, N.C., he married Jean Carolyn, the daughter of Bluma Inex White and Wm. Lewis Cockrell, who was born in Rocky Mount, August 9, 1930.

Mr. Boddie was educated at the University of North Carolina, and is now with A. C. Comer Oil Co.

Children:

I. Benjamin Mayo Boddie, Jr., b. Dec. 29, 1952.
II. William Lewis Boddie, b. Jan. 13, 1954.

Rebecca Boddie, daughter of George Boddie and his first wife, Susan Parham Hill, was born at Rose Hill, Nash County,

N.C., Feb. 7, 1791. She married James Peters of North Carolina.

Children born in Nash County, N.C.
I. Susannah Hill Peters, m. Col. William Arthur. (See later)
II. Thomas Hill Peters.
III. George Boddie Peters, m. (1) Narvelina Williams; (2) Mrs. Evelina McDowell (nee McNeil); (3) Jessie Helen McKissack.
IV. Ann Elizabeth Peters, b. 15 June 1819, m. Benjamin Franklin Young. (See later).
V. John Buxton Peters, b. 15 Mar. 1817, m. Paralee Jackson.
VI. Lucy Peters.
VII. Mary Caroline Peters, b. 1827, m. Robert Archibald Burton. (See later)
VIII. James Peters.
IX. Rebecca Peters.
X. Ellen Pauline Peters, b. 1832; m. Dr. William Green Wright of Pine Bluff, Ark. Children: Mary Arthur, b. April 15, 1858; m. La Fayette Bell Scull; James Peters, b. Jan. 7, 1862; m. Ella Sutherland; Alice Lee, b. Aug. 28, 1861; m. James H. Mann.

Ann Elizabeth Peters was born in Maury County, Tenn., June 15, 1819, and died at Marshall, Texas, February 25, 1912. She married November 21, 1840, at Tippah, Miss., Benjamin Franklin Young, born August 10, 1810 in the Greensville District, S.C., and died May 24, 1863, at Marshall, Tex. Dr. Young was a physician and resided at Marshall, Texas.

Children:
I. James William Young, b. Sept. 5, 1841; m. Nanie Keys.
II. Charles Franklin Young, b. Nov. 4, 1844.
III. Mary Peters Young, b. Nov. 29, 1846; m. Capt. Joseph C. Terrell, who died Oct. 15, 1909. Mrs. Terrell resided at Fort Worth, Texas. She was one of the organizers of the Texas Federation of Womens Clubs of which she was the second president and was instrumental in securing the enactment of the Rural Public Library Law of Texas, by means of which free circulating libraries were introduced in the various counties. Mrs. Terrell was also a director of the General Federation of Womens Clubs in 1902-1906. (See later)
IV. Fannie E. Young, b. Feb. 4, 1849, m. Alfred B. DeLoach.
V. Thomas Peters Young, b. July 20, 1851, m. Katie Knight.
VI. Edward Leonidas Young, b. Mar. 5, 1854, d. Apr., 1855.
VII. Anna Green Young, b. Sept. 18, 1856.
VIII. William Arthur Young, b. June 24, 1859; d. Oct. 27, 1899.
IX. Ellen Rebecca Young, b. March 2, 1863; m. Robert Campbell Martin.

Fannie E. Young was born at Marshall, Texas, Feb. 4, 1849. She married Nov. 22, 1871, at Marshall, Texas, Alfred Burton De Loach, born April 19, 1837 in Lexington, Sumter County, Alabama, died Oct. 21, 1891, at Texarkanna, Texas, son of Etheldra (Roby) and Alfred Burton De Loach. Mr. De Loach was a physician and resided at Texarkana, Texas.

Children:
I. Lawrence Eads De Loach, b. Dec. 1, 1872; m. Margaret Watts. (See later)
II. Etheldra De Loach, b. June 25, 1874; m. William Little-john Martin.
III. Alfred Burton De Loach, b. Jan. 29, 1876; m. Emma Wisdom.
IV. Mary De Loach, b. Jan. 24, 1879.
V. Fannie De Loach, b. June 20, 1881..
VI. Annie Lee De Loach, b. Nov. 16, 1883; m. William Poag Littlejohn.

Lawrence Eads De Loach, born Dec. 2, 1872, at Longview, Texas, died Jan. 28, 1920, at Shreveport, La., married Nov. 7, 1895, at Pine Bluff, Ark., Margaret Watts, born Sept. 3, 1878, at Texarkana, Tex.

Children:
I. Nita De Loach, born Nov. 14, 1900, at Pine Bluff, Ark., married Oct. 7, 1917, David Morrison Lide, Jr., born in Mason County, Tenn., son of Anna T. (Wilson) and David Morrison Lide, Sr., (deceased).

Children:
1. David Morrison Lide, Jr., born July 27, 1918.

Susannah Hill Peters, daughter of Rebecca Boddie and James Peters, was born Dec. 31, 1810, and died Nov. 9, 1866. On Sept. 20, 1831, she married Col. William Arthur, son of Dolly Winn and John Arthur, who was born in Glascow, Ky., July 12, 1809, and died 1882 in Jackson, Miss.

Children:
I. Rebecca Jane Arthur, b. May 9, 1833, m. James Ronald Chambers. (See later)
II. Ann Eliza Arthur, b. July 13, 1835, m. Thos. Henry Mc-Neill. (See later)

Rebecca Jane Arthur, daughter of Susannah Peters and Col. Wm. Arthur, was born May 9, 1833, and died Sept. 23, 1899. On June 7, 1854, she married James Ronald Chalmers, who died April 9, 1898.

Children:
I. Kate Henderson Chalmers, b. June 18, 1857, m. Wm. Boddie Rogers. (See later)
II. and III. Susan and Fannie, both d. s. p.

Kate Henderson Chalmers, daughter of Rebecca Jane Arthur and Jas. R. Chalmers, was born June 18, 1857 and died Feb. 19, 1944. On Feb. 21, 1884, she married William Boddie Rogers, son of Elizabeth Battle and Wm. E. Rogers, who was born in 1857 and died Jan. 13, 1915.

Children:
I. Katharin Rogers, b. Sept. 2, 1886, m. Wm. Omberg. (See later)
II. Irene Turley Rogers.
III. and IV. Rebecca and Ronald Rogers, d. s. p.

Katharin Rogers, daughter of Kate Chalmers and Wm. Boddie Rogers, was born Sept. 2, 1886, and on June 6, 1906, she married William Omberg, who was born Jan. 18, 1881, and died Oct. 16, 1939.

Children:

I. Ramelle Omberg, b. Oct. 16, 1909, m. May 1929 (1) David Phelan; (2) Jan. 20, 1939, Albert Littleton. Children: (1st marriage)
1. Katharin Ramelle Phelan, b. Sept. 7, 1932, m. June 2, 1951, John L. Hudgins, Jr. Child: Ramelle, b. Feb. 16, 1953.
2. (2nd marriage) Albert M. Littleton, b. Nov. 2, 1939.
II. Arthur Chalmers Omberg, b. Nov. 4, 1909, m. Nov. 20, 1934, Helen Phillips.
Children:
1. William Fulton Omberg, II, b. Oct. 11, 1935.
2. Arthur Chalmers Omberg, Jr., b. May 2, 1939.
3. Helen Katharin Omberg, b. Nov. 14, 1943.

Irene Turley Rogers, daughter of Kate Chalmers and Wm. Boddie Rogers, was born August 27, 1894, and on Sept. 25, 1918, married Shuback Treadwell Beasley, who was born Jan. 31, 1888, and died May 8, 1954.

Children:

I. Shuback T. Beasley, Jr., b. Dec. 13, 1919, m. Nov. 20, 1944, Ruth Hazel Jacobs.
Children:
1. Chalmers Zanders Beasley, b. April 20, 1946.
2. Shuback T. Beasley, III, b. Jan. 27, 1949.
3. Allison Carruth Beasley, b. May 30, 1950.
II. William Boddie Rogers Beasley, b. July 23, 1922, m. June 12, 1948, Marion Catherine Goedjen.
Children:
1. Wm. B. R. Beasley, Jr., b. Oct. 27, 1947.
2. Eugenia Gabrielle Beasley, b. Feb. 5, 1951.
3. Battle Alexander Beasley, b. Aug. 29, 1952.

Ann Eliza Arthur, daughter of Susannah Hill Peters and Col. Wm. Arthur, was born July 13, 1835, and died Oct. 3, 1866. Sometime after 1857, when his first wife, Rebecca Tuck, died Ann Eliza Arthur married Thomas Henry McNeill, son of Martha Rivers and Malcolm McNeill, who was born near Lafayette, Christian Co., Ky., August 1, 1821, and died at Dogwood Plantation, Coahoma Co., Miss., in 1866.

Children of T. H. McNeill and 1st Wife -- See Boddie and Allied Families, p. 137.
Children of T. H. McNeill and 2nd Wife, Ann Eliza Arthur:

I. William A. McNeill, b. Aug. 17, 1862, m. Rebecca Park Metcalf. (See later)
II. Alexander C. McNeill, b. Aug. 31, 1864, m. Marietta Humes. (See later)

William Arthur McNeill, son of Ann Eliza Arthur and Thomas Henry McNeill, was born at Dogwood Plantation, Coahoma Co., Miss., Aug. 17, 1862, and died at Memphis, Tenn., Oct. 10, 1935. On Nov. 19, 1887, he married Rebecca Park Metcalf, who was born in Memphis, Tenn., Oct. 7, 1867, and died there April 2, 1944. Child: Margaret Metcalf McNeill, born July 21, 1893, married Willis Edward Ayers.

Margaret Metcalf McNeill, daughter of Rebecca Park Metcalf and Wm. A. McNeil, was born in Memphis, Tenn., in the house built by her great-grandfather, William Park, July 21, 1893, and on Nov. 8, 1917, in Chicago, Ill., in the Fourth Presbyterian Church, she married Willis Edward Ayers, who was born in Osceola, Ark., Nov. 28, 1881, and died in Memphis, Nov. 8, 1936.

Children:
I.   Willis E. Ayers, Jr., b. Sept. 8, 1918, in Memphis, m. Aug. 14, 1951, Evelyn Elizabeth Thompson, b. Aug. 11, 1920, in Haywood Co., Tenn.
     Children:
     1. Evelyn Elizabeth Ayers, b. Dec. 31, 1942.
     2. Ann Arthur Ayers, b. May 4, 1948.
     3. Willis E. Ayers, Jr., b. Nov. 15, 1953.
II. William McNeill Ayers, b. Aug. 17, 1920, m. Apr. 8, 1950, Mildred B. Wilkerson, b. May 7, 1928.
     Children:
     1. Wm. McNeill Ayers, Jr., b. June 17, 1951.
     2. Warren Wilkerson Ayers, b. Aug. 12, 1952.
III. Mary Margaret Ayers, b. Jan. 11, 1932.

Alexander Chalmers McNeill, who died in 1924, married Marietta Humes.
Children:
I.   Marietta Humes McNeill, b. Mar. 29, 1891, m. Samuel Tate Morgan, Jr., of Richmond, Va.
II. Alexandra Chalmers McNeill, b. Nov. 25, 1894, m. Eugene H. Smith, 2 children d.s.p., Robert and James Hopkins Smith.

Mary Caroline Peters, daughter of Rebecca Boddie and James Peters, was born cr. 1826 at La Grange, Tenn., and died June 1852 at El Dorado, Ark. On Nov. 1, 1848, she married Dr. Robert Archiblad Burton, who was born Jan. 20, 1822 in Granville County, N.C., and died at Helena, Ark., in 1872. He was a physician and educated at the University of Pennsylvania.

I.   Mary Lucy Burton, b. Sept. 27, 1851, m. James Cole Davis. (See later)

Judge James Cole Davis was born at Goshen Pass, Va., Oct. 11, 1833, and died at Helenea, Ark, Jan. 6, 1886. On Feb. 8, 1872, at Helena, Ark., he married Mary Lucy Burton, the daughter of Mary Caroline Peters and Dr. Robert Archibald Burton, who was born at El Dorado, Ark., Sept. 27, 1851, and died at Lexington, Va., June 4, 1953.

Judge Davis was an attorney, educated at Washington College, and lived in Helena Ark. He was Judge of the Circuit Court of Arkansas.
Children:
I.   Mary Evelyn Davis, b. Feb. 28, 1879, unm.
II. William Cole Davis, b. Oct. 7, 1882, m. N. M. Christie. (See later)

William Cole Davis, who now resides at 5 Lewis St., Lexington, Va., was born at Rockbridge Baths, Va., October 7, 1882,

On May 10, 1916, at Winnipeg, Canada, he married Norma Mada-
leine Christie, daughter of Elizabeth (Currie) and William John
Christie, who was born March 21, 1892, at Winnipeg, Canada.
　　Children:
I.　　Elizabeth Christie Davis, b. May 15, 1917, m. Stewart
　　　Bowness.
II.　　Margaret Cole Davis, b. Oct. 8, 1919, unm.

　　William Bennett Boddie, son of Lucy (Williams) and George
Boddie, was born at "Rose Hill", Nash County, N.C., June 17,
1814, and died near Jackson, Miss., Jan. 1, 1854. He married
Eliza Ann Alston, born in Halifax Co., N.C., Feb. 14, 1814,
daughter of Margaret (Thomas) and Joseph John Alston. (See
Alston History - 152) Children: 1. Mary, d.s.p. in Memphis,
Tenn.; 2. Elizabeth; 3. Laura, m. Major George C. Sebastian;
4. Ellen, m. Benjamin E. Jones; 5. Lucy, m. Andrew Crudup;
6. Annie, m. Herman Bartels; (for children see Boddie Book,
p. 53); 7. William.

　　John Williams Boddie, born Nov. 30, 1810, son of Lucy
(Williams) and George Boddie, moved to Mississippi with his
brother William Bennett Boddie and settled near Jackson, Miss.
He built a home for his bride who died suddenly about the time
it was finished. He never married. A picture of his home which
was kindly obtained by his great niece, Mrs. Laura Boddie West
Jones, is shown herein. He died during the War between the
States. He made his will Nov. 3, 1863, same probated Aug. 8,
1864, as follows: (Abstract) I desire to be interred in a metal-
lic coffin without show or parade by the side of my brother in
the graveyard at Jackson. I give all my estate both real and personal, except such legacies as I may name, to my nephews,
sons of my brothers, George Boddie, Willie P. Boddie, Nicholas W. Boddie, and of my deceased brothers William B. Boddie
and Van R. Boddie. I give $1000 to each of my nephews, Andrew
Crudup, William Crudup, Bartholomew and George Moore.
$500.00 to my nieces, Lucy Kitrell and Lucy C. Moore. I give
my negro men, Jonas and Corry, and my woman Cesi, $10.00
every year and recommend their good treatment. Wits.: Willie
P. Boddie, John T. Sorsby, and Peter Virden. (Madison Co.,
Book A, 394). As a result of the War, his grave is unmarked.

　　Willie Perry Boddie, the brother who witnessed the will,
had left Kentucky and moved to Mississippi with his family to
escape the dangers of the War. His son John Thomas Boddie,
later of Chicago, Ill., was born in his uncle's home on Feb. 28,
1864. The house is now the home of the President of Tougaloo
College, a Mississippi College for colored people. "John T."
as he was affectionately known, had been gathering material
about the family for 25 years previous to my going to Chicago
to study law. I offered to write the book if he would publish it, so
I compiled the first 190 pages and he compiled his wife's family
and published the book in 1918, while I was in the Army. He was
a very dear friend and a wonderful person.

　　Laura Boddie, daughter of Eliza Ann (Alston) and William
Bennett Boddie, was born in Jackson, Miss., May 5, 1849, and
died in Norwood, E. Feliciana Parish, La., June 8, 1931. On

March 14, 1865, at Jackson, Miss., she married Major George
Calhoun Sebastian, who was born March 27, 1830, and died in
New Orleans, La., Aug. 7, 1897. He was the son of Elizabeth
(Murray) and Dr. Charles Sebastian, and grandson of Amelia
(Broadwater) 1752-Feb. 29, 1832, and Benjamin Sebastian, who
was born in England June 29, 1739, came to America and was
a soldier in the Revolution, later moving to Kentucky, where he
died Nov. 20, 1932. George C. Sebastian was a major in the
Confederate Army.

At the outbreak of the War, 1861-65, Laura Boddie, with
her four sisters and young brother, were living with their mother,
Eliza Ann Boddie, a widow, in Jackson, Miss. General Sherman,
in marching through Jackson to Vicksburgh, burned most of the
city, including their home and they fled to the home of their uncle,
William Boddie. (See photo) Later, they moved to Canton. General Wirt Adams, C.S.A., had his headquarters in Canton, and
one day Mrs. Boddie, who wanted to go elsewhere on business,
sent her daughter Laura to his headquarters to obtain a pass.
The message was taken by a young and handsome officer. The
next day she received the pass and a note expressing pleasure
that it had been granted. It was signed "George C. Sebastian,
Major." It was the old story of love at first sight. Though she
was then only sixteen they were married the next year, March
14, 1865, at Jackson, in the first room to the right of the en-
trance of Colonel Fearn's residence. (See photo)

A

B

C

A. - Home of John Williams Boddie, now Tougaloo College.

B. - Gen. Wirt Adams' Headquarters in Canton.

C. - The Col. Fearn residence on
North State St. in Jackson, Miss.

Children:

I. Mary Fielding Sebastian, b. March 12, 1866, m. Robert Green Campbell.

II. Lily Stuart Sebastian, Mary's twin, m. William Alice West. (See later)

III. Charles Wm. Sebastian, b. Sept. 23, 1867, m. a cousin, Mary Sebastian.

IV. George Garner Sebastian, b. April 1, 1870, died in infancy.

V. Annie Fearn Sebastian, b. Sept. 25, 1871.

VI. Clara Lee Sebastian, b. April 30, 1873, m. Cordill Snyder.

VII. John Tobin Sebastian, b. June 20, 1875, m. Mary Madden.

VIII. Odile Vrendenburgh Sebastian, b. April 27, 1877, m. Davis Gudger Lunsford.

IX. Amelia Broadwater Sebastian, b. Jan. 5, 1879, m. Joe Marrin Bosworth.

X. Nita Preston Sebastian, b. March 20, 1883, m. Will L. Byers.

Lily Stuart Sebastian, who was born in New Orleans, La., March 12, 1866, and died in Canton, Miss., July 31, 1945, was the daughter of Laura Boddie and Major George C. Sebastian. On March 14, 1888, in New Orleans, she married William Alice West, who was born at Evergreen Avoyelles Parish, La., Aug. 2, 1864, and died Nov. 10, 1945, in Norwood, E. Feliciana Parish, La.

Children:

I. George Sebastian West, b. Jan. 25, 1889, m. Lillian Pope and had George Sebastian West, Jr., Capt. Tank Corps, killed in action in Germany, Nov. 6, 1944.

II. Laura Boddie West, b. Jan. 14, 1892, m. Ben H. Jones. (See later)

III. William Alice West, Jr., b. Oct. 7, 1895, m. Estelle Hasfoller, lives at 1624 Arabella St., New Orleans.
   Children:
   1. Margie West, m. Luther Waller, Jr.
   2. Roger B. West, m. Felicia Gayle.

Laura Boddie West, the daughter of Lily Stuart Sebastian and William Alice West, was born in Norwood, La., Jan. 14, 1892, and married there, Sept. 16, 1914, Ben Hamlet Jones, the son of Ellin Boddie Jones and Benjamin Edward Jones, who was born Oct. 13, 1879, in Canton, Miss. Mrs. Jones holds a B.A. degree from Newcomb College, New Orleans.

Children:

I. Laura Boddie West Jones, b. June 24, 1915, m. May 8, 1943, Earl C. Bowers, Jr., Captain of Infantry, killed in Holland Oct. 27, 1944; One child, Earl C. Bowers, III, born Nov. 17, 1944.

II. George William Jones, b. July 11, 1922, unmarried.

III. Ellen Sebastian Jones, b. Feb. 6, 1927; m. Perry Frank Hunter, III. Children: 1. Virginia Howel Hunter; 2. Elizabeth S. Hunter; 3. Perry Frank Hunter, IV.

William Boddie, the fourth son of Mary Bennett and William Boddie, was born in Nash County, N.C., May 10, 1749, and died Jan. 6, 1817. On March 5, 1780, he married Martha Jones of Halifax County.

The Federal Census of 1790 shows William Boddie as residing in Nash County, and as having one son under 16 years of age and four daughters. William Boddie was tax collector for the County of Nash in 1784. (N.C. Col. Rec. Vol. XIX, p. 706)

Children born in Nash County:

I. Judith Boddie, b. Dec. 26, 1780, m. March 1802, Rev. Hill Jones. They had these children: Mary Boddie Jones, 1808-1864, m. Nathan Boddie Whithead, 1801-1861; Martha Boddie Jones, m. Hamilton McCauley; Henrietta Jones, d. s. p.; Elizabeth Jones, m. Judge H. Howcott, they had John Howcott, who lives near Canton, Miss; and Wm. Howcott of 802 Perdido St., New Orleans.

II. Sarah Boddie, b. 1783; m. (1) Nathan Whitehead, (2) Elisha Lott. (See later)

III. Mary Boddie, b. March 7, 1785; m. John Sanders.

IV. Temperance G. Boddie, b. March 24, 1787; m. (1) Feb. 19, 1812, Arthur Whitehead; (2) May 29, 1827, Richard Arrington.

V. William Boddie, b. March 21, 1790, d. Apr. 2, 1806.

VI. William Willis Boddie, b. Dec. 12, 1792, m. Tranquilla Sanders.

VII. Martha Anna Boddie, b. June 30, 1793, m. (1) Bennett Boddie Perry, (2) Rev. Lott.

VIII. Elizabeth Jones Boddie, b. April 2, 1795, m. Dec. 30, 1819, Milton Ison.

Sarah Boddie, the daughter of Martha Jones and William Boddie, was born at Nashville, N.C., Jan. 23, 1873; died at Salem, N.C. June 30, 1830; married first, Feb. 21, 1805, in Nashville, North Carolina, Nathan Whitehead, secondly Elisha Lott, the son of Ann and Solomon Lott, born June 21, 1780, died Sept. 17, 1860.

Children of Sarah Boddie and Nathan Whitehead:

I. Nathan Boddie Whitehead, b. 1801, m. Mary Boddie Jones. (See later)

Children of Sarah Boddie Whitehead and 2nd. husband, Rev. Elisha Lott:

I. William Boddie Lott, b. Oct. 22, 1819, m. Eliza Gray Hill (See later).

II. Elisha Willis Boddie Lott.

Nathan Boddie Whitehead, son of Sarah Boddie and Nathan Whitehead, was born in 1801 and died in 1861. In 1831 he married his first cousin, Mary Boddie Jones, daughter of Judith Boddie and the Rev. Hill Jones, who was born 1808 and died 1864.

Children:

I. Sara Elizabeth Whitehead, b. 1833; m. Wm. S. Heard. (See later)

II. Nathan E. Whitehead, m. Eva Walton.

III. William B. Whitehead.

IV. Martha Rebecca Whitehead, m. A. C. Porter.

Sarah Elizabeth Whitehead, daughter of Mary Boddie Jones and Nathan Boddie Whitehead, was born July 18, 1833, in Hinds

Co., Miss., and died Jan. 4, 1894, at Senatobia, Miss. On July 6, 1854, in Madison County, Miss., she married William Smith Heard, who was born in Wilkes County, Ga., April 14, 1818, and died in Senatobia, Miss., June 10, 1870.

Colonel Heard was a planter, and an officer in the Confederate Army. He was the son of Caroline Wilkinson and Jesse Falkner Heard of Wilkes County, Georgia, who was born June 19, 1785, and died Sept. 6, 1832. His wife was born 1792 and died March 8, 1880. His father was the son of Jesse Heard (1740-1803) said to have been an officer in the Virginia Troops at Augusta, Ga., and his wife Judith Wilkinson. Jesse Heard (1740-1803) was the son of Mary Falkner and Stephen Heard, and the grandson of John Heard who came to Virginia from County Tyrone, Ireland, in 1720.

Children of Sarah Whitehead and Col. Wm. Smith Heard:
I. Nathan Heard, b. Aug. 5, 1855, d.s.p.
II. Jesse Falkner Heard, b. Dec. 29, 1856, d. Sept. 1, 1911; he had one dau., Elizabeth, b. 1893, m. Rawlins Colquitt.
III. Mary Heard, b. Dec. 9, 1858, d. Jan. 14, 1859.
IV. John Wilkerson Heard, b. Mar. 27, 1860, m. Mildred J. Townsend. (See later)

General John Wilkerson Heard, son of Sarah Elizabeth Whitehead and Colonel William Smith Heard, was born in Senatobia, Miss., March 27, 1860, and died Feb. 4, 1922, in New Orleans, La. In June, 1886, in New York City, he married Mildred Jewell Townsend, the daughter of Mildred Anna Parker and George Atwater Townsend, who was born in New York City, N.Y., Dec. 12, 1862, and died in Miami, Florida, Jan. 14, 1943.

General Heard was educated at Vanderbilt University, entered the U.S. Military Academy in 1883. He was Brigadier General in the U.S. Army and was awarded the Congressional Medal of Honor for distinguished gallantry in the Spanish-American War. He also served in World War I.

Children:
I. Jack W. Heard, b. March 6, 1887, m. Ella Agnes McCarthy. (See later)
II. Falkner Heard, b. Oct. 15, 1888; m. Victoria Herff.
III. Amy Mildred Heard, b. Oct. 15, 1890, m. Thomas H. Rees.
IV. Marguerite Jewell Heard, b. May 11, 1893, m. John F. Conklin.
V. Ralph Townsend Heard, b. Aug. 15, 1897; m. Rose Loring.
VI. Jesse Philip Heard, b. Dec. 12, 1901.

General Jack Whitehead Heard, who resides at Silver Lake, N.H., in summer and at 219 Burr Road, San Antonio, Texas in winter, was born March 6, 1887 in New York City. On June 11, 1917, at Eagle Pass, Texas, he married Ella Agnes McCarthy, the daughter of Sybelle Varnell and Jeremiah William McCarthy, who was born in Eagle Pass, March 14, 1901.

General Heard served in the Air Corps 1915-19 in World War I. He continued his service in the Army, was commissioned a Major General in 1941 and commanded an Armored Division in World War II.

Children:
I. John Wilkerson Heard, II, Captain U.S.A., World War II,
b. July 11, 1919, m. Margaret Mahoney.
II. Elizabeth Emily Heard, b. Dec. 3, 1920; m. John R.
Deane, Jr.
III. Ralph Varnell Heard, b. Oct. 4, 1922.
IV. Richard Townsend Heard, b. Sept. 25, 1925; m. Virginia
Lynch.

William Baldwin Lott, the son of Sarah Boddie Whitehead
and her second husband, the Rev. Elisha Lott, was born in Nash
County, N.C., Oct. 22, 1819, and died in Madison County, Miss.,
On September 16, 1843, in Hale County, Ala., he married Eliza
Gray Hill, the daughter of Nancy Ann Bowen and William Wallace
Hill, who was born in Greensboro, Ala., March 15, 1825, and
died at their plantation in Madison Co., Miss., June 27, 1888.

Mr. Lott was a successful planter and owned plantations in
various parts of the state. In the 1850's he built a handsome
white pillared mansion costing $80,000, which was quite a sum
in those days, on his home plantation. This mansion was burned
after the Civil War. He had a wholesale plantation supply business in New Orleans.

Children:
I. Sarah Rebecca Lott, b. Oct. 30, 1844; m. Guston W.
Thomas.
II. Ann Eliza Lott, b. Aug. 24, 1847, d.s.p.
III. Elizabeth Jayne Lott, b. Aug. 27, 1849, d. in infancy.
IV. Mary Whitehead Lott, b. Dec. 15, 1850, died in childhood.
V. Elizabeth Jayne ("Danie") Lott, b. June 14, 1859, m. Dr.
Landon C. Cheek. (See later)

Elizabeth Jayne ("Danie") Lott, the daughter of Eliza Gray
Hill and William B. Lott, was born on the plantation in Madison
Co., Miss., June 14, 1859, and died in Canton, Miss., Jan. 24,
1911. On Sept. 25, 1884, at the plantation in Madison Co., Miss.,
she married Dr. Landon Clanton Cheek, who was the son of William Alston Cheek, who was born in Warren Co., Tenn., Aug.
10, 1825, and died May 30, 1897, in Canton, Miss., and his wife
Angelina Augusta Clanton, the daughter of Martha (Kearney) and
William C. Clanton, who was born in Halifax Co., N.C., Aug.
2, 1825, and died in Madison Co., Miss., about 1880. Dr. Cheek
was born in Warren Co., N.C., Feb. 25, 1847, and died in Canton, Miss., Jan. 2, 1900.

Dr. Cheek received his medical education at Tulane University, which at that time was called Louisiana Medical College.
He served in the Confederate Army, going in at the age of 16.
He practiced medicine in Madison County, he was a linguist, pro-
ficient in eight languages, and a scholar.

Children:
I. Angie Hill Cheek, m. John Ruthven Miller. (See later)
II. William Lott Cheek, b. on plantation, unmarried.
III. Elizabeth Somerville Cheek, born in Canton, Miss., was
graduated from the University of Mississippi with Bach-
elor of Science degree; now teaches at Whitehaven High
School, Memphis, Tenn.

Angie Hill Cheek, daughter of Elizabeth Jayne Lott and Dr. Landon C. Cheek, was born on the plantation in Madison County, Miss., Aug. 30, 1888, and was married at Grace Church, Madison Co., Miss., June 24, 1916, to John Ruthven Cameron Miller, the son of Florence Waller and Ozias Sylvanus Miller. He was born in Canton, Miss., Aug. 2, 1888, and died May 26, 1956.

Children:

I.   Angie Hill Miller, b. June 2, 1917; graduated from Louisiana State University; m. James Cecil Denny. They now reside in Lexington, Ky. Children: 1. Angela Hill Denny, b. July 14, 1943; 2. James Cecil Denny, Jr., b. March 31, 1948.

II. John Ruthven Cameron Miller, Jr., b. Dec. 1, 1919, and was shot down over Japan April 16, 1945. He married Yvonne Oline of New Roads. Children: 1. Trena Alberta Miller; 2. Yvonne Teresa Miller.

Captain Miller enlisted in the Army Air Corps on his graduation from Louisiana State University in 1941; on receiving his Wings he was made a pilot instructor. In Jan. 1945, he went to the Pacific as a B-29 pilot in the 21st Bomber Squadron, based on Guam; and from there was heard on a broadcast March 4. He was a Squadron Commander and first B-29 pilot in the raid on Kobe, Mar. 17, said to have been the finest precision bombing of the war; war installations, docks, and industrial areas of the city demolished; residential areas untouched. A little more than a month later he was shot down. The twelve man crew were buried in Japan, but later brought home and buried in a joint funeral at Jefferson Barracks National Cemetery, Sept. 6, 1949. Captain Miller was awarded the Distinguished Flying Cross for "extraordinary achievements while participating in historic missions against the homeland of Japan". His wife also received a posthumus Purple Heart Decoration.

Captain John C. Miller, Jr. at the time he was an Aviation Cadet at Ellington Field, Texas.

III.   Elizabeth Jayne (Danie) Miller, b. March 26, 1923; attended
Louisiana State University; m. William Brightman Single-
ton, Jr., from North Carolina, who was educated at Davidson College and Georgia Tech. He served three and a
half years in the Army; then did graduate study at Massachusetts Institute of Technology and is a full member of
the American Institute of City Planners.

IV.   Kenner Ozias Miller, b. Feb. 6, 1926, as soon as he was
eighteen enlisted in the Merchant Marine, serving in the
Pacific. In Dec. 1954 he married Patsy Sue Merrill.

Isabelle Boddie, who was born in 1823 and died Dec. 20,
1859, was the daughter of Elizabeth Williams Battle, who died
Jan. 7, 1861 and Nathan Van Boddie of Troup Co., Ga., born
Oct. 17, 1794 and died Oct. 14, 1857. He was the son of Sarah
(Smith) and Bennett Boddie of Wake Co., N.C. In 1846, Isabelle
married Capt. W. C. Bray of Talbot Co., Ga., who died June
2, 1880.   Children: Richard Van Bray, m. Annie E. Seay; Julia
Bray, m. W. J. Dunlap; Nathan Van Bray; Mary Battle Bray,
m. Shepard Heard (See later); Wm. Bray, m. Delilah Carr;
Isabella Boddie Bray.

Mary Battle Bray, daughter of Isabelle Boddie and Capt. W.
C. Bray, married Shepherd Heard of La Grange, Ga., and moved
to White Sulphur Springs. Children: Julia Bell Heard, born July
19, 1884, m. Dr. Martin N.G. Greer (See later); Charlie Heard,
born May 17, 1886, d.s.p.; Ira Sheffield Heard, born Feb. 7,
1894; George Walton Heard, born June 7, 1898.

Julia Bell Heard, who was born July 19, 1884, at Hatche-
chubbie, Ala., was the daughter of Mary Battle Bray and Shepherd Heard. She was married in Washington, D.C., May 12,
1906, to Dr. Martin Nesbitt Grant Greer, the son of Mary Ralston and Samuel Greer, who was born at Euclid, Penn., April
21, 1863, and died at St. Petersburg, Fla., April 23, 1956.
Dr. Greer was educated at the University of Pittsburgh, and
Mrs. Greer at the La Grange Female College. Mrs. Greer now
resides at 295-15th Ave., N. St. Petersburg, Fla.

Copied from Boddie Cemetery near La Grange, Troup Co.,
Georgia.

Nathan Van Boddie, born Oct. 14, 1794, died Oct. 14, 1857.
Married Elizabeth Williams Battle May 15, 1818, born 1787,
died Jan. 2, 1861. To Troup County 1828.

Thomas Alfred Boddie, Physician, born March 3, 1834,
died Feb. 15, 1894. Surgeon C.S.A. April 26, 1861 to Aug. 21,
1864. Married Jan. 5, 1864 Aley Womack Smith.

Chloe Boddie, born Nov. 21, 1836, died April 15, 1901.

Vandalia E. Boddie, born June 15, 1845, died June 10, 1906.

George Van Boddie, born Jan. 24, 1828, died April 23, 1907.
Married Rebecca Scott, b. May 1837, died June 1915.

Bennett Boddie, eldest son of Chloe Crudup and Nathaniel
Boddie, inherited his father's land in Wake County; served with
the Nash County Militia at the Battle of Guildford Court House
March 15, 1781, b. Sept. 9, 1763; m. June 3, 1793, Sarah,
daughter of Capt. Benj. Smith of Wayne County, by his wife
Tabitha, daughter of Colonel Benjamin Exum, who commanded

the Wayne County Regiment at the Battle of Camden, 1780.
Bennett Boddie died Feb. 21, 1809, leaving issue:

I.   Nathan Van Boddie, b. Oct. 17, 1794; m. Elizabeth Battle. They moved to La Grange, 'Troup Co., Georgia. (See ante.)

II.   John Exum, of whom presently.

III. Bennett Boddie, b. July 10, 1800, d. 1832.

IV. George Boddie, b. Nov. 20, 1803, d. 1809.

V.   Chloe Crudup Boddie, m. William Battle.

John Exum Boddie, the second son of Sarah Smith and Bennett Boddie, removed to Marengo County, Alabama, 1828, b. Feb. 20, 1798; m. Dec. 17, 1823, Elizabeth, daughter of Oliver Prince, member of North Carolina Legislature, 1815-18, son of Capt. Nicholas Prince, of the Revolutionary Army, and had issue:

I.   Oliver Bennett Boddie, of whom presently.

II.   Sydney T. Laurence Prince Boddie, b. Jan. 26, 1831, m. Martha Burks.

III. John Exum Boddie, b. 1836, m. Emma Donelson.

IV. Arabella Chloe Elizabeth Boddie, b. Aug. 18, 1833, m. Capt. John Haywood Prince, C.S.A.

Oliver Bennett Boddie, the elder son of Elizabeth Prince and John Exum Boddie, of Spring Hill, Marengo County, b. Apr. 11, 1828, educated at Cumberland University, married Dec. 24, 1844, Josephine Rucker, sister of Gen. Edmund Winchester Rucker, C.S.A., for whom Camp Rucker was named, and grand daughter of Gen James Winchester, U.S.A. Mr. Boddie died July 1859, leaving issue:

I.   John Bennett Boddie, of whom presently.

II.   William Sydney Boddie, b. 1851, d. 1853.

III. George Winchester Boddie, b. 1853, d. 1871.

IV. Thomas Edmund Boddie, b. 1857, moved to Texas.

V.   Mary Boddie, b. 1859, m. as his second wife William C. Patterson, of Gallatin, Tenn., a Confederate soldier who fought at the Battle of Shiloh in the First Tennessee Regiment, C.S.A., commanded by Col. William Bate, afterwards Governor of Tennessee and U.S. Senator. Mr. Patterson died about 1928. Mrs. Mary Boddie Patterson (Aunt Mary) died Feb. 3, 1957, at the age of 98. They had two children:

   1. Mary Boddie Patterson, m. Dr. Ralston Woodward, one of Gallatin's leading citizens. He is a dentist, and they live on his farm on the Cumberland River.
      Children:

     (1) Ralston Woodward, Jr., married and living in St. Louis, Mo.

     (2) Mary Louise Woodward, b. March 13, 1922, m. (1) Oct. 4, 1941, Jeff Atchley, b. June 5, 1916 in Lebanon, Wilson County, Tenn. They were divorced Nov. 7, 1943. They had one child, Mary Ralston Atchley, b. Sept. 18, 1942; Mrs. Atchley m. (2) William Hull of Fairbury, Neb., an aviator in World War II, on Dec. 23, 1943. They were divorced Sept. 1948. They had one child, Carolyn Hull, b.

Jan. 27, 1945. She legally changed her name to Carolyn Woodward. Mrs. Hull m. (3) Nov. 1955, William Garrison of Sumner County, b. March 13, 1913, in Sumner.

2. Rucker Patterson, m. Sept. 13, 1925 Esther Josephine McMahan, b. Aug. 13, 1907, in Sevier Co., Tenn. Dr. Patterson is a dentist of Gallatin, Tenn. They have one son, James McMahan, b. April 26, 1934, who is now taking a pre-dental course at Vanderbilt University.

John Bennett Boddie, the eldest son of Josephine Rucker and Oliver Bennett Boddie, removed to Birmingham, Ala., 1882; b. Oct. 20, 1849, educated University of Mississippi, m. July 19, 1879, Anne, daughter of Mumford De Jarnett Perryman of Monroe County, Ala., and died Oct. 13, 1890, leaving a son, John Bennett Boddie. (Burkes Lan. Gen. 1939-40, p. 2569)

Inasmuch as this family is shown in "17th Century Isle of Wight" it is not necessary to repeat what has been said. So only personal details concerning the family in Alabama will be mentioned.

John Exum Boddie and his wife, Elizabeth M. Prince, with three young children, Elanor, Sarah and Oliver, moved to Marengo County, Alabama in 1828, where he bought a plantation, located on a road three miles straight south of Gallion, Alabama, which, however, is in Hale County. His two daughters died soon after moving to Alabama. It will be noted that the early mortality of this family in this locality was very high. Then it was probably a malaria and fever ridden district. Since then these diseases have been eradicated.

John Exum seems to have acquired a large plantation. Mr. William M. Spencer, of Birmingham, also a friend of mine, owns 2500 acres of our old plantation.

John Exum died of typhoid fever in 1841. He was then 43 years of age. His wife had predeceased him, but one daughter and three sons survived. Oliver, my grandfather, the oldest son, was then thirteen years of age.

Oliver and his brother John attended Cumberland University in Lebanon, Tennessee. There they met their future wives. Oliver married, on December 24, 1844, Josephine Rucker, daughter of Louise (Winchester) and Edmund Rucker of Rutherford County, Tennessee, and a granddaughter of General James Winchester of Sumner County. General Winchester's old home, "Cragfont," near Gallatin, is still standing but long ago has passed out of the family. Camp Rucker, in Alabama, is named for Josephine's brother, General Edmund Rucker.

John E. married Miss Emily Donelson, a granddaughter of Colonel John Donelson and a great-niece of President Andrew Jackson's wife, Rachel Donelson. John died of typhoid fever three years after his marriage. His wife married, secondly, Captain Walton and survived her first husband by more than seventy-five years. They had a daughter, Laura Boddie, who married Mr. Mora Sharpe, of Nashville, Tennessee.

When 92 years old Mrs. Walton gave an account of her first marriage, to a reporter of the Nashville Banner, which is an

excellent description of times that have "Gone with the Wind,"
as follows:

"Mrs. Walton was first married October 28, 1856, to John
E. Boddie, Cumberland Law School graduate and a young planter
of Alabama. Of this marriage the bride of nearly seventy-five
years ago recounts:

"Then came the most interesting part of my life, 'loves young
dreams, courtship and marriage. How can I tell about it, with
everybody invited until the guests at Cleveland Hall numbered
more than a thousand. The caterers came from Nashville and
spent a week baking and preparing for the wedding. My uncle
Dr. John Marshall Lawrence, and his wife, Rachel Lawrence,
spent much time decorating the halls and parlors with vines
and the lawn was brilliant with Chinese lanterns, while torches
flanked the approach from the highway to the mansion. All this
for just a little country girl who had lots to learn from life. The
bridal party descended the winding stairway in couples through
the wide hall taking their places in front of the great open fire-
place under the center chandelier filled with wax candles. The
ceremony was performed by Dr. James Wood Hoyte, then Pastor of the Second Presbyterian Church in Nashville, who also
held services at the Hermitage Church.

"There were six bridesmaids, two dressed in blue, two in
white, and two in pink. They were my school girl friends and
were Mary Bass, Henrietta Cockrill, Martha Johns, Jennie
Lewis, Alice Cheatham and my cousin Rachel Donelson. The
groomsmen were Dr. Pegram, and Mr. Hart of Dayton, Alabama, Mr. William Ewing and Mr. Webb Smith of Nashville,
Mr. William Burton of Lebanon and William Donelson, brother
of the bride.

"The wedding dress was of duchess satin, made with an over-
dress of tulle, very full skirt, short pointed waist, with short
puffed sleeves, low round neck, finished with rose point bertha,
worn with short white kid gloves. My jewels were pearls and
diamonds.

"The groom and groomsmen wore very tight trousers with
cutaway coats and waistcoats of white brocaded satin.

"Then the wedding supper. The table in the dining room was
fashioned in the shape of a Maltese Cross and laden with all
kinds of Southern delicacies, pyramids of jellies and creams.
In the center of the table was a pyramid of egg kisses covered
with a veil of spun sugar, and on each end of the table were
castles of sugar and crystal candies.

"All of the meats and salads were served on the large porch
which was enclosed with canvas and lighted with colored lanterns.
Champagne flowed everywhere. The bride's cake was served in
the parlor, on a marble topped table. At the wedding supper the
gentlemen served the ladies. There was dancing until broad day-
light and as the bridal party spent the rest of the week with us
we had infares given every day. One was at the Hermitage, one
at Tulip Grove, the home of my uncle Andrew Jackson Donelson, and other mansions in the vicinity.

"In those days the bride's second day dress was a very im-

portant toilet, it took the place of a bride's going away gown of
the present day. As travel was very difficult at that time honey-
moon trips were rarely taken. My second day dress was an
ecru morie antique with panels of pink roses and green leaves,
made with a basque and full skirt and trimmed with lace."

Cards of the Day

The bride has one of her calling cards of that day. It is thin
and slick in texture, and has a decorative embossed garland
about the name.

After Mr. Boddie's death and some years of widowhood,
Mrs. Boddie married Captain W. B. Walton and returned to
Nashville to live. A daughter of Captain and Mrs. Walton mar-
ried a Mr. Adams of Birmingham, Ala.

John Exum Boddie was not quite 22 when he died. He is buried in the cemetery at Dayton, Alabama, under a tombstone of
Italian marble with the following inscription:

John E. Boddie
Born Aug. 21, 1837
Died June 18, 1859
Our life how short a groan a sigh
To live and then begin to die
But oh how great a mercy this
That deaths a portal into bliss

Oliver B. Boddie, my grandfather, who also died of typhoid
fever, is buried by his side.

Oliver B. Boddie
Born the 11th day of April 1828
and departed this life on the
23rd day of July 1859.
Blessed be the man that provideth for
the sick and needy. The Lord shall
deliver him in time of trouble.

Sydney Boddie, their brother, left the county when he became sick of typhoid, but also died and is not buried in Dayton.
According to Aunt Mary Boddie Patterson, now 98, of Gallatin,
Tennessee, he had an only son, who, while a boy, was drowned
in the Mississippi River at Memphis and a daughter who married a man living in Memphis.

The old plantation was located in what was called the "Black
Belt." An article on the Black Belt was published not so long
ago, and while its descriptive terms might be somewhat flatter-
ing it may give some idea of what the Black Belt was like.

"The Alabama Black Belt" by the Reverand Renwick G. Kennedy; in the Alabama Historical Quarterly No. 3, Volume 2;
1940, p. 282.

"The Alamama 'Black Belt' is a fair-spoken term...it refers to a belt of twelve counties stretching across the state between Columbus, Georgia, and Meridian, Mississippi. The honored counties are Macon, Montgomery, Lowndes, Autauga, Dallas, Wilcox, Perry, Hale, Greene, Sumpter, Marengo, and
Pickens.

"The Black Belt.... referring to the rich black soil of the
area...corresponds not merely to the 'right side of the tracks'

but to the old, exclusive, best-family streets....if you are from the Black Belt, it is like being from the Low Country in South Carolina, or Tidewater in Virginia, or the Blue Grass in Kentucky.

"Virginians and South Carolinians are still proud of the states that gave them birth. Virginia and South Carolina are the two states in which pre-Confederate, Southern aristocracy reached its zenith. In Alabama, the Black Belt counties achieved the most exalted aristocracy of any section of the state.

"The type is nearly extinct, but not entirely. In the Carolina Low Country, the Mississippi Delta, a few parishes in Louisiana, a few counties in Georgia, and in the Alabama Black Belt the strain still survives, somewhat tainted by the Twentieth Century, but preserved well enough to be recognized. Nowhere is it more authentically intact than in the Alabama Black Belt. Nowhere is it preserved in a larger single area than here. Yet of all the Museum pieces of the Old South that remain, none has received less publicity and none is less widely known. So, unsung and unknown and relatively unexploited, it has gone its calm, quiet way, restoring much of its former grandure."

My grandfather Oliver lived in Dayton not far from the plantation. The home place where I was born was not the main plantation residence. I could not find a trace of this old home 60 years after I was last there. Time flies, but I located the spot about where it stood and looked down the hill at an old "bored well" and a small branch at the foot; across from which was a large green field stretching far away to the woods.

My father carried me to Birmingham when I was a month old. My mother died about two years later. My cousin, Dr. Edmund Rucker, told me only recently that his mother went to my mother's funeral which was on a cold rainy day, caught pneumonia and died ten days afterwards.

The "bored" well was, of course, an artesian well but the darkies never called it by that name. They described the new "board" well to me in such glowing terms that when I went back to the plantation that next spring I looked at the gushing water but with great disappointment said "where are the boards?"

This story of plantation life, is related for my children and grandchildren. However, I must record a few vital facts that have occurred since the Isle of Wight book was published.

I served in the Spanish American War in Company K, Birmingham Rifles, First Alabama Volunteers. My great uncle, Gen. E. W. Rucker, who lived next door to Joseph F. Johnston, then Governor of Alabama, succeeded in having me discharged : after only 9 days service in the U.S. Army; as I was under the enlistment age of 18 years.

I was commissioned a First Lieutenant of Infantry at Fort Sheridan, Illinois, Nov. 20, 1917; transferred to Air Service and served in France during World War I; was honorably discharged Dec. 27, 1918, and given a commission of Captain in the Reserves.

My son William was a soldier in World War II. His honorable discharge as a Master Sergeant shows that he enlisted as a private September 4, 1941, at Fort Sheridan, Illinois, and was

honorably discharged October 26, 1945, at Camp Grant, Illinois.
At time of his discharge he was an airplane inspector for H. Q.
37 Troop Carrier Groups. His campaign ribbons were: Bismark
Archipelogo; East Indies, New Guinea, Papuan and Luzon. His
decorations and citations were: Asiactic and Pacific Theater
Ribbon -- with silver star and citation; Phillipine Liberation
Ribbon; Good Conduct Medal; Distinguished Merit Badge with 2
Bronze Clusters; 2 Air Medals.

Bill went to Australia in February, 1942. He was decorated
by General Kenney with the Air Medal in 1942, for flying more
than 25 missions over the Owen Stanley Mountains in hostile territory. He was then a sergeant with the 22nd Troop Carrier
Squadron. He married January 29, 1944, Kathryn Parson of East
Malvern, Australia. They have one daughter, Jill Kathryn, born
January 5, 1954, and one son, Jeffrey William, born Sept. 16,
1955.

My son Oliver served as a Lieutenant (S. G.) in the Merchant
Marine during World War II. He was on an ammunition ship when
Japanese planes attacked a harbor in the Lauauas and blew up
several distant ammunition ships which only made bright flashes
on the water and disappeared. While serving on oil tanker in the
Mediterranean his ship was blown up by a mine. He was injured
and eventually lost a leg. He married Elinor Hayes of New York
City in May 1946 and has one son, Paul John, born February 8,
1947.

My son John is assistant chief of the Clearing House of the
Commerce Department in Washington, D. C. He was rejected
by the army early in 1942 on eyesight much to his disappointment.
He married Mildred Madison of Jacksonville, Illinois, April 25,
1934. They have two children, John Bennett IV, b. November 7,
1943, and Mary Elizabeth, b. October 27, 1947.

My daughter Anne married Gordon Boice Shattuck of West
Springfield, Massachusetts, May 19, 1933. They have two chil-
dren, Arthur Bennett Shattuck, b. August 1, 1940, and Mary
Anne Shattuck, b. December 29, 1943.

My wife, Emma McCall, served as a postal censor for the
War Department at Honolulu during World War II. She died
September 27, 1947, and is buried in the Golden Gate National
Cemetery at San Bruno, California, in block 3, row 10, section
K, grave no 3180 B.

I married, secondly, July 10, 1949, Mrs. Pearl D. Davis of
San Mateo, California. She died July 17, 1951, and is buried in
the Golden Gate National Cemetery, grave no. 3180 A.

Pearl had two daughters by her first marriage. June Davis
married to Richard Glasgow and they have Susie and Richard,
Jr. Doris Davis, her other daughter, married Allen H. Renton
of Honolulu, and they have one son, Allen Davis Renton, and a
daughter.

I married thirdly, Mrs. Lilian Orr Williams, of Todd County,
Kentucky, July 1, 1953. She owns "Woodstock", near Trenton,
Ky., built in 1830, where Elizabeth Meriwether Gilmer ("Dorothy Dix") was born and also Mrs. Caroline Meriwether Goodlett,
of "Daughters of the Confederacy" fame. She has a son, Harry

Lee Williams, living there, who married Virginia Blake of Birmingham, Ala. They have five children: Harriet Day Williams; David Blake Williams; Harry Lee Williams, Jr.; Lilian Ruth Williams; Virginia Rob Williams. See pictures to follow this page.

Captain John Bennett Boddie

Lieut. (S.G.) Oliver B. Boddie

John B. Boddie III
1940

John B. Boddie IV
Age 13

Aunt Mary Boddie Patterson
of Gallatin Tennessee-Died
February 5, 1957, aged 98

Mildred Madison
1930

Wedding picture of Seargant William Boddie and Kathryn Parsons,
East Malvern Australia, January 29, 1944

Mr. & Mrs. Gordon B. Shattuck and children

Patk. 24; Sallie 24; Sarah 24;
Thos. 24; Wm. 24.

- H -

HADLEY, Julie 177.
HAIGH, Elean. 110; Flora 110;
Mary 110; Jos. 110; Sarah 110.
HALE, Earl 268; Ed. 268; Ger-
ald 268; Jesse 268; Madge 268;
Marg. 268; Mild. 268; Robt. 268;
Sam. 268; Virg. 268; Wm. 268.
HALL, Alex 238; Alf. 289; Dixon.
317; Caroly 274; Claire 138;
Edith 212; Eliz. 317; Eula 115;
Fran. 317; Fred. 138; Helen 138;
Instan. 171; Isaac 171; Jane 138;
Linny 56; Marie 119; Marg. 138;
Sarah 138; Thos. 230.
HAM, Wm. 316.
HAMILTON, Eliz. 176; Everd.
176; Elivr. 176; Fran 176; Geo.
176; Jas. 176; John 175-6; Louisa
288; Marmadke. 176; Mary 176-
317; Sarah. 176; Tab. 175-6;
Thos. 176; Wm. 176.
HAMLETT, John 283; Rich. 283.
HAMLIN, Ann 6-7; C. H. 7; Chas.
171; Ed. 251; Eliz. 6; Frank 251;
John 6-7; Helen 251; Peter 7;
Sarah 251.
HAMMET, Adelia 214.
HAMMIL, Cath. 178.
HAMOR, Thos. 8.
HAMPTON, Ed. 287.
HANCOCK, Doug. 150; Martin
149; Milly 270; Polly 150; Sarah
149.
HANNAH, Eliz. 330; Martha 329-
330.
HARDAWAY, Agnes 174; Doroy.
298; Edith 298; Fran. 298; Jane
298; John 298; Sarah 298; Thos.
171-174-298.
HARDCASTLE, Aman. 84; Kend.
84; Martha 84; Sally 84; Sarah 84;
Walt. 84; Yeatn. 84.
HARDIN, Jane 177.
HARDING, Jas. 190.
HARDY, Benj. 231; Berthea 3;
Charlt. 104; Eliz. 3; Geo. 315;
Hugh 3; Jas. 314; Jane 3; John 3-
300; Lucile 314; Lucy 313-4;
Lunore 314; Martha 314; Mary
314; Robt. 313-4; Sarah 313-4;
Thos. 313-4.
HARDYMAN, John 172.
HARGRAVES, Mary 137; Mr.
137.
HARGROVE, Polly 306.
HARLAND, Ailey 96.
HARMON, Fran. 17; Lawr. 214;
Sarah 214.
HARPER, Ben 108; Cecile 129;
Hillard 314; Mary 314; Meliss.
100-1; Nona 108; Sarah 100; Sill-
bta. 100; Walt. 100; Willete 100;
Wm. 101.
HARRINGTON, Agns. 17; Chas.
17; Demp. 17; Druy. 17; Eliz. 18;
Fran. 17-8; John 17; Larany 17;
Mary 17; Mr. 18; Nan. 17; Pati.
17; Philan. 17-8; Polly 17-8;
Rachel 17; Robt. 18; Sally 18;
Sidnh. 110; Tabitha 17; Thos.
17; Whitm. 17; Wm. 17.
HARRIS, HARRISS, Abrm. 316;
Absolm. 311-316-7; Alice 294-5-
299-300-1-2-6-314-5; Allen 311;
Alma 132; Amos 315; Ann 11-295-
301-2-5-6-313-5-9; Anna 50-189;
Art. 256-311; Asa 307; Augt. 313;
Bedford 319; Benj. 186-9-304-5-
316-7-8; Betsy 58; Brittn. 308-
311-317; Buckner 313; Calvin 58-
311; Carola 256; Cath. 306- 312;
Chas 307-318-9; Cherry 319;
Chloe 58; Claibn. 311; Clara 316-
7-8; Clotilda 185; Dan. 306-7-8;
David 306-311-2; Della 189; Dora

312; Dorothy 293-4-6-8-9-317;
Dred 311; Druy. 307-8; Edith
311; Edity 311; Edm. 317; Ed.
302-3-5-6-7-8-310-1-3-4-5-6;
Eligah 313; Elizha 311-2; Eliz.
50-302-4-5-311-3-5-6-7-9; Emma
309-320; Euge. 313; Evol. 198;
Faithy 316-7; Fran. 127-298;
Fredk. 319; Geo. 296-7-8-9-303-
5-311-3; Gert. 313; Green 311;
Hamlin 189; Hann. 304; Hardy
315-6-7; Harmon 24; Hen. 305-8-
311-5-6-7-8; Herb. 307-8; Howell 306; Hubbd. 306; Inez 189;
Isaac 306; Isabel 189-315; Isbla.
185-9-302; Isham 311; Jack 232;
Jacob 306-315; Jas. 303-6-7-9-
311; Jane 305-7-8-311-2-6-7;
Jennet 311; Jeptha 313; Joel 315
John 393-4-6-8-9-300-1-2-3-4-
5-6-311-4-7; Jordan 307-8; Jos.
208-3-5-7; Josaphe. 318; Joshua
304; Judith 303-4-315-8; Keeney
312; Laura 313; Lewis 315; Lind.
58; Litljohn 313; Louisa 189-198-
318; L. T. 311; Lucile 58; Lucy
234-313; Marg. 57-301-2-312;
Martha 58-186-298-9-302-5-6-
313-5-8; Martin 303-5-311; Mary
189-198-298-9-300-1-2-3-4-5-
6-7-9-311-2-3-5-6-7-8; Matt.
305; Michl. 307-8-316-7; Mild.
305; Miss 57; Molly 308; Mumford
58; Meschld. 316; Nan. 309-317;
Nathan 306-7-310-1-2-3; Nath.
316; Pati. 311-2-319; Patsy 56-
68-311; Peter 306; Pinkney 311;
Polly 275; Prisc. 311-319; Ransom 58; Reb. 178-307-311-3;
Reddin 189; Robt. 298-9-303-5-
6-7-319; Rowland 311; Ruth 189-
302; Sally 306-318-319; Sam. 317;
Samp. 313; Sarah 59-296-7-8-
305-7-311-3-4; Simon 313-9;
Solom. 304; Sterlg. 307-8; Susan
189-315-5-8; Susa. 302-8; Tab.
308; Tappa. 58; Theod. 189; Thos.
85-9-293-4-5-6-7-8-9-300-1-2-
3-4-5-6-311-2-4-5; T. P. 311;
Turner 58-9-311; Viola 312;
West 56-6-304-6-7-310-11-6;
Wm. 189-293-303-5-6-7-311-3-
6-7; Walton 306-312-3; Wilmot
319.

HARRISON, Alice 227; Andw.
222-6-8; Ann 227; Anthy. 227;
Benj. 121-172-205-226; Bruw.
120-1-3; Chas. 161; Cottie 193;
Deb. 185; Dunwoody 125; Eliza
121; Eliz. 222; Eva 121; Fran.
225-6; Geo. 8-222-226; Hann.
224-6-7; Harrt. 287; Hen. 33-
193; Isaac 193; Jas. 121; Jerem.
225; John 46-70-121-5-6-262-304;
Jos. 193-226-7; Lovall 224-6-7-8;
Marg. 185; Martha 121-162; Mary
121-161-222-3-267-8; Mollie 70;
Peggy 226; Reub. 121; Rich. 226;
Robt. 121; Sam. 185; Sarah 121-
136; Susan 119-120-1-3-136; Thos.
170; W. B. 121; Wm. 120-121-
136-185-222.
HART, Mr. 362; Sue 53.
HARTWELL, Hen. 298.
HARVEY, Agnes 149; Ann 149-
150-1; Asenath 28; Barb. 149
Benj. 156; Betsy 150; Billy 150;
Blasingame 149-150-6; Charity
28-70-146-155-6; Chas. 79-149-
150-1-2; Civility 156; Clarm.
154; Druc. 149-150; Eleanor 150;
Elijah 154; Eliz. 28-149-150-2-
7; Epsy 28; Evan 28-69-70-147-
152-3151617; Fran. 149-150-156;
156; Isaac 119-154-5; Isham 149;
Israel 154; Jack 149; Jas. 28-77-
8-9-119-150-1-2-153-4-5-6;
Jane 152; Jerem. 28; Jesse 152;
John 28-84-118-9-149-150-1-2-

153-4-5-6; Jos. 156; Judith 28-
151; Liney 150; Lucy 28; Lydia
152; Marg. 84-118-152-4;Martha
154-7 Mary 28-150-1-2-3-4-5;
Matt. 150; Michl. 28-151-2-3-6-
7; Moses 155; Nan 156; Nathan
149-153; Nehemiah 150; Patsy
154; Penel. 156; Pinckthn. 157;
Polly 150-8; Rachel 28-152-4-7;
Raleigh 151 Reb. 28-156-7-197;
Rich. 28-150-3-6; Ruth 118-153-
4-5; Sallie 149-150-3-4-5; Sarah
26-8-84-149-156; Steph. 157;
Susa 150-6; Thos. 28-149-150-1-
2-3-4-5-6--7; Tryford 151; Ur-
sula 155-6; Verlinda 157; Wm.
149-150-1-2-6-7; Willis 154;
Zephariah 150.
HARVIN, Jessie 310; Lucius 310.
HASFOLLER, Estelle 354.
HATCHER, Mastin 97; Virg. 97.
HAUGHTON, Permelia 32.
HAWES, Mittie 99.
HAWKES, Mr. 300; Sam. 276.
HAWKINS, B. H. 122; John 282;
Judge Kendk. 81; Martha 122;
Mary 81; Pinketheman 156-7; Reb.
156; Sophie 266; Wm. 81.
HAYES, Ange. 177; Ann 201;
Belle 177; Eleanor 309-310-365;
Eliza.177; Eliz. 177-305; Ella
177; Eudora 177; Ewnie 177; Geo.
176-7; Helen 115; Jas. 177; Jane
177; John 177; Julie 177; Marm-
dke. 177; Martha 177; Mary 176-
7; Octav. 177; Rich. 176; Robt.
305; Sarah 176-7; Theoda. 177;
Wm. 177.
HAYWOOD, Cecil 314; Moses
314; Sara 311-2.
HAYNE, Harriet 14.
HAZZARD, Isabella 176.
HEADWORTH, Hannah 170.
HEARD, Amy 356; Chas. 359;
Eliz. 356-7; Falkner 356; Geo.
359; Gen. 356; Jack 356; Jesse
356; John 356-7; Julia 359; Marg.
356; Mary 359; Nathan 356; Ralph
356-7; Rich. 357; Shep. 359; Wm.
355-356.
HEATH, Judith 285.
HEATON, Maude 114.
HEAWARD, Rich. 339.
HEDGEPATH, Charity 266.
HENDERSON, Eliz. 31; Isabela
30; Jas. 30; Judge 31; Lucius 30;
Mr. 30.
HENDON, Capt. Jas. 98.
HENDRICKS, John 335; Susan335.
HENDRICKSON, Jordon 49; Mary
T. 49.
HENNING, Mrs. Julia 79-87.
HENRY, Aman. 31; Civility 31-
46; Cora 31; Emmale. 273; John
31; Susan 31.
HERBERT, Buller 170-3.
HERFF, Victoria 356.
HERNDON, Isabella 288; Miss
54.
HERRING, Dan. 189; Maude 279.
HERRINGTON, Black 274; Eudora
274-5; Hen. 274; John 274; Lav.
274; Wm. 274.
HESSICK, Eunice 312; Fred. 312;
Syd. 312; Wm. 312.
HESS, John 55; Julia 55.
HEWLETT, Anna 287.
HEYS, Ann 117; Ethel 117; Jo
Ann 117; Mary 117; Ruba 117;
Sam. 117; Thos. 117.
HICKERSON, Dorothy 16; Porter
16.
HICKS, Julia 245.
HIERONIMOUS, Benj. 334; Em-
ily 334; Mary 334.
HIGDON, Miss 17.
HIGHTOWER, Lilla 11.
HILLIARD, Fran 315; Jas. 340-
1-3; Mourn. 340-1; Tenp. 341.
HILLEMAN, Benn. 28; Mary 28.